THE REIGN OF THE SERVANT KINGS

A Study of Eternal Security
and
the Final Significance
of Man

THE REIGN OF THE SERVANT KINGS

A Study of Eternal Security
and
the Final Significance
of Man

by

Joseph C. Dillow, Th.D.

Schoettle Publishing Co.
P.O. Box 594
Miami Springs, Florida 33266

Library of Congress Cataloging in Publication Data

Dillow, Joseph C.
   The Reign of the Servant Kings

      Includes bibliography and indexes (scripture and subject)
      1.   Theology, doctrinal
      2.   Eternal Security, Perseverance, Rewards

I. Title. II. Title: A Study of Eternal Security and the Final Significance of Man.

ISBN: 1-56453-095-7

Printed in the United States of America

DEDICATION

This book is dedicated to Jimmy Squires, one of Christ's metochoi. Thank you, Jimmy, for all you have meant to us.

TABLE OF CONTENTS

Forward

It became apparent at the Synod of Dort in 1618 that the Calvinists and the Arminians had reached a stalemate concerning the doctrine of salvation which was destined to last for centuries. The Arminians, in their exegetical approach to certain problem passages, viewed the loss of a believer's salvation as a real possibility for those who fail in a consistent walk with Jesus Christ. On the other hand, the Calvinist with a consistent biblical theology maintained that believers in Jesus Christ could never lose their eternal salvation. For almost four centuries there has been a breech between these two major systems of theology. It may very well be that in both systems, Calvinism and Arminianism, there has been a reductionistic error committed in understanding the meaning of salvation. Each of these theological systems appears to have defined the term salvation narrower than God intended by emphasizing one aspect of salvation at the expense of another.

The concept and meaning of salvation in the Scriptures is multi-dimensional. For example, when we look at salvation with respect to deliverance from sin, there is a past aspect--justification, deliverance from the penalty of sin, and a present aspect--sanctification, deliverance from the power of sin, and a future aspect--glorification, deliverance from the presence of sin. There are many works today explaining in great detail the doctrine of justification salvation. There are a lesser number of works seeking satisfactory explanations of the doctrine of sanctification salvation. There are almost no works in our generation explaining the doctrine of glorification salvation. This area of study has remained a virtual vacuum. Yet it seems that in expanding the implications of the doctrine of glorification salvation and the judgment seat of Christ there is an accurate biblical solution for this four hundred-year debate between the Calvinist and the Arminian. Although a believer can never lose his justification salvation, there are dimensions of glorification salvation that may be lost or gained if we take seriously passages such as Romans 14:10, 1 Corinthians 3:15, 2 Corinthians 5:10, and 2 John 7-8. The danger of loss is real and to be taken with appropriate fear and reverence in light of the eternal implications. The opportunity of reward, on the other hand, with its glories of ruling and reigning with Jesus Christ in His coming Kingdom, are presented in the Scriptures as a great motivation for holy living in the present.

It is precisely at this point that Joseph Dillow has performed a monumental service to the Body of Christ. *The Reign of the Servant Kings* may just be the solution to the debate between the two major systems of theology which have dominated church history for four centuries. I have personally studied through this manuscript several times and found myself most enthusiastic with Dr. Dillow's exegetical clarity and consistent biblical theology. His contribution to the disciplines of soteriology and eschatology are to be applauded. I heartily commend this study to you for gaining growth in accurately understanding your position, practice, and place with Jesus Christ, both now and in His coming kingdom rule. God has spoken and He does not stutter. Therefore, we need to be diligent in our study to come to a clearer meaning of what God meant by what He has spoken in His Scriptures.

Earl D. Radmacher, Th.D.
Western Seminary Phoenix
Scottsdale, Arizona
January 1992

Preface

There are few issues which are as capable of raising the temperature of theological discussion as the issue of whether or not the saints will necessarily persevere in holiness. The Westminster Confession (1647) has taught us that true faith inevitably results in a holy life and that justification and sanctification are always united. Indeed, the magnificent Reformed tradition, which has contributed in no small way to the growth and expansion of the church since the Reformation, has had perseverance in holiness as one of its central tenets.

It is also well known that the Remonstrants (1610) rejected that point of Calvinism and went to another extreme--conditional security. Both were struggling with the relation between faith and works. What do we make of a man who claims to have placed his trust in Jesus Christ but whose present life-style is a complete contradiction of the faith he once acknowledged? The Westminster divines had the ready answer that he was never a Christian to begin with, because the ultimate test of the reality of faith is the perseverance in the faith. The Remonstrants, on the other hand, speaking from the Arminian tradition, viewed the matter differently. To them, while it was possible that the man was never truly born again to begin with, it was also possible that he was genuinely born again but, due to his falling into sin or unbelief, lost his justification.

A large portion of Christendom has accepted variations of the Arminian view. We may note that the Roman Catholic Church has long held to these ideas and so has the Wesleyan tradition, in some form or another. In view of the fact that God has given to the church the gift of teaching, we must not easily dismiss this vast body of exegetical literature simply because it disagrees with the Reformed tradition or with our own personal exegetical conclusions. To do so is to cut ourselves off from the expression of the gift of teaching in the church of Christ for the past two thousand years.

Part of the problem may be that the disputants on the question of perseverance in holiness perceived only two interpretive options when confronted with the many passages which seem to indicate that there is something conditional in the believer's ultimate destiny. The warning passages in Hebrews, for example, have entered prominently into the debate. As might be expected, the exegetical literature, in general, has divided along two lines: either these warnings apply to those who merely professed faith and subsequently fell away from a profession, thus proving that they never "possessed" faith to begin with, or they apply to true Christians who, through the sin of unbelief, forfeited their justification.

Is there a third option? Is there an interpretive stance which can be completely faithful to the text and at the same time draws upon the exegetical contributions which the Holy Spirit has made to the church through the able, scholarly work of men from both traditions? Is there a view of these warnings and others in the New Testament which maintains, with the Calvinist tradition, that justification can never be forfeited and at the same time, allows, with the Wesleyans, that justification and sanctification are not inextricably united and that there is indeed something conditional in the believer's ultimate destiny?

The answer to that question is yes. In the pages to follow, I will attempt to chart a middle road between the traditional Reformed approach and that of the Arminian. I accept the Reformed position that those who are truly born again can never lose their salvation. But I also accept the Arminian position that the warning passages of the New Testament (e. g., Heb. 6) are directed to true Christians, not merely professing Christians. There is a real danger here. However, contrary to the Arminian, the danger is not loss of heaven but loss of our reward there and severe divine discipline in time.

The issue of whether or not the saints will necessarily persevere and whether or not true faith is indestructible is a complex interpretive issue involving numerous passages in the New Testament, indeed one's whole system of theology as well. Because of this, the following discussion will take us into many different areas of biblical theology. An entire view of the Christian life is under consideration in the following chapters.

One final note. Throughout this book I refer to the merit which the believer can obtain by means of his good works. In the theology texts, merit is often used in two different senses. It is either construed as a strict legal relation in which the believer by his works places God in his debt or as a more general term for the notion that God rewards us according to our works but not because of them. Unless stated otherwise, it is the latter sense which is always intended. God is not obligated to reward us at all. That He chooses to do this, and that in accordance with a general correspondence to our faithfulness, is an act of pure grace, not of debt.

Joseph C. Dillow
Vienna, Austria
15 January 1992

ABBREVIATIONS

Scripture Versions

LXX   *The Septuagint Version, With Apocrypha - Greek and English.* London: Samuel Bagster & Sons, 1851; reprint ed., Grand Rapids: Zondervan, 1978. (The Septuagint is the Greek translation of the Old Testament, completed around 200 B.C.)

NASB   New American Standard Bible. La Habra, Calif.: Lockman Foundation, 1971.

NIV   New International Version. Grand Rapids: Zondervan, 1978.

NKJV   Holy Bible, New King James Version. Nashville: Nelson, 1982.

Reference Works

AG   Arndt, William F., and Gingrich, F. Wilbur. *A Greek-English Lexicon of the New Testament and Other Early Christian Literature.* Chicago: University of Chicago Press, 1957.

AS   Abbott-Smith, G. *A Manual Greek Lexicon of the New Testament.* Edinburgh: T. & T. Clark, 1937.

BDB   Brown, Francis; Driver, S. R.; and Briggs, Charles A. *Hebrew and English Lexicon of the Old Testament.* London: Oxford University Press, 1966.

DM   Dana, H. E., and Mantey, Julius R. *A Manual Grammar of the Greek New Testament.* New York: MacMillan, 1955.

DNTT   *Dictionary of New Testament Theology.* Edited by Colin Brown. 3 vols. Grand Rapids: Zondervan, 1975-78.

ISBE   *International Standard Bible Encyclopedia.* Edited by James Orr. 5 vols. Grand Rapids: Eerdmans, 1929.

LS   Liddell, Henry George, and Scott, Robert. *A Greek-English Lexicon.* 1907; reprint ed., revised and augmented by Henry Stuart Jones and Robert McKenzie. Oxford: Clarendon Press, 1968.

MM   Moulton, James Hope, and Milligan, George. *The Vocabulary of the Greek Testament.* One-vol. ed., 1930; reprint ed., Grand Rapids: Eerdmans, 1974.

NISBE   *International Standard Bible Encyclopedia.* Rev. ed. Edited by Geoffrey W. Bromiley. 4 vols. Grand Rapids: Eerdmans, 1980-88.

TDNT   *Theological Dictionary of the New Testament.* Edited by Gerhard Kittel and Gerhard Friedrich. Translated by Geoffrey W. Bromiley. Index compiled by Ronald E. Pitkin. 10 vols. Grand Rapids: Zondervan, 1964-76.

TDNTA   *Theological Dictionary of the New Testament.* Edited by Gerhard Kittel and Gerhard Friedrich. Translated and abridged in one volume by Geoffrey W. Bromiley. Grand Rapids: Eerdmans, 1985.

TWOT   *Theological Wordbook of the Old Testament.* Edited by R. Laird Harris, Gleason L. Archer, Jr., and Bruce K. Waltke. 2 vols. Chicago: Moody Press, 1980.

ZPED   *Zondervan Pictorial Encyclopedia of the Bible.* Edited by Merrill C. Tenney. 5 vols. Grand Rapids: Zondervan, 1976.

Commentaries

BKC   *The Bible Knowledge Commentary.* Edited by John F. Walvoord and Roy Zuck. 2 vols. Wheaton, IL: Victor, 1983.

EGT   *Expositor's Greek Testament.* Edited by W. Robertson Nicoll. 5 vols. Reprint ed., Grand Rapids: Eerdmans, 1967.

Lange's   Lange, John Peter. *Lange's Commentary on the Holy Scriptures.* Translated and edited by Philip Schaff. 12 double vols. 1868-70; reprint ed., Grand Rapids: Zondervan, 1960.

NICNT   Bruce, F. F., gen. ed., *The New International Commentary on the New Testament.* 15 vols. to date. Grand Rapids: Eerdmans, 1959--.

TNTC   Tasker, R. V. G., gen. ed. *The Tyndale New Testament Commentaries.* 20 vols. London: Tyndale, 1957-65.

Journals

BibSac   *Bibliotheca Sacra*

GTJ	*Grace Theological Journal*
JBL	*Journal of Biblical Literature*
JETS	*Journal of the Evangelical Theological Society*
JGES	*Journal of the Grace Evangelical Society*

Other

Schaff	*The Creeds of Christendom*. 6th ed. Edited by Philip Schaff. 3 vols. 1876; reprint ed. of Harper and Row 1931 ed., Grand Rapids: Baker, 1985.

ACKNOWLEDGMENTS

In 1973 the writer was given a set of tapes by Zane Hodges on the book of Hebrews. Those lectures resulted in a change of perspective on that book and ultimately to a different way of looking at the New Testament. I would like to thank Professor Hodges for the profound impact he has had on my understanding of the doctrines of eternal security and rewards.

I would like to express appreciation to Wendall Hollis for his faithful assistance in editing this manuscript. His contribution in helping me to think clearly and critically about the issues involved has been a significant aspect of this project.

Also, special thanks to my secretary, Leslie Smith, for her many hours of proofreading and typing and her many helpful suggestions. Any errors which remain are, of course, my own responsibility.

Prologue

Shrouded in darkness, the early earth lumbered silently through the heavens. Its aimless journey had already consumed aeons of cosmic time. It was before . . . the Beginning.[1] No one could have guessed that this planet would one day become the moral center of the cosmic conflict of the ages.

A universal tragedy had occurred. The Morning Star, known as Lucifer,[2] God's perfect one, full of wisdom and beauty,[3] the angelic being whom God had appointed as ruler over the ancient cosmos,[4] . . . had fallen. The prophet Ezekiel paints a picture of divine grief in his woeful description of this betrayal (Ezek. 28:11-19). Lucifer had been given everything. Yet he became proud.[5] He concluded that God's gifts were more important than the giver, that dependence upon God and obedience to His revealed will were not necessary. He became the Satan, God's adversary.[6] He was cast to the earth, and the earth was judged.[7] At that time the earth, from which he ruled and upon which he lived,[8] became without form and void (Gen. 1:1-2).

As the angels looked on, the Lord declared:

---

[1]The writer is assuming a widely held view that Gen. 1:1 refers not to the absolute but to a relative beginning. The entire known universe, including the sun and stars and atmosphere, etc., came into existence out of nothing in Gen. 1:1ff. The earth itself, however, apparently already existed at this time. The angels were created and some of them fell in the pre-Gen. 1:1 universe. When God begins His creative work, the earth is already in a judged condition. This is not to be confused with the "gap theory" which teaches a gap between Gen. 1:1 and 1:2. Rather, the gap is between the original creation in eternity past (Jn. 1:1-2) and the re-creation of Gen. 1:1 which occurred about six thousand to twelve thousand years ago. In the pre-Gen. 1:1 universe an entirely different set of natural laws prevailed. It is not germane to the purpose of this book nor does the book's central thesis depend upon this view. For this reason the writer will not defend it here. The interested reader is referred to Bruce Waltke, *Creation and Chaos* (Portland: Western Conservative Baptist Seminary Press, 1974), pp. 31-36.

[2]Isa. 14:12-17.

[3]Ezek. 28:12.

[4]Ezek. 28:14.

[5]Ezek. 28:17; 1 Tim. 3:6.

[6]The word "Satan" means "adversary."

[7]Ezek. 28:17.

[8]Ezek. 28:13.

We shall give this rebellion a thorough trial. We shall permit it to run full course. The universe shall see what a creature, even the greatest can do apart from God. We shall set up an experiment, and permit the universe of creatures to watch it, during this brief interlude between eternity past and eternity future called "time." In it the spirit of independence shall be allowed to expand to the utmost. And the wreck and the ruin which shall result will demonstrate to the universe, and forever, that there is no life, no joy, no peace, apart from a complete dependence upon the Most High God, possessor of heaven and earth.[9]

The Lord of Hosts could have destroyed this rebel immediately. He could have answered this challenge with raw power. The Satan has said that pride and independence were acceptable. But instead, Yahweh brought into existence a plan which would forever answer this Satanic alternative--a plan which would involve God Himself in a moral demonstration of His love and grace. The King Himself would one day demonstrate the superiority of His ways--dependence and servanthood.

For millions of years mournful silence and darkness reigned in Satan's world. Had God forgotten? Had He decided to ignore this challenge to His sovereignty? Had He decided to look the other way? The silence of God was deafening. The darkness was universal. The earth belonged to the Satan.[10] The angelic sons of God yearned for the darkness and silence to be broken.[11]

Suddenly--it was!

And God said, "Let there be light," and there was light. God saw that the light was good, and he separated the light from the darkness. God called the light "day," and the darkness he called "night." And there was evening, and there was morning--the first day (Gen. 1:3-5).

"At last!" thought Michael, God's archangel. "Our Lord will once again rule here!"

Then God said, "Let us make man in our image, in our likeness, and let them rule over the fish of the sea and the birds of the air, over the livestock, over all the earth, and over all the creatures that move along the ground (Gen. 1:26).

"But," said Michael, "what is this? A man? This creature is so weak, so inferior to the Satan. Why has the King placed **HIM** in the Satan's world and told **HIM** to rule there? How can such an insignificant creature, much lower than the

---

[9]Donald Barnhouse, *The Invisible War* (Grand Rapids: Zondervan, n.d.), p. 60.

[10]See Lk. 4:6-7; 2 Cor. 4:4; Jn. 16:11; 12:31; Eph. 2:2.

[11]And they shouted for joy when it was (Job 38:7)!

angels,[12] possibly accomplish the divine purpose? Surely a great mistake has been made!"

What is the significance of man? That question has been on the lips of both poet and philosopher since man first began to think about these things. Thousands of years later as the shepherd David gazed upward into the brilliantly star covered sky, he was crushed to the ground with a sense of his own insignificance and exclaimed (Ps. 8:3-4):

> When I consider your heavens,
> the work of your fingers,
> the moon and the stars,
> which you have set in place,

WHAT IS MAN THAT YOU ARE MINDFUL OF HIM

David's mind, apparently reflecting on the divine commission in Genesis, received a flash of illumination (Ps. 8:6-9):

> You made him a littler lower than
> the heavenly beings
> and crowned him with glory and honor.

YOU MADE HIM RULER OVER THE WORKS

OF YOUR HANDS;

YOU PUT EVERYTHING UNDER HIS FEET
> . . . .

> Oh LORD, our Lord,
> how majestic is your name in
> all the earth!

Man was to rule! It was the lesser creature who would be crowned with glory and honor. It was the inferior creature who would be placed in rulership over the Satan's world! The glory, honor, and sovereignty which the Satan had stolen in independence and unbelief would be regained by the inferior creature living in servanthood and faith! In this way pride is rebuked. It was God's purpose that the lesser creature living in dependence upon God would obtain a higher position than the superior creature, who had stolen his by independence and unbelief. Years later the Savior would say, "he who is least among you all-- he is the greatest" (Lk. 9:48).

God intends to humble the proud and independent in a unique way. He intends that the lower creature, man (created lower than the angels and hence

---

[12]Ps. 8:5; Heb. 2:7.

lower than Satan), should achieve the highest position ("all things in subjection under His feet," Heb. 2:8). Thus, the lower creature would achieve by dependence upon God a higher position than the higher creature, Satan, achieved through independence. For "it is not to angels that He has subjected the world to come, about which we are speaking" (Heb. 2:5). Out of the least, God will bring the greatest. It was as MAN that the Savior defeated the enemy. It was as MAN that He silenced the principalities and powers. It will be as MAN that He will reign over the future kingdom of God upon this earth.

This future kingdom is the subject of hundreds of passages in the Old Testament. It is a glorious reign of servant kings which extends to "all the works of His hands." (This may suggest that one day mankind will rule the galaxies!) The lion will lay down with the lamb, universal righteousness will reign, there will be no war. Disease will be abolished, and the world of Satan will be placed under the rule of the Servant King and His companions (Heb. 1:9).

Consistent with His divine purpose, God chose to establish His kingdom through the elevation of an obscure and insignificant Semitic tribe, Israel. It is not Greece, Rome, Egypt, Babylon, France, Germany, Russia, or the United States that will rule the earth. That future glory falls to those followers of Christ both within Israel and within His church, who, like their Master, live in dependence and obedience.

The controlling principle of the biblical philosophy of history rests in the precept of the second before the first. God often chooses the "nothings" (1 Cor. 1:26-27). Only in this way is the self praise of man destroyed. It is a pervading characteristic of the whole course of redemption that God chooses the younger before the elder, sets the smaller in priority to the greater, and chooses the second before the first. Not Cain but Abel and his substitute Seth; not Japheth but Shem; not Ishmael but Isaac; not Esau but Jacob; not Manasseh but Ephraim;[13] not Aaron but Moses;[14] not Eliab but David;[15] not the Old Covenant but the New;[16] not the first Adam but the last Adam.[17] The first becomes last and the last becomes first.[18] The great nations are set aside,[19] and God elects to establish His purposes through two insignificant mediums, the Israel of God (the believing remnant of the last days and the body of Christ (the invisible church).

---

[13]Gen. 48:14.

[14]Ex. 7:1.

[15]1 Sam. 16:6-13.

[16]Heb. 8:13.

[17]1 Cor. 15:45.

[18]Mt. 19:30.

[19]Dan. 2:7ff; Rom. 1:24, 26, 28.

But the first Adam, deceived by the serpent, chose the path of the father of lies, and acting independently, contrary to His design, fell into sin. As a result, the newly created universe was subjected to the universal bondage of decay,[20] and the sons of men were born in need of a redeemer.

It is here that the beauty and symmetry of the divine plan became evident. Not only did God purpose to elevate the role of a servant and the disposition of trust, but He gave His Son, the Second Man and the Last Adam,[21] as a savior. He who is of the essence of God became a servant. He "made Himself nothing, taking the very nature of a servant" (Phil. 2:7). He obeyed finally and completely; "He humbled Himself and became obedient to death, even death on a cross" (2:8). And in this way, living by exactly the opposite set of principles from the Satan, He achieved higher glory:

> *Therefore God exalted him to the highest place and gave him the name that is above every name, that at the name of Jesus every knee should bow, in heaven and on earth and under the earth and every tongue confess that Jesus Christ is Lord, to the glory of God the Father* (Phil. 2:9-11).

Those who would rule with Him must find their lives in the same way: "Your attitude should be the same as that of Christ Jesus" (Phil. 2:5). The future rulers of God's creation must, like their King, be servants now. There will be no room for pride nor hubris, only a heartfelt desire to extend the blessing and glory of God throughout the created order. Unlike the Satan and his modern day followers, they will have no desire to be lord over their subjects. Instead, like their Lord, they will desire only to serve those over whom they rule:

> *Jesus called them together and said, "You know that the rulers of the Gentiles lord it over them, and their high officials exercise authority over them.* **Not so with you.** *Instead, whoever wants to become great among you must be your servant, and whoever wants to be first must be your slave--just as the Son of Man did not come to be served, but to serve, and to give his life as a ransom for many"* (Mt. 20:25-28).

They will be greatly loved and valued by their subjects. Instead of disobedience there will be servanthood, to God and to others. The second Adam put it this way, "Blessed are the poor in spirit, for **theirs** is the kingdom of heaven. . . . Blessed are the meek, for **they** will inherit the earth" (Mt. 5:3-5).

---

[20]Rom. 8:20-22.

[21]1 Cor. 15:45. There are only two "Adams," i.e., two federally representative heads of humanity. Jesus is the last Adam but only the second man; there will be many other men as God intended men to be.

We are to become the servant kings. That is our destiny. This destiny was often called "salvation" by the prophets.[22] This was not a salvation from hell, but the glorious privilege of reigning with Messiah in the final destiny of man. In the eternal plan, only those who strive to be servants now can qualify for this great future privilege then. In order to be "great" in the kingdom of heaven, to rule there, we must first become humble like a little child.[23] "The greatest among you will be your servant. For whoever exalts himself will be humbled, and whoever humbles himself will be exalted" (Mt. 23:11-12).

If God's eternal plan revolves around demonstrating the moral superiority of humility and servanthood, it is of the utmost importance that we learn this lesson now. All Christians are not servants, and only those who are will be great in the kingdom. Only those sons of God who are "sons indeed" will be co-heirs with their coming king in the final destiny of man. Many who have been saved by the King are not presently living for Him. Many who have begun lives of discipleship have not persevered. They risk forfeiture of this great future. But we are "partakers (Gk. **metochoi**) of Christ, [only] if we hold our confidence firmly to the end" (Heb. 3:14). However, those who are obedient and dependent servants now and who persevere in discipleship to the final hour will be among Christ's metochoi, the servant kings, in the thousand-year kingdom of the Son of Man. All Christians will be in the kingdom, but tragically not all will be co-heirs there.

It is by losing our lives that they find their ultimate significance.[24] Each act of service is not only an expression of God's eternal purpose but is preparation and training for our final destiny. Yes, the final answer to the Satan's rebellion, and the ultimate meaning of human existence, is to be found in the future reign of the servant kings. But who are they, and how do we join their company? Let us begin . . .

---

[22]A discussion of the various meanings of "salvation" will be undertaken in chapter 6.
[23]Mt. 18:4.
[24]Mk. 8:35.

Chapter 1

Introduction

$\mathbf{N}$o doubt there are millions who have professed the name of Christ and continue to live in such a way which gives no evidence whatsoever that their profession is real. In fact, a widely reported opinion poll survey indicated that over fifty million people in the United States claim to be born again.[1] Surely, if that many people were true "partakers of the divine nature," the impact on our country would be profound.

In the clearest possible terms the New Testament writers presented the unconditional nature of the gospel offer:

And let the one who is thirsty come; let the one who wishes, take the water of life **without cost** (Rev. 22:17 NASB).

For God so loved the world that He gave His only begotten Son that **whoever believes in Him** *should not perish but have everlasting life* (Jn. 3:16 NASB).

Yet explicit statements such as these are sometimes difficult to accept. Could something as important as our eternal destiny really come to us only through believing and be "without cost"? One cannot profitably speculate on the eternal destiny of many who have acted in a way that brings shame to the gospel. But this type of behavior by people who claim to be Christians certainly makes one anxious that the clearest possible presentation of the gospel be made.

Grace under Fire

There are two powerful influences which have caused this hesitation to accept the unconditional freeness of saving grace.

---

[1]George Gallup, Jr. and David Poling, *The Search For America's Faith* (Nashville: Abingdon, 1980), p. 92.

The Abuse of Grace

The first is the deplorable state into which Western Christianity has fallen as we move to the end of the twentieth century. This has caused many to wonder, Is the teaching of free grace healthy?

There has always been sin in the church, but the presence of the media, television evangelists, and the news and information explosion has highlighted certain hypocrisy as never before. Furthermore, Western culture has become so thoroughly secularized and godless that simply living in it has resulted in many Christians getting mud on their feet. The church, instead of being a beacon of light, has often been penetrated by the very abuses which it speaks against.

A lamentable situation such as this is bound to provoke thoughtful and even angry reactions from some within the church who are understandably upset about empty professions of faith which have not resulted in any change of life.

One such reaction has recently come from the able pen of John MacArthur, pastor-teacher of Grace Community Church. Troubled by the prevalence of "cheap grace" in the church today, MacArthur has turned our attention to *The Gospel According to Jesus*, a book which he says is the product of four years of study on the subject of the definition of the gospel according to Christ.

Why does such a situation like this exist in the church today? In MacArthur's opinion it is due to the well-meaning but misinformed teaching that salvation is being offered without the necessity of accepting Christ as both Savior and Lord at the point of saving faith. He feels that many leading Bible teachers are saying "the only criterion for salvation is knowing and believing some basic facts about Christ."[2] The fallout of this thinking, he says, is a deficient doctrine of salvation; justification is not necessarily and inevitably linked to sanctification. People feel they can pray a prayer, receive eternal life, and then go on sinning.

The answer, MacArthur feels, is to include the notion of submission to the lordship of Christ as the antidote to a defective view of faith. This leads him into some views of the nature of saving faith and of the conditions for salvation which, to many, would seem to be an extreme reaction in the opposite direction from the "easy believism" he so vigorously attacks.

The Theology of the Reformers

The second major influence which has caused many to ask, Is free grace healthy? is a persistent theological tradition going back to John Calvin. Calvin and the Reformers who followed him told their readers and parishioners that

---

[2]John MacArthur, *The Gospel According to Jesus* (Grand Rapids: Zondervan, 1988), p. 17.

faith alone saves, but true faith is a faith which results in a life of works. In fact, the final proof of the reality of faith is whether or not a man perseveres in good works to the end of life. Known as the doctrine of the perseverance of the saints, this teaching emerged in its mature form[3] during the Protestant Reformation.

One has only to read Calvin's *Institutes* to see immediately that he labored under a great burden to defend the Reformation against the criticism that a faith alone, grace alone gospel would lead to moral laxity. When perusing these great volumes, the "atmosphere" is pungent with anxiety to demonstrate that the gospel of free grace will not lead to license but will, to the contrary, result in a life of holiness. However, in order to make his argument "air tight," Calvin went beyond the Scripture and taught that the gospel will necessarily and inevitably guarantee a life of holiness. This subtle change in the gospel was readily accepted by the Reformers because it completely negated the Catholic attack. When a person who claimed to be a Christian and yet was living a carnal life was set up by the Catholics as an example of the product of Reformation theology, the Reformers could now simply say he was not a Christian at all. If he was, he would not live like that. When one was in the midst of a debate which was ripping apart the fabric of Western Europe, one needed powerful arguments like this in his arsenal.

Having successfully separated from Catholicism and established the Reformation churches, the next attack came from within. Pelagianism manifested itself in resistance by Protestants in Holland to the notion that a true Christian can never lose salvation. Convinced that certain passages, such as Heb. 6, taught that falling away from salvation was a real danger, they argued against the Calvinist doctrine of unconditional security. Once again the doctrine of perseverance in holiness was a powerful weapon to fend off this attack. Certainly the Reformers could not be accused of a doctrine which leads to license, if the doctrine guaranteed that true Christians will persevere in holiness to the end of life. When the Arminians pointed to a man who had professed Christ and had never given evidence of a godly life, the Calvinists could simply reply that according to their doctrine he was not a Christian at all. "However much [they] avoided this teaching [their doctrine of temporary faith] in their sermons, it was always around, and they could readily raise it when they needed it to explain an apostasy."[4]

This debate about eternal security has not been a brief affair. In fact, it has gone on for several hundred years and continues to some extent today. When a discussion endures that long, issues are more precisely defined, and positions harden. The very length and intensity of the debate has contributed in no small

---

[3]Traces of this teaching can be found in 1 Clement and the Apostolic Fathers.

[4]R. T. Kendall, *Calvin and English Calvinism to 1649* (Oxford: Oxford University Press, 1979), p. 143.

way to the traditional acceptance of opposing positions. Lest the reader doubt this point, consider the typical seminary student, the future teacher of the sheep. When a position differing from his own background or perhaps from that of the seminary which he attends is presented, he is likely to "check it out" by opening up the standard theology texts which support his view and learning the ancient arguments against his opponents. Thus, traditional arguments are passed on from book to student, from professor to pupil, and from pupil to the parishioner when he becomes a pastor. Pressed for time in the seminary, and without it in the church, he rarely has opportunity for original study which might challenge traditional interpretations.

The Answer to Carnality

To prevent abuse of the gospel, two widely held solutions are offered. Some, harkening back to the Colossian error, insist that the cause of the problem is that man needs more than initial salvation in Christ--a "fullness" beyond our salvation experience, a second work of grace to finish the incomplete beginning. However, some of the most notable examples of the present hypocrisy have appeared within the groups which offer such a solution and by the very leaders who teach it. The other solution, and the one which this book addresses, is the tendency to "front-load" and "back-load" the gospel.

Front Loading the Gospel

Front loading the gospel means attaching various works of submission and obedience on the front end and including them in the conditions for salvation. These works are supposedly created in the heart by God. This is commonly done among those who maintain that submission to the lordship of Christ is a condition of salvation. Faith is redefined to include submission, and a man becomes a Christian not by "hearing" and "believing" but by believing and promising God he will submit his life to Christ. This is not to deny that true faith certainly involves a disposition of openness to God and cannot coexist with an attitude of determination to continue in sin. But that is not what those who teach so-called "lordship salvation" mean. Rather, their view is that a man must resolve to turn from all known sin and follow Christ absolutely. It seems that works enter through the front door, and another gospel is taught. But surely this God-created submission to lordship is a work, and works in the human heart whether from God or man do not save!

Back Loading the Gospel

A far more subtle change in the gospel, however, occurs when some back load the gospel. Back loading the gospel means attaching various works of submission as the means for achieving the final aim of our faith, final deliverance from hell and entrance into heaven. This is what has been done in the more extreme expressions of the Reformed doctrine of the perseverance of the saints. While it is often claimed that a life of works is the necessary and inevitable result of true faith, it is also maintained by some that works are the means of achieving our final destiny. Of course, it is not always stated as blatantly as that. These works, we are told, are different than the works which the unregenerate perform to obtain merit with God. These works are the gifts of Christ and the fruits of regeneration. Calvin resisted a similar theology during the Reformation:

> *The Sophists, who delight in sporting with Scripture and in empty cavils, think they have a subtle evasion when they expound* **works** *to mean, such as unregenerated men do literally, and by the effect of free will, without the grace of Christ, and deny that these have any reference to spiritual works. Thus, according to them, man is justified by faith as well as by work, provided these are not his own works, but gifts of Christ and fruits of regeneration.*[5]

Calvin would no doubt be appalled to learn that there are many in the church today who bear his name who espouse this very sophistry! To the prosaic mind, the doctrine of perseverance in holiness sometimes seems to be expressed in a way that teaches that sanctification is a means of justification. The English Puritans often came close to this, and at least one of their luminaries, William Bradshaw (1571-1618), explicitly taught what others only implied.[6]

More recently, Arthur Pink, has maintained that God requires that true Christians must "keep themselves" or risk eternal damnation.[7] Yet he unequivocally maintains the "absolute and eternal security of the saints."[8]

He is attempting to show that God preserves His children through means--works. He quotes John Owen, that prince of the Puritan expositors, with approval, teaching that works are a means of salvation:

> *But yet our own diligent endeavor is such as* **indispensable means** *for that end, as that without it, it will not be brought about . . . . If we are in Christ, God hath given us the lives of our souls, and hath taken*

---

[5]John Calvin, *Institutes of the Christian Religion*, trans. Henry Beveridge, 2 vols. (Grand Rapids: Eerdmans, 1964), 3.11.14.

[6]See Kendall, p. 89.

[7]Arthur Pink, *An Exposition of Hebrews* (Grand Rapids: Baker, 1968), p. 601.

[8]Ibid., p. 599.

upon Himself, in His covenant, the preservation of them. But **yet we** *may say, with reference unto the* **means** *that He hath appointed, when storms and trials arise,* **unless we use our diligent endeavors, we cannot be saved.**[9]

It seems that Pink, Bradshaw, and Owen, John are simply being honest about their understanding of the Reformed doctrine of perseverance. In their preoccupation with means they have forgotten that God has already told us what the means of salvation are and what they are not. Works are not a means, whether on the front end or on the back end. The only means necessary for obtaining salvation is faith, and faith alone:

He saved us, not because of righteous things we had done, but because of his mercy. He saved us **through** *the washing of rebirth and renewal by the Holy Spirit* (Ti. 3:5).

The "means" are the washing of rebirth and renewal by the Holy Spirit, and not our good works:

For it is by grace you have been saved **through faith,** *and this is not from yourselves, it is the gift of God--not by works, so that no one can boast* (Eph. 2:8-9).

The means are one--faith. This faith is apart from any means involving works. How else can Paul say it? When Pink and his modern followers, reacting to the moral laxity in the church, back-load the gospel with means, they are flatly contradicting Paul, if words have any meaning at all. In so doing, they seem to be preaching "another gospel" (Gal. 1:9).

We might ask, "Has loading the gospel with additional means and conditions achieved any more notable moral results than those who add nothing to it?" The answer seems to be no. There is just as much moral laxity in the history of those confessions who have stressed perseverance as in those who have not. One only has to read the works of the English Puritans to see the burden these godly men felt over these same issues in their churches. This approach has been tried before without success, and it is hardly the answer to our present dilemma. Robert Dabney, an articulate proponent of this very doctrine, laments the deplorable state of the Presbyterian Church in his day (1878). The New Testament saints, he says, "did not, like so many now, sit year after year in sinful indolence, complaining of the lack of assurance, and yet indifferent to its cultivation."[10]

---

[9]John Owen, *Hebrews*, cited by Pink, p. 600.

[10]Robert L. Dabney, *Lectures in Systematic Theology* (1878; reprint ed., Grand Rapids: Zondervan, 1972), p. 707.

The problems of spiritual lethargy and spiritual abuse are widespread. The various proposals for correcting them have been tried before, and there seems to be no useful purpose served in continuing with the old answers such as lordship salvation and perseverance in holiness. It seems to me that these problems are rooted in some very fundamental biblical misunderstandings. Could it be that the Protestant Reformation was incomplete and that this lies at the core of a raging modern controversy concerning the freeness of God's grace? Perhaps this unfinished beginning is also a significant cause of the carnality found in many churches. Here is the key to our modern dilemma. The Reformers feared free grace and, as a result, did not take the Reformation far enough. That is, their doctrine of the saints' perseverance in holiness compromised the free grace of God. Because the doctrine of justification by faith alone was potentially vulnerable to the charge of promoting license, the Reformers simply could not let go of the notion that works played a necessary part in our final arrival in heaven. Unable to accept that a regenerate man could live a life of sin and still be saved, they included works on the back end of the gospel as the means (result?) of salvation.

If the saints must inevitably and necessarily persevere in godliness to the final hour, then the doctrine of rewards and chastisement at the judgment seat of Christ becomes murky. How can a man who has persevered in holiness be chastised? Since all who are regenerate will be rewarded anyway, perhaps many settle into spiritual dullness thinking all is well with their souls and there are no negative consequences to pay. And if the doctrine of punishment for a carnal life is vague and if the doctrine of rewards is reduced to a promise of something that everyone will get anyway, then key motivators for living the Christian life are compromised.

Most important, however, is the fact that the motivation of gratitude for unconditional acceptance is lost. This is because in the Reformed system the most likely possibility for the continually sinning Christian is that he may not be a true Christian at all. While some advocates of this doctrine would not intend this, the practical result is often continual introspection and doubt as to whether or not one is really unconditionally loved and accepted in God's family, apart from any works at all! Yet, paradoxically, those who advocate this view say our motivation should come from gratitude. But how can gratitude emerge from the heart of one who is continually re-examining whether or not he is truly accepted?

A new Reformation may be needed in Western Christianity which sets forth the magnificent freeness of God's grace as the only sufficient motivation for godly living.

The Eternal Security of the Saints

It is obvious that the question of eternal security is inextricably involved with the question of free grace. If eternal life is truly offered "without cost" and salvation once received can never be lost, it might seem that some would take the grace of God for granted and live unfaithful lives. All motivation is lost, it is feared, to persevere in the life of faith. For the man who claims he is a Christian and who lives a sinful life, the Arminian warns him that he is in danger of losing his salvation. The English Puritans, on the other hand, simply say he never had salvation to begin with and he had better re-examine his foundations; he is in danger of hell. Only the man who perseveres in a life of good works to the final hour, they said, is truly saved.

The Reformed doctrine of the perseverance of the saints was an outgrowth of the accusations that the Reformation would logically result in moral laxity. It also provided a powerful means of refuting the Arminian teaching of conditional security. The intent of this book is to demonstrate that this doctrine is not only absent from Scripture but could, if not carefully stated, compromise the freeness of the grace of God. This is a book about the eternal security of the saints, a doctrine which the writer feels has good scriptural support. Yet this doctrine has labored under amazing exegetical contortions at the hands of its advocates. The seeming twisting of numerous Scriptures in order to get them to align with a particular view of perseverance, can only be described (if politically inclined) as "voodoo" exegesis. The history of interpretation must, of course, render the final verdict, but if one had to choose between Arminian and Calvinist interpretations of the relevant passages, the writer's opinion is that the Arminian view is eminently more successful and true to the text. Fortunately, one does not have to choose between either of those interpretations, and it will be the burden of this book to chart a third and mediating path.

This investigation will lead us into many related doctrines, such as the relationship between justification and sanctification, assurance of salvation, and the relevance of the warning passages in the New Testament. Can a true Christian commit apostasy? Does the New Testament teach the existence of the carnal Christian? In addition, we will examine all of the passages commonly brought to bear on the question of eternal security and consider both Calvinist and Arminian exegesis.

The Experimental Predestinarian

It is important at the outset of our discussion that we define our terms carefully. Some, for example, maintain that historically the doctrine of perseverance meant only that no true Christian would ever commit apostasy. While there may have been some who limited the doctrine to this mere continuation of belief, the vast majority of the Reformed confessions and the theological works definitely viewed perseverance as a perseverance in good works.

According to the Protestant creeds. From the earliest post-Reformation creeds, perseverance was always connected with a life of practical victory against sin as well as continuation of faith.[11]

The specific occasion of the discussion of perseverance in the Canons of Dort (1619) was the controversy with the Remonstrants who denied this doctrine. The Canons make it explicitly clear that, even though a believer may lapse into carnality for a time, he will always return to repentance:

> *By such enormous sins, however, they very highly offend God, incur a deadly guilt, grieve the Holy Spirit, interrupt the exercise of faith, very grievously wound their consciences, and sometimes lose the sense of God's favor,* **for a time, until on their returning into the right way by serious repentance,** *the light of God's fatherly countenance again shines upon them.*[12]

A lapse is only an "interruption" and lasts only "for a time until." The doctrine of perseverance guarantees, not just that the believer will not apostatize but that, when he backslides,

> *[God] preserves in them the incorruptible seed of regeneration from perishing or being totally lost; and again, by his Word and Spirit,* **he certainly and effectually renews them to repentance,** *to a sincere and godly sorrow for their sins, that they may seek and obtain remission in the blood of the Mediator, may again experience the favor of a reconciled God, through faith adore his mercies, and henceforward more diligently work out their own salvation with fear and trembling.*[13]

When the believer falls, God "certainly and effectually" renews him to repentance so that he will more diligently work out his own salvation with fear and trembling. The assurance that God will always enable them to persevere in good

---

[11]*The Heidelberg Catechism* (1563), for example, says (Q. 127):
"Since we are so weak in ourselves that we cannot stand a moment while our deadly enemies--the devil, the world, and our own flesh--assail us without ceasing, be pleased to preserve and strengthen us by the power of the Holy Spirit, that we may make firm stand against them, and not sink in this spiritual war, until we come off at last with complete victory" (*The Heidelberg Catechism*," in Schaff, 3:355).

Perseverance is a complete victory in the spiritual war against sin and not just a refusal to commit apostasy. Furthermore, this perseverance is ultimately God's work, not ours. It is God who will "preserve and strengthen" us.

[12]"The Canons of the Synod of Dort," in Schaff, 3:593 (5.5).

[13]Ibid., 3:593-94 (5.7).

works by providing a way of escape when they fall (5.11) stimulates believers to persevere in piety, patience, prayer, and in suffering (5.12) and makes them more careful to continue in the ways of the Lord (5.11).[14]

The Westminster Confession refers to the fact of perseverance in the following manner:

> *They whom God hath accepted in His Beloved, effectually called and sanctified by His Spirit, can neither totally nor finally fall away from the state of grace; but shall certainly persevere therein to the end, and be eternally saved.*[15]

What did the Westminster divines mean by "fall away from the state of grace"? What did it mean to persevere in the state of grace? When we see what they contrasted perseverance with, it is clear that they did not limit it to a mere continuation of believing but to a perseverance in good works:

> *Nevertheless they may, through the temptations of Satan and of the world, the prevalency of corruption remaining in them, and the neglect of the means of their preservation, fall into grievous sins; and for a time continue therein: whereby they incur God's displeasure, and grieve his Holy Spirit; come to be deprived of some measure of their graces and comforts; have their hearts hardened; and their consciences wounded; hurt and scandalize others, and bring temporal judgments upon themselves.*[16]

What is prevented by the Holy Spirit is "final" falling, and falling is clearly a falling into grievous sins, not just apostasy. Furthermore, perseverance guarantees that such falling is only temporary and, as stated in the Canons of Dort, can last only "for a time."

According to the Reformed theologians. When we turn to the discussions of perseverance in the writings of Reformed theologians, it is likewise clear that a perseverance in fruit bearing is the meaning, and not just a perseverance in

---

[14]The French Confession of Faith (The Gallic Confession (1559) makes it clear that the perseverance of the saints is specifically a perseverance in the "right way" (Art. 21). "We believe also that faith is not given to the elect not only to introduce them into the right way, but also to make them continue in it to the end. For as it is God who hath begun the work, He will also perfect it" ("The French Confession of Faith," in Schaff, 3:371).

[15]"The Westminster Confession of Faith," in Schaff, 3:636 (17.1).

[16]Ibid., 3:637 (17.3).

faith.[17] For example, Calvin, in his discussion of perseverance and the good works which God works in us (Phil. 2:13), says that God "supplies the persevering effort until the effect is obtained." The effect is the willing and the working of His good pleasure. In fact, he says, in our perseverance in good works "we go on without interruption, and persevere even to the end."[18] For Calvin, the perseverance of the saints was much more than preventing their apostasy from faith; it was a positive sanctification in good works.

In his chapter on perseverance in *Redemption Accomplished and Applied*, Reformed theologian John Murray, John similarly insists that the doctrine of the saints' perseverance is a doctrine of perseverance in good works. "The crucial test of true faith," says Murray, "is endurance to the end, abiding in Christ, and continuance in his Word."[19] For Murray, the doctrine of perseverance is not just a teaching that the true Christian cannot commit apostasy but that he cannot "abandon himself to sin; he cannot come under the dominion of sin; he cannot be guilty of certain kinds of unfaithfulness." His whole chapter is a sustained argument that perseverance cannot be separated from a life of works. He says, "Let us appreciate the doctrine of the perseverance of the saints and recognize that we may entertain the faith of our security in Christ only as **we persevere in faith and holiness to the end.**"[20] For Murray, as for all the Calvinist creeds which preceded him, the doctrine of the saints' perseverance is the doctrine that those who are truly saints will persevere in faith and holiness to the final hour.

He further argues against the Arminians that such a doctrine cannot lead to antinomianism "because, by definition, it means persevering **in holiness and not in unholiness. . . .** It not only promotes but **consists in strenuous and persevering efforts after conformity to Christ.**"[21]

---

[17]Reformed Baptist theologian Augustus Strong says that the saints' perseverance is "the human side or aspect of that spiritual process which, as viewed from the divine side, we call sanctification." He speaks of it as "the voluntary continuance, on the part of the Christian, in faith and well-doing." In this he is correct. The Reformed doctrine of perseverance is simply another way of saying that justification and sanctification are united and that perseverance is the gradual growth in grace which occurs in the life of all those who are truly regenerate.

John H. Gerstner defines the doctrine of the saints' perseverance in this way:

"Theologically speaking, it refers to the fifth point of the Calvinistic doctrinal system that true Christians will continue in faith and holiness forever. Thus Jonathan Edwards finds the very definition of a Christian to be, according to John 8:31, one who continues in the Word of Christ" (John H. Gerstner, "Perseverance," in *Baker's Dictionary of Theology*, ed. Everett F. Harrison [Grand Rapids: Baker, 1960], p. 403-4).

[18]*Institutes*, 2.3.9.

[19]John Murray, *Redemption--Accomplished and Applied* (Grand Rapids: Eerdmans, 1955), p. 152.

[20]Ibid., p. 155.

[21]Gerstner, p. 404.

The outstanding Reformed theologian of the nineteenth century Charles Hodge clearly asserts the true definition of the Reformed doctrine of perseverance:

> *It must be remembered that what the Apostle argues to prove is not merely the certainty of the salvation of those that believe; but* **their certain perseverance in holiness.** *Salvation in sin, according to Paul's system, is a contradiction in terms. This* **perseverance in holiness** *is secured partly by the inward secret influence of the Spirit, and partly by all the means adapted to secure that end--instructions, admonitions, exhortations, warnings, the means of grace, and the dispensations of his providence.*[22]

The various instructions, warnings, and exhortations in the New Testament have as their object continuance in good works and holy living, not just the prevention of apostasy.

Robert Dabney, the well-known Reformed Presbyterian theologian who lectured at Union Theological Seminary in Virginia, was equally insistent that the Reformed doctrine of the saints' perseverance was not just a teaching that true saints will not commit apostasy but that they will persevere in a life of good works. He begins his discussion with Phil. 1:6 and observes, "We have here the Apostle's plain expression of his belief in the perseverance of the truly regenerate, in a state of repentance, unto the end."[23] For Dabney, the perseverance of the saints is perseverance in holiness.[24]

Similarly, Louis Berkhof defines perseverance as "that continuous operation of the Holy Spirit in the believer, by which the work of divine grace that is begun in the heart, is continued and brought to completion."[25] This, of course, closely approximates the Reformed definition of sanctification. It is not just the prevention of apostasy but the growth in holiness Berkhof intends to convey in his doctrine of the saints' perseverance. Like Hodge, he argues against the Arminians' charge of antinomianism by saying:

> *It is hard to see how a doctrine which assures the believer of a* **perseverance in holiness** *can be an incentive for sin. It would seem that* **the certainty of success in the active striving for sanctification** *would be the best possible stimulus to ever greater exertion.*[26]

---

[22]Charles Hodge, *Systematic Theology*, 3 vols. (London: James Clarke, n.d.; reprint ed., Grand Rapids: Eerdmans, 1977), 3:112-13.

[23]Dabney, *Lectures,* p. 688.

[24]Ibid., p. 692.

[25]Louis Berkhof, *Systematic Theology* (London: Banner of Truth, 1941), p. 546.

[26]Ibid., p. 548.

Like the historic creeds, Berkhof is careful to emphasize that perseverance is God's work, not ours. "It is, strictly speaking, not man but God who perseveres." He gives a formal definition of perseverance as follows: "That continuous operation of the Holy Spirit in the believer, by which the work of divine grace that is begun in the heart, is continued and brought to completion."[27]

So the doctrine of the saints' perseverance is a guarantee of success in the active striving for sanctification. That is why William Shedd discusses perseverance under the topic of sanctification in his *Dogmatic Theology*.[28] It is, in the final analysis, a perseverance in holiness and not just a preventer of apostasy.

Conclusion. This brief survey of the various confessions and theologies of the Reformed faith leads to this definition of the Reformed doctrine of perseverance:

1. All who have been justified by God's grace will never lose their justification.
2. Instead, they will persevere in a life of good works and holiness to the final hour.
3. This perseverance is the work of God in which man co-operates.
4. The amount of good works will vary, but the thrust and direction of the life will always be toward holiness.
5. When they fall into sin, their fall will only be temporary, and they will always (if they are truly regenerate) come to repentance. As Thiessen put it, they will not "fail to return from their backsliding in the end."[29]

In describing the adherents of the Reformed doctrine of perseverance, some ambiguity results. Historically, this doctrine grew up in the Puritan tradition, and they called themselves "experimentalists." This is because they felt that, in order to ascertain whether or not one was a Christian, one must perform an experiment. He must ask, "Have I believed?" and "Are their evidences of works in my life?" If the answer to these questions was yes, he was justified in claiming that he was probably saved. Of course, the final verdict could only be rendered at the end of life when the evidence of final perseverance was compiled. They commonly employed what is called the practical syllogism:

Major Premise: *Those who have believed and give evidence of sanctification are saved.*

---

[27]Ibid., p. 546.

[28]William G. T. Shedd, *Dogmatic Theology*, 3 vols. (New York: Charles Scribner's Sons, 1889; reprint ed., Minneapolis: Klock and Klock, 1979), p. 557.

[29]Henry Clarence Thiessen, *Lectures in Systematic Theology*, rev. Vernon D. Doerksen (Grand Rapids: Eerdmans, 1979), p. 294.

| **Minor Premise:** | *I have believed and have some evidences.* |
| **Conclusion:** | *I am saved.* |

This approach to assurance is "experimental." The hypothesis "I am saved" is being tested by an experiment.

A second distinguishing mark of those within this tradition has been a strong emphasis upon eternal predestination. In addition, these Puritan divines placed unusual emphasis on the doctrines of particular grace and limited atonement, a logical (but not exegetical!) extension of predestination. A helpful label then would include the words "experimental" and "predestination." R. T. Kendall has suggested the label "Experimental Predestinarians," which will be used throughout this book.[30]

The Partaker

This book will discuss three basic theological approaches to the questions of security and perseverance. While labels often import connotations not shared by those designated, they are nevertheless helpful in distinguishing between positions. In this book the term "Arminian" refers to those followers of Jacobus Arminius who have held that it is possible for a true Christian to lose his salvation. For them the warning passages (e.g., Heb. 6) refer to regenerate people. The term "Calvinist" will refer to those who feel that one who is born again cannot lose his salvation and will necessarily and inevitably continue in good works until the end of life (the "Experimental Predestinarian"). The warning passages, according to the Experimental Predestinarian, are addressed to unregenerate people who have professed faith in Christ but who do not possess Christ in the heart. The designation for the third position will similarly be derived from a person, although this person is not mentioned by name but by his distinguishing characteristic:

For we have become **partakers** *of Christ, if we hold fast the beginning of our assurance firm until the end* (Heb. 3:14 NASB).

The word "Partaker" will designate the third theological approach to security. The Partaker is one who, like the Calvinist, holds to the eternal security of the Christian but, like the Arminian, believes the warning passages in the New Testament apply to true Christians. The Partaker is the Christian who perseveres in good works to the end of life. He is the faithful Christian who will reign with Christ in the coming messianic kingdom. He will be one of the servant kings. What is in danger, according to the Partaker, is not a loss of salvation but spiri-

---

[30]Kendall, *English Calvinism*, p. 9.

tual impoverishment, severe discipline in time, and a forfeiture of reward, viz., disinheritance in the future. For the Partaker the carnal Christian is not only a lamentable fact of Christian experience but is explicitly taught in the Bible as well.

A comparison and contrast between these three theological positions--the Arminian, the Experimental Predestinarian, and the Partaker--will constitute a major portion of this book. It will be helpful to state at the outset the precise distinctives of the Partaker doctrine.

The Partaker view of eternal security may be summarized as follows:

1.   Those who have been born again will always[31] give some evidence of growth in grace and spiritual interest and commitment. A man who claims he is a Christian and yet never manifests any change at all has no reason to believe he is justified (Mk. 4:5, 16-17).

2.   The assurance of salvation is found only by looking outward to Christ and not by looking inward to the evidences of regeneration in the life. As the gospel promise and the beauty of the Redeemer are held before the believer's gaze, assurance is the result of such contemplation. The fruits of faith are helpful as secondary confirmations of one's regenerate state, but their absence does not necessarily invalidate a man's salvation. If a believer is looking biblically and dependently to Christ, a life-style of sin will be psychologically, spiritually, and biblically impossible (Rom. 6:1, 11; 8:35-39; Heb. 11:1-2).

3.   It is possible for true Christians to fail to persevere in faith and, in remote cases, even to deny the faith altogether (Heb. 10:26, 35). While initial growth is taught in the New Testament, it is possible for a true Christian to lapse into carnality and finish his course walking as a mere man. The automatic unity between justification and sanctification maintained by the Experimental Predestinarians is not taught in Scripture.

4.   The warning passages of the New Testament are intended by the New Testament writers to address regenerate people, not merely

---

[31]This is true because (1) at conversion a person has repented, changed his perspective about sin and Christ and is therefore predisposed to allow Christ to change him; (2) he has been flooded with the new motivations toward godliness accompanied by the indwelling of the Holy Spirit; and (3) the parable of the soil says of the first man there was growth, a kind of fruit. But he may soon after quench the Spirit, walk by means of the flesh, and thus fail to give visible evidences of these initial inner workings. A life of sanctification will not inevitably and necessarily follow justification.

professing people, and to express real dangers to the regenerate. The danger, however, is not loss of salvation but severe divine discipline (physical death or worse) in the present time and loss of reward, and even rebuke, at the judgment seat of Christ.

5. A life of good works is the obligatory outcome of justification but is not the inevitable outcome (Rom. 8:12).

6. Those whom God has chosen before the foundations of the world and efficaciously called into saving faith and regenerated by His Holy Spirit can never fall away from salvation, but they shall be preserved in a state of salvation to the final hour and be eternally saved. This preservation is guaranteed regardless of the amount of works or lack thereof in the believer's life (Jn. 6:38-40).

7. The motive for godly living is not to be found in either fear of losing salvation (Arminian) or wondering if one is saved (Experimental Predestinarian). Rather, it is to be found, negatively, in the fear of disapproval, and, positively, in gratitude for a salvation already assured and in anticipation of hearing the Master say, "Well done!" The doctrine of eternal rewards usually has a more prominent place in spiritual inspiration toward a life of good works in the Partaker view than in that of the Arminian or Experimental Predestinarian (1 Cor. 9:24-27; 2 Cor. 5:10; Jn. 8).[32]

A conversation recently held with an articulate exponent of the Experimental Predestinarian position revealed once again how difficult communication can sometimes be. Listening to this well-known theologian describe what he thought to be the position of those called Partakers, it was evident how thoroughly our biases and theological background can hinder our abilities to understand one another. We were discussing saving faith. In this scholar's frame of reference there were only two possibilities regarding faith--it was either mere intellectual assent or personal commitment. That there was a third possibility, reliance and inner conviction, did not seem to occur to him. Furthermore, if you did not hold to his view that faith was commitment, this, in his thinking, meant that you believed all that was necessary for salvation was that you pray a prayer or intellectually accept some facts. In addition, this meant that you actively taught that there were two optional classes of Christians, carnal or spiritual, and that it was all right to be either one!

For those who may assume that this is either the direct teaching or the logical implication of the Partaker position, please withhold judgment until you

---

[32]John MacArthur, for example, has only one sentence devoted to the subject in his entire book on discipleship, p. 145.

have finished these pages! Like our Experimental Predestinarian friends, we would have serious doubts about the salvation of a man who claims he is a Christian and gives little or no evidence of it in his life. We would not give assurance of salvation to such an individual. We, too, are concerned about those who seem to think they can pray a prayer and live indifferently to Christ's claims and yet maintain the fiction that they will go to heaven anyway.

There is no question that there seems to be a general lack of vitality in many parts of the Western church today. Whether or not many who profess Christ are truly regenerate, none can say with certainty. However, we can all agree that the problem of spiritual lethargy, lukewarm Christians, and even carnality is widespread and must be addressed. It may be that a major cause of this difficulty is that we have not challenged our congregations with the sobering realities of our glorious future. It is mankind's destiny to "rule and have dominion," and that destiny has yet to be fulfilled. However, if the Partaker view of perseverance is right, only those Christians who persevere in a life of good works will have a share in this future glory. For the unfaithful Christian there will be shame and profound regret when he stands before the Lord at the judgment seat of Christ.

In the Experimental Predestinarian view, all who are Christians will be rewarded, and some more than others. Thus, they have created a version of Christianity where complete commitment is optional and not necessary. All that can be lost is a higher degree of blessedness, but all will be blessed. Could it be that this happy ending has lulled many into thinking they can continue their lukewarmness with no eternal consequences to pay?

To answer this question, we must consider some foundational thoughts. It appears that some interpretive principles are at the root of much of the controversy between the Calvinist and the Arminian.

Chapter 2

Interpretation and Perseverance

In recent years it has become quite fashionable to speak of the power of paradigms. Originally a Greek scientific term, today the word "paradigm" more commonly refers to a perception, a model, or a frame of reference. It is the way we "see" the world. The reason paradigms are said to have "power" is that they determine how we perceive things. They are lurking in the background of virtually every conclusion we make. We seldom question their accuracy, and we are usually unaware that we even have them. We commonly **assume** that the way we see things is the way they really are. Our attitudes, behaviors, and even our theology often grow out of these assumptions. The way we see things unconsciously affects our conclusions. This is why two theologians can look at the same data and come to radically opposite conclusions. It is not that the facts are different, but the paradigms which they bring to the facts determine the interpretations.

Stephen Covey illustrates this phenomenon with an experience which happened to him one Sunday morning on a subway in New York. People were sitting quietly. Some were reading newspapers, some were lost in thought, and some were resting, their eyes closed. It was apparently a calm, peaceful scene. Then suddenly a man and his children entered the subway. The children were so loud and rambunctious that the whole climate changed instantly. People in the subway were distracted and upset.

The man sat down next to him and closed his eyes, apparently oblivious to the situation. The children were yelling and throwing things, even grabbing people's papers. It was quite disturbing. And yet, while all this was going on, the man sitting next to him did nothing. It was difficult not to feel irritated. Covey could not believe that this man could be so insensitive as to let his children run wild like that and do nothing about it, taking no responsibility at all. It was easy to see that everyone else on the subway felt irritated, too. So finally Covey, with what he felt was unusual patience and restraint, turned to him and said, "Sir, your children are really disturbing a lot of people. I wonder if you couldn't control them a little more?"

The man lifted his gaze as if to come to a consciousness of the noise for the first time and said softly, "Oh, you're right. I guess I should do something about it. We just came from the hospital where their mother died about an hour ago. I don't know what to think, and I guess they don't know how to handle it either."

Covey continues: "Can you imagine what I felt at that moment? My paradigm shifted. Suddenly I **saw** things differently, and because I **saw** differently, I **thought** differently, I **felt** differently, I **behaved** differently. My irritation vanished. I didn't have to worry about controlling my attitude or my behavior; my heart was filled with the man's pain. Feelings of sympathy and compassion flowed freely. 'Your wife just died? Oh, I'm so sorry! Can you tell me about it? What can I do to help?' Everything changed in an instant."[1]

In order for some readers of this book to share the author's conclusions, they will need to undergo a paradigm shift. Such a shift often happens after we have reflected on things and sincerely tried to see them from a different point of view. It is that "Aha!" experience we feel when things fall into place for the first time. Our perceptions change and, with them, how we interpret the data of our sensory experience.

All interpreters of Scripture bring certain paradigms to their reading of the Bible. These paradigms are "givens." They are things we do not need to think about. They are "obviously" true. Often we are unaware we have them until data which challenges them is presented. At that point we can either reinterpret that data within the framework of our old paradigm or begin to do some fundamental thinking. Perhaps our paradigm is wrong.

About fifteen years ago the writer underwent such a paradigm shift which has resulted in a different way of understanding numerous difficult and often perplexing passages in the New Testament. He concluded that his theological traditions sometimes hindered, rather than illuminated, his understanding of the Bible. The reader is invited on a journey of discovery. A journey which will take him to familiar passages. Yet as he travels, he will be asked to consider the data from a different point of view.

Such a request is difficult to make due to the very nature of this book. It is a book of polemical theology. From beginning to end the author is attempting to persuade the reader of a particular point of view. Having been exposed to these kinds of books himself, the writer knows full well that his own initial reaction to such presentations is to continue to interpret the data from the perspective of his settled paradigms. It is usually proper and natural that we do this.

As the reader journeys to various sections of Scripture and is asked to see the same data from a different paradigm, he will often have the thought, Yes, but

---

[1]Stephen R. Covey, *The Seven Habits of Highly Effective People* (New York: Simon and Schuster, 1989), pp. 30-31.

what about this other passage and what about . . . ? Those desiring to get the most out of this book will need to hold their opinions until the last page. A complete index to every Scripture reference is included. Hopefully, passages which seem to contradict certain interpretations will be found in this index.

We now commence our journey with a discussion of two exegetical issues which must first be cleared away if we are to correctly understand how the New Testament writers viewed the perseverance of the saints. The paradigm shift begins.

Theological Exegesis

It is widely recognized that differing canons of interpretation play a determinative role in theological discussion. The entire difference between the premillennialist and amillennialist views of Old Testament prophecy, for example, are basically differences in interpretive approach. The amillennialist feels he has New Testament justification for spiritualizing the Old Testament predictions and applying them to the church. He believes the New Testament authors did this. The premillennialist feels that no New Testament author would have spiritualized a prophetic utterance so that its meaning differed from the intended meaning of the original author.

What is not widely recognized, however, is that this same hermeneutical difference underlies much of the dispute on the doctrine of perseverance. What is the ultimate determinant of the meaning of a particular text: the intent of the original author or a comparison of that text with other texts (selected by the interpreter)?

Possibly aware that strict attention to the intended meaning of texts could yield theological conclusions at variance with his, Charles Hodge, Charles vigorously protests, "They [Arminians] seem to regard it as a proof of independence to make each passage mean simply what its grammatical structure and logical connection indicate, without the least regard to the analogy of Scripture."[2] No doubt his Arminian opponents would view this as a caricaturization. They, too, are interested in the analogy of Scripture.

Should the single intent of the original author be the primary determinant in our theological constructs? It seems that the answer to that question is obvious. Yes! If the intent of the original author does not determine meaning, then someone else's intent, that of the interpreter, takes over, and all controls are lost. It is not accidental that the biblical theology movement has tended to agree with the premillennialist in the fact that the Old Testament teaches the future exis-

---

[2]Charles Hodge, *Systematic Theology*, 3 vols. (London: James Clarke, n.d.; reprint ed., Grand Rapids: Eerdmans, 1977), 3:167.

tence of a literal earthly kingdom. Their emphasis upon the will of the writer of the book yields such a conclusion.

The Protestant doctrine of the analogy of faith has, in practice, sometimes become what might be called "theological exegesis." What started as a valid attempt to allow other Scriptures to help interpret the meaning of obscure passages has gradually become a method of interpreting obviously clear passages in a way that will harmonize with a particular theological tradition. Instead of permitting each text to speak for itself, the theological system determines the meaning. For example, consider a common interpretation of Rom. 2:6-7:

> *Who will render to every man according to his deeds: to those who by perseverance in doing good seek for glory and honor and immortality, eternal life; but to those who are selfishly ambitious and do not obey the truth, but obey unrighteousness, wrath and indignation.*

Now there is nothing obscure about this passage at all. It says that those who persevere in doing good will obtain eternal life. However, because that seems to involve a contradiction with the doctrine of justification by faith alone, our theological system is brought in to save the day:

> *A person's habitual conduct, whether good or evil, reveals the condition of his heart. Eternal life is not rewarded for good living; that would contradict many other Scriptures which clearly state that salvation is not by works, but is all of God's grace to those who believe (e.g., Rom. 6:23; 10:9-10; 11:6; Eph. 2:8-9; Titus 3:5). A person's doing good* **shows** *that his heart is regenerate. Such a person, redeemed by God, has eternal life.*[3]

It may be true that a person's "habitual conduct" reveals the condition of his heart, but the text is not addressing that issue. According to Paul, eternal life **is** "rewarded for good living." How else could he say it: "God will render to every man **according to his deeds**"? Shouldn't we let this stand?[4]

Although Turretin demanded that "an empty head . . . must be brought to Scripture,"[5] it is, of course, impossible to remove the analogy of faith from our exegesis; indeed, it would not be proper to do so. All of us approach the Bible with certain theological preunderstandings, certain paradigms. Even when we are conscious of them, it is still difficult to negate their controlling influence. Johnson is correct when he observes:

---

[3]John A. Witmer, "Romans," in *BKC,* 2 vols. (Wheaton, IL: Victor, 1983), 1:445.

[4]How this can be reconciled with Paul's doctrine of justification by faith alone will be considered in chapter 7, "Inheriting Eternal Life."

[5]Turretin, cited by H. Wayne Johnson, "The 'Analogy of Faith' and Exegetical Methodology: A Preliminary Discussion on Relationships," *JETS* 31 (March 1988): 76.

It seems reasonable that the agenda we set for ourselves, the problems for which we seek exegetical solutions, reflect our understanding of tension and harmony with what the rest of what Scripture clearly teaches. And is not the exegetical question that we ask just as important as the exegetical means we use to answer that question?[6]

There is no question that there has been a heavy influence by the analogy of faith in the interpretations to follow. A Reformed background has informed the writer's preunderstanding of numerous passages. The problem is that this background seemed to conflict with the plain sense, thus creating the tension of which Johnson speaks and so setting the exegetical agenda for this book.

The analogy of faith, therefore, should only be viewed as one element of the exegetical process. It should not dictate our exegesis, substitute for exegesis, or simply be subsequent to exegesis. Rather, it is part of valid exegetical procedure, but its use should be postponed until a very late stage.

Illegitimate Totality Transfer

Another exegetical error which has tended to obfuscate the clarity of vision of the disputants over the doctrine of perseverance is what James Barr calls "illegitimate totality transfer":

The error that arises, when the "meaning" of a word (understood as the total series of relations in which it is used in the literature) is read into a particular case as its sense and implication there, may be called 'illegitimate totality transfer.'[7]

Kittel's famous *Theological Dictionary of the New Testament* has been severely criticized from this vantage point by Barr. Kittel, contrary to popular perception, is not just a dictionary. He tells us in the introduction that external lexicography (i.e., meanings derived from dictionaries and concordance usage) is not his purpose. Rather, his burden is what he calls "internal lexicography."[8] By this he means "concept history." His burden is to present the "theological idea" behind a word. The result is that we do not always get from Kittel the meaning of the word but the theology of it as perceived by the writer of the particular article. Users of this dictionary often make the mistake of citing Kittel as a lexical rather than a theological authority. While this is sometimes justified, these volumes need to be read with discrimination.

---

[6]Ibid., 76-77.

[7]James Barr, *The Semantics of Biblical Languages* (London: Oxford University Press, 1961), p. 218.

[8]*TDNT*, 1:vii.

As an illustration of this faulty procedure, it will be helpful to consider its application to one of the key words utilized by Experimental Predestinarians in support of their idea that submission to the lordship of Christ and perseverance in that submission to the final hour are the necessary evidences of the truly re-generate.

Regarding repentance, a person could hold the view that repentance means "turning from sin" and is a necessary ingredient of saving faith and still deny the Reformed doctrine of perseverance. However, it seems that those who believe that repentance is a condition of salvation and that it means "turning from sin" are sometimes guilty of Barr's illegitimate totality transfer.

Most would agree that the basic meaning of **metanoeo** is simply to "change the mind."[9] But often Reformed writers go beyond this meaning and read into it the notion of "turn from sin." In some cases they base their appeal on some stan-dard theological dictionaries. Yet these lexical authorities have often been guilty of a "theological idea" kind of lexicography. They have in mind a theological idea of repentance, that it involves turning from sin and conversion, and they read that theological idea into the various texts they quote.

For example, in support of his idea that repentance is a "repudiation of the old life and turning to God"[10] one writer cites Behm's article in the *Theological Dictionary of the New Testament*. Behm claims that repentance "demands radical conversion, a transformation of nature, a definitive turning from evil, a resolute turning to God in total obedience."[11] Behm seems to be using an incorrect pro-cedure, however, in order to come to the conclusion that **metanoeo**, "repent," means to "turn from sin." Consistent with the stated purpose of the dictionary, Behm is looking for the concept of repentance and not the meaning of the word. In so doing, he has an idea in mind, conversion, and believes that conversion and repentance are interchangeable ideas.

Yet he candidly admits, "The Greek world offers no true linguistic or ma-terial basis for the NT understanding of **metanoeo** and **metanoia** as conversion." Furthermore, he says that "the LXX does not use this word in translating the OT" and that **metanoeo** is "rare in the LXX" and is used for "to regret" and "to change one's mind." When he comes to the Old Testament, he says, "the prophets do not invent a special word for true repentance but make do with the common word for return (**shub**)."[12] The problem is that **shub** is never translated in the LXX as **metanoeo**.

---

[9]John MacArthur, *The Gospel According to Jesus* (Grand Rapids: Zondervan, 1988), p. 162.
[10]Ibid.
[11]Johannes Behm, "**metanoia**," in *TDNT*, 4:1002.
[12]Johannes Behm, "**metanoia**," in *TDNTA*, pp. 639-41.

After admitting that neither the Greek world nor the Old Testament gives him any basis for equating repentance with conversion, or turning from sin, he concludes that he will interpret the New Testament usage of the words in light of the Old Testament **concept** of conversion. He does this even though he has admitted that in no place in the Old Testament are the words used for that concept![13] He says that the usual meaning is "'change of mind' or 'conversion' with the full OT nuance."[14] But he has given no evidence that conversion and repentance are ever equated in the Old Testament.[15]

Goetzman experienced the same difficulty in his frustration over the lack of Old Testament support for the idea that repentance means "to turn from sin." He, like Behm, wants to equate it with conversion but admits that "we are not helped by the LXX. It does not use the noun."[16] In fact, the "thought of turning round, preached especially by the prophets and expressed by the Hebrew verb **shub**, is rendered by **epistrepho** in Greek."[17] So, contrary to Behm, the prophet does **not** "make do" with the Hebrew word **shub.** Behm has a theological idea of conversion in mind and needs an Old Testament word which is consistent with this idea, so he goes to **shub.** Never mind that **metanoeo** is never the translation of **shub**; it must be equated with repentance anyway because the theological idea of repentance is equated with conversion! Basically, his procedure boils down to assuming, before looking at the evidence, that repentance is part of a group of words suggesting the theological idea of turning from sin, then going to the Bible and finding words which speak of turning. He then equates repentance with those words. The justification is that they are all part of the same "idea." But

---

[13]Because he is looking for a theological idea rather than the meaning of the word, Behm feels free to go to any passage in the New Testament which contains his idea--turn from sin--and use it to support his notion that repentance means to turn from sin. For example, he appeals to Mt. 5:29-30 and 10:32 where the words **metanoeo** and **metanoia** are not even used and uses these passages to define the meaning of these words (p. 643)! A pronounced illustration of faulty procedure is his use of Matt 18:3, "Unless you are converted and become like children, you shall not enter the kingdom of heaven." He wants "converted" to be equated with "repent," but it is a different word. Furthermore, the idea of becoming like a little child does not mean to turn from sin but to be humble and trusting like a child. Children normally are not viewed as needing to turn from sin, so this is not the likely meaning of repent when applied to them.

[14]Behm, *TDNTA,* p. 642.

[15]This writer is not the only one who has noted this faulty methodology in Behm's article. Sauer, a very articulate Experimental Predestinarian, in an excellent doctoral dissertation observes, "Behm commits a lexical **faux pas** that has far reaching consequences in his article on repentance" (R. C. Sauer, "A Critical and Exegetical Reexamination of Hebrews 5:11-6:8" [Ph.D. dissertation, University of Manchester, 1981], p. 305).

[16]J. Goetzmann, "Conversion," in *NIDNTT,* 1:357.

[17]Ibid.

how does one know what the idea is unless he first considers each word independently?[18]

It seems that **metanoeo** is used in different ways in the New Testament and in the Greek Old Testament, the LXX.

1.   A change of mind (Heb. 12:17; Jon. 3:9-10; 4:2; Amos 7:3, 6; Joel 2:13-14; Acts 2:38).

2.   As a virtual synonym for reliant trust or faith (Acts 20:21).

In Acts 20:21 repentance and faith are united in the same verse. Because they are both joined by one article, it is possible (but not necessary!) that the essential equality of the two words is stressed with the second simply a further description of the first:[19]

Solemnly testifying to both Jews and Greeks of [the] repentance toward God and faith in our Lord Jesus Christ (NASB).

Thus, repentance and faith can be used in some passages as synonyms. This is easy to explain because any time one shifts his trust from himself to God and believes that Jesus is God, he has changed his perspective; he has repented.

3.   A turning from sin as a preparatory stage prior to saving faith (Mt. 4:17; Lk. 3:3), or possibly, a challenge to "get right with God" (Mt. 12:41).

It is not always clear what Jesus and John meant when they said, "Repent, for the kingdom of heaven is at hand." It could simply mean confess your sins and turn from them and prepare to receive the coming Messiah. This would simply mean that the call to confession is, in this instance, preparation for saving faith. It could also mean what an evangelist today might mean by "get right with

---

[18]Sometimes appeal is made to 1 Th. 1:9 where the conversion experience of the Thessalonians is described as "turning": "You turned to God from idols to serve a living and true God." This then is used as proof that metanoia includes the idea of turning, and yet the word metanoia is not even used in 1 Th. 1:9! Often repentance is connected with epistrepho, "to turn." A study of this word is interesting, but it is irrelevant to the meaning of metanoia. The only possible connection with repentance is a theological tradition that says repentance must mean "turning." Then a Greek word which does mean "turning" is found, equated with repentance, and offered as proof that repentance means turning! This is what Barr means by theological idea kind of lexicography. Interestingly, Goetzmann's article on metanoia is not even listed under "repentance" but, rather, under "conversion." Ignoring Colin Brown's introductory warnings about the dangers of Barr's "illegitimate totality transfer" (p. 10), Goetzmann, like Behm, pursues the theological idea kind of lexicography.

[19]The Granville Sharp rule of grammar. See DM, p. 147. However, this rule does not always apply. For example, note "the Epicureans and Stoics" (Acts 17:18) and "the Pharisees and Sadducees" (Acts 23:7).

God." When confronted with broken lives, he appeals, "Friends, your only hope is to get right with God." If they ask how to do this, he says, "First, you must become a Christian, and then you must live like it." He would then give them the gospel and challenge them to come to Christ through faith alone and receive forgiveness. Then he would challenge them to live the Christian life and give them practical counsel. The entire challenge may be termed repentance. But repentance is not a condition of salvation in this sense but a condition of "getting right with God," which includes faith plus submission to his lordship.

The word "salvation" means "rescue or deliverance." However, the context obviously determines what kind of deliverance is in view. Sometimes it refers to deliverance from hell, sometimes from a temporal danger, and sometimes from a disease, i.e., a healing. Similarly, the semantic value of **metanoeo** is only "to change the mind." Context must determine what the change is about. It could be a change of verdict about who Christ really is (Acts 2:38), or it could refer to a change of mind about sin, and hence a contextually added nuance of a turning from sin.

Now it is clear that, in contexts where the meaning is "to change one's mind about sin," the word is not being used as a condition of final deliverance from hell. We know this must be true for two reasons: (1) in no passage where "repentance" is used in the sense of "to turn from sin" can it be demonstrated that it is a condition of salvation, and (2) it is impossible that it could be because the Bible everywhere attests that salvation is by faith alone, and without cost:

> *I will give to the one who thirsts from the spring of the water of life* **without cost** (Rev. 21:6 NASB).

> *And let the one who is thirsty come; let the one who wishes take the water of life* **without cost** (Rev. 22:17 NASB).

> *But to the one who does not work, but believes in Him who justifies the ungodly, his faith is reckoned as righteousness* (Rom. 4:5 NASB).

> *Did you receive the Spirit by the works of the Law, or* **by hearing with faith** (Gal. 3:2 NASB).

Faith occurs by "hearing" and is the opposite of any work, and so salvation comes to us "without cost." If we have to pledge something to God, such as a life of submission, then how does this differ from a work? Even if God works in us to enable us and motivate us to pledge submission, this is still a work, either God-enabled, or human. One thing is that, whatever the condition of salvation is, it is not a divine work in us or a human work. If we have to pledge something of ourselves to God, such as turning from sin, how can salvation be without cost? If one has to give up something, pledge something, or commit to do something, how can it be said that salvation is a gift and without cost? In fact, it would appear in the

Experimental Predestinarian system that it costs us everything, our entire life. Therefore, repentance, understood as a turning from sin, cannot be included in saving faith or added to it.

The preceding paragraph has alluded to a common Experimental Predestinarian view that repentance is worked in us by God and hence, even though it is a work, it is God's work in us, and not a human work. Apparently thinking that only human works can be prohibited as conditions of salvation, Experimental Predestinarians believe they have escaped the charge of a works salvation. But when does God work this work of repentance? If it is a result of salvation, then repentance is not a condition of salvation. On the other hand, if it precedes salvation, then reformation of life precedes faith and regeneration and so is a condition of receiving it. Indeed, we are then making sanctification (i.e., "turning from sin") a condition of receiving our regeneration.

No doubt our Experimental Predestinarian friends would reply that these events are compressed to a point in time, but there is a logical sequence. That is precisely the problem, the logical sequence and not the time which transpires. As long as repentance precedes salvation, then a work precedes regeneration and is a condition of grace, even though it may be a divine work. If it follows, it is not a condition. It should also be pointed out that few follow the Calvinists on this point--that a man can be saved before he believes. Would it not be better to base our doctrine of the conditions of salvation on something more substantial than this obscure and controversial point of Westminster Calvinism?

It is clear that "turn from sin" cannot be part of the semantic value of the word **metanoia** because there are passages in which that sense is impossible.[20] For example, in Heb. 12:17 the NIV translation reads:

> *Afterward, as you know, when he wanted to inherit this blessing, he was rejected. He could bring about no change of mind* [Gk. **metanoia**], *though he sought the blessing with tears.*

Esau was either unable to change Isaac's mind or unable to change the decision he himself had made. He was unable to reverse the situation. Esau found his act was unalterable. There is no possibility that repentance could mean turn from sin here. It would be a non sequitur to say, "Esau could not turn from sin" and then say, "though he sought the blessing with tears." His tears would seem to indicate that he had changed his mind, but it was too late.

Consider also the LXX use of **metanoeo** in Jon. 3:9-10 and 4:2 where God changes his mind about destroying Nineveh and about laying waste to Israel's

---

[20]Trench agrees, "This is all imported into, does not etymologically nor yet by primary usage lie in, the word" (Richard Chenevix Trench, *Synonyms of the New Testament* [London: 1880; reprint ed., Grand Rapids: Eerdmans, 1953], p. 259).

spring crop (Amos 7:3) and farm land (Amos 7:6; Joel 2:13-14). Now it is clear that turning from sin cannot be part of the semantic value of the word, or God turns from sin. These passages make it clear that repentance is simply to change one's mind.[21]

One writer forcefully insists, "No evangelism that omits the message of repentance can properly be called the gospel, for sinners cannot come to Jesus Christ apart from a radical change of heart, mind, and will."[22] Would it not follow then that the Gospel of John, which never mentions repentance, cannot properly be called the gospel? Nowhere does the apostle present any other means except "believe" as a means for salvation. If repentance and surrender to the lordship of Christ are necessary means of salvation, the gospel of John would be incapable of achieving its intended aim (Jn. 20:31).

When advocates of this position insist that faith includes the notion of repentance, they are again committing the error of the illegitimate totality transfer, this time in regard to faith. Beginning as they do with the theological idea that salvation must involve submission to Christ's lordship and realizing that "faith" does not mean that, they import into it the conclusions of their views on conversion, turning from sin, and repentance, and make faith a very pregnant concept indeed! There is no place, however, in John's gospel where the concept of turning from sin or submission to Christ's lordship is either stated or implied in the gospel offer. The fact that reformation of life may have occurred in the case of the woman at the well does not argue that a commitment to reformation was part of the gospel offer. It only shows that she responded to the free offer in grace with the anticipated gratitude which normally follows the salvation experience. The response cannot logically be assumed to be part of the cause.

However, if we understand repentance in its basic sense as "a change of mind" or "change of perspective," then it is easy to see why the word was not included in John's gospel. Anytime a man believes, a certain change of mind is involved. In fact, the change of mind demanded in the New Testament is to trust in Christ instead of institutional Judaism. That is why repentance can be used by itself, and when it is, it is virtually a synonym for faith. The problem for Experimental Predestinarians is that, even though usage and the standard lexicons admit that the words are primarily mental acts and not volitional surrender, they must be made to mean volitional surrender in order to square them with the Reformed doctrine of perseverance and with the notion that discipleship is a condition for becoming a Christian.

---

[21]See Behm, *TDNTA*, p. 641. That "turn from sin" is not part of the semantic value of the word **metanoeo** is proven by the fact that in the LXX it is said that God repented (Gk. **metanoeo** in 1 Sam. 15:29 and Jer. 4:27-28).

[22]MacArthur, p. 167.

Space cannot be taken here to adequately discuss the question of the meaning of repentance in the New Testament.[23] The point here is simply that the procedure used to settle the question is sometimes faulty. Is it acceptable to combine words like "turn" (Gk. **epistrepho**; Heb. **shub**) and "conversion" and "repentance" into a theological concept of repentance? Can we then invest the Greek word **metanoeo** with all these ideas and then read them into the usages of the word throughout the New Testament? The answer according to James Barr is no. This pregnant meaning of "repentance" is far removed from its semantic value, "change of mind." This new sense, now "great with child," has given birth to a theology of faith and salvation which is far removed from the simple gospel offer.

This practice of going through the concordance, noting usage in various contexts, adding all the usages up, reading them into the semantic value of the word, and carrying that freighted new meaning into other contexts is an illegitimate totality transfer.[24] It is quite common to hear in theological discussion, "The usage is predominantly 'this,' so it is likely that this is the sense in this particular passage." One must be careful when using such a statistical approach. As Louw has pointed out, "A word does not have a meaning without a context, it only has possibilities of meaning."[25]

Frequency of use only suggests a probable meaning which would be suggested to a reader in the absence of any contextual indicators as to what is meant. "Open the trunk" would probably be understood by most Americans as "Open the rear end of the car," unless the context had placed them in the attic of the house. Those from England, however, would probably understand the sentence to mean, "Open the box."

Suppose, for example, an "exegete" had been reading a mystery novel which involved many chapters of discussion regarding the contents of the trunk in the attic. The size of the trunk, the color of the trunk, and, most important, clues to its contents were the subject of pages of intrigue. Then a bit unexpectedly he reads, "He went to the driveway and opened the trunk." Our exegete "knows" theologically that "trunks" refer to boxes in the attic. From usage, therefore, he assumes that it must have been temporarily moved to the driveway. It is statistically more probable that a colored box of a certain size is meant. So theological exegesis is brought in to force the word "trunk" to mean "box," and the illegitimate totality transfer is made to speculate on its color, size, and other characteristics. After the required footnotes, which establish that the author has read and interacted with the "literature," and discussion of the use of the word "trunk" by "this

---

[23]For views similar to those that this writer holds, see Charles Ryrie, *So Great Salvation* (Wheaton, IL: Victor, 1989), pp. 91-100.

[24]Barr, pp. 206-62.

[25]J. P. Louw, *Semantics of New Testament Greek* (Philadelphia: Fortress; Chico, CA: Scholars Press, 1982), p. 40.

particular author in all prior examples," we are told that apparently the box was moved to the driveway even though there is no mention of this in the text. The absurdity of this is at once apparent. The meanings of words are primarily determined by the usage in a particular context and that has more force than a hundred usages elsewhere. Trunks in driveways are the posteriors of automobiles! The context determines the meaning. The study of usages helps determine the range of known meanings but not the meaning in a particular context. A good exegete of the above story would know that usage establishes that the word "trunk," when connected in context with an automobile, regularly signifies a storage area in an auto, not in an attic.

An error related to the so-called illegitimate totality transfer is what Barr calls the illegitimate identity transfer. This occurs when a meaning in one context is made to be the meaning in all contexts. The discussion of "trunk" above illustrates this. But perhaps a biblical illustration will be helpful. James Rosscup appears to commit the error of the illegitimate identity transfer in his attempt to define the meaning of the "overcomer" in Rev. 2-3.[26] In 1 Jn. 5:4 it seems clear that the overcomer is a Christian and that all who are Christians are, in a particular sense, overcomers. Those who know the Lord have, according to John, overcome by virtue of the fact that they have believed and for no other reason. In Revelation, however, the overcomer is one who has "kept the word of My perseverance" (Rev. 3:10) and who "keeps My deeds until the end" (Rev. 2:26). As a result of this faithful behavior, the overcomer receives various rewards. Rosscup, in the interests of the Reformed doctrine of perseverance, wants the overcomer in 1 John (all Christians) to mean the same thing as the overcomer in Revelation. He seems to misunderstand the context of 1 John and feels it refers to tests of whether or not one is a Christian, when in fact, as will be discussed later, it refers to tests of our walk and fellowship with God. This can be twisted, but the natural sense is surely to be found in the purpose statements in the opening verses. All who are overcomers in 1 John, therefore, may or may not be walking in fellowship; all who are overcomers in Revelation are. An overcomer in 1 John is simply a Christian; an overcomer in Revelation is a persevering Christian.

Rosscup reasons that, since the overcomer in 1 John is a Christian, it must be the same in Revelation. This, however, is importing a contextually derived usage, "justified saint," into the semantic value of the word and then taking this pregnant new meaning to another context. An overcomer is simply a "victor," and the word itself does not even imply that the victor is a Christian; he could be a victor in the games.

In summary, meanings are to be derived from context. To use the analogy of the elephant's nose, the context includes such references as Africa and large elephants. In that context, to pull on the trunk clearly refers to pulling on an ele-

---

[26]James E. Rosscup, "The Overcomers of the Apocalypse," *GTJ* 3 (Fall 1982): 261-86.

phant's nose. In another context, a driveway in Dallas, Texas, in which an automobile is parked, yields a different meaning. So when someone says that they are pulling on the trunk in that context, everyone understands that they are trying to open the rear end of their car. Now in 1 John, the context is overcoming the world by faith and, as a result, becoming regenerate. In Revelation, however, the context involves overcoming by deeds of obedience, and the result is merited rewards. All Christians are overcomers in the former sense, but not all are overcomers in the latter. To import the meaning of "become a Christian by faith" from 1 John into the sense of the word in Revelation would be about as accurate as insisting that the man in Dallas who was pulling on the trunk was yanking on an elephant's nose! It is an illegitimate identity transfer.

Theological Science

It was Calvin who first formalized the science of theology. He insisted that interpretations had to have a scientific justification. The allegorizing of the Middle Ages was rejected, and sound canons of hermeneutics were embraced for the first time since Augustine. By scientific justification we mean, first of all, that, in order for an interpretation to be true, it must be grounded in the objective data of history, lexicography, culture, grammar, and context. But secondly, it must submit to a "falsifiability criterion." If contrary data invalidate it, it must be given up.

Karl Popper has made the "falsifiability criterion" a principal pillar of modern scientific investigation. In order for a theory to have any scientific value, it must be capable of being proved wrong. When dealing with an induction, we cannot always be sure that we have collected all the data, so the possibility of invalidation must always be part of a theory, or it is not a scientific theory. Similarly, a theological "theory" which is incapable of falsification is questionable in terms of its explanatory value.

The doctrine of the perseverance of the saints certainly qualifies as a valid scientific theory. It has been argued by capable men on the basis of a particular interpretation of many biblical passages. It qualifies as a scientific theory because it is capable of falsification. If there is one example in the Bible of a person who was born again, fell away from the Lord, and persisted in his disobedience up to the point of physical death, then the theory of the saints perseverance has been disproved and must, if we are honest, be abandoned. Deny this, and all theology is as worthless as straw.

In about A.D. 1300 William of Ockham introduced the scientific principle that whatever explanation involves the fewest assumptions is to be preferred. Called Ockham's Razor, it posits that any theory which, when confronted with contrary evidence, must supply secondary explanations in order to justify its existence is a bad theory. The continued introductions of secondary assumptions in order to explain the theory in the light of seemingly contradictory evidence results in a crumbling house of cards. The efficiency (explanatory value) of any theory is simply the number of facts correlated divided by the number of assumptions made.

In theology, when a particular theological position must be maintained by secondary assumptions, it is worthless. This is preeminently the case in the Experimental Predestinarians' doctrine of the saints' perseverance. When confronted with apparently contradictory evidence that a true saint in the Bible has persisted in disobedience, they will often offer the secondary assumption, based on their system, that he could not really be a true saint at all. Or when warnings are addressed to "little children," "brethren," "saints," and those "sanctified forever," a secondary assumption, not supported by the text, is brought in to say that these terms refer to "wheat and tares" and the specific descriptions are only the language of courtesy, not of fact. This continual addition of ad hoc explanations, which are either not alluded to in the texts in question or are specifically refuted by them, renders the theory useless. It becomes incapable of falsification because any data contrary to it is simply negated by additional assumptions. Text after text is often ignored in this way until the whole edifice verges on collapse like the proverbial house of cards.

Theology is a science; in fact, it was once known as the queen of the sciences. Every science is composed of two things, facts and their interpretation. The facts of astronomy do not constitute astronomy, and the facts of chemistry or history do not constitute chemistry or history. Science is the facts plus their correlation and interpretation. The Bible is no more a system of theology than nature is a system of chemistry or physics

The task of a theologian is to collect, authenticate, arrange, and explain the facts of revelation. The natural scientist does the same to the facts of nature. When he does this, however, he must not modify one experimental fact in order to accommodate it with another apparently contradictory one. Instead, he searches for a higher synthesis, larger than each fact, which will explain both. The Protestant doctrine of the analogy of faith has sometimes been extended to justify the modification of the obvious meaning of a text, the "experimental fact," in view of other facts.

The theologian must show how facts in one part of Scripture correlate and explain facts in another part, but he must not modify the facts in order to do so. The chemist does not manufacture facts; the theologian does not either. He must take them as they are. He will systematically gather all the data from revelation on a certain subject and then draw general conclusions. The Bible is to a theologian what nature is to a scientist. Our duty is to collect the facts of revelation, arrange them, and apply them to the hearts of our students. False theories in science and false doctrines in theology are often due to errors of fact. Furthermore, this collection must be comprehensive. An incomplete induction led men to believe that the sun moved around the earth.

Most important, as the student of nature must be honest, so must the theologian. Recently *Time* magazine reported that an Australian scientist had been found guilty of scientific fraud.[27] When some of his experimental data did not fit his theory, he rejected or falsified or ignored that data. *Time* asks, "Why would such a distinguished researcher fix evidence?" The investigating commission suggested that he "had been overcome by a desire to make the facts fit his theory about the drug." The group's conclusion: "Where a passionately held belief overrides scientific objectivity, and the scientist yields to the temptations to publish as facts things which he does not believe to be true, scientific fraud is committed." Who among us, as students of the Word, has not at one time or another been tempted to make the biblical facts fit into our theological theories?

If we come across biblical data that seem to contradict our system, we must be honest and reassess our system and not reinterpret that fact in light of the system. It is a life-long work. Our goal is not to defend the viewpoint of the denomination but to know the mind of God. This means that the doctrines of the Bible, like the principles and laws of natural science, are not imposed upon the facts but are derived from them.

The theologian, perhaps even more than the natural scientist, is susceptible to the temptation to be dishonest with the facts because his facts are much more important. They concern eternal issues and not just the periodic table of the elements. It is not to be implied here that those who disagree with the writer's particular interpretation are "dishonest." But after twenty years of reading the writings of the Experimental Predestinarians, studying their passages in the Greek New Testament, and interacting personally with their advocates, this writer is convinced that there is something going on here besides exegesis. An interpretive framework has so dominated their minds that their method of exegesis cannot always be called exegesis. It sometimes appears to be an honest attempt to explain away passage after passage in order to sustain a theory of the saints' perseverance at all costs. The motivation for this is pure, if unconscious. It lies in the nagging fear that, if this doctrine is abandoned, there is no answer to the Arminians with their denial of eternal security, and even more important, there is no answer to the charge of being antinomian. Indeed, to give up the doctrine of perseverance is, according to Experimental Predestinarians, to turn the grace of God into lasciviousness.

Now, of course, that does not necessarily follow, but there is no question that in some cases carnal believers will do just that. This is why Paul was charged with antinomianism (Rom. 6:1). But the Partaker's position satisfactorily answers

---

[27]Alan Atwood, "Case of the Phantom Rabbits," *Time* (December 5, 1988): 37.

the Arminian objections to eternal security by allowing the texts to speak plainly. The charge of antinomianism is also easily answered in that there is no greater inducement to godliness than the love of Christ, the unconditional acceptance of the Father, the hope of hearing him say "Well done!" and the fear of millennial disinheritance.

We must derive our doctrine from the Bible and not make the Bible teach what we think is necessary. If a man denies that an innocent man can die for the sins of the guilty, he must deny that Christ bore our sins. If a man denies that the merit of one man can be imputed to another, then he must deny the scriptural doctrine of justification. If he believes that a just God would never allow a heathen to go to hell, then he must do so contrary to the doctrine of Scripture. It is obvious that our whole system of revealed truth is useless unless we commit to derive our theology from it and not impose our theology upon it. If the Bible teaches the existence of the carnal Christian, then our system of theology must be adjusted to accommodate this fact. "It is the fundamental principle of all sciences, and of theology among the rest, that theory is to be determined by facts, and not facts by theory. As natural science was a chaos until the principle of induction was admitted and faithfully carried out, so theology is a jumble of human speculations, not worth a straw, when men refuse to apply the same principle to the study of the Word of God."[28]

---

[28]Charles Hodge, *Theology*, 1:14-15.

Chapter 3

The Inheritance: Old Testament

Stephen Covey has recently written a book which is the result of years of research in the success literature of the past two centuries. In addition, his insights have been gleaned from his twenty years of experience world wide as a management consultant to numerous corporations. He is a recognized expert on principles of personal and organizational leadership development. His experience and studies have led him to the discovery that there is a common denominator among all highly effective people--seven habits. The second habit is "begin with the end in mind."[1]

Imagine yourself driving to the funeral of a loved one. As you get out of the car and enter the funeral parlor, there are numerous flowers, friends, and relatives. Gentle music is playing in the background. The sense of sorrow and grief permeates the air, and there are many tears. As you walk down the aisle to the front of the church to look into the casket, you gasp with surprise. When you look into the casket, you see yourself. All these people are here to honor you! This is your funeral, three years from today. These gathered friends and relatives are here to express their love and appreciation.

Still stunned by what you see, you take your seat and wait for the services to begin. Glancing at the program, you note there are to be four speakers. The first is to be from your family both immediate and extended--representing children, brothers, and grandchildren, nephews, nieces, aunts, uncles, cousins, and grandparents. They have come from all over the country to be present at this event. The second speaker is your best friend. He is someone who can give a sense of who you are as a person. The third speaker is someone from your office. This person will, of course, have perspective on what kind of boss you were and what kind of employee you were. Finally, an elder from your church will be called upon to share a few personal comments.

Now think about this scene! What would you like these speakers to say about you and your life? What kind of husband, father, employee, Christian would you like their words to reflect? What contributions and achievements would you like these people to remember? Look carefully at the people around

---

[1]Stephen R. Covey, *The Seven Habits of Highly Effective People* (New York: Simon and Schuster, 1989), p. 96.

you. What difference does it make to them that you lived or died? What impact have you had in their lives?

Now, Covey counsels, take a few moments and jot down the thoughts which come to your mind--the answers to these questions. If you thought deeply about this scene, you discovered something about yourself that you may not have known before. You discovered some of your deep, fundamental values. To "begin with the end in mind" is to begin today with the image, picture, paradigm of the end of your life as the frame of reference or the criterion by which everything else in your life is examined. By doing this, each part of your life can be examined in the context of the whole according to what you have concluded is most important to you. By keeping the end in mind, you can clearly evaluate whether or not on any given day you have violated your deepest values. You can determine whether that day, that week, that month has or has not contributed toward the vision you have of life as a whole.

People often get caught in the trap of having successes at the expense of things which are really more important to them. People from all walks of life struggle daily to achieve higher income, higher position, higher honor only to find that the achievement of those goals, while not wrong in themselves, blinded them to the things which they feel at a deeper level are more important to them.

If you carefully consider what you want said at your funeral regarding you, you have defined your definition of success. It may be different from the definition you thought you had in mind. Many people have spent their lives climbing various ladders only to discover when they got to the top that the ladder was leaning against the wrong wall.

The biblical writers everywhere counsel the Christian to begin with the end in mind, to see life from the perspective of our final accountability before God. One day, at the judgment seat of Christ, we all hope to hear the words, "Well done, good and faithful servant; enter into the joy of your Lord." The general term for the end in mind used in the Bible is the "inheritance." The more material aspects of it are gradually enriched as revelation progresses through the Old Testament toward the magnificent New Testament challenge to "inherit the kingdom."

It may seem surprising that a discussion of the saints' perseverance should begin with a study of the inheritance in the Old Testament. It is therefore appropriate that at the outset of this discussion the writer set forth his understanding of the inheritance of the saints and its relevance to the doctrine of perseverance. These conclusions may be set forth in the following propositions:

1. There is a difference between inheriting the land of Canaan and living there. The former refers to ownership and the latter to mere residence.

2. While Israel was promised the inheritance as a nation, the condition for maintaining their inheritance right to the land of Canaan was faith, obedience, and completion of one's task. The promise, while national, was only applied to the believing remnant within the nation. Even though many within the nation were not born again, the New Testament writers use the nation as an example (1 Cor. 10:6, Gk. **typos**) of the experience of the born-again people of God in the New Testament.

3. The inheritance is not to be equated with heaven but with something additional to heaven, promised to those believers who faithfully obey the Lord.

4. Just as Old Testament believers forfeited their earthly inheritance through disobedience, we can also forfeit our future reward (inheritance) by a similar failure. Loss of inheritance, however, does not mean loss of salvation.

5. Two kinds of inheritance were enjoyed in the Old Testament. All Israelites who had believed and were therefore regenerate had God as their inheritance but not all inherited the land. This paves the way for the notion that the New Testament may also teach two inheritances. We are all heirs of God, but we are not all joint-heirs with Christ, unless we persevere to the end of life. The former refers to our salvation and the latter to our reward.

6. A child of Israel was both an heir of God and an heir of Canaan by virtue of belief in God and resulting regeneration. Yet only those believers in Israel who were faithful would maintain their status as firstborn sons who would actually receive what had been promised to them as an inheritance.

The relevance of these conclusions to the doctrine of the saints' perseverance is obvious. First, if this is in fact the Old Testament view, it surely must have informed the thinking of the New Testament writers. If that is so, then many passages, which have been considered as descriptions of the elect, are in fact conditions of obtaining a reward in heaven. For example, Paul warns the Corinthians, "Do you not know that the wicked will not inherit the kingdom of God?"[2] If "inheriting the kingdom" means "going to heaven," then Paul is saying

---

[2]1 Cor. 6:9.

no wicked person can go to heaven. Such an interpretation would be consistent with the Experimental Predestinarian system which says that the permanently carnal Christian is a fiction. If, on the other hand, "to inherit the kingdom" refers not to entering heaven but to possessing and ruling in the kingdom as it does in the Old Testament, then an entirely different interpretation of the passage emerges. Instead of warning merely professing Christians that they may not be Christians at all, he is telling true Christians that, if they do not change their behavior, they may be in the kingdom, but they will not rule there.

This chapter is rather complex. It may be that the reader would prefer to tentatively accept the propositions listed above and skip to the next chapter.

The Old Testament Concept of Inheritance

In numerous passages of the New Testament, believers are called heirs. We are told that we will "inherit the kingdom," "inherit eternal life," and that the Spirit is the "earnest of our inheritance." Commonly, these passages have been taken to refer to our final deliverance from hell. A severe problem develops, however, when one carefully examines the usage of the term "inheritance" in the Old and New Testaments. When used of Israel's acquisition of Canaan, it seems to refer, almost without exception, to something which is merited or worked for. Because this contradicts the doctrine of justification by faith alone, no lack of exegetical ingenuity has been exercised in reinterpreting the obvious meaning of certain passages. Calvin, for example, struggled with Col. 3:23-24:

> *Whatever you do, work at it with all your heart, as working for the Lord, not for men, since you know that you will receive an inheritance from the Lord as a reward.*

Because the inheritance in his system is heaven and since we are, according to the passage, to earn it as a reward,[3] Calvin resolved the problem by appealing to Gen. 15:5 (the promise of a seed) and Gen. 17:1 (the seed given based on obedience) and concluded:

> *Did Abraham by his obedience merit the blessing which had been promised him before the precept was given? Here assuredly we see without ambiguity that God rewards the works of believers with blessings which he had given them before the works were thought of, there*

---

[3]The Greek is **antapodosis**, and it means a "recompense" or "repaying, reward"; cf. AG, p. 72. The LXX, for example, used the word in Ps. 19:11: "In keeping them [the words of God] there is great reward."

still being no cause for the blessings which he bestows but his own mercy.[4]

The problem is that Genesis clearly says that there was a cause for the blessing--Abraham's obedience.[5] Calvin has turned the text upside down to mean precisely the opposite of that which the original author intended. What we see is a promise of reward in Gen. 15:1 and a recognition that all of God's promised blessings only go to those who are obedient. An inheritance came to the firstborn son by virtue of his birth. But whether or not he actually secured it depended upon his obedience and the father's choice.

If we are obedient, then God promises to bless us. The content of our obedience varies with the blessing to be received. If the blessing is final deliverance from hell, then the only "obedience" or "work" is that of believing (Jn. 6:29). If, on the other hand, the blessing is a richer spiritual life or reward in the future, the work is faithful perseverance (2 Cor. 5:10).

The New Testament writers frequently refer to the inheritance of the saints by quoting passages referring to the land of Canaan in the Old Testament. How was the inheritance in the Old Testament obtained? Was it viewed as a reward for faithful service, something earned, or was it a free gift? Of what did it consist? Was it heaven, or was it an additional blessing for those who were already saved? Certainly the view of the inheritance of the New Testament was directly informed by the Old Testament world of thought.

An Inheritance Was a "Possession"

Nothing is more fundamental to the meaning of the Hebrew word **nachala**, than the idea of "possession."[6] The land of Canaan was Israel's promised possession.[7] Leonard Coppes commits the error of illegitimate totality transfer when he attempts to add the idea of "permanent possession as a result of succession."[8] The notions of permanence and succession are found in some contexts,[9] but they are contradicted in others and are, therefore, not part of the basic significance of the word.[10] Craston avoids this error when he summarizes:

---

[4]John Calvin, *Institutes of the Christian Religion*, trans. Henry Beveridge, 2 vols. (Grand Rapids: Eerdmans, 1964), 3.18.2.

[5]Gen. 22:18: "[They] shall be blessed, because you have obeyed my voice."

[6]AS, p. 248. The Greek words cited here have the same sense, "possession."

[7]1 Chr. 16:18; Josh. 18:20; Num. 26:53; Dt. 4:38; Ps. 105:11.

[8]Leonard Coppes, "**nahala**," in *TWOT*, 2:569.

[9]E.g., Lev. 25:46.

[10]Coppes himself admits this when he refers to "those many passages where the idea of possession was conceived of as permanent and not entailing the idea of succession (I Sam. 26:19)," 2:569.

The Old Testament terms for heir, inheritance, do not necessarily bear the special sense of hereditary succession and possession, although they are found in laws concerning succession to the headship of the family, with consequent control of the family property (Gen. 15:3-5; Num. 27:1-11; Num. 36:1-13; Dt. 21:15-17).[11]

It is clear, for example, that, when the psalmist says, "Rise up, O God, . . . for all the nations are your inheritance" (Ps. 82:8), he does not mean that God receives the nations upon his death from His parent!

Guaranteed filial succession of property is not part of the semantic value of the word.[12] Leon Morris correctly insists that, even though the word properly denotes property received as a result of death, the Old Testament concept of inheritance has no implication of hereditary succession, as it does in classical Greek. Rather, he says, the term refers only to sanctioned and settled possession.[13] The fact that a son became an heir in no way guaranteed that he would obtain the inheritance. The father had the right to insist that the son meet the conditions of the inheritance or to give it to another. The obvious illustration of this is that the exodus generation was promised an inheritance, the land of Canaan. However, they were also warned about the possibility of losing it and the need to obey God, fight the battle, and live by faith if they were to obtain the inheritance which they were promised.

An Inheritance Could Be Merited and Lost

Nothing could be plainer from the Old Testament presentation of the inheritance than that it was often merited or fought for. Babb comments:

In many instances of Biblical usage, the theological meaning of the word goes beyond the legalistic. Apart from any legal processes, it may characterize the bestowal of a gift or possession upon his people by a merciful God, in fulfillment of a promise or **as a reward for obedience.**[14]

---

[11]R. C. Craston, "Inheritance," in *Evangelical Dictionary of Theology* (Grand Rapids: Baker, 1984), p. 561.

[12]See also Gen. 15:7-8; Dt. 16:20; Lev. 20:24; Isa. 57:13; 54:3. Jeremiah says, "Therefore I will give their wives to other men, and their fields to new owners [Heb. their fields to those who will inherit them]" (Jer. 8:10). Those who inherit are simply "owners."

[13]Leon Morris, *The Epistle to the Romans* (Grand Rapids: Eerdmans, 1988), p. 317, citing, in part, comments from F. J. A. Hort, *The First Epistle of St. Peter* (London, 1898), p. 35.

[14]O. J. Babb, "Inheritance," in *The Interpreter's Dictionary of the Bible*, p. 701.

That the believer's inheritance is his reward in heaven and not heaven itself has been held by many within the Reformed faith.[15] In view of the New Testament doctrine of justification by faith alone, it seems curious that so many have therefore equated the inheritance with final deliverance from hell. This is even more surprising because the New Testament itself, almost without exception, presents the believer's inheritance as something merited or earned.

We see the idea of merit related to the inheritance in its earliest references. Abraham is told that failure to obey the work of circumcision will result in forfeiture of the inheritance (Gen. 17:14). Caleb will inherit the land because he followed God "wholeheartedly" (Num. 14:24):

> **But because my servant Caleb has a different spirit, and follows me wholeheartedly,** *I will bring him into the land he went to, and his descendants will* **inherit it.**

> *I, however, followed the* Lord *my God wholeheartedly. So on that day Moses swore to me, 'The land on which your feet have walked will be your inheritance and that of your children forever* **because you have followed the** Lord **my God wholeheartedly'"** (Josh. 14:8-9).

In contrast to those Israelites who disobeyed, Caleb merited an inheritance, the land of Canaan. Caleb and Joshua, only two out of two million, inherited. But surely that two million was composed mainly of those who were justified! Yet only those who "had a different spirit" and who "followed the Lord wholeheartedly" inherited the land. Numerous passages in the Old Testament demonstrate that the inheritance (the land of Canaan)[16] must be merited by obedience.[17]

They will have success in their battle to inherit the land only on the condition that they are "strong and courageous" and that they "obey all the law" that Moses gave them.[18] Furthermore, they are promised "rest" (victory after the conquest of the land of Canaan), but it will be theirs only as they fight and "take pos-

---

[15]Shedd, for example, writes: "This is proved by the fact that the reward of the Christian is called an inheritance (Mt. 25:34; Acts 20:32; Gal. 3:18; Eph. 5:5; Col. 1:12). The believer's reward is like a child's portion under his father's will. This is not wages and recompense, in the strict sense; and yet it is relatively a reward for filial obedience" (William G. T. Shedd, *Dogmatic Theology*, 3 vols. [New York: Charles Scribner's Sons, 1889; reprint ed., Minneapolis: Klock and Klock, 1979], 2:549). This is not to imply that Shedd teaches that some Christians can be disinherited. Dr. Martin Lloyd-Jones similarly acknowledged, "There is a teaching in the Scripture which suggests that there may be a variation in the amount of the inheritance dependent upon our conduct and behaviour" (D. Martin Lloyd-Jones, *The Sons of God: Exposition of Romans 8:5-17* [Grand Rapids: Zondervan, 1975], p. 40).

[16]The land of Canaan is equated with the inheritance in the Old Testament. See, for example, Dt. 15:4; 19:14; 25:19; 26:1.

[17]See Ex. 23:30; Dt. 2:31; 11:11-24; 16:20; 19:8-9; Josh. 11:23; 1:6-7.

[18]Josh. 1:6-7.

session" (Josh. 1:13-15). Not only is the inheritance of Canaan merited by obedience, but David's reign there is predicated on his obedience and character.[19] We are therefore amazed to read in B. F. Westcott's commentary on Hebrews:

> *From these examples it will appear that the dominant Biblical sense of 'inheritance' is the enjoyment by a rightful title of that which is not the fruit of personal exertion.*[20]

Clearly, "the fruit of personal exertion" is found in scores of passages. It is evident from numerous Old Testament passages that Israel would only be successful in their conquest and acquisition of the land of Canaan if they trusted God and obeyed completely. Because the land of Canaan and the inheritance are equivalent terms, this implies that the inheritance is obtained only by faith plus obedience. The argument could be presented as follows:

Major Premise: The land is the inheritance

Minor Premise: The land will be obtained only on the
                      condition of faith plus obedience

Conclusion: The inheritance will be obtained only on
                      the condition of faith plus
                      obedience.

Not only can the inheritance be merited by obedience, but it can be lost by disobedience. Even Moses was excluded from the land of Canaan (i.e., the inheritance) because of his disobedience (Dt. 4:21-22). Clearly, Moses will be in heaven, but he forfeited his earthly inheritance.[21] Not entering Canaan does not necessarily mean one is not born again.

Even though Israel had become God's firstborn son (Ex. 4:22-23), the entire wilderness generation with the exception of Caleb and Joshua forfeited the inheritance due the firstborn. God disinherited them, and they wandered in the wilderness for forty years.

---

[19]Ps. 37:9-11. "Hope" does not refer to saving faith. David was already a saved man. It refers to the attitude of a saved man who continues to trust and does not give up. A man who perseveres in faith.

[20]B. F. Westcott, *The Epistle to the Hebrews* (London: Macmillan, 2d. ed., 1892; reprint ed., Grand Rapids: Eerdmans, 1965), p. 168.

[21]Nothing is said regarding whether or not he forfeited his heavenly reward which of course he did not. The New Testament uses the experience of Israel as a "type" and not an exact parallel. Just as Old Testament believers forfeited their earthly inheritance through disobedience, we (and they) can forfeit our future reward by a failure to persevere or by unbelief. Although the writer realizes that the case of Moses could be urged as an argument against his thesis, it seems to him that Moses is a special case. The spiritual type comes from the nation as a whole, and not one man.

Another generation of Israelites similarly forfeited their inheritance rights and were sold as slaves into Babylon. Jeremiah laments:

> *Our* **inheritance** *has been turned over to aliens,*
> *Our homes to foreigners* (Lam. 5:2).

Israel's disobedience had resulted in the loss of her inheritance, the land of Canaan.[22]

A classic example of the forfeiture of one's inheritance rights was the case of Reuben, Jacob's firstborn, who lost his inheritance rights.[23] The possibility of the forfeiture of the land of Canaan is clearly presented in David's challenge to the nation and to his son Solomon.[24]

It is instructive to note, when studying the inheritance in the Old Testament, that a distinction was drawn between inhabiting the land and inheriting it or, to put it in other words, between merely living in the land and possessing it. Abraham, for example, inhabited the land, lived there, but he never inherited it (Heb. 11:13). He lived there, but he never owned it (Gen. 21:33; 35:27).[25]

In the Old Testament the **ger**, the alien, was someone who "did not enjoy the rights usually possessed by a resident."[26] The **ger** had, according to the lexicon, "no inherited rights."[27] Moses named his son Gershom in memory of his stay in Midian (Ex. 18:3) where he lived as an alien without inheritance rights. Abraham, Isaac, and Jacob lived as strangers in Canaan (Ex. 6:4), meaning that they had no property rights there.

The Levites, in particular, were told that they would have no inheritance rights in the land:

> *The LORD said to Aaron, "You will have no inheritance in their land,*
> *nor will you have any share[28] among them. I am your share and your*
> *inheritance among the Israelites* (Num. 18:20).[29]

---

[22]Of course, the Abrahamic promise guaranteed the ultimate possession of the land by the final generation of Jews who return to the Lord in faith just prior to the second coming. However, the generation of the Babylonian captivity forever lost their inheritance. An inheritance can be lost.

[23]1 Chr. 5:1-2

[24]1 Chr. 28:8

[25]There is a difference between living in the land and inheriting, owning, the land. "May he give you and your descendants the blessing given to Abraham, so that you may take possession [Heb. **yarash**, "to inherit"] of the land where you now live as an alien" (Gen. 28:4). Jacob did not own the land, i.e., he had not inherited it, but he lived there.

[26]Harold Steigers, "**ger**," in *TWOT*, 1:155-56.

[27]BDB, p. 158.

[28]The parallelism equates "share" with "inheritance."

[29]See also Num. 18:23-24

It is therefore perfectly proper to think of living in a land where one had no inheritance or property.

Two Kinds of Inheritance Are Promised

The Old Testament presents two inheritances (possessions) which the people of God will enjoy. All will have God as an inheritance, but only some will "possess the land." All who know the Lord have Him as "their God." But only those who obey the Lord wholeheartedly, as Caleb did, will have an inheritance in the land of Canaan.

God Is Our Inheritance

First, the inheritance is God Himself. The Levites, in contrast to the rest of the nation, were to have no inheritance in the land (Dt. 14:27):

> *The priests, who are Levites--indeed the whole tribe of Levi--are to have no allotment or inheritance with Israel. They shall live on the offerings made to the Lord by fire, for that is their inheritance. They shall have no inheritance among their brothers; the Lord is their inheritance, as he promised them. (Dt. 18:1-2)*[30]

The prerogative of having God as their inheritance went not just to the Levites but, like the Levites, to all who know the Lord. The psalmist viewed God as his **kleros** ("lot, portion, inheritance," LXX):[31] "The Lord is the portion of **my inheritance** and my cup; thou dost support my lot" (Ps. 16:5 NASB). In other places David says:

> *My flesh and my heart may fail*
> *But God is the strength of my heart*
> *And my portion* [**kleros**, LXX] *forever* (Ps. 73:26).

> *The Lord is my portion* [**kleros**];
> *I promised to keep thy words* (Ps. 119:57).

> *I cried out to Thee, O Lord;*
> *I said, "Thou art my refuge,*
> *My portion* [**kleros**] *in the land of the living* (Ps. 142:5).

God is the people's portion now, and He will be their inheritance in the future as well:

---

[30]See also Josh. 7:14; 14:1-5; 18:7.

[31]J. Herrmann, "**kleronomos, synkleronomeo, kleronomeo,**" in *TDNT*, p. 444.

This is the covenant I will make with the house of Israel after that time," declares the LORD. "I will put my law in their minds and write it on their hearts. I will be their God, and they will be my people (Jer. 31:33).

Not only will God own His people, but they will possess Him. The references to "I am the God of Abraham, Isaac, and Jacob" convey a similar thought. Not only do the people have an inheritance in the land, but God Himself is theirs. This only applies to those within Israel who are regenerate.

The Inheritance Is an
Added Blessing to the Saved

All believers have God as their inheritance, but not all (e.g., the Levites, the alien, and the patriarchs, and those who died in the wilderness) have an inheritance in the land. That inheritance is an added blessing to the saved. The New Testament writers often refer to the believer's inheritance. In so doing, they embrace the imagery of Joshua possessing Canaan or the Hebrews inheriting the land (Heb. 3 and 4).

In addition to the passages mentioned above which show that Canaan was the inheritance that went to the already justified children of Israel, the illustration of Abraham himself forcefully illustrates this point. Abraham was a saved man when the Abrahamic Covenant was made. The condition for receiving the inheritance of the land promised in the covenant was circumcision and the offering of his son Isaac. Because of these conditional acts of obedience, Abraham received the second kind of inheritance. Because he was justified, he already was an heir of God; God was his inheritance. Because of his obedience, he became an heir of the nations and specifically of the land of Canaan.

In Gen. 15:1-6 Abraham is promised an heir and in Gen. 15:18 an inheritance, the land of Canaan. Yet in 15:6 we are told, "Abram believed the LORD, and he credited it to him as righteousness." Ross points out that this verse refers to Abram's conversion which occurred years earlier when he left Ur. The form of the verb "believed" shows that his faith did not begin after the events recorded in Gen. 15:1-5:

Abraham's faith is recorded here because it is foundational for making the covenant. The Abrahamic Covenant did not give Abraham redemption; it was a covenant made with Abram, who had already believed and to whom righteousness had already been imputed.[32]

---

[32]Allen P. Ross, "Genesis," in *BKC*, 1:55.

While Abraham received justification by faith alone, it is clear that he could only obtain the inheritance by means of obedience (Gen. 22:15-18).

For the Israelites, conquering Canaan secured their **earthly** inheritance. This parallels that aspect of the New Testament believer's future which is similarly conditional--his reward in heaven, not heaven itself.

It is sometimes erroneously stated that inheriting the land is to be compared with the believer's entrance into heaven. Canaan, we are told, is the Old Testament analogy to heaven. This notion is unacceptable for two reasons. First, as mentioned above, the inheritance of Canaan in the Old Testament was conditioned upon works and obedience, conditions far removed from the doctrine of the free and unearned entrance into heaven.

But just as important, the inheritance in the Old Testament was offered to those who were already justified, who would receive something in addition to heaven if they would obey. This is seen first of all in the fact that the nation which left Egypt was composed primarily of saved people, and inheriting Canaan was in no way related to their acquisition of heaven.[33] According to the writer to the Hebrews, the exodus generation as a whole was saved. He says:

> *By faith the people passed through the Red Sea as on dry land; but when the Egyptians tried to do so, they were drowned.*

> *By faith the walls of Jericho fell, after the people had marched around them for seven days* (Heb. 11:29-30).

His favorite phrase, "by faith," is applied in 11:30 to the believing generation which entered the land and in the rest of the chapter to Abel, Enoch, Abraham, Moses, and others who are all regenerate.[34] He therefore views the exodus generation as a whole that way. Paul had the same view:

> *[They] drank the same spiritual drink, for they drank from the spiritual rock that accompanied them, and that rock was Christ. Nevertheless God was not pleased with most of them; their bodies were scattered over the desert* (1 Cor. 10:4-5).

---

[33]Surprisingly, some have contended that the absence of a fully developed Old Testament doctrine of heaven is proof that Canaan should be interpreted as a type of heaven. The fact that Canaan is not paralleled with heaven in the Old Testament is explained, they say, by the total absence of a doctrine of heaven in the Old Testament. But what kind of argument is this? Are we to say that the absence of something is evidence that it exists? Just because Old Testament saints do not know about something, does this mean that their statements should not be taken at face value? Is absence of knowledge justification for spiritualization of the text, i.e., reading the word "heaven" into the word "Canaan"?

[34]Heb. 11:4-5, 7-8, 11, 17, 20-24.

The Israelites, as a nation, seemed to reveal their regenerate condition when they promised, "We will do everything the LORD has said" (Ex. 19:8). They had "bowed down and worshiped" and trusted in the blood of the Passover lamb (Ex. 12:27-28), had by faith crossed the Red Sea, and had drunk (i.e., "trusted in," Jn. 4:13-14; Jn. 6:53-56) that spiritual rock which was Christ, yet they never obtained Canaan, their inheritance, because of their unbelief and disobedience. Here two categories of Old Testament regenerate saints are presented: those who inherited the land and those who did not. The inheritance (possession) was dependent upon their obedience. Not all who entered were obedient, just as not all who left Egypt were regenerate, but the nation as a whole was obedient. The Old Testament writers, as is well established, thought in corporate terms.

R. T. Kendall, pastor of Westminster Chapel in London, has observed:

It would be a serious mistake to dismiss the children of Israel in the wilderness by writing them off as unregenerate from the start. To say that such people were never saved is to fly in the face of the memorable fact that they kept the Passover. They obeyed Moses, who gave an unprecedented, if not strange command to sprinkle blood on either side and over the doors (Ex. 12:7). But they did it . . . If obeying Moses' command to sprinkle blood on the night of the Passover was not a type of saving faith, I do not know what is. These people were saved. We shall see them in Heaven, even if it turns out they were 'saved so as by fire' (1 Cor. 3:15).[35]

It would not be surprising then if the New Testament writers similarly viewed the inheritance of the saints from a two-fold perspective. All regenerate men have God as their inheritance, or as Paul puts it, are "heirs of God" (Rom. 8:17; Gal. 4:7). That heirship is received on the basis of only one work, the work of believing. But there is another inheritance in the New Testament, an inheritance which, like that of the Israelites, is merited. They are also heirs of the kingdom and joint-heirs with the Messiah (2 Tim. 2:12; Rom. 8:17).[36]

The Inheritance and Heaven--New Testament Parallels?

Many outstanding commentaries and theological works have attempted to equate entrance into the land of Canaan in the Old Testament with the believer's arrival into heaven in the New. Arthur Pink, for example, in his commentary on Hebrews discusses the inheritance/rest of the believer and parallels the Hebrews' journey from Egypt to Canaan with the Christian's journey from spiritual death to

---

[35]R. T. Kendall, *Once Saved Always Saved* (London: Hodder and Stoughton, 1984), p. 115.

[36]These passages will be developed in the section on inheritance in the New Testament below.

heaven.[37] In a similar vein A. B. Davidson says that the writer identifies the Old Testament rest (the land of Canaan) with the Christian's salvation.[38]

Amillennialists have often drawn the parallel between Canaan and heaven. Hoekema, for example, explains: "Canaan, therefore, was not an end in itself; it pointed forward to the new earth . . . of which Canaan was only a type."[39] Or as Patrick Fairbairn put it:

The occupation of the earthly Canaan by the natural seed of Abraham, in its grand and ultimate design, was a type of the occupation by the redeemed church of her destined inheritance of glory.[40]

A more singularly inappropriate parallel could hardly be found. An inheritance which could be merited by obedience and forfeited through disobedience is hardly a good "type" of heaven. Both aspects are, it would seem, an embarrassment to those of the Reformed persuasion. On one hand, the forfeiture of the inheritance through disobedience contradicts the doctrine of the eternal security of the believer. On the other hand, the works required to obtain the inheritance in the Old Testament contradict the doctrine of justification by faith alone. Pink explains the works problem by viewing Israel's struggle to cross the desert and enter the land as a parable of perseverance in holiness. In this way the problem of works as a condition for entering Canaan is solved by saying that all true believers work. The problem is that this would mean there were only two believers in the entire two million, Caleb and Joshua. Only two persevered and therefore proved their regenerate status. However, this fails to fit the biblical data because the writer to the Hebrews views the nation as saved. If the inheritance is heaven, then all two million Israelites perished in hell. This is extremely difficult to believe. As Farrar put it:

If . . . the **rest** *meant* **heaven**, *it would be against all Scripture analogy to assume that* **all** *the Israelites who died in the wilderness were excluded from future happiness. And there are many other difficulties which will at once suggest themselves.*[41]

---

[37]Arthur W. Pink, *An Exposition of Hebrews* (Grand Rapids: Baker, 1968), p. 196.

[38]A. B. Davidson, *The Epistle to the Hebrews* (Edinburgh: T. & T. Clark, 1959), pp. 91-92. By the term "salvation" Davidson means the Christian's final deliverance from hell, a meaning far removed from the Old Testament world in which the writer to the Hebrews moved.

[39]Anthony A. Hoekema, *The Bible and the Future* (Grand Rapids: Eerdmans, 1979), p. 279. Hoekema gives no evidence substantiating this assertion.

[40]Patrick Fairbairn, *Typology of Scripture* (1845-47; reprint ed., New York: Funk and Wagnalls, 1900), II, 3-4.

[41]F. W. Farrar, *The Epistle of Paul the Apostle to the Hebrews* in *Cambridge Greek Testament for Schools and Colleges* (Cambridge: Cambridge University Press, 1984), p. 67.

Those from the Arminian tradition could immediately point out that the failure to enter the land can refer to a loss of salvation. They too, however, must struggle with the problem of the works involved in obtaining it.

Only by allowing inheritance to mean "possession" and acknowledging that it can be merited can the parallel drawn out by the New Testament authors be explained. The inheritance is not salvation in the sense of final deliverance from hell but the reward which came to the faithful in Israel as a result of whole-hearted obedience. Similarly, in the New Testament the inheritance is a reward. Canaan does not parallel heaven or the new earth but the rewards which the saints will enjoy there. These are earned by faithful obedience and may, like the inheritance of the Old Testament, be forfeited through disobedience or a failure to persevere.

The Inheritance--Promises and Conditions

From the earliest references the inheritance was promised to Abraham and his descendants upon the basis of a divine oath.[42] But a tension is apparent. They were told that, if they "do what is good and right in the LORD's sight" (Dt. 6:18), they would have victory over the Canaanites and possess the land (Dt. 11:22-25). Even though the inheritance has been promised on an oath, it will only come to them if they "carefully follow all these laws" (Dt. 19:8-10). How is this tension to be explained?

The parallel with Abraham may suggest an answer. As pointed out above, Abraham was already a saved man when he received the promise of the inheritance. Therefore, it was not the act of saving faith which guaranteed Abraham an heir (Gen. 15:4-5) or the inheritance of Canaan (Gen. 15:8). Canaan is not parallel with heaven but with additional blessings which are given to believers on the condition of subsequent acts of faith. Abraham began to look for the reward of possession of the land in the afterlife (Heb. 11:8, 16). He already had heaven, but he did not have the fulfillment of the Abrahamic land promise. That inheritance was gained by those who obeyed him and who continued in faith (Gen. 17:1-2). One particular requirement in the Old Testament was circumcision. If Abraham had not been circumcised, neither he nor the members of his household would have inherited the promise (Gen. 17:14). That the appropriation of the blessings of the covenant was conditioned upon obedience is clearly stated:

> *The angel of the LORD called to Abraham from heaven a second time and said, "I swear by myself, declares the LORD, that* **because you have done this** *and have not withheld your son, your only son, I will surely bless you and make your descendants as numerous as the stars in the*

---

[42]Gen. 12:7; 15:18-21; 26:3; 28:13; Ex. 6:8.

sky and as the sand of the seashore. Your descendants will take possession of the cities of their enemies, and through your offspring all nations on earth will be blessed, **because you have obeyed me**" (Gen. 22:15-18).

The passage is instructive in that it clarifies that the inheritance which has been given unconditionally to the descendants by oath will only be obtained by each one personally when he obeys. What is true for the "father of those who believe" is true for his descendants. The unconditional nature of the Abrahamic blessing is available for each generation of Israelites. But only that generation which appropriates it by faith will enter into those blessings. God never promised anything to a generation of rebels. It is to the "Israel of God" (Gal. 6:16), the believing remnant of the last days, that the promises will finally be fulfilled (Rom. 11:26ff).[43]

The inheritance, while given to the descendants in general by promise, was obtained by individuals or groups of people only by obedience. This was seen in the life of Abraham above and is forcefully illustrated in the experience of the Israelites and their attempted initial entrance into Canaan. In Num. 14:14ff several things should be noted: (1) they were forgiven for their unbelief and grumbling (Num. 14:20); (2) they disobeyed and tested the Lord ten times (Num. 14:22); (3) those who disobeyed and who were "men" (accountable), who saw the miracles, would never enter the land of Canaan (vv. 22-23); (4) possessing Canaan is the same as inheriting the land (14:24); and (5) only those believers who have "a different spirit" and who follow the Lord "wholeheartedly" will obtain the inheritance (14:24; cf. Josh. 14:9).

These people as a group are saved people, the people of God. While some may not have been saved, only two of them will inherit because only two out of two million met the conditions. Thus, all the rest will go to heaven but forfeit their inheritance. This thought is in the mind of the writer to the Hebrews in Heb. 3:7ff where obtaining the inheritance is equated with "entering rest." The instant they accepted the Passover, were circumcised, and by faith moved out of Egypt, the inheritance was potentially theirs as children of God. But God has never promised anything to rebels who will not trust him.

Conclusion

It has been seen that the Old Testament notion of inheritance does not always include the idea of a guarantee. The Israelite became an heir by birth, but due to disobedience he could forfeit the firstborn privilege. It was necessary that

---

[43]Walter C. Kaiser, Jr., *Toward an Old Testament Theology* (Grand Rapids: Zondervan, 1978), pp. 93-94. In 1 Ki. 8:25 we see a similar parallel with David.

he obey if he would obtain what was promised. We are therefore alerted to the fact that the inheritance is not something which comes automatically to all who are sons but only to those sons who are obedient. The inheritance was something in addition to salvation and was not equated with it. It was obtained by victorious perseverance and obedient faith.

With this background in mind we are now in a better position to understand the New Testament teaching on inheritance.

Chapter 4

The Inheritance: New Testament

We must begin with the end in mind. Only then can we bring the daily details of life into proper perspective. This lesson is wonderfully taught through the example of a high school junior, Kay Bothwell. Kay was greatly admired by both Christians and non-Christians alike. Not only had she given her life to Christ, but she had also allowed Christ to be formed in her.

One day she was given the following assignment in her English literature class: "State how you would spend your time if you knew this would be the last week of your life." Her essay read as follows:

"Today I live. One week from today I die. If a situation such as this came to me I should probably weep. As soon as I realized there are many things to be done, I would try to regain my composure. The first day of my suddenly short-ened life I would use to see all of my loved ones and assure them I loved them all very much. On the evening of my first day I would ask God, in the solace of my room, to give me strength to bear the rest of my precious days and give me His hand, so that I could walk with him.

On the second day I would awaken early in order to see the rising sun, which I had so often cast aside to gain a few more moments of coveted sleep. I would continue throughout the day to visit family and friends, telling each one, "I love you. Thank you for the part you've played in my life."

On the third day I'd travel alone into the woods, allowing God's goodness and creation to surround me. I would see, undoubtedly for the first time, many things I had not taken the time to notice before.

On the fourth day I would prepare my will; all sentimental things I possess I would leave to my family and friends. I would spend the rest of the day with my mother. We have always been very close, and I would want to especially assure her of my deep gratitude for her tremendous impact on my life.

On Friday, the fifth day, my life almost ended, I would spend the time with my pastor, speaking with him of my relationship with Christ and seeking advice for my final hours. I would spend the rest of the day visiting those who are ill, silently being thankful that I know no pain and yet I know my destiny.

On Saturday morning I would spend my time with a special friend who is going through a difficult time with her broken family and seek to comfort her. The rest of Saturday I would spend with my treasured grandparents and elderly friends, seeking their wisdom and sharing my love. Saturday night I would spend awake in prayer, knowing that God was by my side. I would be at peace now, knowing that because of Christ I was soon going to spend an eternity in heaven.

Upon wakening Sunday morning, I would make all my last preparations, and then taking my Bible, I would go to church to spend my last hours in worship and praise, seeking to die gracefully and with the hope that my life had influence upon others for His glorious name. The last hour would not be spent in agony but the perfect harmony of my relationship with Jesus Christ."

One week almost to the day after she handed in this essay, Kay Bothwell was ushered into eternity when she was killed in an automobile accident just outside her home in Marion, Indiana.

For the last week of her life, at least, Kay Bothwell lived life with the end in mind. Like the imaginary funeral referred to in the preceding chapter, the essay in the literature class helped her think through what was really important in life. For the readers of the Old Testament the "end" was often called the "inheritance." As we move into the New Testament, the revelation becomes more specific, and it is referred to as "inheriting the kingdom" and "entering into rest." The New Testament concepts of inheritance and rest will be the subjects of the next two chapters.

Old Testament usage and understanding necessarily informs the thinking of the New Testament writers. It would be surprising indeed if there was no continuity of thought between their understanding of an inheritance and that found in their Bible.

This chapter will try to demonstrate that just like the Old Testament there are two kinds of inheritance presented in the New. All believers have God as their inheritance but not all will inherit the kingdom. Furthermore, inheriting the kingdom is not to be equated with entering it but, rather, with possessing it and ruling there. All Christians will enter the kingdom, but not all will rule there, i.e., inherit it.

There are four words related to the inheritance idea in the New Testament: the verb "to inherit" (**kleronomeo**) and the nouns "inheritance" (**kleronomia**), "heir" (**kleronomos**), and "lot, portion" (**kleros**). Every usage of these words will be referred to in the discussion below. However, since the conclusions parallel Old Testament usage in a striking way, we will organize them under the same categories.

An Inheritance Is a Possession

Like its Old Testament counterpart a **kleronomia** is fundamentally a possession.[1] How it is acquired or passed on to one's descendants is not intrinsic to the word. The word does not always or even fundamentally mean an estate passed on to a son at the death of a parent, as it does in Gal. 4:7. To include those contextually derived notions within the semantic value of the word itself is, again, to commit an illegitimate totality transfer. Arndt and Gingrich define it as an "inheritance, possession, property."[2] Abbott-Smith concurs that it means "in general, a possession, inheritance."[3] Rarely, if ever, does it mean "property transmitted by will."[4] Vine observes that "only in a few cases in the Gospels has it the meaning ordinarily attached to that word in English, i.e., that into possession of which the heir enters only on the death of an ancestor."[5]

The Inheritance Is Meritorious Ownership of the Kingdom

Also like their Old Testament counterparts the words for inheritance in the New Testament often involve spiritual obedience (i.e., faith plus works) as a condition of obtaining the inheritance. Becoming an heir (**kleronomos**) can occur through filial relationship,[6] through faith,[7] or through some kind of works of obedience.[8] The acquisition of the inheritance (**kleronomia**) is often related to merit.[9] In nearly every instance the verb "to inherit" (**kleronomeo**) includes, contextually, either the presence or absence of some work or character quality as a condition of obtaining or forfeiting the possession.[10] In view of the fact that

---

[1]This seems to be the sense of "inheritance, property" (**kleronomia**) in Mt. 21:38; Mk. 12:7; Lk. 12:13; 20:14; Acts 7:5; and Eph. 1:18.

[2]AG, p. 436.

[3]AS, p. 249.

[4]Ernest De Witt Burton, *The Epistle to the Galatians, The International Critical Commentary* (Edinburgh: T. & T. Clark, 1921), p. 185.

[5]W. E. Vine, *An Expository Dictionary of New Testament Words* (1939; reprint ed., Nashville: Nelson, n.d.), p. 589.

[6]Mt. 21:38; Mk. 12:7; Lk. 20:14; Gal. 4:1, 7; Heb. 1:2; Rom. 4:13-14.

[7]Gal. 3:29; Ti. 3:7; Heb. 11:7.

[8]In Jas. 2:5 the condition for becoming an heir of the kingdom is "to love Him." For James it was possible that a true Christian could cease to love Him and instead become a friend of the world and actually become an enemy of God (Jas. 4:4-5). The apostle John taught the same thing when he warned the church at Ephesus that they had lost their first love (Rev. 2:4).

[9]See Eph. 5:5; Col. 3:24.

[10]See Mt. 19:29; Mk. 10:17; Mt. 5:5; 25:34-36; Heb. 6:12; Rev. 21:7; 1 Pet. 3:9.

works are associated with the acquisition of the inheritance, it is prima facie doubtful that the inheritance could be equated with entrance into heaven as is so often done. Yet in order to sustain the idea of perseverance in holiness, Experimental Predestinarians interpret the passages as descriptions of all true Christians. Theological exegesis is thus brought in to make every one of these texts say something that they not only do not say but that is in fact contradictory to the rest of the New Testament.

It is plain that the New Testament not only teaches the existence of the carnal Christian[11] but of true Christians who persisted in their carnality up to the point of physical death.[12] They will, having been justified, be in the kingdom; however, they will not inherit it.[13] Vine points out that the term is often used of "that which is received on the condition of obedience to certain precepts (1 Pet. 3:9), and of faithfulness to God amidst opposition (Rev. 21:7)."[14] Only the obedient and faithful inherit, not all who are saved. It is a "reward in the coming age" and "reward of the condition of soul which forbears retaliation and self-vindication, and expresses itself in gentleness of behaviour."[15] Vine points out that it is "the reward of those who have shown kindness to the 'brethren' of the Lord in their distress."[16]

A rich young ruler once asked Jesus, "What good thing shall I do that I may have eternal life?" "Having" (echo) eternal life is equated with "inheriting" it in the parallel passage in Mark where the word kleronomeo is used rather than echo, demonstrating to the rich young ruler, at least, the equality of the terms (Mk. 10:17).[17] Jesus understands his question as "how to enter life," i.e., how to go to heaven (v. 17). It therefore appears that Jesus is equating "inheriting eternal life" with "entering into heaven." However, that conclusion is too hasty. Several things should be mentioned.

First, consistent with its usage throughout the Old and New Testaments, the verb kleronomeo in this passage implies obtaining a possession by merit. It cannot, therefore, mean to obtain heaven by faith. Second, the rich young ruler is reflecting first-century Jewish theology and not the gospel of the New Testament. The Rabbis taught that works were necessary in order to inherit eternal life,[18] and they were partially correct. Eternal life could be earned when viewed as an en-

---

[11]See chapter 14, "The Carnal Christian."

[12]Acts 5:1-10; 1 Cor. 5:5; 3:15; 11:30; Heb. 10:29; 1 Jn. 5:16-17.

[13]Gal. 5:21; Eph. 5:5; 1 Cor. 6:9.

[14]Vine, p. 588.

[15]Ibid. See Mk. 10:30; Mt. 5:5.

[16]Ibid., p. 589. See Mt. 25:34.

[17]The parallel passages, Lk. 10:25 and 18:18, also demonstrate that kleronomeo can include the idea of merit.

[18]See William E. Brown, "The New Testament Concept of the Believer's Inheritance" (Th.D. dissertation, Dallas Theological Seminary, 1984) for discussion.

riched experience of that life given at regeneration. The rich young ruler, however, was unaware that eternal life could be had now. One could enter into it immediately by faith and not have to wait until the final judgment, where an enriched dimension of it could be rewarded to faithful discipleship. It is to this possibility that our Lord begins to direct his attention.

Third, Jesus understands what he is really asking. He is asking how he can enter into heaven. Jesus says, "It is hard for a rich man to enter into the kingdom of heaven" (Mt. 19:23). In the rich young ruler's mind entering heaven, inheriting eternal life, and having eternal life were all the same thing, and all meant "go to heaven when I die." Jesus neither affirms or denies this equation here.[19] He understands that the young man wants to know how to enter life, or enter the kingdom. Rather, He moves to the heart of the young man's question . . . and his problem. How good does one have to be to merit heaven? Christ leads him to the conclusion that one would have to be perfect if one wants to obtain eternal life by works. He does this by pointing out to him that, if he wants to get to heaven by being good, then he must keep the commandments. It is true that, if a man could keep the commandments, he would merit heaven. The problem is, of course, that no one can. This is what Jesus wants the young ruler to see.

A modern parallel to the young man's question might help elucidate the story. Consider the common situation of a man enmeshed in Catholicism all his life. When he thinks of going to heaven and achieving rewards there, it is all mixed together in his mind. Both entrance and rewards are based upon works. Impressed with an evangelistic sermon he hears, he approaches the evangelist and says, "How good do I have to be to obtain my heavenly reward?" By "heavenly reward" he means two things: entrance into heaven and rewards in heaven. They are joined in his thinking. The evangelist does not go into distinctions between rewards and entrance because he understands what the man is really after; he wants to know how he can have assurance of going to heaven. So the evangelist says, "If you want to go to heaven by being good, here is what you must do." Now when the evangelist says that, he is not equating "heavenly reward" with "go to heaven"; in a similar way Jesus is not equating "entering the kingdom of God" with "inheriting the kingdom." Unless Jesus explicitly makes this equation, we have no reason to extract this meaning from this story. We have no right because the Old Testament and the rest of the New consistently distinguish between inheriting the kingdom and entering it, a view which is in no way contradicted by this parable.

When the young man says, "All these I have kept from my youth," Jesus sensitively moves to the heart of the matter by pointing out one that he has not kept. "If you want to be perfect, go, sell what you have and give to the poor; and

---

[19]The fact that these terms were synonymous to the rich young ruler does not mean that this is the teaching of Scripture. Error is often accurately repeated under inspiration. Recall the Satan's words, "You will surely not die."

you will have treasure in heaven; and come, follow Me." Had he perfectly kept the commandments, he would be willing to part with his money. But he was not willing to part with all his money and follow an itinerant teacher around Palestine.

At this point some have felt that Jesus was asking the man to submit to the lordship of Christ in order to become a Christian. All interpreters have experienced difficulty here. Why does Jesus not explain the faith-alone gospel He came to offer? An adequate answer is found in the parallel passage in Mark. There the Lord explains, "Children, how hard it is for those **who trust in riches** to enter the kingdom of God!" (Mk. 10:24).[20] It is true that the young man was probably violating the command, "Thou shalt not covet." But this was not really the heart of the matter. He coveted his things because he found security in them; he trusted in them. This is the real reason behind his unwillingness to part with them and be left trusting in God alone as he followed a poor rabbi from village to village. He had trusted in his wealth for his future and even for his entrance into heaven all his life. The rabbis taught that there was a connection between wealth and acceptance with God. Indeed, a man with money often trusted in that money in order to achieve eternal life. Jesus wants him to shift his trust away from money and to the "good" teacher, i.e., Jesus as God. "Why do you call Me good? No one is good but One, that is, God" (Mt. 19:17).

After informing the rich young ruler that he must sell all he has if he would obtain eternal life,[21] the disciples ask; "We have left everything to follow You! What then will there be for us?" (Mt. 19:27). Peter's question deals with rewards. That they saw a connection between leaving everything and obtaining some reward is obvious. And in His thrilling answer Jesus confirms their theology:

> *I tell you the truth, at the renewal of all things, when the Son of Man sits on his glorious throne, you who have followed me will also sit on twelve thrones, judging the twelve tribes of Israel. And everyone who has left houses or brothers or sisters or father or mother or children or fields for my sake will receive a hundred times as much and will inherit* [**kleronomeo**] *eternal life. But many who are first will be last, and many who are last will be first* (Mt. 19:28-30).

A difficulty now arises: since eternal life is usually equated with regeneration, how can it be obtained by abandoning father, mother, home, children, and the other things listed? The answer is, as will be argued below, that every time

---

[20]This reading is not found in the most ancient texts but is found in the majority of Greek manuscripts. Whether it is valid or not, it represents a very ancient view of the Lord's words and is one that fits very well with the context.

[21]Jesus is no doubt using the law lawfully to convict this man of the sin of trusting in riches instead of the good teacher alone for salvation.

eternal life is presented in Scripture as something to be obtained by a work, it is always a future acquisition. It becomes synonymous in these contexts with a richer experience of that life given freely at regeneration. The point here, however, is that "to inherit" can be used of a meritorious acquisition. There will be differences in heaven, some first and some last, and those who are first are those who have inherited, who have left all for Him. Only the reference to eternal life could lead interpreters to forget that the subject matter is discipleship which is based on works, and not regeneration which is based on faith alone.

A major theme of the Sermon on the Mount is rewards. The Savior says, "Blessed are the meek, for they will inherit [**kleronomeo**] the earth" (Mt. 5:5). The subject matter is our reward in heaven: "Rejoice and be glad because great is your **reward** [**misthos**] in heaven" (Mt. 5:12). The idea of rewards is repeatedly emphasized in the Sermon, which is addressed primarily to the disciples (5:1).[22] The word **misthos** basically means a "payment for work done."[23] Jesus is speaking of the inheritance here as a reward for a humble, trusting life. There is no indication that all Christians have this quality of life. In fact, it is possible for a Christian to become "saltless" (Mt. 5:13) and be "thrown out." True Christians can lose their saltiness, their testimony for the Lord. When they do, they forfeit their reward in heaven. Furthermore, He specifically says that the disobedient believer who annuls "one of the least of these commandments" will be in the kingdom (Mt. 5:19) but will be "least" in contrast to "great" in that kingdom.

What is the content of our inheritance reward? He says it involves inheriting the earth. No doubt this goes back to the promises to David and his "greater" Son:

> *Ask of Me, and I will make the nations your inheritance, the end of the earth our possession. You will rule them with an iron scepter; and you will dash them to pieces like pottery* (Ps. 2:8-9).

We can become joint rulers with Christ over the nations according to John:

> *To him who overcomes and does my will to the end, I will give authority over the nations--'He will rule them with an iron scepter; he will dash them to pieces like pottery'* (Rev. 2:26).

> *To him who overcomes I will grant to sit with Me on My throne, as I also overcame and sat down with My Father on His throne* (Rev. 3:21 NKJV).

---

[22]See Mt. 6:2, 4-6, 18. Note especially the immediate context of the Beatitudes, Mt. 5:7, 9-10.

[23]AG, p. 525.

The apostle Paul echoed a similar theme when he said, "If we endure, we shall also reign with Him" (2 Tim. 2:12).

So it is the meek who will be rewarded with rulership with Christ in the coming millennial kingdom.

Another passage which refers to the inheritance as a reward is found in Col. 3:23-24:

> *Whatever you do, work at it with all your heart ... since you know that you will receive an inheritance* [**kleronomia**] *from the Lord as a reward* [Gk. **antapodosis**].

The inheritance is a reward which is received as "wages"[24] for work done. Nothing could be plainer. The context is speaking of the return a man should receive because of his work, as in an employer-employee relationship. The inheritance is received as a result of work; it does not come as a gift. The Greek **antapodosis** means repayment or reward.[25] The verb **antapodidomi** never means to receive as a gift; it is always used in the New Testament of a repayment due to an obligation.[26]

An Inheritance Can Be Forfeited

In several passages Paul speaks of the possibility of not "inheriting the kingdom":

> *Do you not know that the wicked will not inherit* [**kleronomeo**] *the kingdom of God. Do not be deceived: Neither the sexually immoral nor idolaters nor adulterers nor male prostitutes nor homosexual offenders nor thieves nor slanderers nor swindlers will inherit* [**kleronomeo**] *the kingdom of God* (1 Cor. 6:9-10).

> *And that is what some of you were. But you were washed, you were sanctified, you were justified in the name of the Lord Jesus Christ and by the Spirit of our God* (6:11).

While entering the kingdom has often been equated with inheriting the kingdom, there is no semantic or exegetical basis for the equality. Even in English we acknowledge a distinction between entering and inheriting. A tenant, for

---

[24]receive = **apolambano**, to receive, especially as wages, AG, p. 93. The word often means to receive something back that is due, not as a gift. See Lk. 6:34; 18:30; 23:41; Rom. 1:27.

[25]AG, p. 72. They relate it to Rom. 2:5. Paul speaks of our receiving at the judgment a recompense based upon our works.

[26]See Rom. 11:35; 12:19; 1 Th. 3:9; 2 Th. 1:6; Heb. 10:30. See the article by P. C. Boettger, "Recompense, Reward, Gain, Wages," in *NIDNTT*, 3:134-36.

example, may live on or enter a landowner's great estate, but he does not own or inherit it. To inherit simply means to "possess," and the distinction between possession of Canaan and living there was observed earlier.

Similarly, there is no reason to assume that entering the kingdom and living there is the same thing as owning it and ruling in it. The heirs of the kingdom are its owners and rulers and not just its residents. Kendall agrees, "In other words, salvation is unchangeable but our inheritance in the kingdom of God is not unchangeable. Once saved, always saved, but our **inheritance** in God's kingdom may change considerably."[27] Even some Experimental Predestinarians acknowledge this distinction. Lenski, for example, observes that "'shall inherit' should not be reduced to mean only shall participate in. . . . That latter may be done without ownership."[28] The loss of one's inheritance is not the same as a loss of salvation.

Yet there is a real danger. It is possible for Christians to lose their inheritance. The Epistle to the Hebrews illustrates this from the life of Esau:

> *See that no one is sexually immoral or is godless like Esau, who for a single meal sold his inheritance rights as the oldest son. Afterward, as you know, when he wanted to inherit* [**kleronomeo**] *this blessing, he was rejected. He could bring about no change of mind, though he sought the blessing with tears* (Heb. 12:16-17).

Esau forfeited his inheritance, but he was still Isaac's son. He did not forfeit his relationship to his father. Furthermore, at the end of his life Isaac blessed Jacob and Esau regarding their future (Heb. 11:20). As Eric Sauer put it:[29]

> *Doubtless, birthright* [inheritance right] *is not identical with sonship. Esau remained Isaac's son even after he had rejected his birthright. In fact, he received, in spite of his great failure, a kind of secondary blessing* (Gen. 27:38-40b).

A Christian can deny his inheritance rights.[30] This should not come as a surprise because the inheritance in the Old Testament could be forfeited through disobedience. This fact surely informed the viewpoint of the New Testament writers! While this is not the same as losing one's justification, the consequences for eternity are serious. The apostle tells us that at the judgment seat of Christ our works will be revealed by "fire" (1 Cor. 3:13): "It will be revealed with fire,

---

[27]R. T. Kendall, *Once Saved Always Saved* (London: Hodder and Stoughton, 1984), p. 92.

[28]R. C. H. Lenski, *The Interpretation of I and II Corinthians* (Minneapolis: Augsburg, 1963), p. 247.

[29]Eric Sauer, *In the Arena of Faith* (Grand Rapids: Eerdmans, 1966), p. 152.

[30]This interpretation assumes that the readers of this epistle are genuine Christians and not merely professing ones. This point will be established in chapter 19 and 20.

and the fire will test the quality of each man's work." It is possible for a Christian's life work to be burned up because the building materials were wood, hay, and stubble. Only those works done in obedience to the Lord, out of proper motivation and in dependence upon Him (gold, silver, and precious stones), will survive the searing heat! Some will survive with very little to carry with them into eternity. As Paul put it:

> *If it is burned up, he will suffer loss;* **he himself will be saved,** *but only as one escaping through the flames* (1 Cor. 3:15).

Sauer summarizes:

> *The position of being a child of God is, indeed, not forfeitable, but not the total fullness of the heavenly birthright [inheritance]. In this sense there is urgent need to give diligence to make our calling and election sure. "For thus shall be richly supplied unto you the entrance into the eternal kingdom of our Lord and Savior Jesus Christ* (2 Pet. 1:10-11).[31]

We are therefore not surprised to read in 1 Cor. 6:10 that unrighteous Christians will lose their inheritance in the kingdom of God. Such an interpretation of the passage is consistent with the Epistle to the Hebrews and the Old Testament concept of the forfeiture of inheritance rights by disobedience.

But does the passage refer to unrighteous Christians, or does it refer to non-Christians who may have been loosely associated with the church and whose lack of perseverance in holiness has demonstrated that they were not true Christians at all?

We are told in v. 9 that the "wicked" (Gk. **adikoi**) will not inherit this kingdom, and in v. 1 the same word is used for non-Christians (cf. 6:6). In fact, the contrast between the righteous, **dikaioi**, and the unrighteous, **adikoi**, is common in the New Testament,[32] and those whose lives are characterized by **adikia** are in some contexts eternally condemned.[33] But this kind of argument assumes that **adikoi** is a kind of technical term for those lacking the imputed righteousness of Christ. The illegitimate identity transfer is committed to import the contextually derived suggestion of one kind of consequence of being **adikos** into the semantic value of the word. However, it is a general term for those (Christian or non-Christian) lacking godly character.[34] Both Christians and non-Christians can be **adikoi**. In fact, in 6:8 the apostle declares that the Corinthians are acting like **adikoi** (he uses the verb form, **adikeo**) just like the non-Christians of v. 1.

---

[31]Ibid., p. 154.

[32]See 1 Pet. 3:18; Acts 24:15; Mt. 5:45.

[33] See Brown. Cf. Rom. 1:18, 29; 2:8; 2 Th. 2:10-12; 2 Pet. 2:13-15.

[34]See usage in Lk. 16:10-11; 18:11; Heb. 6:10.

Robertson and Plummer are correct when they say, "The word ["wicked" in v. 9] is suggested by the previous, **adikeo** ["you cheat and do wrong," v. 8], and not with the **adikoi**, "the wicked," of v. 1."[35]

Exegetically this seems better for three reasons. First, the verbal form of **adikoi** in v. 8 is the near antecedent and one normally looks there first. And second, the phrase in v. 9 is **not the same** as "the wicked" in v. 1. In v. 1 the noun has the article, and it is definite, referring to a class. But in v. 9 it is without the article. "The articular construction emphasizes **identity**; the anarthrous construction emphasizes **character**."[36] Because the same word is used twice, once with the article (v. 1) and then without it (v. 9), it may be justifiable to press for this standard grammatical distinction here. If so, then the **adikoi** of v. 9 are not "the wicked" of v. 1. They are not of that definite class of people who are non-Christians. Rather, as to their behavior traits they are behaving in an unrighteous manner or character. In other words, the use of "the wicked" in v. 1 signifies "being," but the use of "wicked" in v. 9 signifies not being but "doing," and that was their problem. According to the **adikeo** of v. 8, they continued to walk as "mere men" (1 Cor. 3:4).

Finally, it is highly unlikely that the wicked of v. 9 could be non-Christians because Paul says, "do not be deceived," the wicked will not inherit the kingdom. Why would Christians think that non-Christians would inherit God's kingdom? Lang is surely correct, "Wherever inheriting is in question the relationship of a child to a parent is taken implicitly for granted: 'if children then heirs' is the universal rule."[37]

> *Instead, you yourselves cheat and do wrong* [**adikeo**]*, and you do this to your brothers* (1 Cor. 6:8).

Here Paul uses the verb form, **adikeo**, of the adjective **adikos**. He says in v. 8 that they "cheat and do wrong," and then in v. 9 he warns them concerning the eternal consequences of their behavior. He is not warning non-Christians that they will not inherit the kingdom; he is warning Christians, those who do wrong and do it to their brothers. It is pointless to argue that true Christians could never be characterized by the things in this list when Paul connects the true Christians of v. 8 with the individuals in v. 9. It is even more futile to argue this way when the entire context of 1 Corinthians describes activities of true Christians which parallel nearly every item in vv. 9-10. They were involved in sexual immorality (6:15); covetousness (probable motive in lawsuits, 6:1); drunkenness

---

[35]Archibald Robertson and Alfred Plummer, *A Critical and Exegetical Commentary on the First Epistle of St. Paul to the Corinthians*, 2d ed., *International Critical Commentary* (Edinburgh: T. & T. Clark, 1914), p. 118.

[36]DM, p. 140.

[37]G. H. Lang, *Firstborn Sons: Their Rights and Risks* (London: Samuel Roberts, 1936; reprint ed., Miami Springs, FL: Conley and Schoettle, 1984), p. 110.

(1 Cor. 11:21); dishonoring the Lord's table (1 Cor. 11:30--for this reason some of them experienced the sin unto death); adultery (5:1); and they were arrogant (4:18; 5:6). Yet this group of people that acts unrighteously, **adikeo,** and that is guilty of all these things has been washed, sanctified, and justified in the name of the Lord Jesus Christ (1 Cor. 6:11)! They were washed and saved from all those things, and yet they are still doing them. That is the terrible inconsistency which grieves the apostle through all sixteen chapters of this book. His burden in 6:9-10 is not to call into question their salvation (he specifically says they are saved in v. 11)[38] but to warn them that, if they do not change their behavior, they will, like Esau, forfeit their inheritance. As Kendall put it, "It was not salvation, then, but their inheritance in the kingdom of God these Christians were in danger of forfeiting."[39]

This, of course, does not mean that a person who commits one of these sins will not enter heaven. It does mean that, if he commits such a sin and persists in it without confessing and receiving cleansing (1 Jn. 1:9), he will lose his right to rule with Christ. Those walking in such a state, without their sin confessed, face eternal consequences if their Lord should suddenly appear and find them unprepared. They will truly be ashamed "before Him at His coming" (1 Jn. 2:28).

The parallel passages in Gal. 5:19-21 and Eph. 5:5-6 are to be interpreted the same way. In both passages we see the notion of merit and obedience connected with the inheritance. In neither, however, is there any contextual justification for assuming that those in danger of losing their inheritance are non-Christians who have only professed faith in Christ. That is a theological notion, derived from the doctrine of perseverance in holiness, which must be forced into the text. If inheriting the kingdom in these texts refers to going to heaven, then the apostle's sublime exhortation to these believers is reduced to the banal observation: "Remember, non-Christians do not go to heaven." A profound thought! And one which would have little relevance to these Galatian Christians who "belong to Christ Jesus" (Gal. 5:24).[40] Surely R. T. Kendall is correct when he says:

Are we to say that anybody who **does** *any of these things (e.g. envying, strife) is not going to heaven? Not at all. But such things as*

---

[38]He has said they are "sanctified in Christ Jesus, called to be saints" (1 Cor. 1:2) but that they were carnal (1 Cor. 3:1, 3).

[39]Kendall, *Once Saved,* p. 96.

[40]The fact that these believers "have crucified the sinful nature" can hardly refer to the idea that all Christians have sacrificially negated the impulses of the flesh. The unexpected occurrence of the active voice may be paralleled with 1 Cor. 9:22, "I have become all things to all men in order that by all means I might save some." The passage refers back to Rom. 6:1-11, our joint crucifixion with Christ at initial salvation, which must be put into experience by reckoning and yielding.

'covetousness,' 'foolish talking,' as well as sexual immorality forfeit one's inheritance in God's kingdom. "[41]

In Mt. 25:34 we find once again that inheriting the kingdom is conditioned on obedience and service to the King, a condition far removed from the New Testament teaching of justification by faith alone for entrance into heaven:

> *Then the King will say to those on His right, 'Come, you who are blessed by My Father; take your inheritance* [lit. inherit the kingdom, **kleronomeo**], *the kingdom prepared for you since the foundation of the world.*

And again:

> *Then they will go away to eternal punishment, but the righteous to eternal life* (Mt. 25:46).

Why are they being granted this blessing? Because (**gar**, v. 35) they ministered to Christ's brethren, the Jews, during the terrible holocaust of the great tribulation (25:35-40). Here inheriting should be given its full sense of reward for faithful service as the context requires.[42]

But there are only two categories of people mentioned as being at this judgment, not three. We see only sheep and goats, Christians and non-Christians, and not two categories of Christians and one of unbelievers. Why are there not two kinds of sheep, the faithful and the unfaithful? There are three reasons. First, the unfaithful sheep are not mentioned because our Lord is speaking in broad terms, and the focus is on the reward to the faithful. As a group the believers surviving the tribulation are viewed in terms of their expected and anticipated performance, faithful sheep. That some were faithful and some were not in no way negates the general offer of the inheritance to the sheep. All would understand that not all sheep have been faithful and that technically only the faithful sheep receive the inheritance. It seems to this writer that to argue otherwise is a wooden use of language that would prevent men from ever speaking in general terms or risk being misunderstood.

---

[41]Kendall, p. 96.

[42]"Entering eternal life" in Mt. 25:46 is similar to "inheriting the kingdom" in 25:34. It does not refer to the entrance into life at regeneration; these sheep are saints already. Subsequent to becoming saints, they will enter into eternal life. As will be discussed in chapter 7, they are entering into an enriched experienced of that life which they have already received at regeneration, available to the faithful believer. Alford says, "The **zoe** here spoken of is not bare **existence**, which would have **annihilation** for its opposite; but **blessedness** and **reward**" (Henry Alford, *The Greek Testament*, ed. Everett F. Harrison, 4 vols. (1849-60; reprint ed., Chicago: Moody Press, 1968), 1:257. (Emphases are Alford's.)

Earlier in the context He has told us that there are unfaithful Christians: the wicked hypocritical servant (24:48); the foolish virgins (25:2); and the wicked servant (25:26). All three of these unfaithful Christians are sheep, saved people, as will be argued elsewhere.[43]

Second, there were not many unfaithful sheep there. The persecutions of the Antichrist made one very careful about becoming a believer.

But, third, the separation of the faithful from the unfaithful does not occur at this time but afterward. After the kingdom has begun and all those who are born again have entered it, the wedding feast occurs. At that time the separation of the wise and foolish virgins occurs.[44] Because God does not deal with the unfaithful believer at this time, they are not mentioned.

Is this a case of special pleading? Is it not clear that the term "sheep" is all that is mentioned and that there is no reference to faithful **and** unfaithful sheep? In reply we would say that there are many things about these sheep which are not mentioned which are nevertheless taught elsewhere in the Scripture. It is not mentioned that the sheep are distinguished elsewhere into various classes according to differing degrees of reward, but they will be. Some receive five cities and some ten. It is not mentioned that they will receive resurrection bodies at this time with varying degrees of glory, but they will.[45] It is not mentioned that some will sit on thrones and some will not. It is not mentioned that some will be great in the kingdom and some will be least. Everything does not have to be said in every verse! If the distinctions among sheep are taught elsewhere and not contextually denied here (and they are not!), there is no exegetical reason for not assuming their presence in this passage even if they are not specifically mentioned.

The faithful sheep are now being rewarded with the inheritance. This is the fulfillment of the Lord's promise: "But he who stands firm to the end will be saved."[46] They are those who persevered under persecution unto the end (Rev. 14:12). Jesus has already explained that Christians who annul the least of the commands and teach others to do the same will be in the kingdom but will be "called least" there (Mt. 5:19). On the other hand, "whoever practices and teaches these commands will be called great in the kingdom of heaven." Being called "great" in the kingdom is to be one of the meek who "will inherit the earth" (Mt. 5:5). These are those "who are persecuted because of righteousness" to

---

[43]See chapter 17.

[44]See discussion in chapter 17.

[45]1 Cor. 15:41-42.

[46]Mt. 24:13. As will be discussed below, to be saved here refers to more than mere physical survival; it means to enter into the messianic blessing, the coming of the kingdom, and rule there. It refers to the "fruition" of their salvation, the Davidic salvation, not the beginning of it. David exclaimed regarding this future event, "Will He not bring to fruition my salvation, and grant me my every desire?" (2 Sam. 23:5).

whom belong "the kingdom of heaven" (Mt. 5:5). These are the faithful Christians to whom the Lord Jesus said: "Rejoice and be glad, because great is your reward in heaven, for in the same way they persecuted the prophets which were before you" (Mt. 5:12). These verses from the lips of our Lord in the same gospel make it clear that the sheep in Mt. 25:34 are the faithful sheep; otherwise they would not have inherited the kingdom. The unfaithful are not mentioned because they are not relevant here, since they receive no reward. And because inheriting the kingdom is **conditioned** upon this faithful perseverance, it cannot be equated with justification and theologically interpreted as continuation in holiness because a perfect perseverance and obedience would be necessary for that (Mt. 5:48). George Peters explains:

> *The Savior, therefore, in accord with the general analogy of the Scripture on the subject, declares that when He comes with His saints in glory to set up His Kingdom, out of the nations those who exhibited* **a living faith by active deeds of sympathy and assistance** *shall - with those that preceded them . . . inherit (i.e., be kings in) a Kingdom. It is a direct lesson of encouragement to those who live during the period of Antichrist in the persecution of the Church, to exercise charity, for which* **they shall be rewarded** *[emphasis is Peters's]. Hence it follows that the test presented is precisely the one needed to ascertain,* **not who would be saved** *(for that is not the train of thought, although connected with it),* **but who would inherit a Kingdom or gain an actual, real rulership in it.**[47]

Inheriting the Kingdom

The phrase "inherit the kingdom" has occurred several times in the discussion above. Because of its specific meaning, some additional comment is in order. We find the phrase in Mt. 25:34; 1 Cor. 6:9-10; 15:50; Gal. 5:21; and Eph. 5:5. In addition, the phrase "inherit the land" is found in Mt. 5:5. In each instance we find that, in order to inherit the kingdom, there must be some work done or certain character traits, such as immorality, must be absent from our lives. The fact that such conditions are necessary suggests that the term is not to be equated with entering the kingdom which is available to all, freely, on the basis of faith alone but with something in addition to entering. Indeed, the very use of the word "inherit" instead of "enter" in these passages suggests that more than just entrance is meant.

---

[47]George N. H. Peters, *The Theocratic Kingdom*, 3 vols. (New York: Funk and Wagnalls, 1884; reprint ed., Grand Rapids: Kregel, 1972), 2:376.

Inheriting the Kingdom

SCRIPTURE	PHRASE	CONDITIONS
Mt. 25:34	take your inheritance	caring for brothers by giving food and drink during the tribulation
1 Cor. 6:9	inherit the kingdom	having none of the following character traits: immorality, idolatry, adultery, prostitution, homosexuality, thievery, greed, drunkenness, or being a swindler
1 Cor. 15:50	inherit the kingdom	having a resurrection body
Eph. 5:5	an inheritance in the kingdom	having none of the following character traits: immorality, idolatry, impurity, greed
Gal. 5:21	inherit the earth	not having our lives characterized by the acts of the sinful nature
Mt. 5:5	inherit the land	meekness

But what does it mean to inherit the kingdom? The Lord's teaching in the Sermon on the Mount gives us a helpful starting point for understanding this great theme:

Blessed are the poor in spirit, for **theirs is the kingdom of heaven** (Mt. 5:3).

Blessed are the meek, for they **will inherit the earth** (Mt. 5:5).

Blessed are those who are persecuted because of righteousness, for **theirs is the kingdom of heaven** (Mt. 5:10).

The Lord seems to be equating the terms "theirs is the kingdom of heaven" with "inherit the earth." Eichler, noting this parallelism observed, "In the Beatitudes, Jesus puts side by side the promise of the kingdom of heaven and that of inheriting the earth."[48] That the term "inherit the kingdom" is equivalent to the promise to Abraham that his descendants will inherit the land has been noted by many. Robertson and Plummer say, "'To inherit the kingdom of God' is a Jewish thought, in allusion to the promises given to Abraham."[49] According to Godet "the verb, to inherit, is an allusion to the inheritance of Canaan given to Israel."[50]

"But he who takes refuge in Me, shall inherit the land, and shall possess My holy mountain" (Isa. 57:13). The prophet exults that in the coming kingdom "all your people will be righteous; they will possess [inherit] the land forever" (Isa. 60:21 NASB). Throughout the Old Testament the possession of the earth by the righteous is a common theme and refers to the rule of the saints in the future kingdom.[51]

Now if the functional equivalence of the terms "inherit the kingdom" and "inherit the land" are accepted, then our study of inheriting the land in the Old Testament becomes very relevant to the understanding of the term "inherit the kingdom" in the New. In particular, we noted that the land of Canaan was inherited by Israel on the basis of faith-obedience and that this inheritance was an additional blessing to those who were already saved (e.g., Joshua and Caleb). They obtained the land by being victorious in battle, following the Lord wholeheartedly, and being obedient to all He said in his law. Similarly, in the New Testament, inheriting the kingdom is conditioned upon spiritual obedience and not faith alone. Furthermore, in the Old Testament we saw that entering the land was not the same as inheriting it. There is therefore justification in pressing the

---

[48]J. Eichler, "Inheritance," in *NIDNTT*, 2:300.

[49]Robertson and Plummer, p. 118.

[50]Frederick Louis Godet, *Commentary on First Corinthians* (Grand Rapids: Kregel, 1977), pp. 295-96. Godet, an amillennialist, of course sees this land as a "type of the blessedness to come."

[51]See Prov. 11:31; 10:30; Ps. 136:21-22; 115:16; 37:9, 11, 22, 29, 34. In Ps. 37 the inheriting of the land follows the removal of evildoers in the kingdom.

obvious point that inheriting the kingdom is not the same as entering the kingdom.

The New Testament uses the phrase "enter the kingdom of heaven" eight times.[52] In contrast to the phrase "inherit the kingdom," the conditions for entering are faith alone. Entrance is ours through rebirth (Jn. 3:5) which is ours solely through believing on His name (Jn. 1:12-13). We must have the humble, simple trust of a child if we are to enter God's kingdom (Mt. 18:3), and there is only one work we can do, the work of believing (Mt. 7:21; Jn. 6:40).[53] A perfect righteousness is necessary to obtain entrance, a righteousness which comes by faith alone (Mt. 5:20; 6:48; 2 Cor. 5:21; Rom. 4:3). It is difficult for rich men to enter because they trust in riches rather than in God (Mt. 19:24).[54] We must go through many hardships on the path of life as we journey toward this kingdom (Acts 14:22).

That inheriting the kingdom is different from entering (in the sense of inhabiting) the kingdom seems to be reinforced in the New Testament by Paul's use of the phrase in 1 Cor. 15:50:

> *I declare to you, brothers, that flesh and blood cannot inherit the*
> *kingdom of God, nor does the perishable inherit the imperishable.*

It is quite clear to the apostle Paul that men and women in mortal bodies will be in the kingdom. There will be physical procreation and physical death (Isa. 65:20; Ezek. 36:11). Furthermore, a multitude of unregenerate men in mortal bodies will rebel at the end of the thousand-year kingdom and will be "devoured," hardly an experience of resurrected and immortal saints (Rev. 20:7-10).

Paul's statement, in order to be made consistent with the rest of the Bible, requires that there is a difference between being a resident of the kingdom and inheriting it. Clearly, human beings in mortal bodies do live in the kingdom, but they are not heirs of that kingdom, a privilege which only those in resurrection bodies can share.[55]

When the apostle declares that men in mortal bodies will not inherit the kingdom,[56] this obviously requires that the resurrection and transformation of the

---

[52]Mt. 5:20; 7:21; 18:3; 19:23; 19:24; Mk. 9:47; Jn. 3:5; Acts 14:22.

[53]See discussion on Mt. 7 in chapter 9.

[54]See discussion of the rich young ruler above.

[55]Paul is not saying here that **all** transformed saints inherit the kingdom, only that **only** transformed saints inherit the kingdom. See Peters, 1:602, where he expresses the same view and equates inheriting the kingdom with becoming a ruler in it.

[56]Only resurrected Israel united with a resurrected and transformed church will rule in the kingdom.

sheep occurs prior to their "receiving the kingdom" and must be simultaneous with the judgment of the sheep and the goats. If this is the case, then a problem develops in that there appear to be no saints left in mortal bodies to populate the millennium in contradiction to the Old Testament passages previously discussed.

Since the Scriptures are silent on this problem, one must be careful how he explains the difficulty. It is appropriate at this juncture to invoke the analogy of faith and allow other scriptural examples or teachings to explain what is left unsaid regarding this judgment. We are told that the experiences of the Israelites as they journeyed from Egypt to Canaan were to be examples for us (1 Cor. 10:6, 15). Indeed, the New Testament writers appeal to their journey to teach spiritual truth to the New Testament church (Heb. 3:7-14; 1 Cor. 10:1-15). The writer to the Hebrews in particular parallels their conquest of Canaan, their rest, with our entrance into rest, the completion of our work and subsequent reward in Canaan in the coming kingdom. We might therefore be justified in seeking a solution to this problem from their experience.

An answer at once suggests itself. The entire first generation was judged in unbelief and died in the wilderness, with the exception of those under twenty years of age:

> *In this desert your bodies will fall--every one of you twenty years old or more who was counted in the census and who has grumbled against me. Not one of you will enter the land I swore with uplifted hand to make your home, except Caleb son of Jephunneh and Joshua son of Nun* (Num. 14:29-30).

The passage is instructive in several ways. Even though God "swore with uplifted hand" that He would give them the land, they will not receive the land because of their disobedience and unbelief. But equally important it shows that those who had not reached an age of accountability were exempt from the judgment which prohibited their elders from entering the land.[57] In a similar way, perhaps the believing children of the sheep who have escaped the judgments of the great tribulation will constitute a kind of "second exodus" and will be the mortal believers who enter into the coming kingdom and who are its subjects, if not its owners.[58]

Assuming that "inherit the kingdom" has become a functional equivalent to "inherit the land" in Jewish theology, what precisely does it mean? It appears that the basic meaning of "to inherit" (Gk. **kleronomeo**) is "to possess, to own."

---

[57]Entering the land does not parallel the believer's entrance to heaven; it signifies his willingness to "cross the Jordan" and engage the enemy. In other words, it is a decision by a regenerate saint to submit to the lordship of Christ and trust God for victory in the spiritual battle.

[58]One must be born again to enter the kingdom of heaven, Jn. 3:5.

The lexicons define the word as "to receive as one's own,"[59] "to acquire, obtain, come into possession of."[60] An inheritance (Gk. **kleronomia**) is a "possession, property."[61] Therefore, when Jesus invites the sheep to inherit the kingdom, He is inviting them to possess the kingdom, to receive it as their own, to acquire it.

Many times, when the word "possess" is used with concrete nouns, it includes the notion of "to have authority over," but that is, of course, not part of the meaning of the Hebrew and Greek words for inheritance. Nevertheless, it is difficult to separate this notion from its usage in many contexts. This is particularly obvious when the fundamental notion of inheritance, to receive property, is considered. Normally, when one receives property, we understand that he has the right to do with it what he chooses. He may sell it, build a house upon it, farm it, or rent it out. It is his to do with what he wants; he **owns** it. This prerogative of doing what one wants with one's own is what is normally meant by having authority over one's own possession. For this reason there is justification in saying that inheriting land will result in a degree of authority or sovereignty over that land after it has been received as an inheritance. This is not to say that "inherit" itself means to rule or have authority over.

However, when one begins to consider the theological concept involved in inheriting the land, and not just the semantic value of the word "inherit," a justification begins to emerge for investing the phrase "inherit the kingdom" with more than just ownership. Rather, the notion of having authority becomes more prominent. This is implied in the messianic psalm from which Jesus quotes in Mt. 5:5 ("the meek shall inherit the earth"), the context referring to the coming fulfillment of the Old Testament hope in the messianic kingdom. We are immediately cast into a surrounding sea of ideas about the role of the saints in that future eschaton.

Even a cursory reading of the Old Testament passages will attest that God's final goal for man during that era is not simply to live there and be happy. It is much more than this. His goal is that one day we will rule and have dominion over the earth (Gen. 1:16-28):

> *What is man that you are mindful of him, the son of man that you care for him? You made him a little lower than the heavenly beings and crowned him with glory and honor. You made him ruler over the works of your hands; you put everything under his feet* (Ps. 8:4-6).

Man's destiny is not just to reside in blessedness in the millennial land of Canaan; it is to be "ruler over the works of [God's] hands." It is rulership that comes to the forefront.

---

[59]AS, p. 248.

[60]AG, p. 436.

[61]Ibid.

This seems to receive explicit confirmation when Jesus tells the sheep in Mt. 25:34 to "inherit the kingdom." It appears that Jesus is lifting a phrase right out of Dan. 7:

> *As I watched, this horn was waging war against the saints and defeating them, until the Ancient of Days came and pronounced judgment in favor of the saints of the Most High, and the time came when they* **possessed the kingdom** (Dan. 7:21-22).

The contexts are similar; both refer to the coming of a Son of Man (Dan. 7:13; Mt. 25:31). In both passages we are in the tribulation period just prior to the second coming where the saints are persecuted. Jesus evidently had the book of Daniel in mind in the Olivet Discourse because He quotes from it in 24:15 where He mentions the abomination of desolation of Dan. 9:27. The phrase "possess the kingdom" seems therefore to precisely parallel the phrase "inherit the kingdom" and is the source of this New Testament concept.

But what does it mean? The Aramaic word in Dan. 7:22 translated "possess" is **chasan**, and it means to "take possession." "It emphasizes strength and riches."[62] According to the lexicon it means "to be strong, overcome; take possession of."[63] The choice of the word suggests more than a mere passive receiving but a degree of authority in the kingdom. This idea seems to be confirmed when, in Dan. 7:27 Daniel clarifies what it will mean "to possess the kingdom":

> *Then the sovereignty, power and greatness of the kingdoms under the whole heaven will be handed over to the saints, the people of the Most High. . .* (Dan. 7:27).

Possessing the kingdom is therefore the receipt of sovereignty over the nations. One day the saints will rule the world! Ladd says it refers to "rule over all the earth."[64] The apparent direct borrowing of the phrase by Jesus seems to justify the conclusion that "to inherit the kingdom" means far more than mere residence there; it is to have authority and rulership there. If so, this would fit in well with a broad New Testament theme:

> *If we endure, we will also reign with him* (2 Tim. 2:12).

> *To him who overcomes and does my will to the end, I will give authority over the nations.* (Rev. 2:26).

---

[62]R. Laird Harris, "**chasan**," in *TWOT*, 2:1020.

[63]BDB, p. 1093.

[64]George E. Ladd, *A Theology of the New Testament* (Grand Rapids: Eerdmans, 1974), p. 148.

Do you not know that the saints will judge the world? (1 Cor. 6:2).

There are several phrases which seem to be equivalent to the phrase "inherit the kingdom." For example, when Jesus tells the faithful servant to "enter into the joy of your Lord" (Mt. 25:21), this could be understood as an invitation to share in the messianic rule. As such it is possible to understand it as being something different than an invitation to enter the kingdom; rather, it is entrance into the "master's happiness", the messianic partnership. Similarly, as will be explained in the next chapter, the phrase used by the writer to the Hebrews, "enter into rest," is not to be equated with entrance into the kingdom but with obtaining the inheritance, an honor won on the field of battle.

In conclusion, "to inherit the kingdom" is a virtual synonym for rulership in the kingdom and not entrance into it. George N. H. Peters is correct when he says, "To inherit a Kingdom, if it has any propriety of meaning, undoubtedly denotes the reception of kingly authority or rulership in the Kingdom."[65] All saints will enter the kingdom through faith alone (Jn. 3:3), but only obedient saints who endure, who overcome, and who perform works of righteousness (e.g., ministering to Christ's brethren) will inherit it, i.e., rule there.

The Inheritance in Hebrews

The Inheritance

The verb kleronomeo occurs four times in the book of Hebrews.[66] Its usage there is not inconsistent with its usage elsewhere, a reward for a life of faithfulness. The inheritance can be forfeited because of disobedience, as in the case of Esau (Heb. 12:17), and it is only obtained by persevering, i.e., by "faith and patience" (Heb. 6:12). Jesus has inherited a superior name to that of the angels (1:4). He achieved this inheritance by perseverance in suffering (Heb. 2:10; Phil. 2:9-11).[67] Similarly, His companions (Heb. 1:9, Gk. metochoi) will "inherit salvation" (Heb. 1:14) in the same way. We share in that future glory, the inheritance-salvation, only if we remain faithful to the end:

We have come to share in Christ [i.e., we are metochoi] *if we hold firmly till the end the confidence we had at first* (Heb. 3:14).

So do not throw away your confidence; it will be richly rewarded. You need to persevere so that when you have done the will of God, you will receive what he has promised (Heb. 10:35-36).

---

[65]Peters, 2:573.

[66]Heb. 1:4; 1:14; 6:12; 12:17.

[67]Christ's obedience as the condition of obtaining His new name, LORD JESUS CHRIST (Phil. 2:9-11, "therefore"), seems to be a similar idea to His receiving of His inheritance.

Perseverance to the end, faithfulness, and doing the will of God are the conditions of obtaining the inheritance-salvation in this epistle, conditions which are absent from the Pauline teaching of obtaining salvation (in the sense of final deliverance from hell) on the basis of faith alone. As will be discussed below, a different salvation is in view: co-rulership with Christ in the coming kingdom.

To equate the inheritance with heaven results in a glaring inconsistency. It would mean that believers, by entering the church, are already heirs of the kingdom. Why then are they uniformly exhorted to become heirs by faithful labor when they are already heirs?

The noun **kleronomia** is found in two places in Hebrews (Heb. 11:8; 9:15). In Heb. 11:8 it refers to Abraham's acquisition of the land of Canaan. While that land was guaranteed on oath, it was obtained by spiritual obedience. What is stressed in Hebrews 11 is that Abraham "obeyed and went." Had he not obeyed, he would not have inherited.

The final use of the noun is in Heb. 9:15:

For this reason Christ is the mediator of a new covenant, that those who are called may receive the promised eternal inheritance [**kleronomia**]*--now that he has died as a ransom to set them free from the sins committed under the first covenant.*

How they obtain this inheritance is not affirmed here, but it is affirmed elsewhere. It is by "faith and patience" (Heb. 6:12) and "holding firm to the end" (Heb. 3:14) that we "inherit what has been promised." To what promises is he referring? Sometimes in Hebrews the promise seems to refer to justification by faith. But in this passage, the conclusion of the warning, we are justified in looking back to 4:1 where the promise of the remaining rest is in view. This refers to the completion of our task and subsequent entrance into our reward. It appears to have similar meaning in Heb. 11:9, 13 when it is used of the land promises to the patriarchs. They too were to remain faithful to the end of life, and in so doing, they entered into rest and will one day possess the land. The inheritance should take the meaning it takes elsewhere in Hebrews--ownership of the millennial land of Canaan, the future reign of the servant kings, joint rulership with Messiah in the heavenly country, the millennial land of Palestine. Kaiser insists that the inheritance in Heb. 9:15 is "the firm possession of the land as Heb. 11:9 most assuredly asserts."[68] Christ's mediatorial work has as its aim that His sons should enter into that partnership with Him. Their achievement of that destiny, however, as explained elsewhere in the book, is conditioned upon obedience

---

[68]Walter C. Kaiser, Jr., *Toward an Old Testament Theology* (Grand Rapids: Zondervan, 1978), p. 169.

from the heart. It is an eternal inheritance because we will inherit the land forever.[69]

The Rights of the Firstborn

One of the sternest warnings of the New Testament is found in Heb. 12:12-29. The writer of the Hebrews challenges them to pursue sanctification and cautions that without it no one will "see the Lord." Some have held that this refers to a "beatific vision" which some Christians will enjoy in heaven and some will not.[70] However, in view of the other references in Scripture to seeing the Lord, it may be best to understand the phrase as referring to a deeper Christian experience.[71] Then he warns them regarding the loss of their inheritance rights:

> *See to it that no one comes short of the grace of God; that no root of bitterness springing up causes trouble, and by it many be defiled; that there be no immoral or godless person like Esau, who sold his own birthright for a single meal. For you know that even afterward, when he desired to* **inherit the blessing,** *he was rejected, for he found no place for repentance, though he sought for it with tears* (Heb. 12:15-17 NASB).

Esau was the firstborn son and therefore by birth had the rights and privileges described as belonging to the firstborn. The law of the firstborn sheds great light on the biblical conditions for obtaining the inheritance. Among the sons the firstborn son enjoyed special privileges. When his father died, he received a double share of the inheritance (Dt. 21:17). During his life he was preeminent among his brothers (Gen. 43:33). God had originally intended to make the firstborn of the sons of Israel His priests. However, due to the disobedience in the wilderness He took that blessing from the firstborn and gave it to the Levites instead (Num. 8:14-18).

God often violated His own rule regarding the firstborn blessing. Sometimes this was based upon grace. Isaac was selected ahead of Ishmael, the firstborn; and Jacob was chosen instead of Esau for the blessing of the firstborn. Sometimes the reversal of the firstborn right to the inheritance was based upon merit. To the end of his life it was the father's prerogative to determine the disposal of his property.[72] If the eldest son was not qualified, then the father could

---

[69]Peters, 1:322.

[70]For example, Lang, *Firstborn Sons*, pp. 98ff.

[71]In Mt. 5:8 the peacemakers will "see God," i.e., they will really know Him and walk with Him. In Job 42:5 Job came to "see" God as a result of his trial. The meaning is that he came to know Him more deeply and intimately.

[72]1 Chr. 26:10: Shimri the first (for though he was not the firstborn, his father made him the first).

give it to the son who was. The Scripture only requires that, if the firstborn right is denied to the eldest, that it not be a matter of favoritism (Dt. 21:15-17). Even though Reuben was Jacob's firstborn, the inheritance rights passed to Simeon (Gen. 49:3-4) and ultimately to Judah, the fourth in line, because he saved Joseph's life (Gen. 37:26-27).

The rights and privileges of the firstborn were given, provisionally, at birth. The right to the inheritance was his, but he could lose it. It was necessary that the firstborn son maintain these rights. He must be worthy of the elevated status and honor. All the sons are heirs, but only those who met the conditions of the firstborn achieved the elevated status and authority and retain their inheritance. The many New Testament references to something conditional in the future life of the believer may reflect this Old Testament distinction between the firstborn son who retained his privilege and those like Esau who did not. Those Christians who suffer with Him (Rom. 8:17), who endure (2 Tim. 2:15), and who are the overcomers of the book of Revelation are the firstborn sons.

Esau, although heir to the rights of the firstborn, counted them of little value. In order to satisfy his passing appetite, he sold them for a meal. Later in life he changed his mind and regretted his rash decision. Yet he was unable to change his father's mind.

Whether or not Esau was saved is not relevant to this discussion. The writer uses him as an illustration of the fact that the saved can lose their firstborn inheritance rights. His example is applied to those who have come to the church of the firstborn ones (Heb. 12:23).[73]

True Christians fully parallel the description of Esau. We are children of God and we are firstborn sons. Because of that we possess the rights of the firstborn. We do not have to earn these rights. They are given to us through the grace of God. However, we must value and keep these rights and warned by Esau's example regarding the possibility of not doing so. But even though we cannot forfeit eternal life, we can forfeit our firstborn rights

Two Kinds of Inheritance

Consistent with the Old Testament usage, believers in the New Testament are presented with two different inheritances. As discussed above, we are, if faithful, heirs of the millennial land of Canaan and will reign with Messiah there.

---

[73]The Greek word translated "firstborn" is plural, and therefore the firstborn ones are referred to and not Christ as the firstborn. To come to the "church of the firstborn" means to be called to the privilege of being a firstborn son. All Christians are called to be part of that assembly and by birth have a right to be there. However, they may forfeit that right and never achieve their calling. That is the thrust of all the warnings of the book of Hebrews. See chapters 19 and 20.

But another heirship, which is unconditional, is also presented. As Old Testament believers were heirs of God, so are those under the New Covenant:

> *So that, having been justified by his grace, we might become heirs* [**kleronomos**] *having the hope of eternal life* (Ti. 3:7).

Similarly, Paul tells us in Galatians:

> *If you belong to Christ, then you are Abraham's seed, and heirs* [**kleronomos**] *according to the promise* (Gal. 3:29).

The "promise" refers to Gal. 3:8, "All nations will be blessed through you." It is a reference to that aspect of the Abrahamic promise which referred not to Canaan but to the coming gift of the free justifying righteousness of Christ. Again he declares:

> *Because you are sons, God sent the Spirit of his Son into our hearts, the Spirit who calls out, "Abba, Father." So you are no longer a slave, but a son; and since you are a son, God has made you also an heir* [**kleronomos**] (Gal. 4:6-7).

Here is an heirship which comes to the Christian only because he is a son and for no other reason. There is no mention of work or obedience here. However, there is an inheritance which is conditional as well. It is "kept through faith" and obtained only "if we share in His sufferings." All Christians are heirs of God, but not all will inherit the kingdom.

In 1 Pet. 1:3-5 the apostle exclaims:

> *Praise be to the God and Father of our Lord Jesus Christ! In his great mercy he has given us new birth into a living hope through the resurrection of Jesus Christ from the dead, and into an inheritance* [**kleronomia**] *that can never perish, spoil or fade - kept in heaven for you, who through faith are shielded by God's power until the coming of the salvation that is ready to be revealed in the last time.*

It is probable that Paul had a similar thought in mind in Rom. 8:16-17:

> *The Spirit Himself testified with our spirit, that we are God's children. Now if we are children then we are heirs, heirs of God, and co-heirs with Christ* **if indeed we share in His sufferings,** *in order that we may also share in His glory.*

This passage, in agreement with Gal. 4:7, says we are all heirs of God by virtue of the fact that we are His children. But it says something else. It says we are also co-heirs with Christ "if indeed we share in His sufferings." The second heirship mentioned in this verse is conditional upon our joining with Him in His sufferings. Being an heir of God is unconditional, but being a joint heir of the kingdom is conditioned upon our spiritual perseverance.[74] Full discussion of this passage will be undertaken in chapter 16.

The fact that this heirship is conditional is commonly acknowledged by Sanday[75] and Denny.[76] However, since both these commentators equate these two heirships as one, they labor under the difficulty of explaining how all of a sudden Paul is teaching a salvation from hell which is now conditioned upon the believer persevering in suffering. In fact, Sanday specifically connects v. 17 with a "current Christian saying: 2 Tim. 2:11," which makes rulership in the kingdom the issue and not salvation from hell. Their difficulty would be resolved and the obvious harmony with 2 Tim. 2:11 explained on the simple assumption taught elsewhere of two heirships.

The inheritance is usually conditioned upon obedience, but salvation from hell is always by faith alone. In order to become a joint heir with Christ, one of His metochoi, we must faithfully endure our sufferings to the end.

> *This is a faithful saying:*
>
> *For if we died with Him,*
> *We shall also live with Him.*
> *If we endure,*
> *We shall also reign with Him.*
> *If we deny Him,*
> *He also will deny us;*
> *If we are faithless,*
> *He remains faithful;*
> *He cannot deny Himself* (2 Tim. 2:11-13 NKJV).

As in Rom. 8:17 reigning with Christ seems to be conditioned upon endurance. The converse, to deny Him, will result in His denying us when He rewards His church according to the things done in the body, "good or bad" (2 Cor. 5:10). The possibility of being "denied" does not refer to loss of salvation, because the apostle clarifies that, even when we are "faithless," He will remain faithful to us. But it does mean that we may be "disqualified for the prize" (1 Cor.

---

[74]The translation above has been slightly changed from the rendering in the NIV. In the Greek text punctuation marks were added by later editors, and the writer has placed the comma after "heirs of God" rather than after "co-heirs of Christ," thus implying that two heirships, not one, are taught. Justification for this will be found in chapter 16, "Life in the Spirit." See under Rom. 8:17 in index.

[75]William Sanday and Arthur C. Headlam, *A Critical and Exegetical Commentary on the Epistle to the Romans* (Edinburgh: T. & T. Clark, 1902), p. 204.

[76]James Denney, "St. Paul's Epistle to the Romans," in *EGT*, p. 648.

9:27) and stand ashamed at His coming (1 Jn. 2:28) and be denied a place of co-heirship in the final destiny of man.

The Inheritance and Canaan in Galatians

In the Epistle to the Galatians the apostle refers to the inheritance and to the heirs:

> *For if the inheritance* [**kleronomia**] *depends on the law, then it no longer depends on a promise; but God in his grace gave it to Abraham through a promise* (Gal. 3:18).

> *If you belong to Christ, then you are Abraham's seed, and heirs* [**kleronomos**] *according to the promise* (Gal. 3:29).

The promise referred to in 3:18 is found in 3:8 and 16 and recalls the promise to Abraham that "all the nations will be blessed through you" (Gal. 3:8).[77] It is significant that the inheritance here is connected not with the land promise but with that aspect of the Abrahamic promise which referred to the gift of justification to the Gentiles. The heirs of 3:29 become heirs by virtue of being sons, and for no other reason, and they are heirs of God, i.e., possessors of eternal life. Thus, the inheritance is not the land of Canaan in this instance but the gift of justification into which all Christians enter by believing. Amillennialists, of course, would point to such passages and claim that the apostle is interpreting the Old Testament covenants spiritually. Canaan, they say, was intended as a type, a spiritual anticipation of something higher, entrance into heaven itself. Rendall, for example, explains:

> *The original promise was limited to the possession of the promised land, but was coupled with a perpetual covenant between God and the seed of Abraham: "I will be their God, Thou shalt keep My covenant, thou and thy seed after thee in their generations." Hence Hebrew prophecy imported into it the idea of a spiritual inheritance and the Epistle adopts this interpretation without hesitation.*[78]

The argument is fallacious. As pointed out above, Paul does not even have the land promise aspect of the Abrahamic Covenant in view. He is referring to the universal promises to the Gentiles.

The word "heir" is used again in 4:7:

---

[77]Gen. 12:3; 22:18; 26:4; 28:14.

[78]Frederick Rendall, "The Epistle to the Galatians," in *EGT*, 3:171.

So you are no longer a slave, but a son; and since you are a son, God
has made you also an heir [**kleronomos**].

All Christians are heirs of God by faith alone. But like the Old Testament
there are two kinds of inheritance: an inheritance which is merited and an inheritance which belongs to all Christians because they are sons, and for no other reason. The fulfillment of the land promise, while ultimately certain for the nation,
was conditioned for each generation on the basis of obedience.

Paul's use of **kleronomia** in 4:30 is similarly explained:

But what does the Scripture say? Get rid of the slave woman and her
son, for the slave woman's son will never share in the inheritance
[**kleronomia**] *with the free woman's son.*

It should be noted that this usage is found in an illustration from the Old
Testament (4:24-31). He is using the illustration of Hagar and Sarah to refute
the notion that law and grace can be mixed. He says he speaks "figuratively." He
is using the term "heir" in the general sense of "possessor" to figuratively illustrate
that heirship in general is never appropriated by a mixture of Sinai and the
Jerusalem above, Ishmael and Isaac, law and grace; neither is the inheritance of
heaven.

It might be objected that this interpretation seems to be in conflict with
earlier conclusions regarding Gal. 5:21. There it was claimed that the inheritance
was not equal to heaven but referred to our reward. What justification is there
for changing the meaning in Gal. 5:21 from "heaven" to "reward in heaven"?
Surely it is obvious the same word can have different meanings in the same book,
the same chapter, or even the same verse.

In the book of 1 Timothy the word "save" has different meanings in different chapters. In 1 Tim. 1:15 we read that Christ came into the world to save (Gk.
sozo) sinners. The word means "to deliver from hell." But who would claim that
the word means that in 1 Tim. 2:15 where we are told that the women will be
saved (Gk. **sozo**) through childbearing?[79] An example of different meanings of
the same word in the same chapter is found in 1 Tim. 5. In 1 Tim. 5:1 the Greek
word **presbyteros** is translated "older man." However, in v. 17 it is translated
"elder," meaning an official in the church. Finally, sometimes words change their
meaning even in the same verse! For example, in Dt. 2:31 we are told, "The LORD
said to me, 'See, I have begun to deliver Sihon and his country over to you. Now
begin to conquer [dispossess, Heb. **yarash**] and possess [Heb. **yarash**, "to in-

---

[79]See also 1 Tim. 4:16 where "save" does not mean "deliver from hell."

herit"][80] his land.'" The same word means "dispossess" in the first half of the verse and "possess" in the second half!

Now in regard to "the inheritance," it is not even the same word used in the two differing contexts. The noun **kleronomos** ("heir") is used in Gal. 4:7, and the verb **kleronomeo** is found in 5:21. As pointed out earlier in this chapter, in every use of the verb in the New Testament, and in Gal. 5:21 in particular, conditions of merit are contextually associated with the obtaining of the inheritance. In Gal. 4:7 there are no such conditions. One becomes an heir by faith alone. But one inherits the kingdom by works. Since differing conditions are present in the differing contexts, differing meanings of the word are meant.

In summary, the inheritance of Gal. 3:18 and 4:30 is parallel not with the land promises, Canaan, but with the gift of justification to the Gentiles. This is the major passage in the New Testament used to equate the inheritance of the land of Canaan with heaven, but the land of Canaan is not even the subject of the passage!

Another reference to the inheritance is found in Ephesians:

And you also were included in Christ when you heard the word of truth, the gospel of your salvation. Having believed, you were marked in him with a seal, the promised Holy Spirit, who is a deposit guaranteeing our inheritance [**kleronomia**] *until the redemption of those who are God's possession--to the praise of his glory* (Eph. 1:13-14).[81]

The inheritance here is unmistakably heaven. It is an inheritance which goes to those who have believed. As in the Old Testament there are two kinds of inheritance in the New. All Christians are heirs of God, but not all are heirs of the kingdom and joint-heirs with Christ. The content of the inheritance here is life in heaven with God. Should it be objected that there is therefore no justification for equating the inheritance in 5:5 with our reward in heaven, the author would reply as above.

Conclusion

The concept of the believer's inheritance, as has been seen, is rich indeed. It has been argued that it means much more than "go to heaven when we die." The inheritance in the Bible is either our relationship with God as a result of justification or something in addition to justification, namely, a greater degree of

---

[80]BDB, p. 439, **yarash** = take possession of, inherit, dispossess. It means to inherit or possess especially by force. In this passages they are to disinherit the enemy in order to inherit the land by conquest. They are to dispossess in order to possess!

[81]Eph. 1:18; 1:14; 5:5.

glorification in heaven as a result of our rewards. As is always the case in interpretation, the context of each usage must determine meaning in that context. While Experimental Predestinarians are willing to grant that the inheritance is heaven, and even that the inheritance in many contexts seems to be a reward, they have failed to integrate these two meanings into a comprehensive system of biblical thought. Several factors seem to lead to the conclusion that it is proper in most contexts of the New Testament to understand the inheritance of the saints as their ownership of the coming kingdom rather than their mere residence there.

First, as argued from the Old Testament, Israel's conquest of the land was achieved by spiritual obedience. After the victory they inherited. The inheritance of Canaan was a merited, earned reward for faithful obedience.

Second, in every usage of the verb "to inherit" except one (1 Cor. 15:50), the action implies some work of obedience necessary to obtain the inheritance.

Third, usage in the Old Testament, and the common meaning of the word "inherit" in English, Hebrew, or Greek, implies a distinction between merely being in the land of Canaan and owning it. In a similar way, by extension of thought, we are justified in drawing a distinction between being a resident of the future kingdom and being an owner, an heir, of that kingdom.

Fourth, we are explicitly told in Col. 3:24 that the future inheritance comes to us as a reward for obedience.

Fifth, in every instance the phrase "inherit the kingdom" is consistent with its Old Testament analog, inherit the land. The kingdom is always (except for 1 Cor. 15:50) inherited by means of works. It is always associated with character qualities which come from acts of obedience. In one context specific positive works of obedience (service to Christ's brethren during the tribulation [Mt. 25:34-35]) are the reason for their "inheriting the kingdom."

Sixth, the phrase "inherit the kingdom" is directly borrowed from Daniel's term "possess the kingdom" (Dan. 7:22). It refers to the rulership over the kingdom of the Son of Man given to the saints. In the Jewish rabbinical literature this future inheritance was obtained by works. That aspect of Jewish theology was not corrected by the New Testament writers but seemingly accepted as the above arguments show.

These conclusions now must be developed more fully. The writer of the Epistle to the Hebrews in particular does precisely this. He explains that, when we have obtained the inheritance by means of a life of perseverance in good works, we will have finished our task and hence will enter into rest.

Chapter 5

The Inheritance-Rest of Hebrews

The last words of great men are often significant. Often when a man comes to the end of his life, wisdom is distilled and challenging comments are made. Perhaps one of the most moving illustrations of such a final exhortation came from the lips of General Douglas MacArthur before the corps of cadets at West Point in 1961. MacArthur was, perhaps, the greatest military genius in history. He was without doubt the greatest military strategist and fighting general the United States has ever produced. His brilliant "island-hopping" strategy enabled him to overcome superior Japanese forces in the Pacific war. With enlightened statesmanship and compassion he single-handedly created the new Japan. He is the author of the Japanese constitution. During his tour there he ruled for many years as an American caesar. His final military contribution was in the Korean War where his military maneuvers are still studied as classical examples of battlefield genius.

MacArthur went to West Point and once served as commandant of the corps of cadets. His last and most memorable good-bye was given there. Addressing the corps of cadets, he took as his text the academy's motto: Duty, Honor, Country. Speaking without notes, striding back and forth, he closed his message with a passage that no one who was on that plain that noon will ever forget. There was not a dry eye in the corps as he said:

The shadows are lengthening for me. The twilight is here. My days of old have vanished, tone and tint; they have gone glimmering through the dreams of things that were. Their memory is one of wondrous beauty, watered by tears, and coaxed and caressed by the smiles of yesterday. I listen vainly, but with thirsty ear, for the witching melody of faint bugles blowing reveille, of far drums beating the long roll. In my dreams I hear again the crash of guns, the rattle of musketry, the strange mournful mutter of the battlefield. But in the evening of my memory, I always come back to West Point. Always there echoes and re-echoes in my ears - Duty, Honor, Country. Today marks my final roll call with you. But I want you to know that when I cross the river my last conscious thought will be of the Corps, and the Corps and the Corps. I bid you farewell.

MacArthur had completed his life work and could look back on a career spanning over fifty years and know that he had done his best. Likewise, the desire of God is that every Christian should similarly be able to say at the end of life, "I have finished my work." This accomplishment was termed "entering into rest" by the writer of the Epistle to the Hebrews.

Perhaps no other writer of the New Testament reflected as deeply and profoundly upon the theme of the inheritance as did the author of the Epistle to the Hebrews. Addressing believers undergoing persecution and considering a return to Judaism, he presses upon them the failure of the exodus generation and warns them of a similar fate. With unusual insight he notes that their failure to enter into rest was a failure to finish their work, precisely the danger facing the Hebrews who were considering an abandonment of their confession.

The Rest of God

But what is the content of the inheritance in Hebrews? Does it refer to heaven or our rewards there? To answer that, we must consider the rest described in chapters 3 and 4:

> So I declared on oath in my anger,
> They shall never enter my rest (Heb. 3:11).

The readers of this epistle were in danger of "falling away" (Heb. 6:6) and "ignoring a great salvation" (Heb. 2:3). All five of the warning passages are directed against this peril. To enforce their perseverance in the midst of persecutions, he sets before them the example of Israelites in the wilderness who fell away and did not enter into Canaan. When the Old Testament passages describing the conquest as "entrance into rest" are studied, it seems that the Old Testament writers related the two ideas of "rest" and "Canaan" even if they did not precisely equate them. In what way did they relate these words together? There seem to be a number of passages which equate the terms. "To enter into rest" simply means "to complete the conquest of Canaan." These passages stress the fact that "rest" is a place. However, there also seem to be a number of passages in which rest is an experience. Instead of "rest" being only a place, it also is a condition, or state of being.

The Rest Is the Land of Canaan

Those who argue that the rest is the land of Canaan make two basic points. First, the rest seems to be equated with the land which God swore they would not enter into. The writer of the Epistle to the Hebrews appeals to Ps. 95, "So I declared in My anger, they shall never enter into My rest" (Ps. 95:11). Yet elsewhere it is the land of Canaan which he swore they would not enter into. For example, "As surely as I live . . . not one of them will ever see the land promised on oath to their forefathers" (Num. 14:21-23).[1] On this basis, Davidson concludes, "what appears to be spoken of is simply possession of the land of Canaan."[2]

Second, the terms "rest" and "Canaan" seem to be used interchangeably in many places:

> *You are not to do as we do here today, everyone as he sees fit, since you have not yet reached the* **resting place** *and the* **inheritance** *the* LORD *your God is giving you* (Dt. 12:8-9).

Sun sees in this passage a "theological equation of rest with the secured settlement of the Promised Land":[3]

> *But you will cross the Jordan and settle in the land the* LORD *your God is giving you as an* **inheritance**, *and he will give you* **rest** *from all your enemies around you so that you will live in safety* (Dt. 12:10).

In the future, Zion, the capital of Palestine, will be God's resting place:

> *For the* LORD *has chosen Zion, he has desired it for his dwelling: This is my resting place for ever and ever* (Ps. 132:13-14).

F. F. Bruce comments that "Canaan [is] the 'rest' or home which God had prepared for them." He argues that in the above passage "Canaan is called 'the rest and the inheritance, which Jehovah thy God giveth thee.'"[4] Similarly, Walter Kaiser insists that the land of Canaan is the rest of Dt. 12:9 and that the word is used of a "place," "geographical, material, and spatial" as well as of a "condition."[5]

The interchangeability between the terms "rest" and "land" is suggested by the following passages as well:

> *Remember the command that Moses the servant of the* LORD *gave you: 'The* LORD *your God is giving you* **rest** *and has granted you this* **land***'* (Josh. 1:13).

---

[1]See also Dt. 1:34-36; Num. 32:10-12; comp. Dt. 12:9.

[2]A. B. Davidson, *The Epistle to the Hebrews* (Edinburgh: T. & T. Clark, 1959), p. 99. Davidson, however, while acknowledging that this is the meaning of the Old Testament texts, wants to spiritualize them to mean heaven.

[3]H. T. C. Sun, "Rest; Resting Place," in *NISBE*, 4:143. He cites 3:20; 25:19; and 28:65 as parallels.

[4]F. F. Bruce, *The Epistle to the Hebrews, NICNT*, 14:65.

[5]Walter Kaiser, *The Uses of the Old Testament in the New* (Grand Rapids: Zondervan, 1988), p. 157.

I commanded you at that time: "The LORD your God has given you this land to take possession of it. . . . However, your wives . . . may stay in the towns I have given you, until the LORD gives **rest** *to your brothers as he has to you, and they too have taken over the land that the LORD your God is giving them, across the Jordan. After that, each of you may go back to the possession I have given you* (Dt. 3:18-20).

The Rest Is Our Finished Work

While it does seem that "rest" and "land" are clearly related in the Old Testament, it is difficult to see that the concept of rest is limited to the idea of possession of the land. In Josh. 1:13 God says He is giving them rest **and** the land. In Dt. 12:10 a similar statement asserts that He is giving them the "inheritance (Canaan)" **and** rest. Rest seems to have another meaning different from "land." Its usage elsewhere suggests the experience one enters into when he finishes his work:

But there were still seven Israelite tribes who had not yet received their **inheritance**. *So Joshua said to the Israelites: "How long will you wait before you begin to take possession of* [Heb. **yarash**, "to inherit"] *the land the LORD, the God of your fathers, has given to you?"* (Josh. 18:2-3).

So the LORD gave Israel all the land he had sworn to give their forefathers, and they took possession of [Heb. **yarash**, "inherited"] *it and settled there. The LORD gave them* **rest** *on every side, just as he had sworn to their forefathers. Not one of their enemies withstood them; the LORD handed all their enemies over to them. Not one of all the LORD's good promises to the house of Israel failed; every one was fulfilled* (Josh. 21:43-45).[6]

This passage in Dt. 12:10 referred to above is instructive in that it relates the rest to the inheritance, the land of Canaan. Furthermore, it explains that rest involves completion of the battle and victory over the enemies. A similar theme is echoed elsewhere in Joshua when, after the battles of the conquest are won, the enemies defeated, and the inheritance divided, we are told that "then the land had **rest** from war" (Josh. 14:15). Once again, final victory, a spiritual concept, is included in the acquisition of the rest, the land of Canaan. Similarly, God announced to David that his son Solomon, whose name means "peace," would enjoy a reign of peace and rest:

But you will have a son who will be a man of peace and rest, and I will give him **rest from all his enemies** *on every side. His name will*

---

[6]See also Josh. 22:4; 23:4-5; 24:28; 18:7.

be Solomon, and I will grant Israel peace and quiet during his reign. He is the one who will build a house for my Name. He will be my son, and I will be his father (1 Chron. 22:9-10).

The rest from enemies is immediately connected with the opportunity for peace, for building God's house, and for fellowship with Him there.

Our suspicion that rest is a broader concept than mere land seems to be confirmed by the fact that the word for rest (Heb. **nuah**) is used interchangeably with the word for Sabbath (Heb. **shabat**):

By the seventh day God had finished the work he had been doing; so on the seventh day he rested [Heb. **shabat**] *from all his work. And God blessed the seventh day and made it holy, because on it he rested* [Heb. **shabat**] *from all the work of creating that he had done* (Gen. 2:2-3).

For in six days the LORD made the heavens and the earth, the sea, and all that is in them, but he rested [Heb. **nuah**] *on the seventh day. Therefore the LORD blessed the Sabbath day and made it holy* (Ex. 20:11).

Hebrew word **shabat** (to cease from labor) is used to describe God's rest in Gen. 2:2-3, but the word **nuah** is used in the parallel passage concerning God's rest on the Sabbath in Ex. 20:11. Thus rest includes the notion of completing one's work: "By the seventh day God had finished the work He had been doing."

The particular work which Israel had to complete was the conquest of their enemies and the secure and successful settlement of the land of Canaan. It is here that we may see another meaning of rest. It is not just a place, i.e., Canaan, although the Israelites cannot have rest without obtaining Canaan. It is an experience similar to that which God experienced when He completed His work! God's work was creation; theirs was conquest. This explains the common martial use of "rest" found in many passages:

*The LORD gave them **rest** on every side, just as he had sworn to their forefathers. Not one of their enemies withstood them; the LORD handed all their enemies over to them. Not one of all the LORD's good promises to the house of Israel failed; everyone was fulfilled* (Josh. 21:44-45).

Coppes concludes from this and similar passages[7] that rest included the notion of "to defeat Israel's enemies and give them rest (victory and security) in the land."[8] A definite relationship between land and rest exists because

---

[7]E.g., Dt. 12:10; 2 Sam. 7:1; 1 Ki. 5:4; 1 Chron. 22:9.

[8]Leonard J. Coppes, "**nuah**," in *TWOT*, 2:562.

"possession of the land brings 'rest' (Dt. 12:9; 25:19; Josh 1:13; 21:44), i.e., both freedom from foreign domination and the end of wandering."[9] Rest is the inheritance, but it is also a condition or state of finished work and victory over enemies, which the Israelite entered into when he obtained the inheritance.

This impression is reinforced by the Lord's startling statement in Ps. 95:11, "So I declared on oath in My anger, they shall never enter into My rest." Here He calls the rest, into which the exodus generation should have entered, "My" rest. The thought immediately casts us back to Gen. 2:2-3, "By the seventh day God had finished the work He had been doing; so on the seventh day He rested." God's rest is the experience of having "finished the work." That experience is what God desires for His people of all ages, including ours!

But when did the Israelites enter into rest? It was not when they entered into Canaan, for that is when their battle to obtain the inheritance was joined. They would enter into rest, i.e., the experience of completed work and freedom from enemies, when they received the inheritance. This did not occur when they crossed the river Jordan to attack Jericho (Josh. 3-4) but after the victory had been won and the inheritance was distributed (Josh. 12-22). Between initial entry into the land and the final conquest there were victories to be wrought and battles to win, a task to complete.

They entered into rest in Joshua 12 when they received the inheritance.[10] At that point they enjoyed freedom from enemies and had completed their work, just as God had completed His work in the creation.

There is nothing particularly new about this approach. Indeed, it has been articulated in numerous books on the spiritual life. In these books the journey of Israel from Egypt to Canaan is compared with the Christian life. As it is commonly taught,[11] Israel's time in Egypt pictures the unregenerate man, the wandering in the wilderness is the carnal Christian, and the crossing of the Jordan into Canaan is the spiritual Christian. The victories over the Canaanites are illustrative of the victorious Christian. No longer wandering in the wilderness of unbelief but clothed in the full armor of God, he is fighting the "principalities and powers." Finally, as a reward, he obtains the inheritance in Joshua 12-22 when the land is distributed. The spiritual life books often connect this with the distribution of crowns at the judgment seat of Christ.

There is, however, a persistent notion that the land of Canaan is somehow typical of the future millennial kingdom. Indeed, the numerous Old Testament

---

[9]B. L. Bandstra, "Land," in *NISBE*, 3:71.

[10]The writer to the Hebrews informs us that this was not a complete fulfillment of the promised rest (Heb. 3-4).

[11]See Ian Thomas, *The Saving Life of Christ* (Grand Rapids: Zondervan, 1961); Alan Redpath, *Victorious Christian Living* (Old Tappan, NJ: Revell, 1955).

promises that one day Israel will return to the land[12] (Ezek. 37:21-22), be established as an independent state (Ezek. 37:22), be in possession of the old city of Jerusalem, and become a focal point of global concern (Zech. 12:1-4) do indicate that such a parallel can be drawn. These land promises are all fulfilled in the future kingdom. Does not entering the land equal entering the kingdom? And, if it does, are not all who enter heirs of that kingdom?

To state the question is to answer it. Obviously not! The book of Joshua supplies at least one illustration of an Israelite who in fact entered the land but who never finished the task. As a result, he never obtained the inheritance and never entered into rest. His name was Achan. After the successful conquest of Jericho, this regenerate "son" of God (Josh. 7:19) stole some of the plunder for himself and then lied about it (Josh. 7:10-11). Such impurity among the people of God made them impotent against their enemies (Josh. 7:12).

Precisely the same situation existed in the early church when Ananias and Sapphira lied to the Holy Spirit. They claimed some material things had been given to the church, but they had in fact been held back for themselves (Acts 5:3). The result for Achan was capital punishment (Josh. 7:24-26). The same happened to Ananias and Sapphira (Acts 5:5).

It is therefore evident that a man can enter into the land but not obtain the inheritance there and never enter into rest. The former was available to all Israelites on the basis of a promise, but the latter came only to those who obeyed and won the victory.

In the parallel to which the writer to the Hebrews alludes, all Christians enter into the kingdom at the time of spiritual birth. But not all Christians finish their work. For the writer to the Hebrews the predicted Old Testament kingdom has already begun. He divides history between the "past" and "these last days" (Heb. 1:1-2). He tells us that the New Covenant predicted by Jeremiah (Jer. 31:31-34), which will be fulfilled for national Israel in the millennium, has already been inaugurated by the death of Christ (Heb. 9:15-18). Alluded to here is the commonly held teaching among evangelicals that the kingdom of heaven was inaugurated with the life and death of Christ and will be consummated in its literal Old Testament form at the second coming of Christ.[13] If this conclusion of contemporary evangelical scholarship is valid, then all enter the kingdom at spiritual birth (Jn. 3:3). Our present struggle against the principalities and powers (Eph.

---

[12]In addition, see Jer. 3:11-20; 12:14-17; 16:10-18; 23:1-8; 28:1-4; 29:1-14; 30:1-3, 10-11; 31:2-14, 15-20; 32:1-44; 42:1-22; 50:17-20; Ezek. 11:14-21; 20:39-44; 34:1-16; 35:1-36; 36:16-36; 39:21-29. The sheer number of these promises in nearly every prophet of the Old Testament makes it highly unlikely that the meager return under Zerubbabel was the fulfillment. Indeed, if that was the predicted fulfillment, then why did Zechariah in 518 B.C. continue to predict the future return as if it had not yet occurred?

[13]See, for example, George E. Ladd, *A Theology of the New Testament* (Grand Rapids: Eerdmans, 1974), pp. 57-80.

6:12) is the spiritual counterpart to Israel's struggle against her enemies after having entered the land. Like Achan and the exodus generation before him, some Christians will not finish the battle. They are out of Egypt and in the kingdom (in its present form), but they never obtain an inheritance there and will never enter into rest.

A proper illustration of the relationship between the journeys of the children of Israel and the Christian life is suggested by the following diagram:

From Egypt to Canaan

NATURAL MAN	CARNAL CHRISTIAN	SPIRITUAL CHRISTIAN	REWARDED CHRISTIAN
	Struggle	Victory	Rest
	Exodus Generation	Second Generation	
	In the Wilderness	Across the Jordan	Receiving the Inheritance
Ex. 1-11	Ex. 12 - Dt. 34	Josh. 1-11	Josh. 12-22
NON-CHRISTIAN	CARNAL CHRISTIAN	BATTLE	VICTORY
EGYPT	WILDERNESS	CANAAN	
IN THE WORLD	IN THE KINGDOM		AT THE TABLE
1 Cor. 2:14	1 Cor. 3:1-3	Rom. 12:1-2	2 Cor. 5:10

Paul tells us that "these things occurred as examples" (1 Cor. 10:6) so there is some justification for such speculations. The journey of the exodus generation and their sons to Canaan in a striking way portrays the theology of entering into rest. Those who trusted in the Passover lamb and crossed the river out of Egypt were born again and entered into the kingdom. In a similar manner a believer today enters the kingdom at spiritual birth. That kingdom was inaugurated with the ascension of the King to the throne and will be consummated at His second coming to earth. The journey of the children of Israel illustrates two kinds of Christians, the carnal Christians of the exodus generation and the victorious Christians who entered the land and entered the battle. Entering Canaan is not to be equated with entering the kingdom. A Christian enters the kingdom when he is born again. Rather, entering Canaan pictures the decision by a person who already is a Christian to trust God for victory, submit to His lordship, and engage in the spiritual battle necessary to finish our course as victors and, as a result, enter into rest. When the battle is won and when, unlike Achan, we persevere in obedient faith to the end, we receive the inheritance, our rewards in heaven. We have completed our work, and we enter into rest.

To enter into rest was to possess the land of Canaan by means of spiritual obedience and resultant victory over all who would oppose them. So entering rest was more than just obtaining some real estate; it had a spiritual dimension as well. It involved the completion of their work, a finishing of their God-appointed task to take possession of the land. For that generation that was their purpose and destiny. Similarly, the Hebrews are exhorted to "make every effort to enter that rest, so that no one will fall by following their example of disobedience (Heb. 4:11). It is impossible to enter into rest without entering into the land, but it was possible to enter the land and not enter rest. In a similar way, it is impossible to enter into rest without having first entered into the kingdom which was inaugurated at the ascension, but it is possible to enter into that kingdom and never enter into rest. To enter into rest is to obtain the inheritance of Canaan by faithful obedience, to complete our task and persevere to the final hour.

One day the city of Zion, the central city of Canaan in the kingdom, the capital of the entire globe (Isa. 2:3), will be the "resting place" (Ps. 132:13-14) of God when He pours out His blessings on that heavenly Jerusalem (Heb. 11:10) which is located in the heavenly country, the restored millennial land of Canaan (Heb. 11:16),[14] which is the subject of many Old Testament predictions.[15]

It may be concluded that the rest of Heb. 3 is more than the land of Canaan, although it includes that. The inheritance spoken of in the Old Testament was obtained by faithful obedience and rewarded to merit. It included the experience of having completed one's task, a spiritual dimension. To enter rest was to be victorious over one's enemies through spiritual obedience and to complete the task assigned to them by God, to take possession of the land. This

---

[14]The fact that the heavenly country and heavenly city are called "heavenly" does not mean that they were located in heaven "any more than the sharers in the heavenly calling (3:1) who had tasted the heavenly gift (6:4) were not those who lived on earth." The land of Palestine was called the temple of the Lord. Similarly, the heavenly Jerusalem "was not used to mislead the reader into thinking that Mount Zion was in heaven . . . but to affirm its divine origin" (George Wesley Buchanan, *To the Hebrews, The Anchor Bible*, pp. 192, 222). George Peters agrees: "No Hebrew would be misled by the term 'heavenly country.' They were accustomed to designate the restored Davidic kingdom as a heavenly kingdom and the country enjoying its restoration was a heavenly country. The expression does not mean the third heaven, but something that partakes of or pertains to the heavenly" (George N. H. Peters, *The Theocratic Kingdom*, 3 vols. [New York: Funk and Wagnalls, 1884; reprint ed., Grand Rapids: Kregel, 1972], 1:295).

[15]For example, Amos 9:13-15; Joel 3:17-21; Zeph. 3:14-20; Zech. 14:8-21; Isa. 2:2-5; 11:1-16.

paves the way for the writer's concept of receiving a reward for faithful persever-ance (Heb. 10:36).[16] He wants his readers to finish their work and thus avoid the loss of inheritance experienced by the exodus generation.

The Partakers

This magnificent concept of entering into rest was uniquely appropriate to apply to the readers of the Epistle to the Hebrews who were in danger, like the exodus generation, of a failure to complete their life work by doing the will of God to the end (Heb. 10:36). So He warns them in Heb. 3:14:

> *We have come to share in Christ if we hold firmly till the end the con-fidence we had at first.*

The phrase "for we have come to share in Christ" is literally in Greek, "for we are partakers [**metochoi**] of Christ" (**metochoi gar tou Christou gegonamen**). The perfect tense "have come" (**gegonamen**) takes the most basic sense of the perfect, the intensive perfect. "It is a strong way of saying that a thing is. . . . Usu-ally its closest approximation is the English present."[17] The genitive "of Christ" is the simple genitive of possession. We may therefore translate, "We are partners of Christ" or "we are Christ's partners."

The NIV translation above, "we have come to share in Christ," is some-what ambiguous. The word "partaker" (**metochos**) basically means "partner or companion."[18] How is one a partner "in" another person? Someone could cer-tainly "share with" a person but not "in." Perhaps some of the difficulty is that the translators are attempting to read the Pauline concept of "in Christ" into this Greek word. If the word **metochos** means to be "in Christ" or be "part of Christ," then the verse is suggesting that we are Christians if and only if we persevere to the end. If, on the other hand, the word **metochos** suggests something like "companion" with Christ, then an entirely different kind of relationship is in view. In fact, it is highly unlikely that **metochos** implies the Pauline idea of being "in Christ." Montefiore comments:

> *Most commentators take the phrase to mean that we are **partakers of Christ** or that **we share in Christ**. This Pauline concept, however, is entirely alien to our author who regards Christ not as the new human-*

---

[16]Kendall shares a similar view although he equates the rest with our reward in the spiri-tual kingdom of God (he is an amillennialist). "God's rest is a type of our inheritance in the king-dom of God. Losing our inheritance below is tantamount to losing our reward above and will result in the severest type of chastening, viz. being saved 'so as by fire' (1 Cor. 3:15)" (R. T. Kendall, *Once Saved Always Saved* [London: Hodder and Stoughton, 1984], p. 116).

[17]DM, p. 202.

[18]AG, p. 516. In the LXX it often means "companions," Hermann Hanse, "**echo**," in *TD-NTA*, p. 289.

ity into whom believers are incorporated by faith union, but as head of the Christian family, the son among brothers.[19]

Similarly, Hughes concurs:

There is, indeed, a certain ambiguity associated with the Greek noun used here since it may mean either "partakers with" someone in a particular activity or relationship, in which case it denotes "companions" or "partners," as in 1:9 and Luke 5:7 (the only occurrence of the noun outside the Epistle to the Hebrews in the New Testament), or "partakers of."[20]

Hughes argues that the former interpretation should be favored here. He notes that the Israelites were partners with Moses in the wilderness parallel (and not partakers of) and that the same sense is found in Heb. 1:9 where it is implied that the Christians are the companions of the royal Son.

Farrar has adopted the same view:

But the meaning may rather be "partakers **with** *Christ;" for the thought of mystical union with Christ extending into the spiritual unity and identity, which makes the words "in Christ" the monogram of St. Paul, is scarcely alluded to by the writer. His thoughts are rather of "Christ for us" than of "Christ in us."*[21]

Finally, Martin Lloyd-Jones explains it this way, "It means 'participant' or 'sharer'. It is sometimes used for 'associate', 'partner'. A partner is a man who goes along with another man in a business or whatever it may chance to be."[22]

But being Christ's partner is not the same as being His son. Only sons are partners, but not all sons are partners--only those who "hold firmly to the end the confidence" they had at first. The word **metochos** was used in the papyri for a partner or associate in a business enterprise. One manuscript contains a portion of a sentence which reads, "We Dionysius, son of Socrates and the associate [**metochoi**] collectors of public clothing."[23] Apparently, Dionysius and his associates were partners in a tax collecting business. A man named Sotas was also writing receipts for tax bills paid and collected through his company: ". . . paid to

---

[19]Hugh Montefiore, *A Commentary on the Epistle to the Hebrews* (London: Adam and Charles Black, 1969), p. 78.

[20]Philip Edgecomb Hughes, *A Commentary on the Epistle to the Hebrews* (Grand Rapids: Eerdmans, 1977), p. 149.

[21]F. W. Farrar, *The Epistle of Paul the Apostle to the Hebrews, Cambridge Greek Testament for Schools and Colleges,* (Cambridge: Cambridge University Press, 1894), p. 63.

[22]D. Martin Lloyd-Jones, *Romans Chapter 8:17-39: The Final Perseverance of the Saints* (Grand Rapids: Zondervan, 1976), p. 322.

[23]MM, p. 406.

Sotas and associates [**metochoi**], collectors of money-taxes."[24]   A similar usage is found in the New Testament in reference to Simon Peter's fishing business.   He was a partner of James and John (Lk. 5:10):

> *When they had done so, they caught such a large number of fish that*
> *their nets began to break. So they signaled their partners* [**metochoi**]
> *in the other boat to come and help them* (Lk. 5:6-7).

The word is found in classical Greek for a wife, a member of a board of officials, a partner in business, or the joint owner of a house.[25]

The Hebrew word **chaber** is translated by **metochos** nine times in the Septuagint.[26]   In each case it refers to a "companion" or one in partnership with another.   Its common meaning is "companion, associate, knit together."[27]   It describes a close bond between persons such as the close relationship between Daniel and his three friends because of their common faith and loyalty to God (Dan. 2:13-18):

> *The term **chaber** is also used to express the very close relation-*
> *ship that exists between people in various walks of life. Israelites were*
> *"united as one man" (RSV) in their war against the Benjamites be-*
> *cause of their outrageous crime (Jud 20:11). Men can be very closely*
> *joined together as thieves (Isa 1:23), as destroyers (Prov 28:24), and as*
> *corrupt priests likened to ambushing robbers (Hos 6:9).*[28]

Men may or may not be joined together as thieves, destroyers, or robbers, but they are all still men; only their partnership in a particular enterprise is in question.   Similarly, Christians may or may not be joined together with Christ in the coming "messianic partnership," but they are still Christians.

It was perfectly normal for a king to surround himself with certain associates with whom he maintained a more intimate relationship than he did with all other citizens of his kingdom.   In the Old Testament we might think of David's mighty men (2 Sam. 23:8-39) or perhaps of David's invitation to the crippled Mephibosheth to eat at his table like one of the king's sons (2 Sam. 9:7, 11, 13).   Certainly the disastrous counsel which Rehoboam received from "the young men who had grown up with him and [who] were serving him" (1 Ki. 12:8) could be said to have come from his partners, his **metochoi**.

---

[24]Ibid.

[25]LS, p. 1122.

[26]Edwin Hatch and Henry Redpath, *A Concordance to the Septuagint*, 2 vols. (Reprint ed., Grand Rapids: Baker, 1983), 2:918.

[27]Gerard Van Groningen, "**chabar**," in *TWOT*, 1:260.

[28]Ibid.

In the Roman world it was a great privilege to be known as a "friend of Caesar." Recall Pilate's prompt reversal at the trial of Christ when the Jews questioned whether or not he was a "friend of Caesar" (Jn. 19:12). Suetonius, in his *The Deified Julius,* says:

> *Moreover when he came to power he advanced some of his* friends *to the highest position, even though they were of the humblest origin and when taken to task for it flatly declared that if he had been helped in defending his honor by brigands and cutthroats he would have requited such men in the same way.*

Perhaps, in a similar vein, we might think of the honor of being a member of Caesar's household (Phil. 4:22). The term "Caesar's household" was commonly applied to the imperial civil service throughout the empire. Philo says, "If Agrippa had not been a king, but instead one of Caesar's household, would he not have had some privilege or honor?"[29]

God's King-Son in the Epistle to the Hebrews has likewise surrounded Himself with companions (Heb. 1:9, Gk. metochoi). In the case of David there were many citizens living in his kingdom other than those who ate as his table and his mighty men. Many lived under Rehoboam's sovereignty who were not among those with whom he grew up. There were many in Caesar's kingdom who did not have the official title, "Friend of Caesar" or "Member of Caesar's Household," and probably there were many in the businesses of Sotas, Dionysius, and Peter who were not associates.

Jesus made it clear that only those Christians who "do the will of My Father in heaven" are His "friends" (Mt. 12:48-50). He told them that friendship with Him was conditional: "You are My friends if you do what I command" (Jn. 15:14). He even spoke of Christians who could in no way be considered His friends because He "would not entrust Himself to them, for He knew all men" (Jn. 2:24). Yet these from whom He drew back had "believed in His name" and were therefore born again.[30]

The metochoi of King Jesus then are His co-heirs in the rulership of the messianic kingdom. They are those friends, partners, and companions who have endured the trials of life, were faithful to the end, who will therefore obtain the

---

[29]A. Rupprecht, "Caesar's Household," in *ZPED*, 1:683.

[30] Many people saw the miraculous signs and **episteusan eis to onoma autou** ("believed on His name"). Yet Jesus would not **episteuen auton autois** ("entrust Himself to them") because He "knew all men." The phrase "believe on His name" is used throughout John for saving faith. Note especially John 3:18 where the same phrase is used. The phrase **pisteuo eis** is John's standard expression for saving faith. One believes "on him" or "in His name," 6:40; 7:39; 8:30; 10:42; 11:25; 11:26; 12:11. Therefore, Calvin's claim in the *Institutes* (3.2.12) that they did not have true faith but were only borne along "by some impulse of zeal which prevented them from carefully examining their hearts" is fallacious.

inheritance-rest. The danger in Heb. 3:14 is not that they might lose their justification but that they might lose their inheritance by forfeiting their position as one of Christ's metochoi in the coming kingdom. It is to help them avoid this danger that the writer applies to them the lesson of the failure of the exodus generation to enter rest. They too are in danger of not entering into rest.

Entering into Rest (Heb. 4:1-11)

Having set before their eyes the failure of the exodus generation, he now warns them against the possibility of failure in their Christian lives as well.

The Warning (4:1-2)

Therefore, since the promise of entering his rest still stands, let us be careful that none of you be found to have fallen short of it (Heb. 4:1).

There is no reason for assuming the rest (Gk. katapausis) in Heb. 4 is any different from the inheritance of Canaan obtained by obedience as described in Heb. 3. The transition between the chapters is smooth, the application is precise and without any qualification, and the same word, katapausis, is used. It involved a spiritual victory over all opposing enemies which was achieved by spiritual faith-obedience to the King. It was an inheritance merited on the field of battle:

For we also have had the gospel preached to us, just as they did; but the message they heard was of no value to them because those who heard did not combine it with faith (Heb. 4:2).

What "gospel" was preached to them? It probably was not the good news of forgiveness of sins. There is no reference to such a gospel in the context of this warning passage. The word "gospel" is simply "good news." Our Reformation heritage has perhaps caused us to limit it to only one kind of good news, deliverance from hell. But the good news they received was the promise of the inheritance of the land of Canaan and the possibility of entering into that inheritance by faithful perseverance and faith-obedience (e.g., Dt. 12:10-12). This gospel was not only preached to them, but it has been preached to us! Where? A major theme of the New Testament is that the church has been grafted into Israel's covenants and are now heirs of the same promises (Rom. 11:17). The "good news" in this context seems to be good news about entering God's rest (4:10) and not the forgiveness of sins.

The Present Existence of the Rest (4:3-7)

Now we who have believed enter that rest, just as God has said, "So I declared on oath in my anger, 'They shall never enter my rest.'" And yet his work has been finished since the creation of the world (4:3).

Here he makes it explicit that only those who believe enter into rest. His interest is not in those who have believed at a point in time but in those who continue to believe to the end of life (3:6, 14). It is perseverance in faith, not a one-time exercise of it, which guarantees that we enter into rest.

He quotes Ps. 95:11 again, which is a Davidic commentary on the failure of the exodus generation. This rest, this experience of finished work which comes through meritorious acquisition of the land of Canaan, is God's rest. The significance of the statement, "And yet His work has been finished since the creation of the world" is very difficult to interpret precisely. Why is it included? Our author probably means that God completed His work of creation and has offered the experience of completed work to every generation of man since then. This completed work has yet to be entered into by man but will be when the kingdom of heaven is consummated in the millennium to come. Apparently the Hebrews under Joshua had the possibility of entering into this consummation, but they never fully did so.

In the discussion above it was argued that the meaning of entering into rest included not only the obtaining of the inheritance of Canaan but also signified the completion of one's labor. This possible meaning of the term in the Old Testament is now made explicit by the writer to the Hebrews in the words to follow:

For somewhere he has spoken about the seventh day in these words: "And on the seventh day God rested from all his work." And again in the passage above he says, "They shall never enter my rest" (4:4-5).

The precise connection between God having finished His work and their not finishing theirs by entering the land seems to be as follows. Since God has completed His work, the experience of completed work, rest, has been available to all since the creation of the world. We enter into that experience the same way God did, by finishing the task. Possession of Canaan was the task which they were to complete. The concept of rest is thus enriched to mean finished work.

No Final Rest under Joshua (4:6-9)

It still remains that some will enter that rest, and those who formerly had the gospel preached to them did not go in, because of their disobedience. Therefore God again set a certain day, calling it Today,

*when a long time later he spoke through David, as was said before:
"Today, if you hear his voice, do not harden your hearts" (4:6-7).*

The exodus generation failed to enter the land. They never finished their task, and that task still remains to be completed! Even under Joshua the task was not completed. But, someone might argue, was not the entire promise of the land of Canaan fulfilled under Joshua? Did not the Old Testament say that the conquest of the land was the fulfillment of the promised rest (Josh. 22:4; 23:1)? This kind of eschatology is rebutted with the following words:

For if Joshua had given them rest, God would not have spoken later about another day. There remains, then, a Sabbath-rest for the people of God (4:8-9).

If the experience of Sabbath rest had been fulfilled in Joshua's conquest of the land, David, four hundred years later, would not still be offering the same promise in Ps. 95:11 and saying it is available "today." The writer is evidently setting before his Christian readers the hope of an inheritance in the land of Canaan which was made to Israel. This future inheritance is still to be obtained, and the experience of finished work is still to be achieved!

How the Rest Is Obtained (4:10-11)

He now explains how the rest is to be obtained:

For anyone who enters God's rest also rests from his own work, just as God did from his. Let us, therefore, make every effort to enter that rest, so that no one will fall by following their example of disobedience (4:10-11).

As Christian believers they will have an inheritance in the land of Canaan in the consummation of the present kingdom if they make every effort to finish their course. We are to enter rest the same way the exodus generation should have, by finishing our work. This was how God entered into the experience of rest. That we should make "every effort" to do this proves that entrance into heaven is not meant. Otherwise a salvation by works is taught!

Entering rest is therefore more than obtaining the land of Canaan, although it is also that. It is the fulfillment of man's destiny to "rule and have dominion" (Gen. 1:26-28). It is the finishing of our work: "for anyone who enters God's rest also rests from his own work, just as God did from His" (Heb. 4:10). Or as the writer expressed it in Heb. 10:36:

*You need to persevere so that when you **have done the will of God,** you will receive what he has promised.*

In a similar way Jesus said, "My food is to do the will of him who sent me and to finish his work" (Jn. 4:34).

The conclusion is that the content of the inheritance in Heb. 3 and 4 is the millennial land of Canaan. By being faithful to Christ to the final hour, we finish our course and obtain an inheritance there; our task being finished, we then enter into our victorious rest. This inheritance-rest is participation with Christ in that great messianic partnership, the final destiny of man. It certainly involves owner-ship of the land of Canaan, but obtaining Canaan was more than just obtaining some land. It was to live there in the heavenly country, ruling from the heavenly city with the King. Only Christ's metochoi will reign him in the kingdom. To be invited to rule with Christ on earth in the coming kingdom is synonymous with hearing him say:

> *Well done, good and faithful servant! You have been faithful with a*
> *few things; I will put you in charge of many things. Come and share*
> *your master's happiness!* (Mt. 25:21).

There are many in the kingdom today, but only some will inherit the land in the consummation. That is why the rest must be worked for:

> *Let us, therefore, make every effort to enter that rest, so that no one*
> *will fall by following their example of disobedience* (Heb. 4:11).

Consistent with its usage throughout the New Testament, the inheritance (rest) must be earned. Unlike heaven, it is not a free gift, nor is there anything in this passage about perseverance in holiness as proof of the presence of saving faith. Not all Christians will make that effort or will make equal effort, and those distinctions will be acknowledged by Christ in the coming reign of the metochoi during the millennial kingdom.

Conclusion

We enter into rest only when we persevere in faith to the end of life. When we do this, we will obtain a share in the inheritance, the millennial land of Canaan, and will rule with Christ as one of His metochoi there. Rest is not just the land itself; it also includes the state or condition of "finished work," of final perseverance, into which the faithful Christian will enter. God has not set aside His promises to Israel. The promise of the inheritance, the land, is eternally valid, and those Christians who remain faithful to their Lord to the end of life will share in that inheritance along with the Old Testament saints.

The kingdom predicted in the Old Testament was inaugurated at the as-cension and will be consummated at the second coming. God can accomplish what He has decided to accomplish. The Christian who "labors to enter into rest" will do so and will have a share with that great company of the metochoi in the future reign of the servant kings.

Chapter 6

So Great a Salvation

It would be difficult to find a concept which is richer and more varied in meaning than the biblical concept of salvation. The breadth of salvation is so sweeping and its intended aim so magnificent that in many contexts the words used defy precise definition. Yet these difficulties have not thwarted numerous interpreters from assuming, often without any contextual justification, that the words used invariably mean "deliverance from hell" or "go to heaven when you die." It may come as a surprise to many that this usage of "salvation" (Gk. **soteria**) would have been the least likely meaning to come to the mind of a reader of the Bible in the first century. Indeed, in 812 usages of the various Hebrew words translated "to save" or "salvation" in the Old Testament, only 58 (7.1 percent) refer to eternal salvation.[1]

As will be seen in the following discussion, the tendency to assume that salvation always refers to final deliverance from hell has led many to interpret certain passages incorrectly. When James, for example, says, "Can faith alone save a man," the Experimental Predestinarians understandably are perplexed about the apparent conflict with Paul. However, if salvation means something other than "go to heaven when you die," the apparent conflict evaporates.

Usage outside the New Testament

An adequate discussion of the Greek verb **sozo** ("to save"), and the noun **soteria** could easily consume an entire book. This analysis will summarize its meaning in secular Greek and in the Old Testament, and then it will discuss some of the references to these words in the New Testament (over 150 references). In particular, the burden will be to illustrate those usages which establish meanings other than "final deliverance from hell."

---

[1]Robert N. Wilkin, "Repentance and Salvation, Part 2: The Doctrine of Repentance in the Old Testament," *JGES* 2 (Spring 1989): 14.

Usage in Secular Greek

The noun **soteria** is often found in the papyri in the sense of bodily health or well-being (happiness, health, and prosperity).[2] Moulton and Milligan cite one manuscript which reads, "To all this I swear by Almighty God and by the supremacy, salvation and preservation of our most pious sovereigns, Flavius Heraclius and Aelia Flavia." The citizen is flattering his ruler with wishes of good health and good fortune. It commonly means, "to thrive, prosper or get on well" or "to keep or preserve in good condition" in extra biblical Greek.[3] In fact, the positive notion of "keeping in good health," "benefiting," or "well-being" is common, and the thought of deliverance disappears altogether.[4]

In the Apocrypha the word often means salvation from the afflictions of earthly life; in Qumram it was salvation from temptation or from oppression which was central; and the sense of "blessing" is common in Josephus. Philo often used it for preservation, deliverance, health or well-being (i.e., happiness, prosperity, etc.). In the *Testament of the Twelve* salvation is obtained by prayer and personal piety along with God's help and refers to temporal salvation, i.e., a rich and meaningful life.[5]

In view of this common usage one would not be surprised to find similar thoughts in the Old Testament. In fact, such is the case.

Usage in the Old Testament

The principal Old Testament word, **yasha**, which is translated by **soteria** in the LXX, is used 353 times in the Masoretic text. Apparently the original meaning may have been something like "to make wide or sufficient."[6] White speculates that original meaning was "width, spaciousness, freedom from restraint."[7] Salvation could be from the misery of slavery in Egypt;[8] from adversaries;[9] or from oppression.[10] "It evidently includes divinely bestowed deliverance from every class of spiritual and temporal evil to which mortal man is subjected."[11]

---

[2]MM, p. 622. A similar usage is found in Acts 27:34, where food is needed for "survival."

[3]AG, p. 805.

[4]W. Foerster,"**sozo**," in *TDNT*, 1132.

[5]Ibid.

[6]John E. Hartley, "**yasha**," in *TWOT*, 1:414.

[7]R. E. O. White, "Salvation," in *Evangelical Dictionary of Theology*, ed. Walter A. Elwell (Grand Rapids: Baker, 1984), p. 967.

[8]Ex. 14:13; 15:2.

[9]Ps. 106:10.

[10]Jud. 3:31.

[11]Robert Girdlestone, *Synonyms of the Old Testament* (n.c., n.p., 1897; reprint ed., Grand Rapids: Eerdmans, 1976), p. 125.

Of particular interest are references to salvation from social decay which may parallel New Testament usages of salvation from the filth of the world.[12] It often approaches the meaning of "moral and personal welfare" when it is used for prosperity in Job 30:15, and it regularly means religious blessing in general (Ps. 28:9).[13]

By far the most common usage in the Old Testament is of God's deliverance of his people from their struggles (Ex. 14:30).[14] Scores of passages could be cited.[15] This meaning has been considerably enriched by the New Testament writers when they point out that the salvation of Christ also saves us from our enemies--the world, the flesh, and the Satan. Spiritual victory in life is salvation!

Often, however, the word simply means blessing, health, or happiness;[16] restoration to fellowship;[17] or the future blessings of the messianic kingdom.[18]

Schneider notes that "certain passages in the prophets have an eschatological dimension. In the last days Yahweh will bring full salvation for his people (e.g., Isa. 43:5 ff.; Jer. 31:7; 46:27; Zech 8:7; . . .)."[19] At that time, in the future earthly kingdom, Israel "will draw water from the wells of salvation" (Isa. 12:3), and the entire world will participate in the messianic salvation (Isa. 45:22; 49:6). The enemies of Israel will be put to shame in that future day, "but Israel will be saved by the LORD with an everlasting salvation" (Isa. 45:17). The messianic salvation is called the "everlasting salvation" because the kingdom of Messiah will last forever. The phrase is strikingly similar to the phrase "eternal salvation" in Heb. 5:9. In Isa. 52:10 we are told that "all the ends of the world will see the salvation of our God." In that glorious future era His people will know His name, and the feet of those who proclaim salvation will be called beautiful (Isa. 52:7).

According to Schneider, the theme of the great future messianic salvation was often found in the Qumran literature where the people of God are redeemed out of tribulation, saved for an eternal salvation from the powers of darkness, and the enemy nations of Israel destroyed.[20] That salvation could be considered a future deliverance of the people of God in the last day, and the subsequent blessings of the messianic era will be important in our understanding of the meaning of salvation in the book of Hebrews.

---

[12]Hos. 1:7.

[13]White, p. 967.

[14]See 1 Sam. 22:4.

[15]E.g., Num. 10:9; Ps. 18:3; Isa. 30:15; 45:17; Jer. 30:17.

[16]See Ps. 7:10; Ps. 28:8, 9; 86:16; Jer. 17:4.

[17]See Ps. 51:8; 6:3-6; Ezek. 37:23.

[18]Ps. 132:16; Isa. 43:3, 5, 8, 19; 44:3, 20; Isa. 25:9; Jer. 31:7.

[19]J. Schneider, "Redemption," in *NIDNTT*, 3:208.

[20]Ibid., 3:210-11.

Usage in the New Testament

It is in the New Testament, however, that the full breadth of meaning of salvation comes to the forefront. The verb **sozo** occurs 106 times and the noun **soteria** 46 times. The meaning "deliver from hell," while rare in the Old Testament, is quite common in the New. Statistically, **sozo** is used 40 percent of the time in this way[21] and **soteria** 35 percent.[22] Like the Old Testament it sometimes simply means healing or recovery of health. When this happens, the notion of "deliver" disappears altogether, and the word simply means "to heal." For example, in response to the faith and resultant healing of the woman who had been bleeding for twelve years, Jesus said: "Your faith has healed [**sozo**] you" (Mt. 9:21-22). This sense is quite common (19 percent).[23]

Consistent with its most frequent usage in the Old Testament (LXX), **sozo** often means to deliver from some danger (19 percent). For example, when Jesus prayed in the garden, he asked, "Save [**sozo**] me from this hour" (Jn. 12:27).[24]

Salvation of the Troubled

Similar to the idea of "deliverance from danger," but with a distinctively positive emphasis, are the references in which salvation is viewed as victorious endurance and not just escape.

Paul's concern over the **soteria** of the believers at Corinth may reflect this thought:

If we are distressed, it is for your comfort and salvation [**soteria**]; *if we are comforted, it is for your comfort, which produces in you patient endurance of the same sufferings we suffer* (2 Cor. 1:6).

Salvation seems to be equated with patient endurance, an aspect of sanctification.

It is probable that the idea of victorious endurance is behind a use of **soteria** in Philippians which has often perplexed interpreters:

---

[21]E.g., Acts 4:12; 11:14; Rom. 8:24; 9:27; 1 Cor. 5:5; Jude 23. .

[22]Acts 4:12; 13:26; Rom. 1:16; 10:1; 2 Cor. 6:2; Eph. 1:13.

[23]See Mk. 3:4; 5:23, 28, 34; Lk. 6:9; 8:36, 48, 50; Jn. 11:12; Jas. 5:15. No instance of **soteria** in this sense occurs.

[24]See Mt. 8:25; 14:30; 24:22; Lk. 1:71; 23:35, 37, 39; Jn. 12:27; Acts 7:52; 27:20, 31, 34; 1 Th. 5:9.

Therefore, my dear friends, as you have always obeyed--not only in my presence, but now much more in my absence--continue to work out your salvation [**soteria**] *with fear and trembling, for it is God who works in you to will and to act according to his good purpose* (Phil. 2:12-13).

This salvation must be worked for. The phrase "work out" translates **katergazomai**, which simply means "to effect by labor, achieve, work out, bring about, etc."[25] A salvation which can be achieved by labor is hardly the justification-by-faith-alone kind of salvation offered elsewhere. Neither is any notion of obedience being the evidence of true faith found in this passage; rather, obedience is the condition of salvation.

The salvation to which Paul refers here is related contextually back to his discussion in Phil. 1:27-30 and Phil. 1:19-20:

Yes, and I will continue to rejoice, for I know that through your prayers and the help given by the Spirit of Jesus Christ, what has happened to me will turn out for my deliverance [**soteria**]. *I eagerly expect and hope that I will in no way be ashamed, but will have sufficient courage so that now as always Christ will be exalted in my body, whether by life or by death* (Phil. 1:19-20).

The thought of deliverance from danger is the obvious meaning of salvation here, but more than that, Paul wants to be delivered in such a way that Christ will be honored in his body. A higher deliverance, a victorious endurance, is in view. He desires that his readers similarly will be victorious in their trials as well, following his example:

Whatever happens, conduct yourselves in a manner worthy of the gospel of Christ. Then, whether I come and see you or only hear about you in my absence, I will know that you stand firm in one spirit, contending as one man for the faith of the gospel without being frightened in any way by those who oppose you. This is a sign to them that they will be destroyed but that you will be saved [*of your* **soteria**], *and that by God. For it has been granted to you on behalf of Christ not only to believe on him, but also to suffer for him, since you are going through the same struggle you saw I had, and now hear that I still have* (Phil. 1:27-30).

The apostle aspired to a victorious endurance in which his life or death would magnify Christ, and he exhorts them to aspire to the same goal. Their lack of fear in the face of enemies and their united stand is clear evidence of the reality of their victorious endurance (salvation), which will be evident to all. Their

---

[25]AS, p. 240. See Rom. 4:15; 5:3; Jas. 1:3.

courageous attitude also signifies the temporal and eternal doom of their adversaries.

This salvation is one beyond their initial salvation in Christ. The first salvation was received by simple faith (Eph. 2:8-9), but this one comes by faithful endurance. It consists of Christ being magnified in one's life. This salvation must be "achieved by labor." This is the salvation which he wants them to "work out" in Phil. 2:12. They are to continue to bring honor to Christ as they boldly respond to their trials. He is exhorting them to victorious endurance.

Such an interpretation would not be unexpected by readers in the first century, saturated as they were with the idea of salvation found in their Greek Bible. As mentioned above, the most common usage of the word there was deliverance from trials.[26]

Salvation of a Life

The phrase "save a soul" (Gk. **sozo psyche**) seems to have a technical meaning of "preserve your physical life." Jesus used it in Matthew:

> Then Jesus **said to his disciples,** *If anyone wishes to come after me, let him deny himself, and take up his cross, and follow me. For whoever wishes to save his life* [**psyche**] *will lose it; but whoever loses his life* [**psyche**] *for my sake shall find it. For what will a man be profited, if he gains the whole world, and forfeits his soul* [**psyche**]? *Or what will a man give in exchange for his soul* [**psyche**]?" (Mt. 16:24-26).

It remains for scholars of historical theology to discern how this phrase ever became connected with the idea of deliverance from hell.[27] It is never used that way in the Bible, and such an idea would have been foreign to any Jewish reader of the New Testament. Furthermore, the context requires that works, suffering, and taking up one's cross are necessary conditions for the saving of the soul. This creates obvious problems with the rest of the New Testament where works such as this are distanced as far as possible from the gospel offer (e.g., Eph. 2:8-9; Jn. 3:16). It is either necessary to redefine faith as being equivalent to obedience, which a lexical study will not allow, or reconsider the traditional meaning of "save a soul."

---

[26]See, for example, Ps. 3:8; 18:3, 35, 46, 50; 35:3; 37:39; 38:22; 44:4. In all these references the LXX employs **soteria.**

[27]Lenski, for example, says that to deny oneself in order to save one's soul refers to true conversion. See R. H. Lenski, *The Interpretation of St. Matthew's Gospel* (Minneapolis: Augsburg, 1961), pp. 643-46.

This phrase is found eleven times in the LXX, and in each case it has the notion of preserving one's physical life.[28] In Gen. 19:17 it means to "escape with your life"; and in Gen. 32:30 Jacob, after his struggle with the Angel of the Lord, exclaims, "My life has been preserved." In one passage it seems to refer to delivering the needy from social injustice (Ps. 72:13) by preserving their lives. Even the warrior, declares Amos, will "not save his life" in the coming invasion (Amos 2:14).

Because the meaning is definitely established from other passages, there is no reason to abandon it in the New Testament, no reason except the interests of the Reformed doctrine of perseverance. Here we have a case where the traditional meaning, "deliver from hell," is absolutely without parallel in biblical or extra-biblical literature, and yet it is accepted as the starting point for understanding the meaning in the New Testament.

It is clear that the saying in question was addressed to believers (Mt. 16:24), and therefore Christ is not preaching the gospel to unbelievers to come to salvation but challenging Christians to a life of discipleship. The fact the unbelievers may have heard the message does not mean they were the ones addressed. The message was specifically directed toward and applied to the disciples.

The message can conveniently be broken down into four clauses:[29]

Clause 1:   For whoever should want to save his **psyche**
Clause 2:   will lose it.
Clause 3:   But whoever should lose his **psyche** on
              behalf of me,
Clause 4:   he will save it.

If the saving of the **psyche** in clause 1 is physical, it must also be physical in clause 3, and if it is metaphorical in 2, then it must be metaphorical in 4. It obviously cannot be physical in all four clauses because then a man would be preserving and losing his physical life at the same time (clause 1 and 2). The **psyche** can be "saved" in two senses. The first (Clause 1) refers to physical preservation. But the metaphorical sense (Clause 2) is derived from a common usage of **psyche** where it refers to the inner self within an individual which experiences the joys and sorrows of life, i.e., the person. The rich young fool (Lk. 12:19-23) stored up his goods so that his **psyche** could rest and be joyous.[30] To save the soul in this

---

[28]*The Septuagint Version, With Apocrypha - Greek and English* (Samuel Bagster & Sons, London, 1851; reprint ed., Grand Rapids: Zondervan, 1978). See LXX translation of Gen. 19:17; 32:30; 1 Ki. 19:11; 1 Sam. 19:11; Jud. 10:15; Job 33:28; Ps. 30:7; 71:13; 108:31; Jer. 31:6; 1 Macc. 9:9.

[29]Jerry Lee Pattillo, "An Exegetical Study of the Lord's Logion on the 'Salvation of the *Psyche*'" (Th.M. thesis, Dallas Theological Seminary, 1978), p. 33.

[30]For other passages where a similar thought is expressed, see Mt. 6:25; 12:18; Lk. 14:6; Mt. 26:38; Mk. 14:34; Heb. 10:38).

sense is to secure for it eternal pleasures by living a life of sacrifice now. We are apparently, according to Jesus, developing an inner character which will be preserved (saved) into eternity. There is a connection between our life of sacrifice and our capability to enjoy and experience eternal fellowship with God.

"Gaining the whole world" refers to obtaining the joys and pleasures of this world. This "gain," however, can only be accomplished if a man is willing to "forfeit his soul." To "forfeit the soul" is metaphorical for "forfeit true life now and reward in eternity." The verse is an explanation and expansion of Clause 2 above which was shown to be metaphorical, not literal. As mentioned above, it cannot be physical because Clause 1 is physical in all other uses in the Bible.

So the danger is that, if a man does not become a disciple, he will lose his soul. That is, he will forfeit true life now and reward in eternity. The fact that the context is referring to rewards, and not deliverance from hell, is suggested by Mt. 16:27: "[He] will then recompense every man according to his deeds" (NASB). Clauses 2 and 4 therefore refer to the losing or gaining of rewards for discipleship.

The result of this "saving of the soul" is, according to Jesus, the finding of real life now as well. In fact, in the LXX the Hebrew word **shalom**[31] ("peace, prosperity, well, health, completeness, safety")[32] is often translated by the word **soterios** ("saving"). Jesus seems to have merged the ideas of physical preservation of life and the finding of a meaningful and blessed life.

Saving one's life (Clause 1) means what it means every place else in the Bible, "to preserve one's physical life." There was a temptation among Christ's followers to avoid martyrdom and suffering to save their lives. Paradoxically, when a man schemes to preserve his own life, he will lose the very thing he really wants, happiness and blessing (Clause 2). The paradox, however, is that a man who is willing to even die for Christ (Clause 3) will find the very pleasures and blessings he really sought and an eternal reward as well (Clause 4).

Keeping this in mind helps us understand some passages which are fraught with theological difficulty:

> *Therefore get rid of all moral filth and the evil that is so prevalent, and humbly accept the word planted in you, which can save [**sozo**] you* (Jas. 1:21).

These believers in whom the Word has been planted need salvation! The Word of God is capable of saving them if they will act on it. The word seems to take a meaning very close to sanctification:

---

[31]AS, p. 438.
[32]G. Lloyd Carr, "shalom," in *TWOT*, 2:931.

What good is it, my brothers, if a man claims to have faith but has no deeds? Can such a faith save [sozo] him? (Jas. 2:14).

The form of the question requires a negative answer. No, faith without works cannot save! If salvation in James refers to final deliverance from hell, only with difficulty can he be brought into harmony with Paul, a harmony at the expense of the plain meaning of the text. Works clearly ARE a condition of salvation according to James. But what is the content of that salvation?

James takes us back to the teaching of his Master in 1:21 when he refers to the saving of our lives. The Greek text reads: "Humbly accept the implanted word which is able to save your lives [sosai tas psychas humon]." The expression "save your lives" is the same one used by the Lord Jesus in Mt. 16:25.[33] That salvation does require work and self denying service to Christ. But it does not constitute final deliverance from hell. Rather, it involves the preservation of physical life now, a victorious perseverance through trials, and a glorious reward for our faithful service in the future (Clause 4 above in Mt. 16:25).

There is nothing here about a "saving faith" and one that does not save in the sense of final deliverance from hell. There is no perseverance in holiness taught. Nowhere does James tell us that works are the inevitable result of the faith that delivers from hell, nowhere, unless salvation means deliverance from hell. But then, if it does, James is teaching salvation by works!

In 1 Pet. 1:9 Peter speaks of the salvation of our souls in a similar way. The entire passage is instructive and bears comment.

His burden is to encourage his readers toward steadfastness in trials (1:6). Not only are there external enemies, but there are internal enemies such as "fleshly lusts, which wage war against the soul" (2:11). This warfare against their soul (Gk. psyche) is severe, and they need victory in the battle; they need deliverance, or "salvation" (Gk. soteria). Only by daily obedience to the truth can their "souls" be "purified" so that they can love fervently (1:22).

Peter's method of encouragement is to set their hearts aglow with a vision of the great future. They have, he says, been "born again to a living hope" (1:3). This birth is to "obtain an inheritance which is imperishable" (1:4). This inheritance is the "reward of the inheritance" (Col. 3:24) of which Paul spoke. All are appointed to this at spiritual birth but only those who persevere in faith will obtain the intended goal. He gently reminds them of this in the following verse when he says, ". . . who are protected by the power of God **through faith** for a salvation ready to be revealed in the last time" (1:5). The salvation to be revealed is the consummation of our salvation in the glories of the messianic era. This is the

---

[33]See parallel passages in Mk. 8:25; Lk. 9:24; 21:19; Jn. 12:25.

future tense of salvation. Only those Christians who maintain their faith will experience protection now and have a share in that great future.

In vv. 5 and 7 the word "faith" (Gk. **pistis**) is best rendered "faithfulness."[34] The phrase "are protected" refers to present protection that the life of faithfulness to God provides. Possibly the continuous aspect of the present tense could be pressed here, i.e., "are continually being protected."

Even though they are distressed by various trials (1:7), they rejoice in the prospect that, if they remain steadfast, they will "obtain an inheritance." Indeed, Peter says, the intended result of these trials is that after the suffering they may receive "praise and glory and honor at the revelation of Jesus Christ" (NASB). First comes faithful perseverance under suffering, then comes honor from Christ at the revelation.

As they gaze at this glorious future salvation, this wonderful prospect, they obtain benefits of that great future even now:

Obtaining as the outcome of your faith the **salvation of your souls** (1:9 NASB).

It is customary for Experimental Predestinarians to understand "salvation of your souls" as a reference to final deliverance from hell. However, the starting point for our understanding should not be our system of theology but the usage of the phrase in the Bible and the immediate context.

In the LXX the words are found in the same verse four times. In Ps. 42:11 David's "soul," i.e., "life" (Gk. **psyche**), is in despair because enemies revile him and ridicule his belief in God in the midst of his trials. Yet he turns to God for "help of my countenance," which in the LXX is "salvation (Gk. **soteria**) of my countenance." Salvation of a soul is assistance in the midst of trials. In 1 Sam. 19:5 David took his life (Gk. **psyche**) in his hand and killed Goliath, and this resulted in salvation (Gk. **soteria**) of all Israel, including, of course, David. Salvation from enemies is the meaning. Similarly, in Ps. 3:2 David once again finds many enemies saying God will not save (Gk. **soteria**) him. In Ps. 35:3 He asks the Lord to save to his soul (Gk. **psyche**), "I am your salvation (Gk. **soteria**)." He wants deliverance from those who are his enemies and who fight against him (v. 2).

We conclude, therefore, that this phrase is very similar in meaning to "save a soul" (Gk. **sozo psyche**) studied above. In no instance does it mean "go to heaven when I die" or final deliverance from hell. The starting point for our un-

---

[34]Joseph A. Fitzmeyer, "First Peter," in *The Jerome Biblical Commentary*, ed. Raymond E. Brown, Joseph A. Fitzmeyer, and Roland E. Murphy (Englewood Cliffs, NJ: Prentice-Hall, 1968), under 1:7.

derstanding of this term should be "deliverance from enemies." Unless there are contextual indications to the contrary, there is no reason to depart from this universal sense.

That this is the intended meaning in 1 Pet. 1 seems to be confirmed by the fact that they are receiving this salvation now (present tense). That great future is being experienced now. This is the present "outcome of their faith." As they are steadfast and faithful, they experience the benefits of the future salvation in the present. In other words, v. 9 has sanctification and not justification in view. It is not an act of faith which will give them victory but a life of faith that is needed. Thus, the Greek word pistis is best rendered "faithfulness."

Some have objected that this cannot be true because the next verse begins, "As to this salvation, the prophets. . . ." (1 Pet. 1:10). The salvation referred to in this verse is clearly the future salvation of the soul and not its present salvation. Since the salvation in v. 10 refers back to the salvation in v. 9, it is argued that the salvation in v. 9 must be future as well. In this way some notion of "entrance into heaven" is read into the words. However, in v. 9 the salvation is an extension into the present of the benefits of the future salvation. So both verses are speaking about the same thing. When the future salvation is experienced in the present, it is a salvation from the present enemies of the people of God. When experienced in the future, it is the final and permanent deliverance from all enemies. They are able now, however, to earn this salvation in the future as a reward (Gk. komizo, "receive") and have the benefits extend to the present.

This way of viewing the passage is widely held. Edwin Blum, for example, says:

> *For you are receiving* [komizomenoi, a present causal participle], *giving the reason for the paradoxical joy while stressing that the anticipated salvation is even* now in the process of realization. *The "goal"* [telos] *or consummation of faith is "the salvation of your souls."* . . . *The "soul" is used in the Semitic biblical sense of "self" or "person." Therefore the thought of this section closes with the believer's enjoyment of the future salvation in this present age.* [35]

Selwyn, while also seeing an eschatological element in 1:9, nevertheless observes that the salvation here is present as well: "The doctrine of faith issuing

[35]Edwin A. Blum, "1 Peter," in *The Expositor's Bible Commentary*, ed. Frank E. Gaebelein, 11 vols. to date (Grand Rapids: Zondervan, 1976--), 12:221.

in a salvation realized in part here and now is not uncommon in N.T."[36] Hart insists, "**komizomenoi** implies that already they are receiving what is due to them."[37]

What is the present expression of future salvation which they are receiving? In what way does steadfast faith bring salvation to their souls now? What is the salvation of a life (soul) in the present? It is not deliverance from hell or entrance into heaven! The battle in which their souls were engaged and from which they needed deliverance was the battle against fleshly lusts (2:11), the battle for purity (1:22), and the battle for survival in the midst of trials (1:6). These are the enemies these readers face. As they trust God and set their gaze on the great future and remain faithful to him now, they experience the salvation which consists in victorious perseverance in trials and triumph over the pollutions of the age. They are by this means "protected" (a military term, 1:5) from their "enemies."

A final illustration of a usage of the word "salvation" which seems to equate it with deliverance from the enemies of the people of God in the present is found in Rom. 10:1-14.

Old Testament prophecy has a wonderful richness. Couched in oriental thought, it is often mystifying to Western man. In what is, perhaps, one of the most helpful expositions of prophetic interpretation ever written, Willis Beecher has taught us that the prophetic mode of fulfillment is one of cumulative fulfillment.[38] Simply put, it means that God is fulfilling His promises in many individual historical events which will finally culminate in a complete fulfillment. There is a long line of fulfillment of many predictions. Time cannot be taken here to repeat his excellent discussion, but the Old Testament doctrine of the salvation of the remnant provides a good illustration. Paul refers to this in Rom. 9 and 10:

> *Brethren, my heart's desire and my prayer to God for them is for their* **salvation** (Rom. 10:1 NASB).

But what kind of salvation is in view? To answer that, we must turn to the preceding and following contexts. In the preceding context we discover that a deliverance from temporal devastation was his meaning. Quoting Isa. 1:9 , the apostle directs our attention to the Assyrian invasion (ca. 722 B.C.). Unless the Lord leaves some survivors, the nation will end up being completely destroyed like Sodom and Gomorrah (see Rom. 9:29). But a remnant did survive the Assyrian invasion. And this remnant becomes a fulfillment of the promise that a remnant would one day return to the Lord. Paul refers to this in Rom. 9:27 and 28. There he quotes Isa. 10:22-23 and refers to the remnant that will be saved

---

[36]Edward Gordon Selwyn, *The First Epistle of St. Peter*, 2d. ed. (London: Macmillan, 1947), p. 133. He cites Acts 14:9; 15:11; 2 Th. 2:13; 2 Tim. 3:15; Heb. 10:39.

[37]J. H. A. Hart, "The First Epistle General of Peter," in *EGT*, 5:45.

[38]Willis J. Beecher, *The Prophets and the Promise* (New York: Thomas Y. Crowell, 1905; reprint ed., Grand Rapids: Baker, 1975), p. 376.

(Rom. 9:27). The salvation in view is not deliverance from hell but the fulfillment of the promise to Israel that she would one day be restored to Palestine.

Israel once again faces temporal destruction. The Lord announced it in His predictions of the total devastation of the temple and the people of Israel which occurred in A.D. 70.[39] Because He knew Jerusalem would become desolate, the Lord wept for their failure.[40]

The fact that Paul quotes Scripture related to Israel's temporal destruction and the certain knowledge he had of the Lord's prophecy surely suggests that, when he says he desires Israel's "salvation," he refers to the line of cumulative fulfillment of the remnant doctrine. The terrible devastation that would come upon Israel in A.D. 70 was their judgment for rejecting the free gift of the righteousness of God in Christ, their Messiah (Rom. 10:2-4).

The following context enriches the concept of salvation to include not only deliverance from enemies in time but final deliverance from hell as well. They had not submitted themselves to the righteousness of God and therefore would not receive His free righteousness (10:2). We conclude then that being "saved" in v. 1 refers to full salvation, salvation in time and eternity. It is a salvation from enemies and deliverance from hell.

Passing over the next few verses for the moment, we come to an unusual confession:

If you confess with your mouth Jesus as Lord, and believe in your heart that God raised Him from the dead, you shall be saved (Rom. 10:9 NASB).

This confession is unusual because it is the only place in the New Testament where a condition in addition to faith is added for salvation. The Gospel of John, which was written expressly for the purpose that we might believe and as a result be saved (Jn. 20:30-31), never mentions confession of Christ as Lord as a condition. If we must confess Jesus as Lord in order to be saved, then a man could not be saved by reading John's gospel!

A very simple solution to this difficulty is to return to the definition of salvation in the immediate context. This salvation is not only deliverance from hell but includes deliverance from divine discipline in time, brought about by disobedience, and the enjoyment of Divine favor. This was the deliverance Israel failed to enjoy. Only one thing is necessary, according to the book of Romans, for salvation from hell: belief. But two things are necessary for us to enjoy the full salvation spoken of in this context which includes God's blessing, His individual and

---

[39]Mt. 24:2; Lk. 21:5
[40]Mt. 23:37.

spiritual salvation in this life: (1) faith in Christ and (2) submission to His lordship. Furthermore, it is not inevitable that a man who believes in Christ will also confess Him as Lord. Paul makes this plain in the next verse:

For with the heart man believes, resulting in righteousness, and with the mouth he confesses, resulting in salvation (Rom. 10:10 NASB).

Salvation in this verse refers only to the deliverance in time and not the full salvation of v. 1 which included both. Believing with the heart results in final deliverance from hell, but confession of the lordship of Christ is necessary for the kind of salvation mentioned here, salvation from present enemies. Instead of confession of Jesus as Lord being the inevitable result of salvation as the Experimental Predestinarians teach, Paul, to the contrary, says that salvation is the inevitable result of confessing Jesus as Lord!

Just as a confession of Jesus as Lord results in salvation, so calling upon the name of the Lord has the same effect:

For whoever will call upon the name of the Lord will be saved (Rom. 10:13 NASB).

The phrases "call upon the name of the Lord" and "confess Jesus as Lord" are parallel and explain each other. Both result in "salvation." But the salvation in view must be determined by the immediate context in Romans and the Old Testament citations. This verse (10:13) is a quotation from Joel 2:32 and refers to the physical deliverance from the future day of wrath upon the earth and the restoration of the Jews to Palestine and not deliverance from hell.

Furthermore, in the New Testament, "calling upon the name of the Lord" is something only those who are already justified can do. A non-Christian cannot call upon the name of the Lord for assistance because he is not yet born again.[41]

Paul says to the Corinthians:

To the church of God which is at Corinth, to those who have been sanctified in Christ Jesus, saints by calling, with all who in every place call upon the name of our Lord Jesus Christ (1 Cor. 1:2 NASB).

Wherever Christians met in worship, they would appeal to their divine Lord for assistance by calling upon His name. Christians were known by this title; they were simply those who called upon the Lord (Acts 9:14, 21).

Paul similarly urged Timothy to flee youthful lusts and to "pursue righteousness, faith, love and peace, with those who call upon the name of the Lord"

---

[41]The following discussion follows Zane Hodges, *Absolutely Free* (Grand Rapids: Zondervan, 1989), pp. 193-94.

(2 Tim. 2:22). Peter exhorted the believers, "And if you call upon the Father, . . . conduct yourselves throughout the time of your sojourning here in fear" (1 Pet. 1:17 NKJV).

Stephen, as he was being stoned to death, "called upon the Lord" and asked Him to receive his spirit (Acts 7:59).

The pagans called upon their various gods for assistance. But the early Christians called upon the name of the Lord for divine help in time of need. The Romans would call upon Caesar for assistance, and by invoking that formula, a legal appeal to the highest authority was made by a Roman citizen. Paul himself used this phrase when he said:

> *"I stand at Caesar's judgment seat, where I ought to be judged. To the Jews I have done no wrong, as you very well know . . . I appeal to Caesar"* (Acts 25:10-11).

The word "appeal" is the same Greek word for "call upon" used in Rom. 10:13.

The point is that to call upon the name of the Lord was a distinctively Christian privilege. Non-Christians cannot call upon Him and to call upon Him is not a condition of salvation from hell but of deliverance in time from the enemies of God's people.

Paul makes this explicitly clear in the next verse:

> *How then shall they call upon Him whom they have not believed? And how shall they believe in Him whom they have not heard? And how shall they hear without a preacher?* (Rom. 10:14 NASB).

A chronological sequence is intended here. An Israelite cannot hear unless first there is a preacher. He cannot believe unless first he has heard. And he cannot call upon the name of the Lord **unless he has first believed.**

When a man believes, the result, Paul says, is righteousness. He is delivered from hell. When he confesses Jesus as Lord or calls upon His name, he is saved and delivered from all enemies of the people of God in time.

Therefore, we see an excellent illustration of Beecher's cumulative fulfillment of the remnant prophecy. Each deliverance of God's people in time is part of the line of fulfillment intended by Isaiah. Beginning with physical deliverance from the Assyrian invasion, it progresses through subsequent deliverances of the people in time. Paul desires that the people will be saved from destruction in A.D. 70, but he knows that all will experience the temporal deliverances in the broadest sense as they call upon the name of their divine Lord for assistance in time.

Salvation of a Wife

Another passage which has exercised much exegetical ingenuity is found in 1 Tim. 2:15:

But women will be saved [**sozo**] *through childbearing--if they continue in faith, love and holiness with propriety.*

This is certainly a novel approach for obtaining deliverance from future wrath! The meaning of **sozo** in this passage is once again something like "spiritual health," a full and meaningful life. This fits the context quite well. Paul has just excluded women from positions of teaching authority in the church (1 Tim. 2:9-14). What then is their primary destiny? They will find life through fulfilling their role as a mother IF they continue in faith, love, and holiness with propriety. A salvation which comes only to mothers who persist in faithful service is not the faith alone salvation taught elsewhere. For this reason many interpreters agree with Litfin and understand "saved" as being "preserved from insignificance by means of her role in the family."[42] A woman will normally find her fulfillment and meaning in life not by pursuing the male role but by being a wife and mother. But she must follow this vocation with faith and love.

Salvation of a Christian Leader

Similarly, in the same book Paul exhorts Timothy:

Watch your life and doctrine closely. Persevere in them, because if you do, you will save [**sozo**] *both yourself and your hearers* (1 Tim. 4:16).

Salvation in this passage is conditioned on watching one's life and doctrine and perseverance in this attitude. Yahweh exhorted Ezekiel along the same lines:

But if you warn the wicked man to turn from his ways, and he does not do so, he will die for his sin, but you will have **saved** *yourself* (Ezek. 33:9).

Both Timothy and Ezekiel are regenerate and justified saints who are still in need of being saved, of finding spiritual wholeness, or possibly, as one writer suggested, of "continuous preservation from surrounding evil."[43] Timothy is not to neglect his gift (4:14), and the mothers are not to neglect their calling, mother-

---

[42]A. Duane Litfin, "1 Timothy," in *BKC*, 2:736.

[43]Girdlestone, p. 126. He feels Heb. 5:9 refers to the same kind of salvation.

hood. If both heed this injunction, they will find a rich and rewarding experience of Jesus Christ in this life and a great reward in the future. He will truly "save his life" and the lives of many of this flock who observe his progress and follow his example (4:15).

Reigning with Christ in the Kingdom

Often in the Old Testament salvation has messianic overtones. It refers to the future regathering of the nation of Israel and their establishment as rulers in a universal kingdom under the kingship of David's greater Son. It is not surprising then to find that both **sozo** and **soteria** often have similar connotations in the New Testament: joint participation with Christ in the coming kingdom rule.

It is possible that this is the thought behind our Lord's famous saying: "But he who stands firm to the end will be saved [**sozo**]" (Mt. 24:13). The context refers to the terrors of the future tribulation. While it is possible that the meaning is simply, "he who endures to the end will be delivered at the second coming," that seems a bit tautologous and lacks encouragement. If the content of the salvation here is positive, then a great motive for endurance has been provided. It may be preferable to view the salvation here as the receipt of the kingdom and the right to rule there. The condition of salvation in this passage is steadfast endurance which does not yield under persecution but perseveres to the final hour, i.e., either the end of the tribulation or the end of life. Marshall argues, "It probably indicates not so much endurance to the very end of the period of tribulation but, rather, endurance to the very limit, even to the point of death."[44]

> *Then the King will say to those on his right, "Come, you who are blessed by my Father; take your inheritance, the kingdom prepared for you since the creation of the world" (Mt. 25:34).*

The apostle says:

> *Therefore I endure everything for the sake of the elect, that they too may obtain the salvation [soteria] that is in Christ Jesus, with eternal glory (2 Tim. 2:10).*

While the majority of the commentators understand the "elect" to refer to the unregenerate who have not yet believed (but certainly will), there is good reason to understand the term in this context as a virtual synonym for a regenerate saint. First of all, in **every** usage of the term applied to men, in the New Testament it **always** refers to a justified saint. Conversely, it **never** refers to someone who was elect in eternity past but who has not yet entered into the purpose of

---

[44]I. Howard Marshall, *Kept by the Power of God* (Minneapolis: Bethany House, 1969), p. 74.

their election, justification.[45] Cremer is emphatic on this point. He says that the "view decisively appearing in the N.T [is] that the **eklektoi** are persons who not only are **in thesi** the objects of the divine election, but who are so in fact, *i.e.,* those who have entered upon the state of reconciliation. . . . Thus **oi eklektoi** denote those in whom God's saving purpose . . . of free love is realized."[46] There appear to be no particular contextual indicators against applying this consistent usage of the term to 2 Tim. 2.[47] It is best to understand by "the elect" Timothy and the faithful men of v. 2. Timothy is being exhorted to suffer in his ministry to the faithful men just as Paul has been imprisoned for his ministry to the "elect." The idea of Paul suffering for the sanctification and growth of the churches is a common New Testament theme,[48] and is easily seen in this passage as well.

Here then are saved people in need of salvation! The salvation in view is necessarily sanctification or, perhaps, more precisely, victorious perseverance through trials (1:8; 2:3, 9). Elsewhere in the Pastorals, "salvation" has referred to aspects of sanctification so there is no reason why it cannot have such a meaning here as well (e.g. 1 Tim. 2:15; 4:16). The setting is the dismal situation of apostasy (in 1:15, shortly to be identified, 2:17-18). Paul reminds Timothy that loyalty to the profession of faith (v. 11) does not go unrewarded (Rom. 8:17; 2 Tim. 2:12). If they persevere, they will not only obtain victory but eternal honor (v. 10), reward at the judgment seat of Christ.

Salvation in the Book of Hebrews

Moving as he does in Old Testament context, it is to be expected that the writer of the Epistle to the Hebrews would use the word **soteria** in a sense more akin to its Hebrew background. For him salvation is participation with Christ in the future kingdom rule. He distinguishes his usage of the term from the meaning of final deliverance from hell when he says:

---

[45]The word **eklektos** is used twenty-two times in the New Testament. Jesus says that for the sake of the "elect" the days of the tribulation will be shortened (Mt. 24:22; Mk. 13:21). Even the "elect," He says, can be led astray (Mk. 13:22). Paul tells us the "elect" are the justified (Rm. 8:33) and that they are Christians, "chosen of God" (Col. 3:12). The Christian lady to whom John writes is the "chosen lady" (2 Jn. 1, 13) and the "chosen" of Rev. 17:14 are faithful Christians. In some places it begins to take the meaning commonly found in secular Greek, "choice one," as in Rom. 16:13. See MM, p. 196.

[46]Hermann Cremer, *Biblio-Theological Lexicon of New Testament Greek* (Edinburgh: T. & T. Clark, 1895), p. 405.

[47]Indeed, some of the commentators, perhaps struck by this usage, have understood the term to apply to "those chosen for Christianity, both those already Christians and those not yet converted" (George A. Denzer, "The Pastoral Letters," in *Jerome Biblical Commentary*, ed. Raymond E. Brown, Joseph A. Fitzmeyer, and Roland E. Murphy (Englewood Cliffs, NJ: Prentice-Hall, 1968), on 2 Tim. 2:10. This would then require different meanings of the word "salvation," i.e., for the unsaved, deliverance from hell, and for the saved, sanctification.

[48]Cf. Col. 1:24; 2 Cor. 1:5-6; 4:12.

So Christ was sacrificed once to take away the sins of many people; and he will appear a second time, not to bear sin [Gk. **choris**, "apart from sin"], *but to bring salvation* [**soteria**] *to those who are waiting* [**apekdechomai**] *for him* (Heb. 9:28).

The verb **apekdechomai** commonly means to "wait eagerly" or "wait patiently."[49] This salvation does not deal with the removal of the negative (it is **choris** from sin, "apart" from sin). Rather, it refers to a salvation which will come to those Christians who are waiting eagerly for the Lord's return. The verse seem to precisely parallel Paul's anticipation of receiving the crown of righteousness which goes to those who "love His appearing" (2 Tim. 4:8 KJV). The readers of the epistle would understand to what he was referring. Indeed, the major theme of the book is to exhort them to continue to wait patiently, to endure faithfully in the midst of their trials:

So do not throw away your confidence; it will be richly rewarded. You need to persevere[50] so that when you have done the will of God, you will receive what he has promised (Heb. 10:35-36).

Some of the readers were considering throwing away their confidence, returning to Judaism. They would not be the ones found waiting eagerly, who have "labored to enter into rest" (Heb. 4:11), and who have "done the will of God" (10:36), i.e., finished their work. His meaning becomes transparent in Heb. 1:14, Heb. 2:3, and Heb. 2:10:

Are not all angels ministering spirits sent to serve those who will inherit salvation [**soteria**]? (1:14).

The fact that he is thinking in Old Testament terms, quoting the Psalms, and anticipating this salvation as future ("will inherit") suggests that he is thinking of the messianic salvation proclaimed by the prophets mentioned above. In 1:8-9, for example, he quotes the messianic Ps. 45, which describes the kingdom of Messiah and his companions (Gk. **metochoi**). In 1:13 he cites Ps. 110:1, another messianic psalm, where David says, "Sit at my right hand until I make your enemies a footstool for your feet." This psalm was quite appropriate because it anticipates the day when the enemies of Messiah and His people will be defeated. One day the enemies of the readers, those who were persecuting them and therefore tempting them to cast aside their confession of faith, will likewise be destroyed. Then in the verse immediately following he mentions the great salvation.

Surely, the immediate associations with the quotations from the Psalms would lead us to think of the future messianic kingdom and not redemption from hell. Furthermore, as argued in the previous chapter, the verb "to inherit" always

---

[49]See Phil. 3:20; 1 Pet. 3:20; 1 Cor. 1:7

[50]Note Heb. 12:1-3.

has the sense of "to obtain by works" in the New Testament; therefore, this salvation is obtained by works. That there is a salvation which can be obtained by works is taught elsewhere in Hebrews, 5:9. Believers do not "inherit," "obtain by obedience," the salvation which is from hell. But they do obtain by obedience an ownership in the future consummation. To inherit salvation is simply to obtain ownership with the King of His future kingdom. This is the subject of 2:5ff., where he teaches regarding the co-reigning of our Captain and His many sons.

We are therefore justified in being skeptical of the interpretation which says that salvation here is deliverance from hell. That is why F. F. Bruce says:

> *The salvation here spoken of lies in the future; it is yet to be inherited. . . . That is to say, it is that eschatological salvation which in Paul's words is "nearer to us than when we first believed" (Rom. 13:11), or in Peter's words is "ready to be revealed in the last time" (1 Pet. 1:5).*[51]

The salvation to which he refers is the subject of Heb. 2:5-18, the future reign of David's Greater Son, the Messiah, and of our participation with him in the final destiny of man, to rule over the works of God's hand (2:7-8).

It is commonly recognized that the warnings of Hebrews are parentheses in his argument. From 1:4 to 2:18 he is presenting the superiority of Christ to the angels. It is not to angels that the rulership over God's works has been commissioned but to God's King Son and His companions (1:9; 2:10). In the middle of the argument he inserts a warning, Heb. 2:1-4, in which he exhorts them not to neglect this great future, this great **soteria**. Then in Heb. 2:5 he picks up the argument he momentarily departed from at the end of Heb. 1:14. The "for" (**gar**) refers back to 1:14:

> *For* [**gar**] *unto the angels hath He not put in subjection the world to come,* **whereof we speak** (2:5 KJV).

The subjection of the world to come is the **soteria** "of which we are speaking." He then gives an exposition of Ps. 8:1-9 which is in turn David's exposition of the final destiny of man, set forth in Gen. 1:26-28. To "inherit" that salvation is simply to have a share with Christ in ruling in that kingdom. This contextually is the "great salvation" which they are not to neglect:[52]

> *How can we escape if we ignore such a great salvation* [**soteria**] (Heb. 2:3).

---

[51]F. F. Bruce, *The Epistle to the Hebrews*, NICNT, 14:25.

[52]See Thomas Kem Oberholtzer, "The Eschatological Salvation of Hebrews 1:5-2:5," *Bib-Sac* 145 (January-March 1988): 83-97.

The neglected salvation is not our final deliverance from hell, that is not the salvation "about which we are speaking." Rather, it is the opportunity to enter into the final destiny of man, to reign with Christ over the works of God's hands (Heb. 2:8-9).[53] There is something conditional about entering into this salvation. It is the salvation he has just mentioned in 1:14. He tells us there is a danger from which we cannot escape if we neglect it. For the writer of the epistle the danger to which he refers is not loss of justification, "because by one sacrifice he has made perfect forever those who are being made holy" (Heb. 10:14). Our eternal destiny is secure. What is contingent is whether or not we will be "richly rewarded" and "receive what He has promised" (Heb. 10:36) which is achieved only "through faith and patience" (Heb. 6:12).

The writer says that the Lord announced this salvation. While one could think of the Lord's teaching to Nicodemus regarding salvation from hell, the context of Heb. 2:5-10 suggests another salvation:

> *But seek his kingdom, and these things will be given to you as well. Do not be afraid, little flock, for your Father has been pleased to give you the kingdom* (Lk. 12:31-32).

> *And I confer on you a kingdom, just as my Father conferred one on me, so that you may eat and drink at my table in my kingdom and sit on the throne, judging the twelve tribes of Israel* (Lk. 22:29-30).

> *Jesus said to them, "I tell you the truth, at the renewal of all things, when the Son of Man sits on his glorious throne, you who have followed me will also sit on twelve thrones judging the twelve tribes of Israel* (Mt. 19:28).

> *Repent, for the kingdom of heaven is near* (Mt. 4:17).

The coming kingdom of heaven announced here by Jesus is none other than the predicted kingdom-salvation of the Old Testament. It is the time of the restoration of the kingdom to Israel (Acts 1:6).[54] The miracles which confirmed it (Heb. 2:4) are powers of the coming age (Heb. 6:5).

Such a salvation, joint participation with Christ in the coming kingdom rule, is contingent upon our faithful perseverance and obedience. That is why he says:

---

[53]George N. H. Peters, commenting on Heb. 1:14, puts it this way, "Salvation includes far more than moral and bodily regeneration, for it embraces the covenanted kingdom of God, the inheritance of David's Son, the joint-heirship and reign with Christ" (George N. H. Peters, *The Theocratic Kingdom*, 3 vols. [New York: Funk and Wagnalls, 1884; reprint ed., Grand Rapids: Kregel, 1972], 3:451).

[54]Because of Israel's rejection, the final form of that kingdom, the millennium, was postponed until the second advent but was inaugurated in a mystery form in the present age.

Although he was a son, he learned obedience from what he suffered and, once made perfect, he became the source of eternal salvation [**soteria**] *for* **all who obey** *him* (Heb. 5:8-9).

Here in no uncertain terms he declares that this salvation is based on works of obedience and not just faith alone. There is nothing in the book of Hebrews which suggests that this is a description of all true Christians. This salvation is "eternal" because it is final, complete, and lasts for all eternity. The phrase "everlasting salvation" is evidently borrowed from Isa. 45:17. In both places the reference is not to deliverance from hell but to the unending nature of the messianic kingdom.

Of this salvation Christ becomes the "source" (Gk. **aitia**, "the cause, author").[55] In what sense is He the "cause" of the great future? It seems that His death and resurrection made it possible, and His priestly ministry of comfort and intercession makes it available . . . to those who obey Him. It is Christ as priestly helper, and not offerer of sacrifice, that is in the forefront in this section of the epistle (5:2, but especially 4:14-16; 2:17-18). That kind of priestly ministry is necessary to assist the heirs of salvation along the path which their captain has gone (2:10). The priestly ministry of sacrifice for sins does not come into focus until the next major section of the epistle, where he demonstrates that Jesus is superior to Aaron (7:1-10:39).

The final reference to **soteria** in Hebrews is found in Heb. 6:9:

Even though we speak like this, dear friends, we are confident of better things in your case--things that accompany salvation [**soteria**].

The things to which he refers are defined in the following verses (6:10-12): work and love, diligence to the end, and faith and patience. Salvation is the victorious participation with Christ in the coming kingdom as it is in Heb. 1:14, which only those who persevere as companions of the King will inherit. The writer obviously expects that his readers will persevere to the end, enter into rest, and obtain these blessings.

Conclusion

Salvation is a broad term. However, only with difficulty can the common meaning of "deliver from hell" be made to fit into numerous passages. It commonly means "to make whole," "to sanctify," "to endure victoriously," or "to be delivered from some general trouble or difficulty." Without question, the common "knee-jerk" reaction which assumes that "salvation" always has eternal deliverance in view, has seriously compromised the ability of many to objectively discern what

---

[55]AS, p. 15.

the New Testament writers intended to teach. As a result, Experimental Predestinarian views have gained wider acceptance that they should have.

A similar problem exists in regard to the definition of "eternal life." Once again a kind of instinctive response to this word sets in. Without due consideration of contextual matters, it is often assumed, without further discussion or proof, that the term invariably means "to be born again." As we shall see in the next chapter, this is not always so.

Chapter 7

Inheriting Eternal Life

The positive side of our great salvation is eternal life. By this, of course, our Lord did not mean merely eternal existence but a rich and meaningful life which begins now and extends into eternity.

Given Freely as a Gift

All readers of the New Testament are familiar with the tremendous gospel promise of the free gift of eternal life. That this rich experience was obtained by faith alone was one of the key insights of the Reformation:

For God so loved the world that he gave his one and only Son, that whoever believes in him shall not perish but have eternal life [**zoen aionion**] (Jn. 3:16).

I tell you the truth, whoever hears my word and believes him who sent me has eternal life [**zoen aionion**] *and will not be condemned; he has crossed over from death to life* (Jn. 5:24).

For my Father's will is that everyone who looks to the Son and believes in him shall have eternal life [**zoen aionion**]*, and I will raise him up at the last day* (Jn. 6:40).

Eternal life can be ours, now, on the condition that we believe in Him, and for no other condition. Yes, eternal life is ours on the basis of faith alone.

Earned as a Reward

The phrase "eternal life" (**zoen aionion**) occurs forty-two times in the New Testament.[1] Its common meaning of the free gift of regeneration (entrance into heaven on the basis of faith alone) is well documented. However, many are not

---

[1] *A Concordance to the Greek Testament* ed. W. F. Moulton and A. S. Geden, 4th ed., rev. H. K. Moulton (Edinburgh: T. & T. Clark, 1963), pp. 30-31.

aware that in eleven of those forty-two usages (26 percent), eternal life is presented to the believer as something to be earned or worked for![2] For example:

> *To those who by persistence in doing good seek glory, honor and immortality, he will give eternal life* [**zoen aionion**] (Rom. 2:7).

> *The one who sows to please his sinful nature, from that nature will reap destruction; the one who sows to please the Spirit, from the spirit will reap eternal life* [**zoen aionion**] (Gal. 6:8).

> *The man who loves his life will lose it, while the man who hates his life in this world will keep it for eternal life* [**zoen aionion**]. *Whoever serves me must follow me; and where I am my servant also will be. My Father will honor the one who serves me* (Jn. 12:25-26.).

> *And everyone who has left houses or brothers or sisters or father or mother or children or fields for my sake will receive a hundred times as much and will inherit eternal life* [**zoen aionion**] (Mt. 19:29).

Just as there are two kinds of inheritance, two dimensions to salvation, there seem to be two sides to eternal life. We must remember that eternal life in the Bible is not a static entity, a mere gift of regeneration that does not continue to grow and blossom. No, it is a dynamic relationship with Christ Himself. Jesus taught us that when He said:

> *Now this is eternal life* [**zoen aionion**]*: that they may know you, the only true God, and Jesus Christ, whom you have sent* (Jn. 17:3).

He explained elsewhere that this life was intended to grow and become more abundant: "I have come that they may have life, and have it to the full" (Jn. 10:10). But growth is not automatic; it is conditioned upon our responses. Only by the exercise of spiritual disciplines, such as prayer, obedience, faith, study of the Scriptures, and proper responses to trials, does our intimacy with Christ increase. Only by continuing in doing good does that spiritual life imparted at regeneration grow to maturity and earn a reward.

This is what the apostle Paul referred to when he challenged Timothy to "take hold of eternal life":

> *Fight the good fight of the faith. Take hold of the eternal life to which you were called when you made your good confession in the presence of many witnesses* (1 Tim. 6:12).

---

[2]Mt. 19:16; 19:29; Mk. 10:17, 30; Lk. 10:25; 18:18, 30; Rom. 2:7; Gal. 6:8; Jn. 12:25-26; Rom. 6:22.

Possessing eternal life is one thing, but "taking hold" of it is another. The former is static; the latter is dynamic. The former depends upon God; the latter depends upon us. The former comes through faith alone; "taking hold" requires faith plus obedience (6:14). Those who are rich in this world and who give generously "will lay up treasure for themselves as a firm foundation for the coming age, so that they may take hold of the life that is truly life" (1 Tim. 6:19). Eternal life is not only the gift of regeneration but "true life" which is cultivated by faith and acts of obedience.

This should not surprise us. On page after page of the Bible the richness of our spiritual life is conditioned upon our spiritual obedience. Israel was instructed in this manner:

> *Hear now, O Israel, the decrees and the laws I am about to teach you. Follow them so that* **you may live** *and may go in and take possession of the land that the LORD, the God of your father, is giving you* (Dt. 4:1).

To "live" and to take possession of the land, while not the same, are at least related concepts. Recall the numerous references above to obtaining the inheritance by taking possession of the land. Life, too, is a result of our obedience. However, regeneration, the beginning of that life, cannot be meant, so the fruition or growth of it must be in view.

> *Keep the decrees and commands, which I am giving you today, so that it may go well with you and your children after you and that you may live long in the land the LORD your God gives you for all time* (Dt. 4:40).

A long and prosperous life on earth is the reward for keeping the decrees. Surely the consequences of such a life have eternal results as well. Moses implies that it will:

> *Oh, that their hearts would be inclined to fear me and keep all my commands always, so that it might go well with them and their children* **forever!** (Dt. 5:29).

Again he says:

> *Walk in all the way that the LORD your God has commanded you, so that you may live and prosper and prolong your days in the land you will possess* (Dt. 5:33).

But is this life only material prosperity in the land of Canaan? Surely such a view of life would trivialize the commandments into a mere social contract whereby the Israelite could secure property in return for obedience. Spiritual obedience and the spirituality of the Old Testament religion lifts life far beyond mere material prosperity in Canaan. It is a rich fellowship with God. The writer to the Hebrews confirms this when he says:

> *Moreover, we have all had human fathers who disciplined us and we respected them for it. How much more should we submit to the Father of our spirits and* **live**. *Our fathers disciplined us for a little while as they thought best; but God disciplines us for our good, that we may* **share in his holiness**. *No discipline seems pleasant at the time, but painful. Later on, however, it produces a* **harvest of righteousness and peace** *for those who have been trained by it* (Heb. 12:9-11).

He explains that the life which comes from responding to divine discipline is nothing less than "a harvest of righteousness and peace" and sharing "in His holiness." Yet this passage is a divine commentary on Dt. 8:5 and Prov. 3:11-12:

> *Know then in your heart that as a man disciplines his son, so the LORD your God disciplines you* (Dt. 8:5).

In Dt. 30:15-20 life and prosperity are associated and contrasted with "destruction." If they love the Lord their God and walk in His ways and keep His commands, they will "live and increase, and the LORD your God will bless you in the land you are entering to possess." If they follow other gods, they will not live long but will be destroyed in the land they are entering. God sets before them "life and death, blessings and cursing" and says, "Now choose life so that you and your children will live. The LORD is your life" (Dt. 30:20). Moses is equating life with far more than material prosperity. It is ultimately fellowship with God and the rewards which come from that fellowship.

A similar thought is expressed in Lev. 18:5 where they are told:

> *Keep my decrees and laws, for the man who obeys them will live by them. I am the LORD.*

As Lindsay has observed, life here refers to "a happy and meaningful life."[3]

Similarly, Hab. 2:4 refers to the life of faith of the justified believer:

> *But the righteous will live by faith.*

The Hebrew word for faith, **emunah**, means "firmness, faithfulness, fidelity."[4] Its basic sense is "to be steady" or "have firm hands, be dependable, stable, etc." This meaning fits the context of Habakkuk as well. Faced with the inexplicable tardiness of God in dealing with the corrupt nation and the surprising

---

[3]F. Duane Lindsay, "Leviticus," in *BKC,* 1:200.
[4]Jack B. Scott, "**emuna**," in *TWOT,* 1:52.

revelation that He will bring an even more corrupt nation to judge them, the prophet is instructed to be faithful, steady, and to endure. Thus, Blue comments:[5]

A righteous Israelite who remained loyal to God's moral precepts and was humble before the Lord enjoyed God's abundant life. To "live" meant to experience God's blessing by enjoying a life of security, protection, and fullness.

This meaning is uniquely appropriate to the readers of the Epistle to the Hebrews who were similarly in need of patient endurance in the face of many trials. For this reason the author quotes it in application to their situation in Heb. 10:38, "But My righteous one will live by faith." The justified man must live by faith from beginning to end; he should endure.[6] But if he shrinks back and denounces his profession of faith, God's judgment will be upon him. The judgment here is apoleia and can refer to either a temporal judgment, as the context requires,[7] or eternal condemnation.

There is no reason that the reference in Rom. 1:17 should be taken any differently. He has just explained that the gospel is based upon faith "from first to last" (Rom. 1:16). It is therefore appropriate to quote a passage which refers to the continued endurance in faith of the sanctified man to demonstrate that "last" part of the life of the justified man.

It might seem that Paul uses the quotation slightly differently in Gal. 3:11:

Clearly no one is justified before God by the law, because, "The righteous will live by faith."

Can a verse intended by the original author to apply to faithful endurance in the life of the justified be used to refute the notion that justification itself could be obtained by law? The question answers itself. Of course it could. Surely if a Christian man is to live his Christian life by faith, how could the initiatory event by which he entered that life be based on works!?[8]

---

[5]J. Ronald Blue, "Habakkuk," in *BKC,* 1:1513.

[6]This view of the passage is taken by B. F. Westcott, *The Epistle to the Hebrews* (London: Macmillan, 2d. ed., 1892; reprint ed., Grand Rapids: Eerdmans, 1965), p. 337: "The just--the true believer--requires faith, trust in the unseen, for life. Such faith is the support of endurance." See also Arthur W. Pink, *Exposition of Hebrews* (Grand Rapids: Baker, 1954), pp. 641-42.

[7]Compare Heb. 10:30 where the judgments mentioned are from Dt. 32:36 and Ps. 135:14 and refer to God's judgments on His people in time and not in eternity.

[8]Eadie takes the same view: "The statement, he is justified by faith is the inference, inasmuch as he lives by faith - life being the result of justification, or rather coincident with it" (John Eadie, *Commentary on the Epistle of Paul to the Galatians* [Edinburgh: T. & T. Clark, 1884; reprint ed., Minneapolis: James and Klock, 1977], p. 246).

The Old Testament doctrine of the afterlife and rewards is very vague. That the rich life promised on the basis of obedience could result in rewards in heaven is only faintly intimated (Dt. 5:29). But the idea that obedience could be related to the acquisition and growth of a rich spiritual (as well as material) life is clear. We should not therefore be surprised to find such an equation in the New Testament.

And we do find that equation in the references to eternal life being conditioned upon obedience. As long as we remember that eternal life is fundamentally a quality of life in relationship to God, this should not cause us any difficulty with the numerous passages which stress justification by faith alone. It is extremely important to note that in every place where eternal life is presented as something which can be obtained by works, it is contextually **always** described as a future acquisition. Conversely, whenever eternal life is described as something in the present, it is obtained by faith alone.

In Gal. 6:8, for example, eternal life is something earned by the sower. If this passage is speaking of final salvation from hell, then salvation is based on works. A man reaps what he sows. If we sow to please the Spirit, we will reap (future tense) eternal life. Paul calls it a harvest "if we do not give up." Eternal life is earned by sowing to the Spirit and persevering to the end. It is what we get if we do good works. There is nothing here about the inevitability of this reaping. It depends upon us. We will reap, Paul says, "if we do not give up." Eternal life is no static entity but a relationship with God. It is dynamic and growing and has degrees. Some Christians have a more intimate relationship with their Lord than others. They have a richer experience of eternal life. Jesus Himself said, "I came to give life more abundantly" (Jn. 10:10).

In this sense it is parallel to physical life. Physical life is received as a gift, but then it must be developed. Children often develop to their full physical and mental ability under the auspices of their parents. In order for eternal life to flourish, we must also be obedient to our parents. Whenever eternal life is viewed as a reward in the New Testament, it is presented as something to be acquired in the future. But when it is presented as a gift, it is something acquired in the present. No one can receive it as a reward, i.e., experience it to a more abundant degree, until he has received eternal life freely as a gift to begin with.[9]

Bearing this in mind will help solve another interpretive difficulty: the problem of Rom. 2:5-13. In this passage, like Gal. 6:8, receiving eternal life is conditioned upon works. The passage seems to be arranged in the following manner:

God will give to each person according to what he has done (2:6)

---

[9]Mt. 19:29 is to be explained in the same manner. The eschatological harvest is in view, at which obedient men will reap.

To those who by persistence in doing good seek glory, honor and immortality, He will give eternal life (2:7).

> *But for those who are self-seeking and who reject the truth and follow evil, there will be wrath and anger (2:8).*

> *There will be trouble and distress for every human being who does evil: first for the Jew, then for the Gentile (2:9).*

But glory, honor and peace for everyone who does good; first for the Jew, then for the Gentile (2:10).

The section is introduced by a general principle: God will reward each man according to his works. It is then applied to the regenerate in 2:7 and 2:10 and to the unregenerate in 2:8-9. The literary structure of the passage makes 2:8-9 parallel and 2:7 and 2:10 parallel.

The main problem in the passage, of course, is that vv. 7 and 10 promise eternal life on the basis of works, which is in complete contradiction to Paul in 3:19-22--a contradiction IF eternal life means "go to heaven."

This difficulty has been keenly felt by all interpreters of the epistle. In general, three different solutions have been suggested. Hodge[10] and Haldane[11] propose that Paul is speaking hypothetically. In other words, if there were anyone who by persistence in doing good sought eternal life, God would reward him with heaven for his efforts. However, Paul has stated elsewhere that there is none who seeks God and none who "does good" (Rom. 3:12). Therefore, these commentators conclude that this is a hypothetical offer of heaven.

John Murray objects by pointing out that the principle of being rewarded for doing good is found in many other passages of Scripture as well.[12] "If the solution proposed by the interpreters quoted above were to be applied to Romans 2:6-16, then not only this passage but these other passages would have to be interpreted after this pattern. But examination of these other passages will show the impossibility of this procedure."[13] Furthermore, Paul does not seem to be speaking hypothetically. He is making a specific assertion. He is not talking about what God would do if we perfectly obeyed but what he actually will do.

---

[10]Charles Hodge, *St. Paul's Epistle to the Romans* (Reprint ed., Edinburgh, 1964) on 2:7.

[11]Robert Haldane, *Exposition of the Epistle to the Romans* (Reprint ed., Edinburgh, 1974) on 2:7.

[12]He cites Mt. 16:27; 25:31-46; Jn. 5:29; 1 Cor. 3:11-15; 2 Cor. 5:10; Gal. 6:7-10; Eph. 6:8; Col. 3:23.

[13]John Murray, *The Epistle to the Romans, NICNT,* 6-1:63.

Murray's own solution brings us face to face with the difference between the Experimental Predestinarian (Murray) and the Partaker approach to this and numerous other passages. He correctly observes that the general principle of v. 6 is then applied to the saved in v. 7 and 10 and to the unsaved in vv. 8-9. But then his theological system intrudes, and he says regarding v. 7, "The just are **characterized** first of all as those who 'seek for glory and honor and incorruption.'"[14] Now the passage does not say that the just are **characterized** by those things. None would argue that the just **should be** characterized by those things, but Murray has plainly read his doctrine of perseverance in holiness into the text. Witmer takes the same approach:

> *A person's habitual conduct, whether good or evil, reveals the condition of his heart. Eternal life is not rewarded for good living; that would contradict many other Scriptures which clearly state that salvation is not by works, but is all of God's grace to those who believe (e.g., Rom. 6:23; 10:9-10; 11:6; Eph. 2:8-9; Titus 3:5). A person's doing good* **shows** *that his heart is regenerate. Such a person, redeemed by God, has eternal life.*[15]

It may be true that a person's "habitual conduct" reveals the condition of his heart, but the text is not addressing that issue. According to Paul, eternal life **is** "rewarded for good living." How else could he say it: "God will render to every man **according to his deeds**" (Gk. *erga*, "works," 2:6)? Shouldn't we let this stand?

Once the consistent use of eternal life in the future as a reward to works is accepted, a much simpler solution is evident. It is absolutely true in Pauline thought that no **unjustified** man can obtain eternal life on the basis of works. But it is also true that the **justified** man can! As Murray points out, vv. 7 and 10 refer to justified saints and vv. 8 and 9 to unjustified sinners.

In this future time, the time of "the day of God's wrath when His righteous judgment will be revealed" (2:5), God will judge all men, Christian and non-Christian, on the basis of their works. The general principle in v. 6 is that each person, saved and unsaved, will be rewarded according to their works in this future day. This principle is taught all over the New Testament; Christians and non-Christians will have their lives examined. The Christian will stand before the judgment seat of Christ where he will be judged according to his works:

---

[14]Ibid. See also the recent commentary by Cranfield, who thinks "the reference is to goodness of life, not however as meriting God's favour but as the expression of faith. It is to be noted that Paul speaks of those who **seek** glory, honour and incorruption, not of those who deserve them" (C. E. B. Cranfield, *A Critical and Exegetical Commentary on the Epistle to the Romans*, 2 vols., *The International Critical Commentary* [Edinburgh: T. & T. Clark, 1975-79], p. 147).

[15]John A. Witmer, "Romans," in *BKC*, 2:445.

*For we must all appear before the judgment seat of Christ, that each
one* **may receive what is due him for the things done while in the
body,** *whether good or bad* (2 Cor. 5:10).

The non-Christian will stand before the Great White Throne where he
will be judged according to his works:

*Then I saw a great white throne and him who was seated on it. . . .
And I saw the dead, great and small, standing before the throne, and
books were opened. Another book was opened, which is the book of
life. The dead were* **judged according to what they had done** *as
recorded in the books* (Rev. 20:11-12).

As will be discussed in the pages to follow, the outcome of the Christian's
judgment is either reward or the loss thereof. The outcome of the non-Christian's judgment is always the lake of fire because his works are not adequate to
redeem.

The Christian who perseveres in doing good works can obtain the reward
of eternal life, an enriched experience of that life given to him freely at justification through faith alone. It is true that no unjustified man can obtain rewards in
heaven by works, but the regenerate saint can. The unjustified can never earn
honor, glory, and peace, but the justified can if he shows "persistence in doing
good" (2:7).

Conclusion

The Reformed doctrine of perseverance in holiness has often based its
scriptural appeal upon many of the passages discussed in the preceding chapters.
John Murray, for example, appeals to many of these verses to prove that, just because a person professes faith in Christ, that does not mean he is truly saved.
The way we can tell if a man is truly saved, according to Murray, is whether or
not he continues to the end. He quotes "He that endureth to the end, the same
shall be saved" (Mt. 10:22) and "We are partakers of Christ, if we hold fast the
beginning of our confidence steadfast unto the end" (Heb. 4:14). After citing Jn.
15:6 and Jn. 8:31-32 (which deal with discipleship and not salvation), he concludes: "The crucial test of true faith is endurance to the end, abiding in Christ,
and continuance in his word."[16] Not one of the verses Murray cites proves this at
all because none of them are talking about salvation from hell; instead, they refer
to our potential loss of future reward.

---

[16]John Murray, *Redemption--Accomplished and Applied* (Grand Rapids: Eerdmans,
1955), p. 152.

If salvation, eternal life, and inheritance always refer to final deliverance from hell and entrance into heaven, then scores of these passages can only be "interpreted" by foisting upon them the meaning required by a theological system. It is therefore circular to appeal to these same verses, as Murray does, in support of the very system which was used to give them their meaning.

Experimental Predestinarians are sometimes bemused by the fact that in the Partaker position "distinctions crop up everywhere." They are concerned that any view which has two kinds of heirs, two kinds of eternal life, two kinds of salvation, and two kinds of resurrection is intrinsically unlikely. Surely, they think, a hidden agenda is working behind the scenes which introduces numerous distinctions which do not appear to be "natural" (a term they often use in reference to their interpretations).

No doubt they would also be bemused to note many other distinctions as well:

1. Two kinds of heaven (Gk. **ouranos**) - the sky and the abode of God.
2. Two kinds of teachers (Gk. **paideutes**) - those who instruct and those who correct.
3. Two kinds of children (Gk. **pais**) - the boy, youth, or maiden, and the servant slave or attendant.
4. Two kinds of people (Gk. **demos**) - a crowd or a business assembly.
5. Two kinds of righteousness (**dikaiosune**) - conformity to the divine will in purpose, thought, and action (i.e., imparted righteousness) and justice or even forensic legal righteousness (imputed righteousness).
6. Two kinds of cleanness (**katharos**) - physical and ceremonial.
7. Two kinds of time (**kairos**) - due measure, fitness, proportion or a fixed and definite period.
8. Two kinds of hearts (**kardia**) - the bodily organ and the focus of personal life.
9. Two kinds of fruit (**karpos**) - the fruit of the vine and the works and deeds of believers.
10. Two kinds of swords (**machaira**) - a large knife used for sacrificial purposes and a dagger.
11. Two kinds of wages (**misthos**) - a wage earned by a hired worker and divine reward.
12. Two kinds of mysteries (**mysterion**) - that which is only known to the initiated and a secret of any kind.
13. Two kinds of law (**nomos**) - the Old Testament in general and a usage or custom.
14. Two kinds of ways (**hodos**) - a path or road and a journey.

15. Two kinds of houses (**oikos**) - a physical dwelling and a group of people, i.e., household.
16. Two kinds of crowds (**ochlos**) - a multitude of people and the common people.
17. Two kinds of hope (**elpis**) - any hope in general and a specifically religious hope.
18. Two kinds of commands (**entole**) - a charge, injunction, or order and a tradition.
19. Two kinds of messages (**epistole**) - a simple message and a letter.
20. Two kinds of work (**ergon**) - employment and deed.[17]

Words are constantly being used in different ways in different contexts. To be bemused at "distinctions" betrays a wooden concept of language typical of many Experimental Predestinarians with their penchant for the illegitimate totality transfer. If the word means one thing here, it must, they say, mean the same thing in the passage they use to support their system.

The interpretations discussed above were based instead on the method of biblical rather than systematic theology. Our approach has been to base our conclusions upon philology, semantics, and immediate context. The approach is exegetical rather than theological. This is in no way intended to disparage the "queen of the sciences," systematic theology, but to acknowledge the obvious; it must be based on exegesis.

Making all soteriological references to these words refer to our entrance into heaven requires, if we let the text speak plainly, that the entrance into heaven be based upon works. But if these words often refer to something else, something conditional in the believer's experience--his victorious perseverance and subsequent reward--no "theological exegesis" is necessary to make them consistent with the Reformation doctrine of justification by faith alone.

---

[17]All the definitions in this list are taken from AS, except for **demos**, which comes from AG, p. 178.

Chapter 8

Justification and Sanctification 1

It is taken as axiomatic, even obvious, to Experimental Predestinarians that a life of works is the necessary and inevitable result of genuine faith and conversion. In other words, justification and sanctification are distinct but inseparable. Considerable attention is given to this point in their standard theology texts and will be analyzed in what follows. While no one would argue that this is God's intent, that we should walk holy and blameless before Him in love, such a walk depends upon our responses to God's love and grace. While justification is based on faith alone and is a work of God, sanctification is uniformly presented in Scripture as a work of man and God (Phil. 2:12-13) and is achieved by faith plus works. No useful purpose is served by continuing to teach that Christ "does it all" and that our growth in grace is His work alone. The confusion and unreality which these teachings have produced are now legendary.

Yet in their misguided attempts to preserve at all costs the sovereignty of God (the "predestinarian" aspect of their teaching), they have all but eliminated the contribution made by the new man in Christ to his own sanctification. Indeed, to even speak this way would cause them to cringe with fears that ancient "Pelagianism"1 is creeping into the evangelical church. The inseparable unity of sanctification and justification is argued on many grounds.

The Greater Righteousness

Recently the writer was privileged to spend a week at a seminar taught by one of the most articulate Experimental Predestinarian theologians in the United States. His approach to the Sermon on the Mount leads us into the inner workings of their system. In order to establish that true faith will result in a life of works, he expounded Mt. 5:20:

1In the conflict with Augustine, Pelagius, who stressed free will and moral ability, was the loser. Experimental Predestinarians seem to like to use this term. It gives them a sense of connection with history and with a battle in which they were on the winning side.

*For I say unto you, that unless your righteousness exceeds the righ-
teousness of the scribes and Pharisees, you will by no means enter the
kingdom of heaven (NKJV).*

After explaining that the righteousness of the scribes and Pharisees was
not all bad but was, in fact, very scrupulous in spite of its externals, he concluded
that, unless our lives manifest a practical righteousness which is quite high, we
are not truly Christians at all and will be shut out of the kingdom on that fateful
day.[2]

Now, not only is this interpretation highly unlikely, but imagine the
bondage it would put upon the average Christian. How could anyone possibly
know if his righteousness did, in fact, exceed that of the scribes and Pharisees?
Assurance of salvation would be impossible unless the standards of the Pharisees
were reduced to something less than what God requires. At the end of the lec-
ture the speaker was asked, "Are you more righteous than the scribes and the
Pharisees?" If he said no, then he would have no assurance, and the Bible says
assurance is possible now. If he said yes, then one could only be skeptical of his
integrity.

His somewhat hesitant answer was that their righteousness was, perhaps,
not so high after all. Only by reducing it could he escape the dilemma. But this
will not do. In spite of their hypocrisy, their standards were high and, in many
cases, very pure and noble. If a higher righteousness than theirs is characteristic
of all who are Christians, then it would appear that very few if any are regenerate,
so virtually no one can be sure that he is! How much better must we be? If we
assume they were "foul,"[3] then it would not take much to improve on their righteousness. If we assume their error was that they only believed in external righteousness, which may not be true,[4] then any degree of internal righteousness
would exceed theirs. If we assume their error was that they only practiced part of
the law, then if we practice more than part we exceed their righteousness. It is
impossible for us to fulfill all the law. But these assumptions wouldn't result in
any great improvement in Christian behavior at all.

There is no doubt that the Lord is contrasting the righteousness necessary
for entrance into the kingdom with the righteousness of the scribes and the Pharisees. But what is the point of the contrast? It is not a contrast between two lev-
els of human righteousness but between human and divine righteousness. This is

---

[2]This view is expounded by D. Martin Lloyd-Jones, *Studies in the Sermon on the Mount*
(Grand Rapids: Eerdmans, 1971), p. 208 and Arthur Pink, *An Exposition of the Sermon on the
Mount* (Grand Rapids: Baker, 1974), pp. 61-66.

[3]Pink, p. 66.

[4]See Richard Longenecker, *Paul, Apostle of Liberty* (New York: Harper and Row, 1964),
pp. 23, 71-85, where he gathers much evidence regarding a genuine devotional and prophetic spirit
present in Pharisaic Judaism and also in the Qumran community (e.g., Jn. 3:1; Acts 15:8).

evident when the Lord specifies that the righteousness He requires is not just superior to that of the scribes and Pharisees but must be "perfect":

> *Therefore you shall be perfect just as your Father in heaven is perfect*
> (Mt. 5:48 NKJV).

Only a perfect righteousness is good enough. Our Lord is evidently giving us a veiled reference to the justifying righteousness which is imputed to the believer on the basis of faith alone:

> *For He has made Him who knew no sin to be sin for us, that we might*
> *become the righteousness of God in Him (2 Cor. 5:21 NKJV).*

Only through justification can we be "as perfect as the Father in heaven is perfect." Only through justification can we have a righteousness which exceeds the righteousness of the scribes and the Pharisees. Surely Boice is correct when he insists that Jesus "was saying that if a man was to get to heaven he must somehow have a different and better righteousness than these men were showing. And this meant that he must turn his back on human goodness altogether and receive instead the freely offered goodness of God."[5]

Both Are Part of the New Covenant

Quoting the New Covenant of Jeremiah, Robert Dabney argues that both justification and sanctification are included in New Covenant:[6]

> *"This is the covenant I will make with the house of Israel after that*
> *time," declares the Lord. "I will put my law in their minds and write it*
> *on their hearts. I will be their God, and they will be my people" (Jer.*
> *31:33).*

Dabney is struck by the words, "I will put my law in their minds and write it on their hearts." However, he neglects to quote the next verse which helps us to know WHEN this will be fulfilled:

> *No longer will a man teach his neighbor, or a man his brother, saying,*
> *"Know the Lord," because they will all know me, from the least to the*
> *greatest (Jer. 31:34).*

Now it is obvious that v. 34 is in no way fulfilled at the present time. Certainly it is not true that all know the Lord and that there is no longer a need for

---

[5]James Montgomery Boice, *The Sermon on the Mount: An Exposition* (Grand Rapids: Zondervan, 1972), p. 99.

[6]Robert L. Dabney, *Lectures in Systematic Theology* (1878; reprint ed., Grand Rapids: Zondervan, 1972), p. 664.

personal evangelism. The New Covenant was certainly inaugurated at the cross, and we enter in to some of its benefits at the time we believe. But its final fulfillment has not yet taken place and indeed will not until the coming kingdom and the eternal state. Similarly, the ultimate writing of His law upon our hearts and minds will be characteristic of the believer when he has achieved the goal of his justification, glorification. Complete sanctification comes when we receive our resurrection body and not before.

A Disciple Does the Will of God

It is quite common for Experimental Predestinarians to quote the numerous passages referring to discipleship in the Gospels as proof that a man who is truly a Christian, i.e., a disciple, is one who works and does not fall away. John Murray, for example, says in reference to Jn. 8:30-32, "He [Jesus] set up a criterion by which true disciples might be distinguished, and that criterion is continuance in Jesus' word."[7] This is true. However, a concordance study of the word **mathetes**, "disciple," shows that being a disciple and being a Christian are not necessarily synonymous terms:

> *As He spoke these things, many came to believe in Him. Jesus therefore was saying to those Jews who had believed Him, "If you abide in My word, then you are truly disciples of Mine" (Jn. 8:30-32 NASB).*

Some background on the nature of discipleship is helpful for understanding its meaning in the Gospels. The basic meaning is "a learner" or "student."[8] Included in the idea of disciple was the notion of "physical adjacency."[9] In its uses in secular Greek and among the Jews, physical proximity of the student to the teacher was implied in the meaning of discipleship. An itinerant rabbi, like Jesus, was constantly on the move. To be His disciple in a literal way was to be His follower. The word "to follow" occurs about eighty times in the Gospels, and while sometimes it simply means "to believe,"[10] it often describes the relationship between the earthly Jesus and His men. They literally had to leave their occupation,[11] their parents,[12] and follow Christ till death. The disciple could not be above his master,[13] and as the master traveled, the disciple followed.

---

[7]John Murray, *Redemption--Accomplished and Applied* (Grand Rapids: Eerdmans, 1955), pp. 151-52.

[8]See Mk. 9:31; Jn. 12:42; Lk. 10:23.

[9]G. G. Hawthorne, "Disciple," in *ZPED*, 2:130.

[10]E.g., Jn. 10:27.

[11]Mk. 1:18-19.

[12]Mk. 10:29.

[13]Mt. 10:24.

It is probable that the stringent demands placed upon disciples during Jesus' life reflect this background. One must, in order to be a disciple, be willing to leave family and follow Him (Lk. 14:26).

"Disciple" is never used outside of the Gospels and Acts, and probably, according to Hawthorne, for this very reason.[14] The disciple/teacher relationship with Jesus was no longer possible in the new era because Jesus no longer lived on earth. They did not want the requirements of leaving one's trade and family to become universalized as conditions of discipleship for those after them who would believe in the heavenly Christ.

To say that "every Christian is a disciple" seems to contradict the teaching of the New Testament. In fact, one could be a disciple and not be a Christian at all! John describes men who were disciples first and who then placed their faith in Christ (Jn. 2:11). Judas was called a disciple, but he was apparently not saved (Jn. 12:4). This alone alerts us to the fact that Jesus did not always equate being a "disciple" with being a Christian.

Conversely, a man could be a Christian and not a disciple. Correcting this danger is the intent of most of the passages cited by the proponents of perseverance to teach that all who would become Christians must accept the terms of discipleship to do so. In point of fact, these exhortations to become disciples are often addressed to those who are already Christians or to mixed audiences. When Jesus calls a man to become a disciple, He is in no instance asking him to accept the free gift of eternal life. Instead, He is asking those who have already believed to accept the stringent commands of discipleship and find true life.

It is impossible to become a Christian and at the same time harbor ideas that one is going to "continue in sin." Becoming a Christian involves repentance, a change of perspective about sin, i.e., agreeing with God's perspective about it, that it is sin. Becoming a Christian involves looking to the cross for forgiveness. Now it is biblically, psychologically, and spiritually impossible to look to the cross for forgiveness and have God's viewpoint about sin and at the same time cherish ideas of intending to persist in some known sin in the life. But that is a completely different thing from saying that, in order to become a Christian, one must commit himself to turning from all known sin, hate his father and mother, and be willing to die for Christ! The presence of a purpose to continue in sin is incompatible with saving faith, but the absence of a lordship commitment is not.

Joseph and Nicodemus were saved, but they were secret disciples (Jn. 19:38-39). They feared the Jews and would not publicly declare themselves as disciples of Christ. Nevertheless, John acknowledges them as secret believers.

---

[14]Hawthorne, 2:130.

Many disciples left Jesus (Jn. 6:66). If they were not really Christians, then Experimental Predestinarians must acknowledge that being a disciple is not the same thing as being a Christian (or else give up their doctrine of eternal security!), and if they were Christians, then being a Christian does not inevitably result in a life of following Christ. When Paul and Barnabas went to Antioch, they encouraged the disciples to remain true to the faith. It must be possible for them not to remain true or there would be no point in taking this trip (Acts 14:22). In fact, disciples can be drawn away from the truth (Acts 20:30).

Furthermore, throughout the Gospels Jesus challenges people who have already believed in His name (i.e., who are saved) to become disciples. If being a disciple is a condition for becoming a Christian in the first place, why does Jesus exhort those who are already Christians to become disciples (Jn. 8:31-32)?

Now, if being a disciple is not necessarily the same as being a Christian, then it is not logically or exegetically consistent to select passages that refer to discipleship and assume that they refer to the conditions for becoming a Christian or to the characteristics of all who are truly born again. One writer argues, "The word *disciple* is used consistently as a synonym for *believer* throughout the book of Acts." On this basis, he concludes, "Any distinction between the two words is purely artificial."[15] But then he appears to contradict himself and says, "It is apparent that not every disciple is necessarily a true Christian."[16] So, apparently, this writer has concluded that a distinction between the words is not purely artificial but is grounded in the New Testament itself. But if the words "disciple" and "believer" are synonymous, then every disciple is a true Christian, and if they are not synonymous, then every true Christian is not necessarily a disciple. It is clear, as even that writer is forced to admit, that they are not synonymous.[17]

Many writers commit the illegitimate totality transfer. They gather the passages in Acts in which **mathetes** is used of Christians and passages in the Gospels where certain characteristics or conditions of being a disciple are enumerated, and then they import these contextual nuances into the semantic value of the word itself. This now pregnant term is carried back into various passages of the New Testament in service of a particular doctrine of lordship salvation and perseverance. The meaning of a word is determined by its context. The usage elsewhere helps establish the range of possible meanings but not the meaning in the particular passage under consideration.

---

[15]John MacArthur, *The Gospel According to Jesus* (Grand Rapids: Zondervan, 1988), p. 196.

[16]Ibid., p. 196 n. 2.

[17]As will be discussed in chapter 10, "The Possibility of Failure," it is theologically impossible to hold this view of discipleship because the Bible teaches the existence of the permanently carnal Christian who persists in his rebellion to the point of physical death.

Some feel that "there is no more definitive statement on discipleship" in the New Testament than Mt. 10:32-39. Apart from the fact that in Acts the word **mathetes** is used of believers, this is one of the few proofs given that all Christians are disciples:

> *But whoever shall deny Me before men, I will also deny him before My Father who is in heaven (NASB).*

> *He who loves father or mother more than Me is not worthy of Me (NASB).*

> *He who has found his life shall lose it, and he who has lost his life for My sake shall find it (NASB).*

The man who has "lost his life" is in the context the man who suffered physical death for the cause of Christ. The preceding context contains an exhortation to those who already are disciples (10:1) to persevere in the midst of sufferings. They are warned that some will be "put to death" (10:21). Surely physical death is not a condition of becoming a Christian. The man who finds life is not a man who finds regeneration. The disciples to whom He was speaking were already regenerate! The life he finds is co-heirship with the Messiah in the future reign of the servant kings and true meaning and significance in this life now (cf. Mk. 10:28-31). Seen in this light, the passage says nothing about either the conditions for becoming a Christian or the necessary evidence of all who claim to be born again.

No doubt the warning to the unfaithful, "I will deny him before My Father," has led some to the erroneous conclusion that our Lord is speaking of salvation. Certainly, they feel, a true Christian would never be denied before the Father. Unless, of course, Jesus is teaching precisely that in this passage! The passage is, after all, addressed to "disciples," and these regenerate men need to be warned. If it is necessary and inevitable that all who are born again will persevere to endure martyrdom, why warn them? There is no danger to such men. A warning which everyone obeys to avoid a denial which no one experiences is superfluous! There is real danger here, but not danger of finding out they are not saved or that they have lost their salvation. The danger is the possibility of being denied a part in the co-heirship with the coming Messiah![18]

---

[18]For parallel ideas on the danger of the true believer being "denied before the Father," see 1 Cor. 3:15, "saved through fire"; 2 Cor. 5:10, "recompensed for deeds ... whether good or **bad**"; 1 Jn. 2:28, "shrink away from Him in shame at His coming"; 2 Tim. 11:12; "If we deny Him, He will deny us"; the warning passages in Hebrews; Mt. 25:12, "I do not know [i.e., honor] you"; and Mt. 25:30, "and cast out the worthless slave [a true believer, he is a **servant of his master**] into the darkness outside; in that place there shall be weeping and gnashing of teeth." See discussion elsewhere under the passages cited.

The merger of these terms has often given birth to a theology of legalism, doubt, and harsh judgmental attitudes which has virtually eliminated the grace of God as a basis for personal fellowship with Christ. All depends on the believer's willingness or intent to abandon all, yield at every point, submit totally, and the like. Instead of the wonderful freedom of grace, a burdensome introspection has resulted which has made assurance of salvation impossible. In addition, the terms of the gospel offer itself have been severely compromised. Non-Christians are virtually being asked to become holy as a condition of becoming Christians. This preparatory "law work" was prominent in Puritan theology.

But, most importantly, the conditions for becoming a disciple are different from those for becoming a Christian. One becomes a Christian, according to Jesus, on the basis of faith alone (Jn. 3:16). We are justified "freely" (Rom. 3:24) and receive regenerate life "without cost" (Rev. 22:17). But to become a disciple, something in addition to faith is needed, works. A disciple is one who does the will of God (Mt. 12:49), who denies himself, leaves his family, and follows Jesus around Palestine (Mk. 8:34). A disciple must love Jesus more than his own wife, hardly a requirement ever stated anywhere for becoming a Christian (Lk. 14:26)! The condition for discipleship is to forsake all and follow Christ (Lk. 14:33). Consider Jesus' words:

> *If anyone comes to me and does not hate his father and mother, his wife and children, his brothers and sisters--yes, even his own life--he cannot be my disciple. Anyone who does not carry his cross and follow me cannot be my disciple (Lk. 14:26-27).*

> *In the same way, any of you who does not give up everything he has cannot be my disciple (Lk. 14:33).*

Now if being a disciple and being a Christian are the same thing, as some Experimental Predestinarians maintain, then are they not introducing a serious heresy into the gospel? In order to become a Christian, one must not only believe on Christ, but he must also (1) hate his father, mother, wife, children, and his own life; (2) carry his cross; (3) be willing to follow Jesus around Palestine; and (4) give up everything. Can any amount of theological sophistry equate these four conditions with the simple offer of a free gift on the basis of believing? Being a disciple and being a Christian cannot be the same thing! If we are justified "freely," how can the enormous costs of being a disciple be imposed as a condition of that justification?[19]

The most famous discipleship passage in the New Testament makes it quite clear that becoming a disciple and becoming a Christian are two separate things. The Great Commission is to "make disciples." In explaining how this is to

---

[19]When MacArthur says this is a "paradox," the writer would certainly agree. It appears to be not only a "paradox" but an irreconcilable contradiction (p. 140).

be done, three activities are specified: going, baptizing, and teaching. "Going" means to go to them and explain the gospel. "Baptizing" identifies those who have responded publicly as new converts. "Teaching" is simply instruction in the Christian life. So there are three things involved in the production of a disciple: (1) the man must trust Christ; (2) he must be baptized; and (3) he must be taught to obey all that Christ taught. If being a disciple is the same as becoming a Christian, then in order to be saved, we must trust in Christ, be baptized, and must obey the commands of Christ. In other words, salvation is by works.

In the passage which Murray quotes to prove the doctrine of perseverance in holiness, Jesus is in fact teaching that a disciple will persevere in good works, but since all Christians are not necessarily disciples, the passage cannot be of much help to the Reformed doctrine of perseverance. Murray assumes an unbiblical definition of a disciple and then imports that assumption into his exegesis of Jn. 8:31-32 without any comment.

In this controversy section Jesus is in conflict with the Pharisees in the temple in Jerusalem. Some of His hearers believed on Him and were born again. Jesus, in the verses Murray quotes, speaks to these who have believed and challenges them to discipleship. He then returns to the controversy. The structure can be visualized as follows:

**Controversy with the Pharisees
John 8:12-59**

Controversy with the Pharisees		Aside to Those Who Believe		Continuation of Controversy	
8:12	30	31	32	33	56

After listening to Him for a time, some of the Jews, according to v. 30, "believed on Him." The expression in Greek is **episteusan eis auton.** In every other place in John's gospel where it is used, it always refers to genuine not spurious faith. It is virtually a technical term John uses for being saved:

*Yet to all who received him, to those who **believed in his name,** he gave the right to become children of God, children born not of natural* *descent, nor of human decision or of a husband's will, but born of God (Jn. 1:12-13).*

Everyone who **believes in him** *may have eternal life. For God so loved the world that he gave his one and only Son, that whoever* **believes in him** *shall not perish but have eternal life (Jn. 3:15-16)*

Whoever **believes in me**, *as the Scripture has said, streams of living water will flow from within him (Jn. 7:38).*

Examples could be multiplied.[20] Since these men in Jn. 8 **believed on Him** on the authority of Jesus Himself, we may say they are born again and have eternal life. Now in Jn. 8:31 Jesus turns to the "Jews who had believed in Him" (those mentioned in the preceding verse who had **believed on Him**) and says, "If you abide in My word, then you are truly disciples of Mine" (NASB).[21] Abide in the Word of Christ is the condition for being a disciple. He basically says in an aside to these new believers, "It is good that you have believed and are born again. Now, abide in My words and be a disciple!" It is to those who have already believed that He introduces a conditional relationship with Himself. Later in Jn. 15 Jesus will expand on the concept of abiding and explain that it is the condition of fruit bearing in the Christian life and that it is characterized by obedience to His commands and love for the brothers in Christ.

The Lord now turns back to His critics in v. 33. They, having heard His aside to these new Christians, respond in anger. They claim they are children of Abraham, but they are not willing to believe on Him as these others did. It is to these critics, not to those who have just believed that Jesus addresses the stinging rebuke, "You belong to your father the devil" (Jn. 8:44). It is these critics, not the believers of v. 30, who "picked up stones to stone Him" (Jn. 8:59).

We conclude then that the distinction between being a Christian and being a disciple has good foundation in the thought of the New Testament.

The Tests of 1 John

Few passages of the New Testament have been the subject of more controversy and imaginative theological exegesis than the so-called "tests" of 1 John. Despairing of an exegetically sound interpretation of these passages which could emerge naturally out of the words themselves, interpreters of all theological

---

[20]See also Jn. 2:11; 3:17, 18, 36; 6:29, 35, 40, 47; 7:39; 9:35, 36; 10:42; 11:25, 26, 45; 12:44, 46.

[21]This "aside" is used by John to help explain how Jesus' words were being misconstrued. John did this often in his gospel, and these other examples illustrate what he is doing here. See Jn. 2:21; 8:22; 11:13.

backgrounds have resorted to bringing in their theological system to explain the passages. How does one deal with such absolute statements as, "No one who is born of God sins, because His seed abides in Him; and he cannot sin, because he is born of God" (1 Jn. 3:9)? Advocates of the Reformed doctrine of perseverance apply this sword in two ways. They are, we are told, tests of whether or not a man is truly born again. Once again, the experiment with introspection is conducted. The believer is commanded to look within, to fruits in the life, and not to Christ to examine the basis for his justification. But second, and by implication, since only those who pass these tests are born again, justification and sanctification must necessarily and inevitably be connected.

In order to properly interpret the "tests of life" in 1 John, three introductory considerations must first be settled: to whom was the epistle written, Christians or professing Christians; what was the nature of the Gnostic heresy being confronted; and what is the intended purpose of the book?

The Readers of 1 John

Some have maintained that the readers of this epistle were understood by John to be a group of professing Christians of whom, in some cases at least, the apostle doubts their regeneration. For reasons explained elsewhere[22] this is intrinsically unlikely. Is it not better to take John's statements in the epistle at face value? He says of his readers that they are "little children" whose "sins are forgiven for His name's sake" (1 Jn. 2:12). He calls them "fathers" who "have known Him from the beginning," and he writes to the young men who "have overcome the evil one" and in whom "the word of God abides" (1 Jn. 2:13-14). They are specifically contrasted with the non-Christian Gnostic antichrists who departed from them. Furthermore, these people have received an "anointing," the Holy Spirit (1 Jn. 2:20). This anointing, he says, "abides in you and you have no need for anyone to teach you," because His anointing teaches them (1 Jn. 2:27).

In the clearest possible terms the apostle affirms the regenerate state of his readers when he says, "I have not written to you because you do not know the truth, but because you do know it." He is confident that the truth is presently "abiding" in them, and he wants it to continue to abide in them (1 Jn. 2:24). He specifically affirms of them "that we should be called children of God; **and such we are**" (1 Jn. 3:1). Furthermore, they are now "children of God," and when Christ returns, he affirms of his readers that they "shall be like Him, because we shall seem Him just as He is" (1 Jn. 3:2).

They are, he says, "from God" and have overcome antichrists, because "greater is He that is in you than he who is in the world" (1 Jn. 4:4). In contrast to

---

[22]See chapter 10, "The Possibility of Failure."

his regenerate readers, the next verse refers to those who are "from the world." His understanding of the saved state of his readers is further clarified when he says of them, "These things I have written to you who believe in the name of the Son of God" (1 Jn. 5:13). For John, when a person has believed on the name of the Son of God, he is born again (Jn. 3:15-16). In fact, one who has believed in the Son of God has "overcome the world" (1 Jn. 5:5). Finally, while the world "lies in the power of the evil one," we know that "we are of God" (1 Jn. 5:18).

Throughout the epistle he uses the term "we"[23] and includes himself in the same spiritual state and facing the same spiritual dangers as his readers.

Any system of interpretation which ignores these plain statements in the interests of fitting into a theological scheme must ask, "How else could John say it?" If he wanted to assert that his readers were in fact born again in contrast to the world, how could he make it clearer?

The Gnostic Heresy

The readers were plagued by false teachers who had introduced an incipi-Ent form of Gnosticism into the church. It is still impossible to draw final conclusions as to the nature of the heresy apart from specific references in the text of 1 John itself which strive to refute it. One of the key heresies, however, was that there was a "mixture" in God of good and evil, light and darkness, and therefore the new creation in Christ could similarly have a mixture and still be holy. This justified the Gnostic notion that sin was permissible for the Christian. John reacts in horror to this notion by saying, "God is light, and in Him there is no darkness at all" (1 Jn. 1:5). In the Greek text the sentence structure seems to require an emphatic reading, "God is light, and in Him there is absolutely no darkness, not any whatsoever!"[24] He may be responding to a peculiar Gnostic notion of God in this passage.

What was Gnosticism? It is impossible to classify the varieties, but at its core it was an attempt to combine Christianity with various pagan and Jewish philosophies. It seems to have come from two basic sources: Alexandrian philosophy and Zoroastrianism:[25]

Alexandrian philosophy is seen in the attempt by Philo to expound the Old Testament in terms of Plato's thought. A line was drawn between God and the material world. God does not exert any direct action on the material world; He

---

[23]1:1, 3, 5, 6, 7, 8, 9, 10; 2:1.

[24]The phrase "at all" (Gk. **oudemia**) is sitting in a commonly emphatic position. Apparently the author wants to emphasize God's complete separation from any kind of darkness.

[25]John Rutherford, "Gnosticism," in *ISBE*, 2:1240.

operates only through intermediaries--angels and demons. The soul existed before birth and is now imprisoned in the flesh. In order to be "saved," we must break out of the flesh.

In the ancient eastern philosophy of Zoroastrianism the world was viewed as battleground between the good and the evil spirits. It was a dualistic view of the cosmos, common in many eastern faiths.

Gnosticism took the Greek opposition between spirit and matter and the Persian dualism as the basis for its system.

The essential question for the Gnostic was, What is the origin of evil? He did not ask, What must I do to be saved? but What is the origin of evil? In the answer to his question redemption was to be found. Rutherford lists other essential beliefs:

1.   The initiated have a special knowledge. They were more enlightened than ordinary Christians.

2.   There is a strict separation between matter and spirit, and matter is essentially evil.

3.   The demiurge is the source of evil. He is the creator of the world and is distinct from the supreme Deity. Intermediate beings between God and man formed the universe and were responsible for evil. This, of course, only located the source in the demiurge but does not explain how it got into him in the first place.

4.   Denial of true humanity of Christ. His sufferings were unreal.

5.   Denial of personality of supreme God and of the free will of man.

6.   Teaching of asceticism and antinomianism.

7.   Combination of Christianity with pagan thought.

8.   Old Testament Scriptures were a product of a demiurge, or inferior creator of the world, the God of the Jews.[26]

These teachings led, paradoxically, to both asceticism and antinomianism. The ascetic side developed from the thought that, if matter and spirit are com-

---

[26]Ibid., 2:1241.

pletely separate and matter is evil, then sin and evil are inherent in the material substance of the body, and the only way we can achieve perfection is to punish the body. By the infliction of pain and the mortification of the flesh, the region of pure spirit may be reached, and we may become like God.

The antinomian expression of Gnosticism developed in the following manner. If the soul and body are separate entities and have nothing in common, then let the soul go its own way, the way of the spirit, and let the body go its own way as well. If the soul and the body are completely distinct and separate, then nothing that the body does can corrupt the soul, no matter how carnal and depraved.[27] Ignatius said of them, "They give no heed to love, caring not for the widow, the orphan or the afflicted, neither for those who are in bondage, or for those who are released from bonds, neither for the hungry nor the thirsty." This sounds strikingly like certain references to their teaching in 1 John (2:9; 3:14; 4:7-8). In 1 John many of these tendencies are evident:

1. Higher knowledge - John refers to them claiming to be "in the light," abiding in Christ, and knowing God, and yet they are without love and obedience. Only by walking as Jesus did can we claim to be abiding (2:6).

2. Its loveless nature - They had only intellectual head knowledge and no love for the brethren.

3. Docetism - God cannot have contact with matter. Therefore, the incarnation of the Supreme God is not possible (1 Jn. 2:22-23). Jesus only appeared to have a human body.

4. Antinomianism - The Gnostics alleged that sin was a thing indifferent in itself. "It made no difference to the spiritual man whether he sinned with his body or not."[28]

It is not certain what the precise form of Gnosticism was which John counters. However, from other references in his writings and those of Polycarp, we can be certain of some of its broad outlines. In the book of Revelation John alludes to Satan's so-called "deep secrets" (Rev. 2:24). This phrase, "to know the depths (deep secrets)" was common in the Ophite Gnostic sect. "From this language we may, I think, infer the existence of an Ophite sect, boasting of its peculiar gnosis."[29] Gnosticism, before reaching its full development, was fully repre-

---

[27]Ibid., 2:1242.
[28]Ibid., 2:1243.
[29]Ibid.

sented by the Ophite sects or systems. They were so named because of the word "ophis," serpent, to which they paid honor as the symbol of intelligence. "They held that the creator of the world was an ignorant and imperfect being, Ialdaboth, the Son of Chaos; and that it was a meritorious act when the serpent persuaded Adam and Eve to disobey Him."[30] Some of these sects even chose as heroes persons whom the Bible condemns, such as Cain and the men of Sodom.

We know from Polycarp that the apostle heatedly opposed Cerinthus, a well-known Gnostic heretic of the first century. Polycarp says that they encountered each other at Ephesus and that, when John discovered that Cerinthus was in the same building with him, a public bath, he instantly left, exclaiming that he could not remain while Cerinthus, the enemy of God and of man, was there.[31] Central to Cerinthus's teaching, like that of the Ophites, was that the God who created the world was an inferior power and that the incarnation was docetic. He taught that there would be a millennium of sensuality.

Thus, the Ophites "ascribed the origin and the working of evil to God."[32] That is why John calls their "depth" the depths of Satan. He is being sarcastic.

In addition, the Gnostics taught that the supreme God was without personality and was pure spirit. He is the "unfathomable Abyss." The fullness of deity, **pleroma**, flows out from him in emanations, or "aeons," all of which are necessarily imperfect, each of these emanations or aeons or angels [was] more spiritual than the grade immediately below it."[33] At the end of the chain is the world of man. "Life continues to be unfolded in such a way that its successive grades sink farther and farther from the purity of God, the life is feebler the nearer they come to matter, with which, at length, **they blend**. Such, according to Gnosticism, is the origin of evil."[34]

It is against the background of the notion of an imperfect Creator, a demiurge with a mixture of good and evil, that John's rebuke must be seen. "This is the message we have heard from him and declare to you: God is light; in him there is no darkness at all" (1 Jn. 1:5). There is no blending of good and evil in God!

The Purpose of the Epistle

It is common to seek the purpose of John's epistle in his closing words:

---

[30]Ibid., 2:1246.
[31]Ibid.
[32]Ibid., 2:1243.
[33]Ibid., 2:1244.
[34]Ibid.

These things I have written to you who believe in the name of the Son of God, in order that you may know that you have eternal life (1 Jn. 5:13 NKJV).

According to the Experimental Predestinarian interpretation, then, John writes to give believers several tests by which they can reflect upon whether or not they are saved. If they pass these tests, then they are truly saved. However, such a view of the purpose of the epistle depends entirely on the interpretation of the tests. Are these tests of life, tests of whether or not one is born again, or tests of whether or not one is walking in fellowship with God? One cannot assume the former, which is the very point in question, and then use that to determine the meaning of the purpose clause. To do so is to argue in a circle. In a word, are they tests of regenerate life, or are they tests of abundant life?

The above verse is written to those "who believe," that is, to regenerate people. How do born-again people acquire assurance that they are born again? It is not by reflecting on their works. Rather, as the immediate antecedent to "these things" says, "the one who believes in the Son of God has the witness in himself" (1 Jn. 5:10). He who believes has the Son, and "he who has the Son has the life" (5:12). The exegetical basis for taking the antecedent to "these things" as being the immediately preceding context (rather than the whole book) is that John's usage elsewhere of the same phrase always locates the antecedent in the immediately preceding context.[35] In addition, in Jn. 5:24 John makes it plain that the only condition for knowing that you have eternal life is that you have believed, and it is belief alone that is the subject of the preceding 5:9-12.

What then is the purpose of the writer in writing 1 John? It is found where one would often find a purpose statement in a book or letter, in the opening paragraph (1 Jn. 1:3):

What we have seen and heard we proclaim to you also, **that you may have fellowship with us***; and indeed our fellowship is with the Father, and with His Son Jesus Christ (NASB).*

His purpose in writing to these regenerate people is so that they may walk in fellowship with God! As Braune puts it, "The manifest purpose of the Apostle [is] to preserve his readers in the fellowship with God."[36]

He is not writing to test their salvation; he is writing so that his "joy may be made complete" (1 Jn. 1:4). His joy was present; it had "begun" because they had

---

[35]See 2:1, which refers to 1:5-10, and 2:26, which refers to 2:18-25. Because 2:1 refers only to 1:5-10 and not to all of chapter 1, it will not do to protest that this cannot parallel 5:13 because only chapter 1 had been written before 2:1. The phrase "I am writing" found in 2:7, 8, 12, 13, 14 does not seem to refer to all of the preceding, but to the immediate, verses he is writing.

[36]Karl Braune, "The Epistles General of John," in *Lange's*, 12:15.

been born again. But he wants to complete this joy by seeing them walk in fellowship. The completion of his joy does not refer to his desire to obtain assurance that they are really saved, but as the apostle himself explains, "I have no greater joy than this, to hear that my children are walking in the truth" (3 Jn. 4). He wants to rejoice that his saved children are walking in the truth!

Jesus used the term in the same way when He addressed His regenerate disciples: "If you love Me, keep My commandments. . . . These things I have spoken to you, that My joy may be in you, and that your joy may be made full" (Jn. 15:11-12). To have one's joy "made full" is not to become a Christian but, being a Christian already, to act like it!

How can he know they are walking in the truth, and how can they know it in the face of the confusion introduced into their midst by the Gnostics? The Gnostics were maintaining that a child of God could have sin in his life and still be in fellowship, abiding in Christ! The remaining portions of the book present several tests of whether or not a Christian is walking in fellowship with God, tests by which the falsity of the Gnostic teaching could be discerned. They are not tests of whether or not these born-again children are really Christians.

The Tests of Fellowship with God

If we really know Him, we obey Him. The Gnostics claimed to "know God," and yet their indifference to sin in the body led them to disobey God's commands. How can such people claim to "know God"? John says:

> *And by this we know that we have come to know Him, if we keep His commandments. The man who says, "I have come to know Him," and does not keep His commandments is a liar, and the truth is not in him; but whoever keeps His word, in him the love of God has truly been perfected. By this we know that we are in Him. The one who says he abides in Him ought himself to walk in the same manner as He walked (1 Jn. 2:3-6 NASB).*

> *Whoever does not love does not know God, because God is love (1 Jn. 4:8).*

Experimental Predestinarians have used these passages to prove their doctrine of perseverance in holiness. True Christians, i.e., those who "know God," are those who keep His commands and who have love for their brethren. The absence of obedience or love in the life of a man is, on the authority of these verses, proof that he is not a Christian at all. He does not know God!

But for John in this passage, knowing God is to walk in fellowship with Him. It does not refer to the entrance into eternal life at justification but to the continuing experience with Christ called fellowship. What is in focus here is not whether or not they are regenerate but whether or not God's love has been "perfected in them." God's love cannot be brought to completion in one who does not have it at all! In fact, in 2:4 and 2:6 John equates "knowing God" with "abiding in Him."[37] He is not discussing their justification; he is discussing their "walk" (1 Jn. 2:6).

John's usage here is illustrated by his usage in Jn. 14. There he quotes Jesus as saying to Philip:

> *If you had known Me, you would have known My Father also; from now on you know Him, and have seen Him" (Jn. 14:7 NASB).*

Philip naturally wants to be shown the Father. But Jesus says:

> *Have I been so long with you, and yet you have not come to know Me, Philip? (14:9 NASB).*

What did Jesus mean when He said that Philip did not know Him? Of course Philip did know Jesus in a saving sense. He had believed and followed Christ (1:43). But he did not know Him in some other sense. He did not seem to know how fully the Son had manifested the Father. This knowledge comes only as the disciples obey Him (14:21). In other words, we come to know Him in a deeper sense by means of obedience.

This is the same as John's thought expressed as having "fellowship with Him" in 1 Jn. 1:6-7:

> *If we say that we have fellowship with Him and yet walk in the darkness, we lie and do not practice the truth, but if we walk in the light as He Himself is in the light, we have fellowship with one another (NASB).*

It is also called having His "joy in them" and having their "joy be made full" in Jn. 15:11. It is something which is experienced by those who are already regenerate, the disciples in this case.

A Christian who claims to know God but in whose life there is no evidence is a liar. He may or may not be a Christian, but he definitely does not know God. As John puts it, "the truth is not in him." But can the truth not be "in" a truly regenerate person? There are good reasons to believe that this passage is directed at the regenerate and not just those who profess to be so but are not. In the

---

[37]As will be discussed below, the "abiding" relationship refers to our walk of fellowship and not our experience of regeneration.

opening verses of the epistle John says, "And this is the message **we** have heard from Him and announce to you" (1:5). The "we" manifestly refers to the apostles. Therefore, the next verse must also include the apostles when he states, "If we say we have fellowship with Him, and yet walk in the darkness, we lie and do not practice the truth" (1:6). It is possible for an apostle to lie and not practice the truth! It is therefore possible, according to John, for the truth to not be "in" a regenerate person. This requires that "truth" does not refer to the seed of life but to active application of truth in daily experience. Truth can either be in us or not in us depending upon whether we are obeying. For the truth to be not in us simply means that we are not "practicing the truth" (1 Jn. 1:6, 8, 10).

Does everyone who is born again manifest love? The answer is obviously "no." That is why John goes on to say that everyone who loves is born of God "and **knows** God" (1 Jn. 4:7).

There is a difference between being born again and knowing God. Knowing God is a matter of degrees, while being born again, like physical birth, is an absolute transition from hell to heaven. The word "know" has the same latitude in Greek that it does in English. A wife complains, "Even though we have been married for ten years, he does not know me." Her meaning is not that they have never become acquainted but that her husband never took the time to know her in the sense of intimate fellowship. If a Christian claims to know God experientially but does not obey God's commandments, he is lying. John continues by saying that we know we are "in Him" and "abide in Him" by walking as he walked (1 Jn. 2:5-6). His meaning is simply that we know Christ in our experience; our experience is Christlike, only if we are walking like Jesus walked.

For John, one gets to know God by fellowshipping with Him and abiding in that fellowship. The loveless Cerinthus and his Gnostic followers were legendary for saying that they knew God, yet they did not demonstrate practical love. Obviously, anyone who is born again can in one sense say he knows God. But John is not speaking of an absolute knowing but a developing relationship manifested in gradually increasing works of love for the brethren. When viewed that way, there are certainly some Christians who do not know God, who are not walking in fellowship with Him, even if, like the Gnostics, they claim to be.

Eternal salvation is an either-or affair: you either have it or you do not. Whoever believes in Christ has eternal life. Belief occurs at a point in time; it is not a process. Fellowship with Christ, however, is a process. Knowing Him experientially is not all or nothing. There are degrees. Our fellowship with Christ is not something that happens at a point of time; it is a process which continues over a lifetime and varies in intensity proportional to our obedience.

The apostle Paul used the word "know" in a similar sense when he said, "I want to know Christ and the power of His resurrection and the fellowship of His sufferings" (Phil. 3:10). Paul already knows Christ in the sense of possessing justification, but he wants to know Him intimately, to have continual fellowship with Him.

Also in 1 Cor. 8:1-3 (NASB) the apostle says:

Now concerning things sacrificed to idols, we know that we all have knowledge. Knowledge makes arrogant, but love edifies. If anyone supposes that he knows anything, he has not yet known as he ought to know; but if anyone loves God, he is known by Him.

The carnal Christians at Corinth were puffed up in their knowledge. In contrast to showing off their knowledge, Paul wanted them to show off their love because "love builds up." This was to be a demonstration of their love for their fellow weaker brothers who stumbled at the eating of meat sacrificed to idols. Paul is distinguishing between Christians who love and those who do not. Then he says "The man who loves is known by God." He is saying that the Christian who loves, in contrast to the carnal Christians at Corinth who do not, are known by God. To be known by God, at least in this passage, probably means to be in fellowship with Him. Being "known" by God does not refer to being regenerate, but to a richer walk.

What a beautiful thing, at the end of life, to be known as a man who really "knew" God and who was truly "God's friend!" (Jas. 2:23).

True Christians never depart from us. In 1 Jn. 2:19-20 the apostle declares, "They went out from us, but they did not really belong to us. For if they had belonged to us, they would have remained with us; but their going showed that none of them belonged to us." Lloyd-Jones says, "The fact that they had gone out proves that they had never really belonged; they were merely within the realm of the church, and appeared to be Christian."[38]

Jones is identifying "us" with all Christians. However, elsewhere in the epistle John distinguishes between "us," i.e., the apostolic circle, and "you," the believers to whom he is writing. For example, in 1:3 he says, "We proclaim to you what we have seen and heard." And in 1:5 he asserts, "This is the message we have heard from Him and declare to you that you may have fellowship with us." Finally, he says, "We [i.e., the apostles] are from God, and whoever knows God listens to us; whoever is not from God does not listen to us [like Cerinthus and other false apostles]" (1 Jn. 4:6). It would seem then that the "us" of 2:19-20, to be consistent with John's usage elsewhere, is not to be equated with the readers but with the apostles. In other places where this contrast is found, the "us" is un-

---

[38]D. Martin Lloyd-Jones, *Romans: An Exposition of Chapter 8:17-39, The Final Perseverance of the Saints* (Grand Rapids: Zondervan, 1976), p. 285.

derstood as the apostolic circle. Experimental Predestinarians often correctly point out that the "we" of 1:3, 5, where it refers to the apostles, is also used for all Christians. This, however, misses the point. When "we" or "us" is contrasted with "you," it always distinguishes the apostolic circle from the larger body of Christians. And this appears to be the situation in 2:19 where the "us" is placed in contrast once again to the larger body of Christians in v. 20, "you."

The fact that these antichrists departed from the apostolic circle is proof that they were never truly of the apostles even though they, like Cerinthus, claimed to be true apostles. If they were true apostles, they would have joined with John and "listened to him."

If these false teachers had left the church to which the readers belonged, it is difficult to see why they would be a problem. What would be the need to refute them? They would no longer be there troubling the believers. If, on the other hand, they had left the apostolic circle and yet were claiming to be rooted in it and from Jerusalem, then the verse makes sense.

There is no statement here that true believers will persevere to the end. Nor is there the statement that, if a man departs from the faith, this proves he was never a Christian in the first place. What is taught is that, if these so-called apostles were really apostles, they would have listened to the apostle John and would have continued in fellowship with the Twelve.

There is no sin at all in the new creation. If God is imperfect, if the creator is a demiurge possessing mostly good and some evil, then sin may be a matter of some indifference. For this reason he says, "in Him is no sin" (1 Jn. 1:5). It is very emphatic in Greek, "no sin, none at all!" as if he were countering this Ophite heresy of the imperfect God. If there is a mixture in God, the Gnostic could reason, there is also a mixture of evil and good in the creation which emanates from Him, the new man in Christ, who is at the bottom end of the emanations from the Deity. That new man in Christ then, instead of being the perfect sinless creation of a perfect God, is a "blend" of good and evil. Sin is therefore not of great concern.

Seen in this light, John's absolute statement makes good sense:

*No one who **abides in Him** sins; no one who sins has seen Him or knows Him. Little children, let no one deceive you; the one who practices righteousness is righteous, just as He is righteous; the one who practices sin is of the devil; for the devil has sinned from the beginning. The Son of God appeared for this purpose, that He might destroy the works of the devil. No one born of God sins, because His seed abides in him; and he cannot sin, because he is born of God (1 Jn. 3:6-9 NASB).*

It is better to take the statements as they stand, as absolutes. Then it is saying "anyone born of God does not sin even one time, not at all." Yet since he has already said that a man who says he never sins is a liar (1:8), he must be viewing the sinning Christian from a particular point of view. The "anyone" refers to the person as a whole and not a part of him. The Christian, viewed as a man born of God, and particularly as abiding in Christ, does not sin even once. For the Gnostics, a man could be abiding in Christ and yet sin could still be in his life because sin was from the body and was a matter of indifference. John counters that sin is never a part of the "abiding" experience. The reason he does not sin even once is because "God's seed abides in him." God's seed is the regenerate new nature given to each believer when he is born again (Jn. 1:13). Certainly the parallel holds in physical life. When we are born, we inherit the nature of our parents. Jesus Himself in describing the born-again experience made it analogous to physical birth (Jn. 3). Elsewhere Paul refers to this perfect new nature as the "new self" (Eph. 4:24), or "new man" (Col. 3:10).

This means that sin cannot be a product of regenerate life, as the Gnostics maintained. So when anyone sins, he is responsible for it, but the source of it cannot be the seed of God in him. That seed cannot ever result in the Christian committing even one act of sin.

John is saying that the believer, from his capacity as one born of God and who is abiding in Christ, cannot sin. If he sins, it is not an expression of the character as the new creation. It is as if someone says, "The president cannot break the law." Now it is acknowledged that as a man he can, but in his position as president he cannot. If he does, that is not an expression of his character as the president. If someone says, "A priest cannot commit fornication," one cannot deny that as a man he can commit it; but priests, functioning as priests, do not do those things. The Bible uses language in a similar way, "A good tree cannot produce bad fruit" (Mt. 7:18). Of course a good tree can produce bad fruit, but not as a result of what it really is, a good tree. Also Jesus said, men "cannot" fast while the bride groom is with them (Mk. 2:19). They can fast, but to do so is incongruous and unnatural.[39]

Similarly, when John says, "No one born of God sins," he is saying that the person, as a man born of God, does not sin. If he sins, it is not an expression of who he is as a man who has been born of God. It is not compatible with "abiding in him" (1 Jn. 3:6).

We are not ascribing to John the teaching that a part of a man, such as his new nature, cannot sin but that the total, responsible man, as a born one, cannot sin **as an expression of who he is as the new creation of God.** If he sins, it is not an expression of who he is in Christ; if the president breaks the law, it is not an

---

[39]H. Bonar, *God's Way of Holiness* (Chicago: Moody Press, n.d.), p. 99.

expression of who is he as president; and if the priest fornicates, it is not an expression of who he is as a priest.

Similar notions are found in Pauline thought. Paul says, "I have been crucified with Christ; and it is no longer I who live, but Christ lives in me; and the life which I now live in the flesh I live by faith in the Son of God, who loved me and delivered Himself up for me" (Gal. 2:20). If a Christian sins, his sin cannot be expression of who he really is, because his true life is that of Christ in him. In a similar vein Paul declares:

> *But if I am doing the very thing I do not wish,* **I am no longer the one**
> **doing it,** *but sin which dwells in me. I find then a principle that evil is*
> *present in me, the one who wishes to do good. For I joyfully concur*
> *with the law of God in* **the inner man,** *but I see a different law in the*
> *members of my body, waging war against the law of my mind, and*
> *making me a prisoner of the law of sin which is in my members.*
> *Wretched man that I am! Who will set me free from the body of this*
> *death? Thanks be to God through Jesus Christ our Lord! So then, on*
> *the one hand* **I myself** *with my mind am serving the law of God, but*
> *on the other, with* **my flesh** *the law of sin (Rom. 7:20-25 NASB).*

Paul in some sense understands that the true Paul, the real Paul, "I myself," does not serve sin. If when he sins, the true Paul, the "inner man," the new creation in Christ, is not the one doing it, then who, we might ask, is doing it? The answer is, of course, the whole person is doing the sin and is responsible for it. However, the source of that sin is in the "flesh" and is not in the new creation in Christ, the regenerate new nature.[40] The first step toward victory over sin is to be absolutely convinced as Paul and John are, that it is completely foreign to our true new identity in Christ.

But according to the Gnostics, sinning can be a possible expression of the born-again person, and this is the precise heresy which John is trying to counteract. To them an imperfect demiurge can create an imperfect new creation. Furthermore, sin was a matter of the body anyway and not of the spirit and could be ignored because the spirit was the only thing of importance. Since there is a strong separation between spirit and matter, the sins of the body, according to the Gnostics, do not corrupt the spirit. This interpretation allows us to take the absolutes seriously and fits well with the context and is explainable in light of the Gnostic heresy being refuted.

The new creation, being the product of a sinless and perfect parent, cannot sin even once. The Gnostics, seeing a mixture of sin in God, allowed that the new creation (i. e., the "born again" Christian) inevitably sinned and this was not

---

[40]See chapter 9 for a brief discussion of the terms "nature," "person," "ego," and "new man" and how they relate together in biblical psychology.

a matter of great significance. The Gnostics could derive no justification for antinomianism from the notion of an imperfect God and a resultant imperfect new creation.

The same phrase is repeated in 1 Jn. 5:18 with the qualifying thought, "the one who was born of God keeps him, and the evil one cannot harm him":

> *We know that no one who is born of God sins; but He who was born of God keeps him and the evil one does not touch him* (NASB).

When the Christian is viewed as "one born of God," the reference is evidently to his true identity as a new man in Christ. The new man is sinless (Eph. 4:24; Col. 3:10), and no sin in the life of the Christian ever comes from who he really is, a new creation. In 1 Jn. 3:9 the immediate reason for the absolute absence of sin from the new creation was "because His seed abides in him; and he cannot sin, because he is born of God." Now John explains the ultimate reason for the total absence of sin from the new man in Christ. It is due to the protective activity of THE "one born of God."

Who is the "one born of God"? The Christian is described as "one born of God," but the verb is in the perfect tense. This second reference to one born of God employs the aorist tense and suggests that Christ is the one doing the keeping.[41] This would be consistent with John's view that Jesus was God's "only begotten Son" (Jn. 1:14). The keeping ministry of Jesus Christ absolutely prevents sin in the new creation.

We are also told that the Satan cannot "touch" him. It is obvious that the Satan can touch the new man and the Christian as a whole. A particular kind of influence from Satan must be in view. A satisfactory explanation is the Christian is never touched by Satan in the sense of coming under his power to lead him to damnation and hell. This verse is simply the fulfillment of the Lord's prayer, "My prayer is not that you take them out of the world but that you protect them from the evil one" (Jn. 17:15), and "While I was with them, I protected them and kept them safe by that name you gave Me. None has been lost except the one doomed to destruction so that Scripture would be fulfilled" (Jn. 17:12). The loss from which they are being kept is "destruction," or hell. So John's meaning is that the Christian, as an expression of who he really is, does not sin even once but, on the contrary, or "in fact," is being kept from eternal damnation, the normal consequence of all sin, by Jesus Christ Himself. Thus, Jesus Christ not only keeps the new man from any sin at all but also protects him from ever going to hell. It is a strong verse for eternal security.

The alternative interpretation of this passage, followed by some Experimental Predestinarians and reflected in the translation of the New Interna-

---

[41]See David Smith, "The Epistles of John," in *EGT,* 5:198.

tional Bible stresses the present tense of the word "to sin." The NIV translates, "no one born of God will continue to sin." Thus, these translators, and many Experimental Predestinarians, see John as saying that the Christian may sin once in a while, but he will not continually sin. If he does, this simply proves he is not a Christian at all.

However, as is well known, because the present tense does not have a form for punctiliar action, one cannot tell by looking at the Greek form whether sin at a point in time (no sin at all!) or sin as a continual practice is meant. The durative force of the present tense requires contextual justification. Such a force in this context leads to absurdities which John's Gnostic opponents would readily accept. In fact, the verb cannot take a durative sense in other passages, such as 1:7-10 or 2:1-2,[42] and it makes contextual nonsense in 1 Jn. 3:1-10. The Gnostics argued that one could sin and have fellowship with God. The present tense interpretation agrees and could hardly be a refutation of Gnosticism. It says that a man can sin a little and have fellowship. So a little sin will not destroy fellowship, but a lot will. The Gnostics would laugh at such a "refutation" of their arguments. Furthermore, the reason he does not sin is because "God's seed is in him and he cannot sin." On the present tense view, the seed of God is powerful enough to prevent habitual sin, but it is not powerful enough to prevent a little sin. Surely this cannot be John's meaning. Neither can we say that the seed is only powerful enough to prevent the sin of unbelief but not powerful enough to prevent moral sins of other kinds. That would only mean that the seed of God could prevent a Christian from denying Christ but not from daily acts of sin which are each a denial of Christ by life, if not by words. Yet the Gnostics would have favored that view of the seed. It kept them believing in Christ, which they did anyway, but it did not interfere with committing some acts of sin.

John Murray argues against the present tense interpretation on two grounds: (1) The meaning of "habitual" is not precisely defined; and (2) it leaves too much room for a loophole which contradicts the incisiveness of John's teaching. It allows that the believer might commit certain sins, but not habitually.

---

[42] It would be incorrect to say John's meaning in 1:8 is really "if we say that we do not continually have sin we deceive ourselves and the truth is not in us." Pressing such a distinction between continual and non-habitual sin leads to the absurd conclusion that John means that if we are sinning non-habitually then we are not deceiving ourselves and the truth is in us.

"This would contradict the decisiveness of such a statement that the one begotten of God does not sin and cannot sin."[43]

John concludes his discussion by saying, "By this the children of God and the children of the devil are obvious" (1 Jn. 3:10a NASB). By placing a colon after "are obvious," the NIV translators are signifying that the referent of "this" is the following statement: "Anyone who does not do what is right, is not a child of God; neither is anyone who does not love his brother" (1 Jn. 3:10b). In most other cases in 1 John the phrase "in this," **en touto**, refers to the item following and not the item preceding.[44] The verse becomes a bridge between his discussion of righteousness and the expression of it in practical love in the following section.

The Greek text reads, "By this are the children of God and the children of the devil revealed (Gk. **phanera**)." He is referring to the following statement, "Anyone who does not do what is right is not of God; nor is anyone who does not love his brother." Earlier he said, "He who does what is right is righteous, just as he is righteous. He who does what is sinful is of the devil" (1 Jn. 3:8).

When a Christian is "of the devil," John means that, when he commits even one sinful act, in the doing of that act, the source of it was Satan. He has just said that a Christian is not permitted to sin at all, not even once. Now he continues as if to say, "In fact, the absence of sin in the life of a Christian is one way he reveals by his actions that he is a Christian. Furthermore, the presence of sin in the life of a non-Christian is how he reveals that he is a non-Christian." However, when a Christian sins (and John believes he can and will, 1 Jn. 2:1), in that act he is behaving like a child of Satan. Who he really is is not being made evident. To use Paul's phrase, he is walking like a "mere man" (1 Cor. 3:3).

One way the regenerate nature can become obvious or evident to others is through righteous actions. A child of God reveals his true nature when he performs such actions. The child of the devil, on the other hand, reveals his true nature when he sins. When a Christian sins, even once, he is not revealing the presence of his new nature within. The Gnostics, no doubt, would have been somewhat indifferent to the idea that righteous behavior revealed the presence of a

---

[43]John Murray, *Collected Writings of John Murray*, 2 vols. (Edinburgh: Banner of Truth, 1977), 2:283. Murray's own view is that the absolute terms can, and perhaps do, refer to some specific sin in the Gospel of John. Jn. 9:41 = sin of self-complacency and self-infatuation. Jn. 9:2-3 = some specific sin the man may have committed to result in blindness. Jn. 15:22 = sin of rejecting Him and His Father. Murray points out there must be a radical difference between the sin unto death and the sin not unto death in 1 Jn. 5:16-17. He says it is only the sin unto death that the believer cannot commit. The believer can only commit the sin not unto death. "Since, according to 3:6-9; 5:18, the regenerate do not commit sin, it is surely justifiable to conclude that the sin he does not commit is the sin unto death" (Ibid.) However, John says that a "brother" is potentially capable of committing this sin (cf. 1 Jn. 5:16-17). The "sin unto death," with the death being an act of divine discipline, is illustrated elsewhere Acts 5:5; 1 Cor. 11:30; 1 Cor. 5:5).

[44]See 2:3, 5; 3:16, 19, 24; 4:2, 10, 13.

new nature within and that unrighteous behavior revealed that the person was a child of Satan. The presence or absence of sin revealed nothing to them; they were indifferent to it.

But note that John does **not say** what the Experimental Predestinarians say. He does not say that the presence of sin in the life of a Christian proves that he is not a Christian at all. He says only that, when a Christian does not do what is right, in that act he is not "of God," **ek tou theou** (1 Jn. 3:10b). In other places in John's epistle, when that phrase stands by itself, as it does here, it means that he is not of God in the sense that the source of his behavior is not of God, not that he is unregenerate. For example, the apostle in reference to the apostolic band says, "We are of God . . .," **ek tou theou** (1 Jn. 4:6). He means their source of authority is God.[45] In a similar way we might say today, "That man is of God" or "We really feel this suggestion is of God" or "It seems evident that this situation is of God."

John knew that Christians sin. What he does say is that, when a Christian sins, there is no evidence, at least in that act, of his regenerate nature; it is, in effect, concealed. The only way others can tell whether or not we are born again is if we reveal it by our actions. If we do not reveal it by our actions, that does not mean we are not born again, but it does mean that our true identity is not evident.

Love for the brethren. John introduces the idea that true Christianity expresses itself in love for other Christians and that hatred of a fellow Christian is incompatible with the Christian faith. He does not say that a Christian who hates his brother is not a Christian, but, rather, that he "abides in death" and that he does not have "eternal life abiding in him":

> *We know that we have passed out of death into life, because we love the brethren. He who does not love abides in death. Everyone who hates his brother is a murderer; and you know that no murderer has eternal life abiding in him (1 Jn. 3:14-15 NASB).*

The phrase "passed from death to life" is found elsewhere in John:

> *Most assuredly, I say to you, he who hears My word and believes in Him who sent Me has everlasting life, and shall not come into judgment, but has passed from death into life (Jn. 5:24 NKJV).*

It is possible that passing from death into life in both passages refers to the experience of regeneration. John is saying that we "know" (Gk. **oida**, "recognize") that we are regenerate by the fact that we have love for our brothers in Christ in our hearts. Here in no uncertain terms, love for the brothers is an

---

[45]See also 4:1, 3, 6, 7.

evidence of sonship! But this in no way proves the Experimental Predestinarian assertion that justification and sanctification are inevitably united. The passage does not say what Experimental Predestinarians say. It does not say that an absence of love is proof that one is not a son, only that he is abiding in death, i.e., living in the sphere from which he has been delivered. It does not say that, if a man is born again, he will always manifest love. It does say that the presence of love is a way he can recognize his regeneration. As will be discussed in chapter 12, the work of the Holy Spirit in our life is a secondary confirmation to our hearts that we are born again but is not the basis of our assurance.

John's favorite term for an intimate walk with Christ is "abide." This term is his word for something conditional in the believer's relationship with Christ, fellowship within the family. The conditional nature of the abiding relationship is brought out where Jesus says, "If you keep My commandments, you will abide in My love" (Jn. 15:10 NASB). His foremost command, which must be obeyed if we are to abide in Him, is the command which John discusses in 1 John, the command to love one another (Jn. 15:12). Only if we love one another, do we remain in friendship (fellowship) with Christ! "You are My friends, if you do what I command you (Jn. 15:14 NASB).

> *And the one who keeps His commandments abides in Him, and He in him (1 Jn. 3:24 NASB).*

By this statement John signals clearly that the abiding relationship is conditioned on obedience, in contrast to the regeneration experience which comes through faith alone (1 Jn. 5:10-11).

We conclude that the abiding relationship is not the regeneration experience. Rather, it refers to the degree of intimacy and fellowship with the Lord possible for those who continue to obey His commands. For John, Jesus Christ is "the eternal life" which abides in us (see 1:2). To have Christ abiding in us (1 Jn. 3:15, i.e., "eternal life") is not the same thing as being saved. It is a conditional relationship referring to Christ's being at home in the heart of the obedient Christian who loves his brother. It must also be remembered that these commands are to be fulfilled for a man's Christian brother. If the man is not a Christian, then this term is inappropriate.

Can a true Christian "hate his brother"? Of course he can. The phrase "one who hates his brother" is an articular present participle in Greek, which normally does not have a durative sense. Thus, it is grammatically doubtful to claim that this is the man's habitual life-style. Rather, it may refer only to incidents of murder or hatred at a point in his life.

David is a good example of a justified man who not only hated but followed up the murder in his heart with murder in reality by killing Uriah the Hittite (2 Sam. 12:9). Even Peter acknowledges that it is possible for a true Christian to "suffer as a murderer" (1 Pet. 4:15), and who has not felt anger in his heart at some time and is thus, on the authority of Jesus, a murderer (Mt. 5:21-22)?

When we harbor anger in our heart, John says, we are, in effect, murderers, and we abide in death, the very sphere from which we were delivered when we became Christians. We walk as "mere men" (1 Cor. 3:3), i.e., as if we were still in an unregenerate state. We are "carnal Christians" who are "walking in darkness" (1 Jn. 2:11) and are in danger of losing our reward (2 Jn. 8) and shrinking back in shame at the judgment (1 Jn. 2:28). Jesus Christ is not at home in such a heart. He does not abide there.

Chapter 9

Justification and Sanctification 2

Many other arguments are sometimes offered for the teaching that the New Testament connects justification and sanctification as an inseparable unity.

The New Creation

Experimental Predestinarians are impressed with the fact that Paul says any man in Christ is a new creation:

Therefore if any man is in Christ, he is a new creature; the old things passed away; behold new things have come (2 Cor. 5:17 NASB).

From this Iain H. Murray concludes, "So Calvinism says that Christ's work **for us**--that is the legal, forensic side of salvation--is never without Christ's work **in** us. Wherever there is a true change in a man's relation to God there is also a change in his subjective, moral, personal state. Thus, on this understanding, faced with the question, 'Do I belong to Christ?' the Christian is permitted to argue, 'Yes I do belong to Christ because I find in myself changes which He alone can work and changes which only His unbought love prompted Him to work.'"[1]

What is the new creation? While some, like Iain Murray, have interpreted this to refer to subjective internal moral renewal, it may be fair to say that this is by no means the prevalent view.[2] The fact that Paul connects the new creation with our being "in Christ" points us to a positional status rather than an experiential one.[3] As Martin Lloyd-Jones says, "We must differentiate between what is true of our position as a fact and our experience."[4] By position, Lloyd-Jones

---

[1]Iain H. Murray, "Will the Unholy Be Saved," *The Banner of Truth* 246 (March 1984): 4.

[2]See, for example, George Eldon Ladd, *A Theology of the New Testament* (Grand Rapids: Eerdmans, 1974), p. 479, where he rejects the idea that this passage should be interpreted "in terms of subjective experience."

[3]The "new creation" is commonly interpreted as a kind of proleptic anticipation, an assurance here and now of something which will happen experientially in the last day. Then we are perfect. See H. H. Esser, "Creation," in *NIDNTT*, 1:385.

[4]D. Martin Lloyd-Jones, *The New Man: Exposition of Romans 6* (Grand Rapids: Zondervan, 1973), p. 21.

means what a Christian is as a new man. The crucifixion of the old man (Rom. 6:6) like the creation of the new man is not experiential knowledge. Lloyd-Jones objects strongly to Charles Hodge on this point: "My entire exposition [of Rom. 6:1-11] asserts the exact opposite and says that it is not experimental; and that to take it experimentally produces utter confusion. This is not experimental knowledge; it is the knowledge of faith, it is the knowledge which is revealed in the Scripture, and of which faith is certain."[5]

The new creation of the heavens and the earth (Rev. 21:1; Isa. 65:17 Isa. 66:22) does not refer to a renovation of the old creation, but a new order. Peter tells us to look for the total destruction of the present order (2 Pet. 3:12) and the creation of a new heavens and a new earth (2 Pet. 3:13). Similarly, the "old man" was crucified. He no longer exists, and we are a new man in Christ.

The new man in Eph. 4:24 is the regenerate self (Col. 3:3-4). He is in no sense the old self made over or improved.[6] The new self is Christ "formed" in the Christian.[7] He is the new nature united with the ego.

The new nature is a new metaphysical entity, created perfect by God at regeneration. It is a "creation." In Eph. 4:24 we learn that the new man was created **kata theon**, "according to the standard of God," in righteousness, and in **hosiotes**, "holiness, piety" of truth. It appears that this new self is as perfect as God is. The fact that it has been "created" means that it has no sin in it. God would not create something with sin in it. Does this mean that the person is perfect? No. The person, the "ego" either lives in his new capacity or his old. The person always has both and is always sinful. But when viewed from the single perspective of the person as united to the new creation, i.e., the new man, he is perfect. That union, that identity, is man as God intends man to be. However, no person will ever live life as the perfect new creation until his old nature is experientially as well as forensically gone at the resurrection.

Finally, in Col. 3:10 we are told to "put on the new man which is being renewed."[8] The "new self" is being renewed in knowledge in the image of the creator.[9] How can a perfect new man in Christ be "renewed"? The renewal is "into" knowledge (**eis**) and **kata** "according to" the image of God. The new man while without sin is not mature. In the same way, Jesus, who was perfect, was "made

---

[5]Ibid., p. 61.

[6]2 Cor. 5:17; Gal. 6:15; Eph. 2:10; Col. 3:10.

[7]Gal. 2:20; 4:19; Col. 1:27; 1 Jn. 4:12.

[8]Or "Seeing . . . you have put on the new man."

[9]renewed = **anakainoumenon**, from **anakainoo**, the same word is used in 2 Cor. 4:16, inwardly we are renewed day by day. Paul refers to the new creation in Gal. 6:15 where he says that only walking consistently in the rule of the new creation.

perfect" (Heb. 2:10) through suffering. Like Jesus the new man, who really is in Christ, is renewed through suffering (2 Cor. 4:16).[10]

Paul refers to the perfect new creation in Christ when he says:

So now, no longer am I the one doing it, but sin which indwells me (Rom. 7:17 NASB).

But if I am doing the very thing I do not wish, I am not longer the one doing it, but sin which dwells in me (Rom. 7:20 NASB).

His meaning is transparent when seen in this light. The sin in the believer's life is not a product of the new creation! The new creation is sinless and created according to righteousness. Sin is no longer part of our true identity. Lloyd-Jones finds further evidence for the perfect, sinless, new man in Christ in these verses. He notes that Paul will say, "I am not doing this or that, it is this sin that remains in my members that does so. Sin is no longer in me, it is in my members only. That is the most liberating thing you have ever heard. Our old self is gone, we should never think of ourselves in those terms again."[11]

This helps explain John's perplexing statement in 1 Jn. 3:9, "No one born of God sins." The new man in Christ cannot sin; he is sinless. John is speaking of the believer from the viewpoint of the new creation, and sin, he says, cannot come from that.

Therefore, when Paul says that we are now a new creation in Christ, he is not saying that we have been experientially transformed and will inevitably manifest a life of good works. In fact, he repeatedly asks us to act like who we really are. He tells us to "reckon ourselves dead to sin" and to present ourselves to God "as those alive from the dead" (Rom. 6:13). He commands us to "put on the new man."[12] His meaning is that we are to be in experience what we already are in Christ. If it is automatic and inevitable that this will happen, why command it? More to the point, nowhere does the Bible assert that, just because a man is a new creation, he will act like who he is in Christ to the final hour.

The Christian Cannot Live in Sin

Any discussion of the relationship between God's free gift of the justifying righteousness of Christ and the life of works which should follow cannot ignore the central passage on the subject, Rom. 6. Experimental Predestinarians quote it often in support of their view.

---

[10]Lk. 2:52: Jesus grew in wisdom and stature.

[11]Lloyd-Jones, *The New Man*, p. 83.

[12]Eph. 4:24 and Col. 3:10.

As is generally recognized, the context begins with 5:20, where Paul concludes that sin produces more grace to cover it up. He marvels at the grace of God! As might be expected, however, such a doctrine is open to the charge that it logically leads to a life of license. Paul puts the words of the imaginary objector into his epistle and opens Rom. 6 with his complaint: "What shall we say, then? Are we to continue in sin that grace might increase?" (Rom. 6:1). His opening statement should have alerted the Experimental Predestinarians to their misunderstanding of the passage. He is not discussing whether or not it is possible for a believer to continue in sin but whether or not such a lifestyle is logically derived from the premise that grace abounds where sin increases.

His answer to this objector is one of horror, "May it never be! How shall we who died to sin still live in it?" Once again, he does not say, "How could those who died to sin have the capability (he does **not** use **dunamai**, "to have ability or capacity") to live in sin." Whether or not true believers have this capacity to fall into sin is not Paul's question. He is refuting the notion that a life of sin is a logical outcome of the gospel of grace. Paul's response will be to insist that such a life-style is in no way a logical deduction from his doctrine.

There are three arguments which Experimental Predestinarians derive from this passage (Rom. 6) to justify their notion that sanctification necessarily follows justification. First, they are struck with the words "dead to sin." A "decisive breech" with sin has occurred. Second, Paul assures his readers that "sin shall not have dominion over them." And finally, the contrasts between what they were prior to becoming Christians and what they are now in Christ (6:15-23) imply, it is thought, that Christians cannot be characterized by the things of the old man.

Dead to Sin

Central to the understanding of this important passage is the significance of the concept "death to sin." Many answers have been given as to its real meaning. While some have argued that it means "death **for** sin" and teaches that we died for our own sins in Christ,[13] most have concluded that a break with sin's power, and not sin's penalty, is in view. What is the nature of this death?

Some teach that Paul's meaning is that our death to sin is "positional." By this they mean this is truth not necessarily experienced but absolutely true in the reckoning of God. It is "true" truth.[14] Just as we did not experience dying with

---

[13]Shedd, *Commentary on Romans* (New York: Charles Scribner's Sons, 1879; reprint ed., Grand Rapids: Zondervan, 1967), p. 146.

[14]Watchman Nee, *The Normal Christian Life* (Fort Washington, PA: Christian Literature Crusade, 1961).

Christ, we did not experience our death to sin. The practical effect of this positional death to sin is that we are no longer obligated to obey it as our master.

John Murray likes the word "actual" instead of "positional" in regard to Rom 6:

> *And this victory is actual or it is nothing. It is a reflection upon and a deflection from the pervasive New Testament witness to speak of it as merely potential or positional. It is actual and practical as much as anything comprised in the application of redemption is actual and practical.* "[15]

He says this victory over the power of sin was achieved "once and for all" and is not achieved by a process, nor by our striving or working to that end. Yet he differs from perfectionism in three ways:

1.   They (perfectionists) fail to recognize that this victory is possessed by everyone who is born of God.
2.   They portray it as freedom from sinning or freedom from conscious sin, but the Bible says it is a freedom from the power and love of sin.
3.   They say this victory is a second blessing separable from the state of justification.

Murray hardly makes it clear how an actual, practical, and real break with sin, achieved once for all, can leave us with the daily struggle. The terms used in Rom. 6 describe, as Murray admits, something decisive and total. They are absolute--death to sin. But if this total break is real, actual, and practical, then there should be no daily struggle. Since there is a daily struggle due to indwelling sin according to Murray, how can he claim that the death to sin is "real" in the experiential sense? Murray's "death to sin" is real in the heavenlies but not real on earth unless we act on what is real up there. If it is real here, then there is no indwelling sin that has any power over us. He says that "there must be a constant and increasing appreciation that though sin still remains it does not have the mastery."[16]

He is therefore admitting that it is not real, practical, nor actual "once and for all" in our experience. Could we even say, then, it is potential in our experience? Now that is what many mean by positional truth. Murray is trying to make the text say that believers will never live in sin by using the word "actual" in order to justify his doctrine of perseverance in holiness:

---

[15]John Murray, *Redemption Accomplished and Applied* (Grand Rapids: Eerdmans, 1955), p. 142.

[16]Ibid., p. 145.

> *There is a total difference between surviving sin and reigning sin, the regenerate in conflict with sin and the unregenerate complacent to sin. It is one thing for sin to live in us: it is another for us to live in sin. It is one thing for the enemy to occupy the capital; it is another for his defeated hosts to harass the garrisons of the kingdom.* [17]

This is great rhetoric, but does it really say anything? Apparently our death to sin was sufficient to overcome reigning sin, but our union with Christ was not sufficient to overcome remaining sin. Where is the difference between "reigning sin" and "remaining sin" found in Scripture? Is there really any difference between sin living (i.e., expressing itself in life) in us and our living in sin? The fact that as believers we are no longer complacent to sin does not mean that sin is not very much alive and is incapable of taking the capital again if we do not submit to the Lord of the kingdom.

But why does Paul say, "How can we who died to sin, continue to live in it?" Paul is refuting an objection. His statement is very definite and absolute. He is not saying we partially died but that we completely died to sin. If this death is an experiential death, then a serious problem develops. Who in the Calvinist tradition claims that his experiential death to sin is absolute and total? Only by watering down Paul's absolute statements to say that we died to sin a little bit experientially and that we become more and more dead as we mature can this passage possibly be harmonized with the Experimental Predestinarian doctrine of perseverance. Yet the passage is not saying that. We died to sin (absolute); we have been "justified from sin" (absolute); indeed, our relationship to sin is as total a severance and death as that of Jesus Himself which is absolute (Rom. 6:9-10). As Paul put it, we have died to sin "once for all" (6:10).

Therefore we must ask, "Is this death to sin actual in our experience or actual in the reckoning of revelation?" The fact that Paul says in 6:7 that the man who has died is "justified" from sin implies that for Paul this death to sin is legal, forensic, and positional, and not automatically real in experience; it is absolute, not partial. The Greek word **dikaioo** is his normal word for the legal justification of the sinner. [18] It is a forensic and not a "real in experience" term. In fact, after pages of adjectives describing our "decisive breech" with sin, Murray comes to the same conclusion! When he is finally forced to state exactly what he means by a "real decisive breech" with sin, we are told that on the basis of Rom. 6:7, Paul's meaning is that it is "forensic and juridical." [19] Now this is the common meaning of positional truth, the very doctrine which Murray assails.

---

[17] Ibid.

[18] AG, p. 196.

[19] John Murray, "Definite Sanctification," in *The Collected Writings of John Murray*, 2 vols. (Edinburgh: Banner of Truth, 1977).

Death to sin is real in our position but not necessarily real in life. Paul's commands to present ourselves to righteousness and to reckon ourselves dead to sin certainly imply that we might not necessarily do this. As Howe put it, "If the believer's death with Christ described in Romans 6:1-10 is 'actual,' then exactly what is meant by Romans 6:11? If death means cessation of existence **actually**, then why does Paul urge believers in that verse to reckon (count, consider as true, realize, believe) themselves dead to sin."[20] We should do this, but there is the possibility of negligence. However, if we do this, we will be successful, because we present ourselves "as those who are alive" and because "sin will not have dominion."

Sin Will Not Have Dominion

When Paul tells his readers that "sin will not have dominion over you" (Rom. 6:14), John Murray concludes that this means that sanctification inevitably follows from justification. But is it not obvious that this victory is conditioned on what he has just said? It will not have dominion in the future if we do what Paul says we should do--reckon and yield right now. This is a promise of success if we apply the God-appointed means, and not a statement of reality irrespective of those means.

The text does not say that sin does not have dominion. It says sin will not have dominion (**kyrieusei**, future tense, in contrast to the aorist and perfect tenses of the context), IF we reckon and yield. If we do not reckon and yield, then sin can have dominion in the life of a believer. The fact that we have died to sin does not automatically mean we will reckon and yield. It means that, if we do reckon and yield, we will be successful.

If sin's lack of dominion is automatic, regardless of our choices, then why does Paul continually, in this very context, set choices before them? "For just as you presented your members as slaves to impurity and to lawlessness, resulting in further lawlessness, so now present your members as slaves to righteousness, resulting in sanctification" (6:19). It is true that they "became obedient from the heart" (6:17), but now they must continually make choices regarding which master they will serve, sin or Christ. The victory is that they no longer have to obey sin, and if they choose not to, they will be successful. But if they do not so choose, they will not be successful, and sin will have dominion over them.

Paul is refuting a logical argument against grace. It logically follows, the objector says, that we should continue to sin to make more grace abound. Paul says this is illogical, but not impossible. He asks, "Do you not know?" He appeals to an intellectually apprehensible fact of the divine reckoning. It is illogical be-

---

[20]Frederick R. Howe, "A Review of *Birthright*, by David Needham," *BibSac* 141 (January-March 1984): 71.

cause grace not only includes the forgiveness of sin but the removal of sin's legal dominion and the impartation of life. Because we are united with Christ in His death, sin no longer has the legal right to rule us. Since we are united with Him in resurrection, we have new life within us which gives us the power to overcome it and the motivation to want to overcome it. Because we died to sin, we no longer have to sin, and since we live in Christ, we no longer want to sin. A man who does not have to do what he does not want to do does not normally do it. Thus, the objection is fully answered. The fact that a man could subsequently quench the Spirit, become carnal, stop growing, or fall away does not strengthen the objector's case. Logically, the gospel does not lead to a continuance in sin but cessation from it. Any gospel which breaks a man from sin's power and gives him new life and motivation not to sin is not subject to the charge that it logically results in license, even if an individual Christian resists the positive influences of grace.

Slaves of Righteousness

The fact that a man may not reckon and yield is proven by the existence of the commands to do so. If obedience is automatic and "real," then there is no more need to command it than there is to say, "Be human."

It is in this light that the contrasts in the latter half of the chapter must be seen. They were "slaves of sin," but now they have "become obedient from the heart to that form of teaching to which you were committed" (Rom. 6:17). They were "slaves to sin" and are now "slaves to righteousness" (Rom. 6:18). They have been "freed from sin" and "enslaved to God" (Rom. 6:22). Paul explains that we are only slaves of the person we obey:

> *Do you not know that when you present yourselves to someone as slaves for obedience, you are slaves of the one who you obey, either of sin resulting in death, or of obedience resulting in righteousness (Rom. 6:16 NASB).*

Paul is speaking in general terms, enunciating principles which apply to Christians or non-Christians. Slavery to sin leads to death, and obedience leads to moral righteousness. Death for the non-Christian is, of course, eternal and final. For the Christian, death is temporal judgment and spiritual impoverishment as in Rom. 8:13. The righteousness here comes as a result of obedience, and therefore we may conclude that moral, and not forensic, righteousness is in view. Paul has said earlier that, "if Abraham was justified by works, he has something to boast about" and "to the one who does not work, but believes in Him who justifies the ungodly, his faith is reckoned as righteousness" (Rom. 4:2, 5). Forensic righteousness comes by faith alone; this righteousness comes by works of obedience.

These Roman Christians had not only received the righteousness of Christ through faith alone, but in addition, they had submitted themselves to the lordship of Christ subsequent to saving faith and had become obedient from the heart. Their obedience was producing moral righteousness:

But thanks be to God that though you were slaves of sin, you became obedient from the heart to that form of teaching to which you were committed (Rom. 6:17 NASB).

They were already committed to the "form of teaching," the gospel. They were already Christians. But in addition to being Christians, they **became** obedient from the heart, that is, they submitted to Christ's lordship. They became obedient to truth they had already committed themselves to:

And having been freed from sin, you became slaves of righteousness (v. 18 NASB).

Not only had they committed themselves to the truth of the gospel, and therefore become positionally freed from sin, but they heeded Paul's injunction to "present" themselves "as those alive from the dead, and your members as instruments of righteousness to God" (v. 13). In other words, they had become experiential slaves of righteousness. They had become obedient Christians who obeyed from the heart the truth they were taught.

I am speaking in human terms because of the weakness of your flesh. For just as you presented your members as slaves to impurity and to lawlessness, resulting in further lawlessness, so now present your members as slaves to righteousness, resulting in sanctification (v. 19).

When they were non-Christians, they were slaves to impurity. Now they are Christians, and Paul wants them to keep on presenting (Gk. present durative implied by context) their members to righteousness. If they do, they will be sanctified. This further substantiates the observation that the righteousness referred to in v. 16 is moral righteousness and not forensic justification. This righteousness is a product of sanctification. It is not automatic that they will keep on presenting themselves as slaves. They have made a good beginning, and Paul wants them to continue it:

For when you were slaves of sin, you were free in regard to righteousness. Therefore what benefit were you then deriving from the things of which you are now ashamed. For the outcome of those things is death (vv. 20-21 NASB).

When they were non-Christians, they received no benefits from their profligate life-style. The result of it was death, both eternally and in the sense of spiritual impoverishment and wasted life (e. g., 7:9). He does not want them to return to that:

> *But now having been freed from sin and enslaved to God, you derive*
> *your benefit, resulting in sanctification, and the outcome, eternal life*
> *(v. 22 NASB).*

They were positionally freed from sin when they became Christians (vv. 1-14). They became enslaved to God when they chose, after that, not to "go on presenting the members of [their] bodies to sin" (v. 13). They are freed by the act of Christ, they were enslaved as a result of their own act of "presenting." The former is positional and unconditional, and the latter is experiential and conditional.

Some have been impressed with the fact that Paul says we are "enslaved" (passive voice, Rom. 6:22) to God, as if this is something which is an experiential state intrinsic to Christian experience. However, just as freedom from sin is not automatic unless we reckon and yield, neither is slavery to righteousness experienced unless we obey. The fact that the word "enslave" is in the passive voice is inconsequential. It is a restatement of v. 16, "Do you not know that when you present yourselves to someone as slaves (active voice) you are slaves of the one whom you obey?" The second clause, "you are slaves of the one whom you obey," is equivalent to saying, "You are enslaved to God."

Of course we are all, in one sense, servants of our new master. But we are not necessarily obedient servants unless we chose to be. Paul had already made it clear that this slavery to righteousness is a personal choice, and nowhere does he say it is the necessary and inevitable outcome of their regeneration. He says, "Present yourselves to God, **as those alive from the dead**" (Rom. 6:13). He also says, "Present your members **as slaves** to righteousness" (Rom. 6:19).

If we continue to present ourselves for His service and continue to enslave ourselves to Him, then, and only then, will we receive the benefit, sanctification and eternal life. As discussed elsewhere, eternal life is both a gift to faith and a reward in the future. In this verse it is the reward to sanctification and obedience in the future. In the next verse, however, it is the inception of eternal life, the gift to saving faith which is in view:

> *For the wages of sin is death, but the free gift of God is eternal life in*
> *Christ Jesus our Lord (v. 23 NASB).*

In the preceding verse (v. 22) eternal life was not a gift, but was the outcome of service to Christ and progressive sanctification and obedience. Paul is now summarizing his whole discussion with general principles. Death for the Christian is the wage of sin:

When tempted, no one should say, "God is tempting me." For God cannot be tempted by evil nor does he tempt anyone; but each one is tempted when by his own evil desire he is dragged away and enticed. Then after desire has conceived, it gives birth to sin; **and sin, when it is full-grown, gives birth to death** *(Jas. 1:13-15).*

For both James and Paul, in these apparently parallel passages, death is the spiritual impoverishment or sin unto death which can come upon the carnal Christian.

It is a simple truth that Christians, freed from the slavery to sin, have entered into the slavery of another. But our service as slaves to our new master is not automatic and inevitable. We must be good and obedient slaves. The possibility that we may not be is why he commands, "Present your members as slaves to righteousness, resulting in sanctification" (Rom. 6:19). If we do not obey that command, we may be slaves, but we are not acting like it, and we will not be sanctified!

We conclude there is nothing in Rom. 6 which requires the interpretation that a true Christian will persevere in good works up to the point of physical death. We do learn that a true Christian should do this, will be successful if he pursues it, and is obligated to do so because he is a slave to his new master. But nowhere do we learn that he always will do so or that he will persist in doing so to the end of life.

Faith without Works Is Dead

When James said, "Faith without works is dead" and "A man is justified by works, and not by faith alone" (Jas. 2:24), he no doubt was completely unaware of the volumes which would be written in the history of the church which would attempt to harmonize his words with those of the apostle Paul. He would also, I think, be surprised to learn that many would misconstrue his words to mean that those who have true saving faith will necessarily evidence this by a life of works and that, if they lack works, this proves their faith is dead, i.e., not saving faith.

What Is Dead Faith?

The first question to ask in understanding this passage is to consider what James meant when he used the term "dead faith."[21] The use of the term "death" to describe what can happen to Christians is not uncommon in the Bible:

---

[21]For much of the exposition to follow, the writer is indebted to Zane Hodges, *Dead Faith: What is it* (Dallas: Redencion Viva, 1987).

For if you are living according to the flesh, **you must die;** *but if by the spirit, you are putting to death the deeds of the body, you will live (Rom. 8:13 NASB).*

Therefore, my brethren, **you also were made to die** *to the law though the body of Christ (Rom. 7:4 NASB).*

How can we who **died to sin** *still live in it? (Rom. 6:2 NASB).*

In each of these passages the notion of death included a rather obvious point--they were once alive! Normally, death is preceded by life, and in common biblical usage this is true also. There is no reason to assume that James viewed it any differently. The dead faith to which James refers was most probably alive at one time, or it could not have died! This is not pressing the metaphor beyond its intent. It is an explicit implication of this same metaphor used elsewhere in the New Testament as the above passages reveal. Even the non-Christian, born dead in trespasses and sins (Eph. 2:1), was once alive in Adam. Just as we all died in Adam, we were all once alive in Him (1 Cor. 15:22; Rom. 5:12). "Death came to all men because all sinned." If we "all sinned" in Adam, we were obviously "alive" in some sense in order to do so. Whether we lived federally or representatively in Adam is not important here, but Reformed theologians of all persuasions have agreed that Paul teaches we were once alive in Adam and we died in Him.

But furthermore, James seems to say he precisely intends this idea by the analogy he uses, "For just as the body without the spirit is dead, so also faith without works is dead" (Jas. 2:26). The body dies, according to the Bible, when the spirit departs (Jn. 19:30). Just as the body dies when our spirit departs, even so our faith dies when our works depart! Just as the spirit is the animating principle which gives the body life, so work is the animating principle which gives faith "life."

There is no question that in the absence of works our faith becomes useless and dead. Our Christian experience deteriorates into a mere dead orthodoxy which is evident in many Christian churches. This is the danger which James addresses. This view of the passage has long been held by other expositors. It was the view of Origin, Jerome, and of the Roman Catholic church.[22]

Salvation Is NOT by "Faith Alone"

With this in mind James's comments about the inability of faith alone to save a man take on new meaning:

---

[22]Richard Chenevix Trench, *Notes on the Miracles and Parables of the Lord*, 2 vols. in 1 (n.d.; reprint ed., Westwood, NJ: Revell, 1953), 2:253.

What use it is, my brethren, if a man says he has faith, but he has no works? Can that faith save him? (Jas. 2:14 NASB).

The Greek construction requires a negative answer to James's question. Faith alone cannot save, can it? No, something else is needed--works. At this point the apparent conflict between James and Paul caused Luther to say that the doctrine of justification in James made it "an epistle of straw."

As discussed in chapter 6, Luther's difficulty was caused by the fact that he always equated salvation with salvation from hell. But as Sellers correctly observed, "Death from sin, then, could be physical death, for believers or unbelievers. It could be spiritual death--separating a believer from fellowship with God."[23] In James, to be saved refers to salvation from physical death, the death-producing consequences of sin.[24] In other words, salvation is the finding of a rich and meaningful Christian experience! It is true that faith alone will save us from hell, but faith which is alone will not save us from a dead or carnal spiritual life.

It is evident that James is using the term "salvation" in this sense when we consider the context in which his statement is placed. In Jas. 1:13-16 James describes the deathly consequences of sin in the life of the believer:

Let no one say when he is tempted, "I am being tempted by God"; for God cannot be tempted by evil, and He Himself does not tempt anyone. But each one is tempted when he is carried away and enticed by his own lust. Then when lust has conceived, it gives birth to sin; and when sin is accomplished, **it brings forth death.** *Do not be deceived* **my beloved brethren** *(Jas. 1:13-16 NASB).*

It is the "beloved brethren" who are in danger of experiencing the deathly consequences of sin. These Christians who are alive are in danger of losing the vitality of their faith and experiencing death. As he says later, "Faith without works is dead," but it was once alive.

In view of the possibility of death in our Christian life, what shall we do to prevent this catastrophe? James responds by saying:

Therefore putting aside all filthiness and all that remains of wickedness, in humility receive the implanted word which is able to save your souls (Jas. 1:21 NASB).

These are "beloved brethren" who have been "brought forth by the word of truth" in whom the Word has been "implanted." They are saved people in the

---

[23]C. Norman Sellers, *Election and Perseverance* (Miami Springs, FL: Schoettle, 1987), p. 105.

[24]As discussed in chapter 5, the phrase "save a soul" never means deliverance from hell and always refers to the preservation of one's physical life.

sense of final deliverance from hell. However, these saved people need "salvation." This salvation is the salvation contextually defined as a deliverance from the death-producing effects of sin and a lack of good works in their lives. He goes on to say that to receive with meekness the ingrafted word is simply to apply the Word of God to our lives by acts of obedience:

> *But prove yourselves doers of the Word, and not merely hearers who delude themselves (Jas. 1:22 NASB).*

> *But one who looks intently at the perfect law, the law of liberty, and abides by it, not having become a forgetful hearer but an effectual doer, this man shall be blessed in what he does (Jas. 1:25).*

It is quite likely that James is thinking in Old Testament terms here. Frequently, Solomon, for example, will contrast the life-enriching benefits of righteousness with the death-producing effects of sin:

> *The truly righteous man attains life,*
> *But he who pursues evil goes to his death* (Prov. 11:19).

The terms "life" and "death" are contextually defined in Prov. 11 as "abundant life" and "carnality," to use contemporary terms. In a series of contrasts he defines death as "being trapped by evil desires" (Prov. 11:6); physical death and loss of hope (11:7); overwhelmed with trouble (11:8); destroying one's neighbor (11:9); destruction of a city by evil actions (11:11); a lack of judgment and a deriding of one's neighbor (11:12); and a lack of guidance resulting in the fall of a nation (11:14). Life, on the other hand, is defined as having a "straight way" (11:5); being delivered from evil snares (11:6); being rescued from trouble (11:8); giving blessing to a city (11:11); and sowing righteousness (11:18). Contrasts such as these define life and death not as entrance into heaven and final commitment to hell but as relative qualities of life now, qualities which are dependent upon the faith-vitalizing property of good works.[25]

Salvation here is the deliverance from the spiritually impoverishing consequences of sin and the experiential blessing of God now. In Solomon's terms it is rescue from trouble or the trap of evil desires. It is not final deliverance from hell. The parallelism between Jas. 1:21-27 and 2:14-26 enables us to see how these passages explain each other. In 1:21ff James tells us we will be saved by being doers and not just hearers of the word. In 2:14-16 we can now see that his meaning is the same. They will be saved in the sense of finding deliverance from the spiritually impoverishing consequences of sin, not by faith alone, but by faith plus their works of obedience.

---

[25]See also Prov. 10:27; 12:28; 13:14; 19:16.

James makes it clear that this is what he means by salvation in his closing words:

> *My brethren, if any among you strays from the truth, and one turns him back, let him know that he who turns a sinner from the error of his way will save his soul from death, and will cover a multitude of sins (Jas. 5:19-20 NASB).*

Just as it is possible to "save" one in whom the Word has been implanted (Jas. 1:21), it is also sometimes necessary to "save" one who is of the "brethren" and is "among us." A man who is already saved in the sense of final deliverance from hell needs only to be saved from death. The death here may be the "sin unto death" referred to in 1 Cor. 11:30 and 1 Jn. 5:16.[26] Certainly this is the ultimate consequence of Divine discipline brought upon the sinning Christian. But short of that, the life of the sinning Christian can only be characterized as spiritually dead.

We conclude that the word "saved" in James does not refer to final deliverance from hell. It refers, instead, to deliverance from the terrible consequences of spiritual impoverishment and ultimately physical death, which can come upon the regenerate person if he fails to vitalize his faith with a life of works. Divine discipline is certain, but loss of salvation is not under consideration.

James is well within the theology of the Old Testament when he warns against the shortening of life which occurs when a man lives a life of debauchery or bitterness or sin. Indeed, his point has been commonly observed by mankind throughout the ages and confirmed by modern medical science. Most of our ailments have psychosomatic origins. Emotional stress brought on by a life of guilt and bitterness is, perhaps, the major cause of physical death in the Western world.

The words of an objector are now introduced. The objector's comments apparently extend down to Jas. 2:19. At the outset we must insist that these are the words of someone taking the opposite point of view from James. James introduces his opponent with the phrase "But (**alla**) someone will say." This is the normal way of introducing the opposition, and thus James's objector does not share James's views but in some way disagrees with them.[27] James calls him a "foolish man," who is claiming that faith without works is perfectly acceptable.

---

[26]See Charles Ryrie, *The Ryrie Study Bible: New American Standard Translation* (Chicago: Moody Press, 1978), p. 1863. As pointed out in chapter 5, it always has this meaning in every other use in the LXX or New Testament.

[27]Johnstone attempts to make the objector and James agree with one another and unite in opposition to a man without works in the church. His main argument is that the words of the objector seem to agree with James' view expressed elsewhere. See Robert Johnstone, *Lectures Exegetical and Practical on The Epistle of James* (Oliphant Anderson & Ferrier, 1871; reprint ed., Minneapolis: Klock and Klock, 1978), p. 210.

But someone will say, "You have faith; I have deeds." Show me your faith without deeds, and I will show you my faith by what I do."

You believe that there is one God. Good! Even the demons believe that--and shudder (Jas. 2:18-19).

You will notice in v. 18 how the NIV places the quotation marks. Since the New Testament Greek manuscripts did not use quotation marks, we understand the whole verse to be spoken by the objector, not just the first sentence.

From that perspective we note that the objector says he has good works, deeds, and acknowledges that James has faith. But now the objector challenges James to show him his faith without deeds. The objector knows that James feels this cannot be done. The only way faith can be revealed is by a life of works. But then the objector says he will show James his faith by his works, which, the objector implies, likewise cannot be done!

When the objector says, "I will show you my faith by what I do," he is not saying this is possible. He is saying it is as impossible as showing faith apart from what you do. This involves turning the objector's apparent meaning in this phrase upside down. The justification for this is that he is an "objector," and he must be saying something different from James, not agreeing with him. Lange clearly states the problem:

Difficulties have been found: (1) In James' introducing this proposition as the expression of another person and not as his own; and (2) in his introducing it by **alla** *("but").*[28]

This difficulty may be removed with the simple assumption that the objector is being sarcastic. When he says, "I will show you my faith by what I do," he is being insincere. He is really saying, "You can no more show me your faith without works than I can show you faith by means of works." Dibelius cites several illustrations from Greek diatribe which illustrate this debating technique.[29] In *Ad Autolycu 1.2* a Christian apologist named Theophilus writes: "But even if you should say, 'Show me your God,' I too might say to you, 'Show me your Man and I also will show you my God.'" It was impossible for Theophilus to "show" his opponent his God, and similarly, it was impossible for the opponent to "show" Theophilis his "Man." Similarly, when James's opponent says, "Show me," we are alerted that an item impossible of fulfillment is to follow.

---

[28]J. P. Lange and J. J. Van Oosterzee, "The Epistle General of James," in *Lange's,* 12:83.

[29]Martin Dibelius, *James,* rev. Heinrich Greeven, trans. Michael A. Williams, ed. Helmut Koester, *Hermeneia* (Philadelphia: Fortress, Eng. ed. 1976), pp. 154-55 n. 29, cited by Hodges, *Dead Faith,* p. 31.

In other words, the objector's point seems to be that there is no connection between faith and works at all. Even if one produced the works you keep talking about, it would not prove anything. Just as James cannot show his faith apart from his works, the objector claims he cannot show his faith by means of his works. There simply is, according the objector, no necessary relationship between faith and works at all.

The objector continues his attempt to prove that there is no connection between faith and works by appealing to the fact that demons believe and they have no works:

> *You believe that there is one God. Good! Even the demons believe that--and shudder (Jas. 2:19).*

When the objector says, "Good" (Gk. **kalos poieis**), his meaning is not "Good for you" but literally, "You are doing good works." The same phrase is found in v. 8, "If you really keep the royal law of Scripture, 'Love your neighbor as yourself,' you are doing right" (Gk. **kalos poieite**). This meaning of the phrase is found in several places in the New Testament.[30] The objector is therefore saying, "James, you believe in God and you are doing good works. The demons also believe in God, but they shudder. The conclusion is, there is no necessary connection between faith and good works."

Such an argument is ludicrous, and appropriately James calls him a "foolish man" and tells him that faith, unless it is vitalized and matured by a life of works, is not vital. The objector apparently imagines that faith alone is adequate for an abundant life and for the fulfillment of all obligations to God. However, James counters, faith is useless as far as Christian sanctification and practical victory ("salvation") through trials is concerned (2:20; cf. 1:21; 2:14). There is a connection between faith and works but not the connection imagined by the Reformed doctrine of perseverance.

As proof of the worthless nature of a faith apart from works, James now cites the illustration of Abraham:

> *Was not our ancestor Abraham considered righteous* [Gk. "justified by works"] *for what he did when he offered his son Isaac on the altar? You see that his faith and his actions were working together, and his faith was made complete by what he did. And the scripture was fulfilled that says, "Abraham believed God, and it was credited to him as righteousness," and he was called God's friend. You see that a person is justified by what he does and not by faith alone (Jas. 2:21-24).*

---

[30]Lk. 6:27; Mt. 12:12; Jas. 4:17.

James's readers knew that Abraham had been declared righteous before God long before he offered Isaac on the altar. The offering of Isaac occurred in Gen. 22:9 but he had been declared righteous prior to Gen. 15:6. A different kind of justification was in view in Gen. 22, a justification before men. This justification was based upon works. Abraham's faith was strengthened, matured, and perfected by his obedience. To use James's words, it "was made complete" (**eteleiothe**, "matured," "perfected") by what he did. Abraham was already saved, but the vitality and maturity of his faith could only be accomplished by works. Such an obedient response resulted in his being called God's friend. Similarly, Jesus said, "You are My friends, **if you do what I command**" (Jn. 15:14). There was no question about the disciples' regenerate state, but there was a question about whether or not they would continue to walk in fellowship with their King and be His "friend."

When James says in 2:24 that we are justified by works, he is not disagreeing with Paul. He is simply saying that justification by faith is not the only kind of justification there is. Justification by faith secures our eternal standing, but justification by works secures our temporal fellowship. Justification by faith secures our vindication before God; justification by works secures our vindication before men. It is by works that our justification by faith becomes evident to others and is of use to others, including orphans, and those who are hungry, cold, or thirsty.

James's point then is not that works are the necessary and inevitable result of justification. Rather, he is saying that, if works do not follow our justification, our faith will shrivel up and die. We are in danger of spiritual impoverishment, "death." Nor does he say that the failure to work will result in the loss of our salvation. This is not a passage to prove the inevitable connection between justification and sanctification at all! Rather, it proves the desirable connection.

By Their Fruits You Shall Know Them

Probably the most commonly recognized statement of Jesus thought to support the Reformed doctrine of perseverance is his famous warning, "By their fruits you shall know them" (Mt. 7:16). The assumption is made that Christ means by this that one can discern whether or not another person is truly a Christian by examining the evidence of good works in his life. If there is good work (fruit) present, it must be a good tree, i.e., regenerate. If good character qualities are not obvious, then the tree must be bad, i.e., unregenerate. This initial impression is reinforced by Christ's stinging rebuke to these false teachers, "I never knew you," and His explanation that only one "who does the will of My Father who is in heaven will enter the kingdom of heaven" (Mt. 7:21). Such an interpretation obviously contradicts the clear teaching elsewhere that entrance into the kingdom of heaven is based upon faith alone. In order to resolve this difficulty,

Experimental Predestinarians offer the seemingly plausible explanation that, since all true believers persevere in holiness to the end of life, it is certainly true that only those who do the Father's will enter the kingdom. All true believers will do this, and if a person fails to do this, this proves he was not a Christian at all.[31]

This writer believes that a careful reading of the passage will reveal that another interpretation of Jesus' famous words is more plausible:

> *Enter by the narrow gate; for the gate is wide, and the way is broad that leads to destruction and many are those who enter by it. For the gate is small, and the way is narrow that leads to life and few are those who find it. Beware of false prophets, who come to you in sheep's clothing, but inwardly are ravenous wolves (Mt. 7:13-15 NASB).*

This passage about false prophets who appear in sheep's clothing occurs at the conclusion of the Sermon on the Mount. Although the sermon was directed at the disciples (Mt. 5:1), apparently when Jesus went up to the mountain, the multitudes followed and perhaps overheard at least the conclusion of the sermon. We can imagine that Jesus addresses this portion to the multitudes as well as to His intimate followers.

The references to entering by the gate, the sheep, and the wolves immediately suggest a common theme in Jesus' teaching found elsewhere--entrance into the sheepfold:

> *I am the **door** of the sheep. All who came before Me are **thieves and robbers**, but the sheep did not hear them. "**I am the door**; if anyone **enters through Me**, he shall be saved, and shall go in and out and find pasture. The **thief comes only to steal, and kill, and destroy;** I came that they might have life, and might have it abundantly. I am the good shepherd; the good shepherd lays down His life for the sheep. He who is a hireling and not a shepherd, who is not the owner of the sheep , behold the wolf coming, and leaves the sheep and flees, and the **wolf snatches them** , and scatters them. He flees because he is a hireling and is not concerned about the sheep (Jn. 10:7-13 NASB).*

The gate simply refers to an "entrance," whether to Hades,[32] a city,[33] the temple,[34] a private home,[35] or, as Matthew uses it here in harmony with John, a sheepfold.

---

[31]See Stanley D. Toussaint, *Behold the King: A Study of Matthew* (Portland, OR: Multnomah, 1980), pp. 115-19 for an illustration of this approach to the passage.

[32]Mt. 16:18.

[33]Lk. 7:12; Acts 12:10.

[34]Acts 3:10.

The wide gate leads to destruction, and the narrow gate leads to life. "The gate is small, and the **way** is narrow, which leads to life." We are reminded of another claim of Jesus, "I am the **way** and the truth and the life. No one comes to the Father except through Me" (Jn. 14:6). He is the door, the way, the entrance through which we must pass if we want to enter the sheepfold, the kingdom of heaven.

The wide gate reminds us of the many rival religious claims. The Hindus, the Moslems, and the Jews all enter through a different gate, a gate which leads not into the sheepfold but to destruction.

But there are false prophets who would lead the sheep to the wrong gate. These men come in "sheep's" clothing, but inwardly they are "ravenous wolves." The "hireling" in John did not protect the sheep from these false prophets or wolves. Who are they? In times of religious excitement, such as the time of the teaching of Jesus, there is often an outburst of religious extremism. It is unlikely that the Lord has the Pharisees in mind. In fact, they are probably the "hirelings" who did not protect the people against such extremism.[36] The Pharisees were not viewed as prophetic, charismatic, nor as innovators but, rather, as preservers of the status quo. These men are reminiscent of some of today's television evangelists who claim to prophesy, cast out demons, and heal in Jesus' name but who later are revealed to be "ravenous wolves," living in sexual immorality and in million dollar homes, bedecked with jewelry, and driving expensive automobiles. Yet what a person is on the inside is not obvious, and thus a test is needed to determine his nature.

> *You will know them by their fruits. Grapes are not gathered from thorn bushes, nor figs from thistles, are they? (Mt. 7:16 NASB).*

To what does the "fruit" refer? In Mt. 7 the specific fruit is unspecified, but the parallel passage in chapter 12 suggests that the **doctrine** of the false teachers was in view, and not their life-style:

> *And whoever* **shall speak a word against the Son of Man,** *it shall be forgiven him,; but whoever* **shall speak against the Holy Spirit,** *it shall not be forgiven him, either in this age or, in the age to come. Either make the tree good, and its* **fruit** *good, or make the tree bad, and its* **fruit** *bad; for* **the tree is known by its fruit.** *You brood of vipers, how can you, being evil,* **speak what is good?** *For the mouth speaks out of that which fills the heart. The good man out of his good treasure brings forth what is good; and the evil man out of his evil treasure brings forth what is evil. And I say to you, that every careless*

---

[35]Acts 10:17; 12:13.

[36]Dead orthodoxy can offer little protection because it is not as attractive as the alternatives.

word that men shall speak, they shall render account for it in the day of judgment. **For by your words you shall be justified, and by your words you shall be condemned** *(Mt. 12:32-37 NASB).*

In Mt. 7 their life-style outwardly seems to indicate they are Christians. They are called sheep; they look like Christians; they perform miraculous works in Jesus' name. They do some of the works that Christians do. Therefore, the reason that Jesus "never knew them" is not that their outward behavior is corrupt. Rather, it is because they have not "done the will of My Father who is in heaven." Some of the most gentle and kindly men are workers of many good works, and yet they are not regenerate. It would be impossible to discern them by their works. Only their teaching reveals who they are.

Lange, Calvin, Jerome, and others viewed the fruit as the false teaching of the false prophets.[37] Lange points out that the fruit in view is not that of ordinary professors of Christianity but of false teachers. Their fruit is their destructive doctrine. These are no doubt related at points to their character and may often be revealed by behavioral abnormalities, but frequently that is not obvious for many years, and sometimes never in this life. What is obvious is what they say. Even though their character is clothed in sheep's garments, and they are "gentle and meek in their outward appearance," their incorrect teaching is evident to all.

We should not be surprised that Jesus tells us that the teaching of a false prophet is the fruit by which we can discern his true identity. By asserting this, He is aligning himself firmly with Moses and the prophets who continually stressed that the way one discerns a true prophet from a false one is by giving attention to what he says:

> *If a prophet or a dreamer of dreams arises among you and gives you a sign or a wonder, and the sign or wonder comes true, concerning which he spoke to you, saying, "Let us go after other gods (whom you have not known) and let us serve them, you shall not listen to the words of that prophet or that dreamer of dreams; for the LORD your God is testing you to find out if you love the LORD your God with all your heart and all your soul. You shall follow the LORD your God and fear Him; and shall keep His commandments, listen to His voice, serve Him, and cling to Him (Dt. 13:1-4 NASB).*

Moses commands his readers to listen to what these false prophets say and to compare it with the commands and voice of the Lord, the Torah, and not to pay any attention to what they do. In fact, these false prophets, according to Moses and like those in Mt. 7, performed signs and wonders. Observing the works of a false prophet is not how we determine his true identity.

---

[37]J. P. Lange, "Matthew," in *Lange's,* 12:144.

Isaiah, when faced with a people who sought help in mediums, gave similar advice:

> *And when they say to you, "Consult the mediums and the spiritists who whisper and mutter," should not a people consult their God? Should they consult the dead on behalf of the living?* **To the law and to the testimony. If they do not speak according to this word it is because they have no dawn** *(Isa. 8:19-20 NASB).*

The teaching of these false prophets is to be compared to the law and the testimony. If they do not speak according to this word, that is, if their fruit reveals they are not true prophets, it is because they have no revelation.

The idea that a false prophet can be discerned by comparing what he says with Scripture is widespread in the Bible,[38] and it is surprising that the Lord's comments about fruit are not always read in this light. The fruit by which we may discern these false prophets is their doctrine. Their works were good. They looked and acted like sheep and even performed miracles. An examination of works would have led to the wrong conclusion!

It should also be noted that Jesus says, "By their fruit you shall know **them.**" It is not professing Christians in general who are the subject of discussion but men who openly announce themselves as prophets and who claim to do miraculous works in Jesus' name. The passage has nothing to do with the notion that we can test the reality of the faith of a professing Christian by examining his good works.

The Lord continues:

> *Not everyone who says to Me, "Lord, Lord," will enter the kingdom of heaven; but* **he who does the will of My Father who is in heaven.** *Many will say to Me on that day, "Lord, Lord, did we not prophesy in Your name, and in Your name cast out demons, and in Your name perform many miracles?" And then I will declare to them, "I never knew you; depart from Me, you who practice lawlessness" (Mt. 7:21-23 NASB).*

They now call Him Lord, even though they never confessed Him as God during life. We are reminded once again of the wide gate, entered by many religious leaders and their followers. They all thought they were performing works in behalf of the one true God, but they did not acknowledge Christ as that God. Now confronted with Him at the judgment, they do confess Him as Lord, but it is too late.

---

[38]See Jer. 26; Gal. 1:6-9; 1 Jn. 4:2ff.

*What does it mean to do "the will of My Father who is in heaven"?
For this is* **the will of My Father,** *that everyone who beholds the Son
and* **believes in Him,** *may have eternal life; and I Myself will raise
him up on the last day (Jn. 6:40 NASB).*

For all their outward gentleness and show of Christian profession and miraculous works, this is the one thing these false teachers never did. They never believed on Christ nor trusted Him for their personal salvation. Perhaps their Christianity was a "profession" by which they made money. Perhaps they mouthed some of the Christian truths in order to maintain their position with their sheep, but they themselves never inwardly accepted the meaning. Or, perhaps, they never professed Christ at all here on earth but were followers of another religion all together. Their resistance in the heart to acknowledging Christ as God was at root a moral problem they could have done something about had they chosen to. Because they resisted, they were ravenous wolves, but one day they will confess Him as Lord, although their opportunity for salvation has forever passed! Jesus will look at them and say, "I never knew you." As He said in the parallel passage, "I am the good shepherd, and I know My own, and My own know Me" (Jn. 10:14).

Only Believers Go to Heaven

In support of their contention that justification and sanctification are inextricably related, Experimental Predestinarians often point to the passages in which we are told that "whoever believes in Him" (Jn. 3:16) will have eternal life. This implies, they say, that a person who has believed in the past and then has stopped believing will not go to heaven because only "believers" go to heaven.

Now we would certainly want to doubt the salvation of any person who has believed in Christ in the past and then, for some reason, no longer believes. Furthermore, such an individual, even if he is regenerate, can have no assurance of his salvation because faith is the assurance of things hoped for, and if he no longer believes the things hoped for, he no longer has faith or assurance.

As argued elsewhere, it is possible for a truly born-again person to fall away from the faith and cease believing.[39] He is called a carnal Christian and will be subject to severe divine discipline. If this is not possible, then the warnings are empty of meaning, as will be discussed in chapter 10. However, Experimental Predestinarians are often impressed with the fact that in many of these verses the present tense of the verb "to believe" is used or the participle is an articular present participle meaning "the one who believes." The fact that these verbs are in

---

[39]See chapter 12, 13, and 19.

the present tense, they say, implies that Jesus meant that "whoever **continues to** believe" has everlasting life.

Thus, the simple offer of the gospel on the basis of faith has become, for the Experimental Predestinarian, something entirely different. When Jesus said, "Whoever believes in Him will have everlasting life," we are told that His true meaning was "whoever believes in Him and continues to believe in Him up to the point of physical death and who also manifests evidence of having truly believed by practical works of holiness persevered in to the end of life has everlasting life." The woman at the well, even Nicodemus, the teacher of Israel himself, would have been perplexed.

The argument from the articular present participle is simply wrong. While it is true that the present tense can sometimes carry a durative force ("continue"), it is not intrinsic to the tense and must be established from the context. The articular present participle, however, rarely, if ever, has durative force; it is merely a substantive.

The adherents of perseverance are reading into the term "believe" the meaning "believe at a point of time and continue to believe up to the point of physical death." This is not only foreign to normal Greek usage but to usage in English as well. We might say, "Whoever believes that Rockefeller is a philanthropist will receive a million dollars." At the point in time a person believes this, he is a millionaire. However, if he ceases to believe this ten years later, he is still in possession of the million dollars. Similarly, if a man has believed in Christ, he is regenerate and in possession of eternal life, even if he ceases to believe in God in the future.

The verses which promise heaven on the condition of belief simply do not logically imply that the real condition is that you continue in belief up to the end of life.

The notion that the present tense requires the sense "he who continually and habitually believes has everlasting life" is not only contrary to the normal conventions of any language but is not supported by Greek grammar. For example, Nigel Turner comments, "Thus in Greek, one seldom knows apart from the context whether the present indicative means, I walk or I am walking."[40] Although the present is a tense which takes the durative Aktionsart (kind of action, durative or punctiliar), the "Aktionsart is often difficult to determine in the present because of the lack of a punctiliar stem in the indicative which does not indicate past time."[41] Often the present has a punctiliar meaning.[42]

---

[40]James Hope Moulton, *Grammar of New Testament Greek*, 3 vols. (Edinburgh: T. & T. Clark, 1963), vol. 3: *Syntax* by Nigel Turner , p. 60.

[41]Ibid., p. 64.

Turner calls attention to the fact that the present articular participle "the one who believes" is often used " **where we would expect aorist.**"[43] "Action (time or variety) is **irrelevant** and the participle has become a proper name."[44]

Perhaps 1 Th. 1:10, "Jesus who delivers us from the wrath to come," is relevant here. The intent is to describe deliverance from the tribulation wrath. He is not saying that Jesus is the One who continually delivers us from the tribulation wrath. A deliverance once accomplished does not need to be habitually repeated.

In his discussion of the articular present participle J. H. Moulton makes a similar point.[45] This form has in fact, he says, become a noun and not a verb at all. For example, "the destroyer of the temple" of Mt. 27:40 is not "the one who continually destroys the temple." It even has a conative sense, 'the would-be destroyer' of the temple." It is used as a noun, and nouns do not have Aktionsart. John the Baptist is called, **ho baptizon,** "the baptizer" (Mk. 6:14, 24), not the one who continually baptizes people.

The timeless nature of the present articular participle is stressed by Robertson.[46] In discussing Mk. 6:14, for example, he says, "it is not present time that is here given by this tense, but the general description of John as the Baptizer without regard to time. It is actually used of him after his death." Agreeing with Moulton he observes, "The participle with the article sometimes loses much of its verbal force."[47]

Similarly, Jay acknowledges, "The participle with the article practically becomes a noun: **oi kakos echontes** ... virtually means 'the sick.'"[48] The intent is not to say, "those who are always and continually sick."

While it is horrible to contemplate, possible apostasy and cessation of belief is a very real danger set before the readers of the New Testament, particularly the book of Hebrews. Though it is possible that a man who professes belief

---

[42]E.g., Mt. 5:22, 28; 14:8; 26:63; Mk. 2:5; Mt. 9:2: "Your sins are forgiven"; Lk. 7:8; 12:44; Jn. 5:34; 9:25; Acts 8:23; 9:34: "He heals you," not "is continually healing you"; 16:18; 26:1.

[43]Turner, *Syntax*, p. 150. See esp. Mk. 5:15-16, **ho daimonizomenos**, even after his healing.

[44]Ibid., p. 150. See also Heb. 7:9; Phil. 3:6. He cites several examples of this aoristic punctiliar use of the articular present participle: Mt. 26:46; Mk. 1:4; 6:14, 24; Jn. 8:18; 6:63; Acts 17:17; Rom. 8:34; Eph. 4:28; Jn. 1:29: the sin bearer; Gal. 1:23; Mt. 27:40.

[45]James Hope Moulton, *Grammar of New Testament Greek*, 3 vols. (Edinburgh: T. & T. Clark, 1963), vol. 1: *Prolegomena* by James Hope Moulton, p. 126.

[46]A. T. Robertson, *A Grammar of the Greek New Testament in the Light of Historical Research* (Nashville: Broadman, 1934), p. 1111.

[47]Ibid., p. 892. Acts 2:47, **tous sozomenous**, and Gal. 4:27, **he ou tiktousa, he ouk odinousa**.

[48]Eric G. Jay, *New Testament Greek: An Introductory Grammar* (London: S.P.C.K., 1958), p. 164.

once and then rejects the faith is not a true Christian, it is also theoretically possible that he is genuinely born again. Even though Robert Shank would not agree, it is definitely true that saving faith is "the act of a single moment whereby all the benefits of Christ's life, death, and resurrection suddenly become the irrevocable possession of the individual, per se, despite any and all eventualities."[49] It is certain, however, that if he is born again, what he forfeits when he "falls away" is not his eternal destiny but his opportunity to reign with Christ's metochoi in the coming kingdom. "And he who overcomes and he who keeps My deeds until the end, to him I will give authority over the nations" (Rev. 2:26).

The Implied "All"

There are a number of passages which ascribe to the saints, in apparently inclusive terms, the benefits of the future kingdom. For example:

Do you not know that the saints will judge the world (1 Cor. 6:2).

Then the righteous will shine forth as the sun in the kingdom of their Father (Mt. 13:43 NASB).

You have made them to be kingdom of priests to serve our God, and they will reign on the earth (Rev. 5:10).

And to her it was granted to be arrayed in fine linen, clean and bright, for the fine linen is the righteous acts of the saints (Rev. 19:8 KJV).

Experimental Predestinarians read these passages to mean that "all" the saints will judge the world, that "all" the righteous will shine forth", and that "all" members of the bride are arrayed with "righteous acts."

It is obvious, is it not, that the word "all" must be read into these texts? The word is not there, and there is nothing in the contexts in which these passages are found which requires that it be there. It is true that the saints will judge (reign), but Paul elsewhere clarifies that only those saints who are faithful will reign with Him (2 Tim. 2:12). Only those saints who "overcome" will have authority over the nations.

Furthermore, it is clear that not all believers will function as priests:

Now if you obey me fully and keep my covenant, then out of all nations you will be my treasured possession. . . . You will be for me a kingdom of priests and a holy nation (Ex. 19:5-6).

---

[49]Arminian Robert Shank makes this statement in objection to the view of saving faith advocated here (Robert Shank, *Life in The Son: A Study of the Doctrine of Perseverance* [Springfield: Westcott, 1961], p. 195).

Only those believers who obey Him are priests. It was and is God's intent that we all attain to that privilege both here and in the coming kingdom, but to say that a disobedient believer has obtained that is contradicted by common sense and by the passage above.

With this the writer to the Hebrews agrees:

We are his house, if we hold on to our courage and the hope of which we boast (Heb. 3:6).

Being part of Christ's priestly house is not automatic to all Christians. It is the intent, the ideal, but it is actual only in the lives of those faithful Christians who persevere in holiness.

It is true that the righteous will shine, but nowhere does it say that "all" of them will. Furthermore, to be "righteous" in Matthew does not always mean to be in possession of the forensic legal righteousness of Christ, as in Paul, but to possess a righteous life.[50] It cannot be proved that justifying righteousness is in view in this passage. Only those saints who live righteous lives will shine in the kingdom. The unfaithful will not.[51]

As for the claim that the wedding garment is for "all" the saved, this is simply a misreading of the text. The text says only that the wedding garment, i.e., righteous acts, adorns the bride as a whole and not each individual saint of which she is composed. Each saint makes various contributions (righteous acts) to the bride's wedding garment, and some may or may not make any at all. There is nothing in the passage which teaches otherwise.

Another passage which is sometimes thought to be all inclusive is 1 Cor. 4:5 :

Therefore do not go on passing judgment before the time, but wait until the Lord comes who will both bring to light the things hidden in the darkness and disclose the motives of men's hearts; and then each man's praise will come to him from God (NASB).

Paul's statement in this verse has led some Experimental Predestinarians to the conclusion that all who are saved will be rewarded. When Paul says, "Then each man's praise will come to him from God," they understand this to mean each man without exception will receive praise. Yet Paul has just said that some will enter eternity with their work "burned up" (1 Cor. 3:15). He evidently does

---

[50]See, for example, Mt. 1:19; 5:45; 9:13; 10:41; 13:17; 20:4; 23:28,29; 23:35

[51]The "shining" could simply refer to the glory of the resurrection body which will, of course, be manifested by all saints.

not intend to teach that all without exception will receive praise. Instead, he is telling us that each man who has earned praise will receive it.

Christians Have Crucified the Flesh

Now those who belong to Christ have crucified the flesh with its passions and desires (Gal. 5:24 NASB).

It is common to understand this passage as saying that all true Christians have crucified the flesh. This is, of course, true. However, the event referred to is not self-crucifixion of the believer but the co-crucifixion of the believer with Christ at the point of saving faith. There is nothing here about a believer's determination to subdue the flesh as a part of the saving transaction. It simply refers to the positional crucifixion of the flesh mentioned in Gal. 2:20 and Rom. 6:1-11.

The fact that this is in the active voice rather than the passive voice as in the other passages has led some to believe that the self-crucifixion of the believer is involved. However, Paul elsewhere unexpectedly uses the active when the passive is meant (e.g., 1 Cor. 9:22) and the verb "crucify" is never used of the self-mortification of the believer. In Gal. 6:14 it is a positional crucifixion. Furthermore, the text refers to the **crucifixion** of the flesh, not a daily struggle with it. The word connotes a decisive death and not a continuing battle. The aorist tense is not to be translated "are crucifying" the flesh but "have crucified." The event occurred in the past and was complete and decisive. This makes the notion of an experiential crucifixion intrinsically unlikely here. In view of the fact that nowhere else in the Bible is such an experiential crucifixion referred to and that in many places our once-and-for-all co-crucifixion with Christ is found in Pauline theology, it seems best to take it this way here.

How did they bring about this crucifixion? They did it by believing in Christ. When they did this they took an action which resulted in the crucifixion of the flesh by joining themselves with Christ and His death, burial, and resurrection.[52]

---

[52]It is also possible to take the phrase "belong to Christ" is a genitive of source and not of possession. The Greek is "of Christ." This would mean that those who are of Christ in their behavior crucify the flesh. Some Christians are, and some are not. Paul does use the genitive "of Christ" in the sense of source elsewhere (1 Cor. 1:1, 12; 11:1; 2 Cor. 1:1; 3:3; 4:4; 5:14; 10:7 [see v. 2]; 11:13; 12:9). From this perspective then those who crucify the flesh are those Christians who are led by the Spirit and who walk by the Spirit.

He Who Began a Good Work

Reflecting with joy on the spiritual vitality of his church at Philippi, Paul says of them:

> *[I thank you] for your fellowship* [**koinonia**] *in the gospel from the first day until now, being confident of this very thing, that He who has begun a good work in you will complete it until the day of Jesus Christ* (Phil. 1:5-6 NKJV).

Some Experimental Predestinarians have understood this to teach that God will continually work to sanctify all who are truly born again until the point of physical death or the return of Christ. The lack of the continuing transformation of life is then proof that a man is not born again. Final failure is not possible according to this verse, they say.

However, as many commentators acknowledge, the "good work" to which Paul refers is probably not sanctification or regeneration[53] but financial contributions or a more general assistance and partnership, including financial help, in the cause of Christ.[54] This was their "fellowship in the gospel" (v. 5) for which he thanks them now and also later in the letter (4:15-17). The sense of "financial contributions" fits the context of the epistle well. Elsewhere, Paul speaks of "fellowship" (Gk. **koinonia**) in terms of financial aid,[55] and he certainly refers to this in 4:15-17 where he uses the verb form of **koinonia**, "to share."

If this is the meaning, then Hawthorne's suggestion that the phrase be rendered "fellowship in order to make it possible to spread the gospel" would make good sense. Hawthorne sees the "fellowship" as financial contributions.[56] He also believes that the phrase "a good work,"

> *cannot be shaken loose from its immediate context and be interpreted primarily in terms of "God's redeeming and renewing work" in the lives of the Philippians.*[57]

Rather, he insists, it is the sharing of their resources to make the proclamation of the gospel possible.

---

[53]This is grammatically unlikely. It involves taking an accusative, "the gospel," and rendering it as a genitive, yielding something like, "on account of your participation of the gospel."

[54]John Eadie, *A Commentary on the Greek Text of the Epistle of Paul to the Philippians* (Edinburgh: T. and T. Clark, 1894; reprint ed., James and Klock, Minneapolis, 1977), pp. 8-9. John Lightfoot, *St. Paul's Epistle to the Philippians* (London: Macmillan, 1913; reprint ed., Grand Rapids: Zondervan, 1953), p. 83.

[55]E.g., Rom. 12:13; 15:26; 2 Cor. 8:4; 9:13; Gal. 6:6; 1 Tim. 6:18; Heb. 13:16.

[56]Gerald F. Hawthorne, "Philippians," in *Word Biblical Commentary* (Waco, TX: Word, 1983), p. 19.

[57]Ibid., p. 21.

The "completion" of this "good work" would then be either (1) its continuation; (2) its consummation in being rewarded at the day of Christ; or (3) its achievement of its final aim--multiplied fruit in the lives of others through Paul's defense and confirmation of the gospel.[58] Indeed, Paul tells them that as a result of their contributions they have become partners with him in this defense and confirmation (v. 6). It is easy to see how this latter kind of "completion" could be carried on until the day of Christ. It is difficult to see how Paul could be teaching that their financial contributions could continue until that time. Paul is saying, "I am sure that God will finish what He started. Your financial sacrifice has not been and will not be in vain. God will complete it."

In other words, like many missionaries who followed, Paul is assuring his supporters that the good work of giving which they began will be completed by God with significant impact for Christ through Paul's ministry to others. God will take their contributions and use them mightily!

Conclusion

All of the major passages supporting the teaching that justification and sanctification are necessarily united have been examined. None of these passages require the meaning that sanctification necessarily will follow justification. Since none of them require this meaning and since the rest of the New Testament warns true Christians that they may not complete their sanctification in this life, it appears the Experimental Predestinarian view of perseverance is falsified.

In conclusion, one passage which will be discussed many times in these chapters appears to have conclusive bearing on this subject. Paul speaks of the believer's work as a building which is composed of either wood, hay, and stubble or gold, silver, and precious stones. The former refers to the works done by believers in the flesh, and the latter to works done by believers walking in the Spirit. One day a fire will be applied to this building and will reveal the materials of which it is composed. The wood, hay, and stubble will burn up, and only the gold, silver, and precious stones will remain:

> *It will be revealed with fire, and the fire will test the quality of each man's work. If what he has built survives, he will receive his reward. If it is burned up, he will suffer loss; he himself will be saved, but only as one escaping through the flames (1 Cor. 3:13-15).*

The apostle describes a man whose entire building is consumed by the flames; it is all burned up. That can only mean that there was not one work worthy of reward he performed during his entire life. Yet, Paul says, he will be

---

[58]The result of the cash gift in the lives of others is alluded to in 1 Cor. 9:13 where the result of giving was that men would praise God.

saved. Here then is a complete refutation of the Experimental Predestinarian assertion that justification and sanctification are inevitably connected.

True Christians are warned against the possibility of such a failure. In passage after passage the writers of the New Testament challenge us with a great danger. Unfortunately, our Experimental Predestinarian friends have taught many that the warnings do not apply to true Christians. They are only addressed to those who have professed Christ but have not possessed Him in the heart. This has in no small way contributed to the general loss of a sense of final accountability observed in many of our churches. This will be the subject of the next chapter.

A Note on "that faith" in 2:14

A few comments need to be made about the translation "that faith," representing the Greek definite article and noun **he pistis**. This construction has yielded three most common translations: "faith" (NKJV), "such faith" (NIV), and, as quoted above, "that faith." What is the correct translation, and what significance does it have?

First, it must be said that any one of these translations can be justified on the basis of Greek usage. The NKJV represents the generic use of the definite article. "Such" and "that" are essential equivalents, reflecting the demonstrative or previous reference usage.[59]

The translations "such" and "that" have led some to the idea that James is referring to two different kinds of faith, a faith that saves and a faith that does not.

In Greek, as with many languages, the article is often left untranslated, since in these cases its presence is meant to give the noun a generic sense. On the other hand, context often compels the translation of the article by its usual "the." Thus, the careful exegete must ask the question, when considering this verse, Why is the article translated "that" here? Most would admit that the translation "the faith" does not fit well, but translating it in its other normal manner, "faith" without the article, definitely does not clash with the context and indeed makes very good sense in context. Why not then leave it that way? Are the reasons for the translation "that" contextually or linguistically compelling? Or is it the reflection of a theological bias?

---

[59]For discussions of the use of the definite article in the Greek New Testament, see C. F. D. Moule, *An Idiom-Book of New Testament Greek*, 2d ed. (London: Cambridge University Press, 1959), pp. 106-17; Turner, *Syntax*, pp. 165-84; and DM, 135-53.

A study of the occurrences of **pistis** with and without the article in the book of James reveals that the word "faith" occurs sixteen times, including 2:14. In eleven instances (including 2:14) it occurs with the article,[60] and in five it occurs without it.[61]

In four instances the article is left untranslated. In none of the other instances where the article is translated is the translation "that" or any other word except "the." Although this does not make it impossible that the article in Jas. 2:14 could still be translated by "that," it does make it highly unlikely, with the burden of proof resting on the shoulders of those who translate it that way, especially if a theological point is going to be made on the basis of this translation.

Therefore, the most grammatically and contextually justifiable translation, "faith," shows James making a simple point: faith alone cannot save a man.

---

[60]1:3; 2:1, 14, 17, 18 (two times); 2:20, 22 (two times), 26; 5:15.
[61]1:6; 2:5, 14, 18, 24.

Chapter 10

The Possibility of Failure

The Reformed doctrine of perseverance not only lacks scriptural support for its view of sanctification, it also flies in the face of the numerous warnings against falling away repeated in nearly every book of the New Testament. Arminian theologians have pressed the warning passages vigorously upon their Calvinist friends, and in the judgment of this writer, with telling force. Unless it is possible for a true believer to fall away, it is difficult to see the relevance of these passages which seem to be directly applied to him by the New Testament writers.[1]

It is possible that the widespread acceptance of the Reformed view of perseverance is due, in part, to the fact that certain verses which seem to support it are given more attention than those which seem to deny it. When plausible refutations of a few "problem passages" have been offered in the theology textbooks, an implication is made that the remaining passages can similarly be explained. What many are not aware of, however, is that the entire New Testament is replete with passages which argue convincingly and decisively against the doctrine of the perseverance of the saints.

The New Testament Warnings

In order to set the Experimental Predestinarian difficulty in the full glare of the New Testament witness, it will be helpful at this point to peruse a few of these so-called warning passages and sense their importance for this discussion.

Few passages have entered more frequently into the discussion of perseverance than Jn. 15:6:

---

[1]As will be argued elsewhere, the term "fall away" does not refer to falling away from eternal salvation. It refers, rather, to a falling away from the path of growth, or forfeiture of eternal reward.

If anyone does not abide in Me, he is thrown away as a branch, and dries up; and they gather them, and cast them into the fire, and they are burned (NASB).

The difficulty for the Experimental Predestinarians is that Jesus is referring to branches which are "in Me," who do not bear fruit (15:2). It seems to be possible for men "in Christ" to be unfruitful and be cast into the fire and burned.

Speaking to the Colossians, the apostle Paul warns:

*And although you were formerly alienated and hostile in mind, engaged in evil deeds, yet He has now reconciled you in His fleshly body through death, in order to present you before Him holy and blameless and beyond reproach--***if indeed you continue in the faith firmly established and steadfast, and not moved away from the hope of the gospel** *which you have heard* (Col. 1:21-23 NASB).

There is a real danger here, a danger of not being presented before him! On the Reformed premises, there can be no real danger because all true Christians will continue in faith and will not be moved away from the hope of the gospel. He warns them further about the danger of "not holding fast to the head" (2:19) and of being taken "captive through philosophy and empty deception" (2:8).

The salvation of the Corinthians seems to be conditioned on their holding fast:

Now I make known to you brethren, the gospel which I preached to you, which also you received, in which also you stand, by which also you are saved, **if you hold fast the word** *which I preached to you, unless you believed in vain* (1 Cor. 15:1-2 NASB).

Young Timothy is challenged to guard against the danger of "wandering from the faith":

For the love of money is a root of all sorts of evil, and some by longing for it have wandered away from the faith, and pierced themselves with many a pang. But flee from these things, you man of God; and pursue righteousness, godliness, faith, love, perseverance and gentleness. Fight the good fight of faith; take hold of the eternal life to which your were called, and you made the good confession in the presence of many witnesses (1 Tim. 6:10-12 NASB).

Paul apparently does not feel that perseverance is the necessary and inevitable result of saving faith. Otherwise, why would he warn this regenerate man of the danger of wandering from the faith and need to exhort him to "fight the good fight"?   On Experimental Predestinarian premises all true Christians will necessarily and inevitably fight the good fight, and they will not wander from the faith. They will persevere in faith up to the point of physical death.

According to James, it is possible for a true Christian to stray from the truth:

My brethren, if any among you strays from the truth, and one turns him back, let him know that he who turns a sinner from the error of his way will save his soul from death, and will cover a multitude of sins (Jas. 5:19-20 NASB).

The "sinner" to which James refers is evidently a Christian brother. The conditional clause implies that it is by no means inevitable that he will always be turned back.

Likewise, the apostle Peter makes is clear that true Christians can "fall":

Therefore, my brothers, be all the more eager to make your calling and election sure. For if you do these things, you will never fall, and you will receive a rich welcome into the eternal kingdom of our Lord and Savior Jesus Christ (2 Pet. 1:10-11).

The conditional participle, "if you do" (Gk. **poiountes**), holds forth a real danger to the readers of this epistle. They might "fall" and forfeit their rich welcome into the eternal kingdom. Earlier, he suggested that they can become "ineffective and unproductive" in their knowledge of Jesus Christ (1:8). In fact, he teaches the need to have certain character qualities manifested in "increasing measure" and then teaches that true Christians may not have this increasing measure of growth and are nearsighted, blind, and forgetful of their being cleansed from former sins (1:8-9). Yet according to the Experimental Predestinarians, true Christians will always have an increasing measure growth and will never permanently fall.

The danger of falling away is repeated later in the same epistle:

His [Paul's] letters contain some things that are hard to understand, which ignorant and unstable people distort, as they do the other Scriptures to their own destruction. Therefore, dear friends, since you already know this, be on your guard so that you may not be carried away by the error of lawless men and fall from your secure position. But grow in the grace and knowledge of our Lord and Savior Jesus Christ (2 Pet. 3:16-18).

Once again the danger of falling way is something real for true Christians. Ignorant and unstable people have distorted the epistles of Paul, and this act resulted in their "destruction." That the same result can come upon these "dear friends" seems to be stated when he warns them "not to be carried away by the error of lawless men and fall from your secure position." Why would this warning be addressed to these "dear friends," if in fact it was not possible for them to experience this danger?

Consistent with the other passages studied, the apostle Jude affirms a similar danger:

> *These are men who divide you, who followed mere natural instincts and do not have the Spirit. But you, dear friends, build yourselves up in your most holy faith and pray in the Holy Spirit. Keep yourselves in God's love as you wait for the mercy of our Lord Jesus Christ to bring you to eternal life* (Jude 19-21).

In contrast to the nonbelievers, who do not have the Holy Spirit and who have caused division, these "dear friends" are warned that they must keep themselves in God's love. If being kept in God's love is the necessary and inevitable result of regeneration, why are they commanded to keep themselves? Surely the command implies that they may not. And if they may not, then the Experimental Predestinarian position is fiction.

The danger of failing to abide in Him is clearly in the mind of the apostle John when be writes to his "little children," i.e., his regenerate sons and daughters in the faith:

> *If what you heard from the beginning abides in you, you also will abide in the Son and in the Father. . . . And now little children, abide in Him, so that when He appears, we may have confidence and not shrink away from Him in shame at His coming* (1 Jn. 2:24-28 NASB).

We continue to abide in Him only if what we heard from the beginning abides in us. Failure to continue to abide is very real, not hypothetical, and will result in shrinking away from Him in shame at His coming.

According to the apostle, there is a danger that a Christian can "die":

> *Therefore, brothers, we have an obligation--but it is not to the sinful nature, to live according to it. For if you live according to the sinful nature, you will die; but if by the Spirit you put to death the misdeeds of the body, you will live* (Rom. 8:12-13).

It goes without saying that the possibility that a "brother" could live "according to the sinful nature" is assumed.

In the same book Paul issues another emphatic warning, a warning against the possibility of being "cut off":

> *Granted. But they were broken off because of unbelief, and you stand by faith. Do not be arrogant, but be afraid. For if God did not spare the natural branches, he will not spare you either. Consider therefore the kindness and sternness of God; sternness to those who fell, but kindness to you,* **provided you continue in this kindness.** *Otherwise,* **you also will be cut off** (Rom. 11:20-22).

In no uncertain terms Paul affirms a real danger of being in some sense "cut off" if we fail to "continue in His kindness."

In this famous passage the apostle himself acknowledges the possibility of failure:

> *Do you not know that in a race all the runners run, but only one gets the prize? . . . I beat my body and make it my slave so that after I have preached to others, I myself will not be disqualified for the prize* (1 Cor. 9:24, 27).

He warns them, by inference, concerning the danger of similarly being disqualified.

In 1 Cor. 10:1-21 Paul warns the Corinthians against the danger of failure. The whole passage is instructive. As demonstrated earlier, the majority of the Israelites were born again, and yet the majority did not persevere in holiness. Consider:

> *So if you think you are standing firm, be careful that you don't fall. No temptation has seized you except what is common to man. And God is faithful; he will not let you be tempted beyond what you can bear. But when you are tempted he will also provide a way out so that you can stand up under it* (1 Cor. 10:12-13).

He tells them that the experience of the forefathers was intended as a warning for us (10:11). It is clear that he has Christians in view, and not mere professors in Christ, because he promises them the assistance of God in standing up to temptation.

Few verses seem to have impacted popular consciousness as frequently as Paul's famous warning about "falling from grace":

> *Stand firm, and do not let yourselves be burdened again by a yoke of slavery. . . . Mark my words! I, Paul, tell you that if you let yourselves be circumcised, Christ will be of no value to you at all. . . . You who*

*are trying to be justified by law have been alienated from Christ; you
have fallen away from grace* (Gal. 5:1-4).

Marshalling his full authority as an apostle, he tells these Galatians that it
is possible for true believers to fall from grace, come under the yoke of slavery,
and become alienated from Christ! These strong words fly directly in the face of
the Experimental Predestinarian's claim that true believers cannot fall and could
never become alienated from Christ because they will persevere in faith to the
end of life.

The possibility of failure to "continue" is stressed by Paul in the famous
passage where he worries that he may have labored "for nothing."

*Therefore, my dear friends, as you have always obeyed--not only in my
presence, but now much more in my absence--continue to work out
your salvation in fear and trembling . . . in order that I may boast on
the day of Christ that I did not run or labor for nothing* (Phil. 2:12-
16).

These are "dear friends" who previously have "always obeyed." They are
born again. Yet there is a possibility of their failure to "continue to work out
their salvation," resulting in the apostle's labor among them being "for nothing."
There is nothing inevitable and necessary about their perseverance.

Can a true Christian fail to persevere and thus forfeit the prize?

*Do not let anyone who delights in false humility and the worship of
angels disqualify you for the prize* (Col. 2:18).

A true believer can, by his life, deny the faith and become worse than an
unbeliever:

*If anyone does not provide for his relatives and especially for his im-
mediate family, he has denied the faith and is worse than an unbeliever* (1 Tim. 5:8).

This person who denies the faith is contrasted with the "unbeliever."
Clearly, Paul is saying that a believer can be described in this way.

The love of money can cause true Christians to wander from the faith:

*People who want to get rich fall into temptation and a trap and into
many foolish and harmful desires that plunge men into ruin and destruction. For the love of money is the root of all kinds of evil. Some
people, eager for money,* **have wandered from the faith** *and pierced
themselves with many griefs* (1 Tim. 6:9-10).

The "people" to whom Paul refers include those who have wandered from the faith, i.e., those who have faith but are not in some way persevering in it. The result of this is many griefs. In contrast to these Christians who wander, Timothy is told to "take hold of the eternal life to which he was called" (1 Tim. 6:12).

That there is something conditional in the believer's future and that he faces a danger of not persevering necessarily and inevitably to the end of life could hardly be made plainer than it is in these verses:

> Here is a trustworthy saying:
> If we died with him,
>   we will also live with him;
> if we endure,
>   we will also reign with him;
> If we disown him,
>   he will also disown us;
> if we are faithless,
>   he will remain faithful,
>   for he cannot disown himself (2 Tim. 2:11-13).

The possibilities of failure to endure, of disowning Christ, and of being faithless are stark realities. To say that true Christians do not face these dangers seems contradictory to passages such as this.

Without question, the center of the controversy in theological discussion has swirled around the warnings of Hebrews. Perhaps no other passages of the New Testament more clearly reveal the weakness of Experimental Predestinarian exegesis. Confronted with the stark and drastic nature of these warnings, some of the most ingenious misunderstandings in the history of interpretation have been argued in order to avoid their force. It is sometimes claimed that these verses apply only to those who have professed Christ, and not to those who have really believed. This assertion will be responded to in a later chapter, but first, let us consider the warnings themselves:

> *We must pay more careful attention, therefore, to what we have heard, so that we do not drift away. For if the message spoken by angels was binding, and every violation and disobedience received its just punishment, how shall we escape if we ignore such a great salvation?* (Heb. 2:1-3).

Notice that "we" are in danger. The author includes himself as an object of this warning. Unless there are some contextual indicators to suggest this is an "editorial" we, there is no obvious justification for concluding anything else but that truly born-again people are the subject of the warning. It is possible for these Christians to drift away and as a result receive a punishment.

The apostle exhorts his believers against the danger of a failure to enter rest:

Therefore, since the promise of entering his rest still stands, let us be careful that none of you be found to have fallen short of it (Heb. 4:1).

It is possible that a true Christian will not enter rest. There is real danger, not hypothetical danger, here.

The warning becomes more forceful in this well-known passage:

It is impossible for those who have once been enlightened, who have tasted the heavenly gift, who have shared in the Holy Spirit, who have tasted the goodness of the word of God and the powers of the coming age, if they fall away, to be brought back to repentance, because to their loss they are crucifying the Son of God all over again and subjecting him to public disgrace (Heb. 6:4-6).

These born-again people[2] are in danger of "falling away." That they are born again is evident from the descriptive phrases applied to them.

There is no warning in the New Testament which is more forceful and direct than this caution against sinning willfully:

If we deliberately keep on sinning after we have received the knowledge of the truth, no sacrifice for sins is left, but only a fearful expectation of judgment (Heb. 10:26-27).

But are genuine Christians the objects of this warning or mere professors in Christ who were never really born again? Several things characterize those being warned.

First, they have "received the light" (Heb. 10:32). To be "enlightened" (**photizomai**) means to be born again and to have truly and inwardly experienced the heavenly gift and the personal ministry of the Holy Spirit.[3]

Second, they "stood [their] ground in a great contest in the face of suffering" (10:32). These people had not only responded to the gospel, they had suffered for it and persevered in their suffering for Christ's sake.

Third, they "were publicly exposed to insult and persecution; and at other times stood side by side with those who were so treated" (10:33). The public nature of their confession of Christ resulted in public ridicule and persecution. But

---

[2]That these readers are regenerate will be established in chapter 19.

[3]This will be substantiated in chapter 19.

far from backing away, they pressed on and joined with others who were similarly treated.

Fourth, they sympathized with those in prison (10:34). Risking danger to their own lives, they visited persecuted brothers and sisters in prison, thereby publicly identifying themselves to hostile authorities as Christian sympathizers.

Fifth, they "joyfully accepted the confiscation of [their] property" (10:34). Furthermore, they accepted this confiscation for the right motives, "because you knew that you yourselves had better and lasting possessions." They were focused on the eternal inheritance which the faithful will acquire.

Finally, he specifically says they have been "sanctified":

How much severer punishment do you think he will deserve who has trampled under foot the Son of God, and has regarded as unclean the blood of the covenant **by which he was sanctified,** *and has insulted the Spirit of grace?* (Heb. 10:29 NASB).

Sanctification in Hebrews looks at the imputation of the justifying righteousness of Christ from the vantage point of being qualified to enter the presence of God to worship and seek help in time of need (Heb. 10:10, 14, 19). It is possible for men who have been the recipients of this sanctification to trample under foot the Son of God and insult the Spirit of grace.

Does the writer of this epistle doubt their salvation? No! What he worries about is their loss of reward. He says:

So do not throw away your confidence; it will be richly rewarded. You need to persevere so that when you have done the will of God, you will receive what he has promised (Heb. 10:35).

That he does not consider them mere professors in Christ is proven by the six things he says are true of them. In addition, one does not warn professing Christians about the loss of reward but about their eternal destiny in hell. One does not tell non-Christians to persevere in the faith so that they will receive a reward. Instead, he tells them to believe the gospel.

The exegetical and theological bankruptcy of the Experimental Predestinarian position is clearly seen by the following fact. In their system of assurance a man can know he is a Christian by reflecting on the truth that (1) he has believed; (2) he has the evidences of works in his life; and (3) the internal witness of the Holy Spirit. Now in the case of these people, whom Experimental Predestinarians maintain are not really Christians at all, all three criteria of their own introspective system are fully met. These people have believed (10:35, their "confidence); they have evidenced their belief by perseverance in trials and good works (10:32-34); and they have the inner testimony of the Spirit ("enlightened," 10:32; 6:4). If they are not Christians, then the Reformed view of assurance is false, and if they are Christians, the doctrine of the perseverance of saints is fiction.

Only a few of the many warnings of the New Testament have been considered.[4] This lengthy presentation, however, has been necessary in order to force a consideration of the breadth of the Experimental Predestinarian problem. It cannot be dismissed by plausible exegesis of a few difficult passages. It is contradicted by the entire New Testament.

The Reformed View of the Warnings

The Reformed faith has produced some of the most outstanding Christian scholars in the history of the church. Their contribution to the theological stability and apologetic defense of Protestant Christianity has been enormous. Yet the proverb remains true: "Brilliant men confuse things brilliantly." These brilliant men are not unaware of the numerous passages which can be quoted against their position and have spilt no little amount of ink in attempts to defend their view of the warnings in the light the passages cited above.

In response to these passages which seem to imply that the true Christian is in some kind of danger, that there is something contingent about his future destiny, the Experimental Predestinarians have replied that either (1) the passages are addressed to professing but not true Christians; or (2) they are addressed to true Christians but are simply a means which God uses to guarantee that they will persevere. In this system the evidence of the reality of the faith is perseverance in holiness to the end of life. All who are saved will persevere, and those who persevere, and those alone, are the truly saved. True apostasy is only possible for those who have never entered into a saving relationship with Jesus Christ.

In the discussion to follow, these two pillars of the Reformed response will be analyzed.

They Are a Means of Securing Perseverance

When faced with the many passages referred to above, Calvinists commonly say they are in many instances addressed to true believers, but they are not to be understood as saying that a true Christian can lose his salvation. Rather, they are in the New Testament to secure the obedience of final perseverance

---

[4]Other relevant passages are: 2 Pet. 3:16-17; 2 Jn. 6-9; Rev. 2:7, 11-12, 17, 18-26; 3:4-5, 8-12, 14-22; 12:11; 22:18-19.

which has already been decreed for those who are elect. Robert Dabney explains:

> *The certainty that he will not [apostatize] arises, not from the strength of a regenerated heart, but from God's secret, unchangeable purpose concerning the believer; which purpose He executes towards and in him by moral means consistent with the creature's free agency. Among these appropriate motives are these very warnings of dangers and wholesome fears about apostasy. Therefore, God's application of the motives to the regenerate free agent, proves not at all that it is God's secret purpose to let him apostatize. They are a part of that plan by which God intends to ensure that he shall not.*[5]

He then cites Paul's shipwreck at sea.[6] In this passage the apostle Paul is promised that he will not perish, but he warns the men in the boat that, unless they attend to the means of saving themselves from the storm, they will perish.

Similarly, Shedd maintains that the warnings are consistent with perseverance for two reasons:

1.   The certainty of perseverance is objective in God, but it may not be subjective in man. God knows that a particular man will persevere, because God purposes that that man shall. But the man does not know this unless he has assurance of faith. Believers which do not have assurance are subject to the warnings. "But one who is assured of salvation by the witness of the Holy Spirit would not be required to be warned against apostasy, while in this state of assurance."

2.   Exhortations to struggle with sin and warnings against its insidious and dangerous nature are the means employed by the Holy Spirit to secure perseverance. The decree of election includes the means as well as the end.[7]

But how can there be any warning directed to a believer who is sufficiently biblically informed about perseverance to know that falling from grace is for him an impossibility? How can something be subjectively possible for the person who knows it to be objectively impossible?

---

[5]Robert L. Dabney, *Lectures in Systematic Theology* (1878; reprint ed., Grand Rapids: Zondervan, 1971), p. 697.

[6]Acts 27:22, 23, 24, 25, 31.

[7]William G. T. Shedd, *Dogmatic Theology*, 3 vols. (New York: Charles Scribner's Sons, 1889; reprint ed., Minneapolis: Klock and Klock, 1979), 2:557.

Reformed theologian Louis Berkhof expresses a similar view:

But these warnings regard the whole matter from the side of man and are seriously meant. They prompt self-examination, and are instrumental in keeping believers in the way of perseverance. They do not prove that any of those addressed will apostatize, but simply that the use of means is necessary to prevent them from committing this sin. Compare Acts 27:22-25 with verse 3 for an illustration of this principle.[8]

Experimental Predestinarians argue that God's perseverance of the saints is done through means. Men are not passive. God's preservation of the elect assumes that He has determined from all eternity the final destiny of His people. It also presupposes the way along which and in which believers will reach that end and includes the means which must serve the attainment of the final glory. One of the means is the preaching of the Word, which of course includes the warnings.

The advocates of perseverance argue that, just because there is a cliff along the road and that travelers are warned not to drive over it, that does not mean they won't. God warns simply because human beings require motivation. He therefore appeals to their fears to keep them on the path. But the warnings do not prove that believers can fall. On the contrary, they are God's means of ensuring that they shall not fall.

Several objections may be raised against this Calvinist view of the warnings:

The warnings lose their force. This explanation of the warning passages, obviously directed to believers, is unsatisfactory. Shank observes, "The folly of their contention is seen in the fact that, the moment a man becomes persuaded that their doctrine of unconditional security is correct, the warning passages immediately lose the very purpose and value which they claim for themselves."[9]

Berkouwer attempts to state the value of the warnings for the Christian as follows:

Anyone who would take away any of the tension, this completely earnest admonition, this many-sided warning, from the doctrine of the perseverance of the saints would do the Scriptures great injury, and would cast the Church into the error of carelessness and sloth.

---

[8]Louis Berkhof, *Systematic Theology* (London: Banner of Truth, 1958), p. 548.

[9]Robert Shank, *Life in the Son: A Study of the Doctrine of Perseverance* (Springfield: Westcott, 1961), p. 164.

> *The doctrine of the perseverance of the saints can never become an **a priori** guarantee in the life of believers which would enable them to get along without admonitions and warnings. Because of the nature of the relation between faith and perseverance, the whole gospel must abound with admonition. It has to speak thus, because perseverance is not something that is merely handed down to us, but it is something that comes to realization only **in the path of faith.** Therefore the most earnest and alarming admonitions cannot in themselves be taken as evidence against the doctrine of perseverance.*
>
> *To think of admonition and perseverance as opposites, as contradictories, is possible only if we misunderstand the nature of perseverance and treat it in isolation from its correlation with faith. For the correct understanding of the correlation between faith and perseverance, it is precisely these admonitions that are significant, and they enable us to understand better the nature of perseverance."*[10]

He seems to be saying that the nature of the correlation between faith and perseverance explains the presence of the admonitions. But paradoxically, the admonitions help us understand the nature of the correlation between faith and perseverance! He is arguing in a circle although, typical of Berkouwer, his circularity is veiled in complex language. This is the point at issue. Do the admonitions "enable us to understand better the nature of perseverance" or do they help us to understand the impossibility of this Experimental Predestinarian doctrine!

But, we ask, if we have become sufficiently enlightened to understand that perseverance is inevitable and does not depend upon us in any manner or degree, how are we to become alarmed by these admonitions and warnings?

Berkouwer replies, "Faith always directs itself anew to this confidence. In this perspective it always discovers a fresh consolation, after it has allowed itself to be earnestly admonished."[11]

So we are to be first of all alarmed by the warnings and afterwards consoled by the promise of final perseverance. Therefore, a person cannot accept all of Scripture at face value at the same time. "He must oscillate between two contradictory persuasions, both of which are supposedly equally warranted by the Scriptures."[12] A person cannot be motivated by the warnings until he has abandoned the promise that perseverance is inevitable and apostasy is impossible. And if it is inevitable that a person will heed the warnings and the Christian knows this, then how is he alarmed?

---

[10]C. G. Berkouwer, *Faith and Perseverance* (Grand Rapids: Eerdmans, 1958), p. 110.

[11]Berkouwer, p. 122.

[12]Shank, p. 167.

Berkouwer, like many Calvinists, appeals to irresistible grace. The warnings do not prove that the elect are in danger of apostasy, but they are necessary to prevent the elect from apostasy. The elect cannot fall because they are elect, and God keeps them from falling by giving them exhortations to which they will infallibly respond. However, since this irresistible grace is not powerful enough to keep us from some sins, how can we be confident that it is powerful enough to keep us from falling away? Of course, the grace of God is stronger than temptation, but will it inevitably overcome temptation?

It might also be asked, "How does this Calvinist response differ from the arguments commonly offered for universalism?" The universalist claims that the warnings about hell must be taken seriously by non-Christians, even though all the non-Christians will ultimately end up in heaven anyway! The Calvinist is saying that Christians should take the warnings seriously, even though they will all end up in heaven as well. The Calvinist is treating the warnings with no more seriousness than the universalist is treating the threats of eternal hell.

Arminian writer I. Howard Marshall criticizes Berkouwer along these same lines.[13] Paradoxically, Marshall has a view of the relationship between faith and perseverance that is almost exactly the same as Berkouwer's. The difference is that Marshall's Arminianism allows him to take the warnings seriously, that a real danger exits. The believer perseveres by trust in God for help. If he chooses not to trust God for help, he will not persevere and will therefore lose his salvation. Berkouwer is virtually saying that the true believer always will trust God for help. But how does Berkouwer know this is true, unless he knows before he begins his exegesis that the Reformed doctrine of perseverance in holiness is fact? The Partaker also takes the warnings seriously, but he finds no contextual justification for the Arminian conclusion that these warnings threaten loss of salvation. Rather, in each instance a millennial disinheritance or a judgment in time is forecast.

It is logically contradictory. Not only do the warnings lose their force in the Experimental Predestinarian system, but this view of the warnings is logically contradictory. On the one hand, we are told that our eternal destiny is secure and that we will persevere in holiness to the final hour. On the other hand, we are told that there is no guarantee we will. Otherwise, the warnings would lose their force!

Berkouwer states this plainly. He says there is no factor in man which may determine the issue of perseverance, for "in this way the consolation of perseverance would most certainly be lost, because the final outcome would be put again in the hands of persevering man."[14] Yet later, as quoted above, he has said, "the

---

[13]I. Howard Marshall, *Kept by the Power of God* (Minneapolis: Bethany House, 1969), p. 206.

[14]Berkouwer, p. 220.

doctrine of the perseverance of the saints can never become an a priori guarantee in the life of believers which would enable them to get along without the admonitions and warnings."[15]

Shank summarizes:

But if the "consolation of perseverance" is the assurance that the final outcome is not in the hands of persevering man, does not this "consolation" constitute "an **a priori** *guarantee" of perseverance for all who embrace it? If it does not constitute such a guarantee, just what does it constitute? And if the final outcome is in no way in the hands of persevering man, then how can "the alarming admonitions" be sincere?*[16]

An alarming illustration of this contradiction can be found in the famous commentary on Hebrews by Arthur Pink.[17] Pink seems to border on "another gospel" in his efforts to guarantee that all true Christians will persevere in holiness to the end of life.

First of all, he refutes the Calvinist position that Heb. 10:26 refers to unregenerate professors of Christ.[18] For Pink the fact that the apostle uses "we" proves that regenerate believers are in view. Now he wades in: "If it be impossible for truly regenerated people to ever perish, then why would the Holy Spirit move the apostle to so much in hypothetically describing the irremediable doom **if** they should apostatize."[19] Good question. He now treats us to the "answer." The Christian must always be viewed from two perspectives:

1.   As he exists in the purpose of God--eternally secure.
2.   As he exists in himself--in need of solemn warnings and exhortations

In Heb. 10, according to Pink, we see the Christian as he exists in himself, and not in the eternal purpose of God.

We must consider the relationship between God's eternal plan and the predetermined means to bring it about:

God has eternally decreed that every regenerated soul shall get safely through to Heaven, yet He certainly has not ordained that any shall do so whether or not they use the means which He has appointed for their

---

[15]Ibid., p. 110.

[16]Shank, p. 168.

[17]Arthur Pink, *An Exposition of Hebrews* (Grand Rapids: Baker, 1968), pp. 614-24.

[18]Ibid., p. 615.

[19]Ibid.

*preservation. Christians are "kept by the power of God **through** faith"
(I Pet 1:5) - there is the human responsibility side.*[20]

Looked at in himself, the Christian can apostatize. Such a statement is ridiculous. Look at him anyway you want. If God has ordained him to life, to life he will go.

> *To say that real Christians need no such warning because they cannot possibly commit that sin, is, we repeat to lose sight of the connection which God Himself has established between His predestined ends and the means whereby they are reached. The end to which God has pre-destined His people is their eternal bliss in Heaven, and one of the means by which that end is reached, is through their taking heed to the solemn warning He has given against that which would prevent their reaching Heaven.*"[21]

One is reminded of the two Texas farm boys listening to the expositions of a brilliant theologian. After what appeared to be a thoroughly confusing "explanation" of an objection raised against his position, one boy turned to the other and said, "What'd he say?" And the other replied, "I think he said, 'That dog won't hunt.'" How Pink can offer this as a serious explanation of the objec-tion to Calvinist interpretation is baffling. Apparently we are to hold two contra-dictory ideas in our minds at once: viewed from God's perspective, the Christian is eternally secure, but viewed from the Christians perspective, that is "in him-self," he is not.

If it is true that the readers are true Christians and that they are therefore eternally secure, it is ludicrous to think that the warnings would have any signifi-cant impact.

But Pink then goes on to confuse the issue by attempting to make the warnings real and insisting that the Christian can lose his salvation if he does not heed the warnings! He warns that each of us "need to watch against . . . the first budding of apostasy."[22] Yet earlier he insisted that the Christian is eternally se-cure. So viewed from the standpoint of the purpose of God, he cannot aposta-tize, and yet viewed from the human side, he can! One can only marvel at such a convoluted system of theology, a system which can, with a straight face, teach that a Christian both is and is not eternally secure at the same time.

Instead of calling the contradiction between God's preservation and the necessity of our perseverance a "tension," as Berkouwer does, or "differing per-

---

[20]Ibid., p. 616.
[21]Ibid.
[22]Ibid.

spectives," as Pink does, Tosti likes the word "symmetry."[23] Tosti correctly observes that the Reformed doctrine of perseverance is extremely dangerous. "It requires one to walk along the knife-edge of truth; a path so narrow that even the slightest move to the left or right will cast one into an abyss of pernicious error."[24] To move to the "left," he says, robs the children of God of assurance, and to move to the "right" encourages laxity and slothfulness. The antidote to these dangers is to maintain what he calls "biblical symmetry." It is, however, impossible to maintain symmetry between contradictory concepts. Our eternal security either depends solely upon God's guarantees in Scripture, or it depends upon those guarantees plus our perseverance. If both are necessary, this is not a "tension" or a "symmetry" but a contradiction. If the latter is necessary, it is a salvation by works. Only an eternal security based upon the promises of God and completely unrelated to the necessity of the believer's perseverance in holiness can possibly be reconciled with the scores of passages which state the freeness of salvation in Christ.

Tosti's logic, like Berkouwer's, is curious. He correctly assumes that the Bible promises eternal security on the basis of the promises of God. He then correctly assumes that the warnings are directed to true Christians. However, since Tosti and Berkouwer think the warnings imply a danger of loss of salvation, an obvious contradiction is set up. How can God promise eternal security to faith on the basis of the death of Christ and at the same time warn those He has promised that their eternal security is only secured by their faithful perseverance? They may not, in the end, be saved after all! One would normally think he is either eternally secure or he is not. Also, one would normally think that such an interpretation was open to question. Would the Bible mysteriously contradict itself in so many passages on an issue so fundamental to our Christian lives? Tosti simply leaves the contradiction open and says, "For the Scriptures, then, there is apparently no unbearable tension or opposition between the gracious faithfulness of God and the dynamic life; because it is in the thick of the dynamic of the actual struggle of life that Scripture speaks of perseverance in grace. If this is the way the Word of God treats the subject, **dare we do anything different?**"[25] When our minds naturally revolt at such contorted theology, Tosti reminds us that the reason for these "apparent difficulties" is that our minds are yet fallen! Of course, if this is "the way the Word of God treats the subject," we would have to bow in humble submission. Fortunately for our emotional health and our intellectual integrity the Word of God does not treat the subject in this way. It seems that a contradiction of this magnitude could only be accepted by one who has a prior agenda, a commitment to maintain the fiction of the saints' perseverance in holiness against all logic and Scripture, which teach otherwise!

---

[23]J. A. Tony Tosti, "Perseverance: The Other Side of the Coin," *The Banner of Truth* 259 (April 1985): 13.

[24]Ibid., p. 11.

[25]Ibid., p. 16.

At least the Arminians are consistent. There is no mysterious tension or symmetry (a.k.a. "contradiction") in their theology. The regenerate man, they say, will be saved if he perseveres, but he can lose salvation as the warnings clearly teach.

Neither is there a contradiction in the position of the Partaker. What is in view in the warnings is not a loss of justification at all but a loss of reward at the judgment seat of Christ.

To walk on Tosti's "knife-edge," however, would require a theological degree to achieve. Surely, only those with a doctor's degree in theology would ever be able to believe such contradictory things! The Bible, however, was written to the unlearned and prosaic mind.

It fails the test of human consciousness. Calvinism has often enjoyed the sanctuary of the philosopher's hall. It revels in theoretical speculation and theological argument. When one reads Calvin's *Institutes* on the subject of election and reprobation, one often feels that some of the arguments are abstract and unconvincing. Sadly, but probably consistent with the spirit of the day, when he deals with his opponents, Calvin vitriolically assails their character in direct proportion to the weakness of his arguments. When confronted with the perplexing questions of God's justice in the face of election and reprobation, Calvin gives one strained answer after another, and then in each case, as if sensing the futility of his arguments, he falls back on the standard refrain, "Who art thou O Man who repliest against God" (Rom. 9:20). Indeed, that section of his masterpiece could be appropriately renamed, "One Hundred Ways to Use Romans 9:20 To Refute Opponents of Our System."

However, in contrast to the doctrine of election with its doctrine of perseverance, Calvinism must emerge from the halls of academia and submit itself to the test of the consciousness of men. If it is true that the warnings are to produce sincere alarm, then we must concede that it is impossible for one not to know whether he experiences sincere alarm. And it is equally impossible to be convinced that apostasy is impossible, on the one hand, and yet to be sincerely alarmed by the warnings against apostasy, on the other.

Is it not ridiculous to say that men can be alarmed by warnings regarding something which could never happen to them? Calvinism fails the test of human experience.

Is it not also debatable to say that men are to hold two contradictory sets of Scriptures in their minds at the same time and switch back and forth depending upon whether their need is for consolation or admonition? They are unable, on the Experimental Predestinarian view of the warnings, to view the whole of Scripture with equal sincerity at the same time.

Suppose a believer falls into grievous sin. What happens now? If he remains unrepentant, the Experimental Predestinarian will simply say, "This proves you are not one of the elect." He will say this, even if the believer has had evidences of faith and works in his life before this for many years upon which Experimental Predestinarians formerly taught him to rely for assurance. But this of course logically requires that assurance is impossible. No one can know in advance that he will not fall into some sin which will cast doubt on his election. Furthermore, the biblical warnings never say, "Look out, you may have never been converted." Instead, they encourage believers to "hold fast the confession of our hope without wavering, for He who promised is faithful" (Heb. 10:23).

It subtly redefines the basis of salvation. Those within the Reformed tradition insist that works are the results of regeneration, evidences of life. They are the "fruit," and saving faith is the "root." They are the manifestation which arises out of the essence of the new man in Christ. In this they seem to be correct. If a man is truly born again, he will necessarily and inevitably manifest initial evidence of such rebirth.[26] By this is meant a general openness to God and disposition of trust. However, not all Experimental Predestinarians have been content to leave the matter there. Some seem to have made perseverance virtually a condition of salvation, and not just an evidence of it. In this they are either taking the Reformed doctrine to an unjustified extreme, or they are boldly stating what it really means.

This view of perseverance seems to have a basis in the Westminster Confession itself. The Westminster divines appear to make salvation dependent upon a life of good works. The article on assurance reads this way:

> *This certainty is not a bare conjectural and probable persuasion, grounded upon a fallible hope; but an infallible assurance of faith, founded upon (1) the divine truth of the promises of salvation, (2) the inward evidence of those graces unto which these promises are made, (3) the testimony of the Spirit of adoption witnessing with our spirits that we are the children of God.*[27]

It is proposition 2 which opens the door for some rather extreme views of perseverance. The "promises" there are not the promises of assurance but the promises of salvation in the first proposition. The confession seems to be saying that salvation is promised only to those in whose lives works are manifest. It would not be so serious if they had only said the assurance was promised to those in whose lives works are manifest.

---

[26]What is being argued in this book is that this manifestation is inadequate to base assurance upon and will not necessarily continue to the final hour.

[27]"Westminster Confession of Faith," in Schaff, 3:638 (18:3).

That they mean that salvation is to be achieved by works is confirmed in the Shorter Catechism.

> *Ques. 90. How is the Word to be read and heard, that it may become effectual to salvation?*
>
> *Ans. That the Word may become effectual to salvation, we must attend thereunto with diligence, preparation, and prayer; receive it with faith and love, lay it up in our hearts, and* **practice it in our lives.**[28]

Steeped as we are in the Reformed tradition which teaches salvation by grace alone, we naturally recoil at such words and wonder, "Could they really have meant this?" It appears that they did mean this. Any ambiguity here has been removed in the writings of some Experimental Predestinarians.

For example, Arthur Pink, teaches that God requires that true Christians must "keep themselves" or risk eternal damnation.[29] Yet he unequivocally maintains the "absolute and eternal security of the saints."[30]

He is attempting to show that God preserves His children through means, that is, works. He quotes John Owen, that prince of the Puritan expositors, with approval teaching that works are a means of salvation:

> *But yet our own diligent endeavor is such an* **indispensable means** *for that end, as that without it, it will not be brought about. . . . If we are in Christ, God hath given us the lives of our souls, and hath taken upon Himself, in His covenant, the preservation of them. But* **yet** *we may say, with reference unto the* **means** *that He hath appointed, when storms and trials arise,* **unless we use our diligent endeavors, we cannot be saved.**[31]

There is, it seems, a real danger in presenting perseverance in this manner. In his preoccupation with means to the end he in effect makes works a condition of salvation. They are the means by which the final end, bliss in heaven, is achieved. The only means to bliss in heaven known in the New Testament is faith, and faith alone. Pink has in effect added another condition beyond simple faith for becoming a Christian--persevering, positive responses to the warning passages. It serves no purpose to discuss the correlation between means and ends, God's predestination of means as well as ends, and enablement of the

---

[28]"Westminster Shorter Catechism," in Schaff, 3:696 (Q. 90). See also Schaff, Question 85, 3:694.

[29]Pink, *Hebrews*, p. 601.

[30]Ibid., p. 599.

[31]John Owen, *Hebrews*, cited by Pink, p. 600.

means. Perseverance is not part of the gospel, and when added to it, the gospel is changed.

Sensing the apparent difficulty of his position, Pink then shifts the terms. Those who apostatize are not really Christians at all; they were mere professors![32] He started his discussion by saying that Heb. 10 applies to true Christians, and now, faced with the fact that the warnings are real and that final damnation is in view, he shifts to calling them professing Christians.

He rails against the carnal security offered by "dead" preachers who have led people to believe that "guilt can nevermore rest upon them, and that no matter what sins they commit, nothing can possibly jeopardize their eternal interests."[33] Of course, if they are eternally secure in the purpose of God, which Pink believes, nothing can! He says that some Christians sin with a high hand because all they have to lose is "some millennial crown or reward." Then he declares his views even more clearly: "the blood of Christ covers no sins that have not been truly repented of and confessed to God with a broken heart."

If all he means is that, if Christians do not confess their sins, they will not be restored to fellowship with God, then all would agree. But he does not mean that. He means that a Christian who does not repent is really not a Christian at all and is "hastening to Hell as swiftly as time wings its flight."[34]

Perhaps Mr. Pink has forgotten the promise in the book on which he wrote his commentary, "Their sins and lawless acts I will remember no more" (Heb. 10:17). Indeed, he seems to have forgotten the gospel itself. He would have us believe that Heb. 10:26 applies to true Christians and only to professing Christians at the same time. The only reason for shifting to the fact that they must be professing Christians is the demands of his theology.

It is interesting that an Arminian, Robert Shank, and Pink agree on this point, that salvation must be earned by attention to the means of its attainment-- faithful perseverance.[35]

One of the most blatant statements of perseverance comes from Christian Friedrich Kling. He views **adokimos**, "disapproved," as losing salvation and says:

A sound belief in the doctrine of the saints' perseverance is ever accompanied with a conviction of the possibility of failure and of the absolute necessity of using our utmost endeavor in order to final success. No experiences of Divine favor in the past, no circumstances, however

[32]Pink, 618.
[33]Ibid.
[34]Ibid.
[35]Shank, p. 299.

advantageous, furnish such a guarantee of salvation as to warrant spiritual repose. There is no perseverance without conscious and determined persevering, and the requisite effort can be put forth only under the influence alike of hope and fear. And he who apprehends no danger of being ultimately a castaway through neglect or transgression, will lack the motive necessary to urge him triumphantly to the goal.[36]

If ever a statement of works as a condition of salvation was made, this is it. While we may be saved by faith, we are kept saved by works exactly as the Arminian maintains. Kling thinks that the Christian must be continually in fear of hell if he is to be sufficiently motivated towards a godly life.

Maurice Roberts, a contributor to the Experimental Predestinarian journal *The Banner of Truth* writes, "There are conditions to be fulfilled if Heaven is to be ours."[37] His condition is perseverance. This condition, however, is to be fulfilled by God's effectual work in the regenerate. But we must cooperate with God in this work. So salvation in this system is initial belief coupled with a life-long synergism of human and divine work. Only when the condition is fulfilled, can heaven be ours. But the condition of perseverance cannot be fulfilled until we have persevered. Thus, we can have no certainty of our perseverance, and hence of our salvation, until the final hour. A doctrine leading to this conclusion seems to fly in the face of the numerous biblical statements offering assurance now.

It seems that Pink, Owen, Kling, and Roberts are simply being honest about the real meaning of the Reformed doctrine of perseverance. Their concern about antinomianism and Scriptures which contradict their system have boxed them into a distortion of their own doctrine. They start out by saying that the warnings are the means of securing perseverance and end up by saying that it is our obedience to those warnings which finally saves us. They subtly make this shift because they are undoubtedly aware that merely warning a man will not guarantee he will obey. Thus, one needs to make his actual obedience the necessary ingredient for obtaining heaven. This indeed shuts out all possibility of antinomianism, and for this they are to be commended. However, the price is too high--it is another gospel!

Not only does the fear of antinomianism cause them to make this shift, but the Scriptures themselves present obedience as a means of obtaining the desired spiritual result. If the desired spiritual result is entrance into heaven, as they maintain, then it would appear that works have crept into the gospel through the back door. Faced with such passages as "if you hold to my teaching, you are re-

---

[36]Christian Friedrich Kling, "The First Epistle of Paul to the Corinthians," in *Lange's,* 10:210.

[37]Maurice Roberts, "Final Perseverance," *The Banner of Truth* 265 (October 1985): 11.

ally my disciples"[38] or "if anyone does not hate his father, . . . even his own life, he cannot be my disciple."[39] Experimental Predestinarians teach that not only are the warnings means to salvation, but hating your life, your father, and holding onto the teaching of Christ are, too. These are presented as means for the certain spiritual result--discipleship. Since in their system discipleship is to be equated with salvation itself, they are boxed into explaining how such works can be a means of obtaining salvation.

So, on the one hand, they tell us that the warnings are the means, but then, confronted by the need for an air tight case against the carnal Christian and the fact that the Bible speaks of works as a means of discipleship, they shift to saying that obedience is a means of obtaining eternal life. This is where all this confusing Calvinist double-talk about "biblical symmetry," "walking on a knife edge," "healthy tension," and "paradoxes" comes in. However, discipleship and regeneration are different, and the life of obedience, while obligatory for the Christian, is nowhere necessarily and inevitably united with regeneration as previously discussed. This double-talk simply veils the other gospel that is being presented. When others complain that this must be accepted as a "paradox,"[40] one is reminded of the man who threw dust up in the air, and as it cascaded around him, he cried, "I cannot see." The only reason for these mysterious paradoxes and tensions is a system of theology that will not allow the biblical texts to speak for themselves.

In their preoccupation with means they have forgotten that God has already told us what the means of salvation are and what they are not. Works are not a means, whether on the front end or on the back end. The only means necessary for obtaining salvation is faith, and faith alone:

> *He saved us, not because of righteous things we had done, but because of his mercy. he saved us* **through** *the washing of rebirth and renewal by the Holy Spirit* (Ti. 3:5).

The divine "means" are the washing of rebirth and renewal by the Holy Spirit, and not our good works:

> *For it is by grace you have been saved* **through faith,** *and this is not from yourselves, it is the gift of God--not by works, so that no one can boast* (Eph. 2:8-9).

The human means are one--faith. This faith is apart from any means involving works. How else can Paul say it? When Pink and his modern followers,

---

[38]Jn. 8:31.

[39]Lk. 14:26.

[40]E.g., John MacArthur, *The Gospel According to Jesus* (Grand Rapids: Zondervan, 1988), p. 140.

reacting to the moral laxity in the church, back-load the gospel with means, they are flatly contradicting Paul, if words have any meaning at all. In so doing, they seem to be preaching "another gospel" (Gal. 1:9). They are saying that, if one is truly a Christian, he will inevitably produce a life of works and perseverance. If he does not meet this requirement of being a Christian, then he is not a Christian at all and will not go to heaven. Furthermore, these fruits are not only evidences of regeneration, but they are actual means by which God intends to secure our ultimate arrival in heaven. However, requirements which must be met in order to secure a certain result, going to heaven, are in fact conditions necessary for the attainment of that result. And if a life of works is a necessary condition for obtaining the result of heaven, then salvation is ultimately conditioned upon works and not faith alone, and so the words of Paul have been turned upside down.

The subtlety of the Experimental Predestinarian argument is rarely perceived. Works are not, we are told, a condition of salvation but a necessary result of saving faith. Consider the simple statement, "If you want to arrive in Los Angeles, you must drive a car." A correct understanding of the gospel offer is more like a train. The train carries us to our final destination with no participation from us. We only sit. The car requires our diligent effort.

Condition: drive a car

Result: arrival in L.A.

Now to draw the parallel with gospel, we would say, "If you want to go to heaven, you must believe."

Condition: believe

Result: arrive in heaven

The person who drives a car to Los Angeles knows, however, that driving a car involves many things: turning on the ignition, use of the brakes, turning wheels, filling up with gas, and signaling with hand signals. Now it is true that use of brakes and turning of wheels are necessary aspects of driving a car. However, if one does not use the brakes and does not turn the steering wheel, he will never achieve the intended result, arrival in Los Angeles. All understand, therefore, that these necessary aspects are really conditions of arriving in Los Angeles. They are all assumed as part of the general condition, driving a car.

But the gospel does not include all these additional items in the word "believe." "Believe" is not a general term for a life of good works, even if driving is a general term for a number of works involved in navigating with an automobile. This is the precise point at which the Reformed argument falls. To believe is to trust and includes nothing else. If anything is clear in the New Testament, whatever belief is, it is the opposite of works:

> *Does He then, who provides you with the Spirit and works miracles among you, do it by the works of the Law, or by hearing with faith? (Gal. 3:5 NASB).*

> *Just as Moses lifted up the snake in the desert, so the Son of Man must be lifted up, that everyone who believes in him may have eternal life* (Jn. 3:14-15).

In the latter passage the Lord is equating "belief" with mere "looking." He is referring to Num. 21:8-9:

> *The LORD said to Moses, "Make a snake and put it up on a pole; anyone who is bitten can look at it and live: So Moses made a bronze snake and put it up on a pole. Then when anyone was bitten by a snake and looked at the bronze snake, he lived.*

The intent is obviously that a man should look with the expectation of healing and with belief in God, asking for help. A non-Christian who will not believe will not be healed, even if he looks. But the point is that looking and believing are synonymous terms.

When Paul and Jesus connect faith with hearing and looking, they are trying to throw it into the strongest possible contrast with anything connected with working. Hearing and looking are receptive functions. One sees when light happens upon the eye. One hears when sound happens upon the ear. Trust does not include a life of works! It "happens" to us.

But to pick an even more lucid illustration, let us explore the parallel with physical birth. We might say, "A condition of growing old is to be born." Now on Experimental Predestinarian assumptions, there are certain kinds of results of birth which are necessary for a person to grow old, such as eating. Hunger is a possible result of being born, and satisfying hunger is a necessary condition of growing old. Furthermore, unlike breathing, eating is a result for which we are responsible. We can choose to eat or not to eat. Here we can lay down a self-evident principle: a necessary result for which we are responsible which must be present for another result to occur is no different than an additional condition for the achievement of that second result. In the analogy of physical birth, there are therefore two conditions necessary for growing old, birth and eating, the former making the latter possible and the latter making old age possible. There is no difference between a result for which we are responsible and a condition! Let the reader ponder this, and he will discover that it is impossible to come up with an illustration which contradicts this fact!

Now a man who has been born physically might do a lot of things like brush his hair, shave his beard, and brush his teeth. None of these things, however, are conditions of growing old, and none of them are necessary results of birth. However, any result of birth which is a necessary condition of growing old and for which we are responsible is in fact a second condition, added to birth, for growing old.

Besides physical birth, the other human relationship which the Lord uses to describe salvation is marriage. Consider the marriage requirements in this country. If a man is to get married, he must have a blood test. Now it is clear that someone could break the law or, perhaps, some state does not require this. However, let us create a fictional world where this is always true. Then we can say the condition of getting married is a mutual commitment to do so. Furthermore, the necessary and inevitable result of that commitment is a trip to the hospital to get a blood test. In addition, getting a blood test is a condition of getting married. A necessary result is no different than a condition.

Imagine after reflecting upon the illustrations regarding marriage and birth above, you observe to a friend, "A blood test is a condition of getting married and eating is a condition of growing old." Steeped in Experimental Predestinarian ways of thinking, your friend replies, "No, that is not true. Securing a blood test is not a condition of getting married but a necessary result of a commitment to get married. Furthermore, eating is not a condition of growing old but a necessary result of birth." Your reaction would understandably be one of amazement. The blood test and eating are **both** a result **and** a condition.

Therefore, when Experimental Predestinarians use such phrases as "faith alone saves a man, but the faith that saves is not alone," they are in fact unconsciously speaking nonsense. Terminology like "faith plus works does not save, but a faith that works does" is simply saying that faith plus works saves. The cleverness of the prose serves to conceal the fact. Proverbial sayings like this have been passed on in the theology textbooks for centuries. They seem to have explanatory power, and they certainly left opponents of the Experimental Predestinarian system speechless, but in reality they are not only empty of meaning but contradictory. They are simply ways of saying that true faith necessarily results in works, but it is the faith, not the resulting works, which saves. This, however, is quite confusing. If the works are a necessary result of the faith and if a man cannot be saved without them, then the works are, in fact, a condition of salvation. If they are not present, the man will perish. Necessary results for which we are responsible are the same as conditions.

Notice the above illustrations spoke of necessary results "for which we are responsible." There are, of course, necessary results of spiritual and physical birth for which we are not responsible. Physically we may think of such things as breathing, heartbeat, and transmission of neurons across synapses. Spiritually we may think of the creation of the new man, our death to sin, our justification, and the gift of all spiritual blessings in Christ. But there are many spiritual effects of new birth for which we are jointly responsible with God. The Reformed faith maintains, and we certainly agree, that, while salvation is a work of God, sanctification is a work of God in which believers cooperate.[41] The entire responsibility for our sanctification cannot be laid upon God.[42] He is the source, the motivator, and the One who enables, but we are the ones who must do. We do it and He strengthens (Phil. 4:13). The Bible calls the unbeliever to do one thing, believe (Acts 16:31). But the calls to the believer are to work: we are to flee fornication (1 Cor. 6:18), present our bodies as living sacrifices (Rom. 12:1), and make every effort to enter rest (Heb. 4:11), to mention just three. Yes, the warnings, the commands, and the exhortations of the New Testament make it clear that man is responsible for his sanctification. We must respond to God's promptings and appropriate the help He gives. Berkhof puts it this way, "Though man is privileged to co-operate with the Spirit of God, he can do this only in virtue of the strength which the Spirit imparts to him from day to day."[43]

But if man must cooperate, then he must choose to do this. If he does not choose to cooperate, then he will not be sanctified. The numerous biblical illustrations of failure prove that a man may not so choose. It is therefore incorrect to say, as Berkhof does, that man deserves no credit. He certainly does deserve credit, and the Lord everywhere acknowledges that he will be rewarded for it in the future. Now if a man may not be sanctified, then he will not, according to Experimental Predestinarians, go to heaven.

Now, what shall we call this "cooperation" of man? What shall we call his decisions to pursue godliness? Could we not call them works for which he is responsible? And if we can call them that, then are they not additional works necessary to obtain heaven? If they are not done, the man will perish. If a person is responsible to do these works and if that person may choose not to (and both Scripture and experience confirm that he may), are not these works a condition of his salvation? If works are demanded as an essential part of the agreement which secures our final arrival in heaven, how is this different from works being a condition? Indeed, the dictionary defines a condition as "something demanded as an essential part of an agreement."[44]

It is at this point that the Experimental Predestinarian often feels that the one arguing against his position does not really understand his position. "Do you not believe in mystery?" he will often say. "Are you unaware of the mysterious working of the Holy Spirit with the human will in such a way that the result can be declared God's work and not man's?" In many discussions with Experimental

---

[41]Berkhof, *Theology*, p. 534.

[42]G. Walters, "Sanctification, Sanctify," in *New Bible Dictionary* (Grand Rapids: Eerdmans, 1962), p. 1141.

[43]Berkhof, p. 535.

[44]*Lexicon Webster Dictionary*, s.v. "Condition," 1:211.

Predestinarian friends, there is a tendency to retreat to "mystery" when the arguments against their view become too pointed or logical.

The writer remembers teaching a seminar to a group of Reformed students, and after giving some of the illustrations above, one of the professors asked, "I still don't see why the results of regeneration are necessarily works necessary for salvation. Regardless of what you have just said, it seems to me that these works are merely evidences of true faith, and not conditions of salvation."

The professor was thinking of the Reformed teaching that any evidential works are worked in the believer by God. But if we are responsible for these works and they are partly a result of our own efforts, then it is faith plus human works which are necessary for our arrival in heaven. As John Owen pointedly insists, "But yet our own diligent endeavor is such an **indispensable means** for that end, as that without it, it will not be brought about. . . . **Unless we use our diligent endeavors, we cannot be saved.**" He was not making a careless statement when he said this. He was simply stating the real meaning of the Reformed doctrine of perseverance. If these resulting works are **all** of God, then no human work would be involved, and they might, perhaps, escape the charge of works salvation. But if the resulting works are part God's and part ours (as the Reformed faith and Scripture teach), then a man may choose not to do them as Solomon and other regenerate men in the Bible often did. If he may choose not to do them, then true faith will not necessarily result in a life of works. Even acknowledging that God through "mystery" secures the cooperation of the human will, **man is still responsible and must do good works.** This means that works **ARE** a condition of entrance into heaven whether worked in us or done by divine aid. After all, Paul did not say, "**Christ** can do all things through me," but "**I** can do all things through [Christ]." Paul does the work, and Christ "strengthens." However, in the Experimental Predestinarian view, faith itself includes this life of works for which we are responsible (i.e., driving the car to L.A.), and therefore, faith is not simple reliance and conviction but conviction plus obedience. In other words, salvation by faith is actually faith plus works.

While we must certainly submit to the mysteries of God's providence, that doctrine does not really appear to be relevant to the discussion. The issue is quite simple. According to Experimental Predestinarians:

(1)   Perseverance in works is the means of obtaining heaven

(2)   We are responsible for doing these works

(3)   A commitment to perform these works is included within saving faith

Therefore, a works salvation is taught. If, on the other hand, perseverance in works is not necessary for final entrance into heaven and is not included within the compass of the word "faith," then the gospel of pure and free grace has been maintained.

A problem arises in regard to this doctrine in the way Experimental Predestinarians present it. Because in their view the warnings are addressed to non-Christian professors of Christ, they could be interpreted as commands to obtain salvation by works. Imagine, for example, an unregenerate church member. After observing his life for a period of time, one of the elders observes that he does not manifest the evidences of regeneration in his life. The elder, steeped in Experimental Predestinarian ways of thinking, exhorts him with the New Testament warnings to various fruits and works. Now what is the psychology of this? If the warnings are directed to the unsaved, then they are asking the unsaved to perform certain works in order to prove that they are saved! This is, of course, theologically impossible. The man's psychological response will be that he must do some works, manifest some fruits in order to obtain salvation. The warnings do not direct him to the grace of God and the gospel but to works he must do.

Consider, on the other hand, the psychological impact on the saved. If we are to assume that the warnings are addressed also to the saved and serve as means to achieve their perseverance, then a sense of law and not grace also pervades a man's consciousness. At the practical level a man who is saved is told that he must prove it to himself and others by works. When in his own or someone else's opinion he does not possess adequate works to justify the conclusion that he is saved, what does he do? He immediately begins to focus on doing good works in sufficient number to quiet his conscience and satisfy the opinions of fellow church members. For most no amount of works will be adequate, and any basis for assurance is lost.

An important distinction must be made here. As mentioned in chapter 1, everyone who is born again will necessarily manifest some fruit. What was meant was faith, a consciousness of sin, a sense of conviction or guilt, and a general sense of openness toward God. However, that is not all that is meant by "fruit" in the writings of Experimental Predestinarians. The above mentioned items "happen" to a man. The will of man is entirely passive. He receives these fruits freely, without effort, as a gift from God. This kind of fruit necessarily and inevitably flows from true faith. A life of good works, however, does not. It should, but a believer can quench the Spirit and turn from the Lord, as many biblical illustrations prove.[45] The kind of fruits being objected to here as necessary and inevitable results of justification are the fruits of progressive sanctification. In this kind of fruit the will of man **is** involved and cooperates with God in their production. A continual refusal to grow in the faith will not only inhibit these fruits but

---

[45]See Chapter 14.

will cause the believing "brother" to develop a hardness of heart (Heb. 3:8). When that happens, a man's sense of conviction, openness, and even his faith can be lost.

It makes God to be a liar. If God has decreed that His elect will finally persevere in holiness and if warnings are a means He uses to secure that perseverance, then God is threatening His elect with a destiny He knows will never befall them. He is telling them they might lose their salvation in order to motivate them by fear (read "healthy tension" or "wholesome fear") to persevere. How can a God of truth use lies to accomplish His purpose of holiness in His elect?

Consider how Calvin interprets Paul's famous warning to the Romans:

Behold the kindness and severity of God; to those who fell, severity, but to you, God's kindness, if you continue in His kindness; otherwise you also will be cut off (Rom. 11:22 NASB).

In his commentary on Romans 11 he says:

We understand now in what sense Paul threatens those with excision whom he has already asserted to have been grafted into the hope of life through God's election. For, first, though this cannot happen to the elect, they have yet need of such warnings, in order to subdue the pride of the flesh; which being strongly opposed to their salvation, needs to be terrified with the dread of perdition. As far then, as Christians are illuminated by faith, they hear, for their assurance, that the calling of God is without repentance; but as far as they carry about them the flesh which wantonly resists the grace of God, they are taught humility by this warning, "Take heed lest thou too be cut off."[46]

Calvin's "interpretation" here is not only empty, but borders on blasphemy! He is saying that, even though God knows the sinning Christian is elect and therefore saved, God terrifies him with "the dread of perdition" to teach him humility! Lest this be considered simply an aberration of the sixteenth century, listen to Andrew Fuller as quoted approvingly by Arthur Pink:

It is necessary for those whom the Lord may know to be heirs of salvation, in certain circumstances, to be threatened with damnation, as a means of preserving them from it.[47]

So God, on the one hand, knows this Christian will never go to hell, but, on the other hand, He tells him he might go to hell if he does not respond to the

---

[46]Calvin, Commentary, *Romans*.

[47]Arthur Pink, *An Exposition of the Sermon on the Mount* (Grand Rapids: Baker, 1953), p. 88.

warning! Thus, God is lying to this Christian, telling him something God Himself knows to be false! Experimental Predestinarians sometimes reply, "Well, God threatens the world with damnation, knowing that the elect will never experience it. Is this a lie?" The answer is that God has never promised eternal life to a man who has not accepted Christ. And the elect, prior to their acceptance of Christ, are subject to damnation. But once a man has become a child of God, born into His family, and promised that he can never lose his salvation, an entirely different ethical situation is present. Prior to becoming a Christian, the elect are damned, but after becoming Christians, they are not! It is therefore one thing to warn a non-Christian (even if he is elect) that, if he does not believe, he will perish. That is a true statement. But it is another thing for God to tell that same man, now that he is saved, that, if he does not obey, he will be damned, when God knows this man is now justified and will never be damned for his disobedience. It is true that the elect, if they do not believe (even though they surely will), will be damned. It is not true that the regenerate, if they do not obey, will be damned.

But not only do Calvin and Pink have God telling lies (in order to maintain their doctrine of perseverance), they have the poor Christian in contradictory states of mind. As far as we are "illuminated by faith," we know that the calling of God is without repentance. But in our struggle with the flesh we are to fear going to hell. So, on the one hand, we are to have a consciousness that we are eternally secure, and, on the other hand, because of our flesh we are to have a consciousness that we might go to hell. How can a person hold these two contradictory states in his mind at the same time? A consciousness of either logically and subjectively excludes the other. In psychology there is a term for the ability to maintain two different states of mind at the same time. This used to be called schizophrenia. Now it is called the Reformed doctrine of perseverance!

They Apply Only to Professing Christians

The second way in which Experimental Predestinarians respond to the problem of the warnings is to claim that they are addressed to professing and not possessing believers. As Martin Lloyd-Jones put it, "The primary purpose of the warning passages is to test our profession of faith in order that we may know whether it is true or spurious. They are given to warn us against the terrible danger of having a false profession."[48]

Dabney says the Arminian would conclude from his backsliding that he had fallen from grace and the Calvinist would conclude that he never had any to begin with, a fear which Dabney believes is "much more wholesome and searching that the erring Arminian's":

---

[48]D. Martin Lloyd-Jones, *Romans: An Exposition of Chapter 8:17-39, The Final Perseverance of the Saints* (Grand Rapids: Zondervan, 1976), p. 307.

*For this alarmed Calvinist would see, that while he had been flattering
himself he was advancing heavenward, he was, in fact, all the time on
the high road to hell; and so, now, if he would not be damned, he
must make a new beginning, and lay better foundations than his old
one (not like the alarmed Arminian, merely set about repairing the
same old ones).*[49]

Often Calvinists appeal to the wheat and the tares, the example of Judas,
and the rejection of those who say "Lord, Lord" and yet He never knew them as
proof that the writers of the New Testament viewed their readers as a group
which was mixed, professors and not possessors. However, this approach to the
warning passages is fraught with difficulties.

Differing contexts. First of all, this view ignores the differing contexts intended by the Lord's references to the wheat and tares and the New Testament
house fellowships which were in the mind of the writers of the New Testament.
When the Lord referred to wheat and tares, He was speaking of a theoretical situation in the church in general. When the writers of the New Testament address
their readers as "saints," "brothers," "brethren," and "little children," they are
speaking not to the unknown masses of Christendom at large but to their intimate
friends to whom they have ministered and often led to the Lord. We must not
read the present situation of large twentieth-century churches, many containing
over one thousand people, most of whom are not known well by the preacher on
Sunday morning, into the first-century church. These first-century churches were
small, personal "table fellowships," consisting of several families who knew each
other well. Participation in the Lord's supper involved, therefore, a commitment
to the other families.[50] Additionally, the presence or possibility of persecution
made attendance at these meetings no casual thing. Indeed, they often had to
meet together secretly in order to avoid persecution. Each house fellowship was
presided over by an appointed elder. So the intended audience is more intimate,
definitely Christian, and known by the writers. Richard Lovelace comments:

*Unlike most modern congregations the early Christian church was an
integrated community centered around the worship of God and the
advancement of his kingdom. Economically it was a commonwealth,
which meant that its members were not being pulled apart from one
another by the pursuit of individual goals of success; they were devot-
ing everything they were and owned to the strengthening of one another and the cause of Christ. Worshiping and eating together, the
members were in constant communication. . . . Little time or distance*

---

[49]Dabney, *Lectures,* 697.

[50]Johannes Behm, "**deipnon**," in *TDNT,* 3:801.

separated the members of this body, so there was an unhindered communication of the gifts and graces of each one to the others.[51]

It is emphatically NOT the same situation a Baptist preacher in the twentieth century faces when he climbs into the pulpit before eight thousand professing Christians. We are therefore fully justified in concluding that, when a New Testament writer uses a term like "brethren," he is not thinking that some may and some may not really be brothers, but he assumes and believes that all his readers are in fact born again. He knows these people, has led some of them to the Lord, has discipled them, and has maintained contact over the years by repeated visits and letters.

Requires unusual discrimination. But, second, if all the letters are viewed as addressed to professors and not possessors, then both wheat and tares will be required to be very discriminating in their reading of the epistle. The wheat must come to all the warnings and realize that they apply only to the tares, and the tares must realize that all the commands are only addressed to believers and that the real issue for them is to believe. Such a requirement almost guarantees that the epistles would be frequently misunderstood by their intended audience.

The writers assume regeneration. The writers rarely draw the distinction between wheat and tares in the very epistles supposedly addressed by intent to those kind of groups. In nearly every case the distinction must be read into the text and read into the author's mind. Nowhere, for example, does the writer to the Hebrews say, "How can we who claim to be Christians (and may not really be) escape if we neglect so great a salvation." The writers never qualify the warnings and never introduce the distinction which the Calvinist view specifically requires. Since the writers themselves never explicitly say that they feel their audience is a mixture and since they everywhere make statements to the effect that they are talking to genuine Christians, we have no warrant for reading into their otherwise clear statements qualifications which they themselves never make.

The issue is not the theoretical existence of wheat and tares but to whom is the writer speaking. That he can speak to wheat, tares, or both does not mean that he is. We can only discern his intended audience by studying the terms and themes he discusses in describing them. Everywhere he uses terms like "brethren," "sanctified," "holy brethren," and "children" and describes them as having believed and manifested a life of works (Heb. 10:35ff). While it is possible that mere professing Christians are in audience, he does not seem to have them in his thinking at all. The existence of these kinds of people in the New Testament fellowships was not an issue of conscious concern reflected in the writings of the New Testament writers. The fact that they may exist does not logically require that the writer included them in his intended audience.

---

[51]Richard F. Lovelace, *Dynamics of Spiritual Life: An Evangelical Theology of Renewal* (Downers Grove, IL: InterVarsity, 1979), p. 161.

But do they assume they are talking to genuine Christians and not to a group of professing Christians? Consider the book of Hebrews. Nowhere in the New Testament are the warnings more frequent, and nowhere is it more evident that the recipients of the warnings are truly saved people:

1. We are told that they have been enlightened and have tasted the good Word of God. They had an initial conversion followed by Christian experience as discussed above.

2. He calls them "holy brothers" and "partakers of the heavenly calling" (Heb. 3:1).

3. He warns that an "evil heart of unbelief" can be present in a "brother" (Heb. 3:12 NASB) and that such a person risks falling away from the living God as the born-again nation of Hebrews in the wilderness did.

4. The danger about which he warns them is not that they have not yet become Christians but that as Christians they might fall away (Heb. 3:12; Heb. 4:1).

5. He specifically says he believes they are Christians. He feels they possess the things which accompany salvation (Heb. 6:9-12). He acknowledges "the work and love" which they "have shown toward His name." On Experimental Predestinarian premises they have believed and have demonstrated the genuineness of their faith with works of love following. He does not exhort them to become Christians but, rather, he assumes they are and says, "And we desire that each one of you show the same diligence so as to realize the full assurance of hope to the end." He says that they have "fled for refuge in laying hold of the hope set before us."

The warnings exhort believers not to surrender a faith they already possess. I. Howard Marshall has correctly pointed out that, "if the Calvinist theory were true, the warnings would necessarily take such forms as: 'Make sure that you really were converted.' 'Beware lest what you think is an experience of salvation by faith is really nothing of the kind.'"[52] Instead, the authors of the various warning passages take the salvation of their readers for granted. These warnings, contrary to Martin Lloyd-Jones, cannot be construed as tests to find out if you are saved. They are everywhere presented to saved people, exhorting them to continue in the faith or to face some danger. They are warned against giving up a faith they already possess.

---

[52]Marshall, *Kept,* p. 201.

The warnings are never presented as positive commands to begin to be a genuine believer. They are meant to challenge believers to persevere and continue in the faith which one already has. They are never told to go back to the beginning and start over by becoming true Christians, but they are warned to hold fast to true faith to the end of life. Marshall summarizes:

> *The New Testament takes for granted a present experience of salvation of which the believer is conscious. Here and now he may know the experience of Christian joy and certainty. He is not called to question the reality of this experience on the grounds that it may be illusory because he was never truly converted; rather, he is urged to continue to enjoy salvation through abiding in Christ and persevering in faith.*[53]

Conclusion: Why Are the Warnings Given?

Contrary to the Arminian, we do not believe they are given to raise concerns about forfeiture of one's eternal destiny. Contrary to the Calvinist, they are not the means by which professing believers are to be motivated to examine to see if they are truly regenerate. Nor are they intended to motivate true Christians to persevere by causing them to wonder if they are really saved. God has more sufficient means than fear of hell to motivate His children. Rather, the warnings are real. They are alarms about the possibility of the forfeiture of our eternal rewards and of learning at the judgment seat that our lives have been wasted.

If the Reformed view of the warnings is correct, it would seem that assurance of salvation is impossible. For the warnings to present a real danger, assurance must be doubted. It is to this problematic situation raised in Experimental Predestinarian theology that we must now turn our attention.

---

[53]Ibid., p. 202.

Chapter 11

From Calvin to Westminster

John Duncan was born in 1796 in Aberdeen, Scotland, the son of a shoemaker.[1] Although not well known, his influence upon Jewish missions was great. He was affectionately called "Rabbi" Duncan because of his immense knowledge of Hebrew literature and his espousal of the cause of the Jews. In fact, when he applied for the Chair of Oriental Languages in the University of Glasgow, there was no one who was qualified to examine him. He read fluently in Syriac, Arabic, Persian, Sanskrit, Bengali, Hindustani, and Mahratti, as well as Latin, German, French, Hebrew, and Greek!

While studying in Budapest, he met a brilliant Jewish scholar, whom he led to Christ. This man was later to become the most learned writer on the life of Christ in the nineteenth century, Alfred Edersheim.

Becoming a Christian was not easy for Rabbi Duncan, and believing that he was saved was even harder. He struggled so desperately with doubt concerning his salvation that on one occasion, at a prayer meeting of professors and students, Duncan, who was presiding, broke down and wept, saying that God had forsaken him.[2]

In his quest to find subjective assurance that he was truly born again, Duncan turned repeatedly to Caesar Malan, through whom he was converted. Malan was ordained to the ministry in Geneva and apparently preached with great power and evangelical zeal. Malan's pastoral method of helping Duncan find assurance was through the use of a practical syllogism. He asked Duncan to consider the following logic:

Major Premise: *He that believeth that Jesus is the Christ is born of God*

Minor Premise: *But I believe that Jesus is the Christ*

---

[1]This historical information is from John E. Marshall, "'Rabbi Duncan and the Problem of Assurance (I)," *The Banner of Truth* 201 (June 1980): 16-27.

[2]John E. Marshall, "Rabbi Duncan and the Problem of Assurance (II)," *The Banner of Truth* 202 (July 1980): 27.

Conclusion: *Therefore, I am born of God.*

As the implications of this reasoning dawned upon his consciousness, Duncan said he sat still for hours, without moving, as many sermons he had preached came to his memory. The contemplation of the syllogism transformed his life, for a while. His new joy lasted for only two years and was followed by a time of terrible darkness. He says he prayed for the Holy Spirit and tried vainly to believe in Christ but could not. He then quarreled with God for not giving him His Holy Spirit and then rebuked himself for doing this. He thought that perhaps he was reprobate. He asked that the following words be published after his death:

> *I can't put a negative upon my regeneration. I don't say I can put a positive. Sometimes hope abounds, and at the worst I have never been able dogmatically to pronounce myself unregenerate ... Sometimes I have strongly thought that what is formed between Christ and me shall last forever. At other times I fear I may be in hell yet. But if I can't affirm my regeneration, I can't deny it; my self-examination can go no further.*[3]

He pursued another version of the syllogism. He reasoned that those who are born of God will produce the fruits of regeneration.

Major Premise: *Those who are born again will necessarily produce the fruits of regeneration in their lives.*

Minor Premise: *I have the fruits of regeneration*

Conclusion: *I am born again.*

Duncan's problem was with the minor premise. He simply could not be convinced that there was sufficient evidence of the fruits of regeneration in his life for him to draw the necessary conclusion that he was indeed born of God.

He wrote one more time to his spiritual mentor, Caesar Malan. Once again he told Duncan to reflect upon his faith and scolded him for not believing the promises of the gospel. He told him that the fruits of regeneration can only come after we have received assurance.

This did not help Duncan at all, and his struggles remained with him until his deathbed. In fact, his doubts were renewed with terrifying intensity. "I was in a terrible agony last night at the thought of a Christless state, and that I might be in it. The fear of it exhausted my faculties."[4] No doubt Duncan's healthy fear of

---

[3]Cited by Marshall, p. 27.
[4]Ibid., p. 28.

taking the grace of God for granted (antinomianism) contributed to his emotional state, but the methods employed to secure confidence are foreign to the New Testament. Nowhere are we commanded to look to faith or to fruits to find out if we are born again. We look only to Christ for that kind of assurance.

The incident highlights two things about the Experimental Predestinarian view of assurance. First, in order to know whether or not you are saved, you must employ what they called the practical syllogism. It went something like this:

Major Premise:	*All who have believed and who have the fruits of regeneration are saved.*
Minor Premise:	*I have believed and have some fruits.*
Conclusion:	*Therefore, I am saved.*

The actual implementation of the syllogism occurred during what they called the reflex act of faith, where the soul reflects upon its belief and fruits and concludes that it is among God's elect. This was in contrast to the so-called direct act of faith where the man trusts in Christ for justification.

Second, faith and assurance are separate acts of grace. Assurance is not part of saving faith but a reflex act of faith which comes later. Even though they bear the name of Calvin, they have completely departed not only from him in their view of faith and assurance but, in our opinion, from the New Testament as well.

It is possible that for many within the Experimental Predestinarian position this will be the most important discussion in this book. It would not be surprising if the previous and following chapters were skipped over in the search for the answer to the question, What does the author say about assurance? For the Puritans and their modern followers assurance of salvation is their magnificent obsession, 2 Pet. 1:10 their life verse, and the practical syllogism their chief practice. When Peter wrote, "Be all the more eager to make your calling and election sure," he unwittingly gave them a basis for four hundred years of introspection. Indeed, this verse could aptly be used to summarize the roughly one hundred years between the Reformation and the Westminster Confession (1649).[5]

If God has elected some to salvation and passed over others, how can we be sure we are among the elect? Our churches today are full of people who claim

---

[5]This writer is indebted to R. T. Kendall for discussion of the development of this theme among the English Puritans in *Calvin and English Calvinism to 1649* (Oxford: Oxford University Press, 1979) and in Scotland to Mr. Charles Bell, *Calvin and Scottish Theology: The Doctrine of Assurance* (Edinburgh: Handsel, 1985). Their contributions to this chapter are gratefully acknowledged.

to be Christians. In fact, according to a Gallup Survey over fifty million people in the United States believe they are born again. In view of the seeming lack of influence or cultural relevance of all these people as far as the gospel is concerned, one naturally asks, Are they really saved? It would be a terrible tragedy to "give assurance"[6] to someone who is not truly justified. We would then be assuring a man that all is well with his soul, when in fact he is on the high road to hell. It is this concern which seems to motivate the modern heirs of the Puritan tradition.

This is a book of exegetical, not historical, theology. However, since many who share these views of assurance seem to feel they stand in the tradition of the early Reformers, and of John Calvin in particular, it will be of interest to note that those who bear Calvin's name have widely departed from Calvin in this central fact. For Calvin, assurance was not a reflex act of faith but part of the direct act of saving faith itself. Our assurance, Calvin said, does not come from reflecting upon our faith but from reflecting upon Christ.

The period leading up to the assembly at Westminster produced many notable theologians in both England and Scotland. The contributions of several of these key figures reveal that the Preacher was right, "There is nothing new under the sun." The same struggles with assurance and perseverance which are present today were clearly manifested in their writings.

John Calvin (1509-1564)

Saving Faith

If Calvin were to be asked, "Where do we get faith?" He would have answered that its source is the intercessory prayer of Christ. We receive the gift of faith because Christ prayed to the Father and asked Him to give it to us. Faith is thus located in the mind and is not an act of the will or an initiative which we take in order to become a Christian; it is passively received. With unusual insight this towering theologian of the Reformed faith put his finger on the heart of the matter. Faith and assurance go together and are God's gift to His elect, and neither are the product of human will:

> *We shall now have a full definition of faith if we say that it is a firm and sure knowledge of the divine favour toward us, founded on the*

---

[6]One of the great errors of the Experimental Predestinarian is that he seems to think he has either the responsibility or the right to pronounce upon another man's eternal destiny. Better is the attitude of the apostle Paul, "Do not go on passing judgment before the time" (1 Cor. 4:5 NASB).

*truth of a free promise in Christ, and revealed to our minds, and
sealed on our hearts, by the Holy Spirit.*[7]

A firm and sure knowledge that we are saved is thus of the essence of faith
itself and is not the result of later reflection upon whether we have believed or
whether or not there are fruits of regeneration in our lives.[8] Calvin devotes several sections in the *Institutes* to explain and clarify this definition.[9] For Calvin
faith is knowledge. It is not obedience. It is a passive thing received as a result of
the witness of the Holy Spirit. It is "recognition" and "knowledge."[10] It is illumination[11] and knowledge as opposed to feeling; it is certainty, firm conviction,[12] assurance,[13] firm assurance,[14] and full assurance.[15] In all these descriptions the idea
that faith is an act of the will is absent. Neither are works required to verify its
existence in the heart. Calvin insists, "For, in regard to justification, faith is
merely passive, bringing nothing of ourselves to procure the favor of God, but receiving from Christ everything we want."[16] It is the instrument for receiving righteousness,[17] a kind of pipe through which the knowledge of justification is transmitted.[18] He makes the interesting point that the gift of faith and justification
comes to the elect by means of the intercessory prayers of Christ.[19]

This doctrine of faith leads to a view of assurance which would be quite
foreign to much modern discussion. The idea of "giving assurance" or of obtaining assurance by reflection upon our works would have seemed like entrance to
another culture to Calvin. Assurance is faith and faith is assurance. You cannot
have one without the other. Faith is a feeling of full assurance that God's mercy
applies to us. It is not a matter of rational deduction but something we know
within ourselves.[20] Calvin will go so far as to say that, if a man has no assurance,
he is not a true believer,[21] a view which seems rather extreme.

---

[7]John Calvin, *Institutes of the Christian Religion*, trans. Henry Beveridge, 2 vols. (Grand
Rapids: Eerdmans, 1964), 3.2.7.

[8]Of course there should be fruits of regeneration in our lives, but our assurance is not
based upon their presence or absence.

[9]See *Institutes,* 3.2.14, 15, 28, 29, 32, 33, 31.

[10]Ibid., 3.2.14.

[11]Ibid., 3.1.4.

[12]Ibid., 3.2.2.

[13]Ibid.

[14]Ibid.

[15]Ibid., 3.2.22.

[16]Ibid., 3.13.5.

[17]Ibid., 3.11.7.

[18]Ibid.

[19]Ibid., 3.11.3.

[20]Ibid., 3.2.15; 3.20.12.

[21]Ibid., 3.2.16.

The Basis of Assurance

What then is the basis of assurance according to Calvin? Christ is the source of our assurance. How? It is on the basis of His atoning work. We look for peace "solely in the anguish of Christ our Redeemer."[22] We are to look to Christ who is the "pledge" of God's love for us.[23] When we look to Him, He pledges eternal life to us. Unless we cling steadfastly to Christ, we will "vacillate continually."[24] Bell explains that, while acknowledging that the Scriptures call upon us to examine our lives, Calvin maintains that this is never to discern whether or not we are Christians:

> *When we so examine ourselves, however, it is not to see whether our holiness, our works, or the fruit of the Spirit in our lives warrant assurance of salvation. Rather, it is to determine that such assurance rests on the proper foundation of God's mercy in Christ. Because of the phenomenon of temporary faith, we see that our feelings are an unreliable test of our standing with God. Therefore, if we are to be sure of our salvation, we must always direct our gaze to Christ, in whose face we see the love of God for us fully displayed.*[25]

We ask not, Am I **trusting** in Christ? but Am I trusting in **Christ**? In other words, for Calvin the object of self-examination is not to see if we are saved but to be sure that we are trusting in Christ and not our works for our assurance.

According to Calvin, faith is the principal work of the Holy Spirit.[26] Calvin goes so far as to say that, "unless we feel the Spirit dwelling in us," we can have no hope of our own future resurrection.[27] In this experience the believer understands that the Spirit is God's earnest and pledge of adoption. This, in turn, gives us a sure persuasion that God loves us and is our gracious heavenly Father.[28] In this way the Holy Spirit seals or guarantees our salvation.[29] Calvin conceded that believers struggle against doubts, but the outcome is sure because of the Spirit's work.

Calvin said we should not seek our assurance in the doctrine of election, but the decree of election does bring comfort and confidence in our salvation.

---

[22]Ibid., 3.13.4.

[23]Calvin, *Commentary,* Jn. 15:9.

[24]Ibid., Jn. 17:17.

[25]Bell, *Scottish Theology,* p. 30.

[26]*Institutes,* 3.1.4.

[27]Ibid., 3.2.39.

[28]Calvin, *Commentary,* Gal. 4:16.

[29]*Institutes,* 3.1.3; 3.2.36.

Indeed, he says, until we know of God's decree of election, we will never know assurance of "the free mercy of God."[30] This is so because election means that our salvation does not depend upon us but upon God.

However, we should not involve ourselves in questions as to whether or not we are elect. Bell says, "When concern for our salvation arises, we must not look to God's secret counsel, which is hidden from us. We must not ask whether we are chosen. Rather, our concern must be related to Christ, since all that pertains to our salvation is to be found in him, and while, indeed, we are elect from the foundation of the world, yet this election is 'in Christ'".[31] Thus, Calvin speaks of Christ as the "mirror" of our election:

> *But if we are elected in Him, we cannot find the certainty of our election in ourselves; and not even in God the Father, if we look at Him apart from the Son.* **Christ, then, is the mirror in which we ought, and in which, without deception, we may contemplate our election.** *For since it is into His body that the Father has decreed to ingraft those whom from eternity He wished to be His, that He may regard as sons all whom He acknowledges to be His members, if we are in communion with Christ, we have proof sufficiently clear and strong that we are written in the Book of Life.*[32]

Or as he put it in his commentary on Ephesians:

> *But if we have been chosen in Him, we shall not find assurance of our election in ourselves; and not even in God the Father, if we conceive Him as severed from His Son. Christ, then, is the mirror wherein we must, and without self-deception may, contemplate our own election.*[33]

In other words, if we doubt our salvation, we are not to look to ourselves to find evidences of justification, but we should look to Christ who is a mirror reflecting back to us those persons who are elect. As we look at Him, we see ourselves in the reflection and have assurance of our salvation.

Calvin feels strongly about this. He not only asserts that faith is assurance, but conversely, he states where we cannot find assurance, by examining our works.

> *Doubtless, if we are to determine by our works in what way the Lord stands affected towards us, I admit that we cannot even get the length*

---

[30]Ibid., 3.21.1.

[31]Bell, p. 27.

[32]*Institutes,* 3.24.5.

[33]Calvin, *Commentary,* Eph. 1:4.

of a feeble conjecture: but since faith should accord with the free and simple promise, there is no room left for ambiguity. With what kind of confidence, pray, shall we be armed if we reason in this way--God is propitious to us, provided we deserve it by the purity of our lives?[34]

If we are not to trust in our works for justification, why should we trust in them for our assurance? While acknowledging that regeneration has its fruits, such as love, he avows that the presence in our hearts of love for our neighbor is an "accessory or inferior aid to our faith."[35] He insists that, "if we are elected in Him, we cannot find the certainty of our election in ourselves."[36] In his commentary on 1 Corinthians he says, "When the Christian looks at himself he can only have ground for anxiety, indeed despair."[37]

There is no doubt that Calvin would see good works as helpful to convince the believer that he is among the children of God, but they do so as confirmations of salvation and not as the basis of assurance. They bring secondary encouragement to the mind which already has assurance. He argues that the fruits of regeneration are the evidence that the Holy Spirit dwells in us, but only to the man who is already deriving his assurance from contemplation of Christ. When present, they reveal salvation, but when absent, they prove nothing. The evidences of holiness in our lives have no assuring value except to the mind which has already "perceived that the goodness of God is sealed to them by nothing but the certainty of the promise."[38] He continues:

Should they begin to estimate it [assurance of their salvation] *by their good works, nothing will be weaker or more uncertain; works, when estimated by themselves, no less proving the divine displeasure by their imperfection, than His good-will by their incipient purity.*[39]

While our obedience confirms our adoption, it is not the basis of our assurance. Our good works give a "subsidiary aid to its confirmation."[40] Love is an inferior aid, a prop for our faith. But even with this concession he insists that we must never "look to our works for our assurance to be firm."[41] If we want to know if we are elect, we must be "persuaded" that Christ died for us. We know this by a direct act of faith. We do not look for testimonies of good works in our lives.

---

[34]*Institutes,* 3.2.38.

[35]Calvin, *Commentary,* 1 Jn. 3:19; 3:14.

[36]*Institutes,* 3.24.5.

[37]Calvin, *Commentary,* 1 Cor. 1:9.

[38]*Institutes,* 3.14.19.

[39]Ibid.

[40]Calvin, *Commentary,* Josh. 3:10.

[41]Calvin, *Commentary,* 1 Jn. 3:19.

Thus, Calvin affirms: "If Pighius asks how I know I am elect, I answer that Christ is more than a thousand testimonies to me."[42]

Saving faith in Calvin and in the New Testament is a passive thing located in the mind. It is not mere assent to a proposition but includes the additional element of confidence or assurance. This basic idea is still held today by many within the Experimental Predestinarian tradition,[43] but confusedly. While attempting to hang onto the New Testament doctrine that faith is assurance, they have attempted to add that good works are the necessary and inevitable result of faith, and some even define faith as obedience or submission. As long as any works are **necessary** to establish that a man is of the elect, then works become the basis of his confidence instead of Christ. Calvin himself confused the issue with his doctrine of temporary faith (see discussion below) and with his insistence that repentance necessarily follows faith. As soon as some specific fruit of regeneration is said to **necessarily** follow faith, then it becomes difficult to avoid asking, Do I have this fruit in sufficient degree of manifestation to establish that my faith is real? Clearly, as indicated above, Calvin warned against this, but his doctrine of necessary works compromises his central, and biblically correct, belief: assurance is the essence of faith.

Furthermore, if works are either a basis of assurance or necessary for assurance, then it is impossible for a man to have assurance until works have been manifested in his life. This leads to the absurd conclusion that a man can believe in Christ but not know that he has believed. In fact, he cannot really know if he has believed until he finds himself believing at the "final hour." Then, and only then, have his works finally verified his faith to be that of the elect and not that of the reprobate.

He also taught that the reprobate can have similar feelings and evidences of regeneration as the elect. How then does one know if he is of the reprobate? Some means of discrimination are immediately thrust upon the Christian mind: Is my faith only temporary? How can I know if my faith is saving faith? Wherein do they differ? Having opened the door to a possible separation between assurance and faith (which he himself vigorously denied), his followers drove a truck through it and separated them forever.

It seems that Calvin's stress on the passive nature of faith is a valid biblical insight. It does appear that faith is something that "happens" to us. We are responsible to believe[44] in the sense that we are responsible to look to Christ, not conjure up faith. Clearly, faith is not located primarily in the will, as Calvin observed, for we often are forced to believe things against our will (the death of a

---

[42]John Calvin, *Concerning the Eternal Predestination of God*, 1961, p. 130.

[43]Berkhof, Warfield, Voss.

[44]See also Jn. 5:43; 1 Jn. 5:1; Jn. 3:16, 36.

loved one, for example). Also, it seems that for some people they would give the world to believe, but for some reason they just can't. To tell them that they can is to violate their consciousness.

Calvin's Doctrine of Temporary Faith

The scandal of the Experimental Predestinarian tradition, which the divines at Westminster passed over, was the doctrine of temporary faith. The origin of this odious doctrine is to be traced to Calvin himself. He based it on misinterpretations of the parable of the sower,[45] the warnings in Hebrews,[46] and the Lord's warning, "By their fruits you shall know them."[47]

The central claim of this teaching is that God imparts supernatural influences to the reprobate[48] which approximates, but does not equal, the influences of effectual calling. He is illuminated, he tastes, he grows, and he has similar feelings as the elect. However, it seems God is deceiving this man into believing he is elect so that God can be more than just in condemning him when he finally falls away. After all, the man had these "tastes."

Calvin taught three kinds of grace. Common grace enabled a man to do physics, produce a *Summa Theologica*, a Mass in B Minor, a painting, or a *Hamlet*. This is due to the general grace of God.[49] Effectual grace is that ministry of the Holy Spirit whereby the unregenerate are infallibly acted upon and inclined to believe and be saved. Ineffectual grace (the writer's term) is due to the ministry of the Spirit in imparting "transitory" faith or temporary faith.[50] Calvin argues this from Scripture on the basis of Heb. 6:4-5:[51]

> *I know that to attribute faith to the reprobate seems hard to some, when Paul declares it (faith) to be the result of election. This difficulty is easily solved. For ... experience shows that the reprobate are sometimes affected by almost the same feeling as the elect, so that even in their own judgment they do not in any way differ from the elect.*

---

[45]This will be discussed elsewhere. Each of the last three are regenerate as evidenced by the obvious fact that even the one with "temporary faith," the stony ground, evidenced life and growth.

[46]These warnings are addressed to true Christians and present the danger of millennial disinheritance. This is what they potentially may fall away from. See chapters 19 and 20.

[47]The fruit in view is not the character quality of professing Christians but the false doctrine of the false teachers. False doctrine, not immoral lives, is the fruit. See chapter 9.

[48]Those predestined to damnation.

[49]*Institutes,* 2.2.16.

[50]Ibid., 3.2.11.

[51]Ibid.

He does not think it absurd that the reprobate should have "a taste of the heavenly gift--and Christ" (Heb. 6:4-5), because this makes them convicted and more inexcusable. This is a consequence of a "lower" working of the Spirit which he later seems to term an "ineffectual" calling.[52] "There is nothing strange in God's shedding some rays of grace on the reprobate and afterwards allowing these to be extinguished."[53] This, according to Calvin, was "an inferior operation of the Spirit," the whole purpose of which is "the better to convict them and leave them without excuse."[54]

His discussion is worthy of extensive quotation:

Experience shows that the reprobate are sometimes affected in a way so similar to the elect, that even in their own judgment there is no difference between them. Hence it is not strange, that by the Apostle a taste of heavenly gifts, and by Christ Himself a temporary faith, is ascribed to them. Not that they truly perceive the power of spiritual grace and the sure light of faith; but the Lord, the better to convict them, and leave them without excuse, instills into their minds such a sense of His goodness as can be felt without the Spirit of Adoption. **Should it be objected, that believers have no stronger testimony to assure them of their adoption, I answer, that though there is a great resemblance and affinity between the elect of God and those who are impressed for a time with fading faith, yet the elect alone have that full assurance which is extolled by Paul, and by which are enabled to cry, Abba, Father.** *Therefore, as God regenerates the elect only forever by incorruptible seed, as the seed of life once sown in their hearts never perishes, so He effectually seals in them the grace of His adoption, that it may be sure and steadfast. But there is nothing to prevent an inferior operation of the Spirit from taking its course in the reprobate. Meanwhile, believers are taught to examine themselves carefully and humbly, lest carnal security creep in and take the place of assurance of faith. We may add, that the reprobate never have any other than a confused sense of grace, laying hold of the shadow rather than the substance, because the Spirit properly seals the forgiveness of sins in the elect only, applying it by special faith to their use. Still it is correctly said, that the reprobate believe God to be propitious to them, inasmuch as they accept the gift of reconciliation, though confusedly and without due discernment; not that they are partakers of the same faith or regeneration with the children of God; but because, under a covering of hypocrisy, they seem to have a principle of faith in common with them. Nor do I even deny that God illumines their minds to*

---

[52]Calvin, *Commentary*, Lk. 17:13.

[53]*Institutes,* 3.2.12.

[54]Ibid., 3.2.11.

these extent, that they recognize His grace; but that conviction He distinguishes from the peculiar testimony which He gives to His elect in this respect, that the reprobate never obtain to the full result or to fruition. When He shows Himself propitious to them, it is not as if He had truly rescued them from death, and taken them under His protection. He only gives them a manifestation of His present mercy. **In the elect alone He implants the living root of faith, so that they persevere even to the end.** *Thus we dispose of the objection, that if God truly displays His grace, it must endure forever. There is nothing inconsistent in this with the fact of His enlightening some with a present sense of grace, which afterwards proves evanescent. Although faith is a knowledge of the divine favour towards us, and a full persuasion of its truth, it is not strange that the sense of the divine love, which though akin to faith differs much from it, vanishes in those who are temporarily impressed. The will of God is, I confess, immutable, and His truth is always consistent with itself; but I deny that the reprobate ever advance so far as to penetrate to that secret revelation which Scripture reserves for the elect only. I therefore deny that they either understand His will considered as immutable, or steadily embrace His truth, inasmuch as they rest satisfied with an evanescent impression; just as a tree not planted deep enough may take root, but will in the process of time wither away, though it may for several years not only put forth leaves and flowers, but produce fruit. In short, as by the revolt of the first man, the image of God could be effaced from his mind and soul, so there is nothing strange in His shedding some rays of grace on the reprobate, and afterwards allowing these to be extinguished.*[55]

Aware of the obvious objection that the Spirit of God is lying to the reprobate, leading them to believe they are elect when they are not, Calvin continues:

Nor can it be said that the Spirit therefore deceives, because He does not quicken the seed which lies in their hearts, so as to make it ever remain incorruptible as in the elect.

Which is simply an answer by assertion and no answer at all!

Calvin says (1) the reprobate may have "almost the same feeling as the elect"; and (2) this is "but a confused awareness of grace." He goes on to say that the reprobate "believe that God is merciful toward them, for they receive the gift

---

[55]Ibid., 3.2.11-12.

of reconciliation, although confusedly and not distinctly enough." Moreover, they seem "to have a beginning of faith in common" with the elect.[56]

Calvin recognizes the obvious objection that a true believer could suspect his own faith to be that of the reprobate:

> *Should it be objected that believers have no stronger testimony to as-sure them of their adoption, I answer that there is a great resemblance and affinity between the elect of God and those who are impressed for a time with fading faith, yet the elect alone have that full assurance which is extolled by Paul, and by which they are enabled to cry, Abba, Father."[57]*

This answer would be of little comfort to someone who was struggling with assurance. In fact, it would just add to their fear. Obviously, a true believer can become discouraged and imagine that his faith is simply a "confused awareness" which the reprobate have. Kendall observes:

> *And if the reprobate may experience 'almost the same feeling as the elect', there is no way to know finally what the reprobate experiences. Furthermore, if the reprobate may believe that God is merciful to-wards them, how can we be sure our believing the same thing is any different from theirs? How can we be so sure that our 'beginning of faith' is saving and is not the 'beginning of faith' which the reprobate seem to have?[58]*

Thus, when Calvin bases his doctrine on an inner assurance given by the Spirit and then affirms that the reprobate can have a similar sensation, he ruins his argument.

Calvin has said that the reprobate cannot discern the difference between their experience and that of a born-again Christian. They believe God to be pro-pitious to them and to have given them the gift of reconciliation. Since both the reprobate and the saved can have these feelings, how can one know if he is saved? Calvin seems to be saying that the unsaved man has these feelings, but they are more intense in the elect and enable them to say, "Abba, Father."

He feels, however, that the differences between the reprobate and the elect are more important than the similarities. The primary difference is that the faith of the reprobate is temporary. Eventually it fails and they fall away. The

---

[56]Ibid., 3.2.11.

[57]Ibid.

[58]Kendall, *English Calvinism*, p. 24. (Emphasis is in the original.)

true believer is sustained.[59] A second difference is that the reprobate never enjoy a "living feeling" of firm assurance.[60]

Part of Calvin's problem goes back to his misinterpretation of the parable of the soils. The last three are all true Christians and are not reprobate. Therefore, there is no "temporary" faith taught here. Similarly, Heb. 6 refers to true Christians, not mere professors, and the doctrine of temporary faith is not found there either. Since the Bible does not address the subject of a supernaturally imparted temporary faith, should we speculate about it? Calvin's doctrine of perseverance, to which he was driven in order to defend the Reformation against the Catholic attack that it was antinomian, has forced him to interpret these passages in a way contrary to their obvious meaning. We should assume that those who produce fruit, who take root, who grow, who are illumined, and who have tasted the heavenly gift are genuinely born again even if they do fall away in the future. We will see them in heaven if they genuinely believed. We do not know if they have, but a lack of enduring fruit does not prove they are reprobate.

In the final analysis Calvin has thrown away the possibility of assurance, at least until the final hour. When he grants that the only certain difference between the faith of the elect and the faith of the reprobate is that the faith of the former perseveres to the end, he makes assurance now virtually impossible. As Shank has insisted:

> *Obviously, it can be known only as one finally perseveres (or fails to persevere) in faith. There is no valid assurance of election and final salvation for any man, apart from deliberate perseverance in faith.*[61]

Those who bear Calvin's name in the Reformed faith have, of course, come to a similar conclusion. Charles Hodge, for example, says:[62]

> *Election, calling, justification, and salvation are indissolubly united; and, therefore, he who has clear evidence of his being called has the same evidence of his election and final salvation... The only evidence of election is effectual calling, that is, the production of holiness. And the only evidence of the genuineness of this call and the certainty of our perseverance, is a patient continuance in well doing.*

In other words, the only real evidence of election is perseverance, and our only assurance of the certainty of persevering is--to persevere! So on this ground

---

[59]*Institutes,* 3.2.17-18.

[60]Calvin, *Commentary,* Mt. 13:20.

[61]Robert Shank, *Life in The Son: A Study of the Doctrine of Perseverance* (Springfield, MO: Westcott, 1961), p. 293.

[62]Charles Hodge, *St. Paul's Epistle to the Romans,* (1860; reprint ed., Grand Rapids: Eerdmans, 1950), p. 212, on Rom. 8:29-30.

there is no assurance at all! As John Murray put it, "The perseverance of the saints reminds us very forcefully that only those who persevere to the end are truly saints."

The Experimental Predestinarian cannot really ever offer security and is, in fact, teaching a flat contradiction in this regard, as can be seen by the following:

Proposition A: *It is possible for a man to have assurance before the end of life that he will go to heaven when he dies.*

Yet the following syllogism leads to proposition B:

Major premise: *I am saved now if I persevere in faith to the end of life.*
Minor premise: *It is possible that I will not persevere to the end of life*
Conclusion: *I may not be saved now*

This inevitably leads to:

Proposition B: *It is not possible for man to have assurance before the end of life that he will go to heaven when he dies.*

Since A cannot equal non-A, since both proposition A and proposition B cannot be true at the same time, the Calvinist system flatly contradicts itself. Some Calvinists might reply, "This is not a contradiction, only a healthy tension."[63] The word "healthy" is used to imply that there is value in wondering whether or not one is saved. His doubts and resultant fears may motivate him to live a godly life. The word "tension" is simply a circumlocution for a blatant contradiction.

It is disturbing how Experimental Predestinarians are able to continue to believe these contradictory things. One is reminded of the Red Queen in Lewis Carroll's story of Alice in Wonderland. When Alice protested that there is no use trying to believe impossible things, the Queen said:

I dare say you haven't had much practice. . . . When I was your age I did it for half an hour a day. Why sometimes I've believed as many as six impossible things before breakfast.[64]

Furthermore, the idea that God intends to motivate His children to godly living by desiring that they wonder if they have only temporary faith like the

---

[63]Berkouwer uses the word "tension" as a substitute for the more obvious word "contradiction." See C. G. Berkouwer, *Faith and Perseverance* (Grand Rapids: Eerdmans, 1958), p. 110.

[64]Lewis Carroll, *Alice Through the Looking Glass* (London: McMillian, 1880), p. 100.

reprobate and that they must persevere to the end to find out is so far removed from the apostles' statements of grace and love that one wonders how anyone could ever find it in the New Testament. Such perspectives are not uncommon in Experimental Predestinarian writings.

Maurice Roberts, for example, exhorts his readers to hold two contradictory notions in their minds at the same time: "We may cling tenaciously to the doctrine of Final Perseverance and yet at the same time we may legitimately view our own personal profession of faith with something akin to uncertainty."[65] So we are to believe in the Reformed doctrine of perseverance in a general sense but doubt that we in particular are necessarily saved! Roberts finds justification for this travesty of grace in the apostle Paul's statement that he worries that he himself should be a castaway (1 Cor. 9:26-27). As demonstrated elsewhere, the word translated "castaway" (Gk. **adokimos**) does not mean final rejection to hell but to be disqualified for the prize, to forfeit reward.[66] But then Roberts makes it worse. "More positively we may say that this fear of being **adokimos** or castaway is one of the great hallmarks of those who are elect and who finally do persevere. All who lack it are possessed of a sickly presumption which needs correcting from the pulpit or which--may God forbid--they will have to unlearn by the sad experience of falling."[67]

For most, however, the certainty of their final salvation does not lead to license. On the contrary, it leads to a wonderful security and sense of gratitude which promotes true religion and godliness. Is it not indisputable that our children are more likely to behave well in an atmosphere of unconditional parental acceptance than in an atmosphere of uncertainty? Can it ever be "healthy" for a child to cherish doubts about his parents' long-term acceptance? If it is true that earthly parents must strive to communicate unconditional and permanent acceptance regardless of failure, would it not be even more true of our heavenly parent?

To teach that a "hallmark" of the saved man is that he carries about the "fear of being castaway" is absurd and obviously contradictory to the promises of assurance found in the New Testament. Roberts is simply taking the Experimental Predestinarian view to its logically ridiculous conclusion: there is not only no real certainty of perseverance, because you may not be elect, but to have such certainty is a "sickly presumption." Few thoughtful readers of the New Testament would ever glean such a view from the apostle's letters!

---

[65]Maurice Roberts, "Final Perseverance," *The Banner of Truth Trust* 265 (October 1985): 10.

[66]See verses under 1 Cor. 9:26-27 in index.

[67]Roberts, p. 11.

Theodore Beza (1519-1605)

Calvin grounded assurance in the death of Christ and included it in saving faith itself. However, Calvin's successor at Geneva, Theodore Beza (1519-1605), departed from Calvin and grounded assurance in evidences of fruit in the life. Beza's starting point was his doctrine of limited atonement. Calvin, according to Kendall, held to unlimited atonement.[68] If Christ died for all, Beza argued, then all would be saved. He developed a system which became known as supralapsarianism. In that system the order of elective decrees is:

1. Decree to elect some to be saved and to reprobate all others
2. Decree to create men, both elect and non-elect
3. Decree to permit the fall
4. Decree to provide salvation for the elect
5. Decree to apply salvation to the elect

The view is to be rejected because it assumes that the decrees of election and preterition have reference to an as yet uncreated entity. The Scriptures uniformly represent the decrees of election as involving some actually created beings from which to select, e.g., Rom. 9:18: "On **whom** He will, He hath mercy, and **whom** He will, He hardens." Thus the first decree must be the decree to create. God must bring into existence before He can decide what man will do or what his final destiny will be. The Scriptures represent the elect and non-elect as taken out of an aggregate of beings.[69]

Calvin said men are chosen from a corrupt mass, but Beza says men are chosen from a mass "yet unshapen." By basing his system around predestination, Beza gave election and reprobation priority over creation and the fall. Predestination refers to the destinies of men not yet created, much less fallen.

---

[68]See Kendall, *English Calvinism*, pp. 13-18. He cites *Institutes*, 3.1.1; *Commentary on Isaiah*, 53:12; *Commentary on Hebrews*, 9:28. In both places Rom. 5:15 is referred to, and Calvin says "many" = "all." In his commentary on Mark at 14:24 Calvin says, "The word 'many,' does not mean a part of the world only, but the whole human race." In *Concerning the Eternal Predestination of God*, p. 148, he says, it is "incontestable that Christ came for the expiation of the sins of the whole world." In his commentary on Jn. 1:29 he observes, "And when he says **the sin of the world** he extends this kindness indiscriminately to the whole human race." "For God commends to us the salvation of all men without exception, even as Christ suffered for the sins of the whole world" *(Sermons on Isaiah's Prophecy*, p. 141). See also the extensive comment on this point in Bell, *Scottish Theology*, pp. 13-19, where he negatively critiques Paul Helm's response to Kendall in Paul Helm, "Article Review: Calvin, English Calvinism and the Logic of Doctrinal Development" in *Scottish Journal of Theology* 34.2 (1981).

[69]Jn. 15:19. Also, the elect are chosen to sanctification (Eph. 1:4-6; 1 Pet. 1:2). They must therefore have already fallen and consequently been created. Supralapsarians quote Rom. 9:11 as proof. But birth is not synonymous with creation. Parents are not the creators of their children. Man exists in Adam and in the womb before he is born into the world.

Beza logically works out his system so that Jesus is the savior of the elect before their creation or fall. Assurance is thus grounded in two things: the election of God and the knowledge that we are among the ones who have been offered a redeemer, for not all have. For Beza, if the knowledge that Christ died for us can be obtained, then we may be certain that we will not perish, because God will not demand a double payment for sin.

This doctrine led to the division between assurance and faith which differed from Calvin. For Calvin, Christ was the "mirror" in whom we contemplated our election. By this he meant we look to Christ for assurance and not ourselves. But for Beza we have no certainty that we are elected because we do not know for sure that we are one of those for whom Christ died. If Christ died for all, then we could know that we are elect, but if He died only for the elect, it is presumptuous for us to trust in Christ's death, if not dangerous:

> *We could be putting our trust in One who did not die for us and therefore be damned. Thus we can no more trust Christ's death by a direct act of faith than we can infallibly project that we are among the number chosen from eternity: for the number of the elect and the number for whom Christ died are one and the same. The ground of assurance, then, must be sought elsewhere than in Christ.*[70]

Beza, knowing this, suggests that we should look within ourselves for the evidence that Christ died for us. We cannot comprehend God's eternal decrees, but we can see if He is at work in our lives. "Beza directs us not to Christ but to ourselves; we do not begin with Him but with the effects, which points us back, as it were, to the decree of election. Thus, while Calvin thinks looking to ourselves leads to anxiety, or sure damnation, Beza thinks otherwise. Sanctification, or good works, is the infallible proof of saving faith."[71]

Beza's doctrine requires the use of the practical syllogism in order for one to be persuaded he is one of those for whom Christ died. Conversion includes two works of grace: faith and then sanctification. The first, however, is invalid if not ratified by the second.

He also taught the doctrine of temporary faith which is contradictory to a theology which grounds assurance in works. He says that the unregenerate may receive an ineffectual calling. The reprobate may have the appearance of virtue, called moral virtue, but such are different from the works of the children of God governed by the Spirit of regeneration. According to Kendall, Beza does not state what these differences are. We might justly fear that our good works are simply the moral virtues of the unregenerate. Thus, contradictory to his statement that sanctification yields assurance, our sanctification can yield little com-

---

[70]Kendall, p. 32.
[71]Ibid., p. 33.

fort. Even the reprobate can have the evidences of life. So what is the solution? Ultimately, Beza says the only true evidence that Christ died for you is if you persevere in holiness. He turns to 2 Pet. 1:10 and argues that assurance of election is based on a good conscience. We make our election sure by good works. These works, he says, are a testimony to our conscience that Christ lives in us, and thus we cannot perish, being elected to salvation.

William Perkins (1558-1602)

William Perkins is, according to Kendall, "the fountainhead of the experimental predestinarian tradition." He developed a system of assurance built around an interpretation of 2 Pet. 1:10 which says we must prove our election to ourselves by means of good works. He is the third member of the Calvinist Trinity (Calvin, Beza, and Perkins), and by the end of the sixteenth century his works were more published and read than those of Calvin. He was a supralapsarian, and his famous work *A Golden Chain* brings this out forcefully.

According to him, before one can become a Christian, the heart must be made malleable by four hammers: the Law, knowledge of sin, sense of God's wrath, and a holy desperation. Second Pet. 1:10 teaches us to prove to ourselves that we have faith by means of a good conscience. Justifying faith is that by which a man is persuaded in his conscience. The will to believe does not yield assurance, but the conscience, reflecting on the fruits of regeneration, can.

Because he accepts Calvin's doctrine of temporary faith and since the only way you can know if you are elect is by works, Perkins has to have a way of distinguishing the faith of the reprobate from that of the elect. He concludes that the reprobate believes that some shall be saved but not that he himself shall be saved. The reprobate, however, can acknowledge his sin, feel God's wrath, be grieved for sin and feel he deserves punishment, acknowledge that God is just in punishing him, desire to be saved, and promise God he will repent, and God can even answer his prayers.[72] The problem, of course, is that all these graces are characteristic of the elect as well.

Perkins set the stage for the syllogistic reasoning by saying:

---

[72]Ibid., p. 68.

Major Premise:	*He that believes and repents is God's child*
Minor Premise:	*I believe in Christ and repent: at the least I subject my will to the commandment which bids me repent and believe: I detest my unbelief, and all my sins: and desire the Lord to increase my faith*
Conclusion:	*I am the child of God.*[73]

The minor premise involves the graces of sanctification which Perkins says are essential if you are of the elect. He expands this and lists nine effects of sanctification which must be present:[74]

1. Feelings of bitterness of heart when we have offended God by sin
2. Striving against the flesh
3. Desiring God's grace earnestly
4. Considering that God's grace is a most precious jewel
5. Loving the ministers of God's word
6. Calling upon God earnestly and with tears
7. Desiring Christ's second coming
8. Avoiding all occasions of sin
9. Persevering in the effects to the last gasp of life

Each of these points, except for desiring Christ's second coming, is imputed to the reprobate also. When we read Perkins, we may be drawn to the sincere desire for holiness and attracted to the intense practical concern for assurance. However, it is superficial to be drawn to this without realizing the terrible theological bondage and misunderstanding which underlies his concept of the grace of God. The reprobate are characterized by ineffectual calling. This calling will fail in the end. This is really the only way to tell if you are saved or not, which is no way at all.

Perkins's advice to the troubled Christian is to seek the assurance promised in 2 Pet. 1:10 by practicing the virtues of the moral law, 2:24. For Perkins sanctification is the ground of assurance.

He himself acknowledges that we must "descend into our own hearts" (1:290) to know our assurance. Apart from a special revelation, there is no way to know if we are one of those for whom Christ died. Therefore, we must do certain things, and if we do them, we can reflect upon the fact that we have done

---

[73]Ibid., p. 71. (Spelling modernized.)

[74]William Perkins, *The Works of that Famous and Worthy Minister of Christ in the University of Cambridge, Mr. William Perkins,* 3 vols. (Cambridge: n. p., 1608-1609), 1:115, cited by Kendall, p. 72.

them and from this infer we are of the elect. Apparently, Perkins left this world in a spiritual conflict of troubled conscience. And it is no wonder in view of the doctrine he held.

There are two works of grace necessary: initial faith and perseverance. Only the second ultimately proves that the first is valid. If godliness is the means by which we make our calling and election sure, then the Experimental Predestinarians reasoned we had better give a list of what it means to be godly and how to become godly. This led to the legalism for which Puritanism is noted and the heavy sobriety and lack of joy which is so proverbial in their churches.

Various Puritan divines discerned varying bases for assurance. For some it was keeping a pure heart. Others based it upon a feeling, others on being in love with godliness, others on being sincere, and others in keeping of the law. One thing they all agree on, and seem to think is noble, is that full assurance is not to be obtained easily.

Jacobus Arminius (1559-1609)

Jacobus Arminius studied under Beza at Geneva in 1581. After taking a pastorate in Amsterdam in 1587, he was asked to defend Beza's doctrine of predestination in the light of a pamphlet circulating against it. However, after studying the matter further, he became a convert to the very opinions he had been asked to refute. The general belief was that the man in Rom. 7:14-21 was regenerate. Arminius began to question this. When Perkins's book on predestination appeared in Holland, Arminius read it eagerly because he was an admirer of Perkins. He prepared a refutation but did not publish it out of respect for Perkins's death. He was appointed Professor of Theology at University of Leiden and was made a Doctor of Theology.

His doctrine of predestination was simple: God predestines believers. If one believes, he is elected; if he does not believe, he is not elected. This was a view of faith which was active. Man chooses to believe; thus, faith is an act of the will. Once God has seen that he chooses, then God moves on his heart. Paradoxically, this is precisely the view held by Experimental Predestinarians as illustrated in Perkins. Faith for them follows repentance, and a man prepares himself for Christ by the four hammers and then chooses to believe when the heart has been softened enough. However, Arminius did believe that faith was a gift. He said, "A rich man bestows, on a poor and famishing beggar, alms by which he may be able to maintain himself and his family. Does it cease to be a gift, because the beggar extends his hand to receive it?"[75] "Arminius ties election (though based on foreseen faith) to man's will to believe; the Experimental Predestinarians

---

[75]Jacobus Arminius, *Works of Arminius*, 3 vols. (London, 1875, 1828, 1875), 2:52.

make the will to believe the proof of election."[76] The similarity is in the nature of saving faith.

Arminius believes salvation can be lost. He affirms dogmatically that it is impossible for believers to decline from salvation. What he means, however, is that they cannot decline as long as they remain believers. Thus, both Arminius and the Experimental Predestinarians agree that those who apostatize or reject the gospel are reprobates. "The Experimental Predestinarians explain that believers persevere because they were elected; Arminius says God elects believers whom He foresees will persevere."[77]

Arminius challenged Perkins on his two works of grace. If perseverance must be achieved to prove that faith is real, then there is no practical difference between their positions. Kendall concludes, "If Perkins holds that the recipient of the first grace must obtain the second (perseverance) or the first is rendered invalid, there is no practical difference whatever in the two positions. If the believer does not persevere (whether Arminius or Perkins says it), such a person proves to be non-elect."[78]

The difference between the two is not in the issue of whether men fall but, rather, what is the theoretical explanation behind the event. Like the Experimental Predestinarians, Arminius places faith in the will and says that faith is obedience. He says there are three parts to it: repentance, faith in Christ, and observance of God's commands.[79] His doctrine of assurance is also the same as that of his opponents. Assurance comes from the fruits of faith. Arminius's views were rejected at the international Synod of Dordrecht (Dort) on May 29, 1619.

The Westminster Assembly Theology

Those invited to the Westminster Assembly were completely unified from the beginning in their doctrine of saving faith. No representative of the viewpoint of Calvin was there, and the breech between faith and assurance was now given credal sanction. The assembly is therefore to be seen as the credal conclusion of the Experimental Predestinarian tradition. In addition, the assembly was convened to answer the threat of the antinomianism of John Eaton (1575-1641), Henry Denne (d. 1660?), and others. By "antinomian" they meant a doctrine which did not place faith in the will and thus opened the door for apostasy. Thus, Calvin himself would have been antinomian!

---

[76]Kendall, p. 143.

[77]Ibid., p. 144.

[78]Ibid.

[79]*Works of Arminius*, 1:589.

The theology of Westminster completely reversed the doctrine of Calvin. Calvin often used such synonyms for faith as persuasion, assurance, knowledge, apprehension, perception, or conviction. The Westminster theology used terms like accepting, receiving, assenting, resting, yielding, answering, and embracing-- all active words. Man's will is not eliminated as it was in Calvin. Saving faith is not only believing that God's word is true, but it is "yielding obedience to the commands, trembling at the threatenings, and embracing the promises of God for this life, and that which is to come. But the principal acts of saving faith are accepting, receiving, and resting upon Christ alone."[80] For Calvin faith was an instrument of our justification, but it was **God's** instrument, not ours. It was the instrument of God's act whereby He opens our blind eyes. For the assembly at Westminster, however, faith is **man's** act.

Surprisingly, there is no mention in the Westminster Confession of Calvin's doctrine of temporary faith. Perhaps it was because these divines sensed the latent contradiction such a teaching brings into their Experimental Predestinarian system. It seems obvious that, if assurance is to be grounded in sanctification, the doctrine of temporary faith had to be done away with. The reprobate simply cannot experience the graces of sanctification or there would be no way to distinguish between the reprobate and the saved. Hence, there is no basis for assurance. Therefore, if a man is doing good, he cannot be reprobate.

In regard to assurance, they clearly stated that "assurance of grace and salvation, not being of the essence of faith, true believers may wait long before they obtain it."[81] Calvin asserted that the "least drop of faith" firmly assures. Seeing Christ, even afar off, assures; Christ is the mirror of our election. "But holding out Christ as the ground of assurance as a direct act seems not to have been regarded as an option by the Westminster divines."[82] Rather, our assurance is based on three things:[83]

1. The divine truth of the promises of salvation
2. "The inward evidence of those graces unto which these promises are made"
3. The testimony of the Spirit of Adoption that we are children of God

In the second statement the experimentalists are simply calling a spade a spade. Assurance, and, perhaps salvation also, is ultimately based upon works! Assurance is promised only to those who have evidence of regeneration in their

---

[80]"Westminster Confession of Faith," in Schaff, 3:630 (14.2).

[81]Ibid., 3:638 (18.3).

[82]Kendall, p. 203.

[83]"Westminster Confession," in Schaff, 3:638 (18.2).

life. Surprisingly, when they define faith as "yielding obedience,"[84] they appear to teach salvation by works.[85] But the assurance of salvation, if not salvation itself, is remarkably held out to those who can discover inward fruit in their lives.

When they try to draw a distinction between this and the Old Covenant, their theology gets murky. The Old Covenant promised salvation on the basis of a "perfect and personal obedience," and the new is promised on the condition of faith.[86] Yet when faith is defined as "yielding obedience to the commands," we are left without clear understanding of the difference. Kendall concludes that "the difference seems to be that perfect obedience was required under the old covenant and doing our best is required under the new."[87] Even though they posited faith as the condition of salvation, when they describe faith as an act of the will and submission to the commands of God, they come quite close to making salvation, or at least our personal assurance of it, the reward for doing good. The responsibility for salvation, in the final analysis, is put back upon our shoulders.

Believers can lose their assurance because it is based upon their performance, how one's conscience feels about one's performance as he reflects upon his recent behavior. Assurance is grounded in reflection upon our sincerity. Our good works do not need to be perfect, only sincere.[88] This leads to the inevitable conclusion, however, that perseverance and sanctification are not based upon a response to God's love but upon one's intense desire to insure his salvation. The end result is that salvation is a payment for sanctification.

It is certainly true that the assembly at Westminster could never be charged with antinomianism. That in itself should make its theology suspect. Had the apostle Paul espoused their doctrine, it is inconceivable that he would have ever been misunderstood to be saying "let us continue in sin that grace may abound." Paul was susceptible to the charge of antinomianism, but Westminster could not be. There must be a difference, therefore, between the theology there and that of the apostle.

But such a deviation from Paul and Calvin in the interests of protecting the church against antinomianism has its own dangers, which Calvin often warned against: endless introspection, constant self-analysis, and legalism. When they endorsed the experimental way of thinking, they embraced a much more complex theology than Calvin's simple idea that "Christ is better than a thousand testimonies to me."

---

[84]Ibid., 3:630 (14.2).

[85]Kendall, p. 204. Elsewhere the confession specifically says salvation is by faith and is given freely, apart from works (Schaff, 3:617 [7.3]).

[86]"Westminster Confession," in Schaff, 3:617 (7.2).

[87]Kendall, p. 206.

[88]"Westminster Confession," in Schaff, 3:639 (18.4).

Faith for Calvin was never a condition. He felt it was a passive work to which "no reward can be paid."[89] Calvin would never accept the idea that God gives Christ to us on the condition of faith because for Calvin the very seeing that God gave Christ to us is faith. He pointed men not to personal revelations by the Spirit to know they had faith but to Christ's death. This was God's pledge that we are chosen. To use the language of Westminster, the promise of salvation was "made" to our persuasion that Christ died for us.

The paradoxical thing is that the doctrines of Arminius and Westminster, which are supposedly opposed to one another, are much the same. With Westminster, Arminians would agree that (1) faith is not a persuasion; (2) that there is a separation between faith and assurance; (3) that there is a need for two acts of faith, the direct and reflex acts; and (4) that assurance comes by means of the practical syllogism.

Furthermore, in the question of perseverance there is virtually no practical difference either. If a man who has professed Christ dies in a fallen condition, neither Arminius nor Westminster would grant that he is elect. Both agree that it is only the persevering believer, after all, who can certainly be said to be born again.

Conclusion

The road from Calvin to Westminster was to be expected. Even though he taught that assurance was of the essence of faith, Calvin's doctrine, temporary faith, obviously led to the need for some criteria other than perseverance to determine which faith was temporary and which was real. It was Theodore Beza, with his doctrine of limited atonement, who made the quest for assurance based upon works a necessity. Since Christ did not die for all men, it would not be proper to direct men to Christ for assurance, as Calvin taught, because Christ may not have died for that particular man. Therefore, according to Beza, assurance must be based on works. As he reflected deeply on this problem, William Perkins concluded that the best means of arriving at personal assurance was by means of the practical syllogism. The divines of Westminster codified these conclusions in credal form.

It is now necessary to look more carefully at some of the biblical passages which have been discussed along this journey. What does the Bible say about faith, assurance, and the need to examine ourselves?

---

[89]Calvin, *Commentary*, Jn. 6:29.

Chapter 12

Faith and Assurance

In the previous chapter the relationship between faith and assurance from Calvin to Westminster was described. The complete departure from Calvin's simple idea that faith is located in the mind and is basically "belief" and assurance was noted. Now our attention will be turned to the biblical and theological issues. While historical theology yields interesting perspective, the final issue is: what does the Bible teach, and not what did Calvin, Beza, Perkins, or Westminster teach? This brings us immediately to the relevant texts which have been used to establish the Westminster tradition.

Faith

The Definition of Faith

It is somewhat perplexing how this simple, universally understood, and commonly used term has been so freighted with additional meanings. Notions like obedience, yieldedness, repentance, and a myriad of other terms are continually read into this word in order to make it serve the purpose of some particular theological system. It is perplexing because the lexical authorities are virtually unanimous in their assertion that faith, **pistis**, means belief, confidence, or persuasion. The verbal forms all mean the same--to believe something, to give assent, to have confidence in, or to be persuaded of.[1]

In his extensive philological comment on faith Benjamin Warfield does not offer one suggestion that faith includes obedience.[2] He observes, for exam-

---

[1]The verb **peitho** means to convince, to persuade, to be convinced, to be sure, to come to believe, to be persuaded (AG, pp. 644-45). The remote meaning, to obey, is noted but is not relevant to the soteriological usage in the New Testament, just as the meaning "elephant's nose" is not relevant to a discussion about a box in the attic. Abbott-Smith asserts that it means to apply persuasion, to persuade, to trust, to be confident, to believe, or to be persuaded (pp. 350-51). Otto Michel says the active form of **peitho** "always has the meaning of persuade, induce, and even to mislead or corrupt" ("Faith, Persuade, Belief, Unbelief," in *NIDNTT*, 1:589). "Soon you will persuade [peitho] me to become a Christian" (Acts 26:28). The passive form always means to be persuaded, to be convinced. Similarly, the word **pistis** simply means belief, conviction, or assent, and the verb, **pisteuo**, means to believe (Michel, 1:599-605). Abbott-Smith concurs that the sense is belief, trust, or confidence, and to believe something (pp. 361-62).

[2]Benjamin B. Warfield, "Faith," in *Biblical and Theological Studies* (Grand Rapids: Eerdmans), p. 444.

ple, that **pisteuo** plus the dative in the New Testament "prevailingly expresses believing assent."[3] The constructions with the prepositions lead us to the deeper sense of the word, "that of firm, trustful reliance."[4] "A survey of these passages will show very clearly that in the New Testament, 'to believe' is a technical term to express reliance upon Christ for salvation."[5]

Warfield continually stresses that faith is a mental matter rather than a matter of obedience:[6]

> *The central movement in all faith is no doubt the element of assent; it is that which constitutes the mental movement so called a movement of conviction. But the movement of assent must depend, as it always does depend, on a movement, not specifically of the will, but of the intellect; the assensus issues from the notitia. The movement of the sensibilities which we call "trust," is on the contrary the produce of the assent. And it is in this movement of the sensibilities that faith fulfills itself, and it is by that, as specifically "faith," it is formed.*

This view of faith has strong historical precedent in the Lutheran confessions. Indeed, this is one of the principal areas of disagreement between Lutheranism and the English Puritans. The Puritan view of faith, like that of many modern Experimental Predestinarians, is virtually the same as Rome's. By adding words like "submission" and "obedience" to the concept, they have aligned themselves with their opponents. The Council of Trent declared, "If anyone should say that justifying faith is nothing else than trust (**fiducia**) in the divine compassion which forgives sins for Christ's sake, or that we are justified alone by such trust, let him be accursed."[7] Lutheranism, in agreement with Calvin, has traditionally defined faith as "personal trust, or confidence, in God's gracious forgiveness of sins for Christ's sake."[8] It is viewed as a passive instrument for receiving the divine gift. The will is not involved. Faith, according to Lutheran Theologian Mueller, "merely accepts the merits that have been secured for the world by Christ's obedience."[9] He calls it a passive act or a passive instrument.

In spite of their claims to orthodoxy, Experimental Predestinarians have totally departed from Luther, Lutheranism, and John Calvin himself in their formulations of the meaning of faith. What is being argued here is a definition of

---

[3]Ibid., p. 436.

[4]Ibid., p. 437.

[5]Ibid., p. 440.

[6]Ibid., p. 403.

[7]Session 6, Can. 12 cited by John Theodore Mueller, *Christian Dogmatics* (St. Louis: Concordia, 1955), p. 324.

[8]Mueller, p. 329. For a good discussion of the Lutheran view of faith and how it differs from Experimental Predestinarians, Arminians, and Catholicism, see Mueller, pp. 321-35.

[9]Mueller, p. 327.

faith found at the very core of the Reformation polemics against Rome. How surprising to see some evangelicals today at odds with their theological forebears whom they mistakenly understand themselves to represent!

Bultmann, on the other hand, in his article on "faith" in *The Theological Dictionary of the New Testament* attempts to prove that faith equals obedience, or that at least it includes the idea. But if anything is clear from the New Testament, faith is the opposite of obedience. It is passive "hearing" in contrast to a volitional decision. In Gal. 3:5, for example, Paul speaks of God working miracles among them because "you believe what you heard"[10] and set this in contrast to works of obedience. Whatever faith is, it certainly does not include within its compass the very thing it is contrasted with--obedience! In Romans he is equally clear:

But to one who does not work, but believes in Him who justifies the ungodly, his faith is reckoned as righteousness (Rom. 4:5 NASB).

For we maintain that a man is justified by faith apart from works of the law (Rom. 3:28 NASB).

If faith is the opposite of works of obedience (law) and is the opposite of work, by what mental alchemy can men seriously argue that, while faith is apart from works of obedience, faith itself includes works of obedience![11] If faith plus works does not save, then it is illegitimate to include obedience as a part of faith and then say faith alone saves when you mean that faith plus works saves.

In Bultmann's article[12] he says over and over again that faith is reliance, trust, belief and makes a small reference to the fact that it includes obedience. In a good example of searching for the "theological idea" rather than the semantic value of a word, Bultmann strings three verses together:

Through whom we have received grace and apostleship to bring about the obedience of faith among all the Gentiles (Rom. 1:5 NASB).

What Christ has accomplished through me, resulting in the obedience of the Gentiles by word and deed (Rom. 15:18 NASB).

For the report of your obedience has reached to all (Rom. 16:19).

Now, even though the word **pisteuo** is not used in Rom. 15:18 or 16:19, Bultmann uses these verses to prove that **pisteuo** means to obey. In Rom. 1:5 Paul's efforts resulted in the "obedience of faith among all the Gentiles." Since

---

[10]Gk. **akoes pisteos**, "the hearing which is faith." Faith is totally passive, a "hearing" of the gospel!

[11]The "faith of a mustard seed" is certainly not obedience, nor does it include it (Lk. 17:6).

[12]Rudolph Bultmann, "**pisteuo**," in *TDNTA*, p. 854.

an "obedience" was the result of his ministry to Gentiles in 15:18 and 16:19, Bultmann seems to conclude that the obedience of faith is equal to obedience to the moral precepts of God.

He has a theological idea in mind, that salvation is by means of works, and feels no contextual restraint in equating the three verses. But Rom. 1:5 is properly "the obedience which is faith" and not the obedience resulting from faith.[13]

Paul wanted to bring about both kinds of obedience, the obedience which consists of believing assent and the life of works. But the verb "believe" refers only to the former and not to the latter. Furthermore, only the former, according to the rest of the epistle, is the means of salvation (Rom. 3:28; 4:5).[14] This is the only evidence Bultmann gives that faith is equal to obedience!

John MacArthur similarly misunderstands the nature of faith and, like Bultmann (whom he quotes), wants to equate it with obedience.[15] For example, he quotes W. E. Vine in his discussion of the words **peitho** and **pisteuo**. "**Peitho** and **pisteuo**, 'to trust,' are closely related etymologically; the difference in meaning is that the former implies the obedience that is produced by the later. . . . **Peitho** in the N. T. suggests an actual and outward result of the inward persuasion and consequent faith."[16] MacArthur goes on to say that "the real believer will obey," and he carefully states, "The biblical concept of faith is inseparable from obedience."[17] But possible, or even inevitable, consequences of faith are not to be equated with faith itself. Faith does NOT mean "to obey." It is NOT "the determination of the will to obey the truth."[18] Faith is "reliant trust."[19] As men-

---

[13]"Faith is the act of assent by which the gospel is appropriated" (William Sanday and Arthur C. Headlam, *A Critical and Exegetical Commentary on the Epistle to the Romans* [Edinburgh: T. & T. Clark, 1985], p. 11).

[14]Bultmann also cites Heb. 11; Rom. 1:8; 1 Th. 1:8; 10:3; 2 Cor. 9:13, all of which are irrelevant and suggest only that works are a proper result of salvation but not that obedience is intrinsic to faith or even that obedience is a necessary result of faith.

[15]John MacArthur, *The Gospel According to Jesus* (Grand Rapids: Zondervan, 1988), pp. 172-78.

[16]W. E. Vine, *Expository Dictionary of Old and New Testament Words*, 2 vols. in one (Old Tappan, NJ: Revell, 1981), 2:71.

[17]It is true, as MacArthur maintains, that faith includes the idea of repentance (p. 172), but repentance does not mean "turn from sin" but "to change one's perspective." When the writer to the Hebrews says, "The just shall live by faith," he means that the modus operandi of life of the regenerate man is faith. He does not mean that we must believe (= obey) for the rest of our lives to become Christians or to prove that we already are. It is true that we are only partakers of Christ if we hold firm to the end, but being a partaker and being a Christian are different things. (See discussion in chapter 5 under Heb. 3:14). The work which God will complete in the lives of the Philippians is not sanctification but their participation in the gospel with Him, which will continue up to the Lord's return. Paul expected the Lord to return in his lifetime.

[18]MacArthur, p. 173.

tioned above, to import notions of obedience into the word "faith" is contrary to the teaching of the apostle Paul.

It seems somewhat evasive to argue that this apparent inconsistency is a "paradox"[20] and that, after all, it is not our work but God's work in us which produces both repentance[21] and faith.[22] To say that faith can equal obedience and not equal obedience is not a paradox; it is a contradiction. To define faith and repentance as obedient surrender and then say that salvation is by faith and not by works is confusing, to say the least. Sensitive to the charge of heresy, MacArthur says, "Lest someone object that this is a salvation of human effort, remember it is only the enablement of divine grace that empowers a person to pass through the gate."[23]

But can one escape the charge that such a view contradicts Paul's doctrine that salvation is apart from works by saying that this "faith-work???" is a work of God and not of man? Would it make any difference to Paul whether the work in us is produced by God or produced by man? Do works produced in us save? It is not just salvation by "human effort" which contradicts Paul but salvation by works produced in us, whether worked by God or by man. Furthermore, works in the believer's life are produced both by God and man, and not by man alone, and are meritorious. Paul asserts, "I can do all things through Him who strengthens me" (Phil. 4:13). Paul is the one doing the work, Christ helps (cf. Heb. 4:16), and at the judgment seat Paul can boast about what he has done (1 Th. 2:20).

The Reformed faith has commonly held that the sanctification of the believer involves the work of God and of man. With this the writer agrees. But the only works of obedience which God performs related to our justification **are imputed to us and not worked in us.** These works are known as the active obedience of Christ, his perfect obedience to the requirements of the law on our be-

---

[19]MacArthur quotes passages like Heb. 11, which describe how people accomplished great things by faith, as proof that faith itself is the determination to accomplish great things. He has taken a contextual nuance, obedience, read it into the semantic value of the word **pisteuo** and then interpreted **pisteuo** to mean "to obey" in its other usages in the New Testament. Such a procedure is not exegesis but the reading of theological ideas into words and has no place in legitimate New Testament interpretation. Nor does it have any place in the presentation of the gospel. The gospel according to MacArthur is so confusing that a non-Christian would have to be a theologian to comprehend it. Gone is the simple offer of eternal life on the basis of faith apart from works. Rather, it is a faith which consists of works, and yet does not consist of works, which MacArthur offers.

[20]MacArthur, p. 140.

[21]Ibid., p. 163.

[22]Ibid., p. 173.

[23]Ibid., p. 183. MacArthur quotes Bultmann to support his contention that "to believe is to obey" (MacArthur, p. 175; Bultmann, "**pisteuo**," in *TDNT*, 6:205). However, MacArthur does not seem to realize that Bultmann does not consider this obedience to be a work of God in the heart. Bultmann explicitly denies what MacArthur is at pains to affirm, namely, that faith, and the obedience of which it consists, is a work of the Holy Spirit and gift of God: "**Pistis** is a gift of the Spirit" (6:219).

half. These merits are reckoned to our account in the act of justification (Rom. 10:4;Rom. 5:19;Col. 2:10).[24] When MacArthur speaks of works being worked in us, his doctrine of justification differs not a whit from Catholicism's idea of justification making us righteous. However, the conclusion of the Reformation was that justification is a forensic act of God in which He declares us righteous.

The Role of the Will in Faith

Actions of will arise from faith, but the will itself does not seem to be involved in the production of faith. This may seem surprising to some, but a moment's reflection will substantiate the commonly understood notion that faith is located in the mind and is persuasion or belief. It is something which "happens" to us as a result of reflection upon sufficient evidence. We can no more will faith than we can will feelings of love.

That faith is a passive thing, and not active, is evident when Paul says:

Did you receive the Spirit by works of law, or by hearing with faith? (Gal. 3:2 NASB).

As he often does, Paul throws faith into the sharpest contrast possible with works and describes its function as "hearing." In choosing that word (instead of "obeying"), he is not only stating that faith is a passive reception, but he is aligning himself with his Master who taught that faith was "looking"[25] and "drinking"[26] and with the writer to the Hebrews who described it as "tasting."[27] All these terms assign a passive, receptive function to faith. The will plays no part.

Saving faith is reliance upon God for salvation. It does not include within its compass the determination of the will to obey, nor does it include a commitment to a life of works. To believe is to be persuaded and be reliant and includes nothing else. If anything is clear in the New Testament, whatever belief is, it is the opposite of works:

Does He then, who provides you with the Spirit and works miracles among you, do it by the works of the Law, or by hearing with faith? (Gal. 3:5 NASB).

---

[24]See discussion in chapter 21, "Upon His Substitutionary Life."

[25]Jn. 3:14-15; compare Num. 21:9 where "looking" resulted in living.

[26]Jn. 4:14; 7:37-38. It is true that sometimes "drink" can have ideas such as "surrender" (e.g., Mt. 20:22; Jn. 18:11), but it does not have such a meaning in soteriological passages. It is a figure of speech, and its meaning must be derived from each context in which it is used. In Rev. 5:5 Jesus is called a lion, but in 1 Pet. 5:8 Satan is called a lion. If the intent of a figure is always the same, irrespective of context, we would be forced to say that Jesus is Satan!

[27]Heb. 6:4.

Just as Moses lifted up the snake in the desert, so the Son of Man must be lifted up, that everyone who believes in him may have eternal life (Jn. 3:14-15).

In the latter passage the Lord is equating "belief" with mere "looking." He is referring to Num. 21:8-9:

The LORD said to Moses, "Make a snake and put it up on a pole; anyone who is bitten can look at it and live." So Moses made a bronze snake and put it up on a pole. Then when anyone was bitten by a snake and looked at the bronze snake, he lived.

The intent is obviously that a man should look with the expectation of healing and with belief in God, asking for help. A non-Christian who will not believe will not be healed, even if he looks. But the point is that looking and believing are synonymous terms.

One writer has attempted to negate this by adding a few thoughts to the Old Testament account. Aware that mere looking at the serpent would contradict his obedience view of faith, he simply adds, "In order to look at the bronze snake on the pole, they had to drag themselves to where they could see it."[28] Dragging themselves to see the serpent is, of course, not simply "looking." Neither is it found in the Old Testament text! But this commentator's real point is that the reason Jesus used the illustration of the serpent in the wilderness was to show Nicodemus the necessity of repentance. According to him, Jesus was actually telling Nicodemus that he had to identify himself with sinning and rebellious Israelites, acknowledge his sin, and repent.[29]

While it is true that the Israelites confessed their sin (Num 21:7), Cocoris correctly points out that "there is not a hint of such an application in Jesus's message to Nicodemus."[30] No parallel between Nicodemus and the Israelites is made at all! The parallel was between the serpent and the Son of Man. Nowhere does it say they had to drag themselves to where they could see the serpent. The serpent was lifted up so that they could see it! Nowhere in the story of Nicodemus does the word "repent" occur. In fact, it does not occur anywhere in John's gospel. All that is necessary for Nicodemus to do to escape judgment is what they did, look to the serpent. This is the exact opposite of "dragging" or "repenting," and it is the only point Jesus made from the text as far as application to Nicodemus was concerned.

---

[28]MacArthur, p. 46.

[29]Ibid.

[30]G. Michael Cocoris, "John MacArthur's System of Salvation: An Evaluation of the Book, The Gospel According to Jesus" (Los Angeles, CA: By the Author, 1989), p. 6.

No! When Paul and Jesus connect faith with hearing and looking, they are trying to throw it into the strongest possible contrast with anything connected with working. Hearing and looking are passive functions. Trust does not include a life of works!

The conclusion that faith is a persuasion is completely within the mainstream of the Reformed faith, and there is no better discussion of it than Benjamin Warfield's article "On Faith in its Psychological Aspects."[31]

Warfield eliminates a role for the will in faith when he says:

The conception embodied in the terms "belief," "faith," is not that of an arbitrary act of the subject's; it is that of a mental state or an act which is determined by sufficient reasons.[32]

This, of course, rules out any notion of obedience which is located in the will, not the mind. He continues:

That is to say, with respect to belief, it is a mental recognition of what is before the mind, as objectively true and real, and therefore depends upon the evidence that a thing is true and real and is determined by this evidence; it is the response of the mind to this evidence and cannot arise apart from it. **It is, therefore, impossible that belief should be the product of a volition;** *volitions look to the future and represent our desires; beliefs look to the present and represent our findings.*[33]

He says that faith cannot be created by the will willing it. It is a product of evidence.[34] This statement conforms to common experience. On many occasions this writer has spoken with non-Christians who simply cannot believe. To tell such a man that he can is a mockery. In some cases he sincerely wants to, but for some reason the evidence necessary for such a reflection has not yet been presented to his mind for reflection. No faith is possible without evidence or what the mind takes for evidence.

It is common for Experimental Predestinarians to insist that, anytime we trust in something, there is some kind of obligation to that object. Every time we trust, a willingness to obey is implied in the very meaning of the word "trust." It cannot be denied that we sometimes use the word this way in English and also that somewhere in early Greek it may be possible to adduce examples of the words which could be translated by something like "be loyal." The writer knows

---

[31]Benjamin B. Warfield, "On Faith in its Psychological Aspects," in *Biblical and Theological Studies* (Philadelphia: Presbyterian and Reformed, 1968), pp. 376ff.

[32]Ibid., p. 376.

[33]Ibid.

[34]Ibid., p. 379.

of no such examples in biblical or extra-biblical Greek, but they may be there. The point is that, if the word ever means that, the other meaning is not part of the meaning of persuasion. Similarly, an elephant's nose is not part of the meaning of "box in the attic." Both are trunks. Context determines meaning, and in the New Testament contexts related to salvation, faith is thrown in contrast with works of obedience. How then can obedience or willingness to obey be implied in the word?

Consider, for example, the following statement. A policeman friend of yours makes the following statement, "The President promises to reduce the budget deficit. Do you believe this?" For the sake of argument and because you are incredibly naive, you say, "Yes, I do." You have an inward conviction that he is a man of his word; he can be counted on to do what he says. You have "believed." Now, the next day a policeman notes that you were driving seventy kilometers per hour in a fifty-kilometer-per-hour zone. He approaches you and says, "I thought you said you believe in the President to reduce the budget deficit. How can you say you believe 'truly' when you do not do what he says?" Such a response on his part would be curious, would it not? Having an inward conviction that the President will reduce the budget deficit in no way implies that you have also purposed to turn from your irresponsible past and totally submit to this authority. Neither does being persuaded that Jesus has died for your sins imply a willingness or determination to obey him. Willingness to obey is simply not part of the semantic value of the word. Please note, however, that a determination to disobey or to continue in a known disobedience is contrary to saving faith.

If, indeed, faith is a mental and not a volitional thing, then two problems immediately come to mind. First, if the will is not involved in faith, then why is it that faith is everywhere presented in Scripture as something for which men are responsible? Second, how can such a view of faith be distinguished from mere intellectual assent? Certainly Satan assents mentally to the proposition that Jesus is God. Does this mean that he has faith?

There are, says Warfield, two factors, not one, involved in the production of faith: (1) the evidence, or the ground on which faith is yielded; and (2) the subjective condition by virtue of which the evidence can take effect in the appropriate act of faith:

> *Evidence cannot produce belief, faith, except in a mind open to this evidence, and capable of responding to it. A mathematical demonstration is demonstrative proof of the proposition demonstrated. But even such a demonstration cannot produce conviction in a mind incapable of following the demonstration.*[35]

---

[35]Ibid., p. 397.

Something more is needed to produce faith. Faith is not a mechanical result of the presentation of evidence. Good evidence can be refused because of the subjective nature or condition of the mind to which it is addressed. This is the ground of responsibility for belief or faith: "it is not merely a question of evidence but of subjectivity; and subjectivity is the other name for personality." Warfield continues,

> *If evidence which is objectively adequate is not subjectively adequate,*
> *the fault is in us. If we are not accessible to musical evidence, then we*
> *are by nature unmusical, or in a present state of unmusicalness. If we*
> *are not accessible to moral evidence then we are either unmoral, or*
> *being moral beings, immoral.*[36]

Since this is true, it is easy to see that a sinful heart which is at enmity to God is incapable of the supreme act of trust in God. Arminians resist this conclusion, because they attribute higher abilities to the mind and will of the natural man than Scripture allows. They are therefore tempted to make faith an act of will instead of a response to testimony. It is surprising that many modern Experimental Predestinarians, in their concern to incorporate obedience into the meaning of faith, have inconsistently accepted this Arminian view of faith.

The biblical solution, however, is to admit that for the natural man faith is impossible and to attribute it to the gift of God. This gift is not communicated mechanically. Rather, it is given through the creation of a capacity for faith on the basis of the evidence submitted. It starts with illumination, softening of the heart, and a quickening of the will. As a result, a man freely believes on the basis of the evidence submitted to him in the Gospels. This creation of capacity is called regeneration. The biblical evidence that faith itself is a gift is impressive and has often been repeated. It comes not of one's own strength or virtue but only to those who are chosen of God for its reception (1 Th. 2:13); hence, it is a gift (Eph. 6:23; cf. 2:8-9; Phil. 1:29). It comes through Christ (Acts 3:16;1 Pet. 1:21), by means of the Spirit (2 Cor. 4:13; Gal. 5:5), and by means of the preached word (Rom. 10:17; Gal. 3:2, 5). Because it is thus obtained from God (2 Pet. 1:1;Jude 3), thanks are to be returned to God for it (Col. 1:4; 2 Th. 1:3).

Warfield concludes:

> *If sinful man as such is incapable of the act of faith, because he is in-*
> *habile to the evidence on which alone such an act of confident resting*
> *on God the Saviour can repose, renewed man is equally incapable of*
> *not responding to this evidence, which is objectively compelling, by an*
> *act of sincere faith.*[37]

---

[36]Ibid., p. 398.
[37]Ibid., p. 399.

If Warfield is one of the leading lights of the Reformed faith in the twentieth century, surely Archibald Alexander would be considered by many to be the leading Reformed thinker of the nineteenth century. He was professor of theology at Princeton Seminary from its beginning in 1812 to his death on September 7, 1851. Dr. Charles Hodge, also of Princeton fame, said of Alexander that he was the greatest man he had ever seen. He was known not only for his wide learning but also for his devout piety. In his classic discussion of the practical Christian life, *Thoughts on Religious Experience*, he has a very interesting discussion of faith. Like Warfield he insists that "faith is simply a belief of the truth."[38] Similar to Calvin he explains that faith "is a firm persuasion or belief of the truth, apprehended under the illumination of the Holy Spirit."[39]

Charles Hodge in his commentary on Romans is quite clear as to the meaning of faith in the Reformed tradition:

> *That faith, therefore, which is connected with salvation includes knowledge, that is, a perception of the truth and its qualities, assent or the persuasion of truth of the object and trust or reliance.*[40]

Nowhere does he suggest that faith involves obedience. Rather, it is knowledge of the truth, a correct understanding of that knowledge, and reliance or trust.

Louis Berkhof will be cited as a final illustration. John MacArthur has apparently misunderstood Berkhof and actually quotes him to prove a point which Berkhof not only did not make but with which he would violently disagree. MacArthur says that Berkhof teaches that faith involves a volitional element and defines Berkhof to mean by this that faith is "the determination of the will to obey the truth."[41] The quotation marks, however, are MacArthur's, not Berkhof's. When one reads what this Reformed theologian actually said, we find that what he means by "volitional element" is not obedience but trust.

> *This third element consists in a personal trust in Christ as Savior and Lord including a surrender of the soul as guilty and defiled to Christ and reception and appropriation of Christ as the source of pardon and spiritual life.*[42]

---

[38]Archibald Alexander, *Thoughts on Religious Experience* (1844; reprint ed., London: Banner of Truth, 1967), p. 64.

[39]Ibid., p. 65.

[40]Charles Hodge, *St. Paul's Epistle to the Romans* (1860; reprint ed., Grand Rapids: Eerdmans, 1950), p. 29.

[41]MacArthur, p. 173.

[42]Louis Berkhof, *Systematic Theology* (London: Banner of Truth, 1958), p. 505.

Possibly MacArthur was led astray by Berkhof's use of the word "surrender." But it is clear that Berkhof does not mean "obedience" but a reliant trust in Christ as the only source of pardon and regeneration, because the Latin word he uses to define this volitional element is **fiducia**, which does not mean "the determination of the will to obey the truth" but "to trust."

Berkhof makes his meaning clear when he defines faith as "a certain conviction, wrought in the heart by the Holy Spirit, as to the truth of the gospel, and a hearty reliance (trust) on the promises of God in Christ."[43] Faith is conviction and trust. It is NOT obedience.

Therefore, it may be concluded that, when the Bible teaches that we are responsible for believing (e.g., Acts 16:31), the meaning is plain. We are responsible for directing our sight to Christ and to an openness to consider the evidence. The evidence for faith is good--the revelation of God in the Bible--and to reject it is a moral, not an intellectual, problem. The refusal of man to do this precludes the possibility that he will come to faith. It is in this that the responsibility for faith lies. In this way we can see that faith itself is not a volitional but a mental act, as it is everywhere described.

Faith and Knowledge

But if faith is merely a mental act, a persuasion based upon evidence, how is it distinguished from mere knowledge, which the demons possess? Are we to say that saving faith is simply the acceptance of a set of propositions about the deity of Christ and the atonement?

There are two things which differentiate saving faith from mere knowledge. The first may be summed up in the word "trust." It is one thing to intellectually accept certain propositions; it is another to be in a state of reliant trust. It is one thing to believe that Jesus is God and that He is the Savior, as the demons do; it is another to look to Him as one's personal Savior from the penalty for sin.

The story has been told of a man who pushed a wheel barrow across the Grand Canyon on a tight rope wire. For five dollars one could daily watch his death-defying performance. As the finale he would ask his assistant to get into the wheel barrow, and he would push her across in front of him. Now imagine you are watching this performance and a man turns to you and says, "Do you believe he can push his assistant across the Grand Canyon on the wire?"

"Of course," you reply. I have watched him do it every day for a week."

---

[43]Ibid., p. 503.

"Then, get in!"

To believe that he can push the wheel barrow across without accident is knowledge. To have an inward conviction that you could "get in," is not only knowledge but faith.

This illustration is helpful in highlighting the error of the Experimental Predestinarian view of faith. Note that the story said that "to have an inward conviction that you could get in" is faith. Experimental Predestinarians would say that, unless you "get in," you do not have faith. But faith is, after all, "the conviction of things hoped for." It is not necessary to actually get in in order to have faith. One need only to have the inward conviction that this man could safely carry you across the canyon.

But there is a second characteristic of true faith which separates it from mere knowledge or intellectual assent. True faith, according to Archibald Alexander, is distinguished from historic faith in the differing evidence upon which it is based.[44] The ground of historical faith, or assent, is only the deductions of reason or the prejudices of culture and education. It is based upon cultural familiarity (i.e., "I am a Christian because I am an American," etc.) or intellectual acceptance of logical conclusions based upon reasonable data. Biblical faith, however, differs from this. Faith in the Bible is not based upon cultural convenience or a deduction of reason. It is based upon a perception of the beauty, glory, and sweetness of divine things as revealed in Scripture and the gospel promise. The object of biblical faith is the saving work of Christ and the gospel offer. The evidence upon which it rests is the promises of Scripture.

While a true believer can quench the Spirit and lose his first love, the faith which emerges from our regeneration is more than detached knowledge; it is assent.

Neither Alexander or Warfield nor a host of other Reformed theologians, including Calvin himself, ever taught that faith included obedience. They would all, no doubt, be surprised to learn that some modern-day Experimental Predestinarians view them as unhistoric or antinomian! What they did teach was that true faith always results in obedience, a conclusion which is simply untrue to Scripture, as earlier chapters of this book have shown.

Faith and Profession

Closely related to the question of faith and knowledge is the question, How is a saved man to be distinguished from one who professes to be saved but in fact is not? Or, How is a false profession of faith in Christ to be distinguished

---

[44]Alexander, p. 66.

from a true one? If the preceding train of thought is granted, then it is clear how we do not discern a false profession. We do not discern this by an examination of his fruits or an assessment of his grief over sin or a measurement of his desire to have fellowship with God.[45] Rather, the presence of a false profession is to be discerned by asking questions which will reveal whether or not a man understands the gospel and has Christ as the conscious object of faith. We ask questions which will reveal whether or not a man is trusting in Christ for salvation and whether or not he has accepted the gospel offer. While such an examination can never yield the certainty which the Experimental Predestinarian seems to desire, it should be realized that his method of examining fruit yields no certainty at all. Indeed, the whole quest for certainty is ill-founded. Paul warned us to judge no man before the time.

Only the individual can know if he has believed. We cannot externally know this for him. Certainly the lack of fruit in a person's life raises the question, Does he possess the Spirit at all, or if he does, has he quenched Him? But just as the presence of fruit cannot prove a man is a Christian, neither can its absence deny it.

Additional citation of authorities or of biblical references is unnecessary.[46] Any concordance will abundantly confirm the conclusions of those already referred to. It may be dogmatically stated that Calvin was correct. Faith is located in the mind. It is primarily a mental and not a volitional act. It differs from mere assent in that it has the additional idea of confidence or persuasion and reliance. It is, as the writer to the Hebrews insisted, an inward conviction, "a conviction of things hoped for" (Heb. 11:1).

Faith and Assurance

Since faith is located primarily in the mind and is received as a gift of God, there are no necessary actions of the will (other than the "act" of reliant trust) or good works required to verify its presence. A man knows he has faith in the same way he knows he loves his wife and children. And if he has faith, then he has justification and assurance. He does not have to wait until the will "kicks in" weeks or months later to produce a few evidences of regeneration. Rather, he can accept the gospel promise that "whosoever believes in Him will not perish"

---

[45]As suggested by Darrell L. Bock, "A Review of *The Gospel according to Jesus*," *BibSac* 146 (Jan-Mar 89): 31-32.

[46]MacArthur refers to Jn. 10:27 and says the sheep "follow." This supposedly means that those who are saved follow him to the end of life (p. 178). But "follow" is simply another way John speaks of "believing," just as elsewhere he refers to "eating" and "drinking" (Jn. 6:56) as believing. The illustration of the little child coming to Jesus does not, contrary to MacArthur, illustrate "obedient humility" (p. 178) but naive, simple trust (Mt. 18:3).

and assume at the instant he believes that his eternal security is definite. Yes, all that is necessary is to "believe at a point in time."

Berkhof properly distinguishes objective and subjective assurance. Objective assurance is "the certain and undoubting conviction that Christ is all He professes to be, and will do all He promises. **It is generally agreed that this assurance is of the essence of faith.**"[47]

Warfield insists that faith is given a formal definition in Heb. 11:1, "It consists in neither assent nor obedience, but in a reliant trust in the invisible Author of all good."[48] According to Warfield, assurance is part of saving faith.[49]

Various views of personal assurance have been held in the history of the church. The Roman Catholic view denies that personal assurance belongs to the essence of faith. Believers can never be sure except in special instances where assurance is given by special revelation, such as to Stephen and Paul. This had great impact in keeping people under the control of the church. Only through such means as indulgences, masses, and priestcraft could a person have a chance of heaven.

The Reformers, on the other hand, held, as we have shown, that personal assurance was in the essence of saving faith. They did not deny that true children of God may struggle with doubt.

The Reformed confessions, however, vary. The Heidelberg Catechism teaches that the assurance of faith consists in the assurance of the forgiveness of sin and is included in saving faith. But the Canons of Dort say that assurance comes from (a) faith in God's promises; (b) testimony of Spirit; and (c) from the exercise of a good conscience and the doing of good works and is enjoyed according to the measure of faith.

Westminster Confession similarly affirms that assurance does not belong to the essence of faith. "This infallible assurance doth not so belong to the essence of faith, but that a true believer may wait long, and conflict with many difficulties before he be a partaker of it. . . . Therefore it is the duty of every man, to give all diligence to make his calling and election sure."[50]

For the pietists assurance does not belong to the being but the well-being of faith, and it can be secured only by continuous and conscientious introspection. Like the Experimental Predestinarians they emphasized self-examination.

---

[47]Berkhof, p. 507.

[48]Ibid., p. 422.

[49]Ibid., p. 427.

[50]"Westminster Confession of Faith," in Schaff, 3:638 (18.3.21-32).

Methodists hold that one can have assurance that he is saved now but not assurance that he will be saved ultimately. Wesley and the later Arminians believed that, while final assurance is impossible, present assurance is. A man can be assured of his present conversion and have some hope of his final salvation. This present assurance comes through an immediate impression of the Holy Spirit. This mystical direct witness seems to have come through the Moravians to Wesley. Wesley was also a great admirer of the mystic Thomas a Kempis and may have been influenced by him as well.

The Reformed Presbyterians deny that faith itself includes assurance. Yet Kuyper, Bavink, and Vos **correctly** hold that true faith is trust and carries with it a sense of security, which may vary in degree. There is also an assurance of faith which is the fruit of reflection. It is possible, they say, to make faith itself an object of reflection and thus arrive at a subjective assurance that does not belong to the essence of faith. In that case, we conclude from what we experience in our own life that the Holy Spirit dwells within us.

Berkhof, in alignment with this tradition, seems to be saying that true assurance is of the essence of faith but that there is an additional assurance which can come on the basis of reflection.

The modern Calvinists accept the doctrine of Westminster. The assurance of hope is not of the essence of saving faith. A man may be justified without having it. It is based upon the witness of the Spirit and a comparison of one's life with Scripture and should be the goal sought by every believer.

Robert Dabney and the Assurance of Faith

Robert L. Dabney was one of the best minds the Reformed faith has ever produced. His *Lectures in Systematic Theology*[51] are filled with valuable theological insight. He served under General Stonewall Jackson during the Civil War and was a professor at Union Theological Seminary. This Southern Presbyterian from Virginia was an articulate spokesman for the Experimental Predestinarian views of assurance and faith. One of the best ways then to critique their position is to interact with his discussion.

Dabney acknowledges that Calvin and the early Reformers united assurance and faith as one direct act of faith.[52] It is interesting that in 1878 Dabney attacks this doctrine as an "error" of the "early" Reformers and their "modern imitators."[53]

---

[51]Robert L. Dabney, *Lectures in Systematic Theology* (1878; reprint ed., Grand Rapids: Zondervan, 1972).

[52]Ibid., p. 699.

[53]Ibid., p. 703.

Dabney objects to the doctrine of Calvin on three grounds.[54] First, saints in the Bible often seem to lose their assurance. If assurance is of the essence of saving faith, how, Dabney asks, can these verses be explained (Ps. 31:22; 77:2, 5; Isa. 50:10)? The lack of this assurance can easily be explained by the fact that the Christian is not looking biblically to Christ and the gospel promise. Saved people often lose their perspective and stop relying upon Christ as the conscious object of their faith. They are emotionally troubled. This does not mean they are not saved. It only means that at that moment they are not exercising the biblical faith they did at first and hence have no assurance. This answer would not have occurred to Dabney because his Westminster Calvinism has taught him that any true Christian always believes. Such a position is not only contrary to Scripture but is contrary to Christian experience.

Second, Dabney objects that Calvin's view adds something to the object of saving faith. Thus, a man is not saved until he has come to believe that Christ has saved him, but it is only by believing that he is saved to begin with. This definition of faith, Dabney maintains, requires the effect, being saved, to precede the cause, faith.

Dabney argues that a man knows he is saved only if he meets the conditions.

Major Premise: *All who believe are saved*
Minor Premise: *I have believed*
Conclusion: *Therefore I am saved*

"Now my point is: that the mind cannot know the conclusion before it knows the minor premise thereof."[55]

But is this not theological hair splitting? Calvin would reply that a persuasion that Christ has saved you is saving faith and is therefore not something you must have before you have saving faith. Furthermore, the state of salvation occurs simultaneously with the exercise of this faith and does not occur before it.

It appears that Dabney ignores the teaching which is common not only in the Reformed faith but also among the so-called "early Reformers," that faith is a "gift of God."[56] There surely is an immediate enlightenment and gift of faith to the soul which enables us to know simultaneously that we have believed and are saved. It is called efficacious grace, and Dabney himself teaches it: "The sinner is enabled to believe by being regenerated, not **vice versa**."[57] Part of the enlightenment and the gift of faith bestowed upon the elect is assurance they are

---

[54]Ibid., pp. 702-704.

[55]Ibid., p. 703.

[56]Phil. 1:29; Eph. 2:8; Jn. 4:10; Heb. 6:4.

[57]Dabney, p. 608.

saved. If faith includes assurance (and it does; cf. Heb. 11:1) and if faith is a gift, then assurance is given with faith.

The gift of faith is included in regeneration. In time they are simultaneous; in source, they are of grace. Put in order of production, regeneration precedes faith. Thus, the sinner is able to believe God has saved him, because God has saved him and his regenerate mind testifies to this in the gift of believing.

Finally, Dabney objects to Calvin on the grounds that the scriptural exhortations to self-examination refer not only to our moral life but also whether or not we are truly saved.[58] Dabney argues that, if assurance of grace was an essential part of faith, then believers would not be commanded to examine their faith and settle the question. In fact, if assurance is of the essence of saving faith, then the need to examine faith proves that we are not Christians at all! The biblical calls to self-examination will be examined below. It is sufficient to say here that none of Dabney's proof texts establish his point. Nowhere in the Bible is a Christian asked to examine either his faith or his life to find out if he is a Christian. He is told only to look outside of himself to Christ alone for his assurance that he is a Christian. The Christian is, however, often told to examine his faith and life to see if he is walking in fellowship and in conformity to God's commands.

Assurance Is of the Essence of Faith

That Calvin, Warfield, Berkhof, and the Heidelberg Confession are more in alignment with Paul than the Experimental Predestinarians in the matter of faith and assurance is evident for several reasons.

First, some assurance must always be part of faith. There must always be some hope where there is faith or belief in the heart. Assurance of faith and assurance of hope are therefore both ingredients of faith.[59]

But, second, an assurance which is based upon the believer's own spirituality does not deserve to be called assurance. It is too subjective and uncertain.

In addition, since faith and hope have the same object, the death of Christ for sin, and the same basis, the promises of God, they must be inseparable. Dabney responds:[60]

---

[58]He refers to Rom. 5:4; 1 Cor. 11:28; 2 Cor. 13:5; 2 Pet. 1:10; Jn. 15:14; Jn. 3:14, 19.

[59]Dabney responds that of course there is assurance with all faith, but not **plerophoria elpidos**, full assurance of hope. The assurance of hope, according to Dabney, is grounded on gospel promises, testimony of the Spirit, and evidences of fruit. He answers by assertion, rather than by biblical reference. They say they are united because any true faith requires it, and he simply refuses to accept that, but he gives no reason for the distinction.

[60]Dabney, p. 699.

> *The promises are assuredly mine, provided I have genuine faith. But I know that there is a spurious faith. Hence, although I have some* **elpis** *from the moment I embrace that truth, I do not have the* **plerophoria elpidos** *until I have eliminated the doubt whether my faith is, possibly, of the spurious kind.*

However, Dabney's reference to **plerophoria elpidos** reflects a misunderstanding of this word (to be discussed below). He intends it to mean the "fulfilling of hope," i.e., the finding of assurance, rather than "fullness of hope," as its usage elsewhere suggests. But the way we determine whether or not our faith is spurious is not by examining our faith or our works but by examining the object of our faith and the biblical presentation of the gospel promise. A man looking biblically at the person of Christ as presented in the Scriptures does not have a spurious faith.

Third, if assurance is separate from faith, then the basis of our assurance is not our trust in Christ but our trust in Christ plus reflection upon the fruits of regeneration in our lives. We are therefore ultimately trusting for assurance in self and not in the promises of Scripture.

Dabney's logical syllogism may once again be stated:

Major Premise:	*All who believe are saved*
Minor Premise:	*I have believed*
Conclusion:	*Therefore I am saved*

The troubled believer must focus his attention on the minor premise, how do I know if I have truly believed? It seems obvious that this would cause him to base his assurance on the results of the self-examination of his faith, a point which Dabney elsewhere tells us we must do.[61] Nevertheless, Dabney claims this does not mean we are trusting in ourselves for assurance:[62]

> *When that same God tells him that there are two kinds of believing, only one of which fulfills the terms of that proposition, and that the deceitfulness of the heart often causes the false kind to ape the true; and when the humble soul inspects his own faith to make sure that it meets the terms of God's promise, prompted to do so by mistrust of self, it passes common wit to see, wherein that process is a "trusting in self instead of God's word."*

It may "pass common wit" for Dabney, but most would see a serious problem here which Dabney merely answers by assertion. As Dabney says elsewhere, faith is a product of looking at the object of faith and not at faith itself. If a be-

---

[61]Ibid., p. 704.
[62]Ibid., p. 705.

liever tries to determine whether he is saved by examining his faith, he is, in effect, placing his faith in faith instead of in Christ. His examination will always turn up an impurity, an insincerity, or an incompleteness in his believing. Rather, the Bible calls us to look away to the object of faith, and this act of "looking" **is** faith. It will be true faith if we are looking scripturally and objectively at the God-man who paid the penalty for all sin. As long as we focus our thoughts on Him and His justifying righteousness and rest on that wholeheartedly, we have true faith and the full assurance of faith. Saving faith never comes from a self-examination, but it is part of a "Christ examination." Christ is the mirror in which we contemplate our election. As we look at Him, we see our own image reflected back to us.

Also, it must be remembered that it is not so much the amount of faith (faith the size of a mustard seed will do!) but the existence of faith which "is the evidence of things hoped for." The mere presence of faith in the life is the evidence of regeneration. Yet the Bible never asks us to examine the quality or amount of our faith, as Dabney and the Puritans insist. Rather, like Calvin, it directs us to reflect upon Christ, not faith, in order to find our assurance.

If a man has believed, he knows it, and if he has believed, he has eternal life and therefore knows it, i.e., he has assurance. Consciousness attends all the operations of the soul. Therefore, no man can believe (resulting in salvation) without being conscious that he has believed (resulting in salvation). To say otherwise leads to the absurd conclusion that a man can believe in Christ and not know if he has done this.

Dabney responds by noting that, when the mind is troubled or confused, a remembered consciousness is obscured, or even lost. Thus, it is possible to believe and not be conscious of it. With this the writer agrees, but this is not the point. We are not dealing with the troubled state of a Christian sometime after he has believed but with the gospel offer to the nonbeliever. Is it not generally true, apart from psychological disturbance of some kind, that a man can believe and know that he has done so? If he cannot, then the gospel promise is no promise at all. But, says Dabney, a man can believe falsely, and his faith must be examined. If his faith must be examined, then, says Dabney, so must his consciousness.[63]

> *If a man thinks he believes aright, he is conscious of exercising what he thinks is a right faith. This is the correct statement. Now, if the faith needs a discrimination to distinguish it from the dead faith, just to the same extent will the consciousness about it need the same discrimination.*

[63]Ibid.

But a self-examination of faith once again puts our faith in faith. We do not examine faith, but we look to Christ and rest in Him, and that act is true faith. The Bible nowhere commands us to examine whether or not our faith is true or false faith. It calls upon us to look to Christ, to believe on Him. The act of doing this is faith itself. Assurance is intrinsically involved in such an act if faith and the finished work of Christ are properly understood. Dabney everywhere assumes that a man must struggle with the question of whether or not he has believed correctly. The Bible never raises this issue which dominated three hundred years of English Puritan theological debate and which Dabney vainly tries to defend. Does a man struggle to know if he loves his child? Does he struggle to know if he has trusted the courts of law? Does he struggle to know if he has chosen a particular profession? These things are obvious as soon as the decision is made. We know we have believed aright if we have believed according to biblical truth. We do not know it by the results; we know by the act of believing in the biblically understood object. If the object is correctly understood and we place our faith in the object, then our faith is correct, and we have assurance.

Now the way we come to accurate knowledge of the object of faith is called preaching the gospel. If the gospel is incorrectly preached, as with the Mormons, for example, then the faith in that object is false. But if the object is correctly perceived and trusted in, the faith is correct, the consciousness of having believed is valid, and the assurance associated with trusting in that object is valid assurance. We are not called upon in Scripture to examine our faith but to examine Christ, the object of our faith.

The issue is not a rational examination of our faith as to whether or not we have believed correctly, as Experimental Predestinarians insist. Rather, the issue is a rational examination of the object of faith, Jesus Christ, and the gospel offer.

Finally, the Bible explicitly and implicitly affirms that assurance is part of saving faith. The writer to the Hebrews unambiguously declares this to be true when he says, "Faith is the assurance of things hoped for" (Heb. 11:1). But in addition, the scores of passages which tell us that "whosoever believes has eternal life" surely imply that a person who has believed has eternal life. If he is not assured of that fact, how is it possible that he has believed the promise? Belief and assurance are so obviously inseparable that only the interest of preserving the Experimental Predestinarian doctrine of perseverance can justify their division.

But if assurance is in fact part of true faith, why then does the Bible ask us to examine ourselves to see if in fact we are truly Christians. Surely, if assurance is part of true faith, such examinations would be unnecessary. This will be the subject of the next chapter.

Chapter 13

Self-examination and Assurance

Experimental Predestinarians assume, often without discussion, that the Bible obviously calls upon believers to "examine themselves" in order to discern whether or not they are actually Christians. Yet to this writer's knowledge only four passages (other than the so-called "tests of life" in 1 John) have ever been adduced in support of this contention. Yet these passages lend little support for their doctrine. In this chapter these passages will be discussed.

The Scriptural Admonitions

Hebrews 6:11

The NKJV translation of Heb. 6:11 reads:

And we desire that each one of you show the same diligence to the full assurance of hope until the end.

The text has often been used to establish the notion that we can prove our election to ourselves by means of good works and thus through examination of them become assured of our salvation. Indeed, they say, it is our duty to be diligent to find assurance.[1]

There are several factors in this verse that make this interpretation unnecessary, if not unlikely. First, the word translated "full assurance," Gk. **plerophoria**, is always used in a passive sense in the New Testament,[2] namely, it means "fullness" and not "fulfilling." If it meant "fulfilling," the phrase might be translated, "show diligence for the fulfilling of hope." This would mean that we

---

[1]"These verses [Heb. 6:11; 10:22; Col. 2:2] obviously imply that there are degrees of assurance, and that Christians should never be satisfied with little assurance but should always be striving for greater degrees of grace" (John E. Marshall, "'Rabbi' Duncan and the Problem of Assurance," *The Banner of Truth* 206 [November 1980]: 2).

[2]B. F. Westcott, *The Epistle to the Hebrews* (London: Macmillan, 2d. ed., 1892; reprint ed., Grand Rapids: Eerdmans, 1965), p. 156.

should be diligent to obtain assurance. However, if it is rendered passively, as it is elsewhere in the New Testament, then the translation is: "Show diligence in respect of the fulness of hope." This would mean that we should be diligent regarding something already obtained.

Next, the preposition "to" in the phrase "to the full assurance" is the Greek word **pros**. Based on its spatial sense of motion and direction, it is often used in a psychological sense of "in view of," "with a view to," "in accordance with," and "with reference to."[3] Arndt and Gingrich say the meaning in this verse is "as far as . . . is concerned, with regard to."[4]

Considering only the lexical meanings of **pros** and **plerophoria** together, the author would appear to be exhorting the Hebrews to "show diligence with regard to the assurance of hope that you now have to the end."[5] Or more simply, "Be faithful to the end of life."

But, as is usually the case, it is contextual and biblical factors that ultimately decide an issue. In favor of this rendering of **pros** is: (1) The context of the warning passage is about holding your confidence, your confession of Christ, firm to the end of life (3:6, 14; 6:6, 15; 10:35); (2) the passage seems to be closely paralleled by Heb. 10:32-36. Verse 10 is expanded on in 10:32-34 (the external works) and v. 11 is expanded on in 10:35-36 (the internal maintenance of one's confession); (3) the other usage of **plerophia** in Hebrews refers to an assurance which comes as a result of trusting in the cross for forgiveness, not an assurance which is arrived at later in life through diligent attention to the fruits of regeneration (Heb. 10:22); (4) the word **plerophia** always has a passive, never an active, meaning in the New Testament and is not found in classical Greek; and (5) it appears from 1 Th. 1:5 that this fullness of hope is not the result of a reflex act of faith later in the Christian's life but comes with the gospel to begin with.

His meaning is that, just as they have shown diligence in regard to these external matters--loving others, v. 10--he wants them to show diligence in regard to this internal matter, maintaining their assurance of hope to the end. He is not fearful that they will lose their salvation. He is fearful they will lose their testimony, their faithfulness, their perseverance.

Thus, the meaning of the passage is completely unrelated to finding out if one is a Christian by means of perseverance. Rather, it is an exhortation to be diligent in regard to our sure hope of salvation as we have already been diligent

---

[3]Murray J. Harris, "Prepositions and Theology in the Greek New Testament," in *NIDNTT*, 3:1204.

[4]AG, p. 717.

[5]This use of **pros** is found in Heb. 5:1: "in things pertaining to (God)." Note also Heb. 1:7: "in regard to (the angels)"; Rom. 10:21: "in regard to (Israel)"; Lk. 12:47: "(that slave did not act) in accord with (his master's will)."

in our love for the brothers. In other words, it is an exhortation to persevere to the end.

2 Peter 1:10

The central verse of the Experimental Predestinarian tradition is 2 Pet. 1:10-11:

Therefore, my brothers, be all the more eager to make your calling and election sure. For if you do these things, you will never fall, and you will receive a rich welcome into the eternal kingdom of our Lord and Savior Jesus Christ.

What does it mean to make our "calling and election sure?" Arminians see it as an exhortation to guarantee that we do not fall fatally and lose our salvation.[6] Experimental Predestinarians generally have understood the passage to apply to the conscience. In other words, by the doing of good works, by the adding of the various qualities of the preceding context to faith (1:3-7), we prove to our conscience that we really are saved people. As the troubled conscience reflects upon the presence of these qualities in the life, it is supposedly quieted and assured. Our salvation, they say, is sure from the viewpoint of the counsels of God, but from our side it is "insecure unless established by holiness of life."[7] We must "produce a guarantee of [our] calling and election"[8] or "make your calling and election secure."[9] Others, such as Calvin, do not connect this with conscience but simply with the need for some external evidence as proof we are saved.[10] Thus, no subjective sensation of an assured conscience is meant.

It seems that his interpretation of Peter's words is unlikely. First of all, it suffers from the fact that the immediate context seems to define the sureness as a bulwark against falling, and not a subjective confidence to the heart that one is saved. Peter says that the way we make our calling and election sure is by "doing these things." This evidently refers back to 1:3-7 where he exhorts us to add various virtues to our Christian lives. The result of doing these things is that we will not stumble and fall. This immediately suggests that sureness is a sureness that prevents stumbling and not a sensation of assurance or proof of salvation.

---

[6]For example, R. C. H. Lenski, *The Interpretation of the Epistles of St. Peter, St. John, and St. Jude* (Minneapolis: Augsburg, 1966), p. 277.

[7]Henry Alford, *The Greek Testament,* ed. Everett F. Harrison, 4 vols. (1849-60; reprint ed., Chicago: Moody Press, 1968), 4:394

[8]R. H. Strachan, "The Second Epistle General of Peter," in *EGT,* 5:128.

[9]For example, Alford, 4:394.

[10]John Calvin, *The Epistle of Paul The Apostle to the Hebrews and The First and Second Epistles of St. Peter,* trans. W. B. Johnston, *Calvin's New Testament Commentaries,* ed. David W. and Thomas F. Torrance (Reprint ed., Grand Rapids: Eerdmans, 1963), p. 334.

Furthermore, the general thrust of the book, as summed up at the end in 3:17, is concerned with their perseverance and not their assurance. Third, the Greek word for "sure," Gk. **bebaios**, never has a subjective sense in biblical or extra-biblical Greek. Indeed, it is often used elsewhere in the New Testament of an external confirmation[11] or of something legally guaranteed.[12] A few verses later Peter refers to the prophetic word which is "more sure" (**bebaios**) than the subjective experience Peter enjoyed in witnessing the transfiguration of the Lord on the mountain (1:19). Finally, this interpretation must assume that Peter addresses his readers as professing Christians and not as true Christians. In this view Peter wants his readers to prove that they are Christians by living a godly life. Yet this directly contradicts what Peter has just said in the preceding verse (1:9). There he assured them that, even if they lack these Christian virtues, it means only that they have forgotten they have been cleansed from sin. Would he then in the next verse (1:10) say that if they do lack these virtues, then this means they have not been cleansed from sin?

Though **bebaios** is often a technical term for a legally guaranteed security,[13] that is probably not the sense here. In classical Greek **bebaios** and the related words[14] meant "fit to tread upon" or a "firm foundation." The words are used in two ways in the New Testament.[15] The verb means "to confirm or validate." It is also used in the sense of "to strengthen, to establish, to make firm, reliable, durable, unshakeable."[16] Experimental Predestinarians prefer the former, but the context seems to be strongly in favor of the latter.

Of particular interest is our passage regarding the **metochoi** in Heb. 3:14: "We are partakers (**metochoi**) of Christ if we hold **firm** (**bebaios**) the beginning of our assurance to the end." The similar contexts seem to suggest that "to hold firm" may be a similar idea to "make your calling and election sure." In other words, to make our calling and election sure is simply another way of saying persevere to the end. It has the simple sense of "remain firm," or "strengthen." This is the meaning in Col. 2:7 where Paul exhorts them to be rooted and built up in him and "strengthened" (**bebaioo**) in the faith. "It is good," says the writer of the Epistle to the Hebrews, "for the heart to be strengthened (**bebaioo**) by grace" (Heb. 13:9). It is most important to notice that Peter, himself, in two passages seems to explain what he means by "make sure." We are to make our calling and election "sure" as a protection so that we will never stumble in our Christian lives (1:10). This thought is central to the epistle and is brought out again at the end.

---

[11]Heb. 2:2

[12]Heb. 6:19; 9:17.

[13]MM, p. 107. It is common in the juristic sense: "if I make a claim or fail to guarantee the sale, the claim shall be invalid" or "[I] will guarantee the sale with every guarantee" (p. 108).

[14]**Bebaioo**, "to establish," and **bebaiosis**, "confirmation"

[15]H. Schoenweiss, "Firm, Foundation, Certainty, Confirm," in *NIDNTT*, 1:658.

[16]Ibid.

"You therefore, beloved, knowing this beforehand, **be on your guard** lest, being carried away by the error of unprincipled men, you **fall from your own steadfastness**" (2 Pet. 3:17). To "be on your guard" is a parallel thought to "make your calling and election sure." "Fall from your own steadfastness" is manifestly the same as to stumble in 1:10.

To "make [our] calling and election sure" means to guarantee by adding to our faith the character qualities of 1:5-7 that our calling and election will achieve their intended aim. What is that?

> *But as He who* **called** *you is holy, you also* **be holy in all your conduct** (1 Pet. 1:15 NKJV).

> *But when you do good and suffer for it, if you take it patiently, this is commendable before God.* For **to this you were called** (1 Pet. 2:20-21 NKJV).

> *Not returning evil for evil or reviling for reviling, but on the contrary blessing, knowing that* **you were called to this**, *that you may inherit a blessing* (1 Pet. 3:9 NKJV).

Similarly, we are elected so that we might be holy and blameless before Him,[17] that we might be obedient (1 Pet. 1:1-2), and that we might proclaim His name (1 Pet. 2:9). Because they already knew they were chosen of God, the Thessalonians lived consistently with the intended purpose of the election and became examples to the believers in Macedonia and Achaia (1 Th. 1:4-7).

The aim of our calling and election appears to be holiness in this life, perseverance in suffering, and inheriting a blessing in the life to come. "Calling and election" are united under the same article. This often signifies that they refer to the same thing. Calling and election are very practical and experiential concepts in the New Testament. Our Reformation heritage has perhaps caused us to overemphasize the basic meaning of the words instead of their intended aim. In our discussions we often talk of election rather than election to be holy. We speak of an efficacious call rather than a call to suffer and persevere. In other words, we discuss the initial event, call and election, separately from the intended effect, a holy, obedient life. This writer is not objecting to this. The concepts of calling and election are so profound and problematic that they fully justify such a treatment. But readers of the New Testament would not do this. They saw the ideas of initial event and intended result as all part of the same term, "calling and election." The point is simply that the terms "calling and election" would signify more than what is covered in the chapter on the ordo salutus in our systematic theologies. A first-century reader would have seen the terms as signifying the totality of their Christian experience. To them it is probable that the two words

---

[17]Eph. 1:4.

taken together represent their Christian lives or the intended aim of calling and election.[18]

Peter's meaning is that we must make our Christian lives impregnable against falling into sin by adding the virtues in the preceding context to our foundation of faith. We must strengthen our lives. This will make us unshakable and firm in the midst of suffering. To say it differently, to make our calling and election sure is to purpose that they will achieve their intended aim: a holy life, perseverance in suffering, and inheriting a blessing.

In 2 Pet. 1 the apostle is concerned not with their assurance but with their perseverance and their fruitfulness. He says:

> For this very reason, make every effort to add to your faith goodness; and to goodness, knowledge; and to knowledge self-control; and to self-control, perseverance; and to perseverance, godliness; and to godliness, brotherly kindness; and to brotherly kindness, love (2 Pet. 1:5-7).

Having begun well, he wants them to finish well. He explains why:

> For if you possess these qualities in increasing measure, they will keep you from being ineffective and unproductive in your knowledge of our Lord Jesus Christ (2 Pet. 1:8).

To be effective and productive in our knowledge of Christ will result in our calling and election being "sure," morally impregnable against falling into sin. Rather than call into question the salvation of those who may lack these qualities, as the Experimental Predestinarians do, Peter does just the opposite. He affirms they are saved.

> But if anyone does not have them, he is nearsighted and blind, and **has forgotten that he has been cleansed from his past sins** (2 Pet. 1:9).

The absence of these qualities does not necessarily cast doubt on our justification. It only points out that we have forgotten the motivating benefits of the grace of God.

Elsewhere Peter expressed a similar thought:

---

[18]This phrase has merismic tendencies in that it seems to be looking at the Christian life as a totality by using the words that signify the beginning and the end of the process. For further explanation of merism see A. M. Honeyman, "Merismus in Biblical Literature," *JBL* 71 (1952): 11-18.

> *But resist him, firm in your faith, knowing that the same experiences of*
> *suffering are being accomplished by your brethren who are in the*
> *world.   And after you have suffered for a little while, the God of all*
> *grace, who called you to His eternal glory in Christ, will Himself per-*
> *fect, confirm, strengthen and establish you* (1 Pet. 5:9-10 NASB).

The experimentalists say that to make our calling and election sure is to find out if we are elected by looking at our works. Peter is saying something different. To make our calling and election sure is to add virtues to our faith so that (1) we build a firm foundation, impregnable against falling into sin; and (2) we will obtain a rich welcome when we enter the kingdom.

2 Corinthians 13:5

The exhortation to "examine yourselves" has found a prominent place in the theology texts of the Experimental Predestinarians:

> *Examine yourselves to see whether you are in the faith; test yourselves.*
> *Do you not realize that Christ Jesus is in you--unless, of course, you*
> *fail the test* (2 Cor. 13:5).

Here the apostle tells his readers that a self-examination can result in knowledge as to whether or not one is "in the faith." A failure of this test is proof that Christ Jesus is not "in you." If having Christ "in you" refers to salvation, then this passage would seem to lend credence to the idea that we should examine our lives to find out if there are sufficient evidences present to establish to our consciences that we are in fact among the elect. However, it does not mean this.

"Yourselves" is first in the sentence; it is emphatic. He is referring back to v. 3. They wanted proof that Christ was speaking "in me." Paul now turns it around on them. "You, yourselves, should test yourselves to see if he is really speaking **in you.**"

The object of this examination is not to find out if they are Christians but to find out if they are "in the faith." Why do some assume that being "in the faith" is the same thing as being regenerate? In other uses of this phrase it refers to living according to what we believe. For example, in the LXX it is found in 1 Chr. 9:31:

> *And Mattithiah . . .* **was entrusted with the responsibility** [Gk. **en te**
> **pistei**, "in the faith"] *for baking the offering bread.*

The verse could be translated something like, "And Mattithiah was in the faith for baking the offering bread. To be "in the faith" in this verse is to have responsibility for something.

In 1 Cor. 16:13 Paul says, "Be on the alert, stand firm **in the faith**, act like men, be strong." Being "in the faith" here seems to mean something like "live consistently with what you believe." Paul spoke of fellow Christians who are "weak in the faith" (Rom. 14:1). Doesn't this mean something like "weak in living according to what one believes"? Paul wants believers to be "sound in the faith" (Ti. 1:13), and Peter urges the Christians to be strong in resisting the devil, "steadfast in the faith" (1 Pet. 5:8-9). In each case, being "in the faith" refers to consistency in the Christian life, not possession of it.

Christ "in me" in v. 3 does not refer to salvation but to demonstration of powerful speech and deeds. Similarly, the test they are to perform to find out if Christ is "in them" is not to discover if they are saved but whether or not Christ is manifesting Himself in their words and deeds. Paul, of course, doubts that Christ is in them in this sense. Salvation is not in view at all.

Christ is in them, unless they fail the test, i.e., unless they are **adokimos**, unapproved. This word is used seven times in the New Testament. It is found in the often quoted passage in 1 Cor. 9:27 where the apostle himself fears he might become **adokimos**. Its basic meaning is "not standing the test, rejected."[19] According to Eric Sauer, it "is the technical term for a runner not standing the test before the master of the games and therefore being excluded at the prize-giving."[20] The meaning of **adokimos** is simply "to fail the test." It is used of Christians four times (1 Cor. 9:27; 2 Cor. 13:5-6; Heb. 6:8). The result of their failure is determined by the context. In 1 Cor. 9:27 the message is not loss of salvation but loss of reward in the Isthmian games. In Heb. 6:8 it is used of the unfruitful believer. He is a worthless field because he yields thorns and thistles and is close to being cursed.

Surely Leon Morris is correct:[21]

*"Castaway" is too strong for **adokimos**. The word means "which has not stood the test," and in this context refers to disqualification. Paul's fear was not that he might lose his salvation, but that he might lose his crown through failing to satisfy his Lord (cf. 3:15).*

In 2 Cor. 13:5 to "fail the test" is to fail the test that Christ is mighty in them in the sense of mighty words and deeds. This was their charge against Paul in 2 Cor. 13:3. He now turns it around on them.

---

[19]AS, p. 10.

[20]Eric Sauer, *In The Arena* (Grand Rapids: Eerdmans, 1966), p. 162.

[21]Leon Morris, *The First Epistle of Paul to the Corinthians*, TNTC, p. 140.

1 Corinthians 11:28-32

A command to examine ourselves is also found in 1 Cor. 11:28-32 (NKJV):

> *But let a man examine himself, and so let him eat of that bread and drink of that cup. For he who eats and drinks in an unworthy manner eats and drinks judgment to himself, not discerning the Lord's body. For this reason many are weak and sick among you, and many sleep. For if we would judge ourselves, we would not be judged. But when we are judged, we are chastened by the Lord, that we may not be condemned with the world.*

The passages raises two questions: (1) what kind of self-examination is commanded; and (2) what is the consequence of failure in this test?

In answer to the first question, Paul says that this examination is about judging the body of Christ rightly. The NIV translates, "recognizing the body of the Lord." It seems that to partake of the Lord's supper in a worthy manner is to partake with a consciousness of what it truly signifies: His death for our sins. This should cause us to avoid careless indifference or irreverence. Conversely, to partake in an unworthy manner is to go to the Lord's table with an indifferent attitude about what it signifies. The self-examination here is apparently not for the purpose of finding sin in the life but to determine whether our minds are sufficiently centered on Christ so that, when we partake, we do so with full appreciation for the significance of the elements. They are not commanded to examine themselves to see if they are Christians, or even to see if they have sin in their lives, but to see if they are properly comprehending the body of Christ.

The consequences of failure to do this are severe indeed. Some of them were sick, and some had fallen asleep in the Lord. While it is sometimes said that the judgment which can come upon the believer is the final judgment of hell,[22] that passage seems to say precisely the opposite--it is a discipline in time (11:32).

We go through these disciplines in time "in order that" we might not be condemned with the world. This probably means "in order that we will not be judged in time." If a Christian responds properly to discipline, he will confess and submit to the Lord and avoid the judgments in time which commonly come upon the wicked. Paul is nowhere raising the question of their saved condition. Indeed, even those who die are really "asleep." This is the common Christian

---

[22]See Frederic Godet, *Commentary on First Corinthians* (Edinburgh: T. & T. Clark, 1889; reprint ed., Grand Rapids: Kregel, 1977), p. 597; Archibald Robertson and Alfred Plummer, *A Critical and Exegetical Commentary on the First Epistle of St. Paul to the Corinthians*, 2d ed., *International Critical Commentary* [Edinburgh: T. & T. Clark, 1914], p. 254.

term for the death of a believer (e.g., 1 Th. 4:14). In addition, he is contrasting true Christians with the world.

Conclusion

No part of Experimental Predestinarian teaching is potentially more damaging to Christian growth than their misguided notion that assurance is based upon evidences of works in the life. Their continual insistence on self-examination to verify one's state of salvation cannot be found in the New Testament. It would be a hateful father who entered into the following imaginary conversation with his son:[23]

Son: "Dad, am I **really** your son, or am I only adopted?"

Father: "Well, young man, it depends on how you behave. If you really are my son, you will show this by doing the things I tell you to do. If you have my nature inside of you, you can't help but be obedient."

Son: "But what if I disobey you a lot, Dad?"

Father: "Then you have every reason to doubt that you are truly my son!"

A child's greatest need when faced with doubt about his acceptance is to have the Father's unconditional love reaffirmed. No human father would treat his child as Experimental Predestinarians imagine our divine Father treats His!

Obtaining Assurance

How then is assurance to be obtained, according to the Experimental Predestinarian? If it is not part of the essence of faith and does not come as we look at Christ, then it must come from looking at Christ and something else.

Different writers have different criteria, but all advocates of the Reformed doctrine of perseverance agree that a self-examination of certain fruits of regeneration is necessary in order to verify the presence of saving faith. John Murray insists the finding or obtaining assurance is a duty.[24] By "grounds of assurance" he

---

[23]Illustration taken from Zane Hodges, *Absolutely Free* (Dallas: Zondervan, 1989), p. 17.

[24]John Murray, *Collected Writings of John Murray*, 2 vols. (London: Banner of Truth, n.d.), 2:264. He cites 2 Pet. 1:4-11; 1 Jn. 2:3; 3:14, 18-19, 21, 24; 5:2, 5, 13; Rom. 8:15-16, 35-39; Heb. 6:11, 17-19; 2 Cor. 1:21-22; 13:5; Eph. 1:13-14; 4:30; 2 Tim. 1:12.

means "the ways in which a believer comes to entertain this assurance, not of the grounds on which his salvation rests." He expands the grounds of assurance to five:[25]

First, there must be intelligent understanding of the nature of salvation. Second, we must recognize the immutability of the gifts and calling of God. Our security rests in the faithfulness of God and not in the fluctuations of our experience. Third, we must obey the commandments of God. Fourth, there must be self-examination. He cites 2 Pet. 1:10 and 2 Cor. 13:5. Finally, Murray bases our assurance upon the inward witness of the Holy Spirit.[26]

He concludes by saying that "assurance is cultivated, not through special duties, . . . but through faithful and diligent use of the means of grace and devotions to the duties which devolve upon us in the family, the church and the world."[27]

Martin Lloyd-Jones has a different list. He rests assurance totally on evidences of fruit in the life. He even goes so far as to say that our certainty of salvation is increased according to the number of tests we pass.[28]

His tests are:

1. My outlook on life will be spiritual (1 Cor. 2:12).
2. I will love the brethren.
3. I will seek God's Glory: "A man who is led by the Spirit of God, is, by definition, a man who desires to live to God's glory."
4. A man led by the Spirit always has a desire within him for greater knowledge of God, and a greater knowledge of our Lord and Saviour Jesus Christ.
5. Anyone led by the Spirit is always concerned about his lack of love for God and for the Lord.
6. Anyone led by the Spirit has an increasing awareness of sin within.
7. A man led of the Spirit is increasingly sensitive to every approach of sin and evil and to temptation.
8. Are we putting to death the deeds of the body?
9. He is aware in himself of desires for righteousness and holiness. Do you long to be holy?[29]

---

[25]Murray, 2:270.

[26]Rom. 8:15-16; Gal. 4:6; 1 Cor. 2:12; 2 Cor. 1:21; 2 Cor. 5:5; Eph. 1:13-14.

[27]Murray, 2:274.

[28]D. Martin Lloyd-Jones, *The Sons of God, Exposition of Romans 8* (Grand Rapids: Zondervan, 1973), pp. 185-92.

[29]He misquotes the Beatitudes here, which apply to rewards for perseverance and not tests of holiness.

10.   Are we manifesting the fruit of the Spirit? (Gal 5). [But that only happens to those whose walk which is not automatic. He actually considers this as nine additional tests! How much joy do you have? How much peace do you have, etc., he asks?]

Lloyd-Jones asks, "Are we testing ourselves as we should?" Then he begins to qualify. "I am not asking whether you are perfect with respect to anyone of the questions. I am simply asking - and I do so to encourage you - Do you find in yourself any evidence of these things? If you do, you are Christian. If there is but little, a mere trace, you are a very small infant and you have perhaps only just been formed. That is a beginning. . . . If there are but glimmerings of life in you, it is sufficient."[30] So apparently, only a "little" evidence, even a "trace," is all that is necessary. Of course, traces are found in the reprobate with their temporary faith and in disobedient Christians as well. Therefore, Lloyd-Jones's assurance gives no basis for distinguishing one's faith from that of the non-elect. In other words, his excruciating introspection will yield no assurance at all.

This is the problem: how much evidence do you need? How much is "any evidence"? How much is a "glimmering"? A man might be very carnal for life and have glimmerings and some evidence. If that is all he means, then how is his regeneration to be validated?[31]

Returning once again to Robert Dabney, we learn that there are only three things we must do to obtain assurance: (1) We must be sure we are true Christians. [Why he includes this is perplexing. Obviously if we are sure we are true Christians, we would not need assurance. That is the point of his self-examination!] (2) We should endeavor to live godly lives in accordance with Scripture. (3) We should make a comparison between the Bible description of a Christian and our own heart and life.[32]

---

[30]Lloyd-Jones, p. 193.

[31]Rosscup seems trapped in the same ambiguity which he tries to overcome by forceful assertion rather than logic (James E. Rosscup, "The Overcomers of the Apocalypse," *GTJ* 3 [Fall 1982]: 261-286). He says the demonstration of regeneration must be "in some vital degree" (p. 268), or as he later qualifies, "at least in some degree" (p. 273). So he has reduced the qualifications from a "vital" degree to only "some" degree. But this helps the sensitive soul not at all. What degree is "vital"? What degree is "some"? "He follows in the direction of faith toward God in the thrust of his life" (p. 268). These statements are not only not found in Scripture but give little help. How much following "in the direction of faith toward God" is necessary to establish that the "thrust of his life" is one of "following." Rosscup acknowledges that believers can die in carnal rebellion but then contradicts himself and says, "The truly saved ones are the brand of people who, when they sin, confess, seek God's forgiveness and cleansing, and desire to live in the light with God" (p. 270). Certainly the saved believer who dies in carnal rebellion like the regenerate Solomon did would not fit in this category.

[32]Robert Dabney, *Lectures in Systematic Theology* (1878; reprint ed., Grand Rapids: Zondervan, 1972), p. 708.

This is, of course, the root of the matter. We are to examine our moral attributes and see if they correspond with the Scriptures. Dabney acknowledges, however, that this is an "indirect means of assurance." This is what Calvin called a secondary means and not the basis of assurance. If that is all Dabney means, then he differs from Calvin not at all! Yet throughout his discussion he has emphasized that self-examination is the basis, not the "indirect means," of assurance.

He hastens to warn us of the dangers of introspection:[33]

For a faithful self-inspection usually reveals so much that is defective, that its first result is rather the discouragement than the encouragement of hope. But this leads the humbled Christian to look away from himself to the Redeemer; and thus assurance, which is the reflex act of faith, is strengthened by strengthening the direct act of faith itself.

With this he seems to throw away his whole discussion and informs us that assurance comes only by looking to Christ after all! However, that alone, he confusedly adds, is not sufficient. There must be evidence of fruit in the life. How much? Dabney feels that, if there is "little" evidence, this would not be sufficient.[34] Martin Lloyd-Jones, however, feels that a "trace" or "glimmer" would do the job! How much then? Dabney never answers. He only says that, if the "soul finds evident actings of such graces as the Bible calls for," then he has assurance. But Dabney has already acknowledged the existence of a temporary faith which has similar evidences. How can the believer know whether or not his faith is temporary? How much evidence would be adequate to give him assurance now? Only with Christ in the forefront of the believer's mind and as the direct object of his faith can there be any assurance at all. As soon as we begin to examine our love for Christ, we substitute another object. This results in a reduction of our love for Him by the very act of measuring it. As the love for Christ subsides through self-examination, the introspection is more and more likely to return a negative verdict. How then can assurance ever come via self-examination?

Some Experimental Predestinarians have higher requirements than others for determining the saved condition of another Christian. Consider Arthur Pink's criteria. He tells us the things which are absent in the life of a man who claims to be a Christian but really is not:

We will mention some things which, if they are absent, indicate that the "root of the matter" (Job 19:28) is not in the person. One who regards sin lightly, who thinks nothing of breaking a promise, who is

---

[33]Ibid.
[34]Ibid.

careless in performance of temporal duties, who gives no sign of a ten-
der conscience which is exercised over what is commonly called
"trifles," lacks the one thing needful. A person who is vain and self-
important, who pushes to the fore seeking the notice of others, who
parades his fancied knowledge and attainments, has not learned of
Him who is "meek and lowly of heart." One who is hypersensitive,
who is deeply hurt if someone slights her, who resents a word of re-
proof no matter how kindly spoken, betrays the lack of a humble and
teachable spirit. One who frets over disappointments, murmurs each
time his will is crossed and rebels against the dispensations of Provi-
dence, exhibits a will which has not been Divinely subdued.[35]

Such a list would surely call into question the salvation of every believer since the dawn of time, including even Mr. Pink himself! His listing is completely arbitrary. How careless in our duties must we be? How lightly is sin regarded? How vain is too vain? If the professing Christian is too sensitive, he is not really saved. Yet if he is not sensitive enough, if his conscience is not tender enough, then this proves that "he lacks the root of the matter."

The whole quest for assurance based upon self-examination is doomed for a seemingly conspicuous reason. How can a man know that the works he produces are in fact produced by the Holy Spirit and not by his unregenerate flesh? There is no evident way to distinguish them outwardly, and yet it is to these outward evidences that assurance is promised. The apostle specifically forbids such attempts at discrimination when he commands the Corinthians to postpone such judgments until the judgment seat of Christ (1 Cor. 4:1-5).

If there is no infallible way to discern whether the works are the product of the Holy Spirit or the product of the flesh, then is not assurance based upon works impossible?

Obviously these questions cannot be answered on the premises of the Experimental Predestinarian. Since the premises of the Westminster view of assurance logically make assurance now impossible, those premises must be contrary to Scripture which says it is possible now. The only way to achieve the full assurance which the Scriptures promise is to ground it completely outside the subjective vicissitudes of the believer's experience and emotions and objectively in the person and work of Christ. The Reformation attempt to establish the fact that justification was an external, rather than an infused, righteousness was, according to Richard Lovelace, thwarted in part by Puritan and Pietist legalism and their stress on self-examination. "An unbalanced stress on auxiliary methods of assurance--testing one's life by the inspection of works and searching for the

---

[35]Arthur Pink, *Eternal Security* (Grand Rapids: Baker, 1974), p. 67.

internal witness of the Spirit--obscured Luther's teaching on assurance of salvation through naked reliance on the work of Christ."[36]

To argue that we must derive our assurance by observing qualities in ourselves which could only be wrought by sovereign grace is specious. Experimental Predestinarians already acknowledge the existence of temporary faith which manifests the same qualities and the deceitfulness of the human heart which is, in any case, prone to misinterpretation (both for and against being in a state of grace). The only quality which reliably and finally distinguishes temporary faith from saving faith is that saving faith is not temporary! And we cannot know if our faith is temporary until the final hour. In which case, contrary to Scripture, we can have no true assurance until the end of life.

The major objection to all views of assurance is that they could become occasions of spiritual indolence and carnal security. According to the Partaker view of assurance, the Christian living in sin may or may not be genuinely saved. If he is, the Scriptures give him no comfort. He faces serious warnings of divine discipline now and severe rebuke and disinheritance at the judgment seat of Christ. If he has departed from the faith, he has no assurance of salvation because he is no longer looking to Christ, and assurance comes only from conscious reflection upon the object of faith. Hence, the Partaker view of assurance can never lead to carnal security. Yet, paradoxically, those within the Experimental Predestinarian tradition have promulgated a view of security which lends itself to the carnal security they abhor. By looking to some work in the life, non-Christian professors of Christ might be led to believe they are born again when in fact they are on the highway to hell. He needs only to see Lloyd-Jones's "glimmer" or "trace" and conclude all is well with his soul. But if a man is asked to look biblically to Christ for his assurance, carnal security is impossible because looking biblically to Christ makes a life of sin inconceivable.

In answer to the question, "Would you give assurance to someone who is living a profligate life?" the answer is no. Neither should assurance be given to someone who is living a godly life. There is no illustration or teaching in the Bible of one believer ever "giving assurance" to another, i.e., pronouncing him saved. Only the Holy Spirit gives subjective assurance in the heart, in response to looking to Christ, the mirror of our election ("The Spirit himself testifies with our spirit that we are God's children," Rom. 8:16).

So if a person living an inconsistent life and claiming to be a believer asks, "Am I saved?" The only answer can be, "You can only find your assurance of salvation in looking to Christ. You cannot find it in the subjective opinions of men. However, if you are saved, your present lifestyle is inconsistent with the faith you claim to profess." We cannot pronounce on the eternal destiny of men in this sit-

---

[36]Richard F. Lovelace, *Dynamics of Spiritual Life: An Evangelical Theology of Renewal* (Downers Grove, IL: InterVarsity, 1979), p. 100.

uation, we simply explain the gospel, and leave the conviction to the Holy Spirit. We have not left him with a "carnal security."

External fruit is an evidence **for others** that a man is saved, and it is certainly a secondary confirmation to the believer of the reality of God in his life, but it is never presented in Scripture as a basis for the man's personal assurance. When a person lives a profligate life we have no observable evidence that he is a believer. "This is how we know who the children of God are and who the children of the devil are" (1 Jn. 3:10). Since a life of good works reveals who the children of God are, one can only wonder about the genuineness of a man's faith if that man reveals no good works. However, a total unbeliever can live a loving life full of good works, so this kind of testimony is of little value apart from a knowledge of what the man believes and in whom he trusts for justification.

It must be candidly admitted that a person who has lived for Christ for many years and who one day rejects him could theoretically enjoy a hypothetical assurance. He could reason, "If Christianity is really true, I will be in heaven even though I do not presently believe it." Furthermore, it must be admitted that a man who continues to believe and yet persists in sin could theoretically reason, "I can continue in sin and grace will abound." Indeed, Paul's doctrine was criticized at this very point. Any doctrine of assurance which is not open to this charge is not biblical. This would seem to exclude the Experimental Predestinarian view of assurance.

But, we must ask, would such responses be typical? Would this be a normal response to love and grace? Probably not. It seems that these theoretical possibilities do not represent the normal Christian life. Is it not true that a major objection to the Partaker's view is that it is too narrowly focused on the few who might abuse grace rather than the many who do not want to? Grace can be abused and taken for granted, or it is not really grace, i.e., "without cost."

The secrets of a man's heart are known only by the Spirit of God. We do not know the hidden struggles. Neither can we know of an underlying genuine faith which for a lengthy time does not manifest itself in righteous living. It is not for us to judge. In fact, the entire preoccupation with "giving assurance" is a presumption on our part. The apostle Paul specifically refrained from giving or denying assurance: "Therefore judge nothing before the appointed time; wait until the Lord comes. He will bring to light what is hidden in darkness and will expose the motive of men's hearts" (1 Cor. 4:5). On the contrary, the apostle specifically left the giving of assurance to the Holy Spirit.

The Calvinist can offer no real assurance. A man has no assurance he is saved unless he is in a state of godly living at every moment. He therefore does not derive his comfort from Jesus' death; he derives his real comfort and assurance from his own works. Jesus may have saved him, but he can have no real assurance unless he has good works to show that he has really saved him.

However, nothing more than looking to Christ is required, insofar as assurance of heaven is concerned. If more were required, then we would have to say it is by grace through faith plus works or by grace through faith on the condition of faithfulness. As long as assurance is grounded in an examination of our good works, submitted to our conscience, real assurance will not be possible for many. Yet the gospel promises it to all. A sensitive person will never be persuaded that he is holy enough. Even a mature saint, sincerely agonizing over his sin, would in this system often doubt whether or not his faith is real. How could it be, he will reason, since he is as bad as he is?

How then are we to comfort the troubled soul who lacks assurance of salvation? There is perhaps no better way than to follow the method employed by the apostle Paul in Rom. 8:31-39. Here the apostle asks four questions, each beginning with the word "who":

1. Who can be against us (v. 31)? His answer is **no one**, because Christ gave Himself for all of us, and therefore God will graciously give us all things.

2. Who will bring any charge against those whom God has chosen (v. 33)? His answer is **no one**, because God, the only One who could bring such a charge has already rendered His verdict, justified!

3. Who is he that condemns (v. 34)? His answer is **no one**, because Christ has paid the penalty for sin and is at the right hand of God right now interceding for us.

4. Who shall separate us from the love of Christ (35)? His answer is **no one**, because Christ loves us.

What is striking about all four of these answers is that Paul never asks the believer to look inwardly and test for evidences of regeneration, as the Experimental Predestinarian requires. Rather, in answer to all four questions he directs him to Christ. "How does this bring assurance? It does so objectively because it provides the answers to my deepest doubts and fears. . . . From such a premise, only one conclusion is possible. It is the conclusion of assurance."[37]

A believer may lack subjective assurance due to doubt, trials, or even due to an inconsistent Christian life. But for the sincere Christian the Bible does not ask him to examine his life but to look outwardly to Christ. Attention must be

---

[37]Sinclair B. Ferguson, "The Assurance of Salvation," *The Banner of Truth Trust* 186 (March 1979): 5-6.

focused on Christ and the answers Paul gives to the four questions above. This gives the objective foundation from which subjective feelings of assurance can flow. Assurance can be felt to greater or lesser degrees, but it is the product of looking at the "mirror of our election."

The Bible says, "Faith is the assurance of things hoped for." How else could a biblical writer make it plainer that assurance is the essence of faith?

Chapter 14

The Carnal Christian

Attempting to defend that the Bible actually teaches the possible existence of the so-called "carnal Christian" is sometimes viewed with great concern by Experimental Predestinarians. Yet the Bible is more realistic than some of its modern adherents. It accepts the woeful fact that failure is possible.

By "carnal Christian" the writer means a Christian who is knowingly disobedient to Christ for a period of time. He is a Christian who walks as if he were a "mere man," that is, an unregenerate person (1 Cor. 3:4). Occasional lapses of sin are not the subject of this chapter. The focus is the apparent persistence in sin by regenerate people. In remote cases it is even possible that such people will publicly renounce Christ and persist in either sin or unbelief to the point of physical death. However, if they were truly born again in Christ, they will go to heaven when they die.

It should be noted that the Westminster Confession comes very close to the view in this book with the exception of the length of time a carnal Christian can persist in carnality. The Westminster Confession reads as follows:[1]

> *Nevertheless they may, through the temptations of Satan and of the world, the prevalence of corruption remaining in them, and the neglect of the means of their preservation, fall into grievous sins* [Mt. 26:70, 72, 74]; **and for a time continue therein** [Ps. 51:14 and title]; *whereby they incur God's displeasure* [Isa. 64:5, 7, 9; 2 Sam. 11:27], *and grieve his Holy Spirit* [Eph. 4:30]; *come to be deprived of some measure of their graces and comforts* [Ps. 51:8, 10, 12; Rev. 2:4; Song 5:2, 3, 4, 6]; *have their hearts hardened* [Isa. 36:17; Mk. 6:52; 16:14; Ps. 95:8], *and their consciences wounded* [Ps. 33:3, 4; 51:8]; *hurt and scandalize others* [2 Sam. 12:14], *and bring temporal judgments upon themselves* [Ps. 134:31-32; 1 Cor. 11:32].[2]

---

[1]"Westminster Confession of Faith," in Schaff, 3:637 (17:3).

[2]Scripture references in square brackets in this quote are written as footnotes in the confession itself.

Apparently the Westminster divines believed that the Holy Spirit's power was capable of preventing apostasy or persistence in sin to the point of death. Was He not quite strong enough to prevent it "for a time"? It is interesting to note, however, that they acknowledge that one of the judgments in time is physical death (1 Cor. 11:32). There the length of time in which a person can "continue therein" is for the rest of his life! Here we have the precise position of this book.

Such people, of course, may theoretically enjoy a "carnal assurance." But they cannot enjoy biblical assurance. They may or may not be saved. If faith is a looking to Christ for forgiveness of sin, then a life of sin is psychologically and ethically contradictory to such faith. Since faith includes assurance, such people can have no biblical assurance of their final destiny. Therefore, to assert that the Bible teaches the existence of the carnal Christian is not the same thing as "giving assurance" to a man who has professed faith in Christ but has no evidence of such faith. The only way one can know externally if a man is saved is by his claim that he has believed in Christ and by the evidences of such belief in perseverance. Many who say they are saved are not.

It is possible that Experimental Predestinarians have become unnecessarily preoccupied with this issue because they have assumed it is their responsibility to "judge before the time," to pass judgment on whether or not a man claiming faith really possesses it. Instead of "giving assurance," they should focus on turning people to Christ by asking them to do what the Bible says to do, "Believe on the Lord Jesus Christ and you will be saved." They should set aside the unbiblical and unscriptural practice of the practical syllogism which they inherited from William Perkins and their Puritan ancestors.

Because Experimental Predestinarians ground assurance in observation of works in the life, their churches are prone to have people who have a false assurance. The subjective nature of such a personal examination leads many in their assemblies to believe they are Christians when in fact they are not. Since the precise amount of work necessary to verify the presence of saving faith is impossible to define, many who are not regenerate at all believe, on the basis of some imagined work in their life, that they are saved. No doubt this is why Experimental Predestinarians are so exercised about the carnal Christian. This danger, of course, is not present in those who, like the Partakers, ground assurance in looking to the cross and to Christ. Such a looking is incompatible with a life of sin and the resultant carnal security which Experimental Predestinarians seem to observe in their circles.

The argument for the Reformed doctrine of perseverance has been disputed in the previous chapters. Their claim that a regenerate man will necessarily and inevitably persevere in a life of good works is refuted on all counts.

First of all, they lack any convincing biblical evidence that the Bible teaches this. The passages commonly cited to prove that justification and sanctification are united prove nothing (cf. chapters 8 and 9). Second, the Bible specifically warns true Christians about the possibility of failure. These warnings are a mockery unless the possibility exists, and only the most contorted theological exegesis can assign them to the unregenerate (cf. chapter 10). Third, the Bible promises assurance now, included in faith itself. Yet the Experimental Predestinarians cannot logically grant assurance before the final hour. Thus, their doctrine contradicts Scripture (cf. chapters 11-13).

But the conclusive refutation of the Reformed view is that the Bible cites numerous instances of people who have in fact been born again but who later fell into sin. Some persisted in it to the end of life.

Realizing the threat to over three hundred years of tradition, the discussion of the carnal Christian strikes a "raw nerve" in those committed to works as a means of obtaining final entrance into heaven, that is, to perseverance in holiness. No amount of abuse seems adequate to describe those who deny their doctrine. Their fear that somewhere, somehow, a man who is not a Christian might be assured that he is so dominates their consciousness that the grace of God which saved them seems to be forgotten. Is it possible that some of them have forgotten that they too are presently imperfect? Have they forgotten that there is not a purely sincere motive in their hearts? Have they forgotten that there is no unsullied act which they commit? Have they forgotten their cleansing from former sins (2 Pet. 1:9)? Or is it only the obviously inconsistent Christian which is the subject of their concern, and not themselves? We are all sinful. There is a continuum of sin from the sin in the heart of the sincere saint to the sin in the heart of the Christian who lives inconsistently and persists in it. Indeed, who of us does not "persist" to the final hour in mixed motives, in pride, in hypocrisy, in greed?! The only difference between the most sincere saint and the most carnal one is a matter of degree. To deny this is to teach sinless perfection or the eradication of the sin nature. But listen to the apostle Paul:

> *For that which I am doing, I do not understand; for I am not practicing what I would like to do, but am doing the very thing I hate.*
>
> *For the good that I wish, I do not do; but I practice the very evil that I do not wish* (Rom. 7:15-19 NASB).

The apostle is certainly not a carnal Christian, but he recognizes that in his life there is sin and a mixture of good and evil, and that this persists to the end of life. "If we say that we have not sinned, we make Him a liar, and His word is not in us" (1 Jn. 1:10).

The evident impossibility of drawing a line across this continuum to divide those who are saved from those who only claim to be is, no doubt, what has caused the more consistent advocates of the Experimental Predestinarian tradition to push assurance of salvation to the final hour--a consistency which is invalidated by the fact that the Bible offers assurance now.

The preoccupation with where to draw the line has historically resulted in the need for external objective standards. This explains the legalism present in both Reformed and Arminian circles. Whatever they disagree on, on this one point they are united: a man who is not living the life is not a Christian. This requires an objective definition of "the life" which must be lived. In some circles this has led to such views as a woman who wears make-up is probably not saved and a man who drinks or smokes surely could not be.[3]

Another common error is to confuse the idea of lordship as a condition of salvation with perseverance in holiness. Some seem to think they will solve the problem of carnality in our churches by teaching (1) that obedience is part of saving faith; and (2) that, in order to be saved, we must turn from all known sin and submit ourselves to the lordship of Christ.

But it should be obvious that, even if this is granted, which it is not, the act of submitting to the lordship of Christ at the point of saving faith in no way guarantees that a person will continue to submit to the lordship of Christ throughout the rest of his life. Thus, books written to eliminate the problem of dead Christianity by front loading the gospel with lordship salvation are not only wrong biblically, but logically they provide no answer at all.[4] It is perseverance in godliness which will solve the problem and not a decision at a point in time. If their meaning is that, when a man is truly saved, he will necessarily persevere in holiness, then whatever saving faith is, even if it does not include lordship, it will guarantee the life of works. Therefore, the issue of lordship salvation is logically irrelevant to the whole discussion.

One well-known theologian objects to the existence of the carnal Christian on two grounds. First, it can lead to antinomianism.[5] By this he means that those espousing the carnal Christian believe that one can receive Christ as Savior but not necessarily as Lord. "It assumes faith without obedience." He incorrectly feels that this is what James referred to as a "dead faith," i.e., a non-saving faith. In fact, James is referring to the faith of a believer which is not vital or living.

This theologian feels that "if a person manifests a life of pure and consistent carnality, he is no Christian."[6] Apparently it takes "pure" and "consistent"

---

[3]These viewpoints are common in some parts of the conservative churches in Eastern Europe. Spurgeon is reported to have said, "I will smoke my cigar for the Glory of God."

[4]See, for example, Alan T. Chrisope, *Jesus is Lord* (Hertfordshire, England: Evangelical Press, 1982).

[5]R. C. Sproul, *Pleasing God* (Wheaton, IL: Tyndale, 1988), p. 152.

[6]Ibid., p. 153.

carnality to demonstrate this. How much carnality is "consistent" carnality? If "pure" carnality is required, then a person could have a lot of carnality short of "pure," but he would apparently be willing to acknowledge him as a believer. What of Solomon, what of Saul and many others in the Bible who did live lives of "consistent and pure carnality" and yet were regenerate?

The second danger of the carnal Christian teaching is that "people begin to think that all that is required to be saved is a **profession** of faith."[7] What this theologian apparently intends to imply is that those who are not Christians will think that a profession has saved them. If a Christian did this, it would be a result of an incorrect presentation of the gospel and in no way flow logically out of the teaching of the possible existence of a carnal Christian. The real peril is that those who espouse the Experimental Predestinarian view and who are in fact non-Christians will be in danger of thinking they are truly saved because their carnality is not "pure" and "consistent." Thus, their teaching could possibly promote the very carnality which they reject.

The theory of the saints' perseverance in holiness is, in principle, falsifiable. If the Bible offers illustrations of individuals who have persisted in sin for a lengthy period of time, the theory is simply wrong. No amount of special pleading that these are simply "descriptions of the failure of one man" rather than the "teaching" of Scripture will do. If one man who is born again fails to persevere in holiness, then the Scriptures cannot teach that all who are born again will persevere in holiness. They will be in error.

In fact, there are not just one or two passages which seem to describe such failing believers but scores of them covering the entire range of biblical revelation, Old Testament and New. Only one such illustration would be sufficient to falsify the Reformed doctrine of perseverance, but the existence of many of them leave the theory in shreds.

Spiritual Dullness

A central passage in the New Testament on the subject of the carnal Christian is Heb. 5:11-14. The writer has just referred to the Melchizedekian priesthood of Jesus Christ when he realizes that the spiritual state of his hearers prevents him from explaining it in detail:

Concerning him, we have much to say, and it is hard to explain, since you have become dull of hearing (5:11 NASB).

They had "become" dull. They were not always so. They had fallen from a former state. There are two Greek words for "dull." The first is **bradus**, which

---

[7]Ibid. (Emphasis is Sproul's.)

simply means "slow." It is a person who is not to blame for his dullness, and so he has no moral fault. But the word used here is **nothros**. This word means slowness of perception due to moral laxness or irresponsibility.[8] It goes much deeper and reflects a moral deficiency. In classical Greek it was used as an epithet for the mule.

> *For though by this time you ought to be teachers, you have need again for someone to teach you the elementary principles of the oracles of God, and you have come to need milk and not solid food* (5:12 NASB).
>
> *For everyone who partakes only of milk, is not accustomed to the word of righteousness, for* **he is a babe** (5:13 NASB).
>
> *But solid food is for* **the mature**, *who because of practice have their senses trained to discern good and evil* (5:14 NASB).

Here one of the chief characteristics of the "carnal," (**nothros**) Christian is mentioned, persistence in sin for a period of time, the very thing which many Experimental Predestinarians say cannot happen in the life of a true Christian. The contrast in these verses is not between Christians and non-Christians but between the "babes" in Christ and the "mature" (5:13-14). He wants them to move from infancy to maturity.

In a recent commentary one popular Bible teacher has suggested that "the maturity being called for is not that of a Christian's growing in the faith, but of an unbeliever's coming into the faith--into the full-grown, mature trust and blessing of the new Covenant."[9] However, **nowhere** else in the Bible is the movement from death to life described as a movement from infancy to maturity. This is indeed a novel way of maintaining the Experimental Predestinarian interpretation of Hebrews! The contrast between the "babe" (Gk. **nepios**, 5:13) and the mature (Gk. **teleios**, 5:14) is elsewhere always between the immature and the mature Christian and never between the non-Christian and the Christian (Eph. 4:13-14).

The writer mentioned above bases this on the fact that the biblical writer wants his readers to become "mature," and the Greek word **teleios** in its verb form, **teleioo**, is used in 10:1 and 10:14 of perfect sanctification, or that which is received at salvation. However, the contexts are completely different. In chapter 10 the writer is discussing being made qualified to worship by means of sacrifice. In chapter 5 the subject is becoming mature by means of "eating meat" and the practice of discerning good and evil. This way of handling the text is an illustration of Barr's illegitimate identity transfer. A meaning of **teleios** from another

---

[8]Richard Chenevix Trench, *Synonyms of the New Testament* (London: 1880; reprint ed., Grand Rapids: Eerdmans, 1953), p. 382.

[9]John MacArthur, *Hebrews* (Chicago: Moody Press, 1983), p. 129.

chapter in a different context is read into the semantic value of the word and then carried into Heb. 5. A foreign context is thus imposed on this chapter. The meaning of **teleioo** in chapter 10 has as much relevance to the context of chapter 5 as the meaning of the "stock" purchased on Wall Street has to the cattle sequestered on a cattleman's ranch.[10] The lexicon says that **teleios** in chapter 5 refers to people who are "full-grown, mature, adult."[11] No instantaneous movement from death to life is in view. Instead, the writer to the Hebrews is urging progress to maturity by the proper exercise of spiritual disciplines over a period of time.

The problem with these Christians has apparently been a willful refusal to grow. They have had time to mature but have chosen not to. The carnal Christian is characterized by:

1. Refusal to grow for a period of time
2. A lack of skill in the use of the "word of righteousness"
3. Able to absorb only milk and not solid food
4. Spiritual dullness due to a lack of "meat"

These four things would aptly describe a person whose faith is "dead" (Jas. 2:17). The Bible abounds with illustrations of genuine believers who have become **nothroi**, dull of hearing, carnal Christians.

Biblical Illustrations Contradicting Perseverance

There appear to be numerous biblical illustrations of regenerate people who seem to have lived lives of "total and constant" carnality. In some cases they lived in such a way to the "final hour." In others it characterized their behavior for an extended period of time. In the discussion below several examples will suffice.

Jacob's Sons

The founders of the nation of Israel were in a state of willful sin for over eleven years.[12] They first considered murdering Joseph without any sense of regret (Gen. 37:20). Then at Judah's suggestion they decided to sell him in the slave trade into Egypt (Gen. 37:27). They sold their brother into slavery, told

---

[10]Another term for such cattle is "stock." This example is suggested by J. P. Louw, *Semantics of New Testament Greek* (Philadelphia: Fortress Press; Chico, CA: Scholars Press, 1982), pp. 34-35.

[11]AG, p. 817.

[12]Gen. 39 = 1 yr. + 41:2 = 2 yrs. in prison + 41:30, 53 = 7 yrs. of abundance + 42:3 = 1 yr., trips to Egypt for food during the famine and back, etc. = TOTAL = more than 11 years.

their father he was killed by a ferocious animal (37:33), and then jointly persisted in this lie for eleven years in the face of their parents' intense grief (37:34-35). Today, if we met a man who claimed to be a Christian, and found out that he had sold his sister into the white slave trade, then reported to his parents that she was drowned, pocketed the money, and persisted in this perfidious sin, even in the face of the pain and anguish of the parents, and did nothing to get the sister back and gave no indication of repentance until he was caught, we would, of course, deny he was ever a Christian. Yet this is the state of the born-again sons of Jacob.

Saul

Saul was clearly regenerate. He was anointed by the Lord as ruler over God's inheritance (1 Sam. 10:1; 1 Sam. 10:24), the Spirit of the Lord had come upon him "mightily," and he prophesied and had been "changed into another man" by means of the Spirit (1 Sam. 10:6-11). The Spirit of the Lord came upon him on one occasion, provoking him to a righteous anger (1 Sam. 11:6). He expelled all the mediums and spiritualists from the land (1 Sam. 28:3). Even in his carnality he remembered that God has answered his prayers in the past (1 Sam. 28:15), and he seemed to have some faith and inclination to goodness (1 Sam. 24:16-21). He still prayed (1 Sam. 28:6), and he could still repent. All these things would, of course, indicate to the Experimental Predestinarian that Saul was regenerate (1 Sam. 26:21,25). Yet his continued favor with God was conditioned upon his obedience (1 Sam. 12:14;1 Sam. 12:25). There was the possibility that he would fall away from the Lord. Becoming regenerate was not viewed as a guarantee of his perseverance in holiness.

Now here was a man who met all of the conditions which the Experimental Predestinarian says are necessary for true salvation. He had believed, and he had manifested his faith in a life of good works. Yet Saul became carnal. At first, he was repentant, a further proof of his regenerate state (1 Sam. 15:24-25). But he became disobedient and forfeited his rulership over the kingdom (1 Sam. 13:13-14). This precisely parallels the experience of the carnal Christian who, like Saul, forfeits his inheritance and will not rule over the kingdom, i.e., inherit it. He became deceptive (1 Sam. 18:21). He persisted in his anger and sin to the end of his life (1 Sam. 18:29). There was no perseverance in holiness. The Lord disciplined him by sending an evil spirit upon him (1 Sam. 19:9). He murdered the priests of the Lord (1 Sam. 22:17).

Saul was a regenerate man who became carnal. Furthermore, he persisted in his carnality to the point of physical death. A doctrine which teaches that all who are regenerate will necessarily and inevitably persevere in a life of good works up to the point of physical death is falsified if only **one** regenerate person fails to do so. The life of Saul falsifies the Experimental Predestinarian theory of perseverance.

Solomon

1 Ki. 1-10 describes Solomon's glory and his dedication to God. His request for wisdom was granted by the Lord with discernment between good and evil (1 Ki. 3:9). His childlike humility (1 Ki. 3:7), his intimacy with the Lord (1 Ki. 3:11-12), his prayer of dedication (1 Ki. 8:23-53), and his God-given wisdom and administration all confirm that he was regenerate. He wrote three books of Scripture which reveal divine wisdom available only to the regenerate mind. But beginning in chapter 11, he forsakes the Lord. He began to love foreign wives (11:1), even though God had forbidden intermarriage (11:2). These wives turned his heart to "other gods," and his heart was no longer fully devoted to God (11:2). He became an idolator and worshiped the Ashtoreth, the goddess of the Sidonians, and Molech, the detestable god of the Ammonites (11:5). We are told that he did evil in the eyes of the Lord and did not follow the Lord completely (11:6). The Lord tells him that he did not keep His covenant and His decrees (11:11) and that he became a worshipper of other gods. God begins to bring divine discipline. He tears the kingdom from his house (11:11). He raises up adversaries, Hadad the Edomite (11:14), Rezon , Hadadezer king of Zobah, and others (11:23). Solomon tried to kill Jeroboam (11:40). We find him unrepentant and in carnality up to the point of his death. The kingdom was split because of his sin (12:1-33).

If we met a man today who had professed faith in Christ, been a well-known spiritual leader for years, manifested incredible divine wisdom and published numerous journal articles and Christian books of high spiritual calibre, we would conclude he was a Christian. If that same man then rejected the Lord and began to worship idols, get involved in witchcraft and the New Age Movement, Experimental Predestinarians would say he was never born again to begin with. Yet this is what happened to Solomon who was born again. Once again, the Experimental Predestinarian's theory of the saints' perseverance is falsified.

Lot

Lot was called "just" (Gk. **dikaion**, righteous) by Peter (2 Pet. 2:7). Had Peter not said this, we probably would not have thought him to be saved. He willingly entered a corrupt city, choosing Sodom where the men were "wicked and were sinning greatly against the LORD" (Gen. 13:12-13). He offered his own daughters for the sexual pleasures of its inhabitants in order to save his guests from homosexual attack (Gen. 19:8). The last mention of him in the Bible is in old age, drunk with wine and permitting his decadent daughters to sleep with him (Gen. 19:33). His days are proverbial for sin and corruption (Lk. 17:28). All in all, he was not exactly the kind of fellow that one would want for a neighbor. Yet he was justified! But he did not persevere in holiness to the final hour.

Amaziah

Amaziah did what was right in the eyes of the Lord, but he did not follow the Lord wholeheartedly (2 Chr. 25:2). He turned away from following the Lord and apparently persisted in it unto death. Had he reversed himself, his fortunes would have been changed (2 Chr. 25:27). It is possible then for a true believer to turn away from following the Lord. This is seen in contrast to Asa, who was fully committed to the Lord all his life (2 Chr. 15:17), or in contrast with Jotham, son of Uzziah, who grew powerful because he walked steadfastly before the Lord his God (2 Chr. 27:6).

Uzziah

King Uzziah did what was right in the eyes of the Lord (2 Chr. 26:4), but when he became powerful, because of pride he fell into sin (26:15-16) and became unfaithful to the Lord. As a result, while he was burning incense in the temple, which was only for the Levites, he was struck with leprosy on his forehead (26:19-20). The Lord had afflicted him (26:20). He had leprosy until he died, lived in a separate house, and was excluded from the temple of the Lord. The rulership of his kingdom was given to Jotham, his son.

Fall of a Righteous Man

> *But if a righteous man turns from his righteousness and commits sin and does the same detestable things the wicked man does, will he live? None of the righteous things he has done will be remembered. Because of the unfaithfulness he is guilty of and because of the sins he has committed, he will die* (Ezek. 18:24).

It is stated here that it is possible for a "righteous man," a justified man, to do "the same detestable things that a wicked man does." Once again the Experimental Predestinarians are refuted by the patent meaning of the text. Arminians, understandably, view this as strong evidence that a regenerate person can indeed lose his salvation, that is, "die."

But of course their view depends upon the meaning of the word "die." Does the prophet have eternal or temporal death in view? The context clearly favors a temporal calamity and not an eternal forfeiture of salvation. The man who:

*lends money on interest and takes increase, will he live? He will not
live! He has committed all these abominations,* **he will surely be put
to death***; his blood will be on his own head* (Ezek. 18:13 NASB).

The death in view here is a temporal calamity; eternal destiny is not in
question at all. "Life," on the other hand, is not regeneration in this instance but
a rich walk with God which is based on obedience. It comes to the man who does
not oppress anyone, who gives bread to the hungry (v. 7), who does not lend
money on interest, and who walks in God's statutes and ordinances (v. 9). The
man who does these things "will surely live" (v. 9). Since life in the sense of regeneration comes on the basis of faith alone, we are justified in concluding that
the prophet has life in the sense of physical life or spiritual vitality in view. Its
opposite, death, is not loss of salvation but physical death or spiritual impoverishment.

Here is a regenerate man who fell into sin, who did the same things which
the wicked do, and who persisted in sin up to the point of physical death. This
seems to contradict the central thesis of the Experimental Predestinarian position.

1 Corinthians 5

An extreme case of the "consistently carnal Christian" seems to be found
in 1 Cor. 5:5. Apparently a member of the congregation was involved in an incestuous relationship with his mother-in-law! (5:1). Paul hands this carnal Christian
over to physical death, but he notes that he will be saved at the day of the Lord
Jesus.

*I have decided to deliver such a one to Satan for the destruction of his
flesh, that his spirit may be saved in the day of the Lord Jesus*
(NASB).

In describing this incestuous brother and other immoral Christians like
him, some have emphasized the NIV translation which describes him as one "who
calls himself a brother" (1 Cor. 5:11). The implication, of course, is that this man
is not truly a regenerate person; he only claims to be.[13] This meaning, while possible, seems unlikely. This man is contrasted with the heathen in 5:1 and with
those of the world and outside the church in 5:12 (cf. 5:9, 10, 12, 13). He is therefore being contrasted with non-Christians and not equated with them. His similarity to them is in his behavior.

But second, the Greek word translated "called" (**onomazo**) in no other
passage in the New Testament carries the sense of doubt as to whether the per-

---

[13]For example, G. G. Findlay, "St. Paul's First Epistle to the Corinthians," in *EGT,* 2:813.

son being "named" as something really is what he is being named to be.[14] Regardless of the theological difficulties involved, it seems that the exegetical data is on the side of the view that a regenerate man is in view. Indeed, if it were not for the theological problems, it probably would not be doubted.

We are told that this man was turned over to Satan for the destruction of his flesh "in order that" his spirit might be saved on the day of the Lord. The phrase is difficult to interpret, to say the least. The Greek is **hina** plus a verb in the subjunctive. This is normally a purpose clause. In fact, in the other uses of this phrase with the word "save" in Paul's writings, it is a purpose clause (e.g., 1 Cor. 9:22, 10:33; 1 Th. 2:16). However, this translation yields a very difficult sense in 1 Cor. 5:5. How is a man turned over to Satan for the purpose that he will be delivered from hell at the final hour! A possible explanation is that the turning over to Satan is remedial in nature. It is sometimes pointed out that this was God's purpose in allowing Satan to afflict Job. Paul himself viewed his thorn in the flesh as a messenger of Satan which God used to keep him humble (2 Cor. 12:7). In fact, there is a specific parallel in 1 Tim. 1:20 where Hymenaeus and Alexander were turned over to Satan for a remedial purpose, that they would learn not to blaspheme. If this is the sense, then the passage comes to mean, "Turn him over to Satan for the destruction of his sinful nature in order that through this disciplinary process he might be humbled and repent of his sins and be saved at the day of the Lord."

However, there is a difficulty with this view. While a turning over to Satan for remedial purposes is found in the Bible, this verse specifically says that this turning over is not for instruction but for destruction! Nowhere else does Paul speak of the destruction of the flesh as being a humbling of the sinful nature. In every other use of this word "destruction" (Gk. **olethros**) something final and eternal is in view.[15] It **never** takes a remedial sense.[16] Indeed, such a thought is without parallel in the New Testament. Isn't this reading too much into the text?

Probably the main reason for taking this passage in a remedial sense is the presence of the purpose clause, "in order that." The purpose of this turning over

---

[14]Did Jesus doubt that those He "designated" (**onomazo**) apostles really were (Mk. 3:14)? Of course, one of the apostles was not regenerate, Judas, but he was truly an apostle. Did the Jews in their attempts to drive out evil spirits invoke the "so-called" name of Jesus (Acts 19:13)? When Paul says he wants to preach the gospel in places where Christ is not known (**onomazo**), did he imply that Christ may have been known but he was not sure (Rom. 15:20)? Is Jesus far above every "so-called" title that can be given as if there is some doubt about the validity of these titles (Eph. 1:21)? Is the Father's family only "named" His family but is not really His family (Eph. 3:15)? Is Paul only concerned about a "so-called" hint (**onomazo**) of immortality among the Ephesians or a real and actual hint (Eph. 5:3)? The apostle exhorts that "everyone who confesses the name of the Lord must turn away from wickedness" (2 Tim. 2:19). Is this the "so-called" name of Jesus?

[15]See 2 Th. 1:9; 1 Tim. 6:9; 1 Th. 5:3.

[16]Arndt and Gingrich say that the passage refers to the physical death of the sinner and not a remedial activity (AG, p. 566).

is for the sinner's ultimate salvation. This would seem to require an additional assumption that this turning over was intended to bring about the repentance and ultimate salvation of the sinner. However, this runs aground on the fact that this man is most likely viewed as regenerate already and, in any case, Satan's "ministry" here is specifically declared NOT to be remedial but that of physical destruction. Is there another option?

While not as common, the use of **hina** plus the subjunctive in a sense of result is well established. For example, in Rom. 11:11 Paul says of Israel, "Did they stumble so as to fall beyond recovery?" They did not stumble for the purpose of falling beyond recovery, but that was the **result** of their stumbling.[17] The Gramcord computer program yields the following illustrations in the Pauline literature of **hina** followed by a verb in the subjunctive with a sense of result (Rom. 3:19; 11:11; 15:32; 1 Cor. 7:29; 2 Cor. 1:17; Gal. 5:17; 1 Th. 5:4).[18]

If this is the correct meaning, then the verse would be rendered, "Hand this man over to Satan, so that his body ("flesh") may be destroyed, with the result that at least his spirit will be saved on the day of the Lord." This has the advantage of taking **olethros** in its normal sense of total ruin, "flesh" in a very common sense (physical body), and requires that nothing be read into the passage at all. In fact, it explains nicely the contrast between flesh and spirit. His body will be destroyed, but his spirit will be saved. Furthermore, this fits well into the well-known New Testament teaching of a sin unto physical death (e.g., in the same epistle, 1 Cor. 11:30).

All in all, this seems to be the most plausible interpretation of the apostle's meaning, and it does not require a reading of secondary ideas into the passage. It emerges simply from the words themselves. Here then is another example of a carnal Christian who persisted in his carnality to the point of physical death. He did not persevere in a life of good works to the final hour, yet his spirit will be saved when the Lord returns. We will see him in heaven.

1 Corinthians 8

Two categories of Christians seem to be taught in 1 Cor. 8:11, the weak and the carnal. Paul refers to the carnal man, who is arrogant through his superior spiritual knowledge and ruins his weaker brother. In so doing, he sins against Christ (8:12). His problem is that he is arrogant and sins against the brethren.

---

[17]See also Gal. 5:17; Lk. 1:43; and Jn. 6:7.

[18]The Gramcord Institute, Paul Miller, Director, "Gramcord" (2065 Half Day Road, Deerfield, IL 60015).

Galatians

Can a true Christian lose his joy (4:15)? Yes! Can a true Christian count an apostle as his enemy (4:16)? Yes! Can true Christians put themselves under the law (4:21), fall from the grace way of life, and become alienated from Christ (5:4)? Yes! Is it possible for a true Christian to use his freedom in Christ to "indulge the sinful nature" (5:13)? Yes. If it were not possible, there would be no point in warning them not to do something which they could never do. True Christians can "destroy" each other by their biting and devouring of each other (5:15). The true Christian is capable of expressing the fruits of either the flesh or of the Spirit. The works of the flesh are warned against (5:21). If they persist in them, they will not inherit the kingdom. If there is no possibility of their living like this, why warn them against it?

Now if true Christians can do all these things, how are they to be distinguished from the carnal Christian which many Experimental Predestinarians say do not exist?

If a Christian sows to please his flesh, he will reap destruction (6:8, divine discipline, possibly physical death, and certain loss of reward). If he sows to please the Spirit, he will reap eternal life. When eternal life is put in the future, it is often viewed as something earned, i.e., a reward. The verb is in the future tense here.[19]

John 2:23

Many people saw the miraculous signs and **episteusan eis to onoma autou** ("believed on His name"). Yet Jesus would not **episteuen auton autois** ("entrust Himself to them") because He "knew all men." This phrase, "believe on His name" is used throughout John for saving faith. In fact, the first usage of the phrase in the book contradicts the view that it refers to a spurious faith.

> *Yet to all who received him, to those who* **believed in his name,** *he gave the right to become children of God--children born not of natural descent, nor of human decision or a husband's will, but born of God* (Jn. 1:12-13).

> *Whoever believes in him is not condemned, but whoever does not believe stands condemned already because he has not* **believed in the name** *of God's one and only Son* (Jn. 3:18).

---

[19]See chapter 7, "Inheriting Eternal Life."

The phrase **pisteuo eis**, "believe in," is John's standard expression for saving faith. One believes "on Him" or "in His name."[20] When Calvin [21] says that they did not have true faith but were only borne along by some impulse of zeal which prevented them from carefully examining their hearts, he is therefore flatly contradicting John's consistent usage in the rest of his writings. This illustrates "theological exegesis."

Martin Lloyd-Jones falls into the same error. He feels that those who "believed in His name" "did not truly believe in Him. They gave a kind of intellectual assent, they seemed to believe in Him; but He knew that they had not believed in Him in reality, and that is why He did not commit Himself to them."[22] He cites Jn. 6:60-66 where Jesus says there were some disciples "that believe not" and concludes that this explains the people in Jn. 2:25. But isn't this directly contradicting the very words of John? John tells us that in Jn. 2, contrary to the unbelieving disciples in Jn. 6, these people specifically **did** believe. On what authority does Lloyd-Jones say they did not? How else could John say it if his intent was to indicate saving faith? Nowhere in the New Testament are adverbs, such as "truly" or "really" believed, ever used. These adverbs are frequently inserted in front of the word believe in order to maintain the fiction of the final perseverance of the saints.

The fact that these believers became believers in response to signs in no way requires that their faith was superficial. John makes it clear that he feels that signs are a cause of faith and would be most perplexed to read in many modern commentaries that a faith which is generated in response to signs is not genuine. "Jesus did many other miraculous signs in the presence of His disciples, which are not recorded in this book. But these are written that you may believe that Jesus is the Christ, the Son of God, and that by believing you may have life in His name" (Jn. 20:30-31). In fact, John viewed a lack of response to signs as sinful rebellion! "Even after Jesus had done all these miraculous signs in their presence, they still would not believe in Him" (Jn. 12:37). John would never reject a faith based on signs; in fact, he would applaud it! It is, however, a more mature faith, a more virtuous faith, which does not rest on visible signs (Jn. 20:29).

After the departure of Judas, the Lord turns to the disciples and says, "You are my friends if you do what I command" (Jn. 15:14). Friendship with Christ is **not** a free gift; it is conditional. The result of such friendship is that Jesus commits Himself to His friends. He does this in the sense of imparting to them additional truth. "I no longer call you servants because a servant does not know his master's business. Instead, I have called you friends, for everything that

---

[20]See Jn. 6:40; 7:39; 8:30; 10:42; 11:25, 26; 12:11.

[21]John Calvin, *Institutes of the Christian Religion*, trans. Henry Beveridge, 2 vols. (Grand Rapids: Eerdmans, 1964), 3.2.12.

[22]D. Martin Lloyd-Jones, *Romans: An Exposition of Chapter 8:17-39, The Final Perseverance of the Saints* (Grand Rapids: Zondervan, 1976), p. 282.

I learned from My Father I have made known to you (Jn. 15:15). When Jesus says He did not commit Himself to them, there is no need to conclude they were unregenerate. Rather, it means He was not their friend and did not reveal to them additional truth learned from the Father.

John 12:42

Many of the leaders among the Pharisees **episteusan eis auton**, "believed on Him," and yet they refused to confess their faith for fear of being put out of the synagogue (Jn. 12:42). They hardly had submitted to the lordship of Christ or persevered in a life of good works. In fact, "they loved the praise of men more than praise from God" (12:43). Yet this technical term for saving faith characterizes their state of mind; they believed on Him! If one did not "know" before he came to the text that regenerate people could not be characterized by this, he would assume this applies to true Christians. Only a theological system can negate the consistent usage of this phrase in John. Could not these hypocritical pharisees, these secret Christians, be called "carnal Christians"? Similarly, it is written of Joseph of Arimathea at the time of Christ's burial that he "was a disciple of Jesus, but secretly because he feared the Jews" (Jn. 19:38-42).

Christians Who Have No Part with Christ

Two kinds of Christians are referred to by the Lord in Jn. 13:8:

Peter said to Him, "Never shall You wash my feet!" Jesus answered him, "If I do not wash you, you have no part with Me" (NASB).

He who has bathed need only to wash his feet, but is completely clean (Jn. 13:10 NASB).

Jesus refers to Christians who are "bathed" (Gk. **louo**), who are "completely clean," i.e., regenerate. But a bathed, regenerate person sometimes needs washing (Gk. **nipto**). In fact, if he does not go through this washing (**nipto**) he has no part with Christ. To wash (**nipto**) means to wash in part, but to bathe (**louo**) means "to wash all over."[23] The former refers to cleansing from daily sin by confession (1 Jn. 1:9), whereas the latter refers to regeneration. Christ teaches here that, if a person who has been bathed refuses daily washing, he will have no part with Him. This is what is meant by a carnal Christian.

---

[23]See Trench, *Synonyms*, pp. 161-62.

Simon Magus

Under the preaching of Philip, a magician named Simon Magus believed and was baptized (Acts 8:13). In addition, "he continued on with Philip." According to Luke, if a man believes and is baptized, he is saved (Acts 2:38; 16:31-33). Experimental Predestinarians will simply say he could not have been saved because he did not persevere. Over one hundred years ago James Inglis forcefully rejected this view:

> *Those who regard Simon as a hypocrite must own, that on the supposition that he was a true believer, it would have been impossible to state it more plainly than in the language of the passage, which records not merely the fact of his public profession of the faith, followed by the natural evidence of his sincerity, but the express testimony, "Simon himself believed also."*[24]

The gift of the Holy Spirit, however, was delayed in Samaria until Peter and John arrived. When the Spirit was given, apparently the external manifestations which Simon saw motivated him to try to purchase the gift of being able to impart the Holy Spirit by the laying on of hands (8:18). Because of his sin, the apostle Peter responds:

> *May your silver perish with you, because you thought you could obtain the gift of God with money! You have no part or portion in this matter, for your heart is not right before God. Therefore repent of this wickedness of yours, and pray the Lord that if possible, the intention of your heart may be forgiven you. For I see that you are in the gall of bitterness, and in the bondage of iniquity. But Simon answered and said, Pray to the Lord for me yourselves, so that nothing of what you have said may come upon me* (Acts 8:20-24 NASB).

What was Simon's sin? It was selfish ambition. "Give this authority to me as well, so that everyone on whom I lay my hands may receive the Holy Spirit." Peter concluded that he wanted to buy the power to pass on the gift of the Holy Spirit with money and that his heart was not right with God. Surely the presence of prideful ambition is not a basis for concluding that a man is not saved! Who among us has not at one time or another been tempted in this way? Unholy rivalries and ambitions often plague relationships between true Christians. To say the presence of this sin invalidates the claim to regeneration is unrealistic.

The punishment for Simon's sin is that he will "perish." This refers to physical death. His money is to perish with him, and the perishing of his money is

---

[24]James Inglis, "Simon Magus," *Waymarks in the Wilderness* 5 (1867): 35-50; reprinted in *JGES* 2 (Spring 1989): 45-54.

obviously temporal. This is another illustration of the sin unto physical death.[25]
If Simon repents, "perhaps" he will be forgiven. Is it not difficult to imagine that
there is any "perhaps" in the gospel offer to the unregenerate? We read, "Believe
in the Lord Jesus Christ, and thou shalt be saved," not "perhaps thou shalt be
saved." There is uncertainty, however, as to whether or not the divine parent will
punish (and how severely) his sinning child in time. Often the intent of family
discipline is accomplished best by listening to the cry of the erring child.

Here is a believer who is in carnal rebellion. Peter warns him that he may
perish (die physically) in such a state if he does not repent. Peter is therefore
holding out the possibility of a failure to persevere to the end of life.

Christians Who Sleep

Paul rebukes the Corinthians because many of them were coming to the
Lord's table drunk. He says that because of this many were ill and some were
asleep (1 Cor. 11:29-32). To "sleep" (Gk. **koimao**) was the Christian term for
death.[26] The passage speaks of rebellious believers who were drunks, who apparently failed to respond to other forms of divine discipline ("illness"), and whom
God eventually took to be with Him. That is the meaning of sleep. Remember,
the theory of the saints' perseverance requires that all regenerate people will
necessarily continue in a life of good works until the final hour. If one person
who is regenerate fails in this, then the theory must be wrong. Here was a group
of people who failed and persisted in their failure up to physical death.

Another use of "sleep" (but using a different word) is found in Paul's
words to the Thessalonians:

> *For God has not destined us for wrath, but for obtaining salvation
> through our Lord Jesus Christ, who died for us that* **whether we are
> awake or asleep,** *we may live together with Him* (1 Th. 5:9-10
> NASB).

The wrath in this context is the tribulation wrath of the day of the Lord
(5:2-3). The references to being "awake" and "asleep" do not refer to being alive
and dead but, rather, to being watchful for our Lord's return or being indifferent
to it. In fact, Paul uses a different word for sleep, **katheudo.** Earlier in 1 Th.
4:14, when referring to physical death, he used the word **koimao.** While
katheudo often has an ethical connotation[27] in the New Testament and always
does in every other use in Paul,[28] **koimao** never has an ethical connotation:[29]

---

[25]See also 1 Cor. 8:11 where the perishing of the weaker brother has the same effect.

[26]See Acts 7:60; 1 Cor. 15:51; 1 Th. 4:13-17.

[27]Mt. 13:25; Mk. 13:36

[28]Eph. 5:14; 1 Th. 5:6, 7

> *So then let us not sleep as others do, but let us be alert and sober. For*
> *those who sleep do their sleeping* [Gk. **katheudo**] *at night, and those*
> *who get drunk get drunk at night* (1 Th. 5:6-7 NASB).

Jesus used the same word, **katheudo**, in a similar context in the parable of the doorkeeper (Mk. 13:33-37). Like the exhortation in 1 Th. 5, the exhortation is to spiritual watchfulness in contrast to "sleep" in view of the uncertainty of the Lord's return:

> *Take heed, keep on the alert; for you do not know when the appointed*
> *time is. It is like a man, away on a journey, who upon leaving his*
> *house and putting his slaves in charge, assigning to each one his task,*
> *also commanded the doorkeeper to stay on the alert. Therefore, be on*
> *the alert--for you do not know when the master of the house is com-*
> *ing, whether in the evening, at midnight, at cockcrowing, or in the*
> *morning--lest he come suddenly and find you asleep* [**katheudo**]. *And*
> *what I say to you I say to all, "Be on the alert!"* (NASB).

Apparently Paul has this same parable in mind in 1 Th. 5 when he warns them about the sudden and unexpected nature of the Lord's return (5:2), tells them to be alert (5:6), and warns them against sleeping (**katheudo**), or spiritual insensitivity.[30] The opposite of spiritual insensitivity is to be awake (Gk. **gregoreo**). This is the verb Paul uses of spiritual alertness in 5:6 ("be alert"), and it is the same word he uses as the opposite of **katheudo** in 5:10. Had Paul intended **katheudo** to refer to physical death in 5:10, he would have used the usual word for physical life, **zao**, as its opposite.[31]

It has, of course, been objected that such a view of 5:10 negates the ethical exhortation in the preceding context. The meaning is something like this:

---

[29]See AG, p. 438.

[30]Tracy Howard objects. He feels that Paul's selection of **katheudo** is only due to an un-intentional, unnatural repetition of a word or phrase which was used naturally in the immediately preceding context. He acknowledges that to use **katheudo** for physical sleep would be contradictory to the preceding context. Paul used **katheudo** instead of **koimao** because **katheudo** was still on Paul's mind when he wrote v. 10. See Tracy L. Howard, "The Meaning of 'Sleep' in 1 Thessalonians 5:10 - A Reappraisal" in *GTJ*, 6.2 (1985): 342. However, this kind of reasoning seems to be com-pletely negated by the fact that Paul obviously has the parable of the doorkeeper in his mind, and that parable, with its use of **katheudo** as spiritual insensitivity, would have a far more determinative force in his selection of words. **Katheudo** was the word his Lord used in describing the same situa-tion, spiritual insensitivity at the second advent!

[31]For this reason Hogg and Vine insist that the passage teaches that whether we are spiri-tually alert or not, we will all live with the Lord. They say that **"gregoromen** is not used elsewhere in the metaphorical sense of 'to be alive' and as **katheudo** means 'to be dead' in only one place out of two-and-twenty occurrences in N.T., and never elsewhere in Paul's epistles, there does not seem to be sufficient justification for departing from the usual meaning of the words, i.e., vigilance and ex-pectancy as contrasted with laxity and indifference" (C. F. Hogg and W. E. Vine, *The Epistle To The Thessalonians* [Reprint ed., Grand Rapids: Kregel, 1959], p. 172).

"although I desire you to maintain spiritual alertness in view of the imminent Parousia, Jesus died so that whether or not we are spiritually alert, we might still live with Him."[32] However abhorrent this may be to those steeped in experimental ways of thinking, this is precisely the teaching of the New Testament and is in complete harmony with the rest of Scripture as this book has been attempting to show. The Bible does teach in numerous places that there are believers who will be with the Lord whether they are vigilant or not. The motivation for vigilance is to be found in the desire to hear the Master say, "Well done" and the fear of disapproval when He returns. The sudden and unexpected nature of the Lord's return can leave us unprepared and shrinking away from Him in shame at that day. Paul knows that and his readers know that and we may safely assume that the general teaching of the apostle on this subject had already been imparted to them as he did to the other churches. It is possible to take the grace of God for granted, and that is the very thing he is warning them about!

The passage is a relevant contradiction of the theory of the saints' perseverance because it declares that sleeping Christians will live together with Christ. The sleeping Christian is the carnal Christian, the one who is indifferent to the Lord's return and who spends his time in drunken hedonism.[33]

2 Corinthians 12:21-13:5

As discussed in the previous chapter, 2 Cor. 13:5 is probably not a call to the Corinthians to examine themselves to find out if they are Christians. They are only, but importantly, being exhorted to discern whether or not they are living consistent Christian lives. Yet these regenerate people are carnal. In fact, they are not only carnal Christians, but they refuse to repent of their sin.

> *And I may mourn over many of those who have sinned in the past and not repented of the impurity, immorality, and sensuality which they have practiced* (2 Cor. 12:21 NASB).

It will not do to utilize "theological exegesis" and simply maintain that because they did not repent, this proves, according to the theory of the saints' inevitable perseverance in holiness, that they are not Christians. This will not do because this is the very point in question: do the saints inevitably persevere? Contextual considerations must determine whether or not these people are regenerate, not a theological system which has declared before looking at the evidence that they cannot be!

---

[32]This is Howard's phraseology, p. 344.

[33]See Thomas R. Edgar, "The Meaning of 'Sleep' in 1 Thessalonians 5:10," *JETS* 22 (December 1979): 345-349 for a discussion of a view similar to that taken here.

Paul views them as "beloved" and capable of being "built up" (**oikodome,** 2 Cor. 12:19). The word is always applied to Christians when it is used elsewhere in the New Testament.[34]   In fact, the same word is used of the church as a "building," a holy temple in the Lord (Eph. 2:21). Arndt and Gingrich refer it to "spiritual strengthening" in 2 Cor 12:19.[35] Indeed, the notion of spiritual edification is present in every use of this word in the New Testament. In not one instance are unregenerate people ever considered capable of **oikodome.** This is the language of believers building up one another (Rom. 14:19) and prophesying to one another for the purpose of spiritual growth (1 Cor. 14:3).[36]   In 1 Cor. 3:9 he specifically tells this group of unrepentant carnal Christians that they are "God's building" (**oikodome**).

Here then is a group of people, God's building, who are "in the faith" and yet are impure and immoral and refuse to repent of their sin.

Conclusion

It seems evident that something is amiss with a doctrine seemingly unable to account for what appear to be so many contradictions to its main tenet, the impossibility of perseverance in carnality. But the problem becomes even more acute when we consider the numerous passages which describe not only persistent moral carnality by regenerate people but final apostasy and rejection of the faith altogether.

---

[34]Eph. 4:12, 16, 29; Rom. 14:19; 15:2.

[35]AG, p. 561.

[36]Note also vv. 5, 12, 26.

Chapter 15

Apostasy and Divine Discipline

Within Experimental Predestinarian circles there are variations in how they treat the possible existence of the carnal Christian. Some would not allow that the Scriptures even teach such a thing. Others would say that a Christian can be carnal but only for a limited period of time. If his carnality continues past this subjective limit, this proves he is not truly a Christian at all. What all agree on, however, is that a true Christian will not persist in carnality to the point of physical death and that no true Christian can ever commit the sin of public repudiation of his faith in Christ.

In the last chapter it was seen that the theory of the saints' perseverance was falsified by the many examples of carnality in the Bible. Now, however, we must direct our attention to biblical data which seems to suggest that a true Christian can not only be carnal, but he can actually commit apostasy as well.

New Testament Illustrations of Apostasy

Apostasy of Hymenaeus and Alexander

There are specific cases where the possible became actual!

Keeping faith and a good conscience, which some have rejected and suffered shipwreck in regard to their faith. Among these are Hymenaeus and Alexander, whom I have delivered over to Satan, so that they may be taught not to blaspheme (1 Tim. 1:18-20 NASB).

These two men had "faith" and "a good conscience," but they rejected both and became shipwreck. Experimental Predestinarians, of course, will simply bring their theological system into the passage and say that the fact they rejected the faith proves they never had it to begin with.[1] Once again, however, this is the point in question. The spiritual state of these people must be determined from 1 Timothy 1 and not from a theological system. I. Howard Marshall rejects this interpretation, "The language suggests a violent rejection of the claims of conscience, and the metaphor of shipwreck implies the loss of a faith once held."[2]

Three things are said about these two men: (1) they had believed; (2) they had given the evidence of regeneration in a good conscience; and (3) they need to be taught not to blaspheme. If it were not for the third point, one would conclude on the premises of the Experimental Predestinarian that they were saved people. They had believed, and they had given some initial evidence of it.

However, even the third point paradoxically substantiates the thesis that they are regenerate. When Paul says they must be handed over to Satan, he calls to mind the only other illustration in the New Testament of a man being handed over to Satan, 1 Cor. 5:5. In that passage a member of the congregation was involved in incest (5:1). However, even though he is obviously carnal, he will be saved in the day of Jesus Christ.[3]

Hymenaeus and Alexander needed to be "taught" (Gk. **paideuo**). In its other usages in the New Testament it is commonly used of the divine chastening or discipline of the regenerate (1 Cor. 11:32; Ti. 2:12-13; Heb. 12:5-6).

The exegetical evidence seems to present these men as genuine Christians who have fallen away from the faith. Paradoxically, even Martin Lloyd-Jones, one of the most articulate modern advocates of the Reformed doctrine of perseverance, acknowledges that these men were truly saved, but "with respect to their belief, and their statement of their belief, they were in a state of chaos, shipwreck, utter muddle. The apostle does not say they were reprobate; all he says is that they have got in to this indescribable muddle, a shipwreck, a shambles, call it what you will."[4] We call it a carnal Christian who has denied the faith.

It is possible that this Hymenaeus is the same individual referred to in 2 Tim. 2:17-19 (NASB):

---

[1]Sometimes this is done by translating the word "their" (Gk. **ten**) as "the." Then the sense is that they became shipwrecked in regard to the objective faith and not in regard to their subjectively appropriated faith. However, the subjective sense "agrees better with the previous verse as well as with the stress on faith in the whole Chapter" (J. N. D. Kelly, *The Pastoral Epistles* [London: Adam and Charles Black, 1963], p. 58).

[2]I. Howard Marshall, *Kept by the Power of God* (Minneapolis: Bethany House, 1969), p. 128.

[3]See discussion in chapter 14 under 1 Cor. 5.

[4]D. Martin Lloyd-Jones, *Romans: An Exposition of Chapter 8:17-39, The Final Perseverance of the Saints* (Grand Rapids: Zondervan, 1976), p. 284.

> *And their talk will spread like gangrene, among whom are Hymenaeus and Philetus, men who have gone astray from the truth saying that the resurrection has already taken place, and thus they upset the faith of some. Nevertheless, the firm foundation of God stands having this seal, "The Lord knows those who are His," and "Let everyone who names the name of the Lord abstain from wickedness."*

Hymenaeus had such an impact on the faith of some believers that he actually "upset" the faith of some. The Greek word is a bit stronger than "upset." It means to "cause to fall, overturn, destroy."[5] In direct contradiction to our Lord's words (Jn. 6:39) they asserted that the resurrection had already occurred, and they thereby destroyed the faith of some.

When Paul says, "The Lord knows those who are His," he is not saying that the Lord knows those who are truly regenerate in contrast to those who are not, implying that Hymenaeus was not regenerate. The phrase is quoted directly from the LXX translation of Num. 16:5: "Tomorrow morning the LORD will **show who is His** and who is holy, and will cause him to come near to Him" (NKJV). The incident is instructive. Korah led a rebellion against Moses. The point at issue seems to be that Korah felt that, since Israel was a community, all were in equal authority and that therefore it was only presumption, not God's appointment, which led Moses to assume the leadership of Israel. Furthermore, Moses had taken away the right of the firstborn of every household to be a member of the priesthood of Israel and had instead invested that right in a branch of his own family, the sons of Aaron,[6] his brother.[7] Surely, Korah reasoned, Moses was merely presuming on God.

Three grounds of revolt are stated. Num. 16 records discontent on the grounds, first, that Moses and Aaron have set themselves above the rest of Israel (vv. 3, 13), second, that Moses has failed to bring Israel to the promised land (v. 14), and third, that he and Aaron have arrogated the priesthood to themselves (vv. 7-11).

So Korah gathered many of the leaders of Israel against Moses. These leaders who joined him in the rebellion are called "leaders of the congregation, representatives of the congregation, men of renown" (16:2). They are defined in Num. 1:16 as the distinguished or illustrious. They were renowned for the wisdom of the age and therefore called upon for consultation in matters of importance pertaining to the tribes. They seem to consist of a national council, or diet, of a representative character.[8] They led the nation in the offering of

---

[5]AG, p. 62.

[6]See Num. 3:10.

[7]Moses and Aaron were both Levites and were brothers (Ex. 7:1).

[8]For discussion see George Bush, *Notes on Numbers* (Ivison & Phinney, 1858; reprint ed., Minneapolis: Klock & Klock Pub., 1976), p. 19.

sacrifices Num. 7), were set apart for the work of the tabernacle (Num. 8), and observed the passover (Num. 9). These men are evidently the regenerate leaders of the nation!

They have challenged Moses as to whether or not he is truly appointed by God. Moses replies that God will demonstrate who is appointed by God, Moses or the leaders of the rebellion. The LXX translates the Hebrew as "know," and Paul follows this in 2 Tim 2:19. So when he says that God "knows" those who are His, he is not saying something as banal as "God knows who is truly a Christian." He is saying that God has chosen or appointed His leaders and will actively demonstrate that fact. The Greek word for "know" often carries the sense of "appoint" or "know intimately."[9] To be "known" by God is to enjoy His favor (1 Cor. 8:3) and to be honored or respected by Him (1 Th. 5:12).[10]

Now Korah and his followers experienced the sin unto physical death. The earth opened up and swallowed the lot of them (Num. 16:31-33). Similarly, Hymenaeus and Philetus, like Korah, have usurped authority over God's leader, the apostle. They are contradicting his authority. But, the apostle warns, as in the days of Korah God appoints those in authority and will demonstrate this, i.e., "He knows those who are His." He is intimating that, just as Korah was shown to be false by the judgment of physical death, this could happen to Hymenaeus and Philetus.

So when Paul says that the Lord knows those "who are His," he means "those whom He has appointed in authority." There is no reference to election to salvation in the incident with Korah. Rather, appointment to leadership is in view. The parallel with Korah is precise.

We conclude that Hymenaeus and Philetus were true Christians who like Korah had usurped the authority of Christ and His apostle by teaching false doctrine. But the Lord "knows those who are His," that is, the Lord blesses and favors those whom He has appointed and will make it clear whether a man's authority is truly from God or from himself. Those who do not obey and serve Him risk divine discipline like Korah.

Apostasy in Hebrews

Apostasy is a real danger, just as the writer to the Hebrews warned in chapter 10:

But My righteous one shall live by faith; and if he shrinks back, My soul has no pleasure in him. But we are not of those who shrink back

---

[9]The word is **ginosko**.

[10]The word "know" (Gk. **ginosko**) is translated here as "appreciate" or "respect."

to destruction, but of those who have faith to the preserving of the soul (Heb. 10:38-39 NASB).

The "preserving of the soul" is a common term for the maintaining of physical life (it never means "go to heaven when you die").[11]   Instead of experiencing "destruction," they will live. The word "destruction" (Gk. **apoleian**) is the common term for "loss" or "destruction" in secular Greek.[12] It is not a technical term for hell. Sometimes it means "waste" (Mk. 14:4) and sometimes "execution" (Acts 25:16, Majority Text[13]). The context (10:26-38) refers to the possible execution of judgment in time on the sinning Christian.   The judgment may include physical death or even worse (10:28). In order to avoid the possibility of this sin to physical death, this discipline resulting in ruin of one's physical life, we must persevere in faith. The danger is that they will not. And if that occurs, that is, if "he shrinks back," then God will have no pleasure in him. This is simply an understatement (litotes), for "God will be very angry with the Christian who behaves this way."

Apostasy here is not a theoretical, but a real, possibility. This is the apostasy of God's "righteous one," the regenerate son of God who has received the imputed righteousness of Christ.[14]

Apostasy in Galatians

In Gal. 6:12 Paul seems to refer to those who are true believers who have denied the faith:

Those who desire to make a good showing in the flesh try to compel you to be circumcised, simply that they may not be persecuted for the cross of Christ (NASB).

Submission to circumcision indicated cessation of faith in Christ (Gal. 2:17-21).   In fact, it meant you counted Christ's death as vain, had severed yourself from Christ (Gal. 5:2), had fallen from grace (Gal. 5:4), and were liable to judgment (5:10). To be severed from Christ and to fall from grace logically required a former standing in grace and connection with Christ from which to fall and be severed! It is possible for those who are regenerate to deny the faith and forfeit their share in the coming kingdom. There is no need to assume that they lose salvation, as the Arminian maintains.

---

[11]For proof, see chapter 6.

[12]MM, p. 73.

[13]*The Greek New Testament According to the Majority Text*, ed. Zane Hodges and Arthur Farstad, 2d. ed. (Nashville: Nelson, 1985).

[14]The reference to Hab. 2:3-4 is more of an allusion than a citation. The writer has modified it slightly to fit the context of what he wants to say.

Apostasy in the Last Days

The apostle Paul specifically declares in 1 Tim. 4:1-3 that it is possible for believers to depart from the faith:

But the Spirit explicitly says that in later times some will fall away from the faith, paying attention to deceitful spirits and doctrines of demons.

Now if the Spirit "explicitly says" that apostasy from the faith is possible, by what right do Experimental Predestinarians deny this? These people who fall away are believers and are contrasted with the liars who have a seared conscience (v. 2). It was by means of these non-Christians that these believers were led into apostasy. Marshall observes that the use of **aphistemi** ("fall away") "implies a departure from a position once held and therefore refers to apostasy from the faith by those who once held it."[15]

Denial of the Faith

When a man refuses to care for his household, he has in effect denied the faith:

But if anyone does not provide for his own, and especially for those of his household, he has denied the faith, and is worse than an unbeliever (1 Tim. 5:8 NASB).

It is apparently possible for a true Christian to deny the faith and to be worse than a non-Christian. This is an apostasy in life, if not in lips, and therefore equally serious! If it is possible for a true believer to be worse than an apostate, then could he not be, at least, as bad as one as well?

Apostasy of Widows

Paul specifically says that some younger widows had departed from the faith and followed Satan:

Therefore I want younger widows to get married, bear children, keep house, and give the enemy no occasion for reproach, for some have already turned aside to follow Satan (1 Tim. 5:14-15 NASB).

---

[15]Marshall, *Kept*, p. 129.

Apostasy Due to Gnostic Deception

False teachers are often the cause for the departure from the faith by those who are truly regenerate:

> *O Timothy, guard what has been entrusted to you, avoiding worldly and empty chatter and the opposing arguments of what is falsely called "knowledge"--which some have professed and thus gone astray from the faith* (1 Tim. 6:20-21 NASB).

Some under Timothy's care in the church had gone astray from the faith. It does no good to argue that they could not have been Christians in the first place because Timothy, a Christian, is being warned against this very possibility.

Apostasy of Demas and Others

Toward the end of his life, Paul found himself deserted by many of his fellow-laborers.   Among them were Demas (2 Tim. 4:10), Phygelus and Hermogenes (2 Tim. 1:15), and a number of unnamed people (2 Tim. 4:16).

In 2 Tim. 2:24-26 Paul refers to those who are "in opposition." Who are they?

> *With gentleness correcting those who are in opposition, if perhaps God may grant them repentance leading to the knowledge of the truth, and they may come to their senses and escape from the snare of the devil, having been held captive by him to do his will.*

While the phrase about repentance leading to a "knowledge of the truth" certainly could refer to the conversion of non-Christians, the parallel usage (Ti. 1:1) refers to the knowledge necessary for those who already are Christians, so that they can live godly lives. Furthermore, as Marshall points out,[16] the parallel passage about being ensnared by the devil clearly refers to believers (1 Tim. 3:7). It appears, then, that the lapse of regenerate people are in view. They have fallen from the faith and become opponents of the apostle Paul!

Conclusion

Other passages could be cited which establish the fact that true Christians can become carnal and even persist in their carnality up to the point of physical death.[17]   Reference has already been made to the warnings in the New

---

[16]Ibid., p. 130.

[17]Jas. 1:12-16; 1 Tim. 5:5-6, 11-15; 2 Tim. 2:22-26; Rev. 12:11.

Testament. Each warning implies the possibility of failure, and almost all of them are specifically addressed to regenerate people.[18]

Attempts to evade the force of these and other passages which teach the existence of the carnal Christian seem to be unconvincing. Alan Chrisope, for example, argues that the "permanently carnal Christian" is a figment of the imagination.[19] A Christian may have carnal moments, but if he does not have meaningful character growth, he is not a Christian. By "carnal Christian" Chrisope means "a professing Christian who shows no practical evidence of conversion."[20] If you have one sin, you can apparently still be a Christian. But to have many, or as he says, remain in a state of "constant and total" carnality, you are not a Christian. How do you draw the line? What is constant and what is total? Apparently one sin is not total. How about two or three? In fact, the Corinthians where involved in "constant and total" sin. Paul came to them in A.D. 52 and four years later they are "yet" carnal. They had remained in constant divisiveness for at least four years. The rest of the book documents other aspects of their carnality: jealousy, quarreling (3:3), toleration of incest (5:1), lawsuits against brothers (6:1), fornication (6:18), indifference to weaker brothers (chapters 8-9), drunkenness (11:21), and egotistical use of spiritual gifts (14:4). Certainly the description of these believers is one of "total and constant" carnality. In at least two cases their carnality persisted unto physical death (5:5; 11:30), and their physical death was a divine judgment upon them for their refusal to respond to the exhortations of the apostle.

The Partaker's contention is that the combined weight of the warning passages, the passages illustrating the fact of the carnal Christian, and the specific biblical illustrations of apostasy firmly establish the possible existence of the permanently carnal Christian. We maintain that it is obvious that this is true and that only prior adherence to a theological system could possibly yield another result after careful examination of the biblical data.

It simply cannot be successfully argued that Scripture guarantees that those who believe will be kept in a state of belief to the final hour. What is

---

[18]See chapter 10, "The Possibility of Failure."

[19]Alan Chrisope, *Jesus is Lord* (Hertfordshire, England: Evangelical Press, 1982), p. 89.

[20]He gives the following reasons for rejecting the carnal Christian view: (1) The New Testament teaches that a Christian is one who has made a definite break with the ruling power of sin. As argued elsewhere, however, Rom. 6 is not teaching that this break is automatic and experientially inevitable. Otherwise, why would Paul tell them to reckon and yield? Unless the possibility of not doing it is present, then the command is meaningless. (2) Chrisope also argues incorrectly from 1 John. He camps on the black-and-white portrait of the believer and unbeliever (1 Jn. 1:6; 2:4, 9; 3:6-10; 4:8; 5:18). But 1:6 and 2:4 refer to "know" in the sense of "walk in fellowship with." A Christian who claims to walk in fellowship with Christ and who sins is a liar and is not walking in fellowship with Christ. Any pastor knows of Christians who feign spirituality and who at the same time are engage in acts of disobedience. Their spirituality is a lie, but they are Christians. See chapter 8, "Justification and Sanctification 1," for full discussion.

guaranteed by Scripture is that God's faithfulness is independent from our faith. "If we are faithless, He will remain faithful."[21]

The sense of moral revulsion that God would allow a sinning Christian to enter heaven betrays not only a lack of appreciation for the grace of God in our own lives, as well as those of carnal Christians, but is also the probable motive behind much Experimental Predestinarian exegesis.

Spiritual Consequences

Documenting the moral failures above is an unpleasant but necessary chore. Until the possibility of ultimate failure is clear, the warnings against it have little relevance. Equally distasteful is the task of explaining the consequences of carnality, and they are severe indeed. Once a man is born again in Christ, he is now in God's family, and as any human father would, our divine Father takes a more personal interest in the moral behavior of those who belong to Him than to those who are outside the household of faith. The Scriptures set forth three consequences of sin: discipline, death, and disinheritance.

Divine Discipline

The principle of judgment upon believers is found in many passages of the Old Testament (2 Sam. 7:14-15). If Solomon, for example, is disobedient, he will be disciplined with "the rod of men, with flaggings inflicted by men." This may suggest God will use the instrumentality of men to discipline. But He says He will not remove His love as He did from Saul. To "remove love" refers to 1 Sam. 13:13-14 where Saul is told that, if he had obeyed the Lord, God "would have established your kingdom over Israel for all time. But now your kingdom will not endure." In contrast, David and Solomon's right to the throne will endure even if they disobey. It does not refer to loss of salvation but loss of the right to rule. The principle is that discipline results in judgment in time or forfeiture in eternity but not loss of salvation.

In Ps. 89:30-36 God promises to discipline the sons of David if they refuse to follow His statutes. But "I will not take my love from him [i.e., I will not deny my promise to establish his throne forever]." In 2 Sam. 12:10-12 God disciplines David. He will reap what he has sown (Gal. 6:7-8) and will experience punishment worse than death (Heb. 10:29). God says He will take his wives and give them to someone close to him and that person will lie with his wife "in broad daylight." David repented of his adultery with Bathsheba and murder of Uriah before the baby was born (2 Sam. 12:13), but God took the baby (one reaps what

---

[21]He remains faithful to His promise to save us, not, as some have incredibly stated, "to condemn us"!

one sows). The future of the kingdom went downhill with murder and intrigue as a result of his sin with Bathsheba.

In extreme forms it is possible for a true believer to be forsaken by God:

And if you seek Him, He will let you find Him; but if you forsake Him, He will forsake you (2 Chr. 15:2 NASB).

A true believer can forsake God! These words were addressed to Asa, King of Judah. He is a king who led the people in a brief revival. He responded to Azariah's prophecy with faith and good works. He removed the abominable idols from all the land of Judah and rebuilt the altar of the Lord (15:8). He had believed and manifested his faith in actions. He led the people to seek the Lord, and as a result of the fact that they sought the Lord, they were rewarded (2 Chr. 15:7) and found rest (15:15). Failure to seek the Lord or evidence of forsaking Him resulted in punishment in time (15:12-13), capital punishment. Asa, however, did not continue to seek the Lord and died seeking the help of physicians instead of trusting the Lord for curing of his severely diseased feet (2 Chr. 16:12).

King Uzziah, mentioned above, fell into sin and as a result experienced divine discipline.

Hezekiah was a godly king. He did what was right in the eyes of the Lord (2 Chr. 31:21; 2 Chr. 29:2). Yet in a moment of pride he fell into sin. The Lord disciplined him with "wrath." Hezekiah repented of the pride in his heart and as a result the Lord's wrath did not come upon Jerusalem (2 Chr. 32:24-26).

The central passage in the Bible on the subject of divine discipline is Heb. 12:3-11. Here we are told that God's purpose in discipline is to correct by punishment. He disciplines us for our good that we may share in His holiness (Heb. 12:10). Every child of God will sooner or later experience this. His purpose is always to correct, the definite aim of which is "for our profit, that we might be partakers of His holiness." Without this holiness "no man will see the Lord" (Heb. 12:14). To see the Lord means to fellowship with Him. Job, for example, said, "But now my eyes have **seen** you" (Job 42:5). The parallel is precise. As a result of divine discipline Job came to "see" the Lord. The writer to the Hebrews, steeped in the Old Testament as he was, apparently had this passage in mind.

The Sin unto Death

The second consequence of carnality in the life of a believer is physical death. A number of passages already alluded to suggest that, when a believer fails to respond to discipline, God may take him home. For example:

> *My brethren, if any among you strays from the truth, and one turns him back, let him know that he who turns a sinner from the error of his way will save his soul from death, and will cover a multitude of sins* (Jas. 5:19-20 NASB).

It is apparently possible for a "brother" who is "among" us to stray from the truth and be in danger of death. Truly regenerate people are certainly in view here. The reference to covering a multitude of sins is used elsewhere of covering the sins of the regenerate (1 Pet. 4:8).

These sheep within the fold have "wandered" (Gk. **planao**). The word means to become lost, to lose one's way. Our word "planet" comes from this word and suggests the idea that the planets, in contrast to the stars, were not fixed but wandered about the heavens. The restoration of carnal Christians is in view. The intent is to "save his soul from death," i.e., to intercept his downward path before the Lord brings the discipline of physical death. We recover a "sinner" (a backslidden brother) in this way, by intercession and exhortation (cf. Heb. 3:13; 1 Th. 5:14-15). We are an intercessor with God, as Moses was (Ex. 32:30).

To "save a soul from death" was a way of saying "save a life," i.e., save a man from physical death. No doubt James had a similar concern when he said, "And when sin is accomplished, it brings forth death" (Jas. 1:15). "Death" ultimately refers to physical death, the final consequence of protracted sin. It is probable, however, that James includes all that is involved in the path to death: misery, spiritual impoverishment, and severe divine discipline. All of these things are death as well.

Another passage which refers to the sin unto death is found in 1 Jn. 5:16-17: "There is a sin leading unto death." It appears that physical death is in view. This is suggested by the fact that it is contrasted with physical life. Elsewhere in the epistle, when "eternal" life is meant, the adjective "eternal" is included. Second, John instructs his readers to pray for their "brother" that they might not experience death but "life." How can a brother be prayed for that he might obtain "eternal life." A "brother" already has eternal life. But if abundant life is meant, then the phrase not only makes sense but fits well with the thrust of the epistle: fellowship and joy (1 Jn. 1:3-4). Also it makes good sense to pray that God will spare a sinning brother and restore him to fellowship. There is no reason to suggest that by the term "brother" John means "professing" brother, no reason except a prior commitment to the Experimental Predestinarian view of perseverance! Had John meant professing brother, he could have said so.

Paul explained that some of the Corinthians who had come to the Lord's table drunk were "weak and sick, and a number sleep" (1 Cor. 11:30). The brother in 1 Corinthians who was caught in adultery with his stepmother was turned over to Satan "for the destruction of his flesh, that his spirit may be saved in the day of the Lord Jesus" (1 Cor. 5:5). No doubt Ananias and his wife Sapphira, regenerate members of the early church, experienced the sin unto physical death when they lied to the Holy Spirit (Acts 5:1-11). There are, then, ample biblical parallels to justify the doctrine of the sin unto physical death.

Paul's warnings to the Corinthians in 1 Cor. 10:1-13 contain one of the more obvious refutations of the Experimental Predestinarian's view of the carnal Christian. With warnings from Israel's history he admonishes the Christians at Corinth that they face the possibility of sin unto physical death just as the believing, regenerate nation of Israel did. He addresses this warning to "brothers" (10:1) in whose life God can work and give them a way out of every trial (10:13). These "dear friends" are urged to flee idolatry (10:14). That the wilderness generation is similarly viewed by Paul as mostly regenerate is indicated by the fact that he says they experienced God's leading (v. 1), they were baptized unto Moses (v. 2), and they "ate" and "drank" of Jesus Christ (v. 4). These phrases are used elsewhere of believing appropriation by regenerate people (Jn. 6:55-56).

Yet the wilderness generation experienced the sin unto physical death. The regenerate Corinthian brothers are warned not to set their "hearts on evil things as they did" (v. 6). It is apparently possible for brothers in Christ to set their hearts on evil things! They are warned not to become involved in sexual immorality (v. 8), and not to test the Lord (v. 9), or to grumble (v. 10). Paul says, "These things happened to them as examples and were written down as warnings for us (v. 11). Paul apparently thinks these warnings imply a real danger, a danger which can come upon regenerate "brothers." What was the danger? In each case it was the sin unto death! Due to various acts of persistent rebellion the wilderness generation experienced the death of twenty-three thousand in one day. Some were killed by snakes (v. 9), and some were killed by the destroying angel (v. 10).

When a Christian is judged by God and experiences the sin unto physical death, it is evident that he has not only sinned but that he has persisted in sin unto the final hour, precisely what the adherents of the reformed doctrine of perseverance say cannot happen!

Millennial Disinheritance

The final consequence of protracted carnality is forfeiture of reward and stinging rebuke when the King returns to establish His rule. No tragedy could be greater than for the Christian, saved by grace and given unlimited possibilities, to forfeit all of this and fail to participate in the future reign of the servant kings. The loss of reward at the judgment seat of Christ is often referred to but rarely specifically defined:

For we must all appear before the judgment seat of Christ, that each one may be recompensed for his deeds in the body, according to what he has done, **whether good or bad** (2 Cor. 5:10 NASB).

That there are negative consequences at the judgment seat of Christ is usually glossed over, and then a somewhat nebulous reference to crowns is alluded to in popular presentations. But there are negative consequences too! This is what the apostle Paul referred to when he said:

For we shall all stand before the judgment seat of God. For it is written, "As I live, says the Lord, "Every knee shall bow to Me, and every tongue shall give praise to God." So then each one of us shall give account of himself to God (Rom. 14:10-12 NASB).

It is certainly better for us to deal with our sin now, rather than then.

In the parable of the wedding banquet in Mt. 22:1-14, such a disinheritance is in view. At the marriage feast of the Lamb a great celebration will occur. However, not all will participate in that joy. Jesus describes this lamentable fact in His parable of the unprepared wedding guest. The parable says nothing about those who are not truly Christians being at the wedding banquet. Those who are not truly Christians will never enter the kingdom at all, much less the wedding banquet. Rather, it describes the varying responses different Christians have to the command of their master. The parable teaches that the unfaithful Christian will be excluded from the light and joy of the celebration. It will become painfully evident that there are those who are regenerate slaves who do not persevere in their efforts to be properly attired at the marriage feast.

The parable describes a great banquet, and the Lord invites all of His servants to attend. The invitation to attend is to be understood as an invitation to national Israel to accept Christ as Messiah. Yet some paid no attention at all to this offer:

But they paid no attention and went their way, one to his own farm and one to his business (Mt. 22:5 NASB).

Even more shocking, some of the people of God actually murdered other believers:

And the rest seized his slaves and mistreated them and killed them (Mt. 22:6 NASB).

God sent many of His servants the prophets to His people Israel. They responded by killing His messengers.

The King concludes that many among His people Israel were not worthy to attend the wedding feast. So He opens up the invitation to all, not just those who are descended from Abraham:

The wedding is ready, but those who were invited were not worthy. Go therefore to the main highways, as many as you find there, invite to the wedding feast. And those slaves went out into the streets, and gathered together all they found, both evil and good and the wedding hall was filled with dinner guests (Mt. 22:8-10 NASB).

Salvation is offered to all--Jew and Gentile, good and bad--and many apparently respond, are saved, and are present at the wedding banquet. After the feast begins, however, the King notes that there is one who entered who should not be there:

But when the King came in to look over the dinner guests, He saw there a man not dressed in wedding clothes, and He said to him, "Friend, how did you come in here without wedding clothes?" And he was speechless (Mt. 22:11-12 NASB).

What is the indispensable wedding garment? The answer lies in its function: for sharing a wedding feast. We are not here in a court of law standing before a judge. Instead, we are in the palace of a King at a wedding feast. The garment consists then not of the imputed righteousness of Christ but of deeds suitable to qualify us to participate in the King's banquet. In Isa. 61:10 righteousness is compared to a robe. The garment is not that worn by a criminal being counted righteous but of a bridegroom and bride dressing themselves for a wedding.

The nature of the garment is made explicitly clear in Rev. 19:7-8: "Let us rejoice and be glad and give the glory to Him, for the marriage of the Lamb has come and His bride has made herself ready. And it was given to her to clothe herself in fine linen, bright and clean; for the fine linen is the **righteous acts of the saints.**"

These practical righteous acts (Rev. 15:4) refer not to the act of the Son of God in declaring us righteous (justification). They refer instead to our faithfulness in this life. This practical righteousness, this habitual doing of good deeds, is the fine linen with which the bride is clothed at her marriage. Imputed righteousness is "put on" the believer by God. This garment, however, must be put on by the believer himself.

What the friend at the wedding banquet lacked was not justification but a life of righteous acts. He was a "friend" and a "servant" of his Master, had responded to the invitation (v. 10), and had believed in Him. His failure was to persevere in his life of works. The consequences are terrible:

> *Then the King said to the servants, "Bind him hand and foot, and cast*
> *him into the outer darkness; in the place there shall be weeping and*
> *gnashing of teeth. For many are called, but few are chosen* (Mt.
> 22:13-14 NASB).

Several questions are raised by this striking warning. Is the servant a
saved man? To what does the "darkness outside" refer? What is the meaning of
"wailing and gnashing of teeth"?

Is the servant a saved man? The basis for believing this man is saved is
that (1) he responded to the invitation to salvation (22:10), and (2) he was
apparently not only in the kingdom but actually at the wedding banquet itself.
According to Jesus one cannot enter the kingdom unless one is born again (Jn.
3:3). Since this man has entered the kingdom and even the wedding feast, it
seems justifiable to conclude he is regenerate. In addition, (3) the man is
addressed as a "friend" by the Lord.

It seems that the major reason for denying this man's regeneration is that
he apparently did not persevere in a life of good works! Since that is the subject
in question, it is not a reason to doubt this man's salvation. Because
Experimental Predestinarians do not believe that a true Christian can ever lose
salvation and because they interpret "outer darkness" and "wailing and gnashing
of teeth" as descriptions of hell, they conclude, theologically, that this man could
not have been saved. Their Arminian brethren, however, may be forgiven for
smiling and saying, "This is precisely the point! By what kind of logic can you
conclude that the man was not saved to begin with just because he was not saved
in the end?"

What is the "darkness outside"? The man is said to be bound "hand and
foot" and then cast into "outer darkness." Whatever the illustration of binding
pictures, it must be very severe and causes the cessation of all meaningful activity.
Perhaps the point is that, while the servant kings will participate in man's final
destiny, this bound one will not be free to do so.

The key phrase in Greek is **to skotos to exsoteron**, simply translated "the
outside (or outer) darkness." If there is anything to be made of the word order, it
would be that the adjective is specifying the kind or location of the darkness. It is
not general darkness; it is darkness which is outside. In this discussion we are
choosing to render the phrase as "the darkness outside," rather than "outer
darkness," for two reasons. One is to keep this specifying aspect before us. The
second regards the connotation of the phrase "the outer darkness." Because it
has come to be so strongly associated with judgment in hell, it makes objective
consideration of this passage more difficult. By using the phrase "the darkness
outside," we are freed from traditional usage that might color our thinking to see
what the phrase means in context. When we do that, it becomes highly probable

that this phrase simply refers to the darkness outside the relative light of the banquet hall.[22]

"Darkness" (**skotos**) can refer to simple physical darkness (Lk. 23:44-45).[23] The notion of "judgment" is not part of the semantic value of the word. To necessarily read this idea into it is once again to commit the illegitimate totality transfer. It certainly can and does refer to the judgment of hell elsewhere, but those meanings are due to context, not the intrinsic meaning of the word.

Only Christ uses the term, and it is found only in Matthew (8:12; 22:13; 25:30). The region in view is simply outside some other region, contiguous to it. In two of the references a house of feasting is in view. In these passages the King comes into the banquet hall, and the guests are cast out of it. In the ancient Near East such festivity normally took place at night. The banquet hall is brilliantly lit up but, by contrast, the gardens around them are in black darkness. All that is meant is "darkness which is without, outside the house."[24]

Therefore, when Experimental Predestinarians object and say, "How could there be any darkness in the millennial kingdom for the saved to go into, and how could the saved be in the darkness and yet still shining (Mt. 13:43)?" The answer is, "Every twenty-four hours there will be darkness available for the saved and the unsaved!" The shining of the elect is simply the radiance of their resurrection bodies which characterizes both the faithful and the unfaithful.

In Mt. 8:12 we are told that it is the "sons of the kingdom" who will be cast outside this joyful banquet. **The phrase "sons of the kingdom" refers elsewhere in Matthew's gospel to true believers--the "wheat" in the parable of the wheat and the tares!** (Mt. 13:38).

Yet there are sons, and there are "sons indeed." All are sons by faith in Christ, but Matthew uses the term in some places in the sense of "sons indeed," when he says we must perform good works in order to become "sons of God" (Mt. 5:9, 44-45).

There is evidently a difference between being a son of God and being publicly revealed as such, i.e., "called" a son. Those who are peacemakers and who love their enemies are not only sons but "sons indeed."

This very distinction is implied at the beginning of the Lord's parable on the wedding feast in Mt. 8:10-12. Marveling at the "great faith" of the centurion,

---

[22]Thayer seems to agree when he says the phrase refers to "the darkness outside the limits of the lighted palace" (Joseph Henry Thayer, *Thayer's Greek-English Lexicon of the New Testament* [rev. ed., 1889; reprint ed., Grand Rapids: Associate Publishers and Authors, n.d.], p. 226).

[23]See also Acts 13:11; Mk. 15:33; Mt. 27:45.

[24]G. H. Lang, *Pictures and Parables* (Miami Springs, FL: Schoettle, 1985), p. 306.

He says, "Assuredly, I say to you, I have not found such great faith, not even in Israel!" (Mt. 8:10). Now, our Lord did find faith in Israel. Indeed, thousands believed in Him, many superficially, but nevertheless genuinely. What dismayed Him was that, in comparison with the Gentile centurion, there was rarely an instance of "great faith." There will be those in the kingdom who have shown great faith in contrast to those who, like many in Israel, showed only nominal faith. The latter are the "sons of the kingdom," truly saved Israelites, who of all people should have demonstrated the great faith which the Lord found only outside of the covenant people in the life of the Gentile centurion. These are the sons of the kingdom who will be cast into the darkness outside of the wedding banquet.

A similar truth is taught in the parallel passage in Lk. 13:22-30. Two scenes are presented here. These two events are in response to the question posed in v. 23, "Lord, are there just a **few** who are being saved?"

The first scene is presented in vv. 24-28. Here the fateful destiny of those who professed faith in Christ but who never really trusted Him, is woefully set forth. They apply for entrance into the kingdom, and they are shut out, the Lord's words ringing in their ears, "I do not know you." As a result these unregenerate "workers of iniquity," like the unfaithful Christian, will experience profound regret, "weeping and gnashing of teeth" (v. 28). This experience of regret occurs as these unsaved people observe Abraham, Isaac, Jacob, and all the prophets **in the kingdom of God**. They have, to their eternal shame, been cast out of it! Unlike the parable in Mt. 8:12, we are not at the wedding feast, and there is no darkness outside the banquet hall. They are not even in the kingdom.

But in Lk. 13:29 the scene changes. The tares and the goats have been shut out of the kingdom. What of those remaining? They will now gather at the wedding banquet. "And they will come from east and west, and from north and south, and will recline at table in the kingdom of God." There will be a great multitude of saved people (wheat), who will gather from all over the world. Here the Lord refers to people who are not only in the kingdom, but they **recline at the table** in the kingdom. The phrase rendered "recline at the table" (Gk. **anaklithesontai**) is a technical term referring to reclining at a banquet. Arndt and Gingrich relate it specifically to the messianic wedding banquet in this verse and connect it with Mt. 8:11.[25] In the former scene we were "in the kingdom," but here we are now "at the table." In the former the experience of the nonbeliever, weeping and gnashing his teeth, is described. Here we are concerned with rankings **within** the kingdom. The Lord summarizes the second scene by saying, "And indeed there are last who will be first, and there are first who will be last." This phrase is a common expression found elsewhere in the Gospels of rankings

---

[25]AG, p. 55.

among believers based upon their servanthood in this life.[26] This seems to establish that the wedding feast of Mt. 8:11-12 is parallel with the wedding feast of Lk. 13:29-30 and not with the wider context of Lk. 13:24-28. There is a difference between being "in the kingdom" (v. 29) and being "at the table" (v. 29).[27]

So in answer to the original question, Are there just a few who are being saved? the Lord says that there is a great multitude which is being saved. But many who think they are saved are not (vv. 24-28), and among that great multitude of saved people some will be last, and some will be first (vv. 29-30).

Matthew, therefore, leads us to imagine a great feast of rejoicing. All the faithful Christians in history are there to celebrate victory with their King. This joyful banquet is portrayed by the Lord as occurring in the evening in a brightly lit banquet hall. Outside the banquet where the shining lights of the feast are not present, a relative physical darkness prevails that evening. This is the darkness outside, the darkness outside of the light of the wedding feast! It is not the darkness of hell.

What is the meaning of "wailing and gnashing of teeth." Those Christians who are not "sons indeed," who lack wedding garments at the wedding banquet, will not only be excluded from the joy of the banquet but will also experience profound regret, "wailing and gnashing of teeth." This phrase does not refer to the experience of the unsaved in hell in this passage. It speaks instead of the grief experienced by a true Christian over a wasted life. It must be remembered that this is a parable and contains figures of speech. There is no literal "wailing and gnashing of teeth," just as there will be no literal binding and casting. Rather, these Oriental symbols evoke ideas of a severe rebuke followed by profound regret. These believers will experience great grief ("wailing") and will be angry with themselves, or despairing,[28] because of their wasted lives ("gnashing of teeth").

The Orientals were much more expressive of grief, and strong images were used to portray it. Macalister observes that "the Hebrews did not restrain themselves (as modern Occidentals characteristically do) from expressing

---

[26]Mt. 19:30; Mk. 9:35; 10:31. See also 1 Cor. 4:9; 15:8. M'Neile, for example, on Mt. 19:30 says, "It is more probably a rebuke to Peter, and refers to **ranks** in the Kingdom" (Alan Hugh M'Neile, *The Gospel According to St. Matthew* [1915; reprint ed., London: Macmillan, 1961], p. 283).

[27]The separation in the scene between Lk. 13:22-28 and 13:29-30 is further reinforced by the fact that Luke is here bringing together two separate scenes in Matthew, separated by intervening verses, and combining them in his gospel as one continuous account (i.e., Mt. 7:21-23 = Lk. 13:22-28 and Mt. 8:11-12 = Lk. 13:29-30.) Also Lk. 13:29 is introduced by **kai**, which could be an adjunctive and be translated "also."

[28]In the Old Testament the phrase "gnashing of teeth" referred to the taunts of the wicked (Job 16:9) or despair and envy (Ps. 112:10).

emotion through weeping."[29] In fact, it was customary to hire professional mourners at a burial. The poetic symbolism of the book of Lamentations illustrates this Oriental characteristic. Special clothing was often used. A black garment made of goats hair, coarse in nature and similar to a grain sack, was called a sackcloth (Gen. 37:34; Jer. 6:26).[30] Rending the garments by tearing them from top to bottom was a universal sign among the Hebrews signifying grief and distress. Gregory says, "The capacity of the Hebrew for tears is immense, though the psalmist probably is using hyperbole when he speaks of flooding his bed every night with tears."[31] Loud cries are frequently associated with weeping as a sign of grief (Ruth 1:9; 2 Sam. 13:36), "Alas, alas" (Amos 5:16). Accompanying these cries is the characteristic action of beating the breast. The sprinkling of ashes, dust, or dirt upon oneself and then wallowing in it was a common way to express grief over a personal tragedy (2 Sam. 1:2; 13:19, 31; Ezek. 27:30; Est. 4:1-3).

The point is simply that the Oriental was much more emotional and demonstrative regarding grief and regret. Strong phrases like "wailing and gnashing of teeth" portray extreme pictures to the Western mind which cause us to freight them with meanings such as "hell," when all that is meant is strong remorse.

The phrase "wailing and gnashing of teeth" is found seven times in the New Testament. Even though it is used on three occasions of the experience of the unregenerate in hell,[32] it is also used on four occasions of the regenerate in the kingdom.[33] The notions of heaven or hell are simply not part of the semantic value of the words. The fact that the nonbeliever can experience profound regret in hell in no way implies that the true Christian cannot experience profound regret in the kingdom (there will be no remorse in heaven). We are repeatedly told that, when the Lord comes, He will reward us "good and bad" (2 Cor. 5:10) and that some may draw back in shame at His coming (1 Jn. 2:28). Some Christians are going to be saved "but only as one escaping through the flames" (1 Cor. 3:15). It seems that these verses adequately explain the experience of profound regret for the unfaithful Christian which Matthew calls "wailing and gnashing of teeth."

Lang summarizes well:[34]

---

[29]A. Macalister, "Tears," in *NIBSE*, 4:745.

[30]T. M. Gregory, "Mourning," in *ZPED*, 4:306.

[31]Ibid., 4:304.

[32]Mt. 13:42, 50; Lk. 13:28.

[33]Mt. 8:12; 22:13; 24:51; 25:30.

[34]Lang, *Pictures*, p. 306.

It were but an event to be expected that an Oriental despot, of royal or lesser rank, if offended with one of the slaves, should order that he be bound and thrown into the garden. There the unfortunate man, with the common Eastern emotionalism, would bewail the dark and the cold, and the danger from hungry dogs and jackals, and would gnash his teeth at being deprived of the pleasures forfeited.

This is completely different from the tares, the sons of the evil one (Mt. 13:38), being cast into the furnace of fire, hell, where there will also be wailing and gnashing of teeth (Mt. 13:42). There is no furnace of fire here. "Such obviously distinct pictures must be viewed as distinct, and distinct meanings be sought."[35]

It is not to the unregenerate that this fate occurs but to "sons of the kingdom (Mt. 8:12), who are the "wheat" (Mt. 13:38), to whom the calling naturally belongs. This man is a "friend" who had accepted the invitation and had taken his place. It is the personal slaves of the Lord of the house who are asked to value their rich privileges lest they lose them and fall under his displeasure. The apostles regularly call themselves slaves. It was to his **own** bond-servants (not Satan's!) that the Lord had entrusted his talents.

"What relationship this term ('his own' servant) indicates is not questioned when it is used of the shepherd calling **'his own'** sheep and going before them (John 10:3,4). To avoid this meaning in the former case is to deal deceitfully with the Scripture":[36]

The blessed Lord who loved and redeemed them, made it abundantly plain that one of His own servants may render himself obnoxious to this intensely solemn penalty of being bound and cast forth from the grand reality of the marriage supper, of the joy of the Lord. Nor is the spiritual reality at all unknown now. There are children of God, servants of Christ, who through misconduct have forfeited the once-enjoyed liberty of sons, no more share the joy of their lord, and are in distressing darkness of soul.[37]

We are not to suppose this lasts forever:

Day would dawn, his bands would be loosed, life would be resumed, but he would have missed the joyous festival forever, for the wedding feast would never be repeated. That is to say, the special pleasures, honors, splendors which are to accompany the return of the Lord from heaven and the setting up of His kingdom at the consummation of this

---

[35]Ibid., p. 307.
[36]Ibid.
[37]Ibid., p. 308.

*age, are to be a reward for fidelity, for righteous and dutiful conduct in
His absence, and without this manner of life they may be forfeited.*[38]

According to the Lord, all Christians are called to participate in the
wedding, but only some will enjoy it, i.e., be there. This is apparently the
meaning of the proverb "Many are called but few are chosen." This ancient
proverb, used three times in the apocryphal 4 Ezra, simply means that, while all
Christians are invited to the banquet, only those wearing the wedding garment
are chosen to participate in it. It is not necessary to understand this proverb as
saying that all are invited to be saved, but only the elect will be.

Those Christians who fail to persevere to the end, who are carnal, will
experience three negatives at the future judgment: (1) a stinging rebuke (Mt.
24:45-51);[39] (2) exclusion from the wedding banquet (Mt. 22:1-14; Mt. 25:1-13);[40]
and (3) millennial disinheritance (Mt. 25:14-30).

Confession

The recovery of the carnal Christian requires that he "repent" (2 Cor. 7:10;
Rev. 2:5). Elsewhere this repentance is called confession (1 Jn. 1:9).

While some say that Christians do not need to confess, that God takes no
notice of our sins because they are buried in the sea of forgetfulness, the Bible
seems to speak otherwise. The Lord does not impute sin to us (Ps. 32:1-2; Rom.
4:7-8), but that refers to our eternal standing. If God does not expect confession,
why did the Lord say, "Forgive us our trespasses" (Mt. 6:12)? We would be
confessing what God did not see. Also the Lord said, "If ye forgive not men their
trespasses, neither will your Father forgive your trespasses" (Mt. 6:15).

There are two kinds of forgiveness in the New Testament. One pertains to
our eternal salvation (justification by faith), the other to our temporal fellowship
with the Father. Just as our children may sin within our family, the believer may
sin within God's family. Our child is always our child, but until he confesses, our
fellowship is not good. In God's family the same principle applies. There is a
forgiveness for salvation and a forgiveness for restoration. The Lord referred to
this second kind of forgiveness when He said to Peter, "If I do not wash you, you
have no part with Me" (Jn. 13:8). Peter told the Lord to wash him all over if that
was the case. To this Jesus replied, "He who has bathed needs only to wash his
feet, but is completely clean" (Jn. 13:10). The forgiveness related to restoration
of fellowship is parallel in thought with the cleansing of the feet of the already
bathed, regenerate man.

---

[38]Ibid.
[39]See discussion under Mt. 24:45ff in chapter 17, "Conditional Security: Gospels and Paul."
[40]Ibid.

In 1 Cor. 11:31 we are told, "If we would judge ourselves, we should not be judged." The meaning is plain: if we deal with our sin now, we will be spared from His fierce judgment later on.

Conclusion

The first time that this writer assembled these verses together, he remembered how surprised he was to discover that the Scriptures seemed to teach something that he had always assumed to be impossible: that true Christians can commit apostasy. However, the Bible is quite realistic. It appears to teach that final failure is possible. Indeed, it is constantly warned against in the New Testament.

No doubt this conclusion will be one of the most problematic for many who read this book. It is possible that part of the problem is that many assume that it is faith which saves us. If that is so, then if we stop believing, we would no longer be saved. Imagine a man at the top of a burning building. He notes that the firemen have gathered below with a large net. With a leap of faith (literally!) he trusts himself into the hands of the firemen and jumps off the building. He crashes into the net, it holds, and he is saved. Now did his faith save him? No. It was the firemen holding the net. Leaping into the net did not save him either. Many have jumped to their deaths by leaping out of windows. No! It was not faith, not leaping, but the net that saved him.

After going through an experience like this, the man would probably be encouraged to trust in firemen should he ever find himself again on top of a burning building. Let us imagine, however, that his faith in firemen fails. He has still been saved from crashing to the pavement even if he stops believing.

Even though the man could theoretically be faced with another fire and, due to his loss of faith in firemen and nets, face a deadly peril, the believer in Christ faces no such danger. There are no more fires from which we have to escape!

The danger of apostasy is real. Many readers of this book have known people who once believed, who witnessed, who prayed, who read their Bibles and yet did not finish their course. To say they were never saved to begin with begs the question and in many instances contradicts our personal knowledge of those people.

No! The danger is real, and we must stay close to Christ, or we too can face the prospects of discipline and disinheritance. The Christian life is not easy and believing God in the midst of trials and suffering is hardest of all. Many have abandoned faith due to their disappointment with God.

Fortunately, God has not left us alone. Through the ministry of the Holy Spirit He has provided all the resources needed to avoid this danger and to live abundantly as well. It is to this resource, the power of the Holy Spirit, that we must now direct our attention.

Chapter 16

Life in the Spirit

In Romans, chapter 8, the apostle turns from the struggle in chapter 7 and explains the source and method of living abundantly. It is by the Spirit of God and the use of certain spiritual weapons that our Christian experience can be characterized by "life and peace." Indeed, persistence in using the means of grace will result not only in a vital Christian life but joint-heirship with the Messiah in the final destiny of man. Unfortunately, this wonderful chapter has been woefully misunderstood by Experimental Predestinarians. Instead of seeing it as a contrast between two differing qualities of Christian life, they have usually seen it as a contrast between the Christian and the non-Christian. In so doing, they reduce it to a kind of test of salvation. Paul's intent, however, is not to challenge the Romans to examine themselves to see if they are Christians. Since they are Christians and therefore dead to sin and alive to God, they are obligated to live lives consistent with these facts.

To get a proper view of the argument of the passage, it is necessary to begin in the middle. In Rom. 8:12-13 the apostle declares:

> *So then, **brethren**, we are under obligation, not to the flesh, to live according to the flesh - for if you are living according to the flesh, you must die; but if by the Spirit you are putting to death the deeds of the body, you will live* (NASB).

It seems obvious that it is possible for "brethren" to die. In some sense a true Christian can experience spiritual death. Earlier in the context he has defined death as the opposite of "life and peace" (Rom. 8:6). It is therefore not to be equated with loss of salvation or hell but with emptiness, depression, and spiritual impoverishment.

Freedom from Sin's Power (8:1-7)

In justification of this interpretation some brief comment on the flow of the argument of the Rom. 8:1-11 is necessary. In Rom. 7:14-25 Paul has summarized his experience as a mature Christian.[1] He battles daily with the flesh. The message of the chapter is that the flesh is weak and is unable to win. How then can he be victorious in the daily struggle? In 7:25 he bursts forth in praise that God has provided a means for practical victory. That victory is the subject of Rom. 8:

> *There is therefore now no condemnation for those who are in Christ Jesus* (Rom. 8:1 NASB).

The word "condemnation" (Gk. **katakrima**) is best rendered "penal servitude."[2] It is quite unlikely that the reference is to justification, for that stage of the argument has already been reached in 3:21. Rather, the "therefore" casts us back to the preceding verse, "Thank God." Paul has thanked God that deliverance from the penal servitude to sin is available. He now explains how.

---

[1]Augustine and the Latin Fathers held this view. (1) The language best fits the regenerate man (7:15: I hate what I am doing; 7:21: I desire to do good; 7:22: I delight to do the law of God in the inward man; 7:25b: he serves the law of God with his mind). These expressions are inconsistent with Col. 1:21 where the unregenerate are described as hostile to God. But these verses may refer to the Christian. When he says he serves the law of God with his mind, it seems probable that he has 6:17-18, 20 in view. There, believers are slaves of righteousness. The "inner man" is the human self which is being renewed by God's Spirit, not the self, or any part of the self, of the still unconverted man. "In fact a struggle as serious as that which is here described can only take place where the Spirit of God is present and active (cf. Gal. 5.17)" (C. E. B. Cranfield, *A Critical and Exegetical Commentary on the Epistle to the Romans*, 2 vols., *The International Critical Commentary* [Edinburgh: T. & T. Clark, 1975-79], p. 346). It is objected that the same language is applied by Paul to himself in his unregenerate state in Phil. 3:6, where it is said that he had zeal and was righteous before the law. However, the man in Rom. 7 has no concept that he is experientially righteous before the law. Only a Christian consciousness could come to the conclusions that he was totally sinful. The man in Phil. 3:6 was deluded; he was not really blameless. (2) The language is present tense from 7:14-25. This must refer to a present experience like in 1 Cor. 9:27 where Paul says he disciplines his body and keeps it in subjection. That even the regenerate can have this struggle is proved by Gal. 5:17. (3) The order of the sentences in 7:24-25 is instructive (Cranfield, p. 345). If 7:24 is the cry of an unconverted man or of a Christian living a low quality of life and 7:25a is a thanksgiving that the deliverance has arrived, why does he say in 25b that he is in the same fix he was in 7:24? Apparently it is perfectly possible to have the experience of 25b and 24 even AFTER being delivered. If that is so, then there is no argument left to say that 7:14-25 must refer to the unregenerate state. This is the view of Calvin, Hodge, Shedd, Murray, and most exegetes within the Reformed tradition.

[2]F. F. Bruce, *Romans, TNTC,* p. 159. Arndt and Gingrich say **katakrima** signifies "not condemnation, but the punishment following a sentence." Murray agrees. Condemnation is the opposite of justification but what aspect of justification? He says that the context is talking about sanctification and not expiation. "Hence what is thrust into the foreground in the terms 'no condemnation' is not only freedom from the guilt but also freedom from the enslaving power of sin" (John Murray, *The Epistle to the Romans, NICNT,* 2 vols. in one, 6-1:275).

This deliverance comes by means of a new and higher principle which Paul calls the "law of the Spirit of life."[3] This higher law has set him free from the lower one, the law of sin and death.[4] The problem was not with the law but with the flesh. It was too weak to obey. So God solved this problem by releasing the flesh from its sin master. This was the subject of Rom. 6:1-11 and is now alluded to here:

For what the Law could not do, weak as it was through the flesh, God did: sending His own Son in the likeness of sinful flesh and as an offering for sin, He condemned sin in the flesh (8:3 NASB).

This condemnation of sin is not to be understood as a substitution for sin. He was sent "for sin" (Gk. **peri**) in a general sense. This context is not talking about a sacrifice for sin:[5]

In order that the requirement of the Law might be fulfilled in us, who do not walk according to the flesh, but according to the Spirit (8:4 NASB).

It is important to note that the requirement of the law is to be fulfilled "in us" and not "to us" or "on our behalf." Elsewhere, the requirement which is to be fulfilled is the sum of the law, to love one another (13:8). A perfect fulfillment is not required by the word "fulfill."[6] The condemnation of the sin occurred while Christ was "in the flesh." The condemnation in view is the judgment on the old man (Rom. 6:6) which resulted in our being "freed from sin." This freedom is a legal release from penal servitude to the Sin Master.[7]

---

[3] The term is defined by looking at what it is contrasted with. The law of the Spirit of life is the opposite of the law of sin and death. What is the law of sin and death? In 7:21 it is a principle (same Greek word), law. Bruce says it refers to the principle of the Spirit which is life (p. 160). Murray (6-1:276) says that the law refers to a regulating and actuating power as well as a legislating authority. It is the regulating and actuating power of the Holy Spirit as the Spirit of life. It is the power of the Holy Spirit operative in us to make us free from the power of sin which is unto death.

[4] This cannot refer to the law of Moses because that was holy (7:12) and spiritual (7:14) but to "the inward rule of the sin principle" (H. P. Liddon, *Explanatory Analysis of St. Paul's Epistle to the Romans* [London: Longmans, Green, 1899; reprint ed., Minneapolis: James and Klock, 1977], p. 127).

[5] Cranfield notes that, because the condemnation of sin was in Christ's flesh, the aspect of condemnation against sin related to our struggle with sin in our flesh is in view, i.e., it was the "breaking of sin's power" and not its penalty which is in view (p. 383).

[6] Cranfield says that it "is not to be taken to imply that the faithful fulfill the law's requirement perfectly. Chapter 7 must not be forgotten. They fulfill it in the sense that they do have a real faith in God (which is the law's basic demand), in the sense that their lives are definitely turned in the direction of obedience, that they do sincerely desire to obey and are earnestly striving to advance ever nearer to perfection" (p. 384).

[7] Liddon understands the phrase "He condemned sin" to mean "He condemned the sin-principle to be deposed from its dominion." He did this while he was "in the flesh" (p. 127).

The Two Walks (8:1-4)

Christ condemned sin in the flesh so that the law might be fulfilled in us, but he clarifies who among us will experience the fulfillment of the law, i.e., those "who walk not according to the flesh but according to the Spirit." He therefore presents two possibilities for "us," i.e., Christians: we can walk according to the flesh (i.e., as non-Christians) or according to the Spirit. Paul has told us elsewhere that it is possible for Christians to walk **kata anthropon,** "as mere men" (1 Cor. 3:3).

The phrase "who walk not according to the flesh but according to the Spirit" has been taken in several ways. Some view it as describing the manner in which the law is fulfilled.[8] Others, particularly Experimental Predestinarians, see it as a characteristic of all who are regenerate.[9] But for several reasons it seems best to understand the phrase as a condition whereby the requirement of the law can be fulfilled in us.

First, the immediate context says that true life is conditioned upon "putting to death the deeds of the body" and that this is not automatic. It is possible for true Christians to "die" (8:12). Second, the inclusion of the phrase "who do not walk according to flesh" seems to suggest that there are two possibilities, not one, for the regenerate man. Fitzmyer agrees:

> *The Greek uses a participle with the negative* **me** *which gives almost a proviso or conditional force to the expression, 'provided we walk not according to the flesh.' It thus insinuates that Christian living is not something that flows automatically, as it were, from baptism.*[10]

As Liddon insists, "The condition of retaining this freedom from sin is the cooperation of the regenerate will."[11]

---

[8]Cranfield, p. 385

[9]See, for example, William G. T. Shedd, *A Critical and Doctrinal Commentary on the Epistle of St. Paul to the Romans* (New York: Charles Scribner's Sons, 1879; reprint ed., Grand Rapids: Zondervan, 1967), p. 232. He argues that the clause indicates the necessary effect of justification. He takes the preceding verse to refer to justification. "Those to whom Christ's work is imputed (4:24), and in whom the requirement of the law is thereby completely fulfilled (8:4), and to whom there is consequently no condemnation (8:1), are a class of persons who are characterized by a pious life, though not a sinless and perfect one. The imputed righteousness or justification, spoken of in vv. 3 and 4, is accompanied with the inherent righteousness or sanctification, spoken of in v. 2. The former does not exist without the latter. St. Paul conjoins them and mentions both, in proof that the believer is not in a state of condemnation" (p. 233).

[10]Joseph A. Fitzmyer, "Romans," in *The Jerome Biblical Commentary*, ed. Raymond E. Brown, Joseph Fitzmyer, and Roland E. Murphy (Englewood Cliffs, NJ: Prentice-Hall, 1968), on 8:4.

[11]Liddon, p. 128. F. F. Bruce similarly agrees that two possible kinds of walks for a Christian are being described (Bruce, p. 157).

Third, it seems evident that Paul is referring here to what he has taught elsewhere. "Walk by the Spirit and you will not carry out the desires of the flesh" (Gal. 5:16). There the walk is not automatic for all Christians but is conditional. The contexts appear very similar. Paul also says, "If we live by the Spirit let us also walk by the Spirit" (Gal. 5:25). He is obviously saying that, while all Christians live by means of the Spirit, not all necessarily walk that way.

> *For those who are according to the flesh set their minds on the things of the flesh, but those who are according to the Spirit, the things of the Spirit* (8:5 NASB).

These two kinds of Christians are contrasted in this verse: those believers who walk according to flesh and those who walk according to the Spirit. A Christian can have his mind set either upon what the flesh desires or upon what the Spirit desires.

The following verses up through v. 7, and then in vv. 12-17, continue this contrast. It may be helpful to arrange the descriptions of the two kinds of Christians involved in the following table:

	Spiritual Christian	**Carnal Christian**
8:4	walks according to the Spirit	walks according to the flesh
8:5	sets mind on Spirit	sets mind on flesh
8:6	life and peace	death
8:7		hostile to God not subject to God unable to obey God
8:12	puts to death the deeds of the body	lives according to the flesh
8:13	those being led by the Spirit of God	those who walk according to the flesh
8:17	joint-heirs of Christ	those who do not suffer with him

Paul summarizes the first twelve verses with the statement, "So then **brethren** we are under obligation, not to the flesh, to live according to the flesh" (8:12). He is saying it is possible for "brethren" to walk according to the flesh. It is possible for brethren to be characterized by the things on the right hand side of the table. These verses (8:12-13) summarize the items on the right column and call them "walking after the flesh." The result is that they, Christians, will die. The other alternative summarizes the items on the left side of the table and says they are equivalent to "by the Spirit putting to death the deeds of the body." The result of this activity is that these brethren will "live." Thus, true, abundant life is meant, and not just regeneration.

That it is possible for these brethren not to put to death the deeds of the body is obvious because he says, "if." A failure to do this results in the opposite: death, or walking according to the flesh. Paul's picture here is of a battle, a battle between the flesh and the Holy Spirit. A Christian must choose life or death, fellowship with God or spiritual impoverishment. He evidently has his own struggle in Rom. 7:14-25 in mind.

The Two Minds (8:5-7)

Paul continues and answers the question, What does it mean to walk according to the flesh (Gk. **kata sarka**)? The answer is that it means to set your mind on the things of the flesh. These two kinds of walks begin in the mind:

For the mind set on the flesh is death, but the mind set on the Spirit is life and peace (8:6 NASB).

Now he explains the results of these differing "mind-sets." A mind set upon the flesh is death. By death here he means the opposite of "life and peace." Peace in Romans means either peace with God as a result of reconciliation (Rom. 1:7; 5:1) or peace in the sense of wholeness, harmonious relations, and mental health (2:17; 14:17, 19; 15:13, 33; 16:20). The connection with "joy" and harmonious interpersonal relations (Rom. 14:17, 19) fits well with the sanctification context of Rom. 8 and is the meaning here.

"Life" (Gk. **zoe**) is often used of an abundant quality of life beyond regeneration which is the possession of those who "persevere in doing good" (Rom. 2:7).[12] The "reign in life" of the believer (Rom. 5:17) is called "much more" than the reign in death. Therefore, not just a counterbalance to death is meant, i.e.,

---

[12]See, for example, 1:17: the just shall live by faith--abundant life, vital fellowship with God; 6:2: continue to live in sin--a present experience of life; 7:9-10: he was alive apart from the law once, but when sin came, he died; 10:5: Moses says the man who practices the righteousness based upon law will live by that righteousness--have a rich and meaningful life; 14:8: if we live, we live for the Lord; 2:7: eternal life--enriched experience of it as a result of works; 5:17: reign in life--abundant life; 6:4: we might walk in newness of life--a rich experience of life now, not regeneration; 6:22: the eternal life which comes as a result of works--enriched experience of life; 7:10: the commandment was to result in life--abundant life, but it resulted in death (Murray [6-1:252] admits that life here is life in the path of moral righteousness); 8:2: Spirit of life is Spirit who brings true life--release from the struggle in chapter 7; 8:6: mind set upon Spirit is life and peace.

regeneration, but an abundant life, a vibrant experience with Christ. It is "newness of life" (Rom. 6:4).

Death, being the opposite of life and peace, is not final commitment to hell. It is the life of anxiety and emptiness which comes to any man (believer or nonbeliever) who sets his mind on the wrong things

> *because the mind set on the flesh is hostile toward God; for it does not subject itself to the law of God, for it is not even able to do so* (8:7).

Here we have a key to the seeming inability of many Christians to live consistent, powerful Christian lives. When a Christian sets his mind on the flesh, he is hostile to God and is cut off from the Holy Spirit and therefore unable to obey.

To say that these verses refer to a contrast between Christians and non-Christians rather than between two kinds of Christians not only contradicts the facts of Christian experience but the rest of the New Testament as well. On this view all Christians "walk according to the Spirit" (8:4), have their minds "set upon . . . the things of the Spirit" (8:5), and have their minds "set upon the Spirit" (8:6). This contradicts Paul's teaching elsewhere that walking in the Spirit is not automatic and inevitable (Gal. 5:16). In addition, it is refuted by the condition-ality of this walk in the immediate context of Rom. 8. In v. 13 the possibility of a rich spiritual experience ("life") is conditioned upon putting to death the deeds of the body. It is not the automatic possession of each Christian. Furthermore, what Christian since Pentecost has ever unconditionally experienced this abun-dant life, peace, and the fulfillment of the requirements of the law? To say these things are true of all Christians is a mockery of Christian experience.

Freedom from Sin's Sphere (8:8-11)

In the Flesh (8:8)

Now those who are in the flesh cannot please God (8:8).

The verse opens with the conjunction **de**, variously translated "and" (NASB; RSV), "so then" (NKJV), "moreover" (Wuest), and left untranslated by the NIV. This is a very flexible conjunction and can often express a contrast or a transition to a new subject.[13] It appears here that both a contrast and a transition to a different but related subject are intended. Having spoken of the inability of Christians to obey when their minds are set on the flesh, he now reminds them that, if they were unsaved ("in the flesh"), they would have no possibility of knowing the fulfillment of the law in them. But they ARE saved, and they there-fore not only have the possibility of this experience but the obligation (8:12) to

---

[13]AS, p. 98

live on this new plane. Because v. 9 contrasts sharply with v. 8, they are to be joined together. Thus, v. 8 is not a continuation and exposition of v. 7 but is to be connected to v. 9. It seems the most contextually accurate to translate **de** by "now," or "now then," signifying that a new paragraph has begun.

That a transition to a new subject is intended is further substantiated by Paul's shift from "according to the flesh" to "in flesh" in v. 8. Being "in the flesh" (Gk. **en sarki**) is a different concept that walking "according to the flesh" (**kata sarka**) of 8:1-7. The New Testament avows that it is possible for true Christians to walk as mere men (Gk. **kata anthropon**).[14] It is possible for true Christians to make plans according to the flesh (**kata sarka**, 2 Cor. 1:17). In an instructive non-ethical usage of "flesh"[15] Paul draws a sharp distinction between being "in flesh" (**en sarki**), i.e., in the sphere of bodily existence, and walking "according to the flesh" (**kata sarka**), i.e., walking according to a standard of weakness (2 Cor. 10:2-3). The fact that Paul distinguishes between **en sarki** and **kata sarka** in this non-ethical passage lends support to the distinction that is drawn here. It is one thing to be "in the flesh," to be in that sphere of life with only those weak resources, to be unregenerate. It is another thing to walk "according to the flesh." These terms are not synonymous in the New Testament. Christians can walk according to the flesh, but they are never described in the New Testament as being in that sphere of life, "in flesh," in an ethical sense. They are "in flesh" only in a physical sense.

In v. 13 Paul says that it is possible for true Christians to "live according to the flesh." In that verse he returns to his use of the expression "according to flesh" (**kata sarka**) after the parenthetical contrast between Christians and non-Christians in vv. 8-11. Even if it is possible for true Christians to walk "**according to the flesh**," it is emphatically asserted here that true Christians cannot ever be "**in** the flesh."[16]

In the Spirit (8:9-11)

In sharp contrast to their former life in the flesh, Paul asserts they are no longer in that sphere. They are now in a new sphere and thus able to achieve victory due to the presence of the indwelling Spirit.

But you are not in the flesh but in the Spirit, if indeed the Spirit of God dwells in you. Now if anyone does not have the Spirit of Christ,

---

[14]1 Cor. 3:3.

[15]As far as this writer can tell, the expression is only used in a non-ethical sense outside of Rom. 8 with the possible exception of 2 Cor. 1:17. See Rom 1:3; 4:1; 9:3, 5; 1 Cor. 1:26; 10:18; 2 Cor. 1:17; 5:16; 10:2; 11:18; Gal. 4:23, 29; 5:17; Eph. 6:5; Col. 3:22; 1 Pet. 4:6; Jn. 8:15. The usage in Rom. 8, however, seems to be distinctly ethical in view of vv. 5-7.

[16]The phrase is used in Rom. 7:5 where it means to be a non-Christian.

he is not His. And if Christ is in you, the body is dead because of sin, but the spirit is alive because of righteousness. But if the Spirit of Him who raised Jesus from the dead dwells in you, He who raised Christ Jesus from the dead will also give life to your mortal bodies through His Spirit who indwells you (8:8-11 NKJV).

We would not go astray if we asserted that the apostle is here teaching that not only does the indwelling Spirit revive and revitalize our spirit (8:10), but indeed, it will one day result in our physical resurrection.

Freedom to Really Live (8:12-17)

To this point Paul has taught the Romans that God has released us from our penal servitude to sin and has made that freedom experientially available to those among us who walk according to the Spirit (8:1-7). Then in a parenthetical aside he reminded them that we are no longer unsaved and living in the sphere of the flesh. Indeed, we have the promise that one day we will be done with it altogether in the resurrection (8:8-11).

Returning to his original topic, Paul concludes that we have therefore no obligation to live in accordance with the flesh (**kata sarka**). He introduces **kata** again because he is now back to the subject of Christians walking "according to" either flesh or Spirit. Instead, we are now free to be as God intended us to be. We are free to experience true life.

The Two Obligations (8:12-13)

In order to live abundantly, we must realize that we have no obligation to the sin principle anymore. Furthermore, we must accept our obligation to live according to the Spirit:

So then, brethren, *we are under obligation, not to the flesh, to live according to the flesh--for if you are living according to the flesh, you must die* [**thanatoo**]; *but if by the Spirit you are putting to death the deeds of the body, you will live* (8:12-13 NASB).

If Christians ("brethren") live **kata sarka**, they will die. As Godet says, it is possible that "the regenerate man himself would go on to death."[17] Death is the opposite of life. The life of this verse comes as a result of "putting to death the misdeeds of the body" as Christians live **kata pneuma** (the **kata** must be supplied, but it is necessary from the parallelism with **kata sarka**). As Fitzmeyer has ob-

---

[17]F. Godet, *Commentary on the Epistle to the Romans* (1883; reprint ed., Grand Rapids: Zondervan, 1969), p. 308.

served, "Paul implies that the baptized Christian could still be interested in the "deeds, actions, pursuits" of a man dominated by **sarx**. Hence, he exhorts him to make use of the Spirit received; this is the debt that is owed to Christ."[18] "The life of the flesh is the death of man and the death of the flesh is the life of man."[19]

Experimental Predestinarians have great difficulty with this passage. It seems that "life" comes as a result of perseverance in works. Because they need death to mean "hell," its opposite in their system, "life," must mean heaven. Sellers boldly calls a spade a spade, "The one who does keep his salvation does so by mortifying the deeds of the flesh **through the Holy Spirit**."[20] Thus, ultimately we obtain heaven by means of works. In their system all Christians will put the deeds of the body to death. They do not allow for failure. The plain words of the passage confute this.[21] Nowhere in Romans does Paul suggest that heaven is obtained by means of putting to death the misdeeds of the body. That would, in fact, be contrary to the entire thrust of the epistle where he is trying to separate works as far as possible from the means of obtaining eternal life, which is by faith alone (Rom. 4:5). Death is the spiritual destitution and impoverishment which comes as an ingredient of divine discipline upon the sinning Christian. This is the sense in v. 6 where it is the opposite of "life and peace." This is also the meaning for pre-Christian Paul's experience of death and spiritual depression as a result of his attempts to find life by means of law (Rom. 7:9-11). "Life" here, as in all of Romans, is abundant life, and not regeneration or heaven.[22]

When Paul says we are to put to death the deeds of the body, he says we are to do it "by the Spirit." The ambiguity of the term mocks us. What does Paul mean? The context talks about a warfare, a war between the Holy Spirit and the sin principle within--the flesh. That sin principle is completely foreign to who we are as new men in Christ. We must fight this foreigner, this enemy, by the Spirit. To fight by the Spirit means simply that we must use spiritual weapons against this enemy instead of weak bodily ones. Too often in our thinking of this passage and of similar ones, we have thought in terms of using the Spirit as a person to fight the battle,[23] but the emphasis in the New Testament is normally on using the weapons with which he has equipped us. Consider:

---

[18]Fitzmeyer, on 8:13

[19]Calvin, *Romans*, on 7:9-10.

[20]C. Norman Sellers, *Election and Perseverance* (Miami Springs, FL: Schoettle, 1987), p. 99. (Emphasis is in the original.)

[21]Godet insists that the true believer can refuse to do this and the result will be to renounce life and its privileges (p. 307).

[22]See under 8:6.

[23]"The dative [**pneumati**] is not to be taken to imply that the Holy Spirit is to be a tool in the hands of Christians, wielded and managed by them. A safeguard against such a misunderstanding is afforded by **pneumati theou agontai** in the next verse" (Cranfield, p. 394).

For though we walk in the flesh, we do not war according to the flesh, for the weapons of our warfare are not of the flesh, but divinely powerful for the destruction of fortresses (2 Cor. 10:3-4 NASB).

The "fortresses" are "lofty things raised up against the knowledge of God" (2 Cor. 10:5). In order to fight this battle, Paul says we are destroying speculations and "are taking every thought captive to the obedience of Christ." Once again the spiritual mind is central in our warfare with the enemy, the flesh. To take captive every thought is the same as setting our minds on the things of the Spirit instead of the things of the flesh.

The weapons of our warfare. What are the weapons of this warfare by the Spirit against the flesh? Romans gives us three. First, we attack the enemy by settling in our minds who we really are in Christ and then battle from that viewpoint. We present our bodies as those who are dead to sin and alive in Christ. We are to refuse to present our members as instruments of unrighteousness (Rom. 6:13). Rather, we are to present our bodies as instruments of righteousness. "Instruments" is a military term; these instruments are weapons. We are to present our lives as weapons. We are new men in Christ. The enemy is not part of us. He is foreign to who we really are at the deepest level in Christ. Furthermore, he will not win. He will not have dominion if we war against him from that perspective (Rom. 6:1-11).

The second weapon Paul mentions is the spiritual mind, the mind which fills itself with spiritual thoughts. This suggests that we need to have minds transformed by meditation on Scripture (Rom. 12:1-2). "Out of the heart (mind)," says Solomon, "come the issues of life." We must not have our mind set upon the things of the flesh if we are to win. We must take every thought captive.

Our final weapon for warfare by the Spirit is faith. This is the central theme of the epistle: "But the righteous man shall live by faith" (Rom. 1:17). The meaning is that those who are already justified shall find a rich experience of life only as they trust God. The life of faith is the subject of Eph. 6 where it is called our helmet. Paul tells us that the power of the Spirit, his indwelling presence, is ours by faith

that he would grant you, according to the riches of His glory, to be strengthened with power through His Spirit in the inner man; so that Christ may dwell in your hearts through faith (Eph. 3:16-17 NASB).

These, then, are our weapons: the new man, the new mind, and the new principle--the life of faith. As the flesh attacks, we are to bring this battery to the war. We are to say to ourselves, "I am a new man in Christ. I do not have to obey sin. This flesh is not an expression of who I really am but is a foreigner. I will obey Christ as one who is alive. I reckon myself dead to sin." Then we focus our mind on spiritual things. We set the mind on the things of the Spirit and refuse to allow the mind of the flesh to gain the upper hand. We take every thought captive. Finally, we trust the situation to the Lord in a word of prayer and ask that He might strengthen us in the inner man and that Christ might be the dominate influence in this situation.

These are powerful weapons. The use of them is what Paul means by putting to death the deeds of the flesh.

The Two Sons (8:14-15)

Paul promises that, if we would put the deeds of the body to death, we would find true life. Now he proceeds to explain what true life consists of. He says it involves two things: (1) allowing oneself to be led by the Spirit of God (8:14-15); and (2) being a joint-heir with the Messiah in the final destiny of man (8:16-17).

> *For all who are being led by the Spirit of God, these are the sons of God* (8:14 NASB).

There are three questions which the passage answers: (1) Who is led? (2) Where are they led? and (3) How is this leading accomplished?

Who are the sons of God? Christians can be "sons of God" in two senses in the New Testament. It is, of course, true that all Christians are sons of God by faith in Christ. We are all part of His family. But it is also true that the word **huios** can take a different emphasis depending on the context. In Mt. 5:45 we are to do the work of loving our enemies **in order that we may become sons**. In Mt. 5:9 we need to be peacemakers before we can be called sons of God. In the book of Revelation we are told, "He who overcomes will inherit these things, and I will be his God and he will be My son" (Rev. 21:7). Now obviously these are not conditions for becoming sons of God in the sense of being saved. In fact, the sermon was directed to the disciples so that the disciples could become sons of God. It is possible for those who are already sons, according to these three verses, to "become sons." Is it not obvious that the Lord's meaning in Matthew is something like "sons indeed"? In other words, if we love our enemies and function as peacemakers, we are not only sons in fact, but we act like it and are therefore called sons.

Understandably, most interpreters from the Experimental Predestinarian tradition understand "sons of God" in a restrictive sense, which means these who are led by the Spirit of God, and none other, are sons of God.[24] Many interpreters have understood the phrase in a more general sense. Liddon, for example, says, "This sonship, although a product of God's grace, depends for its con-

---

[24]See Murray, 6-1:295, for comments representing this position.

tinuance on man's passive obedience to the leading of the Holy Spirit."[25] Similarly, Godet argues, "The reference is therefore to a more advanced stage of the Christian life ... You have a right to the title of sons as soon as ye let yourselves be led by the Spirit. Though one becomes a son by justification, he does not possess the filial state, he does not really enjoy adoption until he has become loyally submissive to the operation of the Spirit. The meaning is therefore this: 'If ye let yourselves be led by the Spirit, ye are ipso facto [by that fact itself, in reality, indeed] sons of God.' The verb may be taken as passive, "are driven," or middle, "let themselves be driven."[26]

This meaning fits well with the context of Rom. 8. Those Christians who are "putting to death the deeds of the body" are sons in behavior as well as in fact. Some Christians allow themselves to be led by the Spirit of God, and some do not. Those who do are "sons indeed." They are the Christians who "put to death the things of the body" and as a result enjoy true life. To be led by the Spirit is the same as walking by the Spirit. The sense of the passage is, "For all who are walking by the Spirit are sons indeed."

That Paul may have such a distinction in mind between being a son and behaving as a son is reinforced by the fact that he connects the sonship of v. 15 with being an adopted son, **huiothesia**, which is different from being a son by birth:

> *For you have not received a spirit of slavery leading to fear again, but you have received a spirit of adoption as sons by which we cry out, Abba! Father!* (Rom. 8:15 NASB).

We have received a spirit of adoption, **huiothesia** (Rom. 8:15).[27] The method of adoption intended by Paul is somewhat in dispute. The Roman method of adoption was very severe and binding. The emphasis was on the father's power, and the son was almost a slave. The son was transferred to the power and control of the adoptive father. It was like a sale. All received an equal share of the inheritance. The fact that the epistle was written to the "Romans" has led some interpreters to conclude that the Roman method must be in view.[28]

In the Greek practice, however, a more warm and familial attitude prevailed. If a man desired to extend his possessions or because he had developed a deep affection for a child he had come to know, or even for religious reasons, he might adopt a child. He could in his lifetime or by his will extend to a son of an-

---

[25]Liddon, p. 132.

[26]Godet, p. 309.

[27]For discussion of "adoption" see A. H. Leitch, "Adoption," in *ZPEB*, 1:61-63

[28]D. Martin Lloyd-Jones, *The Sons of God: Exposition of Romans 8:5-17* (Grand Rapids: Zondervan, 1975), pp. 401-2.

other family the privileges of his own family in perpetuity. "There was a condition, however, that the person adopted accept the legal obligations and religious
duties of the new father."[29] Paul used the word in both senses depending upon
what he wanted to emphasize. "He found readily at hand the Roman idea when
he was emphasizing man's release from the slavery of sin and found the Greek
idea congenial when he was emphasizing the relationships and gifts of sonship."[30]
The emphasis on the warm familial relationship with the words "Abba, Father"
and the fact that "the idea, like the word, is native Greek"[31] have led many to
think of the Greek adoptive practices. If that is the case, the sons referred to are
likely those who are fulfilling the conditions of the adoption (Greek inheritance).
The Greek view is also to be favored because the context is referring to obedience by putting to death the deeds of the body and the intent that the righteousness of the law might be fulfilled in us.

In Hebrew practice[32] the firstborn received a double portion.   Even
though they apparently did not have the practice of adoption as a legal act, Cranfield inclines toward the idea that Paul may have had the Jewish view very much
in mind.[33] The Old Testament references to adoption and the rights of the firstborn[34] and Paul's use of the same word in reference to the Israelites "to whom
belong the adoption (Gk. **huiothesia**) as sons" in Rom. 9:4 may suggest that it was
the Jewish practice to which Paul referred. This view is reinforced by the fact
that adopted sons address God using the Aramaic expression "Abba."

All Christians are adopted sons by virtue of our spiritual birth and the legal ransom paid, but not all adopted sons fulfill the requirements of adoption
even though God does His part. Adoption is of grace, and we are adopted regardless of whether or not we fulfill the requirements (Gal. 4:5), but only those
who do so are worthy of the name "son" and will finally obtain the inheritance
rights. The double portion of the inheritance which comes to the firstborn son is
his at birth, based upon grace. But he must value and honor that right. He must
not, like Esau (Heb. 12:16-17), treat it lightly and therefore lose it. In v. 17 Paul
will specify the condition necessary for maintaining the status and honor of being
a firstborn son--we must suffer with him.

Only the faithful Christians are "sons indeed." It is these "sons indeed"
who allow themselves to be "led of the Spirit of God." They are the ones who are
"putting to death the deeds of the body" and who as a result will truly live. It is

---

[29]Leitch, p. 61.

[30]Ibid.

[31]William Sanday and Arthur C. Headlam, *A Critical and Exegetical Commentary on the
Epistle to the Romans* (Edinburgh: T. & T. Clark, 1985), p. 203.

[32]See Lloyd-Jones, p. 401.

[33]According to Sanday and Headlam, p. 203.

[34]E.g., Gen. 14:12-14; Ex. 2:10; Est. 2:7; Ex. 4:22f.; 2 Sam. 7:14; 1 Chr. 28:6; Ps. 2:7; Ps.
89:26f.; Jer. 3:19; Hos. 11:1.

impossible to think of one being led without his submitting to being led. They are two sides of the same coin. An obedient son is one who allows himself to be led, and in so doing, puts to death the deeds of the body.

Where are the sons of God led? As to where this leading takes them, the preceding context makes it clear that it is to holiness. It finds its object in the putting to death the deeds of the body. Indeed, the verse is a kind of summary of deliverance from sin and to "life and peace" just described. When this ministry of the Holy Spirit is viewed with reference to the end of the whole process, we call it sanctification. When we consider it with reference to the process itself, we call it spiritual leading.[35]

The meaning of being led by the Spirit of God is to put to death the deeds of the body:

> *For all who are being led by the Spirit of God, these are the sons of God* (Rom. 8:14 NASB).

As others have observed,[36] vv. 13 and 14 appear to be precisely parallel and explain each other. Therefore:

putting to death the things of the body = led by the Spirit

you will live = to be a Son of God.

In these words we find one of the central passages of the New Testament on the subject of the leading of the Spirit. The introductory "for" goes back to v. 13 and clarifies what Paul means by life, leading us to the first aspect of the meaning of "life." To be led by the Spirit is not the same as our Lord's promise that, when the Holy Spirit comes, He will "guide" us into all truth. Gal. 5:18 gives us a parallel to this passage, "But if you are led by the Spirit, you are not under the law." There the leading is into a holy life:

> *But I say, walk by the Spirit, and you will not carry out the desire of the flesh. . . . But if you are led by the Spirit, you are not under the Law* (Gal. 5:16, 18 NASB).

The phrases are parallel and explain one another. To be led by the Spirit is the same as walking by the Spirit. The difference may be that it throws the emphasis on God's part rather than man's. Both sides are true. A man cannot be led into sanctification unless he allows himself to be, that is, unless he walks by the Spirit.

---

[35]B. B. Warfield, "The Leading of the Spirit," in *Biblical and Theological Studies* (Philadelphia: Presbyterian and Reformed, 1968), p. 546.

[36]John R. Stott, *Men Made New* (Downers Grove, IL: InterVarsity, 1966), p. 92.

This is not to deny that God does not providentially guide His people through Scripture, counselors, and circumstances. But this passage says nothing of this. Nor does it speak of some fancied sporadic supernatural direction someone imagines himself to have received.

How are the sons of God led? Finally, an examination of the word for lead (Gk. **ago**) suggests how these sons of God are being led. Warfield observes that it should be emphasized that in all of the uses of the word "led," the self-action of the object being led is involved. The man may lead the horse to drink, but the horse must under his own energy walk up the hill to the water trough. Had Paul wanted to teach that the leading of the Spirit involved only God's work, he had another word he could have used, "moved" (Gk. **phero**). Peter uses this word to explain how the prophets received their message: "For no prophecy was ever made by an act of human will, but men moved (**phero**) by the Holy Spirit spoke from God" (1 Pet. 1:21). The word "moved" suggests that the power and the work are done completely by the mover, not the will of the prophet. If Paul had wanted to imply that in the sanctification process we are taken up by God and carried to this goal of holiness with no effort or cooperation on our part, he would have used this word. But he passed over it and used "led" (**ago**). This suggests that the Holy Spirit determines the goal and the way of arriving there, but it is by our effort and cooperation that we proceed.

The prophet is "moved," and the child of God is "led." The prophet's attitude in receiving revelation is completely passive and purely receptive; he adds nothing to it and has no part in it. He is only the mouthpiece through which God speaks. The child of God, however, is not passive in the hands of the sanctifying Spirit. He is not "moved" but "led." His own efforts enter into the progress made under the controlling influence of the Spirit. As Warfield put it,

> *He supplies, in fact, the force exerted in attaining the progress, while yet the controlling Spirit supplies the entire directing impulse.*[37]

It is for this reason that no prophet could be urged to work out his own message with fear and trembling. It was not left for him to work out. But the believer is commanded to work out his own salvation with fear and trembling because he knows that the Spirit is working in him both the willing and the doing according to his own good pleasure. This is a

> *leading of an active agent to an end determined indeed by the Spirit, and along a course which is marked out by the Spirit, but over which the soul is carried by virtue of its own power of action and through its own strenuous efforts. . . . It is His part to keep us in the path and to bring us at length to the goal. But it is we who tread every step of the*

---

[37]Warfield, p. 553.

way; our limbs that grow weary with the labor; our hearts that faint, our courage that fails.[38]

We have then in these two verses (vv. 13-14) God's part and man's part in the process of sanctification. In v. 13 we learn that man's part is to "put to death the things of the body" and enjoy true life. In v. 14 we learn that God's part is to lead Christians along the path of sanctification and that those who allow themselves to be so led are sons, or "sons indeed," who enjoy true life.

Another passage which seems to be directly parallel to this is Phil. 2:12-13. To "work out your salvation with fear and trembling" is another way of saying that we should put to death the deeds of the body. And to say that God is "at work in you, both to will and to work for His good pleasure" is to say we are led by the Spirit of God.

The believer who submits to this leading (who is "being led"), who perseveres to the goal is earlier described as a believer who walks according to the Spirit or who sets his mind on the things of the Spirit. He is in the company of the metochoi, a Partaker, and will be a co-heir with Christ, inheriting the kingdom. Furthermore, as he responds to the Spirit's sanctifying leading, he need no longer fear the condemnation of the law.

Finally, Paul says that we "have not received a spirit of slavery leading to fear again" (8:15). There probably is no such thing as a spirit of slavery. Rather, he means simply that the Holy Spirit is not a Spirit of bondage but of adoption.[39] This Spirit does not lead to fear again. This fear can plausibly be understood as the opposite of the certainty of adoption. An adopted son knows he is in the family. He is secure forever. The fear that we are excluded from the family of God and the experience of bondage to sin are no longer necessary to those who are in Christ Jesus. As Godet puts it, "The Spirit which ye have received from God is not a servile spirit throwing you back into the fear in which ye formerly lived."[40]

The Two Heirships (8:16-17)

The Spirit Himself bears witness with our spirit that we are children of God; and if children, heirs also, heirs of God, and fellow-heirs with Christ if indeed we suffer with Him in order that we may also be glorified with Him (Rom. 8:16-17 NASB).

---

[38]Ibid., p. 555.
[39]Cranfield, p. 396.
[40]Godet, p. 309. Compare 2 Tim. 1:7; 2 Cor. 1:12

Paul now introduces the great theme of the inheritance. Cranfield has warned us about the danger of interpreting the inheritance by its parallel usage in Gal. 4:7. He points out that, while there are parallels, there are such significant differences that to ignore them would be to seriously obscure the transcendent significance of what is being said in Rom. 8.[41]

This passage, in agreement with Gal. 4:7, says we are all heirs of God by virtue of the fact that we are his children. But it says something else. It says we are also co-heirs with Christ "if indeed we share in His sufferings." Putting the comma in a different place brings this out clearly, "We are God's heirs, and Christ's fellow-heirs if we share His sufferings now in order to share His splendor hereafter." The second heirship mentioned in this verse is conditional upon our joining with Him in His sufferings. Being an heir of God is unconditional, but being a joint-heir of the kingdom is conditioned upon our spiritual perseverance.[42]

The conditional particle **eiper** regularly takes the meaning "if indeed"[43] as translated in the NIV, and not necessarily "if as is the fact." The difference is significant. If we translate by the latter, then Paul might be saying that all Christians are joint-heirs. If we translate "if indeed," then the conditional nature of joint-heirship is emphasized. In favor of the translation "if indeed" and the placement of the comma after "heirs of God" is the entire flow of the immediate context (Rom. 8:12-14).[44] Furthermore, as Käsemann has pointed out, "The final sentence which follows and the sharp break in thought more naturally suggests a hortatory and conditional understanding. . . . Only those who resist the flesh with suffering can overcome."[45] Both Godet[46] and some Experimental Predestinarians like Denney[47] acknowledge that there is a condition to obtaining the co-heirship

---

[41]Cranfield, p. 405. Cranfield's own view of the passage differs from the writer's, but his warning is appropriate for all.

[42]The translation above has been slightly changed from the rendering in the NIV. In the Greek text punctuation marks were added by later editors, and the writer has placed the comma after "heirs of God" rather than after "co-heirs of Christ," thus implying that two heirships, not one are taught. This punctuation fits better with the flow of the context.

[43]AG, p. 219; AS, p. 130; 1 Cor. 8:5; 15:15. See also 2 Cor. 1:6. Even in Rom. 3:30, where it can be rendered "since," that meaning is suggested by the context. In Rom. 8:17 the context is hortatory. Because it is an exhortation, the basic meaning of which should be accepted.

[44]It is to be observed that Paul has already used a first-class condition at the beginning of v. 17 in the following sense: "If we are children, and we are" (or, "since we are children"). It may be that he shifts to **eiper** specifically to emphasize the conditionality of co-heirship in contrast to the unconditionality of being an heir of God.

[45]Ernst Käsemann, *Commentary on Romans* (Grand Rapids: Eerdmans, 1980), p. 229.

[46]Godet, p. 311: "To reach the possession of the inheritance, there is yet one condition to be satisfied: **if we suffer with Him.**" (Emphasis is Godet's.) Godet may be an Arminian. His position is a bit unclear.

[47] Denney stresses, "The inheritance attached to Divine sonship is attained only on the condition expressed in the clause **eiper** . . ." (James Denney, "St. Paul's Epistle to the Romans," in *EGT*, 2:648).

with Christ. For an Arminian a failure to meet the condition will result in loss of salvation. For Denny such a failure will only prove that the person was never saved to begin with.

But it is not necessary to adopt either of these extremes. Rather, v. 17 introduces two inheritances. If we are sons of God, i.e., children, we are heirs of God, and we will also be joint-heirs with Christ if we suffer for Him. The son of God who puts to death the misdeeds of the body will be a co-heir with Christ.[48] This heirship is earned as a result of the fact that we "share in His sufferings." Certainly, being an heir in the sense of final deliverance from hell is not based upon sharing in His sufferings. Otherwise salvation is earned and based on works. Paul specifically says that we are heirs of God by virtue of the fact that we are sons and for no other reason in Gal. 4:7. Yet in Rom. 8:17 he says that this heirship is conditioned upon works, perseverance in suffering. Contextual considerations suggest that two kinds of Christians are in view, and thus two kinds of inheritances are implied.[49]

The heirship which results in a rich life now and an abundant life in the kingdom, a reward, is based upon a work: putting to death by means of the Spirit the misdeeds of the body and victorious perseverance in suffering with Christ. There is an heirship based solely upon being a son by faith in Christ--the gift of eternal life and final deliverance from hell. All Christians, as discussed above, are heirs of God in this sense: "since you are a son, God has made you an heir" (Gal. 4:6-7). The fact that this heirship is conditional is commonly acknowledged by Sanday[50] and Denney.[51] However, since both these commentators equate these two heirships as one, they labor under the difficulty of explaining how all of a sudden Paul is teaching a salvation from hell which is now conditioned upon the believer persevering in suffering. In fact, Sanday specifically connects v. 17 with a "current Christian saying: 2 Tim. 2:11," which makes rulership in the kingdom the

---

[48]Eric Sauer similarly views the co-heirship with Christ in this passage as conditional and "graduated according to faithfulness" (*In the Arena of Faith*, p. 163). Wilbur Smith punctuates the text the same way and relates the joint-heirship with Christ to Ps. 2:8, "Ask of Me, and I will give you the nations for thine inheritance, and the uttermost parts of the earth for thy possession" (*The Biblical Doctrine of Heaven* [Chicago: Moody Press, 1968], p. 193). The inheritance refers not to heaven but our reward in the kingdom, reigning with Christ. Also this view may be found in G. H. Lang, *Firstborn Sons: Their Rights and Risks* (London: Samuel Roberts, 1936; reprint ed., Miami Springs, FL: Conley and Schoettle, 1984), p. 123. Sweet apparently accepts this interpretation. He says, "The adopted and regenerated children are also heirs, but on the condition that they share the sufferings of the Son" (Henry Barclay Sweet, *The Holy Spirit in the New Testament* [MacMillian, 1910; reprint ed., Grand Rapids: Baker, 1964], p. 219).

[49]Others have noted this possible interpretation. Newell, for example, says, "Here two schools of interpretation part company, one boldly saying that all the saints are designated, and all shall reign with Christ; the other, that reigning with Christ depends upon voluntary choosing of a path of suffering with Him" (William R. Newell, *Romans: Verse by Verse* [Chicago: Moody Press, 1938], p. 318).

[50]Sanday and Headlam, p. 204.

[51]Denney, "Romans," p. 648.

issue and not salvation from hell. Their difficulty would be resolved and the obvious harmony with 2 Tim. 2:11 explained on the simple assumption taught elsewhere of two heirships.

That two contrasting heirships are being discussed seems to be suggested by Paul's use of the Greek particles **men ... de**. Not readily translatable in English, the sense is something like this, "On the one hand (**men ...**) heirs of God, and on the other hand (**de**) joint heirs of Christ." These particles, when coupling two phrases together, are normally disjunctive and imply a contrast between the items compared, not an equality. In fact, in every usage of these particles in this way in Romans, they are **always** contrastive and **never** conjunctive.[52] This suggests that the disjunction comes after the word "God" and not after the word "Christ." In other words, we are all heirs of God, and we will be joint-heirs with Christ if we suffer with Him.

In addition to the immediate context and the normal meaning of **eiper**, the broader context of the New Testament supports the dual heirship view of Rom. 8:17. The inheritance is usually conditioned upon obedience, and salvation from hell is always by faith alone. In order to become a joint-heir with Christ, one of His metochoi, we must faithfully endure our sufferings to the end:

> Here is a trustworthy saying:
> If we died with Him,
>   we will also live with Him;
> **if we endure,**
>   **we will also reign with Him**.
> If we disown Him,
>   He will disown us;
> If we are faithless,
>   but He will remain faithful,
>   for He cannot disown Himself (2 Tim. 2:11-13).

As in Rom. 8:17 reigning with Christ seems to be conditioned upon endurance. The converse, to disown Him, will result in His disowning us when He rewards His church according to the things done in the body, "good or bad" (2 Cor. 5:10). The possibility of being "disowned" does not refer to loss of salvation, because the apostle clarifies that, even when we are "faithless," He will remain faithful to us. But it does mean that we may be "disqualified for the prize" (1 Cor. 9:27) and stand ashamed at His coming (1 Jn. 2:28). Virtually all commentators refer to 2 Tim. 2:12 as explaining or being parallel to Rom. 8:17. It seems that this connection is evident due to the parallel construction and similar theme. Now if there is something contingent in the believer's future in the for-

---

[52]See 2:7-8, 25; 5:16; 6:11; 7:25; 8:10, 17; 9:21; 11:22, 28; 14:2, 5; 16:19.

mer, then this would suggest that there is something contingent in the latter as well.

It must also be remembered that a reader of the New Testament would not have approached Rom. 8:17 with the theological pre-understanding of English Puritanism. When a first-century reader saw a phrase such as "co-heir" of Messiah, he immediately thought in terms of what his Bible, the Old Testament, taught. There are two heirships there, and the joy of reigning with Messiah is a common theme. Indeed, this theme is found all over the New Testament. Furthermore, that co-heirship, as in 2 Tim. 2:12, is always presented as conditional on the believer's faithfulness. Perhaps the fact that we have been influenced by the traditions of English Puritanism leads us to equate the inheritance with heaven and co-heirship with going to heaven with Christ. That seems "natural" to many because the biblical concept of inheritance and heirship has been obscured from view by the widely disseminated creedal definitions of Westminster Calvinism.

The purpose for which we suffer is "in order that we may be glorified with Him." It is not certain that we will be so glorified. A purpose clause describes intent and not necessarily certainty. The presence of the phrase further suggests that **eiper** should be translated "if indeed" rather than "seeing that." Even rendering it "seeing that" necessarily implies something contingent in view of the purpose clause. If they do not suffer with Him, and it is evident from the New Testament that many Christians refuse this gift, then they will not achieve the purpose that such co-suffering was intended to achieve.

What does it mean to be glorified with Him? Some have made the mistake of equating being glorified with Him, which happens only to the faithful Christian, with the glorification referred to in v. 30 which occurs to all Christians. In v. 17, however, it is the glory of the Messiah which is in view and the possibility that we might share in it. In v. 30 it is our own glorification which is in view. That glorification seems to refer to the perfect conformity to the image of Christ referred to in 8:29.[53]

To be glorified with him is to be awarded a share in His glory. The passage is speaking in messianic terms. He has mentioned that we can "suffer with," "inherit with," and "be honored with" the Messiah. "To glorify" is commonly understood as "to honor."[54] It is the Messiah's sufferings, inheritance, and honor we may possibly share in. Sanday and Headlam point out that the inheritance referred to was commonly the secure and permanent possession of the land of Canaan won by the Messiah and ultimately became a symbol for all the messianic

---

[53]Bruce, *Romans*, p. 178. He calls it "perfect conformity to the image of Christ."
[54]See any lexicon.

blessings.[55] Meyer seems to agree: "The **inheritance**, which God . . . transfers to His children as their property, is the **salvation and glory of the messianic kingdom.**"[56]

This future glory of the messianic reign was often referred to in the Old Testament. The "glory of God" in this sense, according to Von Rad, was not so much His intrinsic nature "but the final actualization of His claim to rule the world."[57] Indeed, the equation of the glory of Messiah with His messianic reign and of the need for believers to persevere in order to obtain a share in it is common in the New Testament.[58]

And they said to Him, "Grant that we may sit in Your glory, one on Your right, and one on Your left" (Mk. 10:37 NASB).

When the Son of Man comes in his glory, and all the angels with him, he will sit on his throne in heavenly glory (Mt. 25:31).

The need to persevere in doing good as a necessary pre-condition for sharing in that glory is elsewhere taught in Romans and 2 Corinthians.

To those who by persistence in doing good seek glory, honor and immortality, He will give eternal life . . . but glory, honor and peace for everyone who does good: first for the Jew, then for the Gentile (Rom. 2:7, 10 NASB).

The ccntingent nature of sharing in the future glory of Christ is implied in several of Paul's epistles:

For our light and momentary troubles are achieving for us an eternal glory that far outweighs them all (2 Cor. 4:17).

He called you to this through our gospel, that you might share in the glory of our Lord Jesus Christ (2 Th. 2:14).

It is not insignificant that Paul, in describing us as "heirs of God," uses the word **tekna** ("children)" instead of **huioi** ("sons"). A distinction between the words has often been noted by the commentators. The former refers to a "born one," or simply offspring, but the latter speaks of adult, mature, and understand-

---

[55]Sanday and Headlam, p. 203.

[56]Heinrich August Meyer, *A Critical and Exegetical Hand-book to The Epistle to the Romans* (T. & T. Clark, 1883; reprint ed., Winona Lake, IN: Alpha Publications, 1979), p. 317.

[57]Gerhard von Rad, **"kabod"** in *TDNT*, 2:242. E.g., the whole earth is full of the glory of the Lord (Isa. 6:3), His glory is above the earth (Ps. 57:5, 11), and all the nations will see His glory (i.e., dominion) and declare it to the Gentiles (Is. 66:18f.).

[58]See Mt. 19:28; 24:30; 25:31; Mk. 8:38; 13:26; Lk. 9:26; Col. 3:4; Heb. 2:10; 1 Pet. 4:13.

ing sonship.[59] Alford observes, "**huios** of God differs from **teknon** of God, in implying the higher and more mature and conscious member of God's family (see Gal. 5:1-6)."[60] **Teknon**, according to Cremer, emphasizes the descent, but **huios** emphasizes the relationship.[61] Godet concurs, "In the one what is expressed is the position of honor, in the other the relation of nature."[62] It is, of course, true that Paul sometimes uses "son" in the sense of "offspring," and in those passages the distinction disappears. However, when both words are found in the same context, the presumption would normally be that he probably intends his readers to understand the basic difference in meaning. This distinction seems evident in Rom. 8, and is commonly noted by many commentators.

Thus, all Christians are "born ones," children of God. The Spirit of God testifies to the heart of all that they are His offspring. But not all Christians are sons in the sense of those who go on to maturity, who maintain relationship with Christ, who suffer with Him, and as a result will one day share in His inheritance-kingdom, being honored with Him there.

Our Final Assurance (8:18-30)

The apostle continues,

For I consider that the sufferings of this present time are not worthy to be compared with the glory that is to be revealed to us (8:18 NASB).

The glories of the reign of the Messiah are still in view. The "for" refers back to the salvation and glory of the messianic kingdom. The verse explains why we should suffer with Him in order to be glorified with Him. It is because the blessings of the messianic era are beyond description. What a tragedy it would be not to have a share in all of them!

These glories are to be revealed to us and not "in us" as some translations read. The Greek is clear, **eis hemas**.[63] The wonders of the great future will be revealed to all, but they will be shared in (inherited) only by those who persevere in suffering. Our own resurrection, while certainly included in this glory, is prob-

---

[59]E.g., Newell, p. 314.

[60]Henry Alford, "Romans," in *The Greek Testament*, ed. Everett F. Harrison, 4 vols. (1849-60; reprint ed., Chicago: Moody Press, 1968), 2:391.

[61]Hermann Cremer, *Biblio-Theological Lexicon of New Testament Greek* (Edinburgh: T. & T. Clark, 1895), p. 811.

[62]Godet, p. 311.

[63]This phrase is used nine times in the New Testament: Acts 3:4; Rom. 5:8; 8:18; 2 Cor. 1:5; 1:11; Eph. 1:8, 9; Heb. 2:3 (The Gramcord Institute Computer Concordance, Deerfield, IL, 1989). In each instance the meaning is toward, to, or upon us." It never means "in" in the sense of "within."

ably not yet specifically in view here. The apostle would have used **en hemin**, "in us," had he intended this.

> *For the anxious longing of the creation waits eagerly for the revealing of the sons of God* (8:19 NASB).

The "sons of God" are properly those who have allowed themselves to be led of the Spirit. They are those who have walked by means of the Spirit and who have set their minds on the things of the Spirit. They are the "sons indeed" referred to in v. 14. Not all Christians are sons of God (Gk. **huioi**) in this sense, but all are children of God (Gk. **tekna**). The "revealing of the sons of God" is then the making known to all creation who these faithful Christians are. It refers to their installation as the co-heirs and co-rulers with Messiah in the final destiny of man. The entire creation longs for the future reign of the servant kings!

> *For the creation was subjected to futility, not of its own will, but because of Him who subjected it, in hope that the creation itself also will be set free from its slavery to corruption into the freedom of the glory of the children of God* (8:20-21 NASB).

The introductory "for" informs us that this verse explains why the creation longs for this future reign of Christ's servant kings. When that future reign dawns, it will include a physical transformation of the creation itself. The creation has endured a subjection to futility for many ages. This subjection creates within itself a sense of hope for something better. That "something better" is a transformation similar to that which will occur to all Christians, "the freedom of the glory of the children of God." This glory is part of, but not equal to, the "glory that is to be revealed to us" (v. 18). The former is a general term for the glories of the messianic era. The latter is the glory of a transformed body which all Christians will share in the day of resurrection.

The creation does not share in all aspects of the future glory. It will never be set free to rule with Christ, the revealing of the sons of God. No inanimate thing can share in the reign of Christ's servants. But the creation will share in an aspect of the future glory common to all the children of God, physical transformation. For this reason Paul changes from "sons" (v. 19) to "children" of God in v. 21. All children of God will be transformed, but only the "sons" will rule with Christ.[64]

---

[64]Alford has observed this same distinction here ("Romans," 2:395). Gal. 4:7 is not necessarily in contradiction to this. Paul there uses the word "son" in the sense of adopted child. All adopted children have the full rights of being an heir of God. Only those adopted children who suffer with Christ will be co-heirs of Christ, a subject not addressed in Galatians.

And not only this, but also we ourselves, having the first fruits of the
Spirit, even we ourselves groan within ourselves waiting eagerly for our
adoption as sons, the redemption of our body (8:23 NASB).

The verse presents an interpretive problem in that it seems to be in contradiction with v. 15. There we are told we have been adopted, but here we are
told we await our adoption. The solution seems to be that this verse refers to the
completion of our adoption which consists in the reception of our resurrection
bodies.[65]

Finally, there is good reason for Sanday and Headlam's distinction between the co-glorification with Christ in v. 17 and the glorification of the believer
in v. 30. The former they equate with sharing with Messiah in his inheritance[66]
and the latter with participating in his divine perfection.[67] For Cranfield the former is primarily the outwardly manifest glory of the final consummation, and the
latter is primarily internal, our ultimate conformation to His glory.[68]

That two different aspects of the one future glorification are in view seems
probable due to the contextual contrasts between them. In v. 17 the glorification
is conditional and only for those who suffer with Christ, but in v. 30 it is unconditional and is for all who are justified. In v. 17 it is a sharing in the glory of Messiah, but in v. 30 it refers to our own glorification. In v. 17 the verb is "be glorified with," and v. 30 the verb is "glorified." In v. 17 it refers to the wonders of the
messianic era, but in v. 30 it refers to our ultimate conformity into the image of
Christ at the resurrection of the body. In v. 17 the verb is in a purpose clause implying intent and not necessarily certainty. But in v. 30 it is an indicative implying
the certainty of a presently achieved fact. Verse 17 is in a context which stresses
exhortation. It is a challenge to persevere in order that we might share in Christ's
glory. But v. 30 is a statement of fact that we have already, in a proleptic and an-
ticipatory sense, entered into that glory.

All believers share in the latter aspect of that glory, the final resurrection,
but only those who put to death the deeds of the body will share in the former,
the future reign of the servant kings.

Conclusion

Rom. 8 is a magnificent presentation of the life that is led by the Spirit and
the final outcome of such a life in sharing with Messiah in the final destiny of

---

[65]Sanday and Headlam call it the "manifested, realized, act of adoption, a public promul-
gation," p. 209.

[66]Sanday and Headlam, p. 202.

[67]Ibid., p. 215.

[68]Cranfield, pp. 408, 433.

man. It is a challenge to true Christians to live that life by putting to death the deeds of the body by the use of our spiritual weapons. It contrasts two kinds of Christians and does not contrast the Christian and the non-Christian.

Chapter 17

Conditional Security: The Gospels

Arminians have held as one of their main tenets, distinguishing them from Calvinists, that it is possible for a true Christian to lose his justification. It is our opinion that this point of view, while more plausible exegetically than that of the Experimental Predestinarians, is at odds with not only the major passages on the subject but with the whole thrust of the gospel itself. In their desire to guarantee that no immoral person will ever obtain eternal life and to remove "easy believism" from the church, they have transformed the gospel. Instead of turning the grace of God into lasciviousness, they have virtually rejected it altogether. No matter how they protest otherwise, their doctrine of salvation ultimately throws the burden of achieving our final destiny back on us. It is a salvation based on works which for its ultimate attainment depends on our perseverance to the end of life.

Paradoxically, the Experimental Predestinarians end up in the same situation. It makes no difference whether Calvin or Arminius says it. Those who do not persevere will not be saved. The only difference is the theoretical explanation behind the man's failure to persevere. The Calvinist says he was never born again to begin with, and the Arminian says he was saved but lost his salvation.

Numerous passages have been misconstrued to teach the conditional security of the believer. An attempt will be made here to consider some of those passages in the Gospels which in the history of the church have been thought to support the Arminian position.

Matthew 5:13

Jesus warns His disciples that they can become "saltless," a type of carnal Christian whose testimony and preservative impact or influence on society is completely lost (Mt. 5:13). If that happens, it is difficult if not impossible for them to become salt in society again. They are "good for nothing." Although it may not happen, they are of no further value for the advance of the gospel and might as well, like salt, be thrown out and trampled upon. If this aspect of the metaphor is to be pressed, it would refer not to loss of salvation but to divine discipline and loss of reward at the judgment seat of Christ--a common theme in the Sermon on the Mount (Mt. 5:12).

Matthew 7:16-19

The false teachers, whose unregenerate state is proven by their doctrine, are thrown into the fires of hell (Mt. 7:16-19). The passage is talking about men who never knew Christ (Mt. 7:23), and thus, it has no bearing on the question of eternal security at all.

Matthew 18:21-35

In the parable of the wicked slave the Lord rebukes him for not forgiving "seventy times seven" (Mt. 18:21-35). The master of the household forgave the debt of the slave, but the slave refused to forgive the debt of the one who owed him. As a result, Jesus says, the wicked servant will be handed over to his torturers until he repaid all that was owed him. Arminians then quote v. 35 to prove conditional security. However, the passage is not discussing eternal issues. Temporal relationships are in view. If we fail to forgive our brother from the heart, God will bring severe divine discipline on us in time and withhold temporal forgiveness for fellowship in the family. The apostle John, in addressing his "little children" whose "sins are forgiven" (1 Jn. 2:12), nevertheless told them that to be forgiven by God was conditioned upon confessing their sins (1 Jn. 1:9). If we do not confess, we are not forgiven as far as temporal forgiveness is concerned. But as far as our eternal relationship and forgiveness is concerned, that is unchanging. The bitterness of an unforgiving heart has been discipline enough in many lives.

Matthew 24:13

Christ's famous warning that "he who endures to the end shall be saved" is quoted both by Arminians and Experimental Predestinarians to prove their contradictory points of view (Mt. 24:13). As studied previously, the "salvation" in view is either deliverance from the tribulation or, more likely, entrance into our full reward when we inherit the kingdom (Mt. 25:34). It is a promise that those who are faithful to the end, in the midst of the tribulation persecutions of Antichrist, will be abundantly rewarded with joint rulership with Christ in His coming kingdom.

Matthew 24:45-51

It is probable that this parable of the two servants, as well as the parables following it, refers to Christians, as the Arminian maintains. After describing the taking in judgment which comes upon the unbeliever (Mt. 24:40-41; note 24:39), the Lord begins a series of parables of the faithful vs. the unfaithful householder (Mt. 24:42-44), the faithful vs. the unfaithful servant (Mt. 24:45-51), the wise vs. the foolish virgins (Mt. 25:1-13), and the faithful vs. wicked and lazy servant (the parable of the talents, Mt. 25:14-30). Consistency requires that the unfaithful householder, the evil servant, the foolish virgins, and the wicked servant all refer to the same class of individual. There is nothing in the context which requires us to interpret these four individuals as any other than carnal Christians. Nothing, that is, except certain preconceptions brought to the passage which keep us from believing that a true believer could come under these judgments described.

Indeed, the Lord seems to explicitly distinguish these four parables from the ones preceding. In vv. 36-42 the Lord is emphasizing the point of the suddenness and unexpected nature of the Lord's return. In those verses He is applying this point to the nonbeliever and has the judgment of the sheep and the goats in view. However, in v. 44 He shifts and applies this same principle (i.e., be prepared because of the unexpected nature of the Lord's return) to believers. He says:

Therefore you also be ready, for the Son of Man is coming at an hour when you do not expect Him (Mt. 24:44 NKJV).

Having applied the doctrine of the unexpected nature of His return to the unbeliever, the Lord now applies it to Christians as well. Some Christians, He knows, will be similarly unprepared. It may be diagrammatically set forth like this:

The Unexpectedness of the Lord's Return
Be Prepared!
Matthew 24:36-25:30

Judgment on Nonbelievers	Judgment among Believers	Judgment on Non-believers
	THEREFORE keep watch!	
	So YOU ALSO	
Two men in the field	The householder	The
		sheep
		and
	The faithful/wicked servant	the goats
Two women at the mill; the ten virgins		
	The ten talents	
24:36 41	42 25:30	31 46

In addition, the literary structure of the passage itself supports this view. Using the well-known literary device of chiasm, Matthew develops his argument as follows:

A	-	24:36-41	Judgment on the World
B	-	24:42-25:30	Judgment on God's People
A	-	25:31-46	Judgment on the World

Such a structure enforces the central emphasis that the unexpected nature of the Lord's return is to be applied to the believers. It is the regenerate people of God who are the central focus of this section (Mt. 24:42-25:30), and not the sheep and the goats.

In the parable of the wise servant, the evil servant is after all a "servant." If the wise servant is saved, there is no exegetical basis for implying that the evil servant is not. In fact, the Greek text makes it plain that only one servant, not two, is in view. Then Lord says, "But if that (Gk. **ekeinos**,) evil slave says . . ." (24:48). He is speaking of that same servant, the wise one of the preceding verses. This one servant may conceivably follow two different courses in life.[1]

This servant is not an unbeliever. He genuinely believes in the return of "his" master. Rather, he is a true Christian but has simply become neglectful of his life-style because his Lord's return seems so far away and has been delayed. A non-Christian could hardly be called a "servant" of Christ. An evil son is still a son. Nor is there anything here that says he was a "so-called" servant. Rather, the parable simply acknowledges a common fact of Christian experience. Some servants of Christ are faithful and wise, and some, who start out serving their master, become indolent.

This servant conducts himself in a manner which earns him the title "evil servant." He drinks with drunkards, beats his fellow servants, and is completely unprepared for his master's return. When his master does return, this servant is "cut in pieces" and assigned a place "with the hypocrites" where there is "weeping" and "gnashing of teeth" (Mt. 24:51). It is understandable that interpreters have difficulty in imagining that this could be the experience at the judgment of any truly born-again child of God. Part of the problem is the extreme phrases used: "cut in pieces" and "wailing and gnashing of teeth." The latter is simply Oriental symbolism for profound regret.[2] The former is a metaphor for judgment.[3]

If we were to ask, What is the specific nature of this judgment? the figure "cut in pieces" possibly suggests "the sword of the Spirit, which is the Word of God" (Eph. 6:17). This initial impression is reinforced when we read that, when the Lord returns in judgment, "from His mouth comes a sharp sword" (Rev. 19:15). That the Word of God could be considered an instrument capable of "cutting" in a judgmental sense is further affirmed by Heb. 4:12:

> *For the word of God is living and active and sharper than any two-edged sword, and piercing as far as the division of soul and spirit, of both joints and marrow, and able to judge the thoughts and intentions of the heart* (NASB).

---

[1]Experimental Predestinarians mistakenly parallel this parable with the parable of the two sons in Mt. 21:28-32, wherein one was saved, and one was not. But there are two sons in that parable and one servant with two possible life styles in this one.

[2]See discussion in chapter 15.

[3]AG, p. 159. Arndt and Gingrich say **dichotomeo** is "metaphorical in Luke 12:46, 'to punish with utmost severity,' like the modern threat 'I will tan your hide.'"

When the Lord returns to judge the wicked servant, the instrument of that judgment will apparently be the Word of God. It is able to pierce to the heart of a man, to cut to the inner being, and discern underlying motivations. As a result, all is revealed:

> *And there is no creature hidden from His sight, but all things are open and laid bare to the eyes of Him with whom we have to do* (v. 13).

At this moment the stern warning of our Lord will have pointed meaning:

> *There is nothing covered up that will not be revealed, and hidden that will not be known. Accordingly, whatever you have said in the dark shall be heard in the light, and what you have whispered in the inner rooms shall be proclaimed upon the housetops* (Lk. 12:2-3).

This passage is not teaching that, when we appear before Him, all our sins will be publicly announced to others. To speak in the dark is to speak in the "locked room" (Gk. **tameion**). This was the innermost apartment in contrast to a public room. A roof in the Ancient Near East was often a terrace. From that position one can speak with the greatest possible publicity with those who are in the street. The Lord's point is not that our sins will be published to others but that all sins, even those covered up and in private in our secret rooms, will be fully revealed to the believer and his Lord and will be accounted for at the judgment day.

The servant in Matthew's account is not literally cut in pieces, but his secret motivations are exposed. His "work is burned up" (1 Cor. 3:15), and he draws back "in shame at the Lord's coming" (1 Jn. 2:28). To use Paul's term, he is "disqualified for the prize" (1 Cor. 9:27). We must remember that these ARE parables and full of metaphors which are not to be taken literally. Rather, they symbolically point to literal, sober truths. In a similar way Paul spoke of coming to discipline the carnal Corinthian believers "with a rod" (1 Cor. 4:21). Like the statement about being cut to pieces at the future judgment, this does not speak of a literal rod but of a severe rebuke.

Our Lord affirms that the unfaithful servant will be assigned a place with the "hypocrites" (Gk. **hypokrites**). The word meant one who was an interpreter of riddles and dreams or an actor, one who interprets a poet.[4] He claims to be a servant of his master but does not live like it. It can be used of non-Christians,[5] but it is also used by Christ of true Christians who judge others (their "brother"), while ignoring their own sin (Mt. 7:5). Barnabas and Peter were charged with hypocrisy by Paul (Gal. 2:13), and Peter speaks of "newborn babes" who are to put hypocrisy aside (1 Pet. 2:1-2). The parallel passage in Luke helps us identify

---

[4]Ulrich Wilckens, **"hypokrinomai,"** in *TDNTA*, p. 1235.
[5]Mt. 6:2, 5, 16.

these hypocrites (Lk. 12:42-46). Here they are called "the unbelievers" (Lk. 12:46). The Greek term here is **ton apiston**. It does not mean unbeliever in the sense of "non-Christian." Here it means "unfaithful."[6] This usage is well established[7] and fits the context of the parable well. This man was not an unbeliever; he believed in his "master" and that his master was coming back. The fact that **apiston** is rendered **hypokriton** (hypocrisy) in the parallel passage in Matthew proves that **apiston** should not be translated as "unbeliever" but as "unfaithful." His hypocrisy was not that he professed Christ and inwardly denied Him but that, assuming the role of a servant, he did not take care of the other servants and ended up serving only himself. The servant was not a non-Christian; he was an unfaithful Christian. It is for this that he will be judged.

The parable would have no relevance to those who do not know Christ and who have not begun the process of serving Him. What is of concern is that the servant who begins this service will continue it until his Lord returns. Christians are capable of unfaithfulness and hypocrisy and can lead carnal lives which can be summed up as hypocritical. They will be in the kingdom but not at the wedding feast! The unfaithful servant will not be "at the table," though he is a servant and will be saved.

Matthew 25:1-13

The parable of the ten virgins is to be understood in a similar way. The five foolish virgins, like the unfaithful servant, refused to prepare for the Lord's coming. The foolish virgins are in the kingdom. That is not the issue. They are being shut out of the wedding feast, not the kingdom. The events described here occur after the Messiah has adjudicated the question of the sheep and the goats (Mt. 25:31-46). There is no feast in the kingdom until the judgments are out of the way. Then Messiah sits at table fellowship with His co-heirs in a great wedding feast. The tribulation is over, the judgments on the nonbelievers are executed, and the kingdom has begun. Now it is time to celebrate with His Partakers. No feast had ever been so splendid, and the joy of those faithful servants throughout the centuries is great as they sit at the table with their King.

Experimental Predestinarians have sometimes been misled by Matthew's opening phrase, "The Kingdom of Heaven shall be likened to ten virgins . . ." They conclude that this parable equates the kingdom with the wedding feast. However, it is almost universally acknowledged by New Testament scholars that the words "shall be likened to" are not used by Matthew to draw a precise equivalence of terms between "wedding feast" and "kingdom." Rather, the term is

---

[6]According to Alfred Plummer, *The Gospel According to Luke, The International Critical Commentary* (New York: Charles Scribner's Sons, 1914), p. 333. So also A. T. Robertson, *Word Pictures in the Greek New Testament*, 6 vols. (Nashville: Broadman, 1933), 2:181.

[7]See AG, p. 84.

more general and is used to "illustrate an aspect of" the kingdom, and not the kingdom itself.[8] Thus, the wedding feast is not the kingdom but an aspect of it, and entrance into the feast cannot automatically be equated with entrance into the kingdom. Indeed, to do so would mean, as we shall see below, that entrance to the kingdom was based upon works, a point of view far removed from that of the New Testament:

> *Then the kingdom of heaven will be comparable to ten virgins who took their lamps, and went out to meet the bridegroom. And five of them were foolish, and five were prudent. For when the foolish took their lamps, they took no oil with them, but the prudent took oil in flasks along with their lamps. Now while the bridegroom was delaying, they all got drowsy and began to sleep. But at midnight there was a shout, "Behold, the bridegroom! Come out to meet him." Then all those virgins rose; and trimmed their lamps. And the foolish said to the prudent, "Give us some of your oil, for our lamps are going out." But the prudent answered, saying, "No, there will not be enough for us and you too; go instead to the dealers and buy some for yourselves." And while they were going away to make the purchase, the bridegroom came, and those who were ready went in with him to the wedding feast; and the door was shut. And later the other virgins also came, saying, "Lord, lord, open up for us." But He answered and said, "Truly I say to you, I do not know you." Be on the alert then, for you do not know the day nor the hour* (Mt. 25:1-13 NASB).

Under normal conditions, although there were exceptions, there were four activities connected with marriage: (1) the betrothal, (2) the transfer of the bride to the bridegroom's house, (3) the marriage feast, and (4) the consummation.[9] The first event, the betrothal, was a binding transaction declaring the fact of the marriage and specifying the terms agreed upon by the contracting parties. Although the bride and groom were legally married, they did not usually live together for a period of time. In fact, a delay of up to several years between the betrothal and the celebration of the marriage was common.[10] After this indeterminate time and after the various contractual obligations had been fulfilled, the marriage feast was held, usually at the home of the bridegroom. However, the bride was first transferred to the bridegroom's home. She was accompanied by

---

[8]Alan Hugh M'Neile, *The Gospel According to St. Matthew* [1915; reprint ed., London: Macmillan, 1961], p. 196, on 13:24. Tasker agrees that it would be misleading to literally equate terms connected by this verb. See R. V. G. Tasker, *The Gospel According to Matthew, TNTC,* p. 137. See also Stanley Toussaint, *Behold the King* (Portland: Multnomah, 1980), p. 181.

[9]R. K. Bower and G. L. Knapp, "Marriage," in *ISBE,* 3:264; G. M. Mackie and W. Ewing, "Marriage," in *Dictionary of Christ and the Gospels*, ed. J. Hastings, 2 vols. (Edinburgh: T. & T. Clark, 1913), 2:137.

[10]Mackie and Ewing, 2:137.

maidens who were involved in sword play and dancing and was arrayed in her bridal dress as she rode a horse in the front of a joyous wedding procession.

Normally in an Oriental wedding the bridegroom himself remained absent from the house and stayed with his relatives or friends until all the preparations for the wedding had been made. As he sat among his friends, he had the prerogative of deciding when to begin his procession to his home to meet his bride and her attendants who had already arrived and were waiting.[11] As soon as he signified he was ready, the wedding procession began. Lanterns and torches were lit to guide him and his companions through the dark silent streets. As the bridegroom passed through the streets of the village on his journey to the banquet, a peculiar Oriental cry was raised from the lips of bystanders, "Behold, the bridegroom. Come out to meet him" (v. 6). The time which elapsed between the transfer of the bride to the home of the bridegroom and the bridegroom's decision to begin his own procession to the banquet was up to the discretion of the bridegroom. He could leave his friends immediately or after a matter of hours. This period of uncertainty seems to be the "delay of the bridegroom" (v. 5).

Presumably then the betrothal and transfer of the bride to the bridegroom's home has already occurred.[12] We are to assume that the Lord has already come to receive his bride at the rapture. The ten virgins apparently await the coming of the bridegroom with his bride at the second coming of Christ. At that time the bridegroom brings his bride with Him in a royal wedding procession from heaven to the wedding banquet, where there is a great celebration. During this time the bride is already in heaven with the Lord, and the virgins await the return of Christ to earth for the wedding celebration.

A wedding in Palestine was a great occasion. An entire village would turn out to accompany the bride on her journey to the groom's home and the banquet to follow. In fact, the rabbis agreed that a man might even abandon the study of the law to share in the joy of a wedding feast.[13] When a Jewish couple married, they did not go away for a honeymoon but stayed at home, and for a week they kept open house. They were treated and even addressed as prince and princess. It was one of the happiest weeks in their lives. Only chosen friends were admitted to the festivities of that week. The foolish virgins had not only missed the marriage ceremony but the joyous week as well.

---

[11]Ibid.

[12]It has often been pointed out that this is quite consistent with the pretribulation view of the rapture. The betrothal and transfer of the bride, the church, to heaven has already occurred. Now both the bride in heaven and the virgins on earth await the wedding supper. The bridegroom during the tribulation is executing the judgments on the earth. When he has finished, he will return to the home of the bridegroom to pick up his waiting bride and return with her to earth to the wedding banquet, where he will meet the faithful tribulation saints, the wise virgins.

[13]William Barclay, *The Daily Study Bible, The Gospel of Matthew*, 2 vols. (Philadelphia: Westminster, 1958), 2:352.

As mentioned above, the coming of the bridegroom was heralded by a shout, "Behold the bridegroom. Come out to meet him." When they heard this, the virgins were to take their lamps, make their way to join the procession at some convenient point, and then travel with it to the wedding banquet at the bridegroom's home.[14]

The ten virgins are the regenerate believers of the future tribulation. The word "virgin" means undefiled and is used elsewhere of regenerate people (Rev. 14:4; 2 Cor. 11:12). It is not an appropriate picture for the unregenerate sinner. Since all are designated virgins, there is no reason to doubt that all are regenerate. No reason, that is, except the presuppositions of Experimental Predestinarian theology. One cannot argue that the foolish virgins proved themselves to be unregenerate because they did not persevere unless one knows beforehand that a lack of perseverance is proof that they were unregenerate--the very point in question!

These virgins had all slept. They all had lamps. Even the foolish valued the lamp, for without it they could not find their way to the banquet hall. They were not indifferent to the coming of the Lord. Indeed, all ten had gone out in faith to meet him. All of the virgins also had oil, even the foolish ones, but they did not have enough. M'Neile observes that "they had oil in their lanterns, but not expecting delay had taken no extra oil. The next verse makes this clear."[15] Trench concurs, "Nor is it that they are wholly without oil; they have some, but not enough; their lamps when they first go forth, are burning, otherwise they could not speak of them as on the point of expiring just as the bridegroom is approaching."[16]

It seems that this observation refutes the common Experimental Predestinarian interpretation that the virgins were unregenerate, i.e., had no oil at all. When the Lord says in v. 3 that the foolish "took no oil with them," He means that they took no extra oil with them. It is obvious that they took some oil because their lamps did burn. Due to the uncertainty regarding the time of the bridegroom's arrival, the lamps were normally kept burning during this interlude so that there would be no delay when he returned. It was presumptuous of the foolish virgins, however, to assume that they had enough. They should have prepared for either a short or a long delay in the bridegroom's return.

The lamp in view is probably the so-called "Herodian lamp."[17] It was not a torch but a small clay lamp. These lamps were accompanied by an additional vessel which contained oil to keep the lamp burning after the smaller amount of

---

[14]Richard Chenevix Trench, *Notes on the Miracles and the Parables of Our Lord*, 2 vols. in 1 (Reprint ed., Westwood, NJ: Revell, 1963), 2:248.

[15]M'Neile, *Matthew*, p. 361.

[16]Trench, 2:255.

[17]G. F. Hasel, "Lamp," in *NISBE*, 3:69.

oil in the lamp itself was exhausted. These extra vessels are referred to in v. 4. According to archaeologist Ralph Alexander, it was the custom for the lamp to be lit at dusk prior to the arrival of the bridegroom several hours later. There was, however, only enough oil in these lamps to burn for a few hours. At that time, after the lamps had begun to burn low, they needed to be replenished by the extra oil carried in the auxiliary vessels.[18]

This Herodian lamp is similar to the ones used by the ten virgins (Mat. 25:1-13). These small clay lamps were accompanied by an additional vessel which contained extra oil.

The ten virgins' lamps were lit at dusk and threatened to go out at midnight (v. 6). They had been burning for four or five hours. The foolish, however, did not take an extra vessel of oil along (vv. 3-4). They thought a few hours of burning would be sufficient![19]

They did have spiritual life, and their lamps burned for a while. They are like the rocky and the thorn-infested soils in the parable of the sower. In that case too there was growth and belief but no perseverance. It would seem that the burden of proof is on those who deny the regenerate nature of the five foolish virgins.

---

[18]Dr. Ralph Alexander, former Professor of Old Testament, Western Conservative Baptist Seminary. Personal communication, 18 Aug. 89. M'Neile (p. 361) says the lamps were accompanied by extra vessels of oil (Num. 4:9).

[19]Bernard Ramm observes that the lamps used were "very small and for the foolish virgins to expect them to burn for the three-hour vigil (or longer) was very improvident and therefore foolish" (Bernard Ramm, *Protestant Biblical Interpretation* [Boston: W. A. Wilde, 1956], p. 99).

The fact that the lamps had been burning testifies to their regenerate state. The light emitted from the lamp is elsewhere defined as the good works of regenerate men (Mt. 5:16).[20] It is oil which energizes these works. The meaning of the oil is not specified, but we may surmise it refers to our faith in God, our obedience to Him, and the power and influence of the Holy Spirit in our lives. Specifically, it is the life which is prepared to meet the master. This life has developed a spiritual reserve, or preparedness, by means of good works, by fellowship with other Christians, and by prayer and Bible study. In a word, a supply of oil symbolizes "preparedness."[21]

When a man fails to build up these spiritual reserves, he is unprepared to perform the work which God has called him to do. In the parable the ten virgins were probably part of the wedding festivities and, as was the custom in Oriental weddings, they may have provided some of the entertainment at the wedding banquet. But the foolish virgins discovered that the delay of the bridegroom to come to the wedding banquet meant they had not brought enough oil. The wise virgins counsel them to go and buy some oil. Salvation cannot be bought. It costs nothing. It is free. John said, "Take the water of life without cost" (Rev. 22:17). Clearly, they are not being challenged to become converted! Rather, they are challenged to make preparation immediately by something that does cost, a life of discipleship. However, their good intentions are too late. Even though they set out to secure some oil, the bridegroom comes at the very hour they have decided to get prepared.

In order to be prepared for their participation in the coming wedding banquet, they must take forethought to be sure they had adequate oil. Similarly, the parable teaches we must persist in the things which lead to spiritual preparedness if our lives are to continue to show good works. What had happened apparently is that the foolish virgins did not persist. Their initial works and dependence upon the Holy Spirit had not continued. They had not adequately considered that good beginnings are not all that is necessary to obtain a place at the banquet. We too must "finish our course" because we are "partakers of Christ [only] if we hold fast our confession firm to the end."

What a tragedy to wait until it is too late to prepare! The parable warns us that there are certain things which cannot be obtained at the last minute. A student desiring to pass an examination simply cannot wait until the last minute to prepare. When the bridegroom comes, it will be too late to acquire the character traits, spiritual reserves, and faithful perseverance necessary to participate in the banquet of Christ's metochoi. As Barclay says, "It is easy to leave things so late that we can no longer prepare ourselves to meet with God."[22]

---

[20]Hasel, "Lamp," 3:69. See also Lk. 8:16ff.; Mk. 4:21ff.

[21]Trench, 2:362.

[22]Barclay, 2:354.

The parable also teaches that there are certain things that cannot be borrowed. A Christian cannot live on the association with other Christians and never personally develop intimacy with Christ. A Christian cannot borrow fellowship with God. He must possess it. We cannot substitute fellowship with other Christians for fellowship with God and assume that because we attend Bible studies and go to church that we really know Him.

Like the foolish virgins of the parable there will be some Christians who will not be permitted entrance to the feast! When they seek entrance, the Lord says, "I do not know you." No doubt this has led many to the erroneous conclusion that they were unsaved. Christ refers to "not knowing" the unsaved with **epiginosko** (Mt. 7:23).[23] The Lord used a word similar to **epiginosko, ginosko**, when He spoke of eternal life as being equivalent to "knowing Him" (Jn. 17:3). Here in Mt. 25:12, however, the Lord does not use that word, He uses **oida**. A distinction between these words is commonly recognized by the lexicons.[24] **Ginosko** is to know by observation and experience; it refers to an intimate experiential knowledge. It is used, for example, of sexual intercourse.[25] **Oida**, on the other hand, is to know by reflection; it is a mental process based on information.[26] In fact, it sometimes means "respect" or "appreciate":[27]

> *But we request of you brethren, that you* **appreciate** [or respect, **oida**]*, those who diligently labor among you, and have charge over you in the Lord and give you instruction* (1 Th. 5:12).

The lexicon lists references in extra-biblical Greek where it means to "honor."[28] This apparently is the sense in the parable. When the Lord says He does not know them, He means He does not appreciate, respect, or honor them. It is obvious that He knows them by observation in that He has information about who they are. The word does not mean to know in the sense of personal relationship or eternal life (i.e., **ginosko**). But He does not know them in the sense of honoring them as one of His co-heirs. They are not excluded from all blessing of the kingdom or even with mingling with the saved there. They are excluded only from the joy of the wedding feast and from co-heirship with Christ. The door is

---

[23]In Lk. 13:27 the Lord says to the unsaved, "I do not know (Gk. **oida**) where you are from." This is irrelevant to the usage in Mt. 25:12. Knowing where a man is from and knowing him in a saving sense are not equivalent.

[24]See, for example, Joseph Henry Thayer, *Thayer's Greek-English Lexicon of the New Testament* (rev. ed., 1889; reprint ed., Grand Rapids: Associate Publishers and Authors, n.d.), pp. 174, 118.

[25]This classical distinction between the words still holds in the majority of cases in the New Testament according to Burdick. See Donald W. Burdick, "**Oida** and **ginosko** in the Pauline Epistles," in *New Dimensions in New Testament Study*, ed. Richard N. Longenecker and Merrill C. Tenney (Grand Rapids: Zondervan, 1974), pp. 344-56.

[26]AS, p. 92.

[27]Ibid., p. 311.

[28]AG, p. 559. See also Thayer, p. 174: "to have regard for, cherish, pay attention to."

shut to the joy of the feast, not to entrance into the kingdom. He will not know them as the Thessalonians knew and appreciated the faithful labor of the apostles in their midst. He will not say to them , "Come, you who are blessed by My Father; take your inheritance, the kingdom prepared for you since the creation of the world" (Mt. 25:34).[29]

Finally, we might ask, Why was the servant without the wedding garment in Matt. 22 permitted entrance to the wedding feast, but the foolish virgins found that the door was shut? It seems that both parables are teaching the same thing, the unfaithful Christian forfeits his inheritance in the kingdom. The distinction between the parables is accidental, and such details should not be pressed.

The parable of the virgins has nothing to do with true Christians losing their salvation. It refers to the forfeiture of honor due only to faithful servants when the Lord returns.

Luke 8:11-15

The parable of the four soils in Lk. 8:4-15 presents four differing responses to the gospel. Experimental Predestinarians and Arminians are once again united in their belief that only the person represented by the fourth soil, the one who produces fruit, will ultimately arrive in heaven. The difference is that the Calvinist maintains that the first three soils were never born again in the first place, while the Arminian maintains that the rocky soil and that which was choked by thorns both were saved and then lost their salvation.

One of the central points of the parable is to discern between those who are saved and those who are not. In addition, discrimination among the saved is described. The basis for this conclusion rests particularly upon Matthew's use of the parable. In Matthew, chapters 1 through 12, Jesus presents Himself to Israel as her Messiah. In the twelfth chapter an official delegation is sent by the religious leaders to inspect His claims. Their conclusion: He is a demon from hell! (Mt. 12:24). A natural question arises. If Jesus is truly the Messiah, how do you explain this rejection by His own people? The parables of Matthew 13 seem to be given to answer this question. The first one faces it squarely. The reason for this rejection is that there are various responses to the gospel message, depending upon the heart condition of the recipient.

---

[29]George N. H. Peters, *The Theocratic Kingdom*, 3 vols. (New York: Funk and Wagnalls, 1884; reprint ed., Grand Rapids: Kregel, 1972), 3:306. "The declaration 'I know you not', [is] expressive of exclusion to a position which the others because of their preparation and readiness, obtain. . . . The foolish are only excluded from these marriage festivities, but will ultimately be saved."

Once again John Murray is typical of those holding to the Reformed view of the parable.[30] Murray defines apostasy as falling away from a profession of faith and not from true faith.[31] He supports his doctrine of a false faith from this parable. The man on rocky ground is, according to Murray, a man with false or temporary faith. He is a mere professor but not a true possessor of Christ. Facing the enormous difficulty of his position directly, Murray says:

It is possible to give all the outward signs of faith in Christ and obedience to him, to witness for a time a good confession and show great zeal for Christ and his kingdom and then lose all interest and become indifferent, if not hostile, to the claims of Christ and of his kingdom. It is the lesson of seed sown on rocky ground--the seed took root, it sprang up, but when the sun rose it was scorched and brought forth no fruit to perfection.[32]

Murray ruins his argument when he acknowledges that "there is not only germination; there is growth." How can there be growth and germination if there is no regeneration, new life? Murray tries to explain this as a result of the nearness of the "supernatural forces that are operative in the kingdom of God." This is Calvin's old doctrine of temporary faith. He cites Heb. 6:5-6 as proof. But those enlightened, etc., in Heb. 6 as discussed elsewhere are true Christians. He goes on:

The scripture itself, therefore, leads us to the conclusion that it is possible to have a very uplifting, ennobling, reforming, and exhilarating experience of the power and truth of the gospel, to come into such a close contact with the supernatural forces which are operative in God's kingdom of grace that these forces produce effects in us which to human observation are hardly distinguishable from those produced by God's regeneration and sanctifying grace and yet be not partaker of Christ and heirs of eternal life.[33]

---

[30]John Murray, *Redemption--Accomplished and Applied* (Grand Rapids: Eerdmans, 1955), pp. 151-53.

[31]He cites Jn. 8:31-32 to prove that the only true disciple is the one who continues to the end. We agree. But, as discussed in chapter 8, a disciple is not the same as a Christian. All disciples are Christians, but not all Christians are disciples, as Jn. 8:31-32 proves! He also refers to Mt. 10:22, "He who endures to the end will be saved." Murray does not discuss whether or not "save" means "to deliver from hell" or "preserve physical life." Neither does he discuss his assumption that all Christians are disciples. Since these are the very points at issue, his argument is specious. He also cites Heb. 4:14 as proof that endurance in the faith is the only evidence of the reality of the faith. But this passage refers to loss of rewards. He quotes Jn. 15:6 and misconstrues it. Instead of it dealing with fruit, it deals, according to Murray, with a test of whether or not a man is truly saved.

[32]Murray, p. 152.

[33]See chapter 19.

Confusion abounds in every phrase. There is no scriptural evidence of which the writer is aware that a non-Christian can experience all the supernatural changes and hardly be distinguishable from Christians. Unless, of course, these two passages teach it. Unfortunately for Murray's reasoning, that is the very point in question! The subjects of Heb. 6 seem to be Christians, and it would be questionable to deny the same status to those who have "germinated and grown," i.e., been regenerated. There is nothing in the parable to suggest that this experience of germination and growth was not really germination and growth but only an appearance of it. Isn't this reading a theological view into the parable unsupported by the plain statements of our Lord?

Not only did the individual represented by the rocky soil germinate and grow, but we read that he "received the word with joy" (Lk. 8:13). This can hardly be the description of a superficial profession based on emotion.[34] Elsewhere in the New Testament receiving the word with joy refers to saving faith (e.g., 1 Th. 1:6). In fact, "joy" (Gk. **chara**) is never used in the New Testament of a superficial and insincere excitement. For Luke it is joy the Father feels at finding one of His lost sheep (Lk. 15:5ff.), the joy of true Christians because their names are written in heaven (10:20), and the joy of the disciples after the ascension (24:52).

Furthermore, for Luke and the other gospel writers, the phrase "receive the word" is a virtual synonym for a salvation experience. Luke, as well as Paul, refers to the way in which the Thessalonians "received the word" with great eagerness (Acts 17:11). This was a salvation experience. When Luke argues to prove that the salvation of the Samaritans (Acts 8:14) and the Gentiles (Acts 11:1) was a genuine experience of the Holy Spirit (and not a superficial one), similar to that experienced with the outpouring of the Holy Spirit of Pentecost (see Acts 11:15-18), he says that they "received the word." Indeed, for the gospel writers, "receiving the word" was a virtual synonym for "receiving the kingdom."[35] Luke equates it with saving faith in Acts 2:41 when he refers to the conversion of the three thousand at Pentecost, noting that they had "received His word." Surely most would agree with Link when he says, "In the early Christian communities the phrase **ton logon dechesthai**, to receive the word, became a technical term for **the believing acceptance of the gospel.**"[36]

Luke tells us that in regard to the first soil the devil came and took the word away lest he could believe and be saved (8:12). In contrast to this the second soil did believe and was therefore saved. The meaning of "believe" in v. 12 is clearly "saving faith." Why should the meaning in the next verse be changed to

---

[34]Geldenhuys equates this "joy" with "emotional excitement and superficial enthusiasm" (Norval Geldenhuys, *The Gospel of Luke, The New International Commentary on the New Testament* [Grand Rapids: Eerdmans, 1977], p. 244).

[35]See Mk. 10:15; Lk. 18:17

[36]H. G. Link, "Take," in *NIDNTT*, 3:746. He cites Lk. 8:13; Acts 8:14; 11:1; 17:11; and 1 Th. 1:6 and 2:13 as proof.

"false faith"? The fact that he only believed "for a time" in no way denies that he was truly regenerate (unless one knows before he begins his exegesis that the Experimental Predestinarian doctrine of perseverance is true!).

Sellers is impressed with the fact that the parable says in v. 13 that they "have no root."[37] The rendering of the NASB, however, more correctly catches the sense, "they have no **firm** root." The intent of the phrase is probably not to suggest there was no root at all but only that it was not firm enough and deep enough to sustain a life of perseverance. That is the central point of the parable (Lk. 8:15). Anytime there is germination and growth, there is some root in a plant. This is simply a fact of biology. The Lord's point is that those represented by the second soil believe, are saved, and then fall away due to testing. But all of this is beside the point. The evidence of life in a plant has nothing to do with the presence or absence of a firm root system. The presence of life is indicated by gemination and growth.

In Matthew's version we are told that the man represented by the first soil "does not understand" (Mt. 13:19). In contrast, the fruit-bearing believer, the fourth soil, does understand and produces a crop. Does the fact that it is not said that the second and third soil understand mean that they did not understand the gospel and were therefore not saved? While some have argued this way, such a conclusion is not necessary. We might as well ask: Does the fact that the fourth soil is not said to have "received the word with joy" mean that he had not believed or had no joy? Does a parable have to say everything about each man? Is it not probable that a man who receives the word with joy and believes (Lk. 8:13) has understood the meaning of the gospel and rejoiced in it even if the text does not specifically state that he understood? Is it possible to believe the gospel and yet not understand the gospel? Nowhere are we told that the second two did not understand. It appears that little can be made of this one way or the other.

The issue in the parable is fruit bearing, and not just salvation. The seed which fell on rocky soil produced growth, but the person in view fell away. But from what did he fall? There is not a word about heaven and hell in the parable. There is much about fruit bearing (Lk. 8:8) and progression to maturity (Lk. 8:14). The most plausible interpretation of the phrase is simply to fall away from that progression which leads to maturity, to fruit bearing, and become a dead and carnal Christian. Adherents of perseverance may not like such an interpretation, but it is hardly fair to bring their theological exegesis to play and introduce notions of heaven and hell to which the parable never alludes.

The good fruit comes from lives which hold on to the Word of God and which persevere. But not persevering, i.e., falling away, is not the same as losing

---

[37]C. Norman Sellers, *Election and Perseverance* (Miami Springs, FL: Schoettle, 1987), p. 85.

one's salvation. Arminians who maintain otherwise offer no exegetical evidence for their view of "falling away."

John 8:51

In His conflict with the Pharisees Jesus makes the startling statement, "Whoever keeps My word will not see death" (Jn. 8:51). Arminian writers interpret Jesus to mean that a man must retain the saving Word of Christ if he is to retain his salvation. If a person continually hangs on to the Word of Christ, he will be saved. The word "keep" (**terese**), however, is an aorist, and therefore probably no durative or continuous force is intended. He simply says, "If one keeps (at a point in time kept My word), he shall not see death." The word says nothing about whether or not at some future date a man may cease to "keep." That was not even the subject of the discussion with the Pharisees, and it may be questionable whether a theological discussion over eternal security should even be considered here by responsible exegetes.

What is the sense of "keep"? It does not mean obey, and it does not even necessarily mean "hold on to." Rather, the force here is similar to its meaning in Rev. 1:3 which the NIV translates as follows: "Blessed is the one who reads the words of this prophecy, and blessed are those who hear it and **take to heart** what is written in it." To "keep" in John 8:51 simply means to "pay attention to" or to "take to heart."[38]

In what way are we to "pay attention" and take His words seriously? The parallel passages from Jesus Himself clarify this:

> *I tell you the truth, whoever* **hears my word and believes him who sent me** *has eternal life and* **will not be condemned;** *he has crossed over* **from death to life** (Jn. 5:24).

> *I am the resurrection and the life. He who believes in me will live, even though he dies; and whoever lives and* **believes in me will never die** (Jn. 11:25-26).

The way in which we pay close attention to, and take to heart, what Jesus says is to believe in Him. There is no implied notion of a life of obedience or of continuing to hold on the Word of Christ until physical death in order to be saved.

---

[38]See AG for parallels, p. 823.

John 13:8

The Lord warns Peter that, if he does not allow Him to wash his feet, Peter will have "no part with Christ" (Jn. 13:8). As discussed elsewhere, this refers to a severance of fellowship and end of usefulness in Christ's cause.

John 15

Few passages have been quoted so often and incorrectly as this one. The beautiful and profound analogy of the vine and the branches has been a source of wonderful encouragement to believers throughout the centuries, but it has also become, unfortunately, a controversial passage regarding the eternal security of the saints.

Experimental Predestinarians have been particularly ingenious in their exegesis of this passage. One is reminded of the sign over the old ironsmith's shop, "All kinds of fancy twistings and turnings here."[39]

15:1   I am the true vine, and My Father is the vinedresser.

15:2   Every branch in Me that does not bear fruit, He takes away, and every branch that bears fruit, He prunes it, that it may bear more fruit (NASB).

There is general agreement that the branches which bear fruit and are pruned represent true Christians. However, in order to save the fiction of the saints' perseverance in fruit bearing, Experimental Predestinarians have argued that the branch "in Me" which does not bear fruit is not a true Christian but is only a professing Christian. This is done in two ways. Charles Smith has argued that the phrase "in Me" is simply a reference to being in the kingdom in a general sense. He notes that the future millennium and the present form of the kingdom contain a mixture of true and false believers.[40] As Bishop Ryle put it:

It cannot be shown that a branch in Me must mean a believer in Me. It means nothing more than a 'professing member of My Church, a man joined to the company of My people, but not joined to Me.'[41]

Often justification for this interpretation is found by going outside of John to the analogy of the vine in Isaiah.[42] Here there were branches in the tree who

---

[39]Robert Shank, *Life in The Son: A Study of the Doctrine of Perseverance* (Springfield: Westcott, 1961), p. 44.

[40]Charles R. Smith, "The Unfruitful Branches in John 15," *GTJ* 9 (Spring 1968): 10.

[41]J. C. Ryle, *Expository Thoughts on the Gospels*, 4 vols. (Grand Rapids: Zondervan, n.d.), 4:334.

[42]See Isa. 2:25-29; Rom. 11:16-24; Jer. 5:10a.

were not saved. Surely this is irrelevant to John 15. Isaiah speaks of a **covenant** people. All Jews (saved and unsaved) are in Israel, but not all professing Christians are in Christ! As will be demonstrated below, it is extremely unlikely that "in Me" can refer to an "Israel within Israel."[43] To be "in Me" is not equal to being within professing Israel.

Recently Experimental Predestinarian Carl Laney has suggested a second possibility. He points out that the phrase "in Me" can either be taken adjectivally with the noun "branch" or adverbially with the verb "bearing." If it is rendered adverbially, then the translation is, "Every branch not bearing fruit in Me He takes away." The phrase "in Me" is then the sphere of enablement and fellowship in which fruit bearing can occur.[44] The view is exegetically possible. This rendering seems intrinsically unlikely, however, because it would imply that there are branches not in Christ who bear fruit. Furthermore, it is simply too awkward to be believable even if it is syntactically possible. The majority of the commentators and all of the translations, as far as the writer is aware, translate the phrase as an adjective modifying "branch," so that it is a branch "in Me" which does not bear fruit.

The Meaning of "in Me"

To whom does the branch "in Me" refer? The literature on the "in Christ" relationship is immense. The phrase "in Me"[45] is used sixteen times in John's gospel.[46] In each case it refers to true fellowship with Christ. It is not possible then to take it as "in the sphere of profession." A person "in Me" is always a true Christian. But what is signified by "in Me"? The preposition "in" (Gk. *en*) is often "used to designate a close personal relation."[47] It refers to a sphere within which some action occurs.[48] So to "abide in Me" is simply to remain in close relationship to Me. But what kind of relationship is meant? A review of the sixteen usages in John seem to suggest, that when He used this phrase, the Lord referred to a life of fellowship, a unity of purpose rather than organic connection. It should be noted that this is somewhat different from Paul. While Paul did use the phrase "in Christ" (not "in Me") in this way, he often used it in a forensic (legal) sense referring to our position in Christ or to our organic membership in His

---

[43]I.e., the truly saved within the professing company.

[44]J. Carl Laney, "Abiding is Believing: The Analogy of the Vine in John 15:1-6," *BibSac* 146 (January-March 1989): 64.

[45]Gk. **en emoi**, first person, singular, dative, personal pronoun **ego**.

[46]Jn. 6:56; 10:38; 14:10, 11, 20, 30; 15:2, 4, 5, 6, 7; 16:33; 17:21, 23.

[47]AG, p. 259

[48]Murray J. Harris, "Prepositions and Theology in the Greek New Testament," in *NIDNTT*, 3:1191.

body (e.g., 1 Cor. 12:13). John never does this. For him, to be "in Him" is to be in communion with Him and not organically connected in union with Him.

For example, in Jn. 10:38 it speaks of the fellowship between Christ and the Father:

If I do not do the works of My Father, do not believe Me; but if I do them, though you do not believe Me, believe the works, that you may know and understand that the Father is **in Me, and I in the Father.**

Christ evidently does not mean that the Father is inside of Him and He is inside of the Father. The figure is of a relationship between them. The works that He does enable them to understand the nature of the relationship. Certainly, observation of miracles does not prove to the observer that the Lord is of the same essence as the Father, organically connected with Him. If that were so, then whenever a disciple performed a miracle, it would show that the disciple was also of the same essence. The miracles prove that God is with Him. They prove that what God does, He does, and what He does, God does. They prove that the Son and the Father are like-minded and speak the same things. Therefore, we are to believe what the Son says because what He says is the same as what the Father says. So the "in Me" relationship speaks not of organic connection or commonality of essence but of commonality of purpose and commitment.[49]

This distinctive usage in John's gospel must be carefully noted or his particular contribution to the Christian's walk with Christ will be obscured. John was first of all an apostle of love. He emphasized mystical relationship and oneness with his King. While these elements certainly predominate in Paul's thought as well, most have noted that the great apostle to the Gentiles makes a different contribution to our understanding of the Christian life and walk.

Paul normally proceeds from a doctrinal base in which he sets for the objective, legal, and positional basis of our relationship with Christ. John, however, proceeds from a more mystical and experiential base and from that makes his doctrinal conclusions.

While both Paul and John were Jews, no doubt Paul's Hellenist background and higher education inclined him toward a more systematic and doctrinal method of presenting the Christian faith. This difference in background probably contributed to John's conceptualization of the "in Christ" relationship in terms of fellowship instead of Paul's organic union.

This is borne out in 14:30 where the Lord insists that the ruler of this world has nothing "in Me," that is, he has no relationship or part with Me, no

---

[49]In 14:10 it refers to a close working relationship between Christ and the Father, a unity of purpose.

communion of purpose.[50] He is not teaching that the ruler of this world has not part of His essence but that they are not like-minded. "In Me" does not refer to common essence or organic connection here either.

The experience of peace in the midst of persecution will only come to believers who are obediently walking in His commandments and who are aligned with His purposes (Jn. 16:33). He has spoken these words so that "in Me" they can have peace. This peace comes through fellowship with Him. John's writings and the rest of the New Testament confirm that being "in Him" in a saving way does not automatically result in an experience of peace in the midst of trials. It is only when we are "in Him" in the sense of walking in fellowship with Him that we have peace.

That "in Me" means oneness of purpose and not organic connection is further brought out in 17:21. Here Christ prays for the same kind of oneness among the disciples that He enjoys with the Father, a oneness of love and fellowship. The "in Me and I in you" relationship which Christ enjoys with the Father is explicitly taught to be the same as the experience of oneness, unity, and fellowship for which Christ prays for all His followers.

If the "in Me" relationship referred to organic connection, He would not pray that organic connection be achieved; it already has been! The Father is in Him, and He is in the Father

that all of them **may be one,** *Father,* **just as you are in Me and I am in you.** *May they also be in Us so that the world may believe that you*

---

[50]In 14:20 the Lord says that in "that day" they will know that He is in them and they are in Him. The sense seems to be that, when they see Him in resurrection, they will know again the fellowship they have with Him now. "That day" could refer to either the coming of the Holy Spirit at Pentecost or the appearances of the resurrected Christ to His disciples. The preceding verse seems to connect it with the resurrection appearances. This is confirmed by Jn. 16:16 where He also speaks of the fact that in a little while they will no longer behold Him and then in a little while they will see Him, a reference to His appearance in resurrection. The meaning then is that, when they see Christ in resurrection, they will understand fully some things they do not understand fully now. What they will understand is that Christ is "in the Father" and that they are in Christ and He is in them. It appears that the objective knowledge of the resurrected Christ will bring about this clear perception. At this time they will see clearly that Christ has been operating in complete unity of purpose with the Father and that they are in complete unity of purpose with Him. Apparently they will know something they do not know now. They are already regenerate, but there is something they either do not know at all or only know imperfectly. What brings about the change? The text does not say, but later John informs us that prior to the resurrection the disciples did not understand that He had to rise from the dead (Jn. 20:9). Apparently seeing Christ in resurrection brought a flood of understanding concerning the Old Testament predictions, Christ's unity of purpose and obedience to the Father, and solidified their commitment to Him. The resurrection forever removed doubts regarding who He was and resulted in a change that lasted the rest of their lives. They committed themselves fully to follow Him forever. It was that commitment brought about by their seeing Christ in resurrection on "that day" which resulted in their total unity of purpose and obedience to Him. That is when they knew the experience of unity and fellowship, "you in Me and I in you," with their resurrected Lord.

have sent Me. I have given them the glory that you gave Me, that they **may be one as We are one: I in them and You in Me. May they be brought to complete unity** *to let the world know that You sent Me and have loved them even as You have loved Me* (Jn. 17:21-23).

Again it is not a saving relationship which is portrayed by "in Me" but a life of communion. It is a oneness of purpose and not of organic union which is taught. He wants them to have an experience of unity because that observable unity will prove to the world that they are His disciples, models of Christian love (17:23). If being "in Him" referred only to an organic connection, it would prove nothing. But if it refers to an experiential unity of purpose and fellowship, this would have great testimonial impact. It is a unity they do not yet have but must be "brought to." For John, to be "in Me" is simply to have "complete unity" with Him, not organic connection or commonalty of essence.

In Jn. 3:21 Jesus refers to the fact that His works have been done "in God." Arndt and Gingrich correctly observe that this means that His works were done in communion or fellowship with God.[51] Being "in God" does not refer to an organic relationship but to a relationship of communality of purpose.

In conclusion, then, the use of the phrase "in Me" in John does not require the sense of organic connection often found in Paul. To be "in Me" is simply to be in fellowship with Christ, living obediently. Therefore, it is possible for a true Christian not to be "in Me" in the Johannine sense. That this is true seems evident from the command to "abide in Christ." They are to remain in fellowship with their Lord. If all Christians remain "in Me," then why command them to remain in that relationship? It must be possible for them not to remain. This leads us to a discussion of one of John's favorite terms, "abide" (Gk. **meno**).

The Meaning of "Abide"

According to Webster, the English word "abide" means (1) to wait for; (2) to endure without yielding, to withstand, to bear patiently, to tolerate; (3) to remain stable or in a fixed state, to continue in a place.[52] Thus, it has precisely the same meaning as the Greek word. However, the slightly mystical connotation in American English has freighted it with overtones of faith, dependence.

---

[51]AG, p. 259.

[52]*Webster's Ninth New College Dictionary* (Springfield, MA: Merriam-Webster, Inc. 1987), p. 44.

The lexicons seem to be unanimous in saying the verb **meno** simply means "to remain."[53] It is used often in John, and in **every** instance it simply means to remain, to stay, to continue, or to endure.[54]

It is for this reason that the NIV translates the word as "remain." Christ commands His disciples to remain in Christ. It must be possible not to remain or endure in Christ or He would not command them to remain in that relationship. What does it mean to "remain"?

There are a number of things in different contexts which John says are characteristic of those who remain in Him. First of all, they eat His flesh and drink His blood (Jn. 6:56). When the Lord says, "He who eats My flesh and drinks My blood remains in Me," His meaning is simply that "Whoever eats My flesh and drinks My blood continues in close relationship to Me." The reference to eating His flesh and drinking His blood could refer to the initial act of appropriation of Christ and the resultant gift of regeneration (6:50, 51, 54, 58). When a man believes in Christ, he continues in a close relationship with Christ, i.e., fellowship. The richness of that relationship is determined by the believer's obedience (15:10). However, even though he has believed in Christ and presently remains in fellowship, it is obvious that in the future he might not continue in that fellowship.

The relationship of "remaining in Him" or "continuing in Him" of which it speaks is not a static gift of justification but of life and life abundant (10:10). When Jesus says that the man who believes in Christ remains in fellowship with Christ, He is speaking a general maxim. He knows that there are Christians who will not continue to maintain their fellowship. The proof of this is that in Jn. 15:4 He commands them to continue to abide and puts the verb in the imperative mood instead of indicative present participle as found in Jn. 6:56. If it is not possible to terminate our disposition of remaining in fellowship with Christ, why would He warn us about this possible failure? A warning regarding a danger which no true Christians will ever face and against an action which no true Christian will ever commit is nonsense.

There does not seem to be a compelling reason for equating "remaining" with "believing" in Jn. 6:56. The word "remain" cannot mean "to accept Jesus as

---

[53]For example, Hauck says it means "to stay in a place." Figuratively, "to remain in a sphere," "to stand against opposition, to endure, to hold fast" (Friedrich Hauck, "**meno**," in *TDNT*, 4:574-88). The word is used of the permanence of God in contrast to human mutability. God's counsel "endures" (Rom. 9:11), His Word endures (1 Pet. 1:23, 25), the New Covenant endures (2 Cor. 3:11), and faith, hope, and love endure (1 Cor. 13:13). Paul uses **meno** of the perseverance of believers in the faith (1 Tim. 2:15; 2 Tim. 2:13, 15). If we endure, we will reign with Him. If we are faithless, He "remains" faithful. Karlfried Munzer says it is used metaphorically to mean to hold fast, or remain steadfast, e.g., in a teaching (2 Tim. 3:14; 2 Jn. 9), in fellowship with (Jn. 14:10), to pass the test when one's works are judged (1 Cor. 3:14) ("remain," in *NIDNTT*, 3:224).

[54]E.g., 1:32, 38, 39; 2:12

Savior."[55] We remain in Christ's love by obeying commandments (Jn. 15:9-10). If remaining and believing are equated, then believing is obeying commandments, a thought far removed from John's gospel of faith alone. If **meno** means "believe," a works gospel would be taught, and the verse would be reduced to the absurdity "He who believes in Me believes in Me." And further Jesus would then be saying, "If you believe in Me, and I believe in you, you will bear much fruit." This is hardly a sensible statement! Furthermore, even if one could successfully argue that **meno** in one place could mean "believe," one cannot allow a possible meaning in one place to govern the clear meaning in so many others!

So the first condition of abiding is to believe on Him.

Other conditions for remaining in fellowship with Him are mentioned:

1.   We must love our brothers (1 Jn. 2:10).
2.   We must walk as He walked (1 Jn. 2:6).
3.   We must be strong in the faith (1 Jn. 2:14).
4.   We must do the will of God (1 Jn. 2:17).
5.   We must hold to the truth we learned when we first became Christians (1 Jn. 2:24).
6.   We must not hate our brother (1 Jn. 3:15).
7.   We must keep His commandments (1 Jn. 3:24; Jn. 15:10).
8.   We must love one another (1 Jn. 4:12).
9.   We must publicly confess Christ (1 Jn. 4:15).

The rewards for meeting all of these conditions are great. First, we will truly be His disciples (Jn. 8:31). But most of all, such a life will enable us to stand before Him with confidence when He returns (1 Jn. 2:28).

"No murderer," John says, "has eternal life remaining in him." "Eternal life" in this epistle is metonymy for Jesus Christ. The phrase is precisely the same as saying "No murderer has Jesus Christ abiding in him." As discussed above, this means, "No murderer remains in fellowship with Jesus Christ." This is made clear by the following passages (3:17, 24) which teach that, in order to "remain in Him," we must keep His commandments. Only if we love one another, does the love of God "remain in us" (1 Jn. 4:12). In order for the love of God to remain in us, it must first have been in us to begin with. As elsewhere, "remain" never signifies the initiatory event of saving faith but the enduring relationship of walking in fellowship. The very meaning of the word "remain" implies staying in a position already obtained or entered into and not entering into a position or state for the first time. If a nonbeliever outside of Christ should ask, "What must I do to be saved," only another gospel would answer, "Remain in Christ." We remain in

---

[55]Edwin A. Blum, "John," in *BKC,* 2:325.

Christ (i.e., remain in fellowship) by keeping His commandments **after** we have been saved.

God remains in fellowship with us only if we love one another (1 Jn. 4:12). We become Christians, however, by faith alone. It is through the experience of the Holy Spirit that we enjoy the fellowship of the Father and He with us (4:13). It is literally "out of" (Gk. **ek**) the Spirit that we enjoy this relationship. The Holy Spirit is the source from which we draw to sustain fellowship. This precise wording occurs in 1 Jn. 3:24:

> *And the one who keeps His commandments abides in Him, and He in him. And we know that He abides in us, by the Spirit whom He has given us.*

The condition of remaining in fellowship with Christ is obedience. We know of this fellowship "out of the Spirit He has given us." The Holy Spirit is the energizing source behind this obedience. This same Spirit not only stimulates love and obedience but also public confession of Christ (4:15). A refusal to confess Christ results in Christ no longer remaining in fellowship with us or us with Him.

In 2 Jn. 8-9 the apostle declares:

> *Watch yourselves, that you might not lose what we have accomplished, but that you may receive a full reward.*

> *Anyone who goes too far and does not abide* ["remain"] *in the teaching of Christ, does not have God; the one who abides in the teaching, he has both the Father and the Son* (NASB).

Because "abide" means "remain" or "continue," it is evident that there are those who were once in the teaching of Christ who did not continue in that teaching. John is following up on his warning in the preceding verse about the danger of losing their rewards at the judgment seat of Christ. When he says such a believer does not "have God" when he falls into deviation from the teaching of Christ, he is not saying that he is not regenerate. He simply means that God was not involved in this defection from pure doctrine. There is no exegetical evidence of which this writer is aware that "having God" ever means "be saved" in Johannine literature. It is roughly equivalent to our saying, "He has [a walk with] God" or "He has God with him in this." It is functionally the same as having "eternal life remain in him" which, for John means, "having Jesus Christ remain in fellowship with him" (1 Jn. 3:15).

It is simply not possible, therefore, to equate abiding with believing. Abiding involves all these works such as obedience, avoiding hatred, having love, public confession of Christ, remaining strong in the faith, holding on to truth first learned, and continuing in His word. Whatever belief is, it is not conditioned upon works, nor does it consist of works (Gal. 3:5).

The Analogy of the Vine and the Branches

The analogy of the vine and the branches is therefore intended to signify some kind of relationship to Christ. There are three possibilities: (1) the relationship a professing Christian sustains to Christ; (2) the relation any Christian sustains to Christ; (3) a relation which only mature and growing Christians sustain with Christ. Experimental Predestinarians favor the first; Arminians the second, and the Partakers, the third. As argued above, (1) is impossible and (2) misinterprets the sense of "in Me." That phrase refers not to organic union but to fellowship. Not all Christians walk in fellowship with Christ at all times. The analogy signifies not an organic connection, but a dynamic fellowship. A branch "in Me" is not portraying an analogy of a branch organically connected to Him as a literal branch is organically connected to a vine, rather it is portraying a branch deriving its sustenance from Christ and living in fellowship with Him (as a literal branch derives sustenance from a literal vine). This is proven by the fact that "in Me" means "in fellowship with Me." The analogy is used to illustrate the "in Me" relationship.

In the NIV verse 2 says these branches will be "taken away." This consequence has been understood in at least four different ways.

They are lifted up and encouraged. R. K. Harrison argues that the word translated "takes away" (Gk. **airo**) is best rendered "lifts up" as it is ten times in John's gospel.[56] He says, contrary to Laney,[57] that it was a common practice to lift fallen vines with meticulous care and allow them to heal.[58] The writer has observed this practice himself in the vineyards behind his home in Austria. If that is the meaning, then a fruitless branch in fellowship with Christ is lifted up to put it into a position of fruit bearing. There is no contradiction with v. 6. There we are told that a branch which does not abide is "cast out" (Gk. **ekballo**, a different word). This would suggest that the heavenly vinedresser first encourages the branches and lifts them in the sense of loving care to enable them to fruit. If after this encouragement, they do not remain in fellowship with Him and bear fruit, they are then cast out. So v. 6 and v. 2 do not have to be parallel.

We have here in v. 2 a divine promise that every unfruitful Christian who is not bearing fruit and **yet is walking in fellowship** will receive divine encouragement. It is possible for a true Christian to be in fellowship with God and yet

---

[56]E.g., 5:8-12; 10:18.

[57]Laney, p. 59.

[58]R. K. Harrison, "Vine," in *NISBE,* 4:986.

not be bearing fruit for an extended period of time. The Puritans called it "the dark night of the soul," and their practical treatises on sanctification are full of discussions of how to trust God during this time.

They lose salvation. A second possible destiny of the branches is that they lose their salvation. This is the Arminian view. However, even if the verb means "remove" and not "lift up," salvation and its loss is not in view. The figure of the vine and the branches does not signify regeneration but fellowship. To cease to abide in Him does not mean to cease to be organically in Him but only to fail to remain in fellowship. Thus, the removal here would simply refer to the removal from fellowship of the Christian who fails to obey.

Separation from superficial connection with Christ. A third possibility is that the removal refers to the separation of professing Christians from a superficial connection with Christ. This is Laney's view.[59] But a branch connected to the vine is an illustration of the believer in fellowship with Christ. If "in Me" means to be in fellowship with Me, as Laney says,[60] then the branch connected with the vine must be a branch in fellowship with the vine, a true, not merely professing, Christian. This raises the fundamental problem with Experimental Predestinarian exegesis. To whom is this addressed? Experimental Predestinarians say that the fruitless branches are only professing Christians. On this view the passage has no direct application to the disciples. Rather, Laney argues, it is intended to give them instruction concerning those to whom they would minister and who did not bear fruit.[61] Yet the text itself gives every evidence that in its entirety it was addressed to the disciples to tell them how they could bear fruit in their lives. He tells them in v. 7, "If you [the disciples, not those to whom they would one day minister] abide in Me and My words abide in you, ask whatever you wish, and it will be given to you. This is to My Father's glory that you bear much fruit, showing yourselves to be My disciples." He goes on speaking of the fact that He loves them as the Father loves Him and that He wants them to complete His joy, etc. (15:9-16).

He wants His followers to bear fruit and in this way "be" (aorist, middle subjunctive of **ginomai**) disciples (15:8). The basic difference between **eimi**, "be," and **ginomai**, "come into being," is that the latter suggests a coming into being in contrast to just being. Thus, in the act of fruit bearing, we come into being as a disciple. This is difficult to translate clearly in English, The sense is: when we bear fruit, in that act of bearing fruit, we are becoming a disciple (or better, "proving to be" [NASB]) His disciples.

---

[59]Laney, p. 61.

[60]Ibid., p. 64. Laney calls it being in the sphere of Christ and under His influence.

[61]Ibid.

When Jesus says in v. 3, "You are clean already through the word which I have spoken to you," He is not, contrary to Laney, contrasting the disciples with those in the preceding verse who are only professing Christians. In v. 2 there are two kinds of Christians mentioned: those who are in fellowship with Him who have not yet produced fruit and those in fellowship with Him who have fruit. The former need to be lifted up by the vinedresser so they can become fruitful, and the latter need to be pruned (Gk. **kathaireo**) so that they will bear more fruit. The disciples have already been "pruned" (they are "clean," same Gk. word, **kathaireo**) through the word which was spoken to them. The disciples are now given instruction on how they, not those to whom they will minister, can continue to bear fruit. They will continue to bear fruit if they remain in fellowship with Him (i.e., abide in Him):

> *Abide in Me, and I in you. As the branch cannot bear fruit of itself, unless it abides in the vine, so neither can you* [not those to whom the disciples will minister]*, unless you abide in Me* (15:4 NASB).

There is a warning and an encouragement here to the disciples. In their desire to maintain the doctrine of eternal security and salvage their doctrine of perseverance, Experimental Predestinarians have been forced into the exegetically difficult position that the disciples of Christ are not the subject of the warning. Indeed, this is the only way they can maintain the idea of the saints' perseverance and the truth of eternal security at the same time. If the passage is addressed to true believers, then it must be possible for true believers to be fruitless and be cast into the "fire," as the Arminians and Partakers maintain.

It would seem obvious that it is possible for a Christian through disobedience to remove himself from Christ's influence and enablement. That seems to be the danger the Lord is warning about in this very passage. But that in no way implies that the one being warned is not a Christian. In fact, since he is commanded to remain in that sphere of influence and enablement, we may safely assume he was in it already and hence was regenerate.

Divine discipline in time and loss of rewards. The final possibility is that the destiny of these unfruitful branches is divine discipline in time, possible physical death, and loss of rewards at the judgment seat of Christ. This was the view propounded by Lewis Sperry Chafer and fits the context well.[62] The consequences of the failure of a true Christian to abide in Christ are now explicitly set forth:

> *If anyone does not abide in Me, he is thrown away as a branch, and dried up; and they gather them, and cast them into the fire, and they are burned* (Jn. 15:6 NASB).

---

[62]Lewis Sperry Chafer, *Systematic Theology*, 8 vols. (Dallas: Dallas Seminary Press, 1948), 7:4.

The Lord is saying that, if a true Christian does not remain in fellowship with Him, he will be thrown away (Gk. **ekballo**, "cast out"). The reference is to the severance of branch from the vine. As argued above, the point of the figure of the vine and the branches is not to portray organic connection but enablement and fellowship. This casting out, then, is not from salvation but from fellowship. The result is that these branches, the carnal Christians, are cast into the fire.

To what does the fire refer? Fire is a common symbol in the Bible for the judgment of God's people in time (e.g., Isa. 26:11). Only rarely and exceptionally is it associated with the fires of hell. They are therefore cast out of fellowship with Christ and into divine judgment in time. It is likely that John has an additional thought in mind, that all God's buildings (i.e., believers, 1 Cor. 3:9) will be submitted to fire at the judgment seat of Christ (1 Cor. 3:15). It seems like mere quibbling to say that in 1 Cor. 3:15 the fire is applied to believer's works and in Jn. 15:6 it is applied to the believer himself and therefore that Jn. 15:6 and 1 Cor. 3:15 could not refer to the same event.[63] Paul says that the believer is the building and that the building is built up with various kinds of building materials and that the fire is applied to the building. The apostle obviously sees an intimate connection between the believer and his work. To apply the fire of judgment to the believer is the same as applying it to his work. Indeed the believer's works are simply a metonymy for the believer himself.[64]

Conclusion

Jn. 15 tells us that when a believer is in fellowship with Christ but is not bearing fruit due to immaturity or injury, our Lord lovingly lifts him up so that he can bear fruit. The believer who is in fellowship with Christ and who is bearing fruit is pruned so that he can bear more fruit. The analogy of the vine and the branches signifies fellowship with Christ, not organic connection with Him. The believer who does not remain in fellowship through disobedience is cast out in judgment, withers spiritually, and faces severe divine discipline in time and loss of reward at the judgment seat of Christ. There is nothing in this passage which demands that he loses his salvation. Neither is there anything here to suggest that all believers will always bear fruit. It is only the believer who remains in fellowship who will bear fruit.

---

[63]Laney, p. 61.

[64]A metonymy is a figure of speech consisting of the use of the name of one thing for that of another of which it is an attribute or with which it is associated.

John 17:12

Arminian Robert Shank argues that even the keeping power of Jesus Christ cannot keep a person who does not want to be kept.[65]

While I was with them, I was keeping them in Thy name which Thou hast given Me: and I guarded them, and not one of them perished but the son of perdition, that the scripture might be fulfilled (Jn. 17:12).

Shank wants the word "but" (Gk. **ei me**) to mean that the one who was excepted, Judas, was part of the group which Jesus was keeping, i.e., one of those "Thou hast given Me." This is certainly a possible interpretation. However, this phrase in Greek does not always imply this. For example,

But I say to you in truth there were many widows in Israel in the days of Elijah, when the sky was shut up for three years and six months, when a great famine came over all the land;

*and yet Elijah was sent to none of them, but (*ei me*) only to Zarephath, in the land of Sidon, to a woman who was a widow.*

*And there were many lepers in Israel in the time of Elisha the prophet; and none of them was cleansed, but (*ei me*) only Naaman the Syrian* (Lk. 4:25-26 NASB).

Sellers has pointed out that the widow of Zarephath is not part of the group called the widows of Israel and Naaman was not part of the lepers of Israel. Neither was Judas one of those given to Christ and being kept by Him![66] The group is "those whom Thou has given Me," and the exception is Judas, who was not one of that group. This is proven from Jn. 18:9 (NASB):

That the word might be fulfilled which He spoke, "Of those whom Thou hast given Me I lost not one.

It is obvious from this that in Jn. 17:12 Judas was considered an exception, not included in the group "Thou hast given Me." Judas therefore did not have salvation and then subsequently lose it.

---

[65]Shank, p. 132.
[66]Sellers, pp. 132-33.

Chapter 18

Conditional Security: The Letters of Paul

Romans 6:15-23

Arminians are impressed with the commands to continue to present our bodies as servants of righteousness (Rom. 6:19). They recognize that the consequence of failure to do so is death: "For the wages of sin is death, but the free gift of God is eternal life in Christ Jesus our Lord" (Rom. 6:23). Death here is contrasted with "eternal life." In an earlier chapter[1] the precise meaning of that term was considered at length, and those results may now be applied here. The term "eternal life" is used four times in Romans (2:7; 5:21; 6:22, 23). In two cases eternal life is viewed from the standpoint of abundant life, an enriched experience of life which was begun at regeneration. That rich experience of life is conditioned upon our obedience:

> *Who will* **render to every man according to his deeds***; to those who by perseverance in doing good seek for glory and honor and immortality, eternal life* (Rom. 6:7 NASB).

> *But now having been freed from sin and enslaved to God, you derive your benefit,* **resulting in sanctification, and the outcome, eternal life** (Rom. 6:22 NASB).

The outcome of sanctification, a gradual process involving our faith and obedience, is eternal life. The other reference to the term is in 5:21 where Paul says that "grace might reign through righteousness to eternal life." This may refer to the initial inception of eternal life at regeneration, not the enriched experience of it due to faith and obedience. However, it could also refer to the reign of the believer, an experience beyond regeneration.

Throughout the book of Romans Paul uses the terms "life" and "death" in various ways. Normally "life" refers to a rich present experience of Christ and not

---

[1]See chapter 7.

specifically regeneration. Conversely, "death" is commonly its opposite, spiritual impoverishment, and not hell:

> *For if by the transgression of the one, death reigned through the one, much more those who receive the abundance of grace and of the gift of righteousness will reign in life through the One, Jesus Christ* (Rom. 5:17 NASB).

The reign of death is a reference to the fact that all men physically die, even those who have not disobeyed the law because they have not yet heard of it (Rom. 5:14). In contrast to the reign of death, something "much more" is available to the believer, a "reign in life." If all that was meant was regeneration or resurrection, then a mere balance with the reign of death would be referred to, and not something "much more." It is for this reason that many expositors interpret the reign in life not just with regenerate life but with the rulership in the future age, the "consummation of [our] redemption in the Messianic kingdom in the world to come."[2] Denney parallels this reference to Paul's famous statement:[3]

> *If we endure, we shall also reign with Him; if we deny Him He also will deny us* (2 Tim. 2:12 NASB).

It is likely that Paul refers to the same reign in life, similarly conditioned upon our perseverance in suffering with Him in Rom. 8:17:

> *And if children, heirs also, heirs of God, and* **fellow heirs with Christ if indeed we suffer with Him.**

In Rom. 8:17 Paul makes explicit that this reign in life is contingent upon our sharing with Christ in His sufferings. It was not germane to his point of stressing the "much more" made available to the believer through the death of Christ in Rom. 5:17.

In Rom. 6:4 "life" is "newness of life." He refers not just to regeneration but to the full experience of a "walk" in newness of life.

The life and death contrast is continued in Rom. 7. In his pre-Christian days Paul viewed himself as "alive" spiritually (Rom. 7:9), but when the full implications of the law dawned upon him, he was defeated with guilt and "died" in the sense of depression and defeat in his spiritual struggle. He certainly did not die in the sense of "go to hell" for all men are born dead in that regard.

---

[2]James Denney, "St. Paul's Epistle to the Romans," in *EGT,* 2:630.

[3]Ibid. Ryrie marks the word "reign" in Rom. 5:17 and makes a marginal reference to 2 Tim. 2:12 (Charles Caldwell Ryrie, *The Ryrie Study Bible: New American Standard Translation* [Chicago: Moody Press, 1978], p. 1709).

That "life" refers to "abundant life," and not just regeneration, is also indicated in 8:6 where it is associated with "peace" in "life and peace."

When the apostle affirms in Rom. 8:13 that,

> *if you live according to the flesh you will die; but if by the Spirit you put to death the deeds of the body, you will live* (NKJV),

he is speaking of "life" and "death" in terms of abundant life and spiritual impoverishment, consistent with his predominant usage in the epistle.[4]

No doubt James had a similar idea in mind when he wrote to those born-again Christians in whom the Word had been "implanted":

> *But each one is tempted when he is carried away and enticed by his own lust. Then when lust has conceived, it gives birth to sin; and when sin is accomplished, it brings forth death* (Jas. 1:14-15 NASB).

That James is talking to born-again Christians is obvious. And it is equally obvious that these born-again Christians can in some sense die. The "death" they might potentially experience from a failure to be "doers of the word" is the death of spiritual impoverishment.

It is in this way that contextually "eternal life" and "death" are to be understood in Rom. 6:23. The result of sin in the life of a Christian is spiritual impoverishment (7:15-25). A non-Christian is already dead in trespasses and sin (Eph. 2:1). The wage earned by sin secures the same result as that obtained by the man who lives according to the flesh (8:13), spiritual failure, but in no case is this to suggest that spiritual failure is to be equated with loss of justification. Arminians often assume that "death" means "go to hell" or "lose salvation," but there is no necessary exegetical evidence for this conclusion. In fact, the context argues for "life" being abundant life and "death" referring to spiritual impoverishment. Death cannot mean "go to hell." The apostle emphatically declares just the opposite:

> *For I am convinced that neither death, nor life, nor angels, nor principalities, nor things present, nor things to come, nor powers, nor height, nor depth, nor any other created thing, shall be able to separate us from the love of God, which is in Christ Jesus our Lord* (Rom. 8:38-39 NASB).

---

[4]We do not deny that Paul uses "life" in the sense of regeneration also, only that this is not his normal meaning in the sanctification context of Rom. 5-8. See 5:10 and 18 for the only two places in Romans where life probably means regeneration.

Eternal life is indeed a "free gift." But the growth and full enjoyment of that free gift is the product of faith and obedience (i.e., sanctification, 6:22) and "persevering in doing good" (2:7).

Romans 11:22

In Rom. 11:11 Paul makes a perplexing statement:

Again I ask: Did they stumble so as to fall beyond recovery? Not at all! Rather, because of their transgression, salvation has come to the Gentiles to make Israel envious.

This is a perplexing statement because of the widely held equation of salvation with final deliverance from hell. Such a meaning of salvation here results in the absurd teaching that no Gentiles were delivered from hell until Israel had first been offered such a deliverance and then rejected it. But salvation here does not mean deliverance from hell but rather, "riches for the world."

But if their transgression means riches for the world, and their loss means riches for the Gentiles, how much greater riches will their fullness bring! (Rom. 11:12).

Paul is speaking here of the national promises to Israel, and not of the individual redemption of particular Jews or Gentiles. What is in view is the "greater riches" of joint participation with Messiah in the final destiny of man! The natural branches, Israel, were broken off of the tree of Abrahamic blessing. This means they forfeited their participation in the promises to Abraham. It does not refer to being broken off from heaven but from "riches."

But unnatural branches, the Gentiles, were grafted into the place of Abrahamic blessing, the kingdom rule. This is Paul's teaching in Ephesians when he reveals that Gentiles have been made "fellow heirs" of the promises (Eph. 3:6 ; cf. 2:11-22).

In the last chapter of Acts Paul, after concluding that the Jews were not open to the kingdom of God (Acts 28:23), concludes that the kingdom of God has been taken from the Jews: "Let it be known to you therefore, that this salvation of God has been sent to the Gentiles; they will also listen" (Acts 28:28). He evidently has Ps. 98 in mind:

The LORD has made known His salvation;
He has revealed His righteousness in the sight of the nations.
He has remembered His lovingkindness and His faithfulness to the house of Israel (98:2-3).

The psalm goes on to describe the rule of the coming Messiah:

> *For He is coming to judge the earth;*
> *He will judge the world with righteousness,*
> *And the peoples with equity* (Ps. 98:9 NASB).

The "salvation" of the Lord is not, in this passage, deliverance from hell but the establishment of the messianic kingdom.

These two groups, Jews and Gentiles, who were formerly enemies, have been reconciled in one body in Christ. The enmity between Gentiles and Jews due to the Gentile rejection of the law, has been removed by eliminating the law so that "He himself is our peace, who has made the two one and has destroyed the barrier, the dividing wall of hostility, by abolishing in his flesh the law with its commandments and regulations" (Eph. 2:14-15). Now those who were "aliens" and "far off" and "strangers to the covenants of promise" are brought near (2:12).

Paul refers to this same reconciliation between Jew and Gentile in Rom. 11:15, when he says:

> *For if their rejection be the reconciliation of the world* [removal of enmity between Jew and Gentile], *what will their acceptance be but life from the dead.*

If, due to Jewish national rejection of Messiah, the Gentiles were grafted into the place of blessing, think what will happen when the Jews return to the Messiah. It will be like "life from the dead," magnificent universal righteousness in the coming thousand-year kingdom of God.

Now drawing a lesson from the national loss of Israel and national gain by the Gentiles, Paul applies this in personal terms to individual Gentiles. He warns them that just as the Jewish nation was "cut off" nationally, so they too can be "cut off" individually:

> *Behold then the kindness and severity of God; to those who fell, severity, but to you, God's kindness, if you continue in His kindness; otherwise you also will be cut off.*

> *And they also, if they do not continue in their unbelief, they will be grafted in, for God is able to graft them in again* (Rom. 11:22-23).

There is a real danger here. An individual Gentile can be "cut off" just as national Israel was. But from what was national Israel "cut off"? Certainly not from heaven, because heaven was never offered on national grounds, only individual. One did not go to heaven because he was born a Jew but because he believed. Rather, national Israel was temporarily cut off from their rights to the covenants and promises. Instead of fulfilling their destiny, they are nationally under discipline until the fullness of the Gentiles has come in. Then all Israel will be "saved," i.e., restored to her privileged place of rulership over the millennial earth.

The danger then to which Paul refers is that we may individually, like Israel did nationally, forfeit our opportunity to share in that great future salvation, the kingdom of God, joint rulership with the Messiah in the future reign of the servant kings. The wild olive tree from which we might be cut off and onto which the Gentiles have been grafted is not heaven. It is the privilege of sharing in the Abrahamic promises made to Israel regarding the great land and the great nation. Forfeiture of personal salvation is the furthest thing from Paul's mind. Rather, he worries about their loss of reward.

"God's kindness," His inclusion of us in this great future purpose, is contingent upon our continuing in His kindness (11:22), in other words, upon our perseverance to the end of life. Paul is under no illusion that this perseverance is inevitable, for he warns them of the consequences of failure. They will be "cut off." The Lord Jesus spoke of dead or useless branches being cut off from fruit bearing and communion in Jn. 15 (cf. Jn. 15:2, 6). The writer of Hebrews warns his readers that we are partakers, sharers in the final destiny of man, only if we "hold fast the beginning of our assurance firm until the end" (Heb. 3:14). Experimental Predestinarian exegesis of this passage is severely deficient. In their equation of the wild olive tree with heaven they give the argument away to those of an Arminian perspective. The proof, they say, that a man is truly born again is that he "continues in His kindness." The problem is, however, that, if he does not, he is cut off the wild olive tree. To be cut off from it obviously implies that one was once part of it. In other words, he had salvation and lost it, which is precisely the view of many Arminian interpreters. However, both Arminians and Experimental Predestinarians have missed the point of the context, which has nothing to do with gaining and losing heaven. It has to do with gaining and losing "salvation"joint participation with the Messiah in the rulership of the coming kingdom.

1 Corinthians 3:16-17

In 1 Cor. 3:16-17 the apostle Paul declares:

Don't you know that you yourselves are God's temple and that God's Spirit lives in you? If anyone destroys God's temple, God will destroy him; for God's temple is sacred, and you are that temple.

Some have felt that these verses suggest that there may be some sin that a believer could commit which would result in the loss of his salvation. The sin in question is the destruction of God's temple. Arguing from the use of "temple" in

1 Cor. 6:19, where it refers to individual Christians, it is thought that the sin referred to in 1 Cor. 3:16 is the sin of suicide!

However, the "temple" being discussed in 1 Cor. 3 is the local assembly of believers, not the individual Christian. He has been speaking in the context of the building up of that local assembly by various ministers (3:5-8), Paul, Apollos, and Peter. He is concerned about the divisions in Corinth and how the building up of this local assembly is progressing. He says:

> *For we are God's fellow workers; you are God's field;* **God's building.** *By the grace God has given me, I laid a foundation as an expert* **builder,** *and someone else is building on it. But each one should be careful how he* **builds** (1 Cor. 3:9-10).

He gives a warning, "Be careful how you build this building." The assembly was rife with divisions and carnality. These fights and lawsuits among Christians were disrupting the unity of the believers and threatening the destruction of the "temple," the building, the local church there in Corinth. The city was full of pagan temples, but the local body of believers was the "temple of God." In 6:19 he tells them that their "bodies" are the temple of God. Here it says that they are as a group the temple of God. Scofield, for example, observes:

> *The temple here is the Church, the body of Christ, as distinguished from the temple in 1 Cor. 6:19, which is the physical body of the individual Christian.*[5]

The "temple" in 6:19 is the individual Christian. The temple in 1 Cor. 3 is the building which Paul and the other laborers have been building and which is threatened with division due to the carnal Christians in its membership.

This view of the "temple" is widely accepted because it flows naturally out of the context. For example, Robertson and Plummer have observed, "There is but one Temple, embodied equally truly in the whole Church, in the local Church, and in the individual Christian; the local Church is meant here."[6]

While it is true that each individual Christian is a temple of God, the passage is speaking of the local body. "The context speaks rather in favour of the second meaning, since Paul is addressing the Church as such."[7] Similarly, Ryrie

---

[5]C. I. Scofield, *The Scofield Reference Bible* (New York: Oxford University Press, 1967), p. 1200.

[6]Archibald T. Robertson, *A Critical and Exegetical Commentary on the First Epistle of St. Paul to the Corinthians* (Edinburgh: T. & T. Clark, 1914), p. 66.

[7]Frederick Louis Godet, *Commentary on First Corinthians* (Grand Rapids: Kregel, 1977), p. 192.

concurs, "Here the local church is viewed as a temple of God inhabited by the Spirit; in 1 Cor 6:19 the individual is a temple of God."[8]

The sin of destroying the temple of God is therefore not the sin of suicide but refers to the destruction of the local body of believers. This "destruction" was a real danger in Corinth as the assembly was divided and full of jealousy and quarreling and were behaving like non-Christians:

> *You are still worldly. For since there is jealousy and quarreling among you, are you not worldly? Are you not acting like mere men? For when one says, "I follow Paul," and another, "I follow Apollos," are you not mere men?* (1 Cor. 3:3-4).

Their divisive party spirit was threatening the destruction of the church, the temple of God in Corinth. What are the consequences? Paul solemnly warns, "If anyone destroys God's temple, God will destroy him; for God's temple is sacred, and you are that temple."

Any Christian whose actions result in the disunity and ultimate dissolution of a local church can only face "destruction" from God. To what does this "destruction" refer? In 1 Cor. 5:5 we read of Paul delivering a sinning brother over to Satan for the "destruction of the flesh," i.e., physical death, "in order that his spirit might be saved in the day of the Lord Jesus." It is also possible that Paul has already explained himself in the preceding verses: loss of all his life work at the judgment seat of Christ!

> *If any man builds on this foundation using gold, silver, costly stones, wood, hay or straw, his work will be shown for what it is, because the Day will bring it to light. It will be revealed with fire, and the fire will test the quality of each man's work. If what he has built survives, he will receive his reward. If it is burned up, he will suffer loss;* **he himself will be saved***, but only as one escaping through the flames* (1 Cor. 3:12-15).

The destruction facing the man who destroys the unity of a local church is not eternal. It refers either to the sin unto physical death (1 Cor. 5:5) or the forfeiture of his eternal reward. In any event "he himself will be saved," but all that he has built has been of wood, hay, and straw and will be consumed with fire, destroyed, at the judgment seat of Christ. As a result he will be disinherited by his coming King.

In conclusion, there is no justification in this passage for the teaching that a believer can commit some sin, even suicide, which can in any way affect his eternal destiny. That eternal destiny is secure because it does not depend upon

---

[8]Ryrie, *The Ryrie Study Bible*, p. 1732.

what we do but upon what Christ has done for us. Jesus declared that He will lose "none" of those whom the Father has given to Him (Jn. 6:39-40). If we have "looked to the Son and believed," we have eternal life, and Christ will never lose any of us!

1 Corinthians 8:11

The weak brother can "perish." The same word is used in Jn. 3:16 for eternal damnation. Yet it seems foolish to believe that Paul is teaching that a man can lose his position in Christ because he came under the influence of a carnal Christian. The Greek word **apollumi** means "to come to nought or to lose." A man could lose heaven or a temporal place of usefulness or reward at the judgment seat of Christ. In fact, Jesus uses it in connection with losing one's reward in Mt. 10:42. Paul's meaning, expressed in contemporary language, would be something like "shattered, deeply hurt, crushed." The weaker brother is so shaken by observing the fellow Christian do the "unthinkable" that for a while, at least, he is of no use to Christ. It could even mean that he becomes so demoralized that in the end he forfeits any possibility of reward for himself (Rom. 14:15). It does not mean that he loses his salvation.

1 Corinthians 15:1-2

Paul seems to warn the Corinthians that there is something conditional about their salvation when he says:

> *Now I make known to you brethren, the Gospel which I preached to you, which also you received, in which also you stand, by which also you are saved,* **if you hold fast the word which I preached to you,** *unless you believed in vain* (NASB).

Arminians understandably find evidence here for their doctrine of conditional security, and Experimental Predestinarians find evidence for their view of perseverance in holiness. Other interpretations are possible.

The phrase "hold fast" can, according to Arndt and Gingrich, also be rendered "to take into one's possession," or simply "to possess."[9] In extra biblical Greek the meaning "possess" is quite common.[10] It is used this way in several places in the New Testament including 2 Cor. 6:10 and 1 Cor. 7:30.[11]

---

[9]AG, p. 424.

[10]See MM, p. 336, for numerous illustrations.

[11]See also Lk. 14:9; Acts 27:40

It seems to have a wide range of meanings, and the context would have to determine the precise sense here. If it means "possess," then the verse would mean "you are saved if you possess the word I have preached to you," that is, "if you take the gospel into your possession," referring to the original act of saving faith.

It may be significant that Paul uses the first-class condition when he says "if." The first-class condition assumes the truth of a proposition for the sake of argument. In contexts where the proposition actually is true, it can be rendered "since." If that is the case here, which is likely, then Paul would be saying, "By this gospel you are saved since you possess the word which I spoke unto you." The only reason they would not be saved would be if they had believed in vain, namely, if the resurrection was not really true.

Sellers suggests another interpretation. He correctly points out that salvation has three tenses in the New Testament. The past tense refers to our salvation from sin's penalty (2 Pet. 3:15). The present tense refers to our salvation from sin's power, the process of sanctification by which God daily conforms us to the image of Christ (2 Cor. 1:6). The future tense speaks of the believer's deliverance from the presence of sin at the rapture or death (Rom. 13:11). Sellers suggests that 1 Cor. 15:1-2 refers to the present tense of salvation, our deliverance from sin's power. This deliverance is conditioned upon our continuing to hold fast to Christ.[12]

Galatians 5:4

It is quite common for people to fear that they have "fallen from grace." For some this is the same thing as losing salvation. However, usually people who use the term this way are only vaguely aware of where it came from and to what it originally referred.

In order to understand this phrase correctly, we must first consider the background of the book of Galatians. Paul was dealing with a group of false teachers who had greatly disturbed the faith of his readers. They apparently taught that salvation was to be found by means of faith in Christ coupled with keeping of the law. They seemed to have a particular fixture on the rite of circumcision. The danger his readers faced was not loss of salvation or even lapse into immorality. Rather, it was a return of the bondage of the law.

It is clear that falling from grace is not a reference to loss of salvation. If it was, Paul would have mentioned something about hell or loss of heaven. The only thing Paul stresses is that they are about to return to a "yoke of slavery."

---

[12]C. Norman Sellers, *Election and Perseverance* (Miami Springs, FL: Schoettle, 1987), p. 119.

Even though this passage does not even refer to salvation and its loss, the key phrase of Gal. 5:4, "fallen from grace," has often been misunderstood to teach that regeneration can be lost:

You have been severed from Christ, you who are seeking to be justified by law; you have fallen from grace (NASB).

However, nowhere in this context does Paul say that loss of salvation is possible. Rather, he is trying to prevent the return to a law system as a way of life.

Christ will be of no benefit to you. When Paul warns them thus (Gal. 5:2), he is simply telling them that their Christian lives will be back under the legalistic system of the Mosaic code from which they have been liberated. The whole context, indeed the whole thrust of the epistle, is that the "benefit" in view is the freedom of the Christian man, walking under the grace way of life. To return to the law system forfeits the freedom from law which Christ's death accomplished. It does not forfeit salvation.

You have been severed from Christ. This phrase is literally rendered from Greek as something like "you have been made to receive no effect from Christ, you who are attempting to be justified by law." But what "effect" is he speaking of, sanctification or justification? The following verse presents a righteousness which is to be waited for and which comes through the ministry of the Holy Spirit. Clearly, a moral, and not a forensic, righteousness is anticipated. Thus, sanctification is the effect which they will not receive in v. 4. To return to the law way of life results in their receiving none of the sanctifying effects of the ministry of the Holy Spirit. It is in this sense that they are "severed from Christ." They are in danger of being severed from the sanctifying effects of a relationship with Him, and not from a saving relationship.

You have fallen from grace. It is doubtful that the word "grace" (Gk. **charis**) is ever used in the New Testament of the "state of salvation."[13] A fall from the state of salvation is not necessarily in view. Regardless, two different ways of living the Christian life are being contrasted in Gal. 5, not two differing eternal states. To "fall from grace" is to fall from the grace way of living the Christian life and into a lower, legal way of living it. What has Paul been contrasting? Grace and law. Therefore, to fall from grace is to fall into law, not into damnation.

---

[13]A possible exception is Rom. 5:2.

Colossians 1:23

Both Arminians and Experimental Predestinarians often appeal to this passage in support of their positions:

Yet He has now reconciled you in His fleshly body through death, in order to present you before Him holy and blameless and beyond reproach--if indeed you continue in the faith firmly established and steadfast, and not moved away from the hope of the gospel that you have heard (Col. 1:22-23).

Arminians find support here for their teaching that salvation can be lost if the Christian fails to continue in the faith. Experimental Predestinarians see this as proving that only those who persevere are truly Christians in the first place. The Partakers see the matter differently.

The focus here is on being presented holy, blameless, and beyond reproach. In addition, Paul is laboring to present the Colossians, truly regenerate people, this way. These are people who were "formerly alienated" from God and who are now reconciled (1:21). They are regenerate people who must "continue in the faith." Nonbelievers do not have faith in which to continue.

At issue here is not arrival in heaven but whether or not we will arrive there holy, blameless, and beyond reproach. This is the goal toward which Paul labors. This is a goal of sanctification, not salvation. Throughout the New Testament we are told of a time in which believers will be presented before their King. At that time some will be revealed as faithful and others as unfaithful servants (Lk. 19:16-19).

Probably the major reason for understanding this passage as referring to salvation is that the words "holy," "blameless," and "without reproach" are taken absolutely. Yet elsewhere in the New Testament the terms are used to describe imperfectly holy and imperfectly blameless Christians. Elders of the church, for example, are to be "beyond reproach" (Ti. 1:6). When the 144,000 stand before the throne, they are declared blameless, not because of their justification but because of their experience. There was no deceit in their mouth (Rev. 14:5). A believer is elsewhere exhorted to be holy in both body and spirit (1 Cor. 7:34). This obviously refers to an imperfect experiential holiness, not absolute justification.

In substantiation of this consider Paul's own explanation of this conditional clause:

That we may present every man complete [Gk. **telios**] *in Christ. And for this purpose also I labor* (Col. 1:28-29 NASB).

Most interpreters of the New Testament understand Paul's use of **telios** to refer to maturity. This is the completeness to which James referred when he said we must endure trials joyfully so that we will be "perfect and complete, lacking in nothing" (Jas. 1:4). This is the "mature man" to which Paul refers elsewhere when he says:

> *Until we all attain to the unity of the faith, and of the knowledge of the Son of God, to a mature* [Gk. **telios**] *man, to the measure of the stature which belongs to the fullness of Christ. As a result we are* **no longer to be children***, tossed here and there by waves, and carried about by every wind of doctrine, . . . but speaking the truth in love, we are* **to grow up in all aspects** *unto Him* (Eph. 4:13-15 NASB).

In other words, he does not strive to produce perfect Christians. He knows that is impossible. But he does labor to produce mature Christians, that is, Christians who are relatively holy, relatively blameless, and relatively beyond reproach.

2 Timothy 2:12

The somewhat measured and rhythmical structure of 2 Tim. 2:11-12 has suggested to many that it is a first-century Christian hymn:

> *It is a trustworthy statement:*
> *For if we died with Him we shall also live with Him;*
> *If we endure, we shall also reign with Him;*
> *If we deny Him, He also will deny us;*
> *If we are faithless, He remains faithful; for He cannot deny Himself*
> (NASB).

Here the promise of reigning with Him, being rewarded in the coming millennial kingdom is in the forefront. Those who are victorious in suffering, who persevere to the end will enjoy a joint participation with Christ in the future reign of the servant kings. This theme is taught extensively in the New Testament (Mt. 16:24-27; 19:28-29; Lk. 22:28-30; Rom. 8:17; Rev. 3:21; 2:26-27).

That this is his meaning is clear from the opening word "for," which points us back to v. 10:

> *I endure all things for the sake of those who are chosen, that they also may obtain the salvation which is in Christ Jesus and with it eternal glory* (NASB).

As discussed in Chapter 6, the word "salvation" does not necessarily mean "final deliverance from hell." Indeed, in this context such a meaning would be most inappropriate. He has been discussing the rewards for perseverance: "If anyone competes in athletics, he is not crowned unless he competes according to the rules" (2 Tim. 2:5). This salvation is an additional crown which comes to those who are already saved, the elect. Contrary to final deliverance from hell, there is uncertainty as to its reception. It is not salvation from hell for which Paul labors on behalf of the elect but that they might also possess "eternal glory," i.e., "receive honor." This is the same as receiving the crown mentioned earlier (2:5). Therefore, to "reign with Him" is the reward, the salvation, the crown promised to those who persevere.

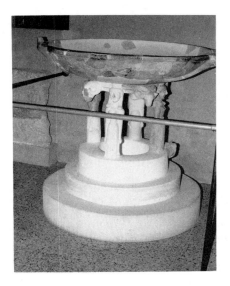

This vase was found in the Temple of Poseidon at Isthmia (6 B. C.). In the Isthmian games held near ancient Corinth, the athletes washed in this basin for ritual purification prior to participating in the games. If a person cheated in the games, his name, his father's name, and the name of his home town was inscribed on the base of the bowl. Paul said there is no reward in the games, unless we "compete according to the rules" (2 Tim. 2:5).

But in what sense can a believer "deny" Him? To deny Christ is the opposite of "enduring" in the preceding phrase. To deny Him then is to fail to persevere in faith to the final hour. The result is that He will "deny us." There is nothing in the context or anywhere else in the New Testament which establishes that his denial of us refers to being excluded from heaven. It is obvious, even though it creates a difficulty for Experimental Predestinarians, that the "we" and "us" refer to true Christians. These regenerate people may actually deny Christ! There is nothing here that says, "This proves they were not Christians in the first place." It is clear that Paul has in mind other warnings made by our Lord to true Christians, such as Mt. 10:33, where the context refers to those who know Christ.

In what sense will Christ deny the believer? That seems to be defined once again by the contrast with the preceding phrase.

> If we endure, we shall also reign with Him;
> If we deny Him, He also will deny us;

If the opposite of enduring is to deny Him, then the opposite of reigning with Him is that He will deny us the privilege of reigning with Him. Christ will deny the unfaithful Christian the reward of reigning with Him. Nothing is said here about loss of salvation.[14]

The Arminians are correct, however, in saying that it is possible for true Christians to deny Christ. This is further brought out in the next phrase when he asserts that it is possible for true Christians to be "faithless." The Greek word is **apisteo** and means either "faithless" or "unbelieving." Yet even when we are like this, "he remains faithful." Paul teaches here that true Christians can become unbelieving but even when this happens, Christ will not be unfaithful to His promises to them of eternal life. As Patrick Fairbairn has observed:

> *Finally* **if we are unbelieving,--apistoumen,** *not merely prove unfaithful in times of trial, shrink from confessing what we inwardly feel to be the truth concerning Him, but, rejecting or quitting our hold of the truth, pass over entirely into the region of unbelief,--if we should thus estrange ourselves from the common ground of faith, still He abides faithful--remaining perfectly true to His declarations and promises, whether we accredit them or not. . . . To disown this, therefore were to deny Himself; and that is impossible.*[15]

An interpretive paraphrase might go something like this:

> If we have died with Him (and every believer has)--
>   then we will live with Him (in His presence after death)
> If we are faithful to Him through the course of our lives
>   then we will also govern with Him in His kingdom.
> If we are unfaithful to Him-
>   then He will deny us the privilege of reigning with Him
> But even if we are unfaithful (forfeiting the privilege of
>   reigning with Him),
> Even then He remains faithful to us - we will live with Him -

---

[14]See Brad McCoy, "Secure Yet Scrutinized--2 Timothy 2:11-13," *JGES* 1 (Autumn 1988): 21-33.

[15]Patrick Fairbairn, *Pastoral Epistles* (T. & T. Clark, 1874; reprint ed., Minneapolis: James and Klock, 1976), p. 341.

For He cannot deny Himself.[16]

Conclusion

It is somewhat ironic that Paul, the apostle of grace, should be interpreted in such a way that salvation could be lost. The great apostle of liberty has given us the clearest possible exposition of the grace of God and the absolute security of the justified. We will explore his teaching on this subject in more detail in chapter 21.

It appears that Arminians, in their zeal to prevent lethargy in the church, have misread Paul. When Paul speaks of death as a possibility for believers, it is not necessary to understand this as always meaning "eternal death." As we argued in this chapter, Romans does not necessarily teach this. Rather, the term "death" can mean "spiritual impoverishment and carnality" or "physical death." We must give careful attention to the context and not assume that eternal death is always in view.

Just as "death" does not always mean eternal death, neither does "salvation" always mean deliverance from hell. When Paul refers to "salvation" coming to the Gentiles in Rom. 11, it is clear that salvation from hell is not in view. Rather, he refers to the future kingdom promised to Israel in the Old Testament. Gentiles can now have a share in this great future. Just as national Israel lost much, so individual Gentiles can also be cut off. But they are not cut off from heaven, only from the privilege of sharing in the fulfillment of the Abrahamic promise, the future reign of the servant kings.

The other passages referred to in this chapter are easily interpreted in ways which are perfectly consistent with the doctrine of eternal security. The famous "if" clause of Col. 1:23 does not cast doubt upon our ultimate arrival in heaven but upon our arriving there mature and pure. When Christ says He will deny the believer who denies Him, He does not mean that that believer will be denied entrance into heaven. He means he will be denied the opportunity of reign with Christ in the kingdom.

Arminians can find little support for their doctrine of conditional security in his writings. In the General Epistles, however, they often feel their case is secure, particularly in the warning of Hebrews, chapter 6. This passage is quoted more than any other by Arminians in defense of their doctrine of conditional security. In the next chapter we want to study this passage in some detail. We will see that the danger of falling away refers not to loss of salvation but, instead, a loss of the opportunity to enter into our inheritance-rest in the coming kingdom.

---

[16]McCoy, p. 33.

Due to the complexity of the passage and the frequency with which it is quoted in defense of the Arminian view, we will devote an entire chapter to it.

Chapter 19

Conditional Security: Hebrews 6

Hebrews 6:4-12

$\mathbf{F}$ew passages have had greater impact on Arminian thinking than this fearful warning about falling away and entering into such a spiritual state that it is impossible to be renewed to repentance. Experimental Predestinarians have exercised great ingenuity in their attempts to maintain the doctrine of final perseverance in the face of the seemingly plain statements confuting it in this passage. Indeed, their exegesis has been widely acknowledged as "theological" rather than "exegetical." If we had only the Arminian and Calvinist views from which to choose, it seems that the Arminian view is much more defensible. However, the Partaker offers another option.

The Exhortation (6:1-3)

> *Therefore let us leave the elementary teachings about Christ and go on to maturity, not laying again the foundation of repentance from acts that lead to death, and of faith in God, instruction about baptisms, the laying on of hands, the resurrection of the dead, and eternal judgment. And God permitting, we will do so* (Heb. 6:1-3).

The opening phrase "therefore" is best taken as referring to the preceding verses (5:11-14) as a whole. Because of their spiritual dullness, they need to commit themselves to learning and applying the truth and to press on to maturity. They need to be able to distinguish "good and evil," and he wants to help them by stretching their minds. He wants them to move from "milk," receiving truth, to "meat," understanding and applying truth.

In the midst of his discussion regarding the Melchizedekian priesthood of the Lord Jesus Christ (Heb. 5:1-10) the author pauses, rebukes them for their spiritual stupor (5:11-14), exhorts them to press on to maturity (6:1-2), warns them about the danger of falling away (6:4-6), illustrates the danger with an analogy from nature (6:7-8), and encourages them regarding confidence in their spiritual status and their need to finish what they have begun (6:9-12). He then returns to his main theme, the Melchizedekian priesthood of Christ in chapter 7.

Now it is plain and almost universally acknowledged that the apostle's burden here is for true Christians to grow to maturity.[1] These people "ought to be teachers," but they are "slow to learn." They "need milk, not solid food." They "live," but they live on "milk." "This is a frequent metaphor in St. Paul, who also contrasts "babes" **(nepios)** with the mature **(teleioi)**, Gal. 4:3; 1 Cor. 2:6; Eph. 4:13,14."[2] Like all these other references in the New Testament, the "babes" here are not non-Christians but "infants" who have refused to grow even though sufficient time for growth to maturity has elapsed. The "maturity" in view is the same as that described in the preceding verses. It is not just spiritual understanding, i.e., advanced mental perception, but it is experiential righteousness and discernment (5:14). The opening word "therefore" connects maturity in 6:1 with 5:14: "But solid food is for the mature, who by constant use have trained themselves to distinguish good from evil." "Therefore," he says, "let us go on to maturity (Gk. **teleioteta**)."

It seems that the apostle here addresses true Christians, as non-Christians cannot grow in their ability to experientially apply the word of righteousness to daily life and have their spiritual senses trained in spiritual discernment.

These true Christians are to go beyond the foundation of repentance and the elementary teachings about Christ and faith in God. But which religious faith is meant, Jewish or Christian? The fact that this is teaching about Christ seems to establish the Christian, and not Jewish background of the six foundation truths.[3] There are three parts to the foundation: repentance, faith, and teaching. The teaching is further defined as consisting of teaching about baptism, laying on of hands, the resurrection, and eternal judgment. He says they have experienced all this. These people have clearly exercised faith toward God (6:1) and have repented and been baptized and are therefore regenerate.

He says, "and God permitting, this we will do." The Greek word order reads "this we will do, God permitting" (6:3). What is it that we will do "God permitting"? The immediate antecedent of "this" is obviously "going on to matu-

---

[1]For example, see Marcus Dodds, "The Epistle to the Hebrews," in *EGT,* 4:292; B. F. Westcott, *The Epistle to the Hebrews* (London: Macmillan, 2d. ed., 1892; reprint ed., Grand Rapids: Eerdmans, 1965), p. 135; F. F. Bruce, *The Epistle to the Hebrews, NICNT,* 14:108.

[2]F. W. Farrar, *The Epistle of Paul the Apostle to the Hebrews, Cambridge Greek Testament for Schools and Colleges* (Cambridge: University Press, 1894), p. 78. See also 1 Cor. 2:6 with 3:1 and 14:20.

[3]R. C. Sauer, "A Critical and Exegetical Reexamination of Hebrews 5:11-6:8" (Ph.D. dissertation, University of Manchester, 1981), pp. 176ff. Sauer has given a full and convincing argument that the foundations of the Christian, not Jewish, faith are in view.

rity."[4] The writer is then telling them that they are to press on to maturity if God permits them to do so. In phrasing it this way, he is preparing them for the warning to follow. God may not permit it just as He did not permit the exodus generation to enter into their inheritance-rest, the land of Canaan![5]

The Warning (6:4-6)

> *[For] it is impossible for those who have once been enlightened, who have tasted the heavenly gift, who have shared in the Holy Spirit, who have tasted the goodness of the word of God and the powers of the coming age, if they fall away, to be brought back to repentance, because to their loss they are crucifying the Son of God all over again and subjecting Him to public disgrace.*

The NIV translation above omits the introductory "for." This word, however, establishes a causal link with what he has just said about going forward to maturity, God permitting. What is the precise nature of this link? It appears to refer back to the phrase "this we will do," i.e., press on to maturity. Thus, the writer explains by this warning why we must press on to maturity. It is because if we do not, we are in danger of falling away, and it will be impossible for us to be renewed to repentance.

Because this warning seems to suggest the possibility of final apostasy of the regenerate man, Experimental Predestinarians have labored to demonstrate that true Christians are not the subject of the warning. For this reason it is important that we pause here to consider the intended recipients--Christian or non-Christian? Typically, Calvinist exegesis consists of an attempt to prove that the phrases ("enlightened," "tasted of the heavenly gift," "become partakers," and "tasted the good Word of God") do not necessarily refer to regenerate people. Instead, they could refer to those exposed externally to the influences of the gospel through association with Christians and through sitting under the preaching of the Word of God. Most commentators in the history of the church have found little difficulty in understanding that these warnings in Hebrews are addressed to regenerate people. Marshall is correct when he says the vast majority of scholars view them as genuine Christians.[6]

---

[4]The antecedent of "this" cannot be "laying again the foundation" because then the writer would be saying, "Let us go beyond the foundation, and we will lay the foundation, if God permits," yielding nonsense.

[5]Marshall objects that this interpretation is in conflict with what follows. In vv. 4ff. it is the impossibility of renewal to repentance which is in view, and not going forward to maturity. But surely this is quibbling. The first step toward restoration of lost love for Christ and progression to maturity is to confess one's sin, i.e., repent (Rev. 2:5). See I. Howard Marshall, *Kept by the Power of God* (Minneapolis: Bethany House, 1969), p. 141.

[6]Ibid., p. 142.

Several things are said of these people who are capable of falling away. The central theme is enlightenment. The last four phrases explain what characterizes those who have been "enlightened." One who has been enlightened is one who has tasted the heavenly gift, who has shared in the Holy Spirit, and who has tasted the goodness of the word of God and the powers of the coming age, and who then falls away.

There are five phrases all united under the word "who" which describe these people "who have" (6:4-5):

1.   once been enlightened
2.   **te** . . . and have tasted the heavenly gift
3.   **kai** . . . and have shared in the Holy Spirit
4.   **kai** . . . and have tasted the goodness of the word of God and the powers of the coming age
5.   **kai** . . . and have fallen away.

Notice that all are united under the same "who" and there is no obvious reason for taking number 5 as conditional (i.e., "if they fall away"), since the first four are not. Furthermore, whenever the Greek word **te** is followed by **kai** . . . **kai**, they must all be taken the same way. In other words, four of the five cannot be circumstantial participles but the fifth one conditional. Therefore, it is not impossible for those characterized by 1-4 to fall away from the faith.

Who have been enlightened. The word **photisthentas** (enlightened) is common in the New Testament. Experimental Predestinarians customarily point to Jn. 1:9. Here the apostle John uses it of Christ Himself as the true light who enlightens every man. However, all this shows is that some kind of general enlightenment short of actual conversion is possible in that passage.[7] In Hebrews, however, this is not likely. The addition of "once for all" and the defining phrases which follow have impressed many that the enlightenment of conversion is probably meant here.

The apostle Paul applies it to true Christians when he prays that the "eyes of your heart may be enlightened in order that you may know the hope to which He has called you, the riches of his glorious inheritance in the saints" (Eph. 1:18).[8] The author of the Epistle to the Hebrews uses it of his readers' initial reception of the gospel: "Remember those earlier days after you had received the light" (Heb. 10:32). Those who received this light are those who have confessed Christ (10:35), who have proven their regeneration by a life of works and hope of heaven (10:32-34), who have been sanctified (10:29), and who possess the im-

---

[7]It may also refer to the particular enlightenment of "every man who is elect."

[8]See also 2:1-5; 8, 11-13, 19; 4:1; 5:8.

puted righteousness of Christ (10:38). In other words, in its only other use in Hebrews, it is clearly used of conversion. Westcott correctly observes:

> *The word **photizesthai** occurs again in 10:32. The illumination both here and there, is referred to the decisive moment when the light was apprehended in its glory.... Inwardly this crisis of illumination was marked by a reception of the knowledge of the truth (10:26) and outwardly by the admission to Christian fellowship.*[9]

Elsewhere in the New Testament receiving the light is commonly used for regeneration:

> *The god of this age has blinded the minds of unbelievers, so that they cannot see the light of the gospel of the glory of Christ, who is the image of God.... For God who said, "Let light shine out of darkness" made His light shine in our hearts to give us the light of the knowledge of the glory of God in the face of Christ. But we have this treasure in jars of clay (2 Cor. 4:4-7).*

The similarity between the phrase "made His light shine in our hearts to give us the light" and "who have once been enlightened" is surely evidence that the latter means the same as the former, and the former is obviously conversion.

In 1 Pet. 2:9, coming out of darkness into light is described as conversion. Indeed, the movement from darkness to light is a popular theme in the apostle John's writings for the movement from death to life, conversion (Jn. 5:24). Jesus called Himself the light of the world and said "I have come into this world so that the blind will see" (Jn. 9:39).

The writer of the epistle to the Hebrews says they have been **hapax photisthentas** ("once for all" enlightened). The word **hapax** often has a sense of finality in it. It is the opposite of "again" (**palin**) in v. 6. It is used by the writer to describe the once-for-all entrance into the Holy of Holies by the high priest on the Day of Atonement, in contrast to the regular and repeated entrances by the priests during the preceding year (Heb. 9:7). He uses it of Christ's "once-for-all" appearance at the end of the age to do away with sin (Heb. 9:26) and of the finality of death which comes upon all men (9:27). It is instructive to note that it is applied to the "once-and-for-all" taking away of sin by Christ's sacrifice (Heb. 9:28). The apostle Jude uses it of the faith, which has been "once and for all" delivered to the saints (Jude 3).

These people then, have been "once and for all" enlightened. This is not a mere mental awareness, a mere first introduction, but a "final" enlightenment. Such language is only consistent with effectual calling.

---

[9]Sauer, p. 142.

This once-for-all inward enlightenment and reception of the gospel is hardly consistent with the thesis that these people were not truly born again. Its use "would be strange if the reference were merely to the reception of a course of instruction" in contrast to actual conversion.[10] Furthermore, assuming that the structural arrangement of the passage outlined above is correct, the word is then defined in the immediate context as "tasting the heavenly gift" and as being a "partaker of the Holy Spirit."[11]

Who have tasted the heavenly gift. This enlightenment is, first of all, explained as involving a "tasting" of the heavenly gift (Gk. **dorea**). The parallel with Jn. 4:10 is noteworthy. In His comments to the Samaritan woman Jesus said:

> *If you knew the gift* [Gk. **dorea**] *of God and who it is that asks you for a drink, you would have asked him and he would have given you living water.*

In every usage of **dorea** in the Bible it refers to the bestowal of some divine gift, spiritual and supernatural, given to man. In each case, unless Heb. 6 is an exception, the receiver of this gift is either regenerate already, or the gift itself is regeneration.[12] In Rom. 5:17 it is the gift of righteousness; in Eph. 3:7 it is the gift of the grace of God; in Acts 2:38 it is the gift of the Holy Spirit. Regeneration is, of course, not part of the semantic value of the word. The precise nature of the gift must be determined from its sense in the context of Heb. 6. There it is qualified as a "heavenly" gift, or a gift which comes from heaven. The phraseology is so suggestive of the numerous other references to the gift of Christ, the Holy Spirit, or righteousness which comes from heaven, that this must surely be the first thought which would come to the mind of a first-century reader.

The gift of God is the gift of regeneration (2 Cor. 10:15) and the gift of the Holy Spirit (Acts 10:44-46). Elsewhere in the New Testament the references to the gift of God refer to true salvation and the forgiveness of sins. "It is the whole gift of redemption, the new creation, the fullness of life eternal freely bestowed, and made known freely, to the enlightened."[13] As Paul said, "The gift is not like the trespass. For if the many died by the trespass of the one man, how much more did God's grace and the gift that came by the grace of the one man, Jesus Christ, overflow to the many!" (Rom. 5:15). To taste the heavenly gift is to experience regeneration, to taste salvation itself.

---

[10]Ibid.

[11]John MacArthur tries to blunt the force of this by referring to a usage of **photizo** in the LXX in Isa. 9:1-2 where we are told that people in darkness saw a great light. See Mt. 4:16. This is irrelevant to the usage in the New Testament where it is specifically the spiritual enlightenment of regeneration and where the context describes it as **hapax**, final, once-and-for-all enlightenment (John MacArthur, *Hebrews* [Chicago: Moody Press, 1983], p. 142).

[12]Jn. 4:10; Acts 2:38; 8:20; 10:45; 11:17; Rom. 5:15, 17; 2 Cor. 9:15; Eph. 3:7; 4:7; Heb. 6:4.

[13]Dodds, "Hebrews," 4:296.

The word **geuomai,** "taste," is not used by our author of an external association but of an internal taste. Some have tried to argue that the choice of the word "taste" means that the gift was not really received; it was only sampled, not feasted upon.[14] Even Calvin "vainly attempts to make the clause refer only to 'those who had but as it were tasted with their outward lips the grace of God, and been irradiated with some sparks of His light.'"[15] Farrar correctly insists, "This is not to explain Scripture, to explain it away in favour of some preconceived doctrine. It is clear from 1 Pet. 2:3 that such a view is untenable."[16]

A contemporary writer pursues the idea of pressing a distinction between "eating" and "tasting." It is only by "eating" that we obtain eternal life, he says, not by tasting. But, on the contrary, the word "taste" includes within its compass the sense of "to eat":

> *He became hungry and wanted something to eat* (**geuomai,** Acts 10:10).

> *Then he went upstairs again and broke bread and ate* (**geuomai,** Acts 20:11).

In both biblical and secular Greek it commonly means to eat or to "partake of" or to "join."[17] One papyri manuscript refers to a man who went to bed without eating his supper (**geuomai**), and another refers to a group who "joined in" (**geuomai**) the praise of another.[18]

Eating and tasting are synonymous terms and imply believing in Christ resulting in regeneration and eternal life. Tiedtke is surely correct when he says:

> *He* [referring to I. H. Marshall] *suggests that the emphasis in tasting is not that of taking a sip, as Calvin thought. In Heb. 2:9 Christ tasted death in the sense that He experienced its bitter taste to the full.* **The amount consumed is not the point, but the fact of experiencing what is eaten.** *The Christians to whom this is addressed have already experienced something of the future age.*[19]

Jesus was not externally associated with death: He experienced it to the full! This was no mere sampling of death. The full experience of death was the

---

[14]MacArthur, p. 143.

[15]Farrar, *Hebrews,* p. 82.

[16]Ibid. "The construction with the Gen. (instead of the Accs. as at ver. 5) does not warrant the interpretation made in the interests of Calvinism, of a mere tasting with the tip of the tongue" (Carl Frederick Moll, "The Epistle to the Hebrews," in *Lange's,* 11:114).

[17]MM, p. 125; AG, p. 156.

[18]MM, p. 125.

[19]E. Tiedtke, "Hunger," in *NIDNTT,* 2:270.

tasting itself and not something which followed tasting. How does one taste death and then fully experience it after dying? Tasting is full experience!

Peter uses it of the experience of true Christians, of newborn babes:

Like newborn babies, crave the pure spiritual milk, so that by it you may grow up in your salvation, now that you have tasted [**geuomai**] *that the Lord is good* (1 Pet. 2:3).

These are not people who have been superficially exposed to external Christian influences. On the contrary, they have internally experienced them through regeneration. As Westcott insists, "**Geusasthai** expresses a real and conscious enjoyment of the blessing apprehended in its true character." He then cites Jn. 6:54 as a parallel.[20]

It is often related to the spiritual experience of the regenerate:

Taste and see that the LORD is good (Ps. 34:8).[21]

The regenerate to whom Peter writes have "tasted (**geuomai**) the kindness of the Lord" (1 Pet. 2:3). The experience of tasting is not that of those who do not know Christ but of those who have come to know Him.

For this reason most recent scholars agree with Behm that the amount consumed is not in mind at all. Rather, the verb points to experiencing the flavor of something.[22]

Who are partakers of the Holy Spirit. The second qualifier of enlightenment is that it includes being "partakers" of the Holy Spirit. This is the same word used in 3:14, metochoi, partners, true Christians.

But in what sense are these people partners with the Holy Spirit? In each reference to metochoi in the book of Hebrews, truly regenerate people are in view.[23] In Heb. 12:8 because they are true sons, regenerate, they are partners (**metochoi**) in discipline. In 1:9 they are regenerate companions (**metochoi**) of the King. In 3:1 they are regenerate "holy brothers" who are partners (**metochoi**) in the heavenly calling. In 3:14, as discussed in chapter 5, they are partakers with Christ in the final destiny of man, ruling over the millennial earth. The ministry of the Holy Spirit in the book of the Hebrews is described in various ways. There is no consistent notion, as Sauer argues, that He communicates information and

---

[20]Westcott, *Hebrews*, p. 149.

[21]See also Job 20:18.

[22]J. Behm, in *TDNT*, 1:675-77; LS, s.v. "**geuomai**."

[23]Heb. 1:9; 3:1, 14; 5:13; 6:4; 7:13; 12:8.

testimony.[24] Rather, He is the Spirit who imparts grace (10:29), i.e., justification and regeneration; He imparts spiritual gifts (2:4) to the **regenerate!** In view of the fact that they are partakers of the Holy Spirit and that in all other references to partakers true Christians are in view, there is no reason here not to assume that it means something like close partnership or true spiritual fellowship, which is possible only to the regenerate.

Who have tasted the goodness of the Word of God. The third qualifier of the word "enlighten" is "tasting the goodness of the word of God." He is summing up their experience to this point. It may be described as a continual tasting of the Word of God (cf. 1 Pet. 2:2-3). Farrar has little patience with Calvin's exegesis on this point. "There is no excuse for the attempt of Calvin and others, in the interests of their dogmatic bias, to make 'taste of' mean only 'have an inkling of' without any deep or real participation."[25]

Who have tasted the powers of the coming age. Furthermore, they had tasted of the powers of the coming age. This refers to the miracles of the New Testament era which are a foretaste, a preview, of the miraculous nature of the future kingdom of God. The ministry of the Holy Spirit in authenticating the gospel with "powers" is mentioned in 2:4. He apparently knows of some of his readers who have fallen away. He writes to warn the rest against the danger of falling away in the future. In what way did these who are in danger of falling away taste these mighty works? Sauer argues that they only externally tasted the Spirit's authenticating ministry through miracles as taught in 2:4. While it is surely true that they experienced this external authentication, it is also possible that they received the spiritual gifts of the Holy Spirit which are given only to the regenerate. At any rate, the taste was not superficial. It was a full taste just as Jesus tasted death. A personal experience with the Holy Spirit is implied, not just the observation of His performing miracles. These people had experienced personally and internally the power of God in their lives.

John Owen objects that the people here are contrasted with true believers later in v. 9. Marshall's view seems more correct, that the contrast "surely is not so much between two different groups of people as between two possibilities which may affect the same people; thus vv. 7ff. describe two possibilities which may arise in the same land."[26]

Who have fallen away. It is difficult to know for sure whether some of the readers have already fallen away or are only in danger of falling away. In either case the writer wants to warn them that they are faced with the danger of "falling

---

[24]Sauer, p. 223.

[25]Farrar, p. 82.

[26]Marshall, *Kept,* p. 144.

away."[27] The Greek word **parapipto** simply means to fall by the wayside. It is used only here in the New Testament. In the papyri manuscripts it is sometimes translated "to wander astray."[28] Its most frequent translation is "to fall in one's way, befall"[29] and is sometimes rendered "to commit sin" with no specific reference at all.[30]

However, in the LXX it seems to have the sense of religious apostasy. In the book of Ezekiel it often takes the sense of turning from God to idols.[31] This meaning fits well with the theme of Hebrews. These believers were considering a relapse into Judaism. Indeed, the whole book was written to demonstrate the superiority of Christianity to Judaism and hence to prevent precisely such a relapse. In addition, the central sin, the sin of willful unbelief, is what is warned about in 10:26. Throughout the epistle he urges them to hold fast to their confession of faith (10:23). It is the danger of final apostasy which is in view.

The writer seems to imply that some of his readers may already have taken this step. He writes to warn others that they too are in danger of doing so (6:9). He is aware, however, that the decisive act of apostasy has precursors. It is the result of a period of hardening of heart which crystallizes at a particular moment. It is preceded by "neglect" of our great salvation, by hardness of heart (3:12), and by refusal to grow (5:11-14). It is likely that the particular reference to "going astray" in Heb. 6 refers not only to apostasy but to the preceding hardness of heart as well.

The context has been speaking of the need to grow from infancy to maturity. They have been exhorted to "go on to maturity." It seems that the meaning of "fall away" here must include the opposite of "going on to maturity." As they "go on," as they press to that goal, there is a danger that some will "go astray, fall away," that they will fail to persevere. He is not speaking of falling away from salvation at all (or falling away from anything else for that matter). He is talking

---

[27]In his attempt to evade the force of these verses, Abraham Kuyper argues, "It is true the apostle declares that the men guilty of this sin 'were once enlightened,' and 'have tasted of the heavenly gift,' and were made 'partakers of the Holy Ghost,' and 'have tasted the good word of God and the powers of the age to come;' but they are never said to have had a broken and a contrite heart" (Abraham Kuyper, *The Work of the Holy Spirit* [New York: Funk and Wagnalls, 1900; reprint ed., Grand Rapids: Eerdmans, 1958], p. 610). Neither is it said of them, of course, that they were born again. Nor did the apostle say they were redeemed or that they passed from death to life. He does not say that they confessed Christ or that they had become new creations. It is true that he does not say many things about them. But what he does say can only be attributed to men who are truly born again. There is no mention of "faith" in the description in 1 Cor. 1:1-10, yet nobody doubts that Christians are there in view.

[28]MM, p. 489, where the untranslated German word **verlorengehen** means "become lost, wander astray."

[29]AS, p. 342.

[30]AG, p. 627.

[31]Ezek. 14:13; 15:8; 18:24; 20:27; 22:4 (LXX).

about wandering from the path leading to maturity, from that progression in the Christian life which will result in their ultimate entrance into rest, the achievement of their life work (Heb. 4:11). Nor is he speaking about falling away from a mere profession of faith. These people possessed true saving faith. They were regenerate. If they did not decide to press on to maturity, they are in danger of denying the faith altogether. At least, this is the real concern of the epistle.

Later he tells them:

So do not throw away your confidence; it will be richly rewarded. You need to persevere so that when you have done the will of God, you will receive what he has promised (Heb. 10:35-36).

He has before his mind the failure of the largely regenerate exodus generation[32] who failed to achieve their intended destiny, entrance into the inheritance-rest of Canaan.[33] A failure to go on to maturity typically results in spiritual lapse, a hardened heart, and unbelief (Heb. 3:7, 12). Just as the wilderness failure to persevere did not result in the loss of salvation of two million Jews, neither would the potential failure of the Hebrews. What is in danger is the forfeiture of their position as one of Christ's metochoi, those who will partake with Him in the future reign of the servant kings.

How does one know when a believer has "gone astray"? It seems that several things are involved in the lives of those who are moving in this direction. There is a "neglect" of our great salvation, that is, a disinterest in our glorious future and a sense of "drift" in their Christian lives (Heb. 2:2-3). A gradual hardness of heart appears. This is associated with an unbelief which results in turning away from, instead of toward, the living God (Heb. 3:12). Spiritual dullness sets in, and there is no evidence of growth (Heb. 5:11). As a natural consequence a person traveling along this road no longer desires the fellowship of other Christians, and he habitually stops meeting with other Christians (Heb. 10:25), refusing to join with those who live by faith and desire to persevere (Heb. 4:1-2). In other words, he finds the company of nonbelievers or carnal believers, more pleasant. If the exodus generation is our parallel, there may be the suggestion that an age of accountability is involved. Only those who were twenty years and older were in danger of the certain severe divine judgment for this behavior pattern (Num. 14:29).

These are only the initial symptoms. The writer to the Hebrews knows of such people to whom he is writing. His concern goes far deeper however. He worries that they will commit apostasy and finally reject the faith altogether. This is his meaning when he warns them "not to throw away their confidence" (Heb.

---

[32]See chapter 3 for proof that the Jews of the exodus were regenerate.

[33]See chapter 5 for discussion of the inheritance rest of Hebrews and demonstration that this refers to the believer's ultimate reward in heaven, not his final deliverance from hell.

10:35) and not to "deliberately keep on sinning" (Heb. 10:26). He does not want them to take this final step and be among those who "shrink back and are destroyed" (Heb. 10:39). It seems evident from these warnings in Hebrews that it is possible for true Christians to commit apostasy, final public rejection of Christ.

The consequence of such an apostasy, however, according to this writer, is not loss of salvation but loss of inheritance, as he illustrates from the example of Esau (Heb. 12:17). Likewise, he warns them extensively through the example of Israel's failure to obtain rest in chapters 3 and 4.

The impossibility of renewal. For those who have "gone astray," "it is impossible to renew them again to repentance."[34] But we must ask, Impossible for whom? To say that it is impossible for God to change them is theologically and biblically unacceptable. "For nothing is impossible with God" (Lk. 1:37) except to lie or otherwise contradict His own holiness (Heb. 6:18).

If it is not impossible for God to do this, then his meaning is that it is impossible for others to renew such a man. He has already told them to "encourage one another daily, as long as it is called Today" (Heb. 3:13). Evidently a person can become so hardened in unbelief that the encouragement and exhortation of his fellow Christians can no longer have any effect on him. It will not always be called "Today." There will come a point in which his opportunity to progress as a Christian may be terminated by God. Encouragement falls on deaf ears. When that happens, they, like the wilderness generation, die in the wilderness and never enter into rest. It must be remembered that God declared "on oath in My anger, they shall never enter My rest" (Heb. 3:11). This is why the writer says that progression to maturity (6:1) can only continue "God permitting" (6:3). God may not permit it. He may draw the line and disinherit them like He did the exodus generation. Once we withdraw from God's house of worship and forsake fellowship with other Christians, we are beyond the opportunity to respond to their encouragement and risk loss of reward at the judgment seat of Christ.

But what is the precise object of "renew"? It is "to repentance." They had experienced repentance before and cannot be renewed again to it. This creates some problems for Experimental Predestinarian exegesis. Normally repentance is viewed as the condition for salvation. If these apostates have repented, then they are saved. Yet on Calvinist assumptions, if they are saved, they cannot be mere professors, as their exegesis of the passage requires. Experimental Predestinarian Roger Nicole is acutely aware of his problem here:

> *This characteristic . . . appears to confront us with greater difficulties than any of the other descriptions. For if the repentance that these*

---

[34]The usage of **adunatos** ("impossible") in other places in the book excludes the idea that it could be rendered "very difficult." It is impossible for God to lie (6:18), impossible for the blood of bulls and goats to take away sin (10:4), and impossible to please God without faith (11:6).

apostates had experienced were not true godly sorrow (2 Cor. 7:10), it is hard to see why it would be desirable to renew it. And if this repentance is the genuine sorrow of the penitent believer, as the word **metanoia** *ordinarily denotes, then regeneration appears presupposed as the only adequate fountain for such an attitude.*[35]

Experimental Predestinarians have adopted two devices to explain this problem. The typical approach, represented by Nicole for example, argues that the repentance which these apostates originally exercised was a false, non-saving repentance,[36] an approach which Nicole himself acknowledges is "not entirely free of difficulty." He admits that the reason he adopts it is that the alternative is that "regenerate individuals may be lost."[37] Hopefully there is a better alternative!

A similar approach, represented by Sauer, is to say that the repentance was real but that repentance plus faith are necessary for salvation and that they are only said to have repented in 6:6:

The fallen had repented. That is, they underwent a change of mind about their sinful life, the validity of Christianity, and the continuing worth of Judaism. . . . This repentance was to be followed up and supplemented by conversion. But the expected **epistrophe**, *or turning to God through faith in Christ is not said to have occurred.*[38]

But it **does** say it has occurred! In 6:1 we are told that they repented and exercised faith toward God. In 10:23 he tells us that they had professed "hope," i.e., trust in Christ. He says they had "confidence" in Christ in 10:35. Furthermore, the descriptive phrases mentioned in 6:4-6, as argued above, are in fact best interpreted as descriptive of regenerate people. Surely the notion that repentance would not result in salvation would sound strange to first-century readers of the New Testament.

Because faith necessarily assumes and includes within its compass the notion of a change of mind or perspective about sin and about who Christ is and about what one trusts in, it is easy to see how the New Testament writers could sometimes have used the terms interchangeably even though the terms by themselves have different meanings.

---

[35]R. Nicole, "Some Comments on Hebrews 6:4-6 and the Doctrine of the Perseverance of God with the Saints," in *Current Issues in Biblical and Patristic Interpretation*, ed. G. G. Hawthorne (Grand Rapids: 1975), p. 361.

[36]Ibid.

[37]Ibid.

[38]Sauer, p. 250.

Arminians have the advantage of viewing repentance in a salvation sense and assuming that they are genuinely saved and have genuinely repented. They simply say that man can lose his salvation.

The Partaker also views the repentance as genuine and resulting in regeneration. He simply notes that both Christians and non-Christians can repent and that the second repentance here is the repentance of Christians in confessing their sin, and thus it is similar in meaning to "confession." The application of repentance (Gk. **metanoia**) to the regenerate is common in the New Testament (cf. Lk. 17:3; 2 Cor. 7:10; 2 Cor. 12:21; 2 Tim. 2:25; Rev. 2:5; Rev. 2:16). His point is that a regenerate man can get into such a psychological and spiritual state that he is hardened; his perspective cannot be renewed and, as a result, he cannot confess his sin or repent. This is not a renewal to salvation from sin's penalty, hell, but a salvation from sin's power. The renewal is a restoration to the state of mind that feels regret and sorrow for sin. This "renewal" is precisely illustrated in 2 Cor. 7:10-11:

> *Godly sorrow brings repentance that leads to salvation. . . . See what this godly sorrow has produced in you: what earnestness, what eagerness to clear yourselves, what indignation, what alarm, what longing, what concern, what readiness to see justice done.*

The salvation here is equivalent to sanctification, moral victory, deliverance from sin's power. But the godly sorrow is the same as the renewal of Heb. 6:6. It is a renewal that produces "earnestness," "eagerness to clear yourself," alarm over sin, and readiness to see justice done, etc. (2 Cor. 7:11). When that state of mind is achieved, a man can repent, change his mind about sin, and confess it. Repentance here is not saving faith but confession of sin by the Christian.[39]

The first time these people repented they changed their minds about sin, trusted God, and were born again. It will be impossible to restore them once again to the state of mind where they are willing to change their minds about their present sins of hardness, unbelief, and lethargy leading to apostasy. It is impossible because the preparatory "renewal" or "godly sorrow" no longer exists due to the hardness of their hearts.

Crucifying the Son of God. The reason given for the impossibility of renewal to repentance is that they crucify the Son of God and subject Him to public shame (Heb. 6:6). First of all, it is likely that the verb "crucify" (Gk. **anastauroo**)

---

[39]Repentance is not always the same as "saving faith" in the New Testament but often means "change of mind." It is used this way of Esau in Heb. 12:17. He sold his birthright for a meal, and afterward he could bring about no change of mind, though he sought it with tears. Even in 6:1, where it refers to the repentance of non-Christians, the meaning is to change one's mind about the value of dead works.

does not necessarily mean "crucify again." Rather, it refers to lifting up on the cross, or simply "to crucify." Any reader of the New Testament would have understood it this way.[40] Furthermore, this crucifixion is not literal but "to themselves," or as the NIV puts it, "to their loss."[41] The thought then is that they will suffer loss at the judgment seat of Christ because of their actions. Those who have drifted into apostasy cannot be renewed to repentance because, due to their life-style and conduct, they have crucified Christ.

There were only two possible interpretations of the death of Christ. He was either crucified justly as a common criminal (the Jewish view), or He was crucified unjustly as the Son of God, an innocent man. When a Christian denies Christ, he is in effect saying that the Jewish view was correct. If He was not the Son of God dying for our sins, then the only other possible conclusion was that He was a blasphemous deceiver who received what He deserved. It is in this sense that the apostate holds Christ up to public shame. His life and denial has testified that Christ was a criminal and that His shameful death was deserved. For the writer to the Hebrews, at least, denial of Christ was a possibility for a true Christian, but loss of salvation was not.

But why is crucifying the Son of God the reason for the impossibility of renewal to repentance? It is possible that the habitual and continuous aspect, which the present tense sometimes carries, should be stressed here. The tenses of the preceding verses were all aorists, so the unexpected switch to the present may be intentional. They cannot be renewed to repentance because they continually crucify the Son of God. In other words, because they have arrived at a state of continuous and habitual sin, they continuously and habitually shame the name of Christ. The hardness associated with any continued state of sin makes repentance psychologically and spiritually impossible. Because of their hardness they are beyond persuasion by other Christians.

It is also likely, as already mentioned, that from the divine side repentance is not allowed while they continue this behavior. He has told us that progression to maturity is only possible if God permits. However, those who have been hardened by sin (3:13) and who have unbelieving hearts which have turned away from God (3:12) are, like the exodus generation, apparently not permitted to go on. They will not advance to maturity and share in the great salvation promised to those who by "faith and patience will inherit the promises" (Heb. 6:12).

---

[40]Dodds, "Hebrews," 4:298. See also Bruce, *Hebrews*, p. 124. Although Arndt and Gingrich favor the view of the older translators, "crucify again," they acknowledge that in Greek it always means simply "to crucify," p. 60. This is also the rendering of E. Brandenburger in "Cross," in *NID-NTT*, 1:397.

[41]This is properly a dative of disadvantage, according to Farrar, p. 84.

The saved condition of the apostates. Before continuing our discussion of the falling away, it is necessary that some summary points regarding the regenerate nature of these apostates be made.

First of all, it seems to be widely acknowledged that the illustration informing the writer's mind is the experience of the exodus generation in the wilderness. Just as they failed to enter rest, so we too are in danger of not entering by "following their example of disobedience" (Heb. 4:11). The majority of the exodus generation was regenerate, but they did not enter rest, i.e., finish their work of possessing Canaan. As stressed in chapter 5, the "rest" of Hebrews is not heaven but the reward of joint participation with Messiah in the final destiny of man. To enter into rest is not to go to heaven when we die but to finish our life work (4:4; 10:36), to persevere to the final hour. Some Christians will and some will not, and those who do are "partakers of Christ," i.e., partners of the Messiah in His messianic purposes.

Since the analogy of the regenerate exodus generation is in his mind and since their failure was not forfeiture of heaven but forfeiture of their reward, there is no reason to assume the lapsed of Heb. 6:4-6 will forfeit more. And . . . there is no reason to assume they are unregenerate.

Second, it is impossible to view the believers of vv. 4-6 as unregenerate because they are being urged to go on to maturity, as unregenerate non-Christians cannot mature in Christ. The maturity of 6:1 is not just advanced doctrine but is defined by the reference to 5:14 as mature character in exercising discernment between good and evil. Even if it was "advanced doctrine," unregenerate professing Christians, lacking spiritual ability to understand spiritual truth (1 Cor. 2:14), being blind (2 Cor 4:4), and being dead in trespasses and sins (Eph. 2:1-3), can hardly be expected or exhorted to understand the Melchizedekian priesthood of Jesus Christ!

Third, the writer assumes their regeneration. He never asks them to examine themselves to see if they are really Christians. If he doubted their salvation, he would certainly have placed this question before them. Instead, he tells them that these "holy brothers" (3:1) are partners of Christ only if they persevere. As most commentators now agree, being a partner and being a Christian are not synonymous. All partners are Christians, but not all Christians are partners. Only those who persevere to the final hour (Heb. 3:14).

Finally, it seems exegetically questionable to detach the references to believers in the warning contexts from the warnings themselves. It is acknowledged by Experimental Predestinarians that believers are obviously being addressed in the broader context of the warning passages.[42] Heb. 6:4-8 is no exception. It is certainly circumscribed by exhortations to believers in 5:11-6:3 and 6:9-12. Is it

---

[42]E.g., 3:1, 12; 6:9; 10:19.

exegetically ethical to switch addressees in the middle of the warning context? There is nothing in the warning itself to suggest that such a change has been made. Indeed, in the other warnings it would almost be impossible to draw such a distinction.[43] Furthermore, even Nicole admits that our "most immediate impulse would be to interpret this cluster of statements [the references to "enlightened," etc.] as describing regenerate persons."[44]

The Thorn-Infested Ground (6:7-8)

The only possible result for such behavior is divine discipline and judgment. The writer now explains this by an analogy from nature in Heb. 6:7-9:

Land that drinks in the rain often falling on it and that produces a crop useful to those for whom it is farmed receives the blessing of God. But the land that produces thorns and thistles is worthless and is in danger [or, "close to being"] of being cursed. In the end it will be burned (Heb. 6:7-8).

The "land" refers to the individual regenerate man, the true Christian. It is not permissible, as some have done, to speak of two lands: one which produces a good crop and one which produces thorns (i.e., regenerate and unregenerate). Only one land is mentioned or discussed here. What is in view is two differing crops which can come from this one land.

That this "land" is a regenerate man is proven from the descriptive phrases applied to him in 6:1-3.[45] As the rain falls upon this land, it stimulates the land to produce a crop, a life of perseverance in good works. Or as he expressed it in v. 10, "your work and the love you have shown Him [God] as you have helped His people and continue to help them." The rain refers to the "free ... bestowal of spiritual impulse; the enlightenment, the good word of God, the energetic indwelling of the Holy Spirit, which the Hebrews had received and which should have enabled them to bring forth fruit to God."[46] In sum, the "rain" points back to the four blessings described in 6:1-3. Furthermore, the land "drank" these blessings. The difference is not in drinking and not drinking but in the kinds of produce which resulted from the drinking. It is clear that the phrase "the land which drinks in the rain often falling on it" is the subject of the verbs "produces" and

---

[43]Note the "we" of 2:1 and 10:19, 26 and the fact that those warned have been "sanctified" in 10:29.

[44]Nicole, p. 356. Nicole honestly admits that he rejects this impulse because he has determined beforehand that it cannot mean this due to the fact that the doctrine of perseverance is "powerfully grounded" elsewhere.

[45]See also 6:10; 10:14, 32-34.

[46]Dodds, 4:299.

"receives" in v. 7, and of "produces" and "is in danger of being cursed" in v. 8.[47] Sauer correctly observes that "the writer's aim is to point out the diversity of results that can arise from the same field under equally favorable conditions."[48] The phrase "which drinks" stresses that the rain does not merely fall upon the ground but is actually absorbed by it. This soil is not hard and unreceptive, as in the case of the first soil in the parable of the soils. There is no picture of the rain simply falling on the surface and not sinking in. It would be hard to find a clearer picture of saving faith. These people not only were enlightened and were partakers of the Holy Spirit and recipients of the heavenly gift, but they drank and absorbed it.

The word "drink" (Gk. **pino**) is commonly used elsewhere of saving faith (Jn. 4:13; Jn. 6:54; Jn. 7:37-38). These "holy brothers" who are in danger of apostasy have all drunk of the water of life (i.e., believed), and on the authority of Jesus will be raised on the last day.[49]

This crop is useful to God, the "owner." Probably Christian ministers and teachers are the farmers (1 Cor. 3:9). However, the same land may not produce this useful crop. It may also produce "thorns." It is clear that this writer does not believe that a life of perseverance is the necessary and inevitable result of regeneration. The Lord taught the same thing in the parable of the soils. The final three soils all represent regenerate people as proven by the fact that even the one with no root did grow and hence manifest regenerate life. But two of the three did not produce fruit.

When the land produces a good crop, it receives blessing from God. This blessing is to be understood as divine approval, our entrance into "rest" (Heb. 4:11), the receiving of our rewards, and various unspecified temporal blessings as well. The only other use in Hebrews is of Esau forfeiting his inheritance (Heb. 12:17). That seems to confirm the interpretation that the blessing from God is reward at the judgment seat of Christ. As demonstrated elsewhere, the inheritance-rest of Hebrews, indeed the inheritance in the New Testament, is always, when conditioned on obedience, a reward in heaven and not heaven itself.[50]

But Experimental Predestinarians insist it is not possible for the same soil to bring forth both a good and a bad crop. It can only bring forth one or the other. But this contradicts the author's plain statements in other parts of the epistle. These regenerate people have produced a "crop" of patience in suffering and commendable good works (10:32-34). But some have also produced the "crop" of dullness and spiritual lethargy (5:11-14), some of these "brothers" are in

---

[47]The verbs are all governed by the definite article preceding "drink" (**te piousa**).

[48]Sauer, p. 273.

[49]The fact that drinking and receiving water elsewhere means regeneration further substantiates the interpretation above that "enlightenment" is not mere mental perception but rebirth.

[50]See chapters 3 and 4.

danger of hardness of heart (3:12), and many have stopped meeting together with other Christians (10:25). The same land that produces a crop of perseverance in patience also produces a crop of initial righteousness that then falls into transgression. That is the whole point of the book.

In order to substantiate their thesis that the same regenerate heart cannot produce righteousness for awhile and then fall into unrighteousness, Experimental Predestinarians have to go outside of Hebrews. They then refer to Mt. 7:16 where the Lord says "by your fruits you will know them" and v. 18 where He says, "A good tree cannot bear bad fruit and a bad tree cannot bear good fruit." Or as James tells us, "Can both fresh water and salt water flow from the same spring? My brothers, can a fig tree bear olives, or a grapevine bear figs? Neither can a salt spring produce fresh water" (Jas. 3:11). But surely little can be argued for their case from these verses.

First of all, these are proverbial sayings. A proverb is a general maxim for which there are exceptions. It is generally true that a good tree cannot bear bad fruit, but a plain fact of agriculture is that sometimes good trees do bear bad fruit. The writer has sixty-seven good apple trees in his back yard that will gladly testify to this fact!

But second, James is hardly saying that regenerate people cannot produce bitter water. He is saying that they are inconsistent with their faith when they do. In the verses immediately preceding he says, "With one tongue we praise our Lord and Father and with it we curse men who have been made in God's likeness. Out of the same mouth come praise and cursing. My brothers, **this should not be**" (v. 10). James's point is not that these things **cannot be** (he has just said they can) but rather, that they **should not be.**

Finally, however, since the entire Bible presents numerous illustrations of truly regenerate people such as Saul and Solomon, who in fact did produce a crop of righteousness and then began to produce unrighteousness, Heb. 6:6-8 cannot be teaching something otherwise, or it is in contradiction with the rest of Scripture.[51] The grammar and syntax of the passage do not require this "either/or" interpretation at all, and since the rest of the Bible prohibits it, there is no reason other than an a priori commitment to the Reformed doctrine of perseverance to accept it!

However, if the heart of the regenerate man produces thorns, three phrases describe his uselessness to God.[52] He is "worthless," "in danger of being cursed," and "will be burned."

---

[51]See chapter 14.

[52]See Thomas Kem Oberholtzer, "The Thorn-Infested Ground in Hebrews 6:4-12," *BibSac* 145 (July-September 1988): 319-328.

They are useless to God. The word **adokimos**, "worthless," means "disqualified" or "useless." Experimental Predestinarians, of course, prefer the translation, "spurious," which, while possible, supplies no opposite for the "useful" of v. 7. The opposite of "useful" is not "false" or "spurious" but "useless" or "worthless." The writer's point is that as thorny ground he is useless to the farmer. The author is not trying to say not that the production of thorns proves that the man's profession of faith was spurious. That Christians can lead useless lives and fail to finish their work is the central warning of the epistle. The exodus generation, which is in the writer's mind, was not unregenerate but useless. They never accomplished the task of conquering Canaan in spite of the many blessings God poured upon them.

Paul used it of himself in 1 Cor. 9:27 when he said that his goal was that at the end of life he would not be found "disqualified (**adokimos**) for the prize." As discussed elsewhere,[53] Paul does not doubt that he might forfeit his salvation. He is burdened that he finish his course and hence receive the reward. Similarly, the believer who produces thorns in Heb. 6 is not subject to damnation, but his disobedient life will disqualify him at the judgment seat and will make him useless for the purposes of God now.

They are in danger of being cursed. The second phrase, "in danger of being cursed" is more literally, "close to being cursed (NASB)." It is possible but unlikely that the curse refers back to Gen. 3. There the thorns were a result of the curse, but here the curse is a result of thorns. We are on safer ground if we remain close to the Jewish background of the readers and look to Dt. 28-30 where Moses taught that obedience resulted in temporal blessing and disobedience resulted in temporal cursing.[54] If this is the meaning, the reference directs us back once again to the temporal curse which fell upon the exodus generation—hardship and physical death. That God sometimes brings this judgment on His regenerate people is taught elsewhere in Hebrews (Heb. 12:5-11), and the sin unto physical death is taught throughout the New Testament.[55]

While the immediate reference is certainly to divine discipline in time, the writer of the epistle probably has the future consequences of this cursing in mind as well. He often speaks of the need to persevere and hence receive our reward[56] and has this thought in view in the immediate context when he says, "Imitate those who through faith and patience inherit what has been promised (Heb. 6:12). Conversely, those who do not persevere in faith and patience will be cursed, i.e., be disinherited like Esau was (12:17). The cursing does not refer to loss of salvation.

---

[53]See discussion under 2 Cor. 13:5.

[54]Note Dt. 29:22-28; 30:15-30.

[55]1 Cor. 5:5; 1 Cor. 11:30; 1 Jn. 5:16-17; Jas. 5:19-20.

[56]10:36; 11:6, 10, 15, 16, 26.

They will be burned. It seems that the antecedent of "it" in v. 8 is "the land" of v. 7. It is the land that is in danger of being burned. What is meant by this burning? Some have argued that the burning is a purifying rather than a destroying fire. Apparently there was a common agricultural practice behind this. When a field was overgrown with weeds and thorns, it was customary to burn it in order to cleanse the field and restore its fertility. If this is the meaning, then the result of the apostate's denial is severe divine discipline with a corrective intent. Justification for this might be found in Heb. 12:5-11.

But the purifying intent is doubtful here. The parallel of the exodus generation's failure and their destruction in the wilderness is the controlling thought of the warnings. It is impossible to renew them to repentance. So the burning is, first of all, divine judgment in time. This is the thought of 10:27 where he speaks of the "raging fire that will consume the enemies of God."[57]

But we are told elsewhere of a burning of the believer's dead works at the judgment seat of Christ (1 Cor. 3:10-15), with negative as well as positive consequences which will accrue to believers at that time (2 Cor. 5:10). So we are not without scriptural parallel if we interpret this passage from that perspective. The burning of the believer then would be a metonymy for the burning of the believer's works.

This would help explain the statement that "in the end" the works of the unfaithful believer (the produce of the field) will be "burned." There is no reference to hell here but rather, to the burning up of the believer's life work at the judgment seat of Christ. Even though the fire consumes his house of wood, hay, and stubble (= "land," metonymy for "thorns and thistles," in Heb. 6:8), yet this carnal Christian "will be saved, but only as one escaping through the flames" (1 Cor. 3:10-15).

Consolation and Encouragement (6:9-12)

Having warned them, his pastor's heart now emerges and he turns to consolation in Heb. 6:9-12. He is confident, he says, that their lives are characterized by the better things which accompany salvation. Salvation in Hebrews, as discussed elsewhere,[58] refers not to final deliverance from hell, which is based upon faith alone, but to the future participation in the rule of man (Heb. 1:14; Heb. 2:5) which is conditioned upon obedience (cf. Heb. 5:9). The inheritance they will obtain refers not to heaven, which is theirs through faith alone, but to their reward in heaven, which only comes to those "who **through** ["by means of"] faith and patience inherit what has been promised" (Heb. 6:12). Since the "promise" in

---

[57]See next chapter for proof that this refers to judgment in time and not the eternal judgment of hell.

[58]See chapter 4.

Hebrews usually refers to the millennium (e.g. 4:1; 6:13, 15; 7:6; 11:9, 11, 13, 17; 12:26), to "inherit the promise" means to rule in the millennium and parallels the phrase "inherit the kingdom," which does not mean merely entering the kingdom but to own it and rule there.[59]

Conclusion

For many years the author has had the privilege of traveling and teaching the Bible in Russia and Eastern Europe. In nearly every Bible conference numerous questions are raised about the doctrine of eternal security. This doctrine is not popular in that part of the world. It is feared, that if it is taught, people will become lax in their Christian lives. On one occasion, while teaching this material, a pastor who was attending the session became quite upset. Even though no reference was made to the doctrine of eternal security, the fact that Heb. 6 was being taught in such a way that removed it as a defense for conditional security caused him great distress. Why? It is quite common for church leaders to use this passage as a kind of club with which they use a fear motivation in order to secure the kind of obedience the scripture requires.

In one situation, after teaching on the book of Hebrews for forty hours with fourteen pastors in Bucharest, Romania, many of them were quite intrigued with the approach to the passage described above. They were so interested that they asked this writer to return for a special three-day conference on the subject of eternal security. They had never been exposed to anyone who believed salvation could not be lost. At the end of three days of wonderful interaction, all of them but one had embraced the doctrines of grace.

An interesting thing happened, however, when they returned to their congregations and began to preach this. One of them was threatened with his job, and another was talked to sternly by the deacons in the church.

People are often afraid of grace. There is a certain security in a system of Christian living bounded by numerous rules and traditions. Everyone understands that, by keeping these rules, you demonstrate to others that you are saved. But equally important, you assure yourself of the fact that you are in a state of grace. Any teaching which upsets this equilibrium must be handled with extreme care and sensitivity.

In conclusion, there is no reference in Heb. 6 to either a falling away from salvation or a perseverance in holiness. Rather, this is a warning to true believers concerning the possible loss of rewards at the judgment seat of Christ and temporal discipline in time. This passage is a dreadful warning to those with a

---

[59]Ibid.

hardened heart, but it is not a passage to apply to the persevering Christian who is "in the battle."

Chapter 20

Hebrews, Peter, and Revelation

Two other warning passages in the book of Hebrews must be considered: the warning about departure from God's house and the warning regarding willful sin. Also Peter warns carnal Christians that their final state might be worse than their earlier one. In addition, the book of Revelation contains a number of warnings about having one's name removed from the book of life and forfeiting one's share in the tree of life. Do these passages refer to the possibility of loss of salvation?

Hebrews 3:1-6

With his well-known statement about being part of the house of God, the writer of this epistle, perhaps unwittingly, gave considerable fodder for both Arminian and Experimental Predestinarian exegesis:

> *But Christ is faithful as a Son over God's house. And we are his house, if we hold on to our courage and hope of which we boast* (Heb. 3:6).

To Arminians the word "if" suggests that it is possible that a true Christian will cease being part of the house of God, the community of the saved, and lose his salvation. Experimental Predestinarians see this passage as further proof of their doctrine of perseverance. Only those who have courage and who hold on to the hope of which we boast are truly members of the saved community.

But does "house" refer to the community of the saved? Most commentators note that the faithfulness of Moses over his house in v. 5 refers to Num. 12. But the house of God in Num. 12:7 is clearly not the community of saved but the place where they worship, the sanctuary. In fact, according to Michel, the term "house of God" (Gk. **oikos theou**) was a fixed term for the sanctuary in the Septuagint.[1] Lange observes:

---

[1]Otto Michel, "**oikos**," in *TDNT*, 5:120.

It is better to understand by "my house" the Tabernacle, including the economy that it represents. The Apostle's reference to this phrase in Heb. 3:2-6 is quite consistent with this, and most of all his words: "whose house we are."[2]

He seems to be speaking of the place where priestly activity occurred. It is Moses' faithful ministry in carrying out, with the Levites, the priestly functions of the old economy in the tabernacle in the wilderness to which he refers. He says, "Moses was faithful in all God's house" (Heb. 3:2). Just as Moses was faithful in the house, we too are to be faithful. We are part of the house of God, if, and only if, we are faithful like Moses was, i.e., if we hold fast our confession. But to be a member of the house of God in the Old Testament was to be a member of the worshiping community in the tabernacle. To be a member of the house of God in the New Testament is to be a member of the worshiping community in the New Testament counterpart to the tabernacle, the gathering of the believers in worship. It is apparent that the readers of this epistle were departing from this house of God because he warns them about this: "Let us not give up meeting together, as some are in the habit of doing" (Heb. 10:25). Moses was faithful in God's house, the gathered community in worship, and Christ is faithful as the Lord over God's house, also the gathered community involved in New Testament worship. To be a member of God's house is not the same as being a member of the mystical body of Christ, the invisible church. Rather, it is membership in the visible body of Christ, the gathered worshiping community. To depart from God's house in this sense then is not loss of salvation or proof that one never had it. It simply refers to the "habit of some" in not meeting together in corporate worship for fear of persecution.

When we withdraw from the exercise of our priestly New Testament worship, we are no longer fellowshipping with the other believers. But this does not mean we are not saved or that we had salvation and lost it.

Hebrews 10

The warning against deliberate sin in Heb. 10:26-39 has understandably given rise to doubt in the minds of some as to whether or not the doctrine of eternal security is found in the Bible. Arminians may be forgiven for being unimpressed with Experimental Predestinarian exegesis which labors under the impossible burden of claiming that the readers to whom the warning is addressed may not be truly regenerate. As mentioned in the discussion of Heb. 6, it is evident that the author of this epistle intends to address his readers as regenerate, and not as merely professing Christians.

---

[2]John Peter Lange, "Numbers," in *Lange's,* 3:39.

The Regenerate Nature of the Readers

That he views them as regenerate is evident from several considerations. First of all, they are the same group addressed in Heb. 6. If the arguments there for the saved condition of these people are valid, then the case is settled. However, in addition, these people are called "sanctified" in v. 29 and are described as "righteous" in v. 38. Furthermore, they have confessed Christ (v. 35) and have demonstrated their faith by remaining true to Christ in the midst of reproach and tribulation (v. 35) by showing sympathy to other Christians who had been imprisoned for their faith, by joyfully accepting the confiscation of their property, and by hoping in a better possession, an abiding one (v. 34). On Experimental Predestinarian premises these people must be saved. They have confessed Christ, are declared to be righteous and sanctified, and have proven it by a life of good works. If they are not saved, then the Experimental Predestinarian view of works as a necessary evidence of salvation is false. If they are, then their view of perseverance is fiction!

The Consequences of Willful Sin (10:26-27)

> *For if we go on sinning willfully after receiving the knowledge of the truth, there no longer remains a sacrifice for sin, but a certain terrifying expectation of judgment, and the fury of a fire which will consume the adversaries* (10:26-27 NASB).

We must consider these words as a real warning to Christians. There is a danger here for all who know Christ. To sin "willfully" (Gk. **ekousios**) means to sin "without compulsion" (1 Pet. 5:2). This willful sinning continues after having received "full knowledge" (Gk. **epignosis**) of the truth. This word is used of the knowledge of salvation in 1 Tim. 2:4. There is no contextual reason to believe that a knowledge less than salvation is intended here.

It is probable that he has a particular sin in view, the sin of not holding fast our confession, which he has just warned against (10:23): "Let us hold fast the confession of our hope without wavering . . . for if we go on sinning willfully," etc.[3] He is warning them against the sin of deliberate apostasy, rejection of our confession. This biblical writer apparently thinks it is possible for righteous ones, who are sanctified, perfected forever (v. 14), and who have proven their confession by works to finally reject Christ and apostatize from the faith. However distasteful such a view is or however contradictory it is to the Reformed doctrine of perseverance, should not biblical data determine our theology rather than the other way around?

---

[3]The verse opens with "for," connecting the thought with 10:23.

When a person takes this step, "there no longer remains a sacrifice for sins." The sacrifice of Christ no longer avails to protect him from the judgment of God. But what kind of judgment is in view? To answer that question, we must turn to the Old Testament passages to which the writer is referring. What was willful sin?

In the Old Testament, sacrifices were provided for unintentional sin (Num. 15:27, 29). However, if an Old Testament believer sinned willfully, no sacrificial protection was provided.

> *But the person who does anything defiantly, whether he is a native or an alien, that one is blaspheming the LORD; and that person shall be cut off from among his people. Because he has despised the Word of the LORD and has broken His commandment, that person shall be completely cut off; his guilt shall be on him* (Num. 15:30-31 NASB).

The Hebrew word translated "defiantly" is a two-word phrase meaning "with a high hand," used in this context of a person "acting in deliberate presumption, pride, and disdain."[4] When the Hebrews left Egypt, they left with a "high hand," i.e., they left boldly and defiantly (Num 33:3). When a man sinned like this, there was no sacrificial protection from the judgment of God. But what kind of judgment is in view? What does it mean to be "cut off"?

To be "cut off" was to undergo capital punishment:

> *Therefore you are to observe the sabbath, for it is holy to you. Every-one who profanes it* **shall surely be put to death***; for whoever does any work on it, that person shall be* **cut off** *from among his people* (Ex. 31:14 NASB; cf. Dt. 17:12).

This phrase, "cut off," is often used of capital punishment or severance from the covenant community but never of eternal hell.[5] Therefore, when the writer of the Epistle to the Hebrews speaks of the consequences of willful sin, he means that there is no sacrificial protection from the **temporal** consequences of sin. He has in view the judgment of God in time, not in eternity, as these Old Testament references show.

While it is acknowledged that the writer cites Old Testament passages which apply to judgment in time, Experimental Predestinarians object that the Old Testament had an underdeveloped doctrine of the judgment in the afterlife. Therefore, they say, these Old Testament passages are to be understood as pointing to a final judgment of which the temporal one was only a type.

---

[4]Ronald B. Allen, "Numbers," in *The Expositor's Bible Commentary*, ed. Frank E. Gaebelein, 11 vols. to date (Grand Rapids: Zondervan, 1976--), 2:830.

[5]See Gen. 17:14; Lev. 20:2, 4, 5; 7:20; 17:4; Num. 19:13, 20.

What kind of argument is this? In essence they are saying that, since there was a poorly developed doctrine of the afterlife in the Old Testament, we must interpret all references to temporal judgment as hell! However, the New Testament writers do not hesitate elsewhere to introduce the doctrine of final judgment on the basis of new revelation not found in the Old Testament. There is no obvious reason why a writer would appeal to passages which admittedly refer to temporal judgment in order to prove eternal judgment, when elsewhere they do not hesitate to assert the doctrine of final judgment on the authority of Jesus and the apostles alone. If the writer of the Epistle to the Hebrews had intended here to teach final judgment, he would have quoted Jesus rather than Old Testament passages which his hearers would have understood as temporal. An argument based upon a textual meaning which contradicts not only the intended meaning of the Old Testament prophet but the understanding of the prophet by the people whom he was trying to exhort would fail miserably.

The context of Heb. 10 is about the application of Christ's death to daily sins for temporal, and not eternal, forgiveness. He has already said they have protection from the judgment of eternal hell: "By this will we have been sanctified through the offering of the body of Jesus Christ **once for all**" (Heb. 10:10). He has already told them that God will remember their sins and lawless deeds "no more" (Heb. 10:17) and that "by one offering He has perfected for all time those who are sanctified" (Heb. 10:14). Would he now turn around and contradict himself in vv. 26-30? Our eternal position before the Father is in view in Heb. 10:17, while 10:26-30 refer to our temporal relationship to Him. The believer today who sins through ignorance and weakness is protected from temporal judgment in time by the blood of Christ. The blood of Christ, however, will not protect the believer who sins willfully. He is in danger of judgment after the Old Testament pattern, a judgment in time that may include physical death or worse.

If we abandon our confession of Christ, there is no place we can go for sacrificial protection from the judgment of God. There is only one thing left--"a certain terrifying expectation of judgment, and the fury of a fire which will consume the adversaries."

What kind of judgment is in view? This judgment is said to be a "fury of fire that will consume the adversaries." This is a quote from Isa. 26:11 which refers to the physical destruction of Israel's enemies in time, not eternity. The mention of "fire" unnecessarily evokes images of hell in our minds. Normally it simply symbolizes some kind of judgment, either in time or eternity. Here, as the Old Testament citations prove, judgments in time are in view.

Very severe consequences may befall a Christian who sins in this way.

The More Severe Punishment (10:28-29)

Anyone who has set aside the Law of Moses dies without mercy on the testimony of two or three witnesses.

How much severer punishment do you think he will deserve who has trampled under foot the Son of God, and has regarded as unclean the blood of the covenant by which he was sanctified, and has insulted the Spirit of grace? (10:29 NASB).

The **more severe punishment** is a punishment even worse than physical death. Death without mercy in the Old Testament came for idolatry on the testimony of two or three witnesses.[6] An example of more severe punishment which comes to mind is the mental anguish that Saul went through. He became mentally ill and was tormented by evil spirits (1 Sam. 16:14-15). Here was a man who was depressed, consumed with hatred, whose fate was far worse than physical death. As discussed previously, he was a regenerate man. A more severe punishment could be a prolonged illness, being kept alive by artificial means, or insanity. Many people in insane asylums today would testify to the truth of this torture. Lacking the courage to take their own lives, they endure a pain far worse than physical death. One thinks of David's sin and the resultant consequence, the loss of his child. David would be the first to affirm that his punishment was more severe than physical death. No doubt the writer views millennial disinheritance and a failure to enter rest as more severe than physical death as well.

The seriousness of this step is described in three ways. First, such a man "tramples the Son of God underfoot." The sinning Christian here obviously does not literally trample on the Son of God, but that is the effect of his life. The term is used of pigs trampling spiritual truth underfoot in Mt. 7:6. In the writings of Homer it apparently referred to the breaking of an oath.[7] This meaning would fit well with the present context, a denial of one's oath expressed in baptism, a denial of Christ. In Zechariah Jerusalem is described as a stone trampled on by all the nations. The city will be scorned. In conclusion then the term "trample under foot" signifies a strong rejection and actual denial of one's confession of faith in Christ either by life or actual verbal denial.

Suppose a family of four is out in a row boat and a terrible storm breaks out. It soon becomes clear that the boat can only hold two people and that two will have to jump overboard to save the other two. Finally, as the water continues to pour into the boat and the danger becomes acute, the parents, in order to save the children, dive overboard and are drowned. Before they did this, how-

---

[6]Dt. 17:2-7. The death penalty in the Old Testament was given for blasphemy (Lev. 24:11-16), murder (Lev. 24:17, Num. 35:30), false prophecy (Dt. 18:20), and rejection of the decree of the court (Dt. 18:20).

[7]F. F. Bruce, *The Epistle to the Hebrews*, NICNT, 14:259.

ever, they asked the older brother in the boat to take care of his little sister. They say, "We love you both. We are going to die so that you can live. Please commit to us that you will take care of your little sister." The older brother tearfully commits to do so. As the years go by, he becomes involved in other concerns and does not want to be bothered with this little child. He renounces his commitment and sends her off to an orphanage. In effect he has just "trampled" his parents under foot. He has scorned the sacrifice they have made. He is, however, still a son. He is in their family. He entered that family by physical birth just as we enter God's family by spiritual birth. Neither process can be reversed!

Second, these sinning Christians regard "as unclean the blood of the covenant." This blood of the New Covenant has made forgiveness of sins available; it is therefore holy blood. There are only two possible meanings of the death of Christ. It could have been the death of a common criminal. He would then have received his just reward. His sin of blasphemy for claiming to be God was, according to the Old Testament, punishable by death. Or it could have been the death of the God-man, a sacrifice for the sins of the world. If Christ was a criminal, then His blood was "unclean." The man who denies Christ by his life or his lips is in effect saying, "Christ's blood is the blood of a common criminal." It is inconsistent to say that Christ's blood is holy blood, shed for the forgiveness of sins, and then to abandon one's confession. If He is not the Son of God, then there is only one other conclusion: the Jews and Romans were right--He was a criminal.

The blood of the covenant has **sanctified** this man. Here is true evidence of his regenerate nature. MacArthur suggests that the one sanctified is Jesus Christ. It could not, he says, refer to a Christian because the apostate is "regarding the blood as unclean." The reference therefore must be to Christ."[8] But is it impossible for true believers to count the blood of Christ as unclean and apostatize from the faith? If they cannot, well then, they cannot. Unfortunately for MacArthur's position, that is the very point in question! MacArthur has already told his readers that there is a positional, as well as a practical, sanctification. The former is perfect, but the latter is not. By MacArthur's own admission the sanctification by the blood elsewhere refers to positional, and not experiential, sanctification.[9] It is therefore possible on MacArthur's premises, and the Bible's as well, to be perfectly sanctified in one's position but still have sin in one's life.[10] There is no need to go to a remotely different context like Jn. 17:19, where Christ speaks of sanctifying Himself to find the meaning of "sanctify" in Heb. 10. The word is defined in the book of Hebrews itself. In this book, to be "sanctified" always refers to Christians made qualified to worship and never to

---

[8]John MacArthur, *Hebrews* (Chicago: Moody Press, 1983), p. 279.

[9]Ibid., p. 263, where he refers to 9:14.

[10]Ibid.

Christ.[11] Why didn't MacArthur go to the use of the word in Hebrews instead of jumping into the Gospels?[12]

Third, this is an insult "to the Spirit of grace." It is presuming on the grace of God. It is taking the grace of God for granted. Severe consequences can be expected.

The Consequences of Willful Sin (10:30-31)

For we know Him who said, "Vengeance is Mine, I will repay." And again, "The Lord will judge His people. It is a terrible thing to fall into the hands of the living God (NASB).

The first phrase "Vengeance is Mine" is quoted from Dt. 32:35. Experimental Predestinarians and Arminians are invited to read that chapter and see if they can find any indications that the punishment of eternal hell is in view. Rather, judgments on the people of God **in time** are the subject. The principle the writer is extracting is that, when a Christian fails to persevere and denies Christ, he is no different than the rebellious people of God in the Old Testament and can only expect a similar fate--judgment in time.

The second phrase "the Lord will judge His people" is taken from Dt. 32:36. In Deuteronomy, however, it reads, "The Lord will vindicate His people." Bruce comments, "This certainly means that He will execute judgment on their behalf, vindicating their cause against their enemies, but also that, on the same principles of impartial righteousness, He will execute judgment against them when they forsake His covenant."[13] Thus, either "vindicate" or "judge" are proper renderings of the Hebrew word rendered "vindicate" in Dt. 32:36, and both are consistent with the context of Dt. 32 and of Heb. 10.

God said of Israel, "You only have I known of all the families of the earth: therefore I will visit upon you all your iniquities (Amos 3:2). Greater privilege means greater responsibility and greater discipline for failure to follow the Lord. This was true with the Old Testament people of God on a corporate level, and it is, according to the writer to the Hebrews, true for individual Christians under the New Covenant. It seems that F. F. Bruce is correct when he says, "These words have no doubt been used frequently as a warning to the ungodly of what

---

[11]See 2:11; 9:13; 10:10, 14, 29; 12:14; 13:12.

[12]T. Hewitt and John Owen grant that the sanctification is of the apostate, but they refer it to an external rather than an internal sanctification (T. Hewitt, *Hebrews*, *TNTC*, p. 167). Marshall correctly objects that this "is to read a subtle meaning into the text which is not there, elsewhere in Hebrews sanctified is a description of true Christians" and not just those who are externally so (I. Howard Marshall, *Kept by the Power of God* [Minneapolis: Bethany House, 1969], p. 149). Note also the references in the preceding footnote.

[13]Bruce, pp. 262-63.

lies in store for them unless they amend their ways, but their primary application is to the people of God."[14] This is how the writer of the Epistle to the Hebrews applies the passage. It is clear, however, that there is nothing here about eternal hell or anything that would suggest that the "more severe punishment" implied a loss of salvation.

Exhortation to Persevere (10:32-39)

It is evident that the writer believes that his readers are Christians. They have confessed Christ and have demonstrated the reality of their faith by many good works:

> *But remember the former days, when after being enlightened, you en-*
> *dured a great conflict of sufferings, partly, by being made a public*
> *spectacle through reproaches and tribulations, and partly by becoming*
> *sharers with those who were so treated. For you showed sympathy to*
> *the prisoners and accepted joyfully the seizure of your property,*
> *knowing that you have for yourselves a better possession and an*
> *abiding one* (10:32-34 NASB).

But there is a danger. It is possible that this great beginning will not be completed:

> *Therefore do not throw away your confidence, which has a **great re-***
> ***ward**. For you had need of endurance, so that when **you have done***
> ***the will of God**, you may receive what was promised* (10:35-36
> NASB).

Entrance into heaven is promised to no one on the basis of doing the will of God. What is promised here refers to the "great reward" for perseverance to the final hour. Facing tremendous persecution, these Christians were contemplating rejecting the faith. The danger is not that they will lose salvation but their reward. They will not be of the metochoi, the Partakers, and will not share in the final destiny of man, to rule and have dominion. There is nothing here about their not having "trusted in His Son fully."[15] In the New Testament a man either believes or he does not. Adjectives such as "fully," "genuinely," or "truly" are never found as modifiers of "faith" in the New Testament. They are only found in the writings of Experimental Predestinarians. These people are clearly regenerate, or language has lost its meaning. To say that "they had not done the will of God fully because they had not trusted His Son fully"[16] is to subvert the obvious meaning of the text and the context in the interest of forcing the passage to fit

---

[14]Ibid., p. 263.

[15]MacArthur, *Hebrews*, p. 282.

[16]Ibid.

into a preconceived system of theology. The text says they had not done the will of God fully **because they had not yet endured**. Their endurance, not their saving faith, is the subject of the passage.

He then cites an Old Testament warning from Habakkuk:

For yet in a very little while, He who is coming will come, and will not delay. But **My righteous one***, shall live by faith; and* **if he shrinks back***, My soul has no pleasure in him* (10:37-38 NASB).

It is possible for God's "righteous one," the regenerate Christian, to "shrink back." But the writer encourages them away from that option:

But we are not of those who shrink back to destruction, but of those who have faith to the preserving of the soul (Heb. 10:39 NASB).

The "preserving of the soul" is a common term for the maintaining of physical life (it never means, "go to heaven when you die"). Instead of experiencing "destruction," they will live. The word "destruction" (Gk. **apoleian**) is the common term for "loss" or "destruction" in secular Greek.[17] It is not a technical term for hell. Sometimes it means "waste" (Mk. 4:4) and sometimes "execution" (Acts 25:16 Majority Text). The context (10:26-38) refers to the possible execution of judgment in time on the sinning Christian. The judgment may include physical death or even worse (10:28). In order to avoid the possibility of this sin to physical death--God's discipline resulting in ruin of one's physical life--we must persevere in faith. The danger is that they will not. And if that occurs, that is, if "he shrinks back," then God will have no pleasure in him. This is simply an understatement (litotes) for "God will be very displeased with the Christian who behaves this way."

Conclusion

It is best to interpret Heb. 10 as a warning against the failure to persevere to the end. The consequences of this failure are, according to the Old Testament references quoted, not a loss of salvation but severe divine discipline in time. The God of grace may not always execute these judgments, but common experience shows that the results of willful sin in emotional life can be more severe than death. The most severe punishment, however, is that God will have "no pleasure in Him." When the carnal Christian stands before His Lord in the last day, he will not hear Him say, "Well done, good and faithful servant. Enter into the joy of your Lord."

---

[17]MM, p. 73.

2 Peter 2:20-21

2:18   *For speaking out arrogant words of vanity they entice by fleshly desires,*
by sensuality, those who barely escape *from the ones who live in er-*
ror,

2:19   *promising them freedom while they themselves are slaves of corrup-*
tion; for by what a man is overcome, by this he is enslaved.

2:20   *For if they have escaped the defilements of the world by the knowledge*
of the Lord and Savior Jesus Christ, they are again entangled in them
and are overcome, then the last state has become worse for them than
the first.

2:21   *For it would be better for them not to have known the way of righ-*
teousness, than having known it, to turn away from the holy com-
mandment delivered to them.

2:22   *It has happened to them according the true proverb, "A dog returns to*
its own vomit," and, "A sow, after washing, returns to wallowing in the
mire" (NASB).

Peter seems to be speaking of true believers in these verses. The fact that
they escaped (Gk. **apopheugontas**) the corruptions of the world "by knowing (Gk.
epiginosko) our Lord and Savior Jesus Christ" certainly points in that direction.
In addition, they knew the way of righteousness. This word "know," as Shank correctly points out, often suggests a full saving knowledge.[18]

Throughout the context Peter has been talking about false teachers who
deny the Lord (2:1) and who are unbelievably corrupt. It seems that vv. 2:10-19
show that these are the people whom Jude was talking about in Jude 4. They
"deny Jesus Christ" and their condemnation was written about "long ago" (Jude
4). They are non-Christians, never saved in the first place.

The real question is, Who are the "they" at the beginning of v. 20? A natural answer is that the word "they" refers to the false teachers of v. 19. However,
there is good reason to suggest that it refers to the new Christians who have been
corrupted and led astray by the false teachers in v. 18b.

They entice people who are just escaping [Gk. **apopheugontas**] *from*
those who live in error (2:18b).

Here the reference is to people who are "just escaping," i.e., new converts.
The new believers have been led astray by the immoral libertines described in the
preceding verses of the chapter. The connection between v. 20 and v. 18 seems
certain because Peter brings us back, after a parenthesis in v. 19, to the fact that

---

[18]Robert Shank, *Life in The Son: A Study of the Doctrine of Perseverance* (Springfield:
Westcott, 1961), p. 175. But not always or necessarily. See Bultmann, **"ginosko,"** in *TDNT*, 1:703.

they "escaped" using the same Greek word in both verses (**apopheugeo**). Furthermore, the false teachers do not know Christ, as argued above, yet those addressed in v. 20 have "knowledge of our Lord and Savior Jesus Christ." It is not possible to find an explicit example of a person having "knowledge" (Gk. **epignosis,** "a full and accurate knowledge") who is unregenerate in the New Testament.[19] This suggests that the new Christians of v. 18 are in view.

Peter says "the last state has become worse for them than the former" (2:20). If "last" and "former" are to be taken absolutely, then the meaning is "their final condemnation to hell is worse than their former life of sin." This is banal. It is better to take the terms as "latter" and "former." Then "latter" refers to their current condition, a condition which is in some sense worse than the condition they were in before they were saved.

When he says, "For it would be better for them not to have known the way of righteousness," we must ask, "Why would it be better?" Dunham has suggested that the verb "be" is best rendered by what Moule calls a "desiderative imperfect." It expresses a wish, a potential.[20] So the translation would be "It would almost be better." If this is the rendering, then Peter is saying that in a final sense it is not better, but in terms of this present life, it is better.

The new believers, who have been led back into the worldly life from which they had escaped would have been better off as far as their experience **in this life** was concerned if they had never known Christ at all. They will experience severe divine discipline such as that which came upon Saul. That he refers to their misery in this life, and not eternal damnation, is clear from Peter's quotation of Proverbs 26:11:

> *Of them the proverbs are true: "A dog returns to its vomit," and, "A sow that is washed goes back to her wallowing in the mud"* (2:22).

These newborn babes, who were washed by the bath of regeneration, have returned to the "mud." The most miserable people are sometimes Christians under severe divine discipline. As far as their enjoyment of this life is concerned, they would be far better off never to have known Christ than to endure such correction.

Peter opens his chapter warning that the church will face severe difficulties when and if false teachers enter their congregations (2:1-3). He then describes the characteristics and behavior of these teachers (2:4-17). Finally, he

---

[19]Note usage in 1 Pet. 1:2, 3, 8, 20 and of the verb in 2:21. They all seem to refer to the regenerate.

[20]Duane A. Dunham, "An Exegetical Study of 2 Peter 2:18-22," *BibSac* 140 (January-March 1983): 49. See also C. F. D. Moule, *An Idiom Book of New Testament Greek*, 2d. ed. (Cambridge: University Press, 1959), p. 9.

applies the warning to those most likely to fall into their clutches, new Christians who have just recently escaped the pollutions of the world (2:18-22). He warns them that they will find misery in returning to sin after having enjoyed knowledge of the way of righteousness. Indeed, they will be more miserable than they were before as far as their happiness in this life is concerned. It would almost be better for them not to have known the way of righteousness at all than to fall into a life of carnality after having known the joy of walking with Christ. Turning back to such a state of affairs is like a dog eating its own vomit or a washed pig wallowing in mud.

The passage is a severe warning to those being enticed to return to their former ways of sin, but there is nothing here about loss of salvation.

Revelation 3:5

The Overcomers

In Rev. 2:26 a thrilling promise is held out to those Christians who remain faithful to Christ to the end of life:

And he who overcomes, and he who keeps My deeds until the end, to him I will give authority over the nations (NASB).

In seven other places in this final book similar promises are made to this select company. But who are they?

The Greek word translated "to overcome" is **nikao**. It is found in a legal sense of "winning one's case." It was commonly used of the victor in the games or of the Caesars, "of our all victorious masters the Augusti."[21] The noun **nike** means "victory." **Nike** was the name of a Greek goddess who is often represented in art as a symbol of personal superiority. To be an overcomer was to be victorious in both military and legal combat.[22]

There are three views of the overcomer. Arminians view him as a Christian if he continues in the faith and perseveres under trial. However, if he falls away, he forfeits salvation.[23] Experimental Predestinarians view him as simply a true Christian and as such he will necessarily and inevitably overcome. For them

---

[21]MM, p. 427.

[22]W. Guenther, "Fight," in *NIDNTT*, 1:650.

[23]Marshall, *Kept,* pp. 174-75.

all Christians are overcomers.[24] The Partakers view the overcomer as the faithful Christian, in contrast to one who is not.[25]

The Identity of the Overcomers

There are four reasons given by Experimental Predestinarians for their view that all Christians are overcomers.

The overcomer in 1 John. In 1 Jn. 5:4-5 we are told:

For whatever is born of God overcomes the world; and this is the victory that has overcome the world--our faith. And who is the one who overcomes the world, but he who believes that Jesus is the Son of God? (NASB).

You are from God, little children, and have overcome them (1 Jn. 4:4 NASB).

I am writing to you, young men, because you have overcome the evil one (1 Jn. 2:13 NASB).

It appears that in John's first epistle the overcomer is simply the true Christian.[26] The particular kind of overcoming is believing in Christ (1 Jn. 5:1). The meaning of the phrase in Revelation, however, must be determined from the book of Revelation where it is used in a decidedly different way. There John has in view a victorious perseverance in the midst of trials by which a Christian merits special rewards in eternity, not the initial act of becoming a Christian in which sense all Christians have "overcome the world" by believing.

One Experimental Predestinarian argument used to get around this apparent fact is to appeal to the present tense of the participle "he who overcomes." This supposedly means that the man in view continually and habitually overcomes as a life-style, and not just at a point in time, i.e., saving faith. This device enables them to equate overcoming with an entire life, as in the book of Revelation. However, this is grammatically unlikely. As discussed in chapter 9, the articular present participle is rarely durative in Greek. It acts simply as a noun. So when John refers in 5:1 to "everyone who believes," it is simply a misuse of Greek grammar to insist that John means "everyone who continues to believe." That Experimental Predestinarians have to hang so much of their argument on the

---

[24]James E. Rosscup, "The Overcomer of the Apocalypse," *GTJ* 3 (Fall 1982): 261-86.

[25]Donald G. Barnhouse, *Messages to the Seven Churches* (Philadelphia: Eternity Book Service, 1953), p. 38.

[26]The "whatever" that is "born of God" is evidently the new divine nature.

supposed durative force of the present tense can only be a source of concern. A theological system which depends on such things is leaning on a broken reed.

The fact that all Christians in 1 John are overcomers in no way implies that all Christians in Revelation are. The word **nikao** does not imply "true Christian," only "one who overcomes." To import the contextually derived sense of "regenerate one" from 1 John into the semantic value of the word and then carry this fuller sense into Revelation is simply an illegitimate identity transfer. The meaning and conditions for becoming an "overcomer" in Revelation are completely different. The meaning of overcomer in 1 John has as much relevance to its meaning in Revelation as pulling on the rear end of an automobile has to tugging on an elephant's nose.[27]

The overcomer inherits these things. In Rev. 21:7 the apostle tells us:

He who overcomes shall inherit these things, and I will be his God and he will be My son (NASB).

The advocates of perseverance connect this inheritance with eternal life which comes to all who know Christ. However, consistent with its usage throughout the Bible the word "inherit" is once again a reward for faithful service (e.g., Col. 3:24). Contrary to Rosscup, the context does not "convey the natural impression that blessings the overcomer inherits are for any saved person."[28] Rather, "these things" are those obtained by merit, and not given without cost. To inherit is to own or to possess. The things which the overcomer possesses refer to ownership in contrast to residence in the New Jerusalem. The New Jerusalem will be inhabited by all the saints, but only the overcomers rule there. They are the ones who receive special honor. Clearly, as Lang has suggested, there are three classes of people being compared here.[29]

The first class is specified in v. 6 where we read of a promise to all the saints:

I am the Alpha and Omega, the beginning and the end. I will give to the one who thirsts from the spring of the water of **life without cost** (Rev. 21:6 NASB).

Eternal life is free, a gift which comes solely by means of believing in Christ. John employed similar imagery in recounting the Lord's offer of the free gift of life to the woman at the well (Jn. 4:10, 14) in response to thirst. This offer is of grace; it is a gift; it is, as John says, "without cost." Throughout Revelation

---

[27]Both are trunks.

[28]Rosscup, p. 265.

[29]G. H. Lang, *Firstborn Sons: Their Rights and Risks* (London: Samuel Roberts, 1936; reprint ed., Miami Springs, FL: Conley & Schoettle, 1984), p. 122.

eternal life is offered to the believer freely, without cost (1:5; 7:14; 21:6; 22:14, 17), but the reward which comes to the overcomer costs him everything. This is consistent with the rest of the New Testament, as has been argued in the preceding chapters.

Yet in v. 7 he addresses a second group within those of v. 6, to whom he holds out the possibility of inheriting, of earning a reward by victorious perseverance:

> He who overcomes shall inherit these things, and I will be his God and he will be My son [**huios**, mature son] (Rev. 21:7 NASB).

This outcome costs much, a life of discipleship. Eternal life is absolutely free, but a life of discipleship costs us everything. Is it not obvious that the reference is to those among the saints of v. 6 who have not only received the free gift without cost but have, in addition, persevered faithfully to the final hour?

This thought is consistent with the rest of the book of Revelation. While John occasionally contrasts Christians with non-Christians,[30] his major burden in the book is to challenge Christians to become overcomers by laying before their gaze the magnificent future they can inherit if they are faithful to the end. Repeatedly, the contrasts in this book are between the faithful overcomer and the unfaithful Christian.[31] Since this is so, is not such a contrast to be expected here in this way as well?

The phrase "I will be his God and he will be My son" is defined elsewhere as a statement of special honor, not of regeneration. The Davidic Covenant promised to David's son, Solomon, "I will be a Father to him and he will be a son to Me" (2 Sam. 7:14). The intent of the phrase was to signify a special, intimate relationship. Upon His resurrection from the dead, Jesus was invested with the title "Son" (Acts 13:33), and the reason for this was His humility involving total obedience to the Father's will (Phil. 2:5-10). Similarly, we arrive at the state of full sonship (**huioi**, mature sons, not **tekna**, children) by a life of obedience. All Christians are children (Gk. **tekna**), but not all are obedient mature sons (Gk. **huioi**).[32] The notion that Jesus taught that there are sons and "sons indeed" is discussed elsewhere.[33] Our union with Him, according to the writer of the Letter to the Hebrews means that our path to glory is the same as His. It was because of

---

[30]For example, 22:14-15; 21:26-27.

[31]For example, 2:1-6 vs. 2:7; 2:14-16 vs. 2:17; 2:18-23 vs. 2:24-29; 3:1-3 vs. 3:4-6; 3:11 vs. 3:12; 3:14-19 vs. 3:21.

[32]It may be significant that even though Paul mixes "children" (Gk. **tekna**) and "sons" (Gk. **huioi**), John does not. In every other place in his writings he always uses the term **tekna** to refer to believers. But here he uses **huioi**, full adult sons, in contrast to children. All Christians are, for John, **tekna**, but only the faithful are **huioi**.

[33]See chapter 16. Also note Mt. 5:45, etc.

His obedience that He was entitled to the designation "Son of God," King of Israel. "Thou hast loved righteousness and hated lawlessness; therefore God, thy God, has anointed thee with the oil of gladness above thy companions" (Heb. 1:9).

A similar thought regarding sonship is expressed in Heb. 11:16, "Therefore God is not ashamed to be called their God." God will of course be the God of all in the heavenly city, faithful and unfaithful Christians (Rev. 21:3), but it is apparently possible for us to live life in such a way that God is **proud to be called** our God. Evidently the writer has the title "I am the God of Abraham, Isaac, and Jacob" in mind. This sense fits well the conditional aspect of sonship in Revelation. John's meaning is simply: "Because you have lived a life of constant fellowship with Me," God will say, "I am proud to be known as your God."

The idea here is that God is "proud" to be known as "our God," because we have persevered to the final hour in contrast to other Christians who are sons but not obedient ones and who will draw back from Him in shame at His coming (1 Jn. 2:28).

Finally, in contrast to the two classes of believers in vv. 6 and 7, he describes the fate of the nonbeliever:

But for the cowardly and unbelieving and abominable and murderers and immoral persons . . . their part will be in the lake that burns with fire and brimstone which is the second death (Rev. 21:8 NASB).

There is no evidence here that everyone who is saved overcomes.[34] Rather, he who overcomes is a person who has merited an eternal inheritance, ownership of the heavenly city.[35]

Believers and overcomers partake of the tree of life. In Rev. 22:14 John asserts that all believers will partake of the tree of life. This is the reward to the overcomer in 2:7. If the overcomer does not equal all believers, then a contradiction exists.

---

[34]Rosscup, p. 265.

[35]Some Experimental Predestinarians object that there are no distinctions among believers in the heavenly city mentioned in 21:3-4. But is this not an argument from silence? The fact that these distinctions are not mentioned in these verses does not necessarily imply that they are not real. Many who hold their position acknowledge that there are distinctions in terms of greater and lesser degrees of reward. Are we to deny this truth, too, simply because it is not mentioned? Every verse cannot say everything. In fact, it is common in Hebraic literature to make a general statement and then repeat the same discussion with more detail following. The most obvious illustration of this are the so-called "two creation accounts." But Genesis, chapter 1, is a general statement and Gen. 2 covers the same ground and develops numerous details about the creation of man. Similarly, Rev. 21:3-6 gives a survey of the new order. Then 21:6-8 reviews the survey but gives us more detail.

The phrase "tree of life" is found first in Gen. 3:22, 24. All of its other uses in the Old Testament are confined to the book of Proverbs. There the fruit of the morally upright (Prov. 11:30), a desire fulfilled (Prov. 1 3:12), a gentle tongue (Prov. 15:4), and wisdom (Prov. 3:18) are all called a "tree of life." This usage suggests a quality of life--rich fellowship with God--rather than the notion of regeneration. This fits well with the context of Revelation. Regenerate life comes to all "without cost" (Rev. 22:17), but the "tree of life" is presented as a conditionally earned and merited reward going to those who have not only re-ceived eternal life without cost but who also at great cost to themselves have overcome and persevered to the final hour.

Partaking of the tree of life in 2:7 and 22:14 is a conditional experience of the Christian:

> *Behold, I am coming quickly, and My* **reward** *is with Me, to* **render to** **every man according to what he has done.** . . . *Blessed are those who wash their robes, that they may have the right to the tree of life and may enter by the gates into the city* (Rev. 22:12, 14 NASB).

Because the right to eat of the tree of life is conditional, it is highly un-likely that this experience refers to regeneration, which several verses later is pre-sented by John as offered to all "without cost" on the basis of believing (22:17). Obtaining the right to eat of the tree of life is conditioned upon works. Since eating is commonly a symbol for "fellowship" (Rev. 3:20), it is probable that all that is meant is that those who live godly and pure lives now will enjoy a special fellowship with Christ throughout eternity.

The tree of life yields fruit monthly throughout all eternity:

> *And on either side of the river was the tree of life, bearing twelve kinds of fruit, yielding its fruit every month; and the leaves of the tree were for the healing of the nations* (Rev. 22:2 NASB).

It seems possible therefore to understand participation in the tree of life as a regular experience of fellowshipping with God, i.e., eating of this monthly fruit.

Thus, both verses simply refer to special privileges reserved only for faith-ful believers. Surely Barnhouse is correct:

> *Some have said that eating from the tree of life was the equivalent of receiving eternal life, but this is most evidently a false interpretation. Eternal life is the prerequisite for membership in the true Church. Eating of the tree of life is a reward that shall be given to the over-comer in addition to his salvation. . . . He receives over and above his*

entrance into eternal life, a place in the Heavens in the midst of the paradise of God.[36]

The phrase "wash their robes" is used only two times in Revelation (7:14; 2:14). In Rev. 7:14-15 we read:

"These are the ones who come out of the great tribulation, and they have washed their robes and made them white in the blood of the lamb. For this reason, they are before the throne of God and they serve Him day and night in His temple" (NASB).

Because these people cleaned their own robes, by confession and appropriation of the blood of the Lamb, their garments are not soiled. They have lived faithful and persevering lives. The washing of the robes does not refer to regeneration and justification, which depends upon God, but to progressive sanctification, which depends upon God and us.

Returning to Rev. 22:14, the majority of extant Greek manuscripts read "Blessed are those who keep My commandments" (NKJV). While this may not be the most reliable reading, nevertheless it does reveal that a common ancient understanding of the passage had nothing to do with the cleansing from sin necessary for regeneration. Rather, it reveals that the passage was understood as requiring obedience to His commands in order to obtain his promised reward.

Because it depends upon them, they are being rewarded for their obedience. The "garments" in Revelation refer not to the imputed righteousness of Christ but to the "righteous acts of the saints" (Rev. 19:8).

The church at Sardis had a few people who had "not soiled their garments" (Rev. 3:4). That true Christians are in view is evident from his command to "wake up and strengthen the things that remain, which were about to die; for I have not found your deeds completed in the sight of My God" (3:2). One does not tell non-Christians that their deeds are incomplete and that they are to become Christians by strengthening the things that might remain which were about to die. The death here is, as elsewhere (Rom. 8:13), a possibility for true Christians. It refers to spiritual impoverishment and sin which needs to be repented of. Probably the corporate death of the congregation, the lampstand's removal, is in view. That is why he tells them to repent in v. 3. Many of these true Christians had apparently soiled their garments. They had not "washed their robes" by confessing their sin and performing the righteous acts of the saints.

---

[36]Donald G. Barnhouse, *Revelation: An Expository Commentary* (Grand Rapids: Zondervan, 1971), pp. 43-44. For a similar view see Richard Reagan Benedict, "The Use of Nikao in the Letters to the Seven Churches of Revelation" (Th.M. thesis, Dallas Theological Seminary, 1966), p. 11.

The context of Rev. 22 is similarly conditional. Christ says He is "coming quickly, and My reward is with Me, to render to every man according to what he has done" (Rev. 22:12). Having a right to the tree of life then is a reward to those who have washed their robes, who have walked according to the Spirit, and is not the portion of all who are saved. It is a reward to those among the saved who are faithful. It refers to special fellowship "at the table."

The apostle John spoke of those "who may enter by the gates into the city" (Rev. 22:14). It is probable that he had in mind the victory arches which towered over the main thoroughfares entering into Rome. Through these gates the triumphant Roman generals and their soldiers would march. This is the Arch of Titus near the Forum in Rome. It was constructed after his victory over Jerusalem in A.D. 70. Engravings on it show Roman soldiers bringing back treasures for the temple in Jerusalem. Similarly, those Christians who remain faithful to their King will enter the city in victory and will be likewise honored.

Some have argued that since only those who wash their robes can enter the city, and since entering the city will be a blessing conferred on all Christians, therefore, all Christians are those who have washed their robes and are overcomers (22:14). However, John is placing the emphasis not upon entering the city, but entering "by the gates" into the city. All will enter the city, but only some will come in through the gates. In the Greek text this is emphatic and would be best rendered, "and may **by the gates** enter into the city. The sentence structure suggests that John is giving emphasis to the way of entrance, i.e., by the gates, and not the fact of entrance.

Gates of ancient cities had a purpose of defense or honor or both. To be known "in the gates" was to sit among the "elders of the land" and have position of high honor and authority (Prov. 31:23). Since defense is not a function of these "gates" into the heavenly city, they are to be regarded as places of honor and authority. The overcomer was promised "authority" over the nations (Rev. 2:26). These gates are memorials. Indeed, this is precisely how John describes them elsewhere, as memorials to the twelve tribes of Israel (21:12, 14). We are reminded of the Roman victory arches which sat astride the main thoroughfares entering into Rome. There were thousands of entry ways into Rome, but Caesar entered by the gates, by the victory arch. Through these gates, according to John, "the honor and glory of the nations" will enter (Rev. 21:27). As Lange has suggested, to enter by the gates means to enter "as conquerors in triumphal procession."[37]

It seems that the expression "enter by the gates" is simply a functional equivalent for "enter with special honor." If this is the sense, then no literal gates are in view at all. Some will enter the New Jerusalem with special honor, and some will not. This privilege goes to those who "wash their robes." This refers to confession of sin in the life of the believer and removal of all that is impure, such as sorcery, immorality, murder, idolatry, and lying (Rev. 22:15). The need to "wash" the robes can be paralleled with the Lord's instruction concerning the need to wash the feet, daily confession (Jn. 13:10).

Perhaps the only thing that can properly be alleged against this interpretation is that those who partake of the tree of life are contrasted in the next verse with nonbelievers who are outside the city (Rev. 22:15). It could legitimately be argued that the opposite of a non-Christian is any Christian, not just overcomers. However, that would depend upon the intent of the contrast. Is it not evident that the intent of the contrast here is moral righteousness versus unrighteousness? When making contrasts, it is appropriate to point to the extremes and not items located on a continuum between the extremes. It would therefore be quite natural to contrast the nonbeliever with the victorious overcomer and not with, for example, the lukewarm Christians of Laodicea whom God will spew out of His mouth (Rev. 3:16). Carnal Christians would simply not supply the suitable contrast John has in mind.

It is clear that John attaches different conditions to becoming regenerate and to becoming an overcomer. He tells us that "the water of life is without cost," (Rev. 22:17), and yet a few verses later he explains that becoming an overcomer, obtaining a reward, and securing the right to eat of the tree of life will cost everything (22:11). It depends upon continuing to practice righteousness, remaining holy, and giving attention to our works (22:12). The very chapter under consideration then sets two kinds of Christians before us.

---

[37]John Peter Lange, "Revelation," in *Lange's,* 12:446.

It is possible, like the Ephesian believers, to become so preoccupied with the Lord's work that we forget our devotional relationship to the Lord. We too can lose our first love (Rev. 2:4).

All believers rule. It is sometimes argued that the book of Revelation teaches that all believers will rule and therefore all believers are overcomers.[38] However, the book of Revelation does not teach that all believers will rule over the millennial earth. Only the crowned and rewarded church in heaven rules (cf. 4:10 and 5:10). It is true that all believers will in one sense "reign forever and ever" (22:5), but this is a reference to the eternal state. All believers will not reign over the millennial earth and participate in the final destiny of man. In the three other uses of this word "reign" (Gk. **basileuo**), when applied to Christians, it refers to the rulership in the kingdom.[39] This usage is different and marks the eternal fellowship with Christ in eternity future which all saints will enjoy, although in varying degrees.

Only Faithful Christians Are Overcomers

The teaching that all Christians are overcomers lacks, it seems to this writer, adequate Scripture base. It is better to see the overcomer as the faithful Christian in contrast to those who fail to persevere to the final hour. Several factors suggest this conclusion.

The relevance of the warnings. If the overcomer refers to all Christians, it is difficult to see how the warnings have any relevance to them. Lang objects:

> *It avoids and nullifies the solemn warnings and urgent pleadings of the Spirit addressed to believers, and by depriving the Christian of these, leaves him dangerously exposed to the perils they reveal.*[40]

Rosscup responds that true faith gives a heart to heed God's warnings, "gain victory (1 John 5:4, 5), and forge on with Him."[41] This is no answer at all. If they are truly saved and will, according to Rosscup, receive the reward anyway, how does the warning that they might not receive it have any relevance? A warning about a failure which no one can experience is ludicrous! There is no warning with any "teeth" unless the possibility of failure is real. And if the possibility of failure is real, not only is the overcomer a special class of Christian who perseveres, but the Reformed doctrine of perseverance is fiction.

---

[38] For example, Marshall, p. 254.

[39] Rev. 5:10; 20:4, 6.

[40] G. H. Lang, *Revelation* (Miami Springs: Schoettle, 1985), pp. 91-92.

[41] Rosscup, p. 270.

Rosscup, perhaps sensing the obvious objection to his views, then says that his view "allows the possibility" that some are non-Christians.[42] He wants the warnings to be real and realizes they are not real if there can be no failure. So he shifts to the standard response that those who do not respond to the warnings are revealing that they are not truly saved. He then quotes Mt. 7:23 which helps him not at all. As demonstrated elsewhere, the "fruit" in Mt. 7:23 is not heeding warnings but doctrine. He cites 1 Jn. 2:19, but this refers only to departure from apostolic company by nonbelieving false teachers, and not departure from profession of the faith by non-Christian professors of Christianity.

But Rosscup's view that all Christians are overcomers would yield a different gospel message. The message to non-Christians would not be "believe on the Lord Jesus Christ and you will be saved" but "overcome by returning to your first love (2:5), suffering for Christ (2:10), and keeping Christ's deeds unto the end (2:26)." In other words, Rosscup logically should end up saying that John, the apostle of belief, is now offering salvation to non-Christians on the basis of works.

He says that the word "believe" in John's writings "usually refers to true faith," but he also says the term "can be used for a superficial belief that does not turn out to be properly based and genuine" (Jn. 2:23; 7:31; 12:42; cf. 6:66). However, we only know that the faith was not genuine in these passages if we know that the Experimental Predestinarian view of perseverance is valid. Just because a person does not continue in the faith does not mean he is unregenerate, unless you know before you begin your exegesis of these passages that all true believers will continue in the faith. The circularity of his argument is evident. For John the word "believe" is **always** a term for genuine faith resulting in regeneration.

Rosscup continues his circular reasoning as follows, "Often New Testament passages which address believers weave in warnings that . . . appeal even to the unsaved."[43] But how does one know that the **intent** of the New Testament authors is to do this unless one knows that the doctrine of the saints perseverance is true? He says, "Failure to inherit the kingdom due to tolerating a sinfully indulgent life-style must mean that one will turn out not to be saved."[44] He cites 1 Cor. 6:9-10; Gal. 5:21; and Eph. 5:3-5, which do not prove his point unless we already know that "inherit the kingdom = enter the kingdom." As has been demonstrated elsewhere, this equation is simply false.[45]

If all are overcomers, then none can lose the crown. Now, if it is true that all the saved will receive the crown, as Rosscup argues, then what danger is there of losing it? Indeed, how can the specific warning "I am coming quickly; hold fast

---

[42]Ibid.

[43]Ibid., p. 271.

[44]Ibid.

[45]See chapter 4.

to what you have, in order than no one take your crown" (Rev. 3:11) have any meaning if one cannot in fact lose the crown? Rosscup responds, "Rev. 3:11 more probably refers to an unsaved persecutor who can take the crown from a person who has only a professed relationship with Christ and His church."[46] This seems to be refuted by the plain words of the text, "hold fast to what you have." Surely he is not asking non-Christian professors of Christ to hold fast to their false profession, lest even that be taken from them. Rather, he is talking to true Christians and telling them to hold fast to their genuine faith so that they will receive the reward of perseverance.

If all Christians are overcomers, then John is teaching salvation by works. If these warnings are addressed to non-Christian professors of Christianity, the readers of the book would not only have to be very discriminating but also understand that non-Christians become Christians by works. This is incompatible with the gospel offer and would certainly confuse the supposedly non-Christian readers. Rosscup suggests that this is not incompatible because John the Baptist called upon non-Christians to bring forth fruit in keeping with repentance.[47] But the Baptist **first** asked them to "repent" and **then** live lives of fruitfulness. His command is clear: become a Christian and then live like it. Yet in Rosscup's interpretation of the overcomer, the overcomer is asked to live like a Christian and therefore become one!

If all Christians are overcomers, there is no room for failure. Finally, if all true Christians are overcomers, there is no room for failure in the Christian life. Yet the New Testament presents failure of such magnitude that a true Christian can persist in it to the point of physical death. Such a man is hardly an "overcomer" in the sense which John describes it in Revelation (1 Jn. 5:16; 1 Cor. 11:30, etc.). Rosscup seems to water down John's definition of the overcomer when he tries to draw distinctions between overcomers. The overcomer in Revelation is a man who either does or does not overcome in relation to certain tests. What is in view is not relative degrees of maturity or fruit but overcoming or not overcoming. A man has either repented of his lack of love for Christ or he has not (Rev. 2:5). He has either kept the faith to the point of death or he has not (Rev. 2:10). He has either rejected the teaching of the "depths of Satan" or he has not (Rev. 2:23). They have either repented of sin (3:3) or they have not. They have either persevered under trial or they have not (3:10), etc. Now are we to say that any man who under pressure denies Christ in order to escape torture and persecution and who therefore has not "overcome" is not truly saved? Such a view could only flourish in the pristine purity of the halls of the academy and preferably in a free country like America, not in countries where Christians are persecuted for their beliefs. Yes, we can say that a man who fails like this will

---

[46]Rosscup, p. 272.
[47]Ibid., p. 273.

forfeit his reward, but he surely does not reveal by his failure that he is unregenerate.

The Overcomer in Revelation 3:5

In Rev. 3:5 the overcomer is promised that his name will not be blotted out of the book of life:

He who overcomes will, like them be dressed in white. I will never blot out his name from the book of life, but will acknowledge his name before my Father and his angels.

This raises three questions: Who is the overcomer, what is the book of life, and what is meant by being removed from the book of life? Needless to say, Arminians find in this passage evidence that a true believer can lose his salvation. They have understood that the passage implies it is possible for a believer to have his name removed and hence lose his justification.[48]

Who is the overcomer? As discussed above, the overcomers in Revelation are a separate class of Christians who persevere to the final hour. They are the ones who do God's will to the end, either physical death (2:10; 12:11) or the second coming. As a reward they are given authority over the nations. The singular "he" (2:26) suggests this is an individual thing. Nowhere are we told in Revelation that all Christians will overcome and receive this reward. If that were true, it would eliminate all the motivations for faithfulness. As Fuller put it, "A command that everyone keeps is superfluous, and a reward that everyone receives for a virtue that everyone has is nonsense."[49]

The burden of proof is surely on those who would claim that the warnings are only to professing, and not genuine, believers (as they seem to be) and that the promises are addressed to all believers (as they do not seem to be). The overcomer is the individual Christian who enjoys special benefits in eternity for refusing to give up his faith in spite of persecution during life on earth.

What is the book of life? In the Ancient Near East the book of life was simply a list of the members of a community. Apparently in all Greek and Roman cities of the time, a list of citizens was maintained according to their class or tribe. Those unworthy of the city were removed from the book, and new citizens

---

[48]J. B. Smith, *A Revelation of Jesus Christ* (Scottsdale, PA: Mennonite Publishing House, 1961), pp. 329-31.

[49]J. William Fuller, "I Will Not Erase His Name from the Book of Life (Revelation 3:5)," *JETS* 26 (1983): 299.

were continually added.[50] When a criminal's name was removed from this book, he lost his citizenship.[51]

In ancient Israel it was often the legal register. To "erase his name" meant either (1) physical death (Dt. 29:20) or (2) removal of the memory of a person (Ex. 17:14; Dt. 25:19). It never referred to the loss of salvation. In Ex. 32:32 Moses asks to be blotted out of the book that God has written if He will not forgive Israel.

This is an emotional outburst expressing his deep love for his people. He is asking that God take his physical life, not that he forfeit his eternal destiny. In Ps. 69:28 David asks that the nonbelievers be blotted out of the book and not be listed with the righteous. David asks that they be physically put to death.

Dan. 12:1 says that everyone who is recorded in the book will be delivered from the great tribulation of the end time. This seems to refer to the elect and, in contrast to the other references, seems to refer to direct teaching about their eternal security.

And at that time your people, everyone who is found written in the book, will be rescued.

However, in Revelation it seems to refer to the elect whose names have been recorded in the book since the foundation of the world (13:8; 17:8; 21:27).

What is meant by removal from the book of life? The answer to that question depends upon the meaning of "name." The lexicon lists five usages of **onoma**:[52] name, title or category, person, reputation or fame, and office. They ascribe the meaning "reputation" to **onoma** in Rev. 3:1,[53] and that is how it is translated in the NIV. It is possible that the removal from the book of life refers to the removal of one's reputation, not his person.

The overcomer is promised a new name:

To him who overcomes, to him I will give some of the hidden manna, and I will give him a white stone, and a new name written on the stone which no one knows but he who receives it (Rev. 2:17).

Eric Sauer relates this to a custom of the Greek athletic games. A victor's prize at the games often included objects of value and gifts of gold. According to Plutarch, winners at the Isthmian games were given one hundred drachmas and

---

[50]W. M. Ramsay, *The Letters to the Seven Churches of Asia* (London: Hodder and Stoughton, 1904), p. 385.

[51]Robert H. Mounce, *The Book of Revelation, NICNT,* 18:113.

[52]AG, pp. 573-77.

[53]Ibid., p. 577.

at the Olympics, five hundred. The winner received a certificate of victory which was a small tablet of white stone in which the name of the victor was inscribed by an expert carver.[54]

The believer possessing this white stone with a name on it will submit it to the heavenly judge and will be recognized as a victor in the battle. Even though despised on earth, he will be honored in heaven. The sentence of rejection is reversed. Those hated and expelled here will be honored with heavenly riches and eternal glory.

Christ will give to each overcomer a new name, a name of honor. Yet this name is known to no one but Christ and the one to whom He gives it. Each believer has his own particular life message, his own particular history of struggle and demonstration of God's life in his. God is a God of the individual as well as of the church. The secrecy of the name implies a special relationship between Christ and each overcomer.

The giving of a "new name" was a Jewish custom of assigning a name at a point in life which characterizes the life.[55] In the early church James was called "camel knees" because of the callouses on his knees from so much praying. Joseph, a Levite of Cyprian birth, was called "Barnabas" which means "son of encouragement." James and John were known as the "sons of thunder" and Saul of Tarsus preferred to be known as "Paul" ("little"), remembering that he was the least of the apostles and the greatest of sinners.

But perhaps the greatest illustration of the gift of the new name was the name given to a carpenter's son who grew up in a military camp town, Nazareth. Because He was obedient, even to the death of a cross, He was given a new name, "THE LORD JESUS CHRIST."[56] Just as His new name was earned by faithful obedience, so it is with the many sons He is leading to glory.[57]

What then does it mean to have one's name blotted out of the book of life? There are two suggestions which do not require the interpretation that it refers to the loss of one's justification.

First, this could refer to a promise that the overcomer's reputation will not be blotted out. This view is suggested by William Fuller. He points out:

(1) If name always means "person," then a difficult tension is set up between Rev. 3:5 and Rev. 13:8, Rev. 17:8, and Rev. 21:27. In 13:8, 17:8, and 21:27

---

[54]Eric Sauer, *In the Arena* (Grand Rapids: Eerdmans, 1966), pp. 64-65.

[55]See Jud. 6:31-32, where Gideon was renamed Jerub-Baal which means "Let Baal contend with him" because he took a stand against Baal and cut down his altars.

[56]Phil. 2:9.

[57]Heb. 2:10.

we are told that, if our name is recorded in the book of life, it was so recorded from the foundation of the world. In other words, it is an absolute and unchanging thing. But in Rev. 3:5 we are told that a person's name can be present at one time and absent at another. One emphasizes the permanence of the name and the other the possibility of temporal removal. This is easily harmonized by the simple assumption that "name" means "person" in Rev. 13:8, 17:8, and 21:27, and "reputation" in 3:5.

(2) The overcomer can achieve a new name, 2:17; 3:12, i.e., a spiritual reputation in the sight of God. He will have a reputation in heaven which conformed to his earthly faithfulness. Here "name" cannot mean "person," and the theme of "reputation" is clearly the subject of Rev. 3:1-12.

(3) In Rev 3:1 a name is a reputation. It is descriptive of the person's life and faithfulness. Why should the meaning be different in Rev. 3:5?

(4) Throughout Revelation the life of good works produces a reputation in heaven (2:2, 19; 3:1, 8, 19). The good reputation results in turn in an honorable eternal identity, a new name (2:17; 3:12).

(5) The Old Testament often referred to the name of a man as his reputation and honor. In Prov 22:1 a good name is to be desired more than great riches.[58] Job 30:8 notes that those who had a bad reputation were called "nameless." Being nameless is to be compared with having one's name blotted out of the book of life.[59]

If "name" in Rev. 3:5 refers to a reputation or title, then God is saying, "I will not blot his title or reputation out of the book of life." A name in the sense of "title" or "reputation" may be blotted out but not in the sense of person. God will remember and preserve the **onoma** of the Christian who overcomes, implying a peculiarly close relationship between God and the believer. The quality of eternal life is determined by our faithfulness.

Should it be objected that God has promised He will not forget our labor of love (Heb. 6:10), it could be replied that He WILL forget it in the lives of those who have not overcome. Final failure cannot be reversed. There is no second chance:

> *But if a righteous man turns from his righteousness and commits sin*
> *and does the same detestable things the wicked man does, will he live?*

---

[58]See Isa. 56:4-5. Isaiah speaks of "eunuchs" who (1) keep the Sabbath; (2) choose what pleases God; and (3) hold fast to God's covenant (Isa. 56:4). As a reward for these works of obedience, God says He will give them a memorial and a name within His temple and its walls: "I will give him an everlasting name that will not be cut off" (Isa. 56:6). "Name" is used here in the sense of "reputation" or "memorial." This reputation will be eternal, as a memorial to a faithful life.

[59]Fuller, pp. 299ff.

None of the righteous things he has done will be remembered (Ezek. 18:24).

I tell you that to everyone who has, more will be given, but as for the one who has nothing, even what he has will be taken away (Lk. 19:26).

What may be promised then in Rev. 3:5 is a unique and honorable eternal identity. It is this promise which makes endurance through these trials conceivable. The unfaithful Christian will find, however, that at the second coming, he will be ashamed of his name (Mt. 10:33; 2 Tim. 2:12). John is simply saying that, even if we are ridiculed and ultimately killed for our faith here on earth so that our name is dishonored and forgotten, we will, if we persevere, enjoy a heavenly reputation for all eternity. Our name will never be blotted out in heaven. No Christian will ever have his person blotted out of the book of life, even carnal ones. The overcomer is being reminded that, even though they can destroy him on earth, they cannot ever ruin his heavenly name.

But there is a second way of interpreting this verse. Martin Lloyd-Jones has approached the passage from the assumption that "name" always means person throughout the book.[60] This has the advantage of consistency over the previous interpretation. He explains the apparent contradiction between 13:8 and 3:5 by saying 3:5 is an illustration of a figure of speech known as litotes. In this figure "an affirmative meaning is expressed by denying its opposite."[61] When we say, "an artist of no small stature," we mean he is an outstanding artist. When Paul says of the rebellious wilderness generation, "God was not pleased with most of them" (1 Cor. 10:5), he means that God was extremely displeased with all of them but two! When Paul says, "I am not ashamed of the gospel," he really means that he is very proud of it. Or when Luke says the believers were "not a little comforted" at the restoration of Eutychus to life (Acts 20:12), he means they were "exceedingly" comforted.[62]

These examples reveal the key to understanding a litotes. The negative idea is not central. Rather, the interpreter must focus on the positive idea to which the negative refers. Thus, when the Lord says, "I will not blot his name out," He is not implying that there is such a possibility, but He is saying emphatically that He will keep his name in the book. The point is that what happens in

---

[60]D. Martin Lloyd-Jones, *Romans Chapter 8:17-39: The Final Perseverance of the Saints* (Grand Rapids: Zondervan, 1976), pp. 314ff.

[61]*The Lexicon Webster Dictionary*, s.v. "litotes."

[62]Cited by AS, p. 289, as an illustration of litotes. As futher illustrations, when the writer to the Hebrews says, "God is not unjust to forget your work and labor of love" (Heb. 6:10), he is saying that God most certainly will not forget it. When Jim Elliot said, "He is no fool to give up what he cannot keep to obtain what he cannot lose," the phrase "is no fool" means "is very smart."

Greek and Roman cities, i.e., removal of one's name, can never happen in regard to the book of life.

Not only will his name be kept in the book, not only is his eternal security guaranteed, but his name will also be acknowledged by Christ before His holy angels.

The statement is surely parallel to our Lord's famous words:

I tell you, whoever acknowledges me before men, the Son of Man will also acknowledge him before the angels of God (Lk. 12:8)

Whoever acknowledges me before men, I will also acknowledge him before my Father in heaven. But whoever disowns me before men, I will disown him before my Father in heaven (Mt. 10:32-33).

Only those Christians who acknowledge Christ now will be acknowledged by Him then. Only those Christians who are overcomers now will have their names acknowledged before the Father and His angels (Rev. 3:5). But having one's name "acknowledged" is not the same as being declared saved. Rather, it refers to the public testimony by the Son of God to the faithful life of the obedient Christian. Conversely, not having one's name acknowledged is to forfeit the Master's "Well done."

In summary, then, we note that three blessings accrue to the overcomer: (1) he will be dressed in white; (2) his name will never be blotted out of the book of life; and (3) his name will be acknowledged by Christ to the Father in the presence of the holy angels. The first is a special honor to those who are worthy (3:4). It may consist of some special token of the purity of their lives. In other uses it refers to righteous acts and not justification (19:8, 14). The second is a reminder that no matter what they do to him on earth, he will emphatically not lose his eternal security. And finally, he is assured that he will be publicly acknowledged before the Father in contrast to the unfaithful Christian who will not.

Both interpretations are exegetically sound, and Arminians can therefore find no necessary argument here for their doctrine of conditional security.

Revelation 22:18-19

The apostle John's solemn warning about not adding any words to the book of Revelation has understandably been put into the service of the doctrine of conditional security:

I warn everyone who hears the words of the prophecy of this book: If anyone adds anything to them, God will add to him the plagues de-

scribed in this book. And if anyone takes words away from the book of prophecy, God will take away from his share in the tree of life and in the holy city, which are described in this book (Rev. 22:18-19).

To have a share in the tree of life and in the holy city does not, as discussed above, refer to going to heaven. Rather, it refers to the privileged position of the metochoi. The danger is disinheritance and not loss of salvation. A share in the tree of life is always in Scripture an additional blessing which comes to those who are already saved.

Chapter 21

Eternal Security

We come at last to the specific biblical evidence for the eternal security of the believer. The Arminian denies that the true child of God is eternally secure, and the Experimental Predestinarian insists that, if he does not persevere in holiness, he was never regenerate in the first place.

The Partaker, however, teaches that, if he is a true child of God, he is "obligated" to persevere (Paul's word, Rom. 8:12), but he may not. If he does not, he does not forfeit salvation but faces divine discipline in time and loss of reward at the judgment seat of Christ.

R. T. Kendall put it this way, "A man who is truly saved will go to heaven when he dies no matter what work (or lack of work) may accompany such faith. This is not unbecoming of the gospel, **it honors it!**"[1]

This doctrine is called eternal security, or the preservation of the saints. While the Experimental Predestinarians prefer the term perseverance, the Partaker favors "preservation." The former implies that our ultimate arrival in heaven is dependent upon our faithfulness and the latter that it depends upon God.

It is important to stress some points of clarification:

1.   This doctrine does not teach that a person who prays a prayer, walks down the aisle, or folds the corner of an invitation card at an evangelistic meeting is necessarily going to heaven. Mere intellectual acceptance of Christ with no acknowledgment of one's sinfulness before God is not saving faith.

2.   This doctrine does not teach that those who act like believers outwardly, who attend church, are necessarily going to heaven. We only assert that among those who have outward Christianity are those who have it inwardly as well. Those and only those who have

---

[1]R. T. Kendall, *Once Saved Always Saved* (London: Hodder and Stoughton, 1984), p. 41.

this principle of life within them will be finally saved and will never lose it.

3.   This doctrine does not condone the existence of carnal and dead Christians in our churches. On the contrary, the doctrine of eternal security includes the highest motivation for godly service--unconditional acceptance, and the desire to hear the Master's "Well done!" The fact that some may take advantage of the grace of God does not nullify that grace. Our doctrine stresses that God will discipline the child of God who persists in sin and that sinning child risks severe punishment in this life and the fearful possibility of future disinheritance (Heb. 12:3-15). This is a powerful incentive toward a faithful life.

4.   This doctrine does teach that those whom God has chosen before the foundations of the world and efficaciously called into saving faith and regenerated by His Holy Spirit can never lose salvation but shall be preserved in a state of salvation to the final hour and be eternally saved.

Can a man lose his salvation? Yes! If it depends upon him. A belief in conditional security necessarily leads to consideration of what sin or sins are necessary to forfeit salvation. If we entertain even the remotest possibility that there is something we can do or not do which can nullify the value of the blood of Christ, we will focus our attention on our obedience, and not Christ's blood. This is the way human nature works. This explains the high degree of legalism in Arminian circles. If 99 per cent of saved people cannot be lost, but one percent can, we have no sense of security, ever. We would constantly be worried as to whether or not we were one of the 1 per cent. We would need to know what kind of sin or disobedience it is that catches out the one percent. Whatever that sin may be, we would live in constant horror that we just might, one day, commit such a sin. We are no different than anyone else (1 Cor. 10:13).

From Genesis to Revelation salvation is presented as a work of God. God the Father purposes, calls, justifies, and glorifies those who believe on Christ. God the Son became incarnate that He might be a Kinsman-Redeemer and die a substitutionary death. He rose to be a living Savior, both as Advocate and Intercessor, and as Head over all things to the church. God the Holy Spirit administers and executes the purpose of the Father and the redemption which the Son has wrought. Therefore, all three persons of the Godhead have their share in preserving to fruition that which God has determined.

Salvation depends upon God. Since it depends upon Him and not upon us, it cannot be lost. First of all, our eternal security . . .

Depends upon God the Father

From eternity past God's firm purpose has been established. The Scriptures tell us that before the foundations of the world He elected us to salvation in Christ and predestined us to glory. It is therefore clear that our eternal security depends, first of all:

Upon His Sovereign Purpose

Predestined to glory. God's eternal purpose cannot be defeated in the realization of all He intends, and bringing His redeemed to glory is a major aspect of His divine purpose. That eternal purpose is declared in Eph. 1:11-12:

> *In Him also we have obtained an inheritance, having been predestined according to His purpose who works all things after the counsel of His will, to the end that we who were the first to hope in Christ should be to the praise of His glory* (NASB).

Eph. 1:4-6 adds:

> *Just as He chose us in Him before the foundation of the world, that we should be holy and blameless before Him. In love He predestined us to adoption as sons through Jesus Christ to Himself, according to the kind intention of His will, to the praise of the glory of His grace, which He freely bestowed on us in the Beloved* (NASB).

If we have been predestined to adoption as sons and to an inheritance, it is therefore not possible that we can lose it. Otherwise God's predestination will fail. It depends upon whether or not God can accomplish His intentions. "When anyone is born again of the Holy Ghost and justified in Christ, it is because God had formed, from eternity, the unchangeable purpose to save that soul. The work of grace in it is the mere carrying out of that unchangeable purpose. As the plan is unchangeable, so must be its execution."[2]

Arminian writer I. Howard Marshall attempts to blunt the impact of this by asking whether God's predestination simply outlines a purpose for those who believe or also includes "the predestination of certain individuals to an inevitable final salvation." His argument is somewhat unclear. He says "all that we are told is that God foreordains those who believe to become holy and to be His sons." He then adds, "It [predestination] does not automatically guarantee the response

---

[2]Robert Dabney, *Lectures in Systematic Theology* (1878; reprint ed., Grand Rapids: Zondervan, 1972), p. 690.

of those called or the final salvation of those who do respond."[3] But it does! To predestine is to preplan. If God has preplanned that some will have the inheritance of heaven (1:11), to heaven they will go unless God does not have the power or intention of carrying out His plans! As far as we can tell, Marshall is giving no answer at all. He is simply looking at the text, asserting the precise opposite of what it says and then moving on to his next point.

We have an anchor within the veil. The writer of the Epistle to the Hebrews makes this point in Heb. 6:17-20:

> *Because God wanted to make the unchanging nature of his purpose very clear to the heirs of what was promised, he confirmed it with an oath. God did this so that, by two unchangeable things in which it is impossible for God to lie, we who have fled to take hold of the hope offered to us may be greatly encouraged. We have this hope as an anchor for the soul, firm and secure. It enters the inner sanctuary behind the curtain, where Jesus, who went before us, has entered on our behalf.*

God wanted to show the unchangeable nature of His eternal purpose to give us an anchor within the veil (v. 19) and confirmed it by an oath. Now if He purposed before the foundation of the world to save His elect, His elect will be saved.

Even if the election of God was based on the foreseen knowledge of the believer's faith, the same argument applies. If God knew that we would believe and be saved, then we cannot do otherwise than believe and be saved. If we do believe and then for some reason unknown to God are not saved, then God did not know, and His foreseen knowledge was false. If God does not certainly know that an event will take place, then He does not know it at all. But if He knows certainly that an event will occur, then the occurrence of that event must be without failure.

The golden chain. Theodore Beza, Calvin's successor at Geneva, argued persuasively that Rom. 8:28-30 describes an unbreakable chain consisting of five links:

> *For whom He* **foreknew,** *He also* **predestined,** *and these He also* **called;** *and whom He called, these He also* **justified;** *and whom He justified, these He also* **glorified.**

Note the terms, "whom" and "these also." They link, as in a chain, the history of the same group of people from foreknowledge to glorification. The same group which was foreknown, will also ultimately be glorified.

Foreknowledge

Predestination

Calling

Justification

Glorification

The word "foreknowledge" is most probably a reference to the prior choice of God, and not merely His advance knowledge. For example, in Amos 3:2 God says of Israel, "Only thee have I known of all the nations of the earth." Obviously God has knowledge of the other nations, but only Israel was chosen. It is a personal, loving, and intimate prior choice.

To predestine is simply to plan in advance.

The call referred to here is the efficacious call to come to Him. Jesus said, "My sheep hear My voice and they follow Me." All those who are foreknown are predestined. All those who are predestined are called, and all of those who are called are justified. This calling is an effectual calling. And all those who are justified will be glorified. This refers to the redemption of our bodies at the last day (Rom. 8:23).

The two-verse chain with its five-fold unbreakable links, "those ... he also," is a clear statement of the eternal security of the saints.

John Wesley, in the face of such a passage, finally resorted to reading phrases into the text which are not there in order to salvage his doctrine of conditional security. Listen:

> *And whom He justified -* **provided they continue in His goodness,**
> *Romans 11:22, He in the end glorified - St. Paul does not affirm, either here or in any other part of his writings, that precisely the same number of men are called, justified and glorified. He does not deny that a believer may fall away and be cut off between his special calling and his glorification, Romans 11:22. Neither does he deny that many*

are called who are never justified.   He only affirms that this is the method whereby God leads us step by step towards Heaven.[4]

But God certainly does affirm that "precisely the same number of men are called, justified, and glorified." He affirms it in this passage. To deny it is like looking at the sun and saying there is no light! Wesley is deliberately contradicting the clear intent of the passage in the interests of his pet doctrine that the justified can lose salvation. He offers absolutely no exegetical proof whatsoever for his view. Paul **does** say that all who are called in this sense are justified. That there is an ineffectual call is acknowledged by all, including Wesley, but this one is effectual!

His solemn promise. Now all that He has purposed, He unconditionally promises to His elect. Our salvation depends upon His promise, and not our faithfulness:

> *It is by faith* [nothing on man's part] *that it might be by grace* [everything on God's part]*, to the end the promise might be sure* (Rom. 4:16 KJV).

If the intended end depended at any point on human ability to continue to believe, then the promise could not be sure. The promise that those who believe will be saved is found all over the Bible (Gen. 15:6; Jn. 3:16; Acts 16:33; Rom. 4:23-24):

Some Arminians attempt to make a point out of the present tense of "does not come into judgment." They want this to mean that there is no judgment in the present as long as we continually believe. However, this is a use of the present tense called the futuristic present. "It is the present in a vivid lively sense projected into the future."[5] It takes a future event and places it into the present tense to give heightened certainty and vividness to it, precisely the opposite of how they want to interpret it.

But our eternal security depends not only upon His sovereign purpose, but also . . .

Upon His Infinite Power

He is free to save us. If we can lose salvation, then we must conclude that there is some sin which is sufficiently serious to cause us to forfeit it--perhaps adultery, drunkenness, or denial of Christ.

---

[4]John Wesley, *Explanatory Notes upon the New Testament*, 1754, cited by Marshall, p. 103.

[5]A. T. Robertson, *A Grammar of the Greek New Testament in the Light of Historical Research* (New York: Hodder and Stoughton, 1914), p. 353.

This assumes that we were less worthy of salvation after having committed this sin than before, and it reduces salvation down to human ability to merit it. Our eternal security does not depend upon our moral worthiness. If it did, none of us would be saved. Rather, it depends upon the fact that Christ's death has rendered God free to save us in spite of moral imperfection and that God's power is capable of keeping us saved.

No Arminian claims that normal sins are sufficient to "unsave" a man. Only very wicked sins are adequate. Which ones? How long must they be persisted in in order to forfeit salvation? The impossibility of answering this question has left generations of Arminians turning in the wind regarding the final outcome of their lives.

Because Christ is the propitiation for our sins (1 Jn. 2:2), God is not only able to keep us saved, but He is free to do so in spite of the moral problem of the imperfection in each Christian.

We all have imperfections. If salvation can be lost because of a high decree of imperfection, then we have to draw arbitrary lines of difference between sins which are able to damn and those which are not. Who therefore is worthy? Not Augustine, Paul, you, or this writer.

He has purposed to keep us saved. In no uncertain terms our Lord declares:

> *And this is the will of him who sent me, that I shall lose none of all that he has given me, but raise them up at the last day. For my Father's will is that everyone who looks to the Son and believes in him shall have eternal life, and I will raise him up at the last day* (Jn. 6:39).

It is not God's will that Christ will lose any of all the Father gave to Him.[6] Consider:

> *My sheep listen to my voice; I know them, and they follow me. I give them eternal life, and they shall never perish; no one can snatch them out of my hand. My Father, who has given them to me, is greater than all; no one can snatch them out of the Father's hand* (Jn. 10:27-29).

Arminians customarily evade the force of all these passages by asserting that all gospel promises have an implied condition. That is, it is to be understood that the promises will be fulfilled only if the believer remains faithful to the final hour. This, however, is simply an assertion not supported by the texts. One can read all kinds of conditions into these precious promises, but the promises them-

---

[6]Judas was a "son of perdition" and was never "given" but was unregenerate.

selves, as stated, are unconditional, and one is dangerously close to adding words to the Scripture when he argues this way.

Robert Shank points out that v. 27 must be included in the promise. Only those who hear and follow will never perish. He wants "follow" to imply life of obedience.[7] The context, however, is not speaking of obedience but of belief and unbelief.

> *But you do not believe, because you are not of My sheep* (v. 26 NASB).

The opposite of not believing is found in v. 27--to hear and follow. To follow is not to obey but to trust and believe. This is suggested by the fact that sheep will not follow the voice of an unknown shepherd. They fear the voice of strangers (vv. 4-5). The act of "following" is the act of reliant trust. This is supported by the fact that eternal life is the result of following. It would therefore seem intrinsically unlikely that "follow" is a metaphor for obedience because elsewhere in John eternal life is the result of faith alone.

Experimental Predestinarians are similarly confounded by the passage. Their doctrine states that He first gives eternal life and as a result the sheep follow. Here it is the reverse! Furthermore, if "follow" means to obey Christ all one's life, then it is not possible to obtain eternal life until one has obeyed all his life. In other words, it cannot be received as a gift now, contrary to the gospel promise (Jn. 17:3).

The use of "hear and believe" in Jn. 5:24 seems to further support this interpretation:

> *Truly, truly, I say to you, he **who hears My word, and believes** Him who sent Me, has eternal life; and does not come into judgment, but has passed out of death into life* (Jn. 5:24 NASB).

Hearing and believing there result in eternal life. "Hearing and following" in Jn. 10:27 result in eternal life. Therefore "hearing and believing" equals "hearing and following." This means that "to follow" is simply another of John's metaphors for "to believe." He has also used "look," "taste," "eat," and "drink." Are literal eating, looking, tasting, and drinking necessary for eternal life? Hardly! Neither is literal following. To follow the shepherd is to believe on Him.

The phrase "shall never" is a double negative in Greek. It is very emphatic. It is often claimed that the text only promises that someone else cannot snatch the believer out of the Father's hand. The believer, it is said, can snatch

---

[7]Robert Shank, *Life in The Son: A Study of the Doctrine of Perseverance* (Springfield: Westcott, 1961), p. 56.

himself out of the Father's hand, however, by unbelief or sin. But is that all these precious words mean? If so, then they mean nothing. To any man who really knows his own heart, these implied conditions would nullify the promises. What kind of security is it that offers no security against our own weakness?

> *I find then the principle that evil is present in me, the one who wishes to do good* (Rom. 7:21 NASB).

Both Arminians and Experimental Predestinarians agree that we are only kept by faith, as Peter tells us:

> *Blessed be the God and Father of our Lord Jesus Christ, who according to His great mercy has caused us to be born again to a living hope through the resurrection of Jesus Christ from the dead to obtain an inheritance which is imperishable and undefiled and will not fade away, reserved in heaven for you who are* **protected by the power of God through faith** *for a salvation ready to be revealed in the last time* (1 Pet. 1:3-5 NASB).

Arminian Robert Shank sees this as proof that our final arrival in heaven is dependent upon our persevering in faith.[8] Experimental Predestinarian Norman Sellers sees it the same way, but he adds the idea that God will sustain the believer's faith.[9] If we had to choose between these two options, at least Shank sticks with the text and adds nothing through theological exegesis. Nothing is said here about God supplying the faith which his own perseverance requires.

However, we do not have to choose between these two extremes. The salvation to be revealed in the last time is not deliverance from hell as both Shank and Sellers assume. Rather, it is the glorious reign of the metochoi in the coming kingdom. Those Christians who persevere in faith keep themselves for this great privilege.

If our enjoyment of the promises of eternal security is dependant upon our continued ability to persevere, as Arminians maintain, then the loss of our justification is not only possible but probable. Are we to suppose that Christ's meaning is that no one can snatch us out of the Father's hand provided we do not choose to allow ourselves to be snatched away? Are we to suppose that Christ did not know the common biblical truth that the only way any spiritual danger can attack a soul successfully is by persuasion, that unless the adversary can get the consent of the believer's free will, he cannot harm him? Is there any other way a soul can be snatched away other than by the consent of the soul itself? Dabney observes, "Surely Jesus knew this; and if this supposed condition is to be understood, then

---

[8]Ibid., p. 272.

[9]C. Norman Sellers, *Election and Perseverance* (Miami Springs, FL.: Schoettle, 1987), p. 180.

this precious promise would be a worthless and pompous truism." It would then mean only this:

> *You can never be snatched away except by the only way anyone can be snatched away.*

or

> *No one can take you out of the Father's hand except, of course, by the only means anyone can take you out of the Father's hand.*

or

> *You can never fall unless, of course, you do.*

or

> *You can never fall as long as you stand up.*

God's purpose to ultimately save His elect is not based only upon His infinite power but it also depends . . .

Upon His "Much More" Love

The preservation of the saved flows from the free and unchangeable love of the Father. It was God's love, not the Christian's worthiness, which was the reason for his salvation in the first place. The Scriptures make it plain that God saved no man because he observed some good, attractive, or meriting attribute in an individual sinner. Rather, He saved us for reasons independent of us and outside of us. He was motivated by His electing love, and not by observation of good in the sinner.

> *Not only that, but Rebecca's children had one and the same father, our father Isaac. Yet, before the twins were born or had done anything good or bad--in order that God's purpose in election might stand: not by works but by Him who calls--she was told, "The older will serve the younger." Just as it is written: "Jacob I loved, but Esau I hated"* (Rom. 9:10-13).

Now since the cause of the sinner's salvation had nothing to do with any imagined merit or goodness in the sinner, neither does the preservation of the saint. Since God was not motivated to impart saving grace based on foreseen good works, the subsequent absence of those works would be no new motive for Him to withdraw His grace. God knew when He saved us that we were totally depraved, and therefore any new manifestation of sin in our lives after our conversion cannot be any motivation to God to change His mind and withdraw salvation. God knew about all our subsequent sinfulness before He saved us.

Consider:

For the gifts and call are irrevocable (Rom. 11:29 NASB).

He who did not spare his own Son, but gave him up for us all--how will he not also, along with him, graciously (freely) give us all things? (Rom. 8:32).

For I am convinced that neither death nor life, neither angels nor demons, neither the present nor the future, nor any powers, neither height nor depth, nor **anything else in all creation,** *will be able to separate us from the love of God that is in Christ Jesus our Lord* (Rom. 8:38-39).

That God's intent to bring His elect to glory is grounded in His infinite love for them is clearly brought out in Rom. 5:6-10:

You see, at just the right time, when we were still powerless, Christ died for the ungodly. Very rarely will anyone die for a righteous man, though for a good man someone might possibly dare to die. But God demonstrates his own love for us in this: While we were still sinners, Christ died for us. Since we have now been justified by his blood, how much more shall we be saved from God's wrath through him! For if, when we were God's enemies, we were reconciled to him through the death of his Son, how much more, having been reconciled, shall we be saved through his life!

If God will do all this for us when we were His enemies, He will surely do much more now that we are His friends. If He did the harder thing (die for us) when we were His enemies, He will surely do the easier thing (save us from the coming wrath) now that we are His friends. Love has removed every barrier to eternal security which sin had erected, and the "much more" love will surely keep those whom He has chosen before the foundation of the world.

Finally, eternal security is grounded in the Father's faithfulness; it does not depend upon us. Rather, it depends . . .

Upon His Answer to the Prayer of His Son

The saved are called many things in Scripture: saints, believers, sheep, Christians, partakers of the heavenly calling, etc. But the title most dear to the heart of Christ is repeated seven times in His high priestly prayer--"those whom

You have given Me."[10] This phrase, according to Jn. 17:20, includes all who would believe in Him throughout the ages:

Holy Father keep them in Thy name, the name which Thou has given Me, that they may be one, even as We are. While I was with them, I was keeping them in Thy name which Thou has given Me; and I guarded them and not one of the perished but the son of perdition (Jn. 17:11-12 NASB).

The keeping is from perishing. Christ kept them from this while He was on earth, and He now asks the Father to keep us. The prayer that they may be one is no doubt a prayer for the organic unity of all believers. No member shall be absent.

Judas was not kept because he was never one whom the Father had given Him; he was a son of perdition. Jesus specifically says of him, "There are some of you who do not believe." That He had Judas in mind is clear from the following phrase, "For Jesus knew from the beginning who they were who did not believe, and who it was that would betray Him" (Jn. 6:64).

The Son asks the Father to keep those saved whom the Father has given to the Son. Even if the Father had no personal interest in keeping them saved, which He does, He must respond to the prayer of the Son, whose prayers are always answered (Jn. 11:42). Jesus prays that we will be kept from hell (Jn. 17:15) and that we will be with Him in heaven (Jn. 17:20, 24). Will not the prayers of the Son of God be answered?

It is thus the prayer of the Son of God to the Father that becomes one of the major factors in the believer's security. To deny the safekeeping of the believer is to imply that the prayer of the Son of God will not be answered.

Not only has God the Father committed Himself by oath to guarantee the eternal security of His elect, but God the Son, through His active and passive obedience has made our final arrival into heaven certain. Our eternal security does not depend upon us, but it ...

Depends upon God the Son

The apostle Paul specifically raises the question of eternal security in his magnificent conclusion to Rom. 8:

What, then, shall we say in response to this (8:31).

---

[10]Jn. 17:2, 6, 9, 11-12, 20, 24.

Paul has just finished presenting the "golden chain" (8:29-30). These five unbreakable links guarantee the believer's eternal destiny. What shall we say in response to this "golden chain," he now asks?

> *If God is for us, who can be against us? He who did not spare his own Son, but gave him up for us all--how will he not also, along with him, graciously give us all things? Who will bring any charge against those whom God has chosen? It is God who justifies* (Rom. 8:31-33).

Paul's argument is that, if God has already justified the man who believes in Jesus (Rom. 3:26; 8:30), how can He lay anything to the charge of His justified one? God, of all people, sees the Christian's failures and imperfections. He does not shut His eyes to these failures but disciplines His children because of them.

However, His justification comes from the imputed righteousness of Christ and is legally ours. It is not a subject of merit, and its loss cannot be a subject of demerit. Like a human father, God can and does correct His earthly sons, but they always remain sons.

The truth is that God, having justified the ungodly (Rom. 4:5), will not and cannot contradict Himself by charging them with evil. To do so amounts to reversing their justification. Christ either died for our sins and has paid the penalty or He has not. The Arminian cannot have it both ways. God is the only one ultimately who could bring a charge against His elect, and as Paul says, God has already rendered His verdict--justified. Therefore, none can, or ever will again, bring a charge of guilt against the believer as far as his eternal standing is concerned.

In his answer to the second question, Who is the one that condemns? (Rom. 8:34), Paul gives four answers. Each of the answers affirms the absolute security of the believer as unconditionally safe forever: (1) Christ died, (2) He is risen, (3) He advocates, and (4) He intercedes. Because of these four ministries of Christ, "nothing will be able to separate us from the love of God" (8:39), that is, cause us to forfeit our justification. These four ministries of Christ are taught elsewhere in Scripture, but all are gathered together in one verse here to support the unconditional security of the believer. Paul declares, first of all, that our eternal security depends . . .

Upon His Substitutionary Death

His first answer is "Christ has died!" Who can condemn us, he says, if the penalty for our sins has already been paid? The greatest proof of eternal security is justification by faith. Justification refers to how God sees us, and not the way we ourselves or others see us. Justification is "exterior" to us. It lies utterly outside us. The interior change is due to regeneration. Justification is forensic; it is entirely a legal matter. This is how God will judge us. We have been declared righteous. It was on the basis of the Christ's death for sin that we were saved in the first place, and it is now on that basis that no one can condemn us.

By Christ's death a holy God was freed to pardon every sin that was or ever will be, with respect to its power to condemn.

In Col. 2:14, Paul refers to the accumulation of sin as a "certificate of debt":

He forgave us all our sin, having cancelled the certificate of debt, with its regulations, that was against us and that stood opposed to us; he took it away, nailing it to the cross.

In the ancient world when a prisoner was incarcerated, a "certificate of debt" was nailed to the door of his prison. On it the crime he had committed and the duration and nature of the punishment was written. Over a lifetime every man accumulates a massive "certificate of debt." Imagine an extremely pious man who sins only five times a day. Then his certificate of debt would record

5 sins/day x 365 days x 70 years = 127,750 sins!

Now God knew about all these sins against us when He saved us in the first place. All these sins, past, present and future, were paid in full by the death of Christ. When the weary prisoner had paid his debt, the prison guard came to his cell, tore down the certificate of debt, and wrote a Greek word across it, **tetelestai**, which means, paid in full.[11] Then the cell door was opened and the man was free.

Recall our Lord's last words from the cross. Just before He died He looked to heaven and screamed to the Father, "It is finished" (Jn. 19:30). The Greek word is **tetelestai**, "It is paid in full."

Either Christ's death for sin actually paid the penalty or it did not. If it did, then the believer cannot be condemned for the very sins for which Christ died. All sins which we would ever commit were future to the death of Christ. If our sins are a ground of judgment against us, then Christ's death was not propitious. If it was propitious, then our sin is no longer a ground of condemnation. It is either one or the other, and the Bible is quite clear that Christ has paid the penalty.

---

[11]MM, p. 630, "to pay." In Jn. 19:30 is past tense and takes the sense "paid in full." See Hal Lindsay, *The Liberation of Planet Earth* (Grand Rapids: Zondervan, 1974), pp. 100-102.

However, when Christ paid the certificate of debt, it was not just for sins prior to our imprisonment but for all sin. In contrast to the temporary atonement we might make for our own sin by imprisonment or that a priest might make by offering sacrifices, Christ made an eternal redemption. The writer of the Epistle to the Hebrews says:

> *He did not enter by means of the blood of goats and calves; but he entered the Most Holy Place once for all by His own blood, having obtained* **eternal redemption** *(Heb. 9:12).*

> *But when this priest had offered* **for all time** *one sacrifice for sin, he sat down at the right hand of God (Heb. 10:12).*

> *Because by one sacrifice* **he has made perfect forever** *those who are being made holy (Heb. 10:14).*

Dabney asks:

> *Can one who has been fully justified in Christ, whose sins have been all blotted out, irrespective of their heinousness, by the perfect and efficacious price paid by Jesus Christ, become again unjustified, and fall under condemnation without a dishonor done to Christ's righteousness?*[12]

When Christ our Priest finished His sacrificial work, it is declared that He "sat down." The notion of a seated priest was foreign to the Jewish economy. In fact, there were no chairs in the tabernacle because a priest's work is never done. But here is a Priest who has finished His work. He sat down! There is nothing more to do as far as paying the penalty for sin is concerned. We have an eternal redemption. Our sin has been paid for all time, and we have been perfected forever!

Shank attempts to put vv. 10 and 14 together and say that the phrase "once for all" in v. 10 and "for all time" in v. 14 both refer to Christ's offering, and not to the believer's permanent status before God.[13] However, it is obvious that the recipients of the perfection in v. 14 are "those who are sanctified," and not the "one offering." In v. 14 the phrase "those who are sanctified" is an accusative participle and the phrase "one offering" is dative singular. The accusative case is the case of a direct object. It is those who are sanctified who receive the action of the main verb, "made perfect." The dative is properly rendered, "by means of." Thus we translate: "by means of one sacrifice He made those who are sanctified perfect

---

[12]Dabney, p. 691.

[13]Shank, p. 122. "By this will we have been sanctified through the offering of the body of Jesus Christ **once for all**" (Heb. 10:10).

forever." Shank's version would read something like, "one sacrifice has been made perfect forever, for those who are being sanctified." This is simply impossible from Greek grammar.

Christ guaranteed our eternal security not only by means of His substitutionary death but also by means of His substitutionary life. Our eternal security depends . . .

Upon His Substitutionary Life

Paul does not bring in this aspect of Christ's substitutionary work in Rom. 8:31-34, but it is the subject of a large body of Scripture. Christ was our Substitute by His death, His so-called passive obedience, but He was also our Substitute by His life, His so-called active obedience. The law required both a penalty for disobedience and a standard of perfect obedience. We can and could do neither. But by His righteous life Christ obeyed for us. In fact, we have been saved, according to some interpreters, by the faith **of** Christ as well as by faith **in** Christ.[14]

There is a material cause and an instrumental cause of our salvation. The material cause is the active and passive obedience of Christ, His death and His faith. The instrumental cause is our faith. We are justified by His blood and saved by His life (Rom. 5:9-10). The righteousness which the law required is imputed to us when we believe.

Christ's active obedience is His perfect performance of the requirements of the moral law. There is atoning, or expiatory, value in the active obedience in the sense that His obedience was part of His humiliation. However, His active obedience relates mainly to the law as precept, and not as penalty. The chief function of His active obedience was to win the reward of heaven for the believer.

This is necessary because to merely atone for past sin would not be a complete salvation. It would save a man from hell but not make him fit for heaven. He would be delivered from the law's punishment but not entitled to the law's reward. The law required perfect obedience. The mediator then must both pay the law's penalty, as well as obey the law in man's stead if he is to do for man everything the law requires:

Christ is the end of the law for righteousness to everyone who believes (Rom. 10:4 NASB).

---

[14]Kendall, for example, argues that we receive the active righteousness of Christ from Rom. 1:17: from faith **of** Christ to faith **in** Christ; Rom. 5:10: saved by His life; and Rom. 3:22: the righteousness of Jesus Christ is by the faith **of** Jesus Christ (also Gal. 2:16). Had Christ not justified us by HIS faith, the onus would be on us to keep the works of the law (p. 64, on Rom. 3:22).

This means that Christ completely fulfilled the law for the believer, but the law requires obedience to its precept as well as endurance of its penalty:[15]

For as through the one man's disobedience the many were made sinners, even so through the obedience of the One the many will be made righteous (Rom. 5:19 NASB).

And in Him you have been made complete (Col. 2:10 NASB).

This is another basis of eternal security. If Christ has already perfectly obeyed the law for us and if His obedience has been imputed to us, then our eternal destiny is secure. However, if we base our eternal security upon the degree of holiness or the perseverance in it in this life, we will be filled with the fear of uncertainty:

If I am a Christian for fifty years and have become increasingly godly with every passing year (which I hope would be true) I will still be judged by the same righteousness that was imputed to me when I first believed.[16]

"If only Christ's passive obedience is put to our account, it follows that we must produce sufficient works on our own in order to be finally saved. This would mean that the death of Christ forgives our sins but, since Christ's active obedience is not imputed to us, we must, from the moment of our conversion, live a life worthy of eternal life to be saved in the end. It therefore becomes absolutely crucial to know whether the active obedience of Christ, as well as the passive obedience of Christ, is imputed to us."[17] Because Christ has already obeyed for us, we have a right to eternal life. Our own obedience secures reward but not life. Christ's obedience secures our right to heaven, and our obedience determines the degree of our reward there.

Christ died for us, but He also lives today to intercede for us. Paul emphasizes this in Rom. 8:34 when he mentions that Christ is seated in heaven. There is a man in heaven today! Because of His work of intercession, our eternal security depends . . .

Upon His Present Session

Paul also bases our eternal security on the fact that Jesus rose from the dead and is seated at the right hand of God. He is our Advocate and Intercessor (Rom. 8:34). This is sometimes called the present priestly ministry of Christ, or

---

[15]William G. T. Shedd, *Dogmatic Theology*, 3 vols. (New York: Charles Scribner's Sons, 1889; reprint ed., Grand Rapids: Klock and Klock, 1979), 2:430-33.

[16]Kendall, p. 73.

[17]Ibid., p. 71.

His present session. In this role Jesus pleads our case as our Advocate, our defense attorney in the heavenly courtroom:

> *My little children, I am writing these things to you that you may not sin. And if anyone sins, we have an Advocate with the Father, Jesus Christ the Righteous, and He Himself is the propitiation for our sins; and not for ours only, but also for those of the whole world* (1 Jn. 2:1-2 NASB).

Arminians have feared that this doctrine will tend to sin. John says there is a motivation in this doctrine not to sin. The heavenly courtroom is opened. Satan, "the accuser of the brethren" (Rev. 12:10), brings the sinning Christian before the divine tribunal. In his role as prosecuting attorney he presents a compelling and irrefutable case before the bar of justice. This Christian has sinned, and justice requires the penalty be paid. His accusations are correct. God is just. As the gavel is about to sound "Case closed" and the sinning Christian dismissed to punishment, our Advocate, Jesus Christ the Righteous, approaches the bar and begins His wonderful work of intercession:

> *"Father, it is correct, as the Satan says, this brother of Mine has sinned and Your justice requires his condemnation. But Father, remember, I am the propitiation for his sin. By My death on the cross I have forever satisfied the claims of Your justice."*

When the Father hears this intercessory prayer, He responds:

"Case dismissed!"

Christ could argue our case in various ways. He could make excuses. He could plead for leniency, but the Father, being holy and just, cannot be lenient with sin. However, our Attorney argues differently. Rather, than make excuses or plea for mercy, He reminds the Father of the work He performed which earned Him the title, Jesus Christ the Righteous.

The title refers, first of all, to the fact that He is made to us the righteousness of God. He is the source of the imputed righteousness of Christ, the one by whom the Christian is saved and in whom he stands forever:

> *He made Him who knew no sin to be sin on our behalf, that we might become the righteousness of God in Him* (2 Cor. 5:21 NASB).

But, second, in 1 Jn. 2:2 we are told that this Righteous One is righteous because of His work for us, He is the propitiation for our sins. Thus, when the Father withholds condemnation, He is just. Jesus the Righteous has satisfied every claim against the sinning Christian. His advocacy is presented under the picture of His entrance into the heavenly sanctuary in Heb. 9:24:

For Christ did not enter a holy place made with hands, a mere copy of the true one, but into heaven itself, now to appear in the presence of God for us (Heb. 9:24 NASB).

It is obvious that, while God will exercise parental discipline (Heb. 12:3-15), His child will never be condemned because our Advocate has satisfied the claims of justice. Satan can never again bring a case to the bar of justice which will win. It is Christ who bore our sin who appears in heaven on our behalf, and Christ is the very righteousness in which the Christian is accepted before God. There is therefore no sin we can ever commit which will cause us to lose our salvation because of the advocacy and propitiation for all sin provided by Jesus Christ the Righteous One:

And the former priests, on the one hand, existed in greater numbers, because they were prevented by death from continuing, but He, on the other hand, because He abides forever, holds His priesthood permanently. Hence, also, He is able to **save forever** *those who draw near to God through Him, since He always lives to make intercession for them* (Heb. 7:23-25 NASB).

He is able to save forever, or to the "uttermost," because He lives forever to pray for us. Our eternal security is made to depend upon the advocacy and intercession of Christ.[18]   Through His offering for sin and intercession we are "perfected for all time" (Heb. 10:14).

Not only does the eternal security of the believer depend upon God the Father and God the Son, but it also . . .

Depends upon God the Holy Spirit

The ministry of the Holy Spirit toward the believer in Christ is also devoted to keeping him saved forever. Three specific works of the Holy Spirit are related to the issue of eternal security. Our eternal security depends, first of all, . . .

Upon His Ministry of Regeneration

The ministry of the Holy Spirit in regeneration results in the birth of a new man and the gift of eternal life. Both of these effects imply irreversible change and a permanent new condition.

---

[18]"Forever" is **panteles** in Greek and can mean "for all time" or "completely" (AG, p. 63).

Spiritual birth. When Jesus told Nicodemus, "you must be born again," He taught that there are certain similarities between physical and spiritual birth. In each a new thing is created:

He saved us, not on the basis of deeds which we have done in righteousness, but according to His mercy, by the washing of regeneration and renewing by the Holy Spirit (Tim. 3:5 NASB).

When this happens, a new thing is produced, the new creation:

Therefore if any man is in Christ, he is a new creature; the old things passed away; behold new things have come (2 Cor. 5:17 NASB).

This new creation is His workmanship and unites us with the Divine nature itself:

For we are His workmanship, created in Christ Jesus for good works (Eph. 2:10 NASB).

Arminians, of course, point out correctly that there are important differences between spiritual birth and physical birth and conclude from the differences that none of the similarities can be pressed. However, this surely takes the matter too far. It is obvious that the subject of physical birth has no prior knowledge of his birth. It is also obvious that in physical birth the subject receives a nature independent of his parents. But the subject of spiritual birth partakes of the nature of the divine parent.[19] The real question, however, is, Are there aspects of the physical birth analogy which do carry over into spiritual birth? If so, which ones? It seems that the fundamental idea of the creation of a new thing, a new creation (2 Cor. 5:17) called a "son" (Gal. 4:6) who is an heir of God (Rom. 8:17) allows us, indeed requires us, to stress the point that a son cannot become a non-son and a created new man cannot be uncreated. New birth is clearly irreversible.

In the case of human generation a being comes into existence who did not exist before, and this being will go on living forever. An earthly parent imparts a nature to a child, and that nature endures forever. Thus, to a much higher degree, our divine parent similarly creates a new man in Christ who will live forever. The earthly nature we inherit from our earthly parent never dies but endures forever. Logic requires that the divine nature we inherit from our heavenly parent will similarly endure forever.

Can a man be unborn? Of course he can die, but this in no way reverses the fact of his sonship and his birth. Both physical and spiritual birth are one-time events with permanent consequences. Even death does not reverse it. Our

---

[19]Shank, pp. 171-72.

conscious existence never ends, and one day all will be raised from the dead (Jn. 5:28-29).

The son of a human parent may rebel and disobey, but he is still of the nature of his parent. That never changes. God similarly has created a new man; He gave birth to us. We may rebel, and God may disinherit us, as an earthly father can, but we will never cease to be His sons.

There is nothing then that can be done to reverse regeneration. Even if we decided we did not want to be God's children any longer, it would do no good. Spiritual and physical birth cannot be reversed. Furthermore, we cannot give salvation back. Is it not obvious that one cannot give his physical birth back to his human parent? Neither can he give his spiritual birth back to his divine parent. If that were possible, then the gospel promise would be contradicted. Then a person who had believed in God's Son would perish and not have everlasting life after all (Jn. 3:16). Then a person who possesses eternal life **would** come under judgment in direct contradiction to Jn. 5:24.

Eternal life. Not only are we born into His family, but through regeneration we receive the gift of eternal life. Eternal life implies endless existence. Shank counters by stressing that eternal life is a quality of existence.[20] With this, of course, all would agree. But that in no way diminishes the obvious biblical testimony to the fact that eternal life is eternal, endless. All of the lexicons include the notion of "endless existence" in the semantic value of the word.[21]

Shank insists, however, that eternal life can only be shared with men, not permanently possessed by them.[22] However, if a man has eternal existence, he will live endlessly. Eternal life is owned permanently the moment it is given. It is a characteristic of the new creation. To be given the gift of eternal life, according to Shank, is to be given the gift of living forever until you die and no longer live forever! This is an absurdity. Jesus Himself argued that eternal life was first of all the promise that a believer will rise from the dead after he physically dies (Jn. 11:25-26). But He also says that a Christian has eternal life right now and this means he cannot cease to live:

> *Jesus said to her, "I am the resurrection and the life, he who believes in Me shall live even if he dies, and everyone who lives and believes in Me shall never die* (NASB).

He says we have eternal life now and as a result (1) we will rise from the dead in resurrection, and (2) we will **never** die. For Jesus, at least, the gift of eternal life meant far more than sharing the life of God now. It was a virtual

---

[20]Ibid., pp. 21-22.

[21]E.g., see AG, p. 28; MM, p. 16.

[22]Shank, p. 52.

guarantee of endless existence with Him. We will never die! Over and over again the Savior stresses the permanent nature of the gift of eternal life. He told the woman at the well that, after drinking the water He would give, she would "never thirst" (Jn. 4:14). He said, "I am the bread of life; he who comes to Me shall never hunger, and he who believes in Me shall never thirst" (Jn. 6:35). Eternal life is permanent. "All that the Father gives Me shall come to Me, and the one who comes to Me I will certainly not cast out" (Jn. 6:37). The Christian will "certainly not" be cast out! How else could the Lord say it? Eternal life is not only "without cost," but it is permanent!

Second, our eternal security depends . . .

Upon His Baptizing Ministry

In 1 Cor. 12:13 Paul tells us:

For by one Spirit we were all baptized into one body (NASB).

Through the baptizing ministry of the Holy Spirit we are brought into organic union with Christ. Paul develops this further in Rom. 6:

Or do you not know that all of us who have been baptized into Christ Jesus have been baptized into His death? (Rom. 6:3 NASB).

In this famous passage on sanctification Paul explains that Christ's history has become ours. His death to sin has become ours. But there are permanent effects of this union:

*Now if we have died with Christ, we believe that we shall also live with Him, knowing that Christ, having been raised from the dead, is **never to die again**; death no longer is master over Him. For the death that He died, **He died to sin, once for all**; but the life that He lives, He lives to God* (Rom. 6:8-10 NASB).

Because of the baptizing work of the Holy Spirit, uniting us to Christ, what is true of Him has become true of us. One thing that is true of Him is that He died to sin "once and for all" and that He will "never die again." Paul specifically tells us that this is true of us as well:

Even so consider yourselves to be dead to sin, but alive to God in Christ Jesus (Rom. 6:11 NASB).

What is true of Him is declared to be true of us. We are eternally secure because we are in a permanent union with Christ.

But, finally, our eternal security depends . . .

Upon His Sealing Ministry

There are three references to the sealing ministry of the Holy Spirit:

Who also sealed [**sphragizo**] *us and gave us the Spirit in our hearts as a pledge* [**arrabon**] (2 Cor. 1:21-22 NASB).

In Him, you also, after listening to the message of truth, the gospel of your salvation--having also believed, you were sealed [**sphragizo**] *in Him with the Holy Spirit of promise, who is given as a pledge* [**arrabon**] *of our inheritance, with a view to the redemption of God's own possession, to the praise of His glory* (Eph. 1:13-14).

And do not grieve the Holy Spirit of God, by whom you were sealed [**sphragizo**] *for the day of redemption* (Eph. 4:30 NASB).

Two things stand out in these verses: (1) the Holy Spirit has sealed us (**sphragizo**), and (2) the Holy Spirit is the pledge (**arrabon**).

The ancient practice of using seals is behind the figurative use of the word here. A seal was a mark of protection[23] and ownership. The Greek word **sphragizo** is used of a stone being fastened with a seal to "prevent its being moved from a position."[24] In fact, this was apparently the earliest method of distinguishing one's property. The seal was engraved with a design or mark distinctive to the owner. The seal of ownership or protection was often made in soft wax with a signet ring. An impression was left on the wax signifying the owner of the thing sealed. When the Holy Spirit seals us, He presses the signet ring of our heavenly Father on our hearts of wax and leaves the mark of ownership. We belong to Him. He certifies this by His unchangeable purpose to protect and own us to the day of redemption.[25]

In Eph. 1:13-14 we are told that the Holy Spirit Himself is the seal. He is impressed upon us, so to speak. His presence in our lives is thus a guarantee of God's protection and that we are owned by God. A broken seal was an indication that the person had not been protected. The Holy Spirit cannot be broken. He is the seal of ownership. In Eph. 4:30 we are told that we are sealed **unto the day of redemption**. This sealing ministry of the Spirit is forever and guarantees that we will arrive safely for the redemption of our bodies and entrance into heaven (Rom. 8:23). He is the seal that we are now owned and protected by God until the day redemption.

---

[23]E.g., Mt. 27:66, where the tomb of Christ was made secure by sealing it with a stone.

[24]AG, p. 803.

[25]F. B. Huey, "Seal," in *ZPED*, 5:319.

We are forever protected from wrath. We cannot lose our salvation any more than we can break the seal. We would have to have greater power to lose salvation than the Holy Spirit has to keep us saved. About all Arminian Robert Shank can do is to weakly object, "But the Holy Spirit can do nothing for those who refuse His ministry."[26] But He certainly can! That is precisely what these verses are saying. It seems that Shank is looking right at the verse and simply refusing to accept what it says and actually reverses its plain meaning. Shank lists various experiential ministries which the believer can refuse to accept as proof, such as filling (Eph. 5:18) and points out that we can grieve the Spirit (Eph. 4:30). "But," as Sellers correctly points out, "those ministries are experiential ministries; sealing and pledging are not."[27] Nowhere are believers asked to allow the Spirit to seal them or to become their pledge. These are things which happen to all believers at the point in time they believed, "having also believed, you were also sealed (Eph. 1:13)."

Along with being our seal, the Holy Spirit is our pledge (Gk. **arrabon**). The word refers to a "first installment, down payment, deposit, pledge"[28] which "obligates the contracting party to make further payments."[29]

It is a legal concept from the language of business and trade:

1. An installment, with which a man secures a legal claim upon a thing as yet unpaid for.
2. An "earnest," an advance payment, by which a contract becomes valid in law.
3. A pledge in one passage (Gen. 38:17ff.)[30]

Similarly, in Rom. 8:23 Paul speaks of the "first fruits" of the Spirit, a down payment to be followed by more. We await the redemption of our bodies. We are sealed unto that day.

God, so to speak, has legally bound Himself to our eternal security. The choice of the legal term (**arrabon**, "earnest") implies that God has legally and morally obligated Himself to bring His children to heaven. A down payment was a statement of one's honor, one's word. When God makes a down payment, He has obligated Himself morally and legally to make the final payment as well. The word takes the sense of a pledge or promise.

If one person who was born again in Christ ever fails to enter into heaven when he dies, then God has broken His pledge. His word of honor has been

---

[26]Shank, p. 186.

[27]Sellers, p. 187.

[28]O. Becker, "**arrabon**," in *NIDNTT*, 2:39.

[29]AG, p. 109.

[30]Becker, 2:39-40.

voided. No human conditions are mentioned. This, like other aspects of security, is a work of God and depends upon Him alone.

Conclusion

If our eternal security depends upon anything in us, it is certain that it is not secure. However, the Scriptures teach that our final entrance into heaven is guaranteed by the work of the Father, the Son, and the Holy Spirit. Since it depends upon an infinite person, who is faithful and true, it is inconceivable that the salvation of any child of God could ever be lost.

Chapter 22

Tragedy or Triumph?

"**A**t last!" cried Michael's colleague as he rushed into the archangel's presence.

"Did you hear the trumpet?"[1]

Excitedly, Michael replied, "Of course, my friend. It is time for the beginning."

For centuries the long and arduous course of human history had unfolded. It had been the Father's purpose during that time to prepare a race of servant kings who would fulfill the final destiny of man. During that brief moment between eternity future and eternity past called Time, the futility of independence had been made evident to all. The Satan's lie had been answered. It was now time for the righting of all wrongs, the final accounting. The reign of the metochoi was about to begin.

"We have been preparing for this moment for thousands of years," said Michael. "We have constructed the city exactly according to the King's specifications."[2]

"And what a magnificent structure it is," his angelic helper replied. "The King Himself supervised every detail in anticipation of the ultimate arrival of His servants. Did you see the joy on His face as He saw the completed project?"

"Yes, it thrilled my heart. He has devoted centuries to preparing these mansions for His followers on earth."

Suddenly there was a sound like the rush of a great wind. In an instant millions of people abruptly appeared in the heavenly city. The dead in Christ had risen. Those still living had received resurrection bodies, and all had been trans-

---

[1]1 Th. 4:16
[2]Heb. 11:16

ported to heaven in the twinkling of an eye.[3] But the hosts of heaven were ready; their work was done. Dwellings for each were ready to be inhabited.

"Yes, our King has kept His promise to them; it is now time to honor those who have kept their promise to Him."[4]

"Come, let us proceed to the square in the center of the city."

Upon arrival Michael and his colleague saw multitudes of men and women surrounding a raised platform in the city square. Brilliant lights splashed outward in all directions. Beautiful music created a sense of anticipation. The atmosphere was electric with expectation. Seated upon the jewel-studded throne, the King named Wonderful[5] gazed smilingly and compassionately upon the hushed throng. It was the judgment seat of Christ.[6]

For centuries the angels had been preparing for this event. Not only had they labored to build the city, but each had been assigned to assist a particular man or woman in his personal struggle to inherit salvation.[7]

One by one the members of the vast multitude were summoned to the Judge's throne. A man appeared before the King. He had wasted his life, and it was now all too evident that he had searched for meaning in the wrong places. He had become a Christian at an early age but had never followed the path of discipleship. "Next year," he had always said. "Next year, I will get serious about my Christian faith." But "next year" had finally come, and it was too late. He had married a committed Christian girl, but his real marriage was to his work and himself. For years he had thought of nothing but material success and high position on the corporate ladder. His Christian commitment extended to avoidance of gross sin. He had attended church regularly and had often gone to various Christian meetings. His heart, however, was never focused on eternity. Instead of laying up treasure in heaven, he had chosen to lay up treasure on earth. Bible reading was boring, and his prayer life was non-existent.

"Come, servant of Mine," thundered the voice from the throne. The eyes of the Wonderful Counselor were no longer smiling.

There was a shuffling among the throng. Suddenly everyone was quiet, and many were looking down unable to endure the searing eyes of the King.

---

[3]1 Cor. 15:51-52
[4]Rom. 8:17
[5]Isa. 9:6
[6]2 Cor. 5:10
[7]Heb. 1:14

"Yes, Lord, I . . . ." For the first time in his life he was speechless. All the excuses which had so easily postponed serious commitment no longer mattered. In an instant his entire life was somehow miraculously paraded in front of his mind.

As he remembered all the opportunities he had wasted, he winced in pain. This was heightened in intensity due to the greater sensitivity to sin of the resurrection body. He thought of the great Christian home from which he had come and how his mother had taught him to live for eternity, but the things at school always seemed more attractive. He thought of God's gift to him of a loving wife who had truly modeled Christianity before him. He had never joined her in her desire for a truly spiritual relationship in marriage. Yet outwardly he appeared Christian, and the underlying inconsistencies were not evident.

"Servant of Mine," the voice from the throne interrupted his thoughts. "I warned you often that there is nothing covered up that will not be revealed and hidden that will not be known."[8]

"Lord, I am so sorry," he cried, realizing that momentarily he would face the eternal consequences of his life.

"You have presumed upon My grace and have lived for yourself," the King continued. "I have given you much and told you that to everyone who has been given much, much will be required.[9]

Turning His face upward, the one called The Word of God said, "Father, I bring this servant of Mine before You. He has denied Me by his life on earth, and I now deny him before You. He will not join with My metochoi as one of My servant kings. He has lost his inheritance!"

Then with a stern look on His face, the King rebuked His unfaithful follower, "Depart from Me, you wicked, lazy slave."[10]

"Noooo . . . ," the lazy servant screamed. But the angels came and led him to the darkness outside the city square where he began to weep and gnash his teeth in profound regret.[11]

Another man appeared before the judgment seat. This one stood with joyful countenance and tearful expectation. The eyes of the King called Wonderful softened with compassion and delight.

---

[8]Lk. 12:2
[9]Lk. 12:48
[10]Mt. 25:26
[11]Mt. 25:30

"Come, servant of Mine," said the King.

Jimmy had faithfully served his master throughout his eighty years. It had been the King's purpose that this man would uniquely display God's power and grace. The King had allowed terrible skin cancer to ravage his body for all of his adult life. Over two hundred painful operations had grotesquely lacerated his once handsome face. No one knew the silent, daily humiliation Jimmy had felt having to conduct business appointments and teach Sunday School classes and otherwise be exposed to the public eye. Yet he had never complained nor doubted God's sovereign purpose in his life.

Once when a non-Christian friend was provoked by Jimmy's pain and appearance to doubt the existence of God, Jimmy responded, "Could it be that God allowed this to happen to me so that I would have the privilege of revealing to others how a true Christian deals with tragedy?"

Yet now he stood before his King without pain and whole. His once handsome face had been restored and now radiated with exhilaration at being in the presence of the Master he had so greatly pleased. There were no more tears and no more pain.

Once again with tears in His eyes, the King called Wonderful summoned the man, "Come, servant of Mine."

"Why is he hesitating," said Michael's colleague. "If I were him, I would be bounding upward to join the King."

"This has been typical of Jimmy all his life," Michael replied. "In every case those servants who are most worthy of the King's honors are the most humble and self-effacing."

Then the multitude gasped. The King did something He only rarely did. He got off the throne and came down to the man and embraced him.

"Jimmy," the King said, "I want to thank you for never complaining and for fulfilling the purpose I have designed for your life. You have been faithful in little things. I am now going to make you ruler over many."[12]

"Thank you for the many cups of water you have given to Me."

"But, Lord," Jimmy replied, "When did I ever give you a cup of water."

"Do you remember when you used to take food to the poor on Christmas day? Do you remember the young Korean girl you took into your home? Do you remember the many gifts you gave to charity and to world evangelization? Do

---

[12]Mt. 25:21

you remember the young couples you and Mallory adopted as spiritual children and before whom you modeled My life? Do you remember the many destitute people who came to you for financial and practical counsel and how you were always available and always helpful in representing My view of life? Do you not remember the wise counsel you gave as a board member of many Christian organizations and how you participated at your own expense, even though you were physically in great pain and very weary?"

Jimmy was now very embarrassed but quietly pleased that the One for whom he labored remembered everything.

"Lord," Jimmy replied, "thank you for remembering all that, but I am just your unworthy servant. I have only done my duty."[13]

"Jimmy, what you say is true," the King called Wonderful replied, "but whatever you did for one of the least of these brothers of Mine, you did for Me."[14]

"Because you have honored Me on earth, I will now honor you in heaven. Your new name shall be 'Courageous.'[15] You have been courageous in faith in the midst of personal difficulty. You have lived courageously and faithfully to the end. You have fought a good fight. You have kept the faith. You have now finished your course. You have longed for My return. I now give you the crown of righteousness."[16]

Then, taking Jimmy by the arm, the King escorted him up to the platform to join Him around the throne.

Turning His face upward, the King called Wonderful said, "Father, I now bring before you My faithful servant Jimmy. He has finished his life with his flag at full mast. He has been faithful in the small things. I will now honor him with many things."[17]

With joy in His eyes the King turned to His faithful servant and said, "Well done, good and faithful servant, enter into the joy of your Lord. You will now inherit the kingdom."

---

[13]Lk. 17:10
[14]Mt. 25:40
[15]Rev. 2:17
[16]2 Tim. 4:7-8
[17]Lk. 19:17

The New Testament everywhere avows that each of us will one day face an accounting for the stewardship with which we have been entrusted. Apparently, and fortunately for us, our lives will not be evaluated according to the world's criteria of success but God's. At issue will be our faithfulness.[18] For those who have been faithful to their Lord throughout life, it will be a day of great triumph, of reward, and of hearing the Master say, "Well done."

However, a different fate awaits those Christians who have failed to persevere, who have not remained faithful to their Lord. In an instant, as they stand before their King, their entire lives will be seen to have been wasted. There can be no greater tragedy than to hear the words, "too late."

Yes, the judgment seat of Christ will be a time of either tragedy or triumph.

What is the nature of the judgment seat of Christ? Will there be distinctions in heaven? How can those for whom Christ died receive any negative consequence at the final tribunal? How can the New Testament doctrine of rewards be reconciled with the doctrine of unmerited favor? It is to these and other questions we must now direct our attention.

The Judgment Seat

Travelers to the archaeological excavations of the city of Corinth have all seen the famous judgment seat in the town square. There is little doubt that this was the very forum in the apostle's mind when he wrote:

> *For we must all appear before the judgment seat of Christ, that each one may receive what is due him for the things done while in the body, whether good or bad* (2 Cor. 5:10 NASB).

The judgment seat (Gk. **bema**) in Corinth was a large richly-decorated rostrum, centrally located in the market place. It was the place where rewards were given out for victory at the Isthmian games. These rewards consisted of garlands, trophies, crowns, and special social benefits, such as exemption from income tax. But punishments were also administered here as well.

Apparently this judgment deals with negative as well as positive. Paul says we will be judged according to both the good and the bad things we have done while in the body. We tend to gloss over this, yet the Lord warned, "For there is nothing covered that shall not be revealed; neither hid, that shall not be known" (Lk. 12:2-3).[19] Paul spoke of God bringing to light the hidden things of darkness

---

[18]1 Cor. 4:1-2.

[19]Note also Lk. 8:17; Mt. 10:26; Mk. 4:22.

(1 Cor. 4:3-5), and Peter spoke of the fact that judgment must begin with the household of God (1 Pet. 4:17-18). Paul's reaction to the judgment seat of Christ was, "Knowing therefore the terror of the Lord" (2 Cor. 5:11).

From this very judgment seat, the Bema, Gallio passed judgment on the apostle Paul (Acts 18:12). It was to this raised platform that Paul referred when he said, "We must all appear before the judgment seat of Christ" (2 Cor. 5:10).

Many sermons are preached on the judgments which fall upon the nonbeliever, but the New Testament everywhere emphasizes that the believer faces a final accounting as well.

Paul refers to our life work as a building which will be subjected to a careful examination (1 Cor. 3:14-15). He warns us that all will appear for this accounting (Rom. 14:10-12). Therefore, we should not judge others now, for the Lord will judge the hidden motives then (1 Cor. 4:5). He often compared the Christian life to that of the athlete who pursues the victor's crown (1 Cor. 9:24-27; 2 Tim. 2:5).

Jesus continually exhorted His fellows to full discipleship by reminding them that one day they would face an accounting for their stewardship.[20] He challenged them to pursue rewards[21] and treasure in heaven.[22]

---

[20]Mt. 10:26-42; 16:27; 24:45-51; Mk. 8:38; Lk. 12:42-48

[21]Mt. 5:11,46; 6:1-6, 16-18.

[22]Mt. 6:19-21; 19:21; Mk. 4:24-25; Lk. 12:13-21; 16:1-13.

Throughout the New Testament this theme repeatedly emerges:

My brethren, let not many of you become teachers, knowing that we shall receive the stricter judgment (Jas. 3:1 NKJV).

For the time has come for judgment to begin at the house of God; and if it begins with us first, what will be the end of those who do not obey the gospel of God? (1 Pet. 4:17 NKJV).

Love has been perfected among us in this: that we may have boldness in the day of judgment (1 Jn. 4:17 NKJV).

The Criteria of Judgment

It is vitally important that we understand precisely what Christ will look for in lives. If we are to be evaluated, what are the criteria for passing the test? There seem to be three: our deeds, our faithfulness, and our words.[23]

Our Deeds

In the Partaker view of eternal security it is impossible to take lightly our responsibility to perform good works. The Scriptures everywhere stress their importance:

Each one's work will become manifest, for the Day will declare it, because it will be revealed by fire, and the fire will test each one's work, **of what sort it is** (1 Cor. 3:13 NKJV).

For we must all appear before the judgment seat of Christ, that each one may receive the things done in the body, **according to what he has done, whether it is good or bad** (2 Cor. 5:10 NKJV).

And I will give to each one of you **according to your works** (Rev. 2:23 NKJV).

It is vital to note that the issue will be not just the amount of work but "of what sort it is" and whether it is "good or bad." How does one determine whether his work is good or bad. The Scriptures give two criteria.

They must be according to Scripture. No work will be accepted which does not pass this test:

Do you not know that those who run in a race all run, but one receives the prize? **Run in such a way that you may obtain it** (1 Cor. 9:24).

---

[23]The following discussion is borrowed from Ken Quick, "The Doctrine of Eternal Significance" (D.Min. thesis, Dallas Theological Seminary, 1989).

And if anyone competes in athletics, he is not crowned unless he
competes according to the rules (2 Tim. 2:5 NKJV).

In some instances there may be differing interpretations of Scripture. This introduces a degree of ambiguity. Suppose our interpretation was wrong, and we did a work consistent with an incorrect interpretation? This is why the Lord looks deeper than the interpretation, to our inward motives. Who among us has not been guilty of interpreting the Bible to fit what we wanted to do? Who of us has not been guilty of twisting the Bible to fit into our doctrinal system as well? The purpose here is not to discuss the various social issues of the day. But we are all aware of the new interpretations of the Bible being given by evangelicals regarding women's roles, abortion, government (viz., theonomy), and the definition and nature of the church.

When deeds are performed based upon a particular interpretation of Scripture, the Lord will look to the person's motive in arriving at that interpretation. Was the true motive to discern the single intent of the original author of Scripture? Was the true motive to find out what the Bible truly said and do it no matter what the cost? Or was the person making the Bible fit into a belief system he had accepted elsewhere? Was he, in reaction to something about the Christian community that hurt him in his past, using the Bible falsely? These questions lead us to the second criterion used to test "what sort of work" we have done: motivation.

They must emerge from a motivation to bring honor to God. A work done has two aspects to it: the deed itself and the motive behind it. Is it not true that we often begin good projects for the Lord but they become total failures? Conversely, sometimes some of the works which outwardly are the biggest and most public were done for the wrong motives. When our Lord evaluates our lives, He will look deeper than the works themselves. He will search "the minds and hearts" (Rev. 2:23).

Consider:

Therefore judge nothing before the time, until the Lord comes, who
will both bring to light the hidden things of darkness and reveal the
counsel of the hearts; and then each one's praise will come from God
(1 Cor. 4:5 NKJV).

Jesus too emphasized that it was the inner motivation which determined the value of a deed:

Take heed that you do not do your charitable deeds before men, to be
seen by them. Otherwise you have no reward from your Father in
heaven. Therefore when you do a charitable deed, do not sound the
trumpet before you as the hypocrites do in the synagogues and the

streets, that they may have glory from men. Assuredly I say to you, they have their reward. But when you do a charitable deed, do not let your left hand know what your right hand is doing, that your charitable deed may be in secret; and your Father who sees in secret will Himself reward you openly (Mt. 6:1-4 NKJV).

In one of the most sobering passages of the book of Hebrews, we are told that one day we will have to give an accounting. At this time "the thoughts and intents of the heart" will be the crucial issue:

For the word of God is living and powerful, and sharper than any two-edged sword, piercing even to the division of soul and spirit, and of joints and marrow, and is a discerner of **the thoughts and intents of the heart.** *And there is no creature hidden from His sight, but all things are naked and open to the eyes of Him to whom we must give account* (Heb. 4:12-13 NKJV).

The Word of God is able to penetrate to the very core of a man and will reveal to all what his real motivations have been!

The Lord will primarily want to reveal whether or not what we did was motivated by a desire to bring honor to Christ and out of a sincere heart which fears ("honors") God:

Servants obey in all things your masters according to the flesh, not with eye service, as men-pleasers, but in sincerity of heart, fearing God. And whatever you do, do it heartily, as to the Lord and not to men, knowing that from the Lord you will receive the reward of the inheritance, for you serve the Lord Christ. But he who does wrong will be repaid for the wrong which he has done, and there is no partiality (Col. 3:22-25 NKJV).

Therefore, whether you eat or drink or whatever you do, do all to the glory of God (1 Cor. 10:31 NKJV).

To our ears the word "glory" communicates a somewhat resplendent and even mystical aura. Perhaps a word like "honor" is more understandable. Was our motive in what we did or said to bring honor to God?

This is of course, difficult to discern. We all operate with mixed motives, and this leads us to the issue of faithfulness. In the final analysis the overriding consideration seems to be how faithful we have been. Have we given God our best?

Our Faithfulness

> *Who then is a faithful and wise servant, whom His master made ruler over His household* (Mt. 24:45 NKJV).

> *His Master said to him, "Well done, good and faithful servant; you have been faithful over a few things, I will make you ruler over many things. Enter into the joy of your Lord* (Mt. 25:23 NKJV).

> *He who is faithful in what is least, is faithful also in much* (Lk. 16:10 NKJV).

> *Moreover it is required in stewards that one be found faithful* (1 Cor. 4:2 NKJV).

> *Be faithful until death, and I will give you the crown of life* (Rev. 2:10 NKJV).

A faithful man is of high value to God. Solomon asks, "Who can find a faithful man" (Prov. 20:6). In the final analysis this will be the "bottom line." God will not judge us on the basis of our success but on the basis of our faithfulness. This is an excellent approach to mental health. We cannot all be successful, but we all can be faithful.

Here is a man who struggles with emotional problems that were either chemically or environmentally induced. His struggle against sin in certain areas may never be as successful as the struggle in that area that another man has. But God knows the heart. He looks at faithfulness and not only victory. Thus, even though he was less successful, it is conceivable that he will be more highly rewarded. There will be many reversals in heaven. The first will be last, and those seemingly destined for high honor will be distant from the throne. Those unknown to history, who were perhaps insignificant in this life but who were faithful servants, will reign with the servant kings in the coming kingdom.

Our Words

The third major criterion which the Lord will employ to evaluate the worthiness of our lives is the words we have spoken. This is appropriate because words are often reflections of the motives and attitudes in our hearts:

> *But I say to you that for every idle word men may speak, they will give account of it in the day of judgment. For by your words you will be justified, and by your words you will be condemned* (Mt. 12:36-37).

> *For there is nothing covered that will not be revealed, nor hidden that will not be known. Therefore whatever you have spoken in the dark*

*will be heard in the light, and what you have spoken in the ear in the
inner rooms will be proclaimed on the housetops* (Lk. 12:2-3 NKJV).

This is a sobering thought. We should be ever mindful of the fact that
there is a third party present in every conversation, the Holy Spirit. The Scriptures have much to say regarding the tongue and the impact of our words. Control of the tongue is presented as evidence of depth of character in the books of
James and Proverbs. But, as the apostle says, it is a fire and difficult to tame.
Those who succeed in taming it, however, God will reward greatly.

Rewards and Merit

Perhaps no issue was of greater import to the Reformers than the question
of merit. Having broken with the works-righteousness of Rome, they were very
sensitive to any intrusion of merit into the system of theology they were fashion-
ing. Given this strong aversion to works-righteousness, it is easy to see how they
may have been troubled with the many passages in the New Testament which
seem to offer rewards on the basis of merit.

Apparently the Catholics used the many Old Testament passages which
teach blessing as a result of obedience to the Law.[24] "Motivated by fear of the
meritoriousness of good works," says Abraham Kuyper, "the promised rewards
are suffered to lie in the death-like silence, whereby the goad to piety, given by
the Scriptures in the forms of the rich and many-faceted promise of reward, is
blunted."[25] Calvin was concerned to prove that justification by works could not be
inferred from the doctrine of rewards, and so the motivation of rewards was
blunted in his system.

When Calvin deals with passages where we are told that God will render
to everyone of us according to our deeds,[26] he confuses them as passages
referring to the judgment on non-Christians. He mixes the Great White Throne
passages with the passages about reward to believers.[27]

He feared the use of the word "reward" because it harkened back to the
system of works-righteousness which he and the other Reformers were attacking.
If he could have acknowledged that the reward of the believer's works is in view

---

[24]John Calvin, *Institutes of the Christian Religion*, trans. Henry Beveridge, 2 vols. (Grand
Rapids: Eerdmans, 1964), 3.17.1. See also Dt. 7:12; 9:26; Jer. 7:5-7.

[25]Cited by C. G. Berkouwer, *Faith and Justification* (Grand Rapids: Eerdmans, 1953), p.
113.

[26]*Institutes*, 3.18.1-10. For example, see Mt. 25:34; 5:12; Lk. 6:23; Jn. 5:29; Rom. 2:7; 1 Cor.
3:8; 2 Cor. 5:10; Rev. 20:12.

[27]*Institutes*, 3.18.1.

in these passages, and not entrance into heaven, then he would have in no way surrendered justification by faith alone. He could have simply said that the reward of the believer is a matter of faith and works, but the salvation of the believer is a matter of faith alone.

Berkouwer says, "If we were to distinguish eternal life from special rewards, we would be forced to contend that the earning of rewards has an independent significance side by side with the merits of Christ."[28] This is apparently why he copies Calvin's view and makes rewards identical with eternal life. He then of course finds himself in the midst of an impossible tension. On the one hand, like Calvin he is at pains to emphasize that there is a correspondence between work and reward, but on the other hand, every merit which could accrue to good works must be denied.[29]

Dabney ultimately resorts to Calvin's perseverance in holiness to solve the problem of merit in rewards.[30] He answers all the passages which seem to give merit to works by saying that "good works are the only practical and valid test of the genuineness of faith." When we have genuine faith, we receive the "merits of Christ." These merits include eternal life, final deliverance from hell, and Dabney's "degrees of blessedness," i.e., extra rewards. Dabney does not satisfactorily explain the passages which seem to imply that differing degrees of blessedness are dependent in some way on the believer's service in this life.

This Calvinist reasoning is very complex, but it seems they are arguing like this: God in eternity past has purposed that some believers would have greater reward than others. He therefore purposed that they would do more works in this life to "earn" them. He then enabled them to do the works which were consistent with the reward which He had already purposed. The reward was not based on works but on Christ's merit. God disposed these merits before anyone worked. They are therefore of grace.

Calvinism, while logical and symmetrical, is often scholastic. It is true that Scripture speaks of the predestination of some to eternal life, but it nowhere speaks of the predestination of various degrees of blessedness. Therefore, while such a notion could logically follow from the doctrine of decrees (indeed all is predestined), we should not speculate on these inner workings of works and rewards from the framework of a theological system and at the expense of numerous texts which somehow connect the believer's future reward with his present service. While it is true we must stand with Scripture that faith alone saves, we must also stand with Scripture that faith plus works sanctifies and rewards even at

---

[28]Berkouwer, p. 121.

[29]Ibid., p. 122.

[30]Robert L. Dabney, *Lectures in Systematic Theology* (1878; reprint ed., Grand Rapids: Zondervan, 1972), p. 684.

the expense of a theological system and a point granted to the Catholics. The ascribing of merit to our works for rewards in no way requires us to ascribe merit to our works in order to obtain justification. Calvin's argument fails anyway, because even though God purposed that we would do works, He purposed that these works would be done jointly by the believer and God. On the other hand, God purposed that the gift of salvation would be His work alone. In other words, God purposed that rewards would come as merit and salvation as a gift.

If the Bible teaches that the believer can merit a reward, so be it. This implies no necessary contradiction to the doctrine of justification by faith alone. It simply ascribes more to the new man in Christ than the adherents of perseverance can allow. But the Scriptures clearly allow this and in fact assert it in scores of places. If our Calvinist friends feel this smacks of evil "Pelagianism," our reply is that in this instance then the Arminians are more consistent with Scripture than the heirs of the Beza and Perkins.

Faithful Work Is Our Duty

Perseverance in holiness is not the necessary and inevitable result of justification. It is necessary for rewards in heaven but not for entrance into heaven itself. It is, however, our "obligation" (Rom. 8:12) and our "duty":

Suppose one of you had a servant plowing or looking after the sheep. Would he say to the servant when he comes in from the field, "Come along now and sit down to eat"? Would he not rather say, "Prepare my supper, get yourself ready and wait on me while I eat and drink; after that you may eat and drink"? Would he thank the servant because he did what he was told to do? So you also, when you have done everything you were told to do, should say, "We are unworthy servants; we have only done our duty" (Lk. 17:7-10).

When we have done all that we can do, when we have been faithful to the end, we have still only done what it is required of all servants, that they be faithful. "Now it is required that those who have been given a trust must prove faithful" (1 Cor. 4:2). So the reward we receive is still a matter of grace. That God should reward us for our work is not an obligation on His part, for we have only done what we should. It is a further manifestation of His unmerited favor!

We should not conclude from this, as Dabney does, that the believer's works are the result only of generosity and not merit. The believers works, according to Dabney, "contribute nothing essential to earning the inheritance; in that point of view it is as wholly gratuitous to the believer as though he had been all the time asleep."[31] He asserts that the merit which earned the reward was

---

[31]Ibid., p. 683.

Christ's, but it is never clear how the passages describing the believer's meriting it himself are to be explained. While it seems clear that there is no legal connection between work and reward, it is equally clear that, if there was no work at all, there would be no reward. To say, as Dabney does, that a believer could sleep through life and do nothing is just as absurd as the other extreme; namely, that for everything he does, God is legally placed in the believer's debt.

This, however, does not mean that we obey God only because it is our duty. That is the atheistic ethic, not the Christian one. The atheist maintains that good should be done only for the sake of good and with no reward for the doing of it. This is supposedly "higher" than the Christian view. Yet the Scriptures repeatedly hold out eternal rewards as a central motivation in Christian living.[32] When they are set in the context of gratitude for forgiveness of sins and the desire to say "Thank you, Lord, for dying for me," it is hard to see how this is "selfish."

Rewards Are Dispensed on the Basis of Grace

Part of the problem the Reformers had in regard to the place of merit in eternal rewards is that they construed "merit" in the Catholic and legal sense--a precise, legal obligation. The believer would in this sense put God in his debt, and for every work done God was legally obligated to measure out some degree of reward. However, the Scriptures present the matter in a different light in the parable of the vineyard workers (Mt. 20:1-16):

For the kingdom of heaven is like a landowner who went out early in the morning to hire men to work in his vineyard. He agreed to pay them a denarius for the day and sent them into the vineyard.

About the third hour he went out and saw others standing in the marketplace doing nothing. He told them "You also go and work in my vineyard, and I will pay you whatever is right. So they went (Mt. 20:1-5).

Three hours later the landowner employed some more workers. Now the question of equal payment is raised. At the end of the day we would expect that each man would be paid according to the number of hours he worked, in other words, according to legal merit. Surprisingly, however, the landowner paid each worker exactly the same amount. This evokes a vigorous protest from those who were hired first:

When they received it, they began to grumble against the landowner. "These men who were hired last worked only one hour," they said, "and you have made them equal to us who have borne the burden of the work and the heat of the day" (Mt. 20:11-12 NKJV).

[32]Col. 3:23-24; Heb. 6:10; 11:26 where reward is presented as a praiseworthy motivation.

If rewards were a matter of placing God in our debt and a strict legal recompense for each amount of work done, we would expect the landowner to say, "You are correct. I should pay you more." However he says:

Friend, I am not being unfair to you. Didn't you agree to work for a denarius? Take your pay and go. I want to give the man who was hired last the same as I gave you. Don't I have the right to do what I want with my own money? Or are you envious because I am generous? (Mt. 20:13-15 NKJV).

Therefore, there is not a precise correlation between work and reward as in a labor contract. The idea of legal merit is excluded; only mercy is emphasized. Moreover, the point of the parable is to demonstrate that it is God's sovereign prerogative to do as He pleases with each of us. The parable also teaches that anyone may be saved and fit for heaven just before he dies, just like the thief on the cross (Lk. 23:43). But also it is possible for a young Christian in terms of his time of service to receive the same crown as the aged who has served the Lord for fifty years. The crown of righteousness, according to Paul, is not for him only but for all those who love His appearing (2 Tim. 4:8). Samson's finest hour was his death (Jud. 16:30), and it earned him a place in the faith hall of fame (Heb. 11:32).

The variety of gifts and rewards given in heaven is striking. It is important to note that all of these rewards are given because we faithfully persevere to the end, even in the midst of trial and difficulty. The rewards are given to the overcomer who perseveres in the midst of heresy, idolatry, immorality, pressures, and stresses. Rewards are given for being in the world but not of it.

Temporal rewards are dangled before us like shiny new trinkets that gleam and glow with hypnotizing allurement. We are taught by the world's secularists and 'success seminarists' to visualize our achievements and rewards. Biblically, the Lord tells us this is vanity and chasing after the wind. The Lord challenges us to visualize the rewards in the future and chase after Him alone.

The Duration of the Remorse

In the next chapter we will discuss in detail the theological implications of negative judgment falling upon the believer at the judgment seat of Christ. As discussed above, for some it will be a time of great remorse. However, the Scriptures give us no reason to assume that these unfaithful Christians will spend their eternity in remorse and regret. We are told that Christ will "wipe every tear from their eyes. There will be ... no more mourning or crying or pain" (Rev. 21:4). Those unfaithful Christians who did not repent in life will repent now. In fact, at His name every knee will bow (Phil. 2:10).

Paul specifically applies this very saying to Christians in Rom. 14:10-12:

You, then, why do you judge your brother? Or why do you look down on your brother? For we will all stand before God's judgment seat. It is written:

"As surely as I live," says the Lord, "every knee will bow before me; every tongue will confess to God." So then, each of us will give an account of himself to God.

And, having confessed their sin, they like the prodigal son will be restored to eternal fellowship with their King. Just as an earthly father rejoices over the repentance of his rebellious son (Lk. 15:21-24), so we have every right to expect that the Lord will rejoice in the tardy repentance of those for whom He died. If Christ will redeem lost sinners, how much more will He do for His born-again sons: "Much more then, having been justified by His blood, we shall be saved from the wrath of God through Him. For if while we were enemies, we were reconciled to God through the death of His Son, much more, having been reconciled, we shall be saved by His life" (Rom. 5:9-10). Furthermore, God has promised that "no eye has seen, no ear has heard, no mind has conceived what God has prepared for those who love Him" (1 Cor. 2:9).

The exclusion from the banquet is a temporary act of divine discipline and cannot be an eternal exclusion from fellowship with the King. Paul assured us of this when he said, "Who will bring a charge against God's elect? . . . Who shall separate us from the love of Christ? . . . For I am convinced that neither death nor life, nor angels, nor principalities, nor things present, nor things to come, nor powers, nor height, nor depth, nor any other created thing, shall be able to separate us from the love of God, which is in Christ Jesus our Lord" (Rom. 8:33-39). Not even "things to come" can separate us from the love of Christ.

Yet it is true that we will reap what we sow (Gal. 6:7). There will be for some a time of profound sorrow.

However, this sorrow cannot be absolute, for even the finest of Christians will find things in their lives for which they are ashamed and for which they feel remorse when seen in the light of God's unapproachable holiness. If the sorrow was absolute, this would mean that the finest of Christians could be sorrowful throughout eternity. This is definitely not the picture of heaven.[33] Whatever the time period of remorse in the kingdom, when the eternal state begins, every tear is wiped away. Eternity future will be like a graduation ceremony. There is some measure of disappointment and remorse that one did not do better and work harder. However, the central emotion at such an event is joy, not sadness. The graduates did not leave the auditorium weeping because they did not receive bet-

---

[33]Consider Rom. 8:18-25; 1 Cor. 2; Rev. 21:4.

ter grades. Rather, they are thankful they graduated, and they are grateful for what they did achieve. Hoyt is correct, "To overdo the sorrow aspect of the judgment seat of Christ is to make heaven into hell. To underdo the sorrow aspect is to make faithfulness inconsequential."[34]

How long will this period of remorse and regret last? The Scriptures do not specify. The wiping away of every tear occurs at the end of the millennium, but the experience of remorse need not last that long. We suspect that the duration of this period of self-examination is equal to the duration of the banquet. We can imagine the Lord exiting the banquet hall and restoring to fellowship all those unfaithful Christians for whom He died and for whom His loving heart still desires. However, they will miss the joy of the fellowship of the metochoi, and they will forfeit the right to "reign with him" in the thousand-year kingdom to follow.

We must not forget that, when we stand before Him at that day, we will be in resurrection bodies. Because of the absence of sin and the experience of the maximum fullness of human potential, our ability to deal with the emotion of grief will be heightened and immeasurably more mature. At that time we will finally exist as man was intended to be, mature and without sin. There is a cycle to all grief--it is dealt with, and then it passes. There is no reason that this would not be the case in the kingdom. However, due to our heightened state the cycle will be abbreviated in comparison to our present experience.

Differences in authority and intimacy with Christ will, however, remain throughout eternity. Nevertheless, everyone's cup will be full, but the cups will be of different sizes. This is GRACE!

---

[34]Hoyt, "Negative Aspects," p. 131.

Chapter 23

Negative Judgment and the Believer

The possibility that some will not overcome and hence will have their names removed from the book of life and will not partake of the tree of life and will not rule over the nations raises a troubling theological question. How can carnal Christians whose sins have been paid for, whose trespasses forgiven, ever experience a negative judgment from God again? In the discussion to follow, it must be stressed again that the sober warnings of the New Testament are addressed to the carnal and hardened Christian and not those who are persevering in their sanctification. The Christian who persists in willful, unconfessed sin faces negative judgment both in time and at the judgment seat of Christ and exclusion from the inheritance in the kingdom. However, these negative consequences will not last into eternity. When we enter the eternal state, God will wipe away every tear (Rev. 21:4).

First of all, the Bible makes it clear that God has judicially removed sin from the believer and has done it completely. For example, He says, "I have blotted out, as a thick cloud, thy transgressions, and, as a cloud, thy sins" (Isa. 44:22). Or hear the psalmist, "As far as the east is from the west, so far has He removed our transgressions from us" (Ps. 103:12). Micah assures us, "Thou wilt cast all their sins into the depths of the sea" (Mic. 7:19). The writer to the Hebrews affirms, "For I will be merciful to their unrighteousness, and their sins and their iniquities will I remember no more" (Heb. 8:12).

With regard to sin, Scripture affirms that the child of God under grace shall not come under judgment (Jn. 3:18; 5:24). Our sin, past, present, and future, has been born by a perfect Substitute, and we are therefore forever placed beyond condemnation (Col. 2:10), accepted as perfect in Christ (1 Cor. 1:30; Eph. 1:6; Col. 2:10; Heb. 10:14), and loved as Christ is loved (Jn. 17:23).

The perplexing thing is that the Scriptures affirm in many other passages that God **does** judge us when we become carnal and **does** remember our sin. Consider:

Unless I wash you, you have no part with me (Jn. 13:8).

If we confess our sins, he is faithful and just and will forgive us our sins (1 Jn. 1:9).

If the Christian does not confess, he is not forgiven. This certainly appears to be a penalty for willful sin.

If you obey my commands, you will remain in my love (Jn. 15:10).

If the Christian refuses to obey, he will apparently no longer remain in Christ's love. This is true even though Paul has declared elsewhere that "nothing shall be able to separate us from the love of God" (Rom. 8:39):

So, because you are lukewarm--neither hot nor cold--I am about to spit you out of my mouth (Rev. 3:16).

Who will render to each one according to his deeds (Rom. 2:7 NKJV).

And behold, I am coming quickly, and My reward is with Me, to give to everyone according to his work (Rev. 22:12 NKJV).

These last two passages are clearly universal and assert that every man, Christian and non-Christian, will be judged according to his work.

Apparently, true Christians, due to their sin, can "have no part" with Christ, can be unforgiven, and can be outside of His love. Scores of other passages can be cited. We are also told that we will reap what we sow. We have been warned that there is no sacrificial protection from judgment in time (Heb. 10:26) for willful sin. Paul tells us that at the judgment seat of Christ we will be rewarded for both the good and the bad things we have done. For the persistently carnal Christian a dreadful experience awaits him at the last day. He will suffer the loss of everything but will be saved as through fire (1 Cor. 3:15):

If any man builds on this foundation using gold, silver, costly stones, wood, hay or straw, his work will be shown for what it is, because the Day will bring it to light. It will be revealed with fire, and the fire will test the quality of each man's work. If what he has built survives, he

will receive his reward, if it is burned up, he will suffer loss; he himself
will be saved, but only as one escaping through the flames.[1]

In addition, we have Christ's stern warning to the wicked servant that he
would be cast into the place of weeping and gnashing of teeth. The foolish virgins are excluded from the wedding banquet, and the man without the proper at-
tire for the banquet was cast into the darkness outside. The exegetical data in
these passages argues well for the regenerate state of the individuals undergoing
these punishments. We cannot say they are unregenerate just because our theological system teaches that these punishments could not come upon the regenerate. That is the point in question.

As mentioned in chapter 15, there are three negative consequences for the
consistently carnal Christian at the judgment seat of Christ. First, for some there
will be a stinging rebuke. This is the meaning of the Lord's warning that some
will be "cut in pieces" (Mt. 24:51) and of His stern denunciation, "You wicked,
lazy, servant" (Mt. 25:26). Second, such unfaithful Christians face millennial
disinheritance. When the Lord declares that He will "deny" those who are
ashamed of Him and when Paul says, "If we deny Him, He will deny us," disinheritance is in view. A father may disinherit his son, but that son remains his son.
To be disinherited is simply to forfeit our share in the future reign of the servant
kings. And finally, the carnal Christian faces exclusion from the joy of the wedding banquet, "Friend, how did you get in here without wedding clothes?" (Mt.
22:12).

These passages all seem to teach that Christ does remember our sin and
does take it into account. This raises a perplexing theological problem. But
there is an even more troubling practical problem. For many these conflicting
bits of data cloud their view of the love and unconditional acceptance of God.
Instead of being perceived as a merciful and forgiving Father, He begins to appear more like a stern judge, and the biblical picture of His love retreats from
view.

---

[1]To "suffer loss" in 1 Cor. 3:15 means to "experience forfeiture, to suffer loss, to forfeit" (W.
E. Vine, *An Expository Dictionary of New Testament Words*, 4 vols. in 1 [Westwood, NJ: Revell,
1940], 2:121). The word is from **zemia** which appears with its antonym in Phil. 3:7: "But what things
were gain to me, those I counted loss (**zemian**) for Christ." Robertson and Plummer suggest that
the verb has reference to the reward mentioned in 1 Cor. 3:14 rather than the definite subject "he."
Thus, the verses should read, "If any man's work abide which he hath built thereupon, he shall receive a reward. If any man's work shall be burned, it (the reward) shall be forfeited, but he himself
(**autos**) shall be saved." "Himself" is in contrast to the reward. The reward will be lost, not the
worker (Archibald Robertson and Alfred Plummer, *A Critical and Exegetical Commentary on the
First Epistle of St. Paul to the Corinthians*, 2d ed., *International Critical Commentary* [Edinburgh: T.
& T. Clark, 1914], p. 65).

How are we to deal with these apparently contradictory strains of biblical teaching?[2] The writer does not claim to have a final answer to this difficult problem, but hopefully the following suggestions will give helpful perspective.

Since Paul, who taught the imputation of righteousness, also anticipated that one day we will be judged according to our bad works as well as our good, the ideas cannot be incompatible. Kendall correctly insists, "We must deduce from this that there is no contradiction between Paul's doctrine of justification and his conception of the judgment of God; and that being declared righteous so as to escape the wrath of God (Rom. 5:9; 1 Thess. 1:10) does not exempt us from rewards or punishment in the Last Day."[3] Jesus said every idle word will be judged (Mt. 12:36). This is frightening, but we have been warned. This is why Paul could say, "For if we would judge ourselves, we should not be judged" (1 Cor. 11:31). If we repent now, we will not be judged later.[4]

The Experimental Predestinarian Solution

Because of the clear fact that believers have had the penalty for sin already paid, Experimental Predestinarians argue that any negatives accruing to the believer at the judgment seat of Christ **are not judicially punitive in nature.**[5] This solution is commonly found in Reformed[6] and Lutheran[7] theology texts and is certainly plausible.

Experimental Predestinarians correctly maintain that a primary purpose in the judgment on the believer is disclosure. Every careless word will be revealed (Mt. 12:36). Hidden motives will be brought to light (Rom. 2:16). When it is ar-

---

[2]The Catholics have used these two strains of biblical thought to prove their doctrine of purgatory. They argue that Scriptures such as these establish that the death of Christ did not completely satisfy the justice of God. The believer must assist in this satisfaction in purgatory. For a good discussion see Dabney, pp. 538-45. Purgatory must be rejected. The Scriptures teach the saint is made perfect at death and there is therefore no room for a "purgatorial cleansing." Furthermore, satisfaction of Christ is complete in regard to providing eternal unconditional acceptance and immediate entrance to heaven at death. Therefore, whatever befalls the glorified saint at the judgment seat cannot exclude him from immediate entrance into heaven.

[3]R. T. Kendall, *Once Saved Always Saved* (London: Hodder and Stoughton, 1984), p. 123.

[4]Martin Luther reportedly claimed he would have three surprises in heaven: that some would be there he didn't expect to see, that some would be missing that he thought would be there, and that he was there himself. We should expect to see some saved by fire and some having "abundant entrance" (2 Pet. 1:11).

[5]Samuel L. Hoyt, "The Negative Aspects of the Christian's Judgment," *BibSac* 137 (April-June, 1980): 125.

[6]E.g., Dabney, p. 543.

[7]E.g., "The appearance of the believers before God's judgment-seat will therefore not have the nature of a condemnatory judgment since their sins are forgiven through faith in Christ (Matt. 25:34)" (John Theodore Mueller, *Christian Dogmatics: A Handbook of Doctrinal Theology* [St. Louis: Concordia, 1955], p. 630).

gued that the sins of believers will never be mentioned at the judgment, Experimental Predestinarians properly object that, if this judgment concerns our deeds, words, and thoughts, surely the sins of believers will be revealed on that day. "But," Hoekema stresses, "and this is the important point, the sins and shortcomings of believers will be revealed as **forgiven sins**, whose guilt has been totally covered by the blood of Jesus Christ."[8] Surely this is an incomplete view of the judgment. More is involved than a revelation of God's grace.

Starting from the premise that the death of Christ was designed by God to satisfy all the claims of justice against the believer's sin, Hoekema is led to deny that this is truly a judgment. It is only a revelation of forgiven sins. It is difficult to see that in the texts in question. After all, the sins which have not been repented of are not forgiven according to 1 Jn. 1:9.

The problem with this is that the above Scriptures seem to require a penal sense both in time and at the judgment seat of Christ.

The Dispensational Solution

The above view is also common in dispensational circles,[9] albeit in a more developed form in regard to the judgment seat of Christ. For example, Lewis Sperry Chafer argued as follows:

> *At the Judgment Seat of Christ sin will not be the subject of consideration. At that time believers will be perfect, with no sin nature, and will never sin again in thought, word, or deed. Therefore any concept of discipline because of previous sins is unnecessary and would be unfruitful. The question of righteousness before God was settled when they were justified by faith. The Judgment Seat of Christ deals with works, not with sin. Believers will be judged on whether their works were good (worth something) or whether they were bad (worthless), as stated in verse 10.*[10]

---

[8]Anthony A. Hoekema, *The Bible and the Future* (Grand Rapids: Eerdmans, 1979), p. 259. See also Louis Berkhof, *Systematic Theology* (London: Banner of Truth, 1941), p. 732.

[9]When we refer to a "dispensational" solution to the problem, we do not intend to imply that there is anything intrinsic to dispensationalism that results in a certain solution. Rather, we are referring to the fact that the views described below have been common in dispensationalist circles. The writer himself is a classical dispensationalist in the Pentecost-Ryrie-Walvoord-McClain mold. After a number of years of considering various forms of realized eschatology, the writer finds that the old dispensationalist solutions to the problem of the kingdom offer, rejection, and postponement are very satisfying.

[10]Lewis Sperry Chafer, *Systematic Theology*, abridged ed., ed. John F. Walvoord, 2 vols. (Wheaton, IL: Victor, 1988), 2:474.

John Walvoord similarly affirms that the child of God under grace shall not come into judgment[11] because the penalty for all sins, past, present, and future, has been paid by his Substitute. The believer is therefore beyond condemnation, perfect in Christ, and loved as Christ is loved. Walvoord says that, when we stand at the judgment seat of Christ, the only issue is rewards which will be reckoned on the basis of merit. The believer's "good works are distinguished from his bad works, and on the basis of good works the believer is rewarded."[12] This is not, says Walvoord, a matter of sin being judged, "because the believer is already justified." Furthermore, it is not a matter of sanctification such as is "experienced in present chastisement for failure to confess sin, because the believer is already perfect in the presence of God." He concludes that "the only remaining issue, then, is the quality of the believer's life and the works that God counts good in contrast with works that are worthless."[13]

Experimental Predestinarians would not allow that there is any significant loss or rebuke to a child of God at the judgment seat of Christ. Since all will necessarily persevere in holiness, how can there be any real loss? Dispensationalists such as Walvoord are more realistic, but they both would conclude that, whatever degree of negative consequences are experienced by the believer, it cannot be a penalty for sin. The view one takes, they argue, must depend upon the intent of the Judge. Now in this case the Judge has already declared that at the judgment seat of Christ we are not dealing with satisfaction for sin but rebuke for failure, not retribution but loss of reward.

The Partaker Solution

While there is much to commend in the Experimental Predestinarian and Dispensational solution to this problem, this writer prefers a slightly modified view.

Before proceeding, however, we need to remember that the warnings of the Bible are addressed to those who refuse to repent, who refuse to confess. The Partaker view of this issue is quite similar to that of the Dispensational view. A major difference, however, is that, while the Partaker does not see negative judgment coming upon the persevering Christian, he does see numerous passages speaking of such a judgment on those Christians who persist in willful, uncon-

---

[11]Lewis Sperry Chafer, *Major Bible Themes*, rev. ed., ed. John F. Walvoord (Grand Rapids: Zondervan, 1974), p. 283. Walvoord cites Jn. 3:18; 5:24; 6:37; Rom. 5:1; 8:1; 1 Cor. 11:32 as proof.

[12]Chafer, p. 285.

[13]Ibid., p. 286. Pentecost likewise affirms, "To bring the believer into judgment concerning the sin question, whether his sins before his new birth, his sins since his new birth, or even sins unconfessed since the new birth, is to deny the efficacy of the death of Christ and nullify the promise of God that 'their sins and iniquities will I remember no more'" (J. Dwight Pentecost, *Things to Come* [Grand Rapids: Dunham, 1958], p. 222).

fessed sin. The church in the West is much in need of these warnings, and it is unfortunate that many have taken them out of the Bible as far as their application to the truly regenerate saint is concerned.

In proof of this assertion we might point to (1) the explicit scriptural statement of this point (Heb. 10:26) and (2) the numerous biblical illustrations where God does seem to punish justified saints, e.g., Ananias and Sapphira, the sickness that came upon drunk believers at the Lord's table in 1 Cor. 11, or the punishment David received for his adultery and murder. Peter tells us that judgment must begin with the family of God (1 Pet. 4:17). And the writer to the Hebrews says the Lord will judge His people (Heb. 10:30). When Adam sinned, the penalty was physical and spiritual death (Rom. 5:12-14). The Lord made it clear that we cannot be counted as his friend unless we obey Him (Jn. 15:14). Failure to respond to discipline can result in a believer being condemned with the world (1 Cor. 11:32-33). These judgments can include sickness and death. It is difficult to remove the notion of judgment and penalty from the stern exhortation of the writer to the Hebrews, "And he punishes everyone he accepts as a son" (Heb. 12:6). Hymenaeus and Alexander are punished and turned over to Satan (1 Tim. 1:20). Throughout the Old Testament there are numerous judgments which come upon the people of God. Moses warns of many curses which will come upon the disobedient (Dt. 28:9-26). Saul was punished by God by being rejected as the king (1 Sam. 15:23). God punishes Solomon by taking the kingdom from him and raising up many adversaries (1 Ki. 11:11). King Uzziah was punished by God with leprosy (2 Chr. 26:20). These inflictions are clearly penal in nature even though Christ is the propitiation for all sin and the justice of God has been satisfied!

If it can be shown from Scripture that any believer experiences a penal judgment either in time or eternity, it cannot be argued that the Bible teaches that no believer could ever experience a penal judgment. And it seems that it can be shown that the Bible teaches this. The judgment of physical death is a penal judgment upon sin (Rom. 5:12-14).[14] If all believers are exempt from any kind of condemnation without exception, then why do all believers undergo the penal judgment of physical death (Rom. 5:14-18)? Experimental Predestinarians, such as Berkhof, argue that, because Christ is the propitiation for all sin, the experience of physical death cannot be penal in nature.[15] The problem with this response is that nowhere in Scripture does it say that "the penal element is removed from death."

---

[14]See John Murray, *The Epistle to the Romans* (Grand Rapids: Eerdmans, 1959), pp. 181-182. Also William G. T. Shedd, *A Critical and Doctrinal Commentary on the Epistle of St. Paul to the Romans* (New York: Charles Scribner's Sons, 1879; reprint ed., Grand Rapids: Zondervan, 1967), p. 122.

[15]Berkhof, *Theology*, p. 671.

If God can bring condemnation upon believers in time as these illustrations prove, there is no necessary reason to believe He cannot condemn believers at the judgment seat of Christ. Indeed, there seem to be numerous Scriptures which indicate that this is the case. The wicked servant was warned that he would be cut in pieces. Elsewhere we are warned that every man will be judged according to deeds. It must also be remembered that the central passage on the judgment seat of Christ is set in a legal context. The judgment seat referred to was a raised platform in the middle of the city where judgments were passed and penalties announced. Paul tells us that we will all stand before God's judgment seat (Rom. 14:10) where we must all give an account. Even describing the negative judgment as "loss of reward" is only a circumlocution for penalty. A loss of reward is one kind of penalty! The man in the parable of the talents who buried his money will lose what he has and will be cast into the darkness outside. The foolish virgins will hear the terrifying words, "I do not know you." The condemnation, however, has nothing to do with the believer's eternal salvation. The atonement has forever settled that issue.

The difficulty is obvious. If Christ is truly the satisfaction for sin and has therefore satisfied the justice of God, why then do believers still have to satisfy that justice by undergoing more penalties?

The Intent of the Atonement

The atonement of Christ is either a satisfaction for the sins of some men (limited atonement) or a satisfaction for the sins of all men without exception.[16] It cannot be the former because the Scriptures say it was a satisfaction for the sins of the whole world (1 Jn. 2:2). The atonement must therefore be a satisfaction for the sins of all men without exception.

Now this satisfaction for all must be either provisional (Ryrie)[17] or actual. If it is provisional, then the passages which say it is a satisfaction and redemption and reconciliation must be qualified to mean it is provisionally a satisfaction. This seems to be adding words to the text to help explain a theological difficulty.

It is simpler to say it is an actual satisfaction, redemption, and reconciliation for all men without exception. Granting this, we must then ask, "In what respect is it a satisfaction?" It is either a satisfaction for sin in all respects or a satisfaction for sin in some limited respect. It cannot be a satisfaction in all respects because then all men would be saved. If the claims of justice have truly been satisfied in all respects, then no man should have to satisfy those claims himself

---

[16]See Robert P. Lightner, *The Death Christ Died: A Case for Unlimited Atonement* (Des Plaines, IL: Regular Baptist Press, 1967) for a discussion of the case for unlimited atonement.

[17]Charles Ryrie, *Basic Theology* (Wheaton: Victor Books, 1986), p. 323.

by suffering the penalty of hell. But men do go to hell. Therefore, the atonement must be a satisfaction for sin in a special sense.

What then was the atonement intended to accomplish? The intent of the atonement is not to completely satisfy the claims of justice in all respects or to save all men. Rather, the intent of the atonement is to completely satisfy the justice of God in a limited and specific sense. The atonement has freed God to unconditionally accept those who believe.[18]

Specific support for this view is surprisingly obvious. When we are told that God has reconciled the world to Himself and that he no longer counts their trespass against them (2 Cor. 5:10), we are also told that not all men go to heaven. When we are told that Christ's death is a propitiation for the sins of the world (1 Jn. 2:2), we are reminded that those who do not believe on him are condemned (Jn. 3:18). How can God's justice be satisfied and the world be reconciled and men still go to hell? Either the term "world" refers only to the "world of the elect" or the reconciliation, satisfaction, and redemption of Christ have a more limited intent. To limit the term world to "world of the elect" seems a bit contrived. But a limitation on the atonement is clearly taught in the Bible. We are told, for example, that false teachers, who have denied the Lord, were nevertheless redeemed by Him (2 Pet. 2:1). It is therefore clear that the redemption of Christ does not automatically cover the sin of the unsaved. What then is the atonement intended to do? Its purpose, says Paul, is that God might "be just and the one who justifies the man who has faith in Jesus" (Rom. 3:26). In other words, the death of Christ freed God to confer justification upon those who believe.

If it is permissible to argue for a limitation on the atonement in regard to its extent, as the Reformed theologians do, is it not permissible to argue for a limitation on the atonement in regard to its intent when it is explicitly taught by numerous Scriptures? In fact, Reformed theologian Robert L. Dabney takes virtually the same position when he tries to explain why believers still pay the penalty of physical death. He argues that the satisfaction of Christ does not obligate God to cancel our whole indebtedness, precisely the view of this writer. Rather, His acceptance of Christ's death as a legal satisfaction "was, on His part, an act of pure grace; and therefore the acceptance acquits us just so far as, and no farther than God is pleased to allow it."[19] The man who does not believe is condemned to hell because God apparently did not extend the atonement to be a satisfaction as far as condemnation to hell. Rather, it was designed to satisfy the

---

[18]This line of thinking was first suggested to this writer by Zane Hodges, analyst and writer for Kerugma, Inc. Personal communication 27 June 1991. The true starting point regarding the atonement, according to Hodges, is to realize that its purpose was to remove all barriers to God's acceptance of the sinner. God's justice is satisfied in the sense that He can now confer acceptance upon those sinners who believe.

[19]Dabney, p. 819.

justice of God in the sense of freeing Him to unconditionally accept those who believe. When a man does believe, he is not only unconditionally accepted by the Father, but the benefits of the atonement are extended in his case to protect him from hell. This extension occurs through the free gift of justification, acquittal at the divine bar of justice

What kind of justice accepts a penalty for sin and then extends its benefits only far enough to grant acceptance before the judge to those who believe but not far enough to acquit the sin of those who do not? Can the benefits of a pardon be variously applied and extended at the discretion of the judge? Consider the recent case of Leroy Strachan, who killed a police officer in 1946 and was not caught until February 1990, over forty years later.[20] In the intervening forty years, Leroy had become a Christian and a model citizen. He sang in the church choir and neighbors could not believe he could ever have killed anyone. "That's not the Leroy Strachan we know--he wouldn't hurt a fly." After being imprisoned again, he prayed with and ministered to some of the city's toughest criminals. Most people who followed the case were not eager to see a 63-year-old man, with a loving family and aura of grace about him, spend his last days in jail. "He lived a Christian, decent life," says Pauline Brown, Leroy's great-great grandniece. "He sent money to his family. He made something out of himself. He didn't get into any trouble after all these years."

The Miami police, however, saw the matter differently. They felt that to let him go would send the wrong message.

Strachan's lawyers argued that in view of extenuating circumstances Strachan should be freed. What were those circumstances? Leroy had lived openly and publicly for forty-five years, not as a fugitive. Second, the courts realized that even if he was once a killer, he had become what he pretended to be his whole adult life: a model citizen. He had therefore paid his debt to society without society ever even presenting the bill. As a result (1) the courts reduced the charge to manslaughter and (2) asked for a one-year prison term and probation. Since Leroy had already spent nineteen months in jail in New York, he had already served his time and was a free man.

The extenuating circumstances motivated the court toward mercy, and they counted forty years of good works and nineteen months of penalty serving in jail as sufficient.

This sort of thing happens all the time in human law courts. The judge is free to take various circumstances into consideration which effect how far he will extend the penalties of the law. Now, transferring our human courtroom back to the heavenly forum, we may make a spiritual parallel. Before the human judge would release Leroy from prison, he required two things: (1) forty years of good

---

[20]Cathy Booth, "An Act of Forgiveness," *Time* (Sept. 16,1991), p. 38.

works and (2) a payment of one year in jail for his sin. This is precisely the position of the Roman Catholic Church. They accept the atonement only to the point that, if a man is willing to do good works and to pay off the balance in purgatory, he can have the benefits of the atonement extended to cover all penalties and go to heaven. The biblical picture is radically different. The only requirement placed upon the condemned sinner is the requirement to believe. At that point, the divine judge confers righteousness, i.e., justifies the sinner, and the benefits of the atonement are extended to pay for all his sin. He will never face the penalty of hell again. As Paul put it, "His faith is reckoned as righteousness" (Rom. 4:5).

The extenuating circumstance which inclined the judge to mercy was Leroy's forty years of life as a model citizen. The extenuating circumstance which has inclined our Heavenly Judge toward mercy is the satisfaction of Christ. However, like the earthly judge, our Heavenly Judge can extend the benefits of that "extenuating circumstance" as far or near as He chooses. God is not obligated by the atonement to save anyone. He is freed by it to save whomever He pleases. He is also freed by it to extend the benefits of that satisfaction as far as He chooses.

All of this means that the only thing standing between the unsaved and entrance to heaven is faith in Jesus Christ. Their sin is not a hindrance to entrance, only their unbelief in Christ. Jesus taught this explicitly when He said:

> *He who believes in him is not judged; he who does not believe has been judged already, because he has not believed in the name of the only begotten Son of God* (Jn. 3:18).

The only reason men are excluded from heaven is unbelief in Christ. This is true because two things are required for entrance into heaven: (1) a satisfaction for sin and (2) the gift of righteousness and a new nature. The former has been provided for all men without exception (in a limited respect), but the latter is available only to those who believe. A failure to believe excludes one from the gift of righteousness and justification. He is therefore not acquitted at the heavenly bar of justice and is condemned for his sins. However, when he is condemned, he is not paying a penalty for sins for which Christ already paid. Christ's atonement only paid the penalty for sin in a limited and specific sense: removal of the bars to heaven. It was an actual provision and propitiation in this sense. It was, however, a provisional propitiation whose benefits could be extended to cover the penalty of hell for those who believed. We argue then that the atonement was both actual, as the adherents of limited atonement argue, and provisional as the advocates of unlimited redemption maintain.

Two Kinds of Relationship with God

The understanding of the intent of the atonement explained above clarifies how God can punish believers for sins when Christ is the satisfaction for sin. The answer is that Christ's atonement was not intended to cover the sins of believers for sins within the family of God. It only renders God free to accept unconditionally into His family those who believe. Like all children we enjoy two kinds of relationships with our father. We are forever safe and secure in his family, but our fellowship with our father can vary depending upon our behavior. With God our eternal relationship is secure and unchanging because it depends upon Him; it was secured by the atonement. But our temporal fellowship is variable because it depends upon us. We must confess our sins and walk daily in the light of His Word.

Imagine, for example, that you are a teacher in a classroom. Your son is one of the students in your English class. One day you catch him cheating on the final examination. Will he not pay penalties? Is he not still your son? Or suppose you are the owner of a small business. Your son is employed at the cash register. One day you catch him stealing money out of the cash register. The fact that he has stolen money in no way affects the fact that he is your son. It does, however, mean that, even though he is your son, he will pay penalties for his crime.

True sons of God can likewise pay penalties. The intent of the atonement was obviously not to remove all penalty from the life of the Christian. The atonement was intended by God to free Him so that He can confer unconditional acceptance upon those who believe.

The Partaker's solution to this problem of judgment on the believer is to recognize that we have two kinds of relationship with God: eternal and temporal. Consider the example of David. As a result of David's adultery and murder, Nathan the prophet rebukes him and announces judgment. Then he says, "The LORD has taken away your sin. You are not going to die" (2 Sam. 12:13). David's eternal relationship with God is forever safe and secure. But Nathan also says that David's son will be taken by death and that David's house will experience terrible trouble (12:10-12). It is evident that this is a penalty, a punishment, even though the propitiation of Christ has satisfied the Father's justice and David has been removed from all condemnation. The text suggests two relationships with God: eternal and temporal. In regard to his eternal relationship he is without condemnation, but in regard to this temporal fellowship he can come under condemnation.

The fact that Christ has paid the penalty for the believer's sin, forensically, forever, in no way implies that He automatically grants forgiveness for fellowship within the family irrespective of our behavior. We say "forgiveness for fellowship within the family" because, as discussed elsewhere, the Bible speaks of two kinds of forgiveness: eternal and temporal. The sacrifice of Christ gives sacrificial protection from the former on the basis of faith and the permanent gift of regeneration and justification. But it does not give sacrificial protection to unconfessed temporal sin subsequent to our justification. Our eternal forgiveness depends upon Him, but our temporal fellowship depends upon us.

Unconfessed sin relates not to forensic forgiveness but to familial forgiveness. Any sin is a barrier to fellowship but does not endanger our eternal relationship. "Daily forgiveness of those who are within the family of God is distinguished from the judicial and positional forgiveness which was applied forensically to all of a person's sins the moment he believed in the Lord Jesus Christ."[21] Forensic forgiveness is the subject of Col. 2:13, but familial forgiveness is in view in 1 Jn. 1:9.

Thus, in Jn. 5:24 when we are assured that we will not come into judgment and yet in 2 Cor. 5:10 we do, the resolution is that John is referring to judgment with respect to one's eternal destiny and Paul is referring to the wages for work. John speaks of forensic justification, and Paul refers to familial forgiveness. John speaks of our escape from retribution; Paul speaks of our rewards and punishments within the family of God. The satisfaction of Christ unconditionally and irrevocably covers the former but only provisionally covers the latter. We must confess daily to obtain the benefits of having the atonement extended to forgive sin within the family of God.

In summary, we may observe that sin has three powers over us: the power to bar us from heaven and send us to hell, the power to enslave, and the power to exclude us from vital fellowship and friendship with Christ. Through the atonement God dealt with all three powers. Through propitiation the barriers to heaven were removed for all men. God's justice has been satisfied. God is legally free to confer unconditional acceptance upon those who believe. Through redemption God has purchased us out of slavery to sin. Through reconciliation we are restored to friendship. Yet even though God is now free to confer acceptance, we must appropriate it by faith. Similarly, we appropriate the benefits of redemption from sin by reckoning that we are truly free from sin (Rom. 6:11). We appropriate the benefits of reconciliation by walking in the light, confessing our sin so as to remain in constant fellowship (1 Jn. 1:9). The following chart summarizes these various aspects of the atonement:

---

[21]Samuel L. Hoyt, "The Judgment Seat of Christ and Unconfessed Sins," *BibSac* 137 (January-March 1980): 38.

Work	Purpose	How Obtained
Propitiation	To free God to accept those who believe	Believe
Redemption	To purchase us out of the slave market of sin	Reckon
Reconciliation	To establish friendship be- tween former enemies	Confess

Practical Concerns

But it is asked, "What is the purpose of such a negative judgment against the believer at the judgment seat of Christ?" The final chapter has been written, so why punish him? Throughout Scripture God uses warnings of negative conse- quences in the future to motivate us toward sanctification in time. Why must God punish him? For two reasons: (1) He warned him, and He must honor his Word, and (2) justice requires that sin be punished. Using this objection, one might as well say that there is no purpose in punishing the nonbeliever either. We reap what we sow. So God must punish the carnal Christian, or He is not just and fair.

It is also asked, "How can a negative judgment come upon a completed and perfected saint?" The assumption behind this question is that, since no con- demnation can come upon a believer, all indications of condemnation are in re- ality "discipline" and the intent is correction rather than punishment. What pur- pose would there be for correction in a completed and perfected saint?

We reply that (1) penalties and judgments do come upon saints in time as argued above; (2) the Scriptures teach that such judgments can come upon per- fected saints at the judgment seat, their purpose being punitive not corrective; and finally (3) they came upon the "perfect" angels who sinned and upon Adam who was without sin. Apparently, just being perfect and sinless does not exempt us from judgment.

Will God judge us for sins we have confessed? The answer is yes. However, this judgment would only be loss of reward and not rebuke or disinheritance. We must remember that Scripture speaks in a threefold sense of the judgment of believers.[22] Eric Sauer points out that we are judged as sinners, children, and servants. As sinners we were judged at the cross. There the sentence of damnation was fully executed upon our Substitute. As children we are judged in the present. It is a penalty (1 Cor. 11:32), but its purpose is to

---

[22]Eric Sauer, *From Eternity to Eternity* (Grand Rapids: Eerdmans, 1963), p. 79.

advance our sanctification (Heb. 12:10). Finally, we are judged as servants in the future at the judgment seat of Christ. Here believers can "suffer damage."[23]

A believer who sins an extended period of time and then confesses cannot expect to receive the same reward as one who lives a godly life. While the sins are forgiven, the rewards that could have been obtained are lost. What about the man who lives a carnal life for years and then on his deathbed sincerely decides to confess his sin. Will this man be punished? The answer is yes. Once he confesses, he is forgiven, but he will still be held accountable as a servant. Indeed, when he wakes up in heaven, in the full power of his glorified body, no restraint from sin will be felt. Any failure in the past will be instantly repented of, and he will enter the kingdom in complete fellowship with the Savior. However, he will suffer loss at the judgment seat of Christ. Here he is judged, not as a sinner or a child but as a servant. His reward will be minimal. His loss will be great.

We must remember in all these kinds of questions that God knows everything in our hearts[24] and always deals fairly and with respect to our deepest motivations.[25] In addition, the parable of the vineyard workers should remind us that God does not dispense His blessing on the basis of legal merit and that He can, and does, bring blessing and reward to those who have been in the battle for fewer years than others.

Conclusion

We may say four things about the negative consequences which come upon the believer at the judgment seat of Christ.

First, God's love and acceptance of the sinning Christian is not affected in terms of the Christian's eternal relationship to God and permanent membership in His family. We are forever perfectly accepted in Christ and perfectly loved. However, God does not approve of our sins, and we can lose our fellowship in time and our share in the great future in the kingdom if we persist in them.

Second, the negative consequences for believers at the judgment seat of Christ may be viewed as the final chastisement which the Lord has ordained for His people. The fact that some of the punishments are experienced in eternity rather than in time enhances their value for sanctifying us now. The anticipation of negative chastisements serves to keep us humble, to pursue faithful lives, and to live spiritually in the present. While they are a punishment for an unfaithful life, their main purpose is to effect sanctification now.

---

[23]Ibid.

[24]1 Jn. 3:20.

[25]1 Chr. 29:17; 1 Sam. 16:7; Prov. 16:2.

It is sometimes asked, "How can future chastisement have any motivational influence upon our lives now?" We answer that throughout Scripture God has used warnings about the future to promote the sanctification of His people in time.[26] He has deemed the warnings of these judgments necessary for motivating the indolent and carnal. As their meaningless lives progress, the force of these warnings has more and more impact on them. Having warned them, He must of course carry out the chastisement. For those disciples who feel no motivation toward godliness when faced with these warnings, we would say that the warnings are not addressed to the faithful Christian who is persevering. They are addressed to the Christian who is not persevering, who is carnal. Perhaps for that Christian these warnings will have more pertinent impact. At any rate, for many the sobering reality of final accountability in this matter serves as a goad to perseverance and a barrier to backsliding.

Third, this view of the judgment seat should not lead to introspection. For most of us our inner life is confusing and full of mixed motives. How can we have any confidence to stand before Christ if we know that every word will be recalled and every deed evaluated? We can all identify with the apostle Paul when he said, "For I know that in me . . . nothing good dwells." This being true, the expectation of being punished for our sin can be a frightening and disheartening prospect. How can we quiet the claims of conscience? For the Christian who is walking in the light, even though he fails repeatedly, he has no need for concern. While even persevering disciples will have regrets and loss at the judgment seat, their predominant sense will be of joy and gratitude.

The apostle John says that a condemning heart can be silenced only by resting in the fact of God's omniscience: "For if our heart condemns us, God is greater than our heart, and knows all things" (1 Jn. 3:20 NKJV). Specifically, John counsels us to love other Christians. He says that, if we are demonstrating practical love (v. 18), then we can know that we are practicing the truth (v. 19) even if we do not do it perfectly. Indeed, Peter has assured us that our love for one another will cover a multitude of sins (1 Pet. 4:8). Surely God's love for us will do no less. This in turn should give us confidence that God approves our practical Christianity. With this we can face the future judgment with anticipation and joy.

At this point Experimental Predestinarians object that the Partaker system of motivation leads to as much unhealthy introspection as theirs. However, unhealthy introspection is generally problematic only for unusually introspective people. No matter how the doctrine is presented, these sensitive souls will likely to be troubled. It is, however, astounding that Experimental Predestinarians can equate the introspection of the Partakers with that of their own system. The believer caught up in the doctrine of the Experimental Predestinarians is continu-

---

[26]E.g., Jer. 7:28; cf. 17:23; Isa. 8:11; Job 33:16.

ally worried about his eternal damnation! Surely this a wretched perversion of the grace and assurance offered in Scripture. It is one thing to be introspective regarding our eternal salvation. It is entirely another to be introspective regarding our rewards or the loss thereof.

Finally, God's motive in these future chastisements is merciful and loving. It is His desire that all His children enjoy the fullness of co-heirship with His Son in the final destiny of man. He knows more than anyone how grieved we will be to miss out on the reign of Christ's metochoi in the coming kingdom. He, more than anyone, wants us to have the richest possible experience of heaven. He is not to be viewed as angrily, sternly, rejecting His child as He casts him to the darkness outside. Rather, Jesus weeps with pain that His children must be excluded from the joy of the great future. We are specifically told that "the Lord disciplines those whom he loves" (Heb. 12:4). Another illustration is found in Christ's grief over Jerusalem. As He approached the city at the beginning of the last week of His life, He weeps in anticipation of the terrible judgment which will befall its people in A.D. 70: "And when He approached, He saw the city and wept over it, saying, 'If you had known in this day, even you, the things which make for peace! . . . For the days shall come upon you when your enemies . . . will surround you, and hem you in on every side'" (Lk. 19:41-43 NASB). "How often I have longed to gather your children together, as a hen gathers her chicks under her wings, but you were not willing. Look, your house is left to you desolate" (Mt. 23:37-38). We must never view God as cold and uncaring when He carries out these chastisements. The Father's heart weeps with the full knowledge of what His child is about to undergo and to forfeit. Furthermore, we must remember that the duration of this chastisement is momentary and the subsequent remorse does not last into eternity. We are told that Christ will wipe away every tear. When we arrive in eternity future, everyone's cup will be full, but the cups will be of different sizes.

Chapter 24

The Final Significance of Man

The guardian angel was troubled. His charge, an American military policeman stationed in West Berlin, was in imminent danger.

"Come quickly," he said to the archangel. "One of the heirs is unaware of what faces him."

With instant speed Michael and his colleague rushed to the scene.

A middle-aged man nervously approached Checkpoint Charlie, the border crossing between East and West Berlin, from the Western side. Apart from his darting eyes, he seemed no different than the thousands of others who had to brave this former relic of the cold war. As he fumbled for his papers, the American military policeman on duty that day became suspicious and took time for a more careful examination of the travel documents. Little did he know that the nervous man before him carried automatic weapons and was capable of inflicting instant death. He was a seasoned intelligence agent for the Soviet Committee for State Security, the KGB.

He carried a small microfilm canister of sensitive Western intelligence which could have dramatic impact on the outcome of the cold war.

As the delay lengthened, the man realized he must make a quick decision: Should he break and run? With intuition developed from years of experience, he knew the moment was critical and that the proper decision was obvious.

Suddenly and decisively he made his move. With a burst of energy he raced along the barbed wire and concrete barricade.

"Halt!" the American MP shouted.

Immediately the sirens came on, and the floodlights bathed the area. With years of espionage work hanging in the balance, he began to claw his way over the barricade.

"If you do not stop, we will open fire," said the voice booming out of the speaker system over the area.

Ignoring the final warning, the intelligence officer continued his desperate attempt to salvage his mission.

As he climbed over the wall, the Americans opened fire. Scores of machine gun bullets riddled the man's body, and he fell face downward on the ground.

The MP who had first talked to him ran to the agent and, putting a hand on his shoulder, rolled him over on his back. With his last dying words and with hatred in his eyes the KGB official looked at the American and said,

"I'm dying for communism. What are you living for?"[1]

What is the final significance of human life. What are we living for? Or, better, what should we be living for?

Materialist scientist Carl Sagan begins his book on cosmic evolution with the confident words, "The Cosmos is all that is or ever will be."[2] Throughout the book he spells cosmos with a capital "C." An aura of mystical wonder akin to what the religious man calls worship pervades his description of his Cosmos. He is so impressed with what is "out there" that at times he almost seems to ascribe the attributes of deity to the organized mass of atoms known as the universe. He has, in fact, given us a modern-day nature myth.[3] Of its own accord these atoms have organized themselves into the enormously complex universe which invokes Sagan's reverence.

But is this really all that will ever be? Some modern cosmologists seem to think so. As he concludes his scientific account of this modern nature myth, the big bang theory, Stephen Weinburg, professor of physics at Harvard, turns to the questions of final significance. His theory has led him to the depressing conclusion that the universe is without purpose or design. We are, he concludes, merely specks in an overwhelmingly hostile universe. "The more the universe seems comprehensible, the more it also seems pointless."[4]

---

[1] This story is true. It was told to this writer in 1966 by a professional football player, a committed Christian, who was the MP at Checkpoint Charlie on that fateful day.

[2] Carl Sagan, *Cosmos* (New York: Random House, 1980), p. 4

[3] A "nature myth" is a pantheistic theory of matter found in ancient civilizations like Babylon, Egypt, Persia, and Canaan. God pervades and lives in the stuff of which things are made, and hence the cosmos itself is God.

[4] Stephen Weinburg, *The First Three Minutes* (New York: Basic Books, 1977), p. 154.

What solace does he offer? What is the significance of man? What are we to do with the pointless situation which his hostile cosmos has thrust upon us? Listen:

> *The effort to understand the universe is one of the very few things that lifts human life a little above the level of farce, and gives it some of the grace of tragedy.*[5]

One can sympathize with the pain Weinburg must feel at having to summarize the final significance of his life in such pointless terms. We can also appreciate his honesty. On materialist presuppositions not much more can be said.

In this chapter the writer wishes to discuss the biblical answer to Weinburg's dilemma. According to the Bible the universe is not hostile to man but was created to be ruled by him. The original edenic commission, "rule and have dominion," has yet to be fulfilled. Our purpose in life is not found by making the best of a bad situation but by striving mightily to obtain the high honor of ruling with Christ in the final destiny of man. That destiny is called "the inheritance." This is the future reward the writers of scripture everywhere exhort us to pursue:

> *Since you know you will receive an inheritance from the Lord as a reward* (Col. 3:24).

Many writers have attempted to discern various rewards which the believer can obtain: crowns, co-rulership, participation in the heavenly priesthood, special honor, etc. However, it has always seemed that these things are not viewed by the New Testament writers as separate rewards with separate conditions for their acquisition. Rather, they are various facets of the single reward, the inheritance.

The idea of our future inheritance is a central theme of the Bible. As demonstrated elsewhere, all Christians are heirs of God but not all are co-heirs with Christ.[6] All will have God as their inheritance but not all will "receive an inheritance from the Lord as a reward." It is this latter inheritance which is the subject of this chapter.

While the Old Testament prefigured this inheritance, the New Testament writers enriched the concept immeasurably. At least six separate facets of this great reward are described:

1.   Participation at the wedding banquet

2.   The prize to the overcomers

---

[5]Ibid., p. 155.
[6]See chapters 3-5.

3.   A special class of resurrection

4.   Co-reigning with Christ

5.   Treasures in heaven

6.   Praise and honor from Christ

The atheistic ethic instructs us not to seek reward. We should, according to the atheist, do something only because it is right and not because some benefit will accrue to us if we do it. Such was not the view of the New Testament writers. From Matthew to Revelation the prospect of an inheritance in the kingdom is set before the believer's eye. We are to strive mightily to obtain these heavenly benefits.

The way in which we live our lives now will apparently determine our degree of enjoyment of eternity. Our closeness to Christ now will exactly parallel our closeness to Him then. As we are now, so we will be then.

Participation at the Wedding Banquet

The first aspect of the inheritance is the joy of the final gathering, the wedding feast of the lamb. This event occurs at the onset of the millennial kingdom. The wedding feast and its joys and opportunities have been discussed elsewhere. It will be a time of honor or dishonor. Some will be excluded from the feast, but they will still be in the kingdom.

The Prize to the Overcomer

To those who are victorious in some specific test, the Lord promises a special prize. Each of these prizes could properly be categorized under one of the six aspects of the inheritance. However, due to the uniqueness of the theme it may be best to assemble all the passages regarding the overcomers under one heading.

Rev. 2:7. The overcomer merits a right to eat from the tree of life:

He who has an ear, let him hear what the Spirit says to the churches.
To him who overcomes, I will give the right to eat from the tree of life,
which is in the paradise of God (Rev. 2:7).

Because it is a reward based on works, no thought of salvation can be associated with eating of the tree of life. Indeed, the people who overcome already are believers, persevering under trial. It is inconceivable that a Christian in whom eternal life dwells, must continually eat from a tree to sustain eternal life. Therefore, eating of the tree of life cannot refer to regeneration. To eat of the tree must refer to a special intimacy with the Lord (eating = fellowship) which will be enjoyed in heaven by faithful Christians. Those who do not eat are not non-Christians but regenerate people who have "lost their first love" (2:4). The danger is that they will lose their share in the tree of life as well. The Lord, speaking of the church as a whole, says they will be removed (Rev. 2:5). The removal of the lampstand is not the loss of salvation of individual Christians. It is the removal of the corporate church as a light and witness. The church as a whole is the lampstand (Rev. 1:20). To lose that first love or lose one's share in the tree of life, however, refers to individual Christians who had a first love and a share to lose, i.e., that they are regenerate. How could unregenerate professing Christians lose their share in the tree of life if they never had it to begin with?

Rev. 2:11. The overcomer here endures suffering to the point of martyrdom. He is faithful to death (Rev. 2:10). As a result, his reward is the crown of life. This is not a crown of life given at regeneration, because regenerate life is rewarded to faith, not faithfulness under persecution:

> *Be faithful, even to the point of death, and I will give you the crown of life. He who has an ear, let him hear what the Spirit says to the churches. He who overcomes will not be hurt at all by the second death* (Rev. 2:10-11).

The word for crown, **stephanos,** was used of the victor's wreath, something earned and merited by effort in the games.[7] This crown speaks of a special degree of enjoyment of eternal life. After all, eternal life is a quality more than a duration, and the degree of its experience is dependent upon our faithfulness to Him. It means to know Him, and a personal relationship is developed and enhanced by faithful perseverance.

Their reward is that they will not be hurt by the second death (Rev. 2:11). It is very emphatic in Greek, a double negative (**ou me**) is used. This expression is used to express categorical and emphatic denials.[8] (The second death evidently refers to the lake of fire [Rev. 20:14].) Of course, no believer will be harmed by the second death so how is this a reward for overcoming? He is simply saying that, even if they take your physical life, they can never touch your eternal destiny.

---

[7]1 Cor. 7:24-27; 1 Tim. 6:12; 2 Tim. 4:7.
[8]DM, p. 267.

This is an illustration of the use of litotes.[9] When John says we will not be hurt by the second death, he is actually expressing the positive idea of a rich reward in the future world. John tells his readers, "Be faithful until death, and I will give you the crown of life" (Rev. 2:10 NASB). This is the positive idea negated by the litotes, "you will not be hurt by the second death."

The certainty of heaven makes the Christian bolder under persecution. The enemies of the church can kill the body but not the spirit. The overcomer will be richly rewarded for whatever sacrifices he is called upon to make in the present. In effect, John is saying, "The first death may hurt you, but only briefly, but the second death will not harm you at all."

Rev. 2:17. The "new name" refers to a Jewish custom of assigning a name at a point in life which characterizes the life:

He who has an ear, let him hear what the Spirit says to the churches. To him who overcomes, I will give some of the hidden manna. I will also give him a white stone with a new name written on it, known only to him who receives it (Rev. 2:17).

We cannot be certain what the "hidden manna" promised the overcomer is. Because it favors his view of the wedding banquet, the writer is inclined to Ladd's suggestion that it is a figure depicting admission to the messianic feast.[10] Ladd, of course, is not drawing a distinction between entering the kingdom and entering the banquet. The parable of the virgins and the wedding banquet, however, draw just such a distinction. The danger of forfeiting the manna then is the danger found in those parables, of exclusion from the wedding banquet of the Lamb.

Since the hidden manna is a reward which only the faithful Christian receives, it is likely that the white stone is too. Some have suggested that the stone refers to the victory stone given at the games.[11] If so, this fits well with a theme of the book of Revelation which challenges believers to persevere to obtain the victory, and hence reward, in contrast to those believers who will not and will then forfeit reward.

Rev. 2:26. The overcomer is one who does His will to the end, either physical death (12:11; 2:10) or the second coming. As a reward, he is given authority over the nations:

---

[9]D. Martin Lloyd-Jones, *Romans Chapter 8:17-39: The Final Perseverance of the Saints* (Grand Rapids: Zondervan, 1976), pp. 314ff. Litotes, you will recall, is a figure of speech in which a positive statement is made by negating its opposite. Explanation and illustrations of litotes were given in chapter 20.

[10]George Ladd, *A Commentary on the Revelation of John* (Grand Rapids: Eerdmans, 1972), p. 49.

[11]Eric Sauer, *In the Arena of Faith* (Grand Rapids: Eerdmans, 1966), pp. 63-64.

> *To him who overcomes and does My will to the end, I will give au-*
> *thority over the nations--he will rule them with an iron scepter; he*
> *will dash them to pieces like pottery--just as I have received author-*
> *ity from My Father, I will also give him the morning star. He who has*
> *an ear, let him hear what the Spirit says to the churches* (Rev. 2:26-
> 29).

The singular "him" suggests this is an individual thing. Nowhere are we told in Revelation that all Christians will overcome and receive this reward. As quoted previously, "A command that everyone keeps is superfluous, and a reward that everyone receives for a virtue that everyone has is nonsense."[12] The burden of proof is surely on those who would claim that the warnings are only to pro-fessing and not genuine believers, as they seem to be, and that the promises are addressed to all believers (as they do not seem to be). The overcomer is the indi-vidual Christian who enjoys special benefits in eternity for refusing to give up his faith in spite of persecution during life on earth.

This passage clearly confounds the Experimental Predestinarian. If it refers to Christians, then only those Christians who overcome, in contrast to those who do not, will rule, and their doctrine of perseverance in holiness is lost. If it refers to professing Christians, then John is offering rulership to non-Chris-tians on the basis of works, keeping Christ's deeds unto the end, and thus contra-dicting the rest of the New Testament.

The promise of giving them the morning star is a promise of giving them an experiential knowledge of Christ (Num. 24:17; Rev. 22:16). The promise is not of an eschatological reward in the future but of Christ's comforting and sus-taining presence now in the midst of trials.

Rev. 3:5. As discussed elsewhere, the overcomer is promised that his name will not be blotted out of the book of life. This means either that his eter-nal reputation is secure no matter what they do to his body under persecution, or it is another example of litotes, emphatically reminding them of their eternal se-curity even if they are physically killed:

> *He who overcomes will like them, be dressed in white. I will never*
> *blot out his name from the book of life, but will acknowledge his*
> *name before my Father and his angels. He who has an ear, let him*
> *hear what the Spirit says to the churches* (Rev. 3:5-6).

---

[12]William Fuller, "I Will Not Erase His Name from the Book of Life (Revelation 3:5)," *JETS* 26 (1983): 299.

This act of persevering is to be equated with being clothed in white garments. The "white robes are the righteousness of the saints, not the [imputed] righteousness of God."[13]

To have one's name confessed before the Father is to have his service and worth praised.

Rev. 3:12. The overcomer will be a pillar in God's temple, i.e., he will have intimate association with God:

I am coming soon. Hold on to what you have, so that no one will take your crown. Him who overcomes I will make a pillar in the temple of my God. Never again will he leave it. I will write on him the name of my God and the name of the city of my God, the new Jerusalem which is coming down out of heaven from my God; and I will also write on him my new name. He who has an ear, let him hear what the Spirit says to the churches (Rev. 3:11-13).

The overcomer will never leave the temple. This is best explained as another illustration of litotes, an emphatic statement of the eternal security of the saints. On the other hand, however, those who persecute us can, in a sense, "take our crown." This happens when we yield to persecution and fail to persevere. The Lord spoke of the same danger when He said, "I tell you that to everyone who has, more will be given, but as for the one who has nothing, even what He has will be taken away" (Lk. 19:26).

Rev. 3:21. The overcomer will sit on the Father's throne:

To him who overcomes, I will give the right to sit with Me on My throne, just as I overcame and sat down with My Father on His throne. He who has an ear, let him hear what the Spirit says to the churches (Rev. 3:21).

The reference is once again to joint participation with Messiah in the kingdom rule. It is evident that John's intent is to address them not as "wheat and tares" but as regenerate Christians, because he refers to them as "those whom I love" and says he will "reprove and discipline" (Rev. 3:19) them. This is proof of their regenerate state "for what son is not disciplined by his father? If you are not disciplined then you are . . . not true sons" (Heb. 12:8).

Rev. 21:7. The overcomer is promised meritorious ownership over the new Jerusalem, and God will be proud to be known as his God:

---

[13]G. Campbell Morgan, *A First Century Message to Twentieth Century Christians* (New York: Revell, 1902), p. 149.

> *He who overcomes will inherit all this, and I will be his God and he
> will be my son* (Rev. 21:7).

As discussed in chapter 20, the correct sense of "inherit" must be pressed
here. An inheritance is not something which comes by virtue of birth but by
virtue of faithful perseverance as chapters 3-5 have attempted to demonstrate.
Seen in this light, there is a difference between Christians who dwell in the New
Jerusalem and those who inherit it, own it, i.e., rule there.

In every reference to the overcomer in the Revelation, he is one who is a
victor in battle.[14] The central theme of the entire book is to exhort the saints to
persevere and to be victorious. If all saints persevere and are victorious, the exhortations and promises of rewards are pointless. An exhortation to do something everyone does anyway to obtain a reward which all will receive anyway is
absurd.

A Special Class of Resurrection

In one of the most personal and motivating passages in the New Testament, the great apostle to the Gentiles lays bare his heart:

> *I want to know Christ and the power of his resurrection and the fel-
> lowship of sharing in his sufferings, becoming like him in his death,
> and so, somehow to attain to the resurrection from the dead* (Phil.
> 3:10-11).

His supreme goal in life is to know Christ more intimately, to know the
power of Christ in his life, and to share in Christ's sufferings. He wants this so
that "somehow" he might "attain" to the "resurrection" from the dead. The apostle feels that there is something uncertain about his attaining to the resurrection.
Did Paul doubt his final salvation? Of course not! This verse and those following are speaking of the "prize," the rewards to the faithful at the judgment seat of
Christ.

In this verse he refers to the resurrection by the Greek word **exanastasis**.
This is the only time this word for resurrection is used in the entire New Testament. The normal word is **anastasis**. The fact that Paul would switch to such an
unusual word causes us to wonder if he meant some particular kind or aspect of
the resurrection. Because the word is used so rarely, there is no convincing evidence to help us determine exactly how, if any, this word might have differed
from the regular word. We are therefore thrust upon the context and the word's
basic meaning. Rather than being translated "resurrection," this word could be
literally rendered "out-resurrection." This might suggest a "resurrection out from

---

[14]See also Rev. 12:11; 13:7; 15:2; 17:14.

among the resurrected ones" in contrast to a mere "resurrection from among the dead." In other words, a special category or class of resurrected saints is referred to in this verse.

It does appear, as Lang has suggested, that the phrase is an emphasized repetition of words previously used by Christ.[15]

But those who are considered worthy to attain to that age and the resurrection from the dead, neither marry, nor are given in marriage (Lk. 20:35).

All Christians will obtain the resurrection, but only some will be worthy of it. To be worthy of the resurrection and to "attain to the out-resurrection" appear to be parallel concepts and explain one another. This interpretation fits very well with the following verses and would explain why Paul selected this word instead of his usual word for resurrection, **anastasis**. The following verses read:

Not that I have already obtained [Gk. **katalambano**] *all this, or have already been made perfect, but I press on to take hold of that for which Jesus took hold of me* (Phil. 3:12).

Christ has taken hold of us for a purpose, to attain to the "out-resurrection." Those who strive toward that goal will rule and have dominion" (Heb. 2:5-10). Paul says he has made it his goal to take hold of the same thing. In other words, he wants to make it his purpose in life to achieve Christlikeness and as a result to share with Christ in that final victory. Elsewhere he said there was a special crown reserved for those who have "loved His appearing" (2 Tim. 4:8).

Interestingly, he pictures this goal as a prize to be won. The word **katalambano** is found in 1 Cor. 9:24ff. where it is used for the striving of the athlete to attain the prize in the Isthmian games. In Phil. 3:14 Paul uses another word out of 1 Cor. 9:24-27, which refers to the prize won in the games, the **brabeion**:

Brothers, I do not consider myself yet to have taken hold of it. But one thing I do: Forgetting what is behind and straining toward what is ahead, I press on toward the goal to win the prize for which God has called me heavenward in Christ Jesus (Phil. 3:13-14).

What is the prize for which God has called him heavenward? The use of the Greek word **brabeion** is significant. It signifies a prize in an athletic contest, something earned.[16] The similarity of the two contexts suggests that they inter-

---

[15]G. H. Lang, *Firstborn Sons, Their Rights and Risks* (London: Samuel Roberts, 1936; reprint ed., Miami Springs, FL: Conley and Schoettle, 1984), p. 72.

[16]AG, p. 146.

pret each other. If so, then the prize in Phil. 3:14 is the reward received by the faithful believer when he finishes his race. What is the prize? What is the goal? Phil. 3 does not tell us precisely, but based on the rest of the New Testament, it is entrance into rest and, with that great company of the metochoi, inheritance of the kingdom. This is what he means when he says he hopes to attain to the "out-resurrection." He hopes to earn a place among that special class of resurrected saints who have been faithful to their Master to the final hour and will hear Him say, "Well done!"

Reigning with Christ

The fourth aspect of the inheritance is our future reign with Christ. One day, the Scriptures everywhere affirm, the struggle of fallen man will finally come to an end. This consummation will not be achieved by social engineering or by the successful implementation of any human ideology. Rather, it will be accomplished by a supernatural intervention of God in history, the second coming of Christ. Finally, history will achieve a worthy outcome--the kingdom of God. Page after page of Scripture speaks of this glorious future and the possibility that those who are Christ's servants now can achieve positions of honor in that future glory then. These positions of honor are an important aspect of the believer's future inheritance.

The Extent of the Kingdom

The divine drama of universal history has been played out upon a stage called "earth." It was on earth that the fall of man occurred. It was on earth that the Satan lived and ruled. It was on earth the Son of God came and answered the Satan's lie. It is therefore fitting that it will be on earth that the final resolution of universal history will occur.

However, there are intimations in Scripture that the future reign of the servant kings will embrace the universe as well. We are told, for example, that the saints will one day not only rule the world but will also rule over the angels (1 Cor. 6:1-3):

Do you not know that the saints will judge the world? . . . Do you not know that we shall judge angels?

Since the domain of the angels extends far beyond terrestrial boundaries, we may assume that the kingdom of those who rule over them does so as well.

David reflected upon the divine commission in Genesis to "rule and have dominion,"

What is man that You are mindful of him?

You have made him a little lower than the angels and You have crowned him with glory and honor.

You have made him to have dominion **over the works of Your hands.** *You have put* **all things** *under his feet* (Ps. 8:4-6 NKJV).

While David specifies that the "all things" refers to things on earth, the writer to the Hebrews expands that concept when he says:

You have put all things in subjection under his feet.

For in that He put all in subjection under him. He left nothing that is not put under him (Heb. 2:8).

It is clear that the reign of the Messiah extends to heaven and earth. Since the metochoi are co-heirs with Him (Rom. 8:17), their reign by virtue of association with Him will therefore extend to the cosmos itself:

At the name of Jesus every knee should bow, **of those in heaven,** *and those on earth* (Phil. 2:10 NKJV).

Now when **all things are made subject to Him,** *then the Son Himself will also be subject to Him who put all things under Him, that God may be all in all* (1 Cor. 15:28 NKJV).

God . . . in these last days . . . has spoken to us by His Son whom He appointed heir of all things (Heb. 1:1-2 NASB).

We are told that the entire creation awaits the future reign of God's servant kings:

Now if we are God's children, then we are heirs--heirs of God, and co-heirs with Christ if indeed we share in his sufferings in order that we may also share in his glory.

I consider that our present sufferings are not worth comparing to the glory that will be revealed to us. The creation waits in eager expectation for the sons of God to be revealed.

For the creation was subjected to frustration, not by its own choice, but by the will of the one who subjected it, in hope that the creation itself will be liberated from its bondage to decay and brought into the glorious freedom of the children of God (Rom. 8:17-21).

It is evident that this future kingdom embraces the entire created order. One day mankind will conquer the galaxies! While it is true that one purpose of the heavens was to "declare the glory of God," it seems that they were also created to be placed in subjection to man. Perhaps the future kingdom with its reign of universal righteousness and perfect government will result in a technological explosion as well as a spiritual one. Then, and only then, in submission to the King will man be able to achieve his fondest dreams, to rule and have dominion. The future kingdom will witness the greatest explosion of human creativity and useful work in the history of man. Man will finally be what God intended him to be.

When man first began to understand the enormity of the universe in the late eighteenth century, an intellectual revolution of the first order occurred. Prior to this new knowledge man always viewed himself as having a central role in the cosmos. This gave him a sense of identity and significance. But when scientists discovered that the universe was twenty billion light years in diameter, a profound change occurred. How could man be considered significant anymore? To learn that he is located on the edge of a minor galaxy among billions of similar and larger galaxies caused modern man to lose his sense of significance. Unless . . . his final significance is to rule this vast created order. Instead of demeaning man, these discoveries, when viewed through the biblical promise, magnify him. His importance is far greater than had been formerly supposed. Instead of merely being destined to rule a small planet, mankind has been chosen to subdue something far greater, the vast cosmos itself. No challenge could be greater than to be placed over all the works of God's hands!

Co-regency with the King

It is the kingdom of the Son of God of which we are speaking. "He is the head over all rule and authority" (Col. 2:10). Our future is closely linked with His. Those Christians who are faithful to Him now will reign with Him then:

> *Peter answered him, "We have left everything to follow you! What then will there be for us?" Jesus said to them, "I tell you the truth, at the renewal of all things, when the Son of Man sits on his glorious throne, you who have followed me will also sit on twelve thrones, judging the twelve tribes of Israel"* (Mt. 19:27-28).

> *You are those who have stood by me in my trials. And I confer on you a kingdom, just as my Father conferred on me, so that you may eat and drink at my table in my kingdom and sit on thrones, judging the twelve tribes of Israel* (Lk. 22:28-30).

Conditions for Greatness

The notion that the future kingdom is a kind of classless society where all are equal and rewarded equally has contributed in no small way to the laxness witnessed in the lives of many in the twentieth-century church. Many have sub-consciously reasoned that, since all are equal, my life has no particular eternal significance. In the final analysis my life will be rewarded as much as those who labored more diligently.

The writer well remembers the time when as a new Christian he had just learned about the doctrine of eternal rewards. In youthful fervor he rushed to visit his pastor only to have his new enthusiasm crushed. "Do you mean to tell me," he replied, " that there will be distinctions in heaven? God does not show partiality!"

But there will be distinctions in heaven, and God **DOES** show partiality. He is, however, justly partial. In the kingdom there will be those who are great and those who are least:

> *But many who are first will be last, and the last will be first* (Mt. 19:30).

> *Whoever therefore breaks one of the least of these commandments and teaches men so, shall be called least in the kingdom of heaven; but whoever does and teaches them, he shall be called great in the kingdom of heaven* (Mt. 5:19 NKJV).

There will be authority granted over varying numbers of cities (Lk. 19:17-24). Some will have responsibility for many things, and others will have responsi-bility for nothing (Mt. 25:20-30). As discussed above, only the overcomers will achieve a share in the reign of Christ and have authority over the nations. Some will even have the high honor of sitting at Christ's right hand during the kingdom (Mk. 10:35-40).

Jesus specified three basic conditions for positions of high honor in the kingdom.

We must be faithful to use the gifts we have been given. In the parable of the minas (Lk. 19:11-27) Jesus describes a nobleman who gave his servants ten minas each and then departed. When he returned, the first servant had doubled the number of minas. The Lord makes this an illustration of the final judgment on believers and says:

> *Well done, good servant; because you were faithful in a very little, have authority over ten cities* (Lk. 19:17 NKJV).

The second servant who was also given ten minas had earned less: five mi-nas. He was honored with less:

And the second came saying, Master, your mina has earned five minas. Likewise he said to him, "You also be over five cities" (Lk. 19:18-19 NKJV).

Each had been given the same amount but one had produced more with what he had been given and was rewarded accordingly.

The last servant produced nothing and kept his minas hidden in a handkerchief. The Lord severely rebukes this lethargic Christian and takes the mina away from him and gives it to the servant who had been given ten cities. He summarizes:

"He replied, 'I tell you that to everyone who has, more will be given, but as for the one who has nothing, even what he has will be taken away'" (Lk. 19:26).

We may lay it down as a spiritual axiom that the more opportunities, gifts, money, and training that a Christian receives will result in greater accountability at the judgment seat:

For everyone to whom much is given, from him much will be required, and to whom much has been committed, of him they will ask the more (Lk. 12:48 NKJV).

We must become servants now. The second condition for high honor is that we must strive to be servants of all. Jesus Himself modeled this when He took the form of a servant and became obedient to death. As a result God highly exalted Him (Phil. 2:5-11). Paul says, "Let this mind be in you":

The kings of the Gentiles exercise lordship over them, and those who exercise authority over them are called 'benefactors.'

But not so among you; on the contrary, he who is greatest among you, let him be as the younger, and he who governs as he who serves.

For who is greater, he who sits at the table, or he who serves? Is it not he who sits at the table? Yet I am among you as the One who serves (Lk. 22:25-27 NKJV).

Whoever wishes to become great among you shall be your servant. And whoever of you desires to be first shall be slave of all (Mk. 10:43-44 NKJV).

We must be faithful when suffering. In passage after passage the New Testament writers invest human suffering with high dignity. It is through suffering with Christ that we are trained and equipped to join the great company of the metochoi. Consider:

*Therefore, among God's churches we boast about your perseverance and faith in all the persecutions and trials you are enduring. All this is evidence that God's judgment is right, and as a **result you will be counted worthy of the kingdom of God,** for which you are suffering* (2 Th. 1:4-5).

An eternal honor is being achieved for those who persevere in suffering:

*For our light and momentary troubles **are achieving for us an eternal glory** that far outweighs them all* (2 Cor. 4:17).

In order for us to experience great joy at the appearing of Christ, we must rejoice (i.e., respond in faith) to the sufferings we experience now:

Dear friends, do not be surprised at the painful trial you are suffering, as though something strange were happening to you. But rejoice that you participate in the sufferings of Christ, so that you may be over-joyed when his glory is revealed (1 Pet. 4:12-13).

A major purpose of the incarnation was, according to the writer of the Epistle to the Hebrews, the bringing of many sons to the place of honor, the final destiny of man. This was achieved by the suffering of the Son and His many brothers.

God's intention was to place man over the works of His hands. This was called "salvation" by the Old Testament prophets:

Are not all angels ministering spirits sent to serve those who will inherit salvation (Heb. 1:14).

That this salvation to be inherited is not deliverance from hell is made clear when he says:

It is not to angels that he has subjected the world to come about which we are speaking (Heb. 2:5).

The "salvation" to be inherited is not entrance into heaven but the subjection of the world to come. God has not yet fulfilled His intention. Out of the lesser He will bring the greater. Man will rule the angels! We see Jesus as a kind of promissory note:

In putting everything under him, God left nothing that is not subject to him. Yet at present we do not see everything subject to him. But we see Jesus, who was made a little lower than the angels, now crowned with glory and honor because he suffered death, so that by the grace of God he might taste death for everyone (Heb. 2:8-9).

"We do not see everything subject to him." That statement is an apt summary of human history. How visibly true this is. Man attempts to exercise dominion, but he cannot do it. This desire was planted in man's heart in the Garden, and the vestige of it remains today. That is why men throughout history have dreamed of having dominion over the planet. That is why we cannot keep off the highest mountain. That is why we want to go to the stars.

Man consistently manifests this remarkable racial memory. Our problem is that the more we attempt to exercise dominion, the more frustrated we are because it is beyond our reach. We try to control the insects eating our crops, and it turns out that the pesticides contain poisons that harm us in various ways. We try to begin an energy conservation program, but private interest groups are treated unfairly. We attempt to distribute food to the poor, and it rots in shipyards. The history of man is one of continually precipitating a crisis by attempting to exercise dominion.

This applies not only on a universal scale but to individual men as well. Who among us has achieved all our dreams? When we try to achieve gain from our labor, we are attempting to fulfill the God-given urge to have dominion. When a man attempts to lead his family, he is doing the same. Yet too often we never exercise the dominion. Our objectives are not accomplished. Our dreams are shattered. This is simply part of the human condition and will be until the kingdom.

We have only one hope today. We see one man who has forged the path. This man, like us, had His dreams shattered. He suffered, and yet He presently exercises dominion. Furthermore, through His incarnation we have become united with Him so that, if we are faithful to Him, we can share in His ultimate victory.

It is God's purpose to bring many sons to glory:

In bringing many sons to glory, it was fitting that God, for whom and through whom everything exists, should make the author of their salvation perfect through suffering (2:10).

The great theme of Christ's union with his many sons is close to our writer's heart. Here Christ is our "leader" in other places he is our priest. We are told that he will give us help in time of need. We are to imagine Christ right next to us in our suffering. He has his left arm around our shoulder and his right arm is lifted up to the Father. He says, "Father, I now bring my brother before you. He is in great suffering and needs your help. For the sake of your glory and because I have died, for him I ask that you would strengthen him in the inner man. Give him the courage to face his suffering and the power to endure it. Most of all, Father, let him know your comfort."

The "glory" to which the many sons will be brought is evidently subjection of the world to come (2:5). They will be brought to this destiny, this high honor, by the "author" of their salvation. The Greek word **archegos** means "leader, ruler, prince, founder, author, or originator," depending on the context. In the three other places in the New Testament where it is used, Christ is called "the author of life" (Acts 3:15), "the Prince and Savior" (Acts 5:31), and "the author and perfecter of our faith" (Heb. 12:2). In the ancient world he was the leader, the one at the front, the hero of the city, its defender.[17] If we were to dramatize these ideas and pictures a little, words like "pioneer" or "captain" would be fitting.

In every respect Jesus is the one out front, our supreme leader and example in the life of faith. Whenever we experience difficultities, He knows what we are going through and is there to lead us through them victoriously. When we face temptation, He knows what that is like, and He is ready to strengthen us and leads us away from it. Whatever our needs and weaknesses, He knows them and is able to help, to lead, and to win. As the Author of life He gave us earthly and eternal life. As the Captain of life He leads us now in and through life. And as the Prince of life He is the one who will lead us into the final destiny of man--dominion over the creation.

He alone is qualified to achieve this for mankind. His commitment to us is total. He has died for us and He lives for and in us.

His leadership includes suffering. For Christ to become a sympathetic priest, He must experience the suffering of those He has come to represent:

> *For this reason he had been made like his brothers in every way, in order that he might become a merciful and faithful high priest in the service God. . . . Because he himself suffered when he was tempted, he is able to help those who are being tempted* (Heb. 2:17-18).

Jesus gained honor and learned sympathy by the things that He suffered. His way is to be the way of the "many sons" He is leading to the same glory:

> **Therefore** *I will allot Him a portion with the great . . .* **because He poured out Himself to death** (Isa. 53:12).

> *And being found in appearance as a man,* **He humbled Himself by becoming obedient** *to the point of death, even death on a cross.* **Therefore** *also God highly exalted Him, and bestowed upon Him the name which is above every name* (Phil. 2:8-9 NASB).

---

[17]Gerhard Delling, **"archegos,"** in *TDNT*, 1:487.

*But we see Jesus, who was made lower than the angels, now crowned
with glory and honor* **because He suffered death,** *so that by the grace
of God He might taste death for everyone* (Heb. 2:9).

There are two truths which unite in the exaltation of God's King Son.
First, He had been appointed by God to be the heir of all things (Heb. 1:1). But,
second, it was necessary that Christ vindicate His appointment by showing Himself worthy of it through victorious suffering. "And it is upon precisely the same
double condition that Christ's people will share with Him His honours":[19]

*And you are those who have stood by Me in My trials; and just as My
Father has granted Me a kingdom, I grant you that you may eat and
drink at My table in My kingdom, and you will sit on thrones judging
the twelves tribes of Israel* (Lk. 22:28-30 NASB).

Authority in the kingdom and the honor of sitting at the table at the final
gathering and enjoying the royal feast are plainly promised as superior rewards
for superior devotion. His way is to be our way.

The goal of obtaining glory (i.e., "honor") in the future kingdom is a principal intent of the suffering we endure. God purposes to equip us for rulership in
the great future by preparing through suffering a race of servant kings. God does
not grant this honor to anyone except those who have suffered with Him. We
must first learn obedience and service:

*Although he was a son, he learned obedience from what he suffered
and, once made perfect, he became the source of eternal salvation for
all who obey him* (Heb. 5:8-9).

Treasures in Heaven

The fifth aspect of the inheritance was called "treasure in heaven" by Jesus. Jesus taught about a different kind of wealth, a wealth that could not be seen
in this life:

*Do not store up for yourselves treasures on earth, where moth and rust
destroy, and where thieves break in and steal. But store up for yourselves treasures in heaven, where moth and rust do not destroy, and
where thieves do not break in and steal. For where your treasure is,
there your heart will be also* (Mt. 6:19-21).

The issue seems to be the attitude of heart. If a man's heart is really focused on the future kingdom, then he will naturally want to make any sacrifice
necessary to place as much wealth there as possible.

---

[19]Lang, p. 63.

It is proper that God have some system for compensating those followers of His who are willing to make unusual sacrifices. He promises them an enhanced inheritance in the kingdom, i.e., treasure in heaven.

Therefore, throughout the New Testament, Christians are exhorted to do things which will result in enlarging their eternal storehouse with what they send ahead:

> *Command those who are rich in this present world not to be arrogant nor to put their hope in wealth, which is so uncertain, but to put their hope in God, who richly provides us with everything for our enjoyment. Command them to do good, to be rich in good deeds, and to be generous and willing to share. In this way they will lay up treasure for themselves as a firm foundation for the coming age, so that they may take hold of the life that is truly life* (1 Tim. 6:17-19).

> *Do not be afraid, little flock, for your Father has been pleased to give you the kingdom. Sell your possessions and give to the poor. Provide purses for yourselves that will not wear out, a treasure in heaven that will not be exhausted* (Lk. 12:32-33).

Investing for the future is as old as man himself. It requires faithfulness, self-denial, and patience--all worthy qualities. Furthermore, the man who lays up material treasures in this way is trusting that the money he is denying himself now will one day result in a large profit. But that profit is not yet seen. When a man does this, he is exercising faith. It is not faith in God but faith in the economy of his country. But faith is "the assurance of things hoped for and the evidence of things not yet seen."

But what businessman was ever promised an absolutely guaranteed 10,000% return on his investment? Listen:

> *And everyone who has left houses or brothers or sisters or father or mother or children or fields for my sake will receive* **a hundred times as much** *and will inherit eternal life* (Mt. 19:29).

The result is completely unseen, and hence greater faith is required. We will not receive our return until we arrive in the kingdom. But the object of our trust is infinitely more reliable than the economy of our country; it is the promise of Jesus the Christ.

The ability to connect present decisions with future consequences is a major component of maturity. When we are young, we are commonly very inept at this. Our future horizon often extends no further than getting out of school on Friday afternoon. As we mature, however, we begin to realize that what we do now has definite effects on our future happiness. A mature man is one who understands this and lives accordingly.

The Content of the Treasure

When Jesus promised us treasure in heaven, there is no necessary reason for excluding actual material treasure from His words. Indeed, we are specifically told that we will have the wealth of five or ten cities and that in this age we will receive up to a hundred fold return on our efforts. Christ is said to be preparing a place for us to live. Perhaps the treasures in heaven refer, in part at least, to literal wealth such as enhanced eternal dwellings and greater numbers of cities over which to rule.

It is also possible that Jesus' reference to treasures is to be understood as spiritual treasures such as enhanced relationship to Him.

We cannot be dogmatic, but we can affirm that these treasures are greatly to be desired and sought after in this life.

Conditions for Obtaining Treasure

Jesus says there are two conditions. First, we must do deeds of charity:

So when you give to the needy, do not announce it with trumpets, as the hypocrites do in the synagogues and on the streets, to be honored by men. I tell you the truth, they have received their reward in full. But when you give to the needy, do not let your left hand know what your right hand is doing, so that your giving may be in secret. Then your Father, who sees what is done in secret, will reward you (Mt. 6:2-4).

In order to be rewarded with wealth in heaven, we must give to the needy now. Furthermore, this giving should be in secret and not publicly announced. The main point is probably that it should be given with the intent to help, for Christ's sake, and not for the purpose of obtaining the praise of man.

The second condition for obtaining heavenly treasure is that we must make sacrifices to follow the Lord as a disciple:

If you want to be perfect, go, sell your possessions and give to the poor, and you will have treasure in heaven. Then come, follow me (Mt. 19:21).

A person who parts with his money for Christ's sake is not really losing it. He is simply sending it ahead, transferring it to a more secure place where there are no robbers or rust to ruin it. It takes great faith to believe that the eternal benefits we will receive are worth the sacrifices we must make now to obtain them.

Praise and Honor from Christ

The sixth and final aspect of our inheritance is praise and honor from Christ. With glowing words the enraptured apostle Peter longed for the day when we would be honored for our faithful work:

> *In this you greatly rejoice, though now for a little while you may have had to suffer grief in all kinds of trials. These have come so that your faith--of greater worth than gold, which perishes even though refined by fire--may be proved genuine and may result in praise, glory and honor when Jesus Christ is revealed* (1 Pet. 1:6-7).

If our faith is "genuine," we will receive praise, glory, and honor from Christ. The word "genuine" (**dokimion** = "without mixture"[20]) does not mean a saving faith in contrast to one that is not. It means a saving faith which is without mixture versus a saving faith which is. Peter refers to the man whose faith is unsullied and who steadfastly trusts God in the midst of trials. The sense seems to be: "These have come so that what is genuine in your faith may result in praise, glory, and honor."[21]

This honor and praise from God is what Peter refers to when he says:

> *For if you do these things, you will never fall, and you will receive a* **rich welcome** *into the eternal kingdom of our Lord and Saviour Jesus Christ* (2 Pet. 1:10-11).

The Christian who suffers faithfully and who adds virtues to his faith (1:5-9) will not just barely make it into the kingdom or be saved only as one escaping through the flames (1 Cor. 3:15). He will be welcomed "richly" into the kingdom. The metaphor of a rich welcome no doubt goes back to the honors which were paid to the victor in the Olympic games.

The praise and honor which Christ will bestow upon His metochoi seems to be divided into two categories in the New Testament: verbal praise and specific honors.

---

[20]AG, p. 202.

[21]According to Hort as cited in MM, p. 168.

General Honor: Verbal Praise

We all have needs to receive recognition from those who matter when we have done a good work. The Scripture everywhere testifies that God will affirm the faithful Christian in this way:

Well done, good and faithful servant! You have been faithful with a few things; I will put you in charge of many things. Come and share your master's happiness (Mt. 25:21).

Therefore judge nothing before the appointed time; wait till the Lord comes. He will bring to light what is hidden in darkness and will expose the motives of men's hearts. At that time each will receive his praise from God (1 Cor. 4:5).

These [trials] have come so that your faith . . . may result in praise, glory and honor when Jesus Christ is revealed (1 Pet. 1:7).

It is God's desire to bestow honor upon those believers who have deserved it:

Whoever serves Me must follow Me; and where I am, My servant also will be. My Father will honor the one who serves Me (Jn. 12:26).

The passage does not say that anyone who has believed on Christ shall be with Christ and be honored by Him. Having fellowship with Christ (i.e., being "with Christ") and being honored by Him are benefits conferred only upon those Christians who serve and follow Him.

This verbal praise can be forfeited:

Be careful not to do your acts of righteousness before men, to be seen by them. If you do, you will have no reward from your Father in heaven (Mt. 6:1).

And when you pray, do not be like the hypocrites, for they love to pray standing in the synagogues and on the street corners to be seen by men. I tell you the truth, they have received their reward in full (Mt. 6:5).

When you fast, do not look somber as the hypocrites do, for they disfigure their faces to show men they are fasting. I tell you the truth, they have received their reward in full (Mt. 6:16).

When a Christian seeks the approval or praise of men instead of God, he forfeits praise from God. "What he does must be for God to see, not men."[22]

Specific Honors: Crowns

When Romania became a kingdom in 1881, King Charles realized that there was no crown for him to wear. He instructed his soldiers to go to the arsenal and secure some iron from a canon which had been captured from the enemy. They then melted it and fashioned it into an iron crown. His intent was that this crown would be a token of that which was won on the field of battle. It had been bought and paid for with many Romanian lives.[23]

The second form in which praise will be obtained is in the bestowal of various crowns as honors for particular acts. The crown which the believer obtains is the victor's crown (Gk. **stephanos**). This was the crown of exaltation given for victory in the games, achievement in war, and places of honor at the feasts.[24] "In the N. T. it is plain that the **stephanos** whereof St. Paul speaks is always the conqueror's and not the king's."[25] This crown is not like the royal crown. It is a crown which is given on the basis of merit. It was woven of oak, ivy, spruce, myrtle, or olive. It is the crown of thorns that Jesus wore, a crown of ultimate victory (Mt. 27:29). There are five specific crowns mentioned in the New Testament.[26]

The crown of rejoicing. This crown consists in the people whom we have led to Christ:

> *For what is our hope, our joy, or the crown in which we will glory in the presence of our Lord Jesus when he comes? Is it not you? Indeed, you are our glory and joy* (1 Th. 2:19).

> *Therefore, my brother, you whom I love and long for, my joy and crown* (Phil. 4:1).

It is apparently not a literal crown but people. Apparently Christ will in some way give special honor to those who have faithfully labored at bringing people to Christ.

---

[22]Some of this material is borrowed from Ken Quick, "Living for the Kingdom" (D.Min. thesis, Dallas Theological Seminary, 1988), p. 134.

[23]Sauer, p. 66.

[24]William Edward Raffety, "Crown," in *NISBE*, 1:831.

[25]Richard Chenevix Trench, *Synonyms of the New Testament* (London: 1880; reprint ed., Grand Rapids: Eerdmans, 1953), p. 78.

[26]See Quick, pp. 223-39, for good discussion of the crowns. Also Sauer, pp. 59-67.

The crown of glory. Christ will bestow special recognition upon those who have labored faithfully to care for and disciple other Christians. It is significant that these first two crowns have been designated as awards for those who have given their lives to evangelism and discipleship:

> *To the elders among you, I appeal as a fellow elder, a witness of Christ's sufferings and one who also will share in the glory to be revealed. Be shepherds of God's flock that is under your care, serving as overseers, not because you must, but because you are willing, as God wants you to be; not greedy for money, but eager to serve; not lording it over those entrusted to you, but being examples to the flock. And when the Chief Shepherd appears, you will receive the crown of glory that will never fade away* (1 Pet. 5:1-4).

Here the faithful pastor and elder who works in the church is honored.

In this squalid, wet, and isolated prison cell, the apostle Paul wrote, "I have fought the good fight, I have finished the course, I have kept the faith; in the future there is laid up for me the crown of righteousness, which the Lord, the righteous Judge, will award to me on that day; and not only to me, but also to all who have loved His appearing" (2 Tim. 4:7-8 NASB). Here in the Mammertine prison he spent his last days, triumphant in Christ. He was beheaded by Nero shortly after writing these words.

The crown of righteousness. Paul's second epistle to Timothy exhorts him to evangelize and probably contained Paul's last words. He was beheaded by Nero shortly thereafter. Sensing that the end was near, he penned these moving phrases:

For I am already being poured out like a drink offering, and the time has come for my departure. I have fought the good fight, I have finished the race, I have kept the faith. Now there is in store for me the crown of righteousness which the Lord, the righteous Judge, will award to me on that day--and not only to me, but also to all who have longed for his appearing (2 Tim. 4:6-8).

For those Christians who long for Christ's return, who live their lives in view of this event, there will be special honor. The crown may be symbolic of the righteous life lived. It is "like a soldier's medal for valor in the face of battle. The medal does not contain valor, but it does declare that its possessor is valorous."[27]

The crown of life. For some Christians the purpose of God includes severe testing, even martyrdom. This high honor will be duly compensated with a special distinction; the crown of life:

Blessed is the man who perseveres under trial, because when he has stood the test, he will receive the crown of life that God has promised to those who love him (Jas. 1:12).

Be faithful even to the point of death, and I will give you the crown of life (Rev. 2:10).

Throughout the centuries many Christians have been called upon to give their lives for the sake of the Christ. This honorable heritage was pioneered by Christ and His apostles. James was beheaded in Jerusalem in A.D. 44. Philip was cruelly scourged and afterwards crucified. Matthew was claimed by the sword in Parthea in A.D. 60. Mark was dragged through the streets of Alexandria by his feet, then burned to death the following day. Luke was hanged on an olive tree in Greece. James the Less was thrown from a pinnacle of the temple in Jerusalem and beaten to death down below. Matthias was stoned and beheaded. Andrew was crucified on a cross where he hung for three days and constantly told people around him of the love of Jesus the Christ. Peter was scourged and crucified upside down. He chose this posture himself because he did not think he was worthy to suffer in the same manner as his Lord. Thomas was thrust through with a spear in India. Jude was crucified in the year A.D. 72. Bartholomew was beaten to death with clubs. John was condemned to a caldron of boiling oil, though he escaped death and later died in exile on the island of Patmos. Barnabas was stoned to death by Jews in Salonica. Paul was beheaded in Rome by Nero.[28]

---

[27]Quick, p. 227.

[28]John Foxe, *Foxe's Christian Martyrs of the World* (Chicago: Moody Press, n.d.), pp. 24-35.

What is this "crown of life." Since it is the reward given for an accomplishment subsequent to initial faith, it is probable that it refers to a higher quality of life in the kingdom. It would be the same as the eternal life which can be earned, the special richness of eternal life merited by faithful service on the field of battle.

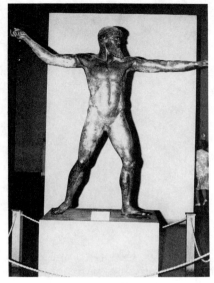

The Isthmian games were held in honor of the god Poseidon, a god of the sea and naval triumph. Held every two years, they were like the Olympics. Paul refers to these games as an illustration of the Christian life (1 Cor. 9:24-27).

The crown of mastery. The apostle Paul also spoke of receiving such honor and praise in terms of the athletic metaphor (1 Cor. 9:24-27):

Do you not know that in a race all the runners run, but only one gets the prize? Run in such a way as to get the prize.

The "race" to which Paul refers is the competition at the Isthmian games held every three years in honor of Poseidon, the god of the sea.[29] Their site was a spruce grove dedicated to him on the Isthmus of Corinth.[30] Vast crowds attended these ancient Greek Games. The Olympiad hosted fifty thousand at the Coliseum in Rome. That of Saurus held eighty thousand persons. A total of over 270 Roman amphitheaters are known.[31] The prize at Corinth was a spruce wreath,

---

[29]Archibald Robertson and Alfred Plummer, *A Critical and Exegetical Commentary on the First Epistle of St. Paul to the Corinthians*, 2d ed., *International Critical Commentary* [Edinburgh: T. & T. Clark, 1914], p. 194.

[30]Sauer, p. 36.

[31]Ibid., p. 39.

the tree sacred to Poseidon.[32] In order to participate in the Games one had to be a freeborn Greek.[33]

This starting gate for the foot race in the Isthmian games dates about 700 B.C. The grooves in the track were lines where string connected to the starting gates. They slid under small metal nails to release all the gates at precisely the same time.

Everyone who competes in the games goes into strict training. The word "strict training" is the Greek **agonizomai**. We get our word "agony" from it. It was a technical Greek athletic term for getting in shape to participate in the games. The athletes were selected by local elimination trials, after which they submitted for ten months to rigorous training under professional trainers. After their arrival for training they were examined by the officials, and they took an oath swearing to obey all the rules.[34] If an athlete left the gymnasium once during the ten months of training, he was disqualified and could not participate in the games. His diet consisted of cheese, figs, and dried meats. No wine was allowed. If he was caught violating the diet, he was disqualified.

Every morning there were two trumpet calls. The first was the warning trumpet. When it blew, the athlete's personal trainer came and rubbed him down with oil. The second trumpet was the signal to begin the daily workout in the exercise square called the agony. As he exercised, there were "marshalls" observing

---

[32]Ibid., p. 48.

[33]Will Durant, *The Story of Civilization*, vol. 2: *The Life of Greece* (New York: Simon and Schuster, 1966), p. 213.

[34]Ibid.

his effort. If he caught an athlete loafing just once during this entire ten months, he was disqualified. If an athlete missed one trumpet call the entire ten months, he was disqualified from the games. The athletes trained and competed naked,[35] regardless of the weather or temperature.

The stadium sprint was the most popular event at the games. This race course, supposedly the length of one footprint of Hercules, was 192 meters or 1/7 of a mile. Only free men (no slaves) could participate. An athlete trained for eleven months in his home town and for one month at Isthmia.

Now why did they do all this? First and foremost, they did it to obtain a spruce wreath on their head! Each winner bound a woolen cloth about his head, and the judges placed the crown upon it. Then a herald announced the name and the city of the winner, a custom continued in the Olympiads of our day. This wreath was the only prize given at the games, yet it was the most eagerly contested distinction in Greece.[36]

However, there was more to it than that. After the victory celebration great honors were heaped on the athlete when he returned home.

A breach in the city wall was cut. This was to signify that the protection of the wall was no longer needed now that an athlete of this stature had returned home. The winner was then placed on a chariot and led through the city in a festive procession.[37] Many cities voted substantial sums of money to the victors.

[35]Ibid., p. 214.
[36]Ibid., p. 216.
[37]Sauer, p. 59.

Some made them generals, and the crowd idolized them so openly that the Greek philosophers complained. Poets were hired by the victor and his parents to pen odes to his greatness. They were sung to by a chorus of boys in the procession that welcomed him home. Sculptors were paid to capture the athlete in his most athletic pose.[38] Some cities fed the athlete's children and wife at public expense for the rest of their lives. The children were allowed to enter the best university in the ancient world, all at civic outlay. The athlete was given a seat of honor on the City Council and a box seat at the Isthmian games for the rest of his life.[39] Last, but definitely not least, he was exempt from all income tax![40]

These are the remains of an ancient "locker room" where the athletes at Pergamum trained in preparation for the games. Usually eleven months were spent in training at this ancient gymnasium under very careful scrutiny of the referees.

They do it to get a crown that will not last; but we do it to get a crown that will last forever (1 Cor. 9:25).

Paul says Christians also will receive a reward if they, like the athletics, are willing to sacrifice and live the life of discipleship, a life which similarly requires strong self-discipline. It is like entering the city. It is this magnificent reward which is referred to as entering "through the gates into the city" in Rev. 22:14. To enter through the gates was to enter in the victory procession of the returning champion.

---

[38]Durant, p. 216.
[39]Sauer, p. 59.
[40]Ibid.

Paul continues:

Therefore I do not run like a man running aimlessly (1 Cor. 9:26).

The race to which he probably refers was the most popular contest at the games, the stadium sprint, usually about two hundred meters.[41] Another race was a four-hundred-meter run and another went for about four kilometers. We have no knowledge of the records, but one ancient Greek writer avows that the athletes jumped over fifteen meters. This only proves that one cannot believe everything he reads![42]

This victor's monument from the Isthmian games dates from the time of the apostle Paul. On it the names of the victors and their judges were inscribed.

For a runner to run "aimlessly" is to run without focusing on the goal. Paul says that our lives must always be "run" with a clear view of the final accounting we will all face. All decisions must be made in view of this coming event. A Christian who lacks this perspective or who ignores it is simply living life without purpose:

I do not fight like a man beating the air. No, I beat my body and make it my slave so that after I have preached to others, I myself will not be disqualified for the prize (1 Cor. 9:26-27).

---

[41]Durant, p. 214.
[42]Ibid.

Boxing was another popular sport at the games. The Greek boxers did not hit straight out from the shoulder like our modern boxers. They fought by swinging their arms in a kind of windmill fashion.[43] Furthermore, the Romans introduced weighting the leather gloves with iron, lead, and metal studs. Terrible wounds were often inflicted. This naturally caused the boxers to adopt evasion as their chief strategy.[44] The Christian life, however, must be lived aggressively, not avoiding danger but challenging it. Not beating the air, windmill fashion, but using our fists in dead earnest, intending to make every blow count. In other words, the Christian is not to practice a life of evading his Christian responsibilities. He is to aggressively pursue them. He is to make every blow count for Christ. He is to live his life with purpose and intensity.

When Paul says "I beat my body," he uses a technical Greek athletic term for what we would call a "knockout." The word, **hypopiazo**, literally means "to give a black eye by hitting."[45] This was the decisive blow which won the fight, the "first blow under the eye."[46] He means that as Christians we must defeat our bodies. We must exercise strong discipline. The self, the "I," must be dealt a knockout blow. It is the self which is our real enemy, and that is what he means by "body." The self with its longings for convenience, its desire to be spared at all costs, its wishes and longings is the real opponent.

Though he does not give this crown a name, it is a crown awarded to those who have fought the battle with the flesh and through self-discipline have emerged victorious. They have dealt the "I" a "knock-out blow." It is a crown for those who have mastered the body

How tragic it would be for one who has instructed others in the rules for obtaining the prize to find that, when the race was over, he should be disqualified for the prize for failing to keep the rules he himself taught.

It should be noted, in conclusion, that these crowns can be lost (Rev. 3:11). We must be faithful to the end of life if we are to obtain these tokens of special honor.

In the book of Revelation the twenty-four elders, perhaps signifying the church, are pictured as casting their crowns to the feet of the Lamb:

Whenever the living creatures give glory, honor and thanks to him who sits on the throne and who lives for ever and ever, the twenty-four elders fall down before him who sits on the throne, and worship him

---

[43]G. F. Hasel, "Games," in *NISBE,* 2:397.

[44]Ibid.

[45]Robertson and Plummer, p. 196.

[46]Sauer, p. 53.

who lives for ever and ever. They lay their crowns before the throne
(Rev. 4:9-10).

This verse reveals that a major purpose of the crowns is as tokens of worship. The rewarded believers are here pictured as worshiping God by laying at His feet the very honors He gave them. This process is not a one-time event but goes on "whenever the living creatures give glory, honor, and thanks to Him who sits on the throne." Throughout eternity these tokens of honor will be laid at Christ's feet in acts of worship. Each time the rewarded believer approaches the throne, he will remove his crown, lay it at the feet of Jesus the Christ, and worship. A central motivation for obtaining these crowns is to be found in the desire to have these tokens of worship.

After a vigorous workout the athletes at the gymnasium at Pergamum would take their "showers" in these wash basins. In these basins all the olive oil was washed off their bodies.

Conclusion

Man's life on this earth does have ultimate significance. There can be no greater purpose than to live our lives in such a way that the one before whom we will one day give an account will say, "Well done!" History is moving toward the final destiny of man--the inheritance. Those faithful to Him to the end of life will share in that great salvation.

Chapter 25

The Partakers

It was a most impressive gathering. Nothing had been spared to celebrate the victory of those in attendance. The King Himself had taken off His robes and was serving them.[1] The roll call of those present consisted of those millions unknown to history but who were proven in battle. No conclave had ever been more magnificent, more rejoicing had never been witnessed. They gathered to remember and to give thanks. It was the "Final Gathering," the wedding feast of the Lamb!

The writer to the Hebrews designated those gathered as the "Partakers," those who had been faithful to Christ to the final hour, the great company of the metochoi. They are the "overcomers" of the book of Revelation. To this elite group rewards were now being given, and they were being invited to share with their king in the future reign of the servant kings, to rule and have dominion over the created order.

The Company of the Metochoi

In this final chapter the writer wishes to speak to some of the practical considerations which such a magnificent vision of the future raises. For sensitive readers there is a likelihood that the possibilities of rebuke and exclusion from millennial joy are an occasion for unnecessary introspection and discouragement. What Christian has been as obedient as he should? What Christian has believed God as he should? The answer is "no one." Who then are the objects of the Lord's displeasure when He returns? We must remember that the parables of the wise and foolish virgins, the good and the wicked servant, and the faithful and unfaithful believer are sharp contrasts. The warnings and parables do not deal with the daily lapses and failures to which all who know the Lord are subject. They deal with those who willfully persist in such unfaithfulness. Many in our day do not really want permanent solutions to their emotional stresses. Rather, they seek a temporary relief. It is to those who refuse to grow, who sin willfully, who

---

[1]Lk. 12:37.

spurn exhortation, and who dismiss their need to repent and change that these sober warnings are given. This seems contextually evident in nearly all of them.

A number of years ago the writer lived in Philadelphia. Many who lived outside the city commuted to work by a network of trains. One morning a young family awoke late and rushed frantically so that the father might catch the 8:05 AM commuter train to the central city. As they dashed around the kitchen making breakfast, young Johnny, their five year old son, was continually underfoot and slowing the process down. Finally, the father put him out the front door and asked him if he would play in the front yard for awhile. As Johnny walked down the front steps, his eye beheld a wonderful sight! It had rained the night before, and there was a gigantic mud puddle in the middle of the front yard. He straightaway walked into it and gleefully began to roll in the mud.

About this time his father, hurriedly looking at his watch burst out the front door on his way to the 8:05, it was now 8:00. He took one look at Johnny and in horror picked him up, brought him inside, and deposited him into his mother's care. Even later now, he rushed out the front door again and to save time, cut across the front yard. As he passed the beautiful mud puddle, he suddenly slipped and fell right into it. "Ugh," he moaned, "how disgusting." He immediately got up out the mud and ran into the house for a change of clothes. Realizing that he had no time, he decided to go to work covered with mud anyway and brush it off when his suit dried. With that, he rushed off to his goal, the 8:05.

Now there are a number of similarities and differences between Johnny and his dad. They both fell into the mud, it was the same mud, and they both got dirty. The difference, however, was that Johnny liked it in the mud and had no particular desire to get out. His dad, on the other hand, when he slipped, was disgusted and immediately got out. An even more significant difference, however, is that Johnny's father had a goal, the 8:05. He was going some place. Johnny, however, had no goal; he just wanted to have fun in the mud.

This parable illustrates the two sides of the sharp contrast drawn by the warning passages and the parables of the New Testament. All Christians fall in the mud. Sometimes it is the same mud, the same sins, into which non-Christians fall. The difference is that the metochoi don't like it there and want to get out. Furthermore, they are on their way to a goal, to hear the Lord say, "Well done." To use the words of Paul, they "love His appearing."

Teddy Roosevelt once said, "It is not so important what a man is as what he is becoming, because he shall be what he is now becoming." Perhaps the Lord echoed a similar sentiment when He looked at unstable Simon, and said, "You are Peter." Simon the unstable was to become Peter the rock!

We all bring a lot of emotional patterns into our Christian lives. This background includes genetic and environmental factors which, in part at least, determine what we are. It is therefore easier for some to live victoriously than others. It appears, however, that the issue is not success but faithfulness!

> *Let a man regard us in this manner, as servants of Christ, and stewards of the mysteries of God. In this case, moreover, it is required of stewards that one be found faithful* (1 Cor. 4:1-2 NASB).

Faithfulness means getting back up out of the mud, asking forgiveness, and persevering to the end of life. God is not so concerned with our success as He is with our hearts. We have a human priest in heaven to represent us. There is a man at the throne of God today! He has been tempted in all ways just as we have and therefore understands our pain. He bids us to "draw near with confidence to the throne of grace, that we may receive mercy and may find grace to help in time of need" (Heb. 4:16). There is no rejection here, no lack of compassion, only sympathy and understanding.

Some of us come from broken homes, alcoholic homes, or some of us have certain genetic predispositions to stress, anxiety, and other emotional difficulties that often make trusting God more difficult than for others. While Scripture never allows us to use these things as an excuse for disobedience, our great High Priest knows about these things and takes them into account now and surely will at the final reckoning. At that time many who are first will be last, and the last will be first. Just because a man struggles with persistent failure now does not mean he forfeits his reward; in fact, it means just the opposite. The fact that he stays in the struggle and returns to the battle is evident proof that he is one of the partakers. Remember, David committed adultery and murder, and yet at the end of his life God said of him that he was a "man after God's own heart." Success is not the only issue; faithful perseverance, even after failure, is!

What then is necessary to become one of Christ's metochoi? In its most general statement the requirement is "to hold fast the beginning of our assurance firm until the end" (Heb. 3:14). Those who have actively kept on believing and trusting God to the end of life are all included in this company. Lest anyone think, Is that all? it seems that Jerry Bridges was certainly correct when he said, "It often seems more difficult to trust God than to obey Him. The moral will of God given to us in the Bible is rational and reasonable. The circumstances in which we must trust God often appear irrational and inexplicable."[2] The Hebrews were not troubled with problems of disobedience so much as trust. It was the seeming distance of God in the midst of their troubles, His lack of apparent involvement in their difficulties which caused them to doubt. It is for this reason that the writer sets before their vision the great heroes of faith in chapter 11, who

---

[2]Jerry Bridges, *Trusting God* (Colorado Springs: NavPress, 1988), p. 17.

"died in faith, **without receiving the promises**" (Heb. 11:13). It is difficult to "trust God when it hurts." While ultimately the life of faith cannot be separated from the life of obedience, God seems to particularly exalt the man who persists in faith: "And without faith it is impossible to please Him, for he who comes to God must believe that He is, and that He is a rewarder of those who seek Him" (Heb. 11:6). When the storm was over and the sea had been stilled, Jesus was still greatly troubled. "How is it that you have no faith?" He asked His disciples. It was the development of their faith that seems to have been most important to Jesus.

Holding fast our confession does imply more than steadfast trust, but steadfast trust is of the greatest importance. It is of higher importance because it requires dependence, humility, and humble submission to the sovereignty of God. Having said that, however, the life of discipleship, practical obedience to His commands, is also necessary for those who would be numbered with the metochoi. Here the stern challenges of Jesus to be willing to leave father and mother, to sell all that we have, to deny ourselves, take up our cross and follow Him come to the forefront. They are not challenges to become Christians but to those who have become Christians to become "overcomers."

All who have persevered to the final hour will be Partakers. But even among the Partakers, Jesus taught there will be distinctions:

A certain nobleman went to a distant country to receive a kingdom for himself and then return. And he called ten of his slaves, and gave them ten minas, and said to them, "Do business with this until I come back."

But his citizens hated him, and sent a delegation after him, saying, "We do not want this man to reign over us."

And it came about that when he returned, after receiving the kingdom, he ordered that these slaves, to whom he had given the money, be called to him in order that he might know what business they had done. And the first appeared saying, "Master, your mina has made ten minas more." And he said to them, "Well done, good slave, because you have been faithful in a very little thing, **be in authority over ten cities.**"

And the second slave came, saying, "Your mina, master has made five minas." And he said to him also, **"And you are to be over five cities."**

And another came, saying "Master, behold your mina, which I kept put away in a handkerchief; for I was afraid of you, because you are an exacting man; you take up what you did not lay down; and reap what you did not sow."

He said to him, "By your own words I will judge you, you worthless slave. Did you know that I am an exacting man, taking up what I did not lay down, and reaping what I did not sow? Then why did you not put the money in the bank, and having come, I would have collected it with interest?"

And he said to the bystanders. **"Take the mina away from him, and give it to the one who has ten minas.** *"*

And they said to him, "Master, he has ten minas already."

"I tell you, that to everyone who has shall more be given, but from the one who does not have, even that what he does have shall be taken away. But these enemies of mine, who did not want me to reign over them, bring them here and slay them in my presence" (Lk. 19:12-27 NASB).

The first servant returned ten minas, a thousand percent return and received ten cities. The second servant, however, still faithful, returned less, five minas, a five hundred percent return and received five cities. The third servant forfeited what he had and was excluded from the right to reign at all! All three are servants, all three looked for the coming of their master, but only two are rewarded. The third will be in the kingdom, but he will not reign there.

A distinction is to be noted between the first two servants. The Lord commends the first with the words, "Well done." The second is rewarded with less. Both will reign with Him, and both therefore have endured and been faithful, but the first more so, and that will be acknowledged when the King returns. Both will have a share in the final destiny of man, and both will rejoice and look forward to the coming of the King.

It is most interesting to note that in a similar parable, the parable of the talents in Mt. 25:14-30, a slightly different truth is emphasized. In that parable the first two slaves did equal work; they doubled the Lord's investment. However, the Lord gave them differing amounts of money to begin with "according to his ability" (Mt. 25:15). God never entrusts us with responsibilities which exceed the abilities He has given! Yet in the final day, even though the servant with greater ability (i.e., more talents) returned more money to his master, both received exactly the same reward. It is not how much we produce, but whether or not we have been faithful with the abilities He has given. This means that the faithful but uneducated Auca Indian could possibly receive greater rewards than a Billy Graham!

Spiritual Motivation

The Motivation of Joint-Rulership

When Jesus offers the joy of reigning over "ten cities" or when Paul says, "If we endure, we will reign with Him," no doubt many readers will think to themselves, even if they do not say it out loud, I am not particularly motivated by the thought of reigning with Christ or having rulership in the future world.

Several things may be said about this. While it is apparently true that for many Christians this is no particular motivation now, it is plainly stated that they will feel differently about it then. When we stand before the Lord in perfect resurrection bodies, our capacity to understand the significance of our Lord's gracious death on our behalf will be heightened to a sublime degree. We will feel many things then that our sin nature clouds for us today. One thing that we will feel strongly is gratitude! We will see as we have never seen that the sinless Son of God loved us and died that we might live. We will be overwhelmed with GRACE.

For those who have not persevered in faith, who have denied their King now, they too will have heightened feelings. They will have feelings of deep shame and regret because they took Him for granted and wasted their lives. The pain will be acute, and there will be weeping and gnashing of teeth.

Furthermore, the notion of reigning with Christ, or ruling over cities, should not be trivialized as if it means various administrative positions in a kingdom. The theme is much broader, and the vision more glorious. What is signified by these expressions is not so much administrative positions as the joy of participating with the Messiah in the final destiny of man, to rule and have dominion. We aspire to higher position because we can then be more effective in the service of our King. To have ten cities instead of five means that we will have greater opportunity to serve Him, to demonstrate our love and gratitude to Him, and to extend the knowledge of His love and goodness throughout the cosmos.

We may not all want specifically to rule a city, but we will all want to be part of that glorious future. We may not know exactly what our role will be, but we can assume it will be consistent with the uniqueness with which He created each of us, and it will be wonderful. To miss that is to miss much.

Also it should be stressed that the motivation behind our perseverance in holiness is not just the crowns we receive but why we want these crowns. We do not want crowns so in carnal hubris we can compare ours with others throughout eternity! There will be no sin nature, no selfishness, no envy, and no pride there.

Rather, we want these crowns so we will have much to lay at His feet! When John describes the victorious metochoi as twenty-four elders surrounding the heavenly throne, he says they "will cast their crowns before the throne" (Rev. 4:10). The crowns are ours to use as tokens of worship and gratefulness. This casting of the crowns at His feet is our way of saying, "Thank you, Lord Jesus, for dying for me." Each crown with which we are rewarded is a token of our gratitude for eternal salvation.

A Mercenary Motive?

Perhaps the greatest objection we feel to the notion of joint-rulership is that it seems to be an unworthy motivation for spiritual living. Surely to be motivated toward faithfulness by offering reward is completely backward in the economy of grace. Are we not told that we are to obey because of the mercies of God (Rom. 12:1) and that "the love of Christ controls us" (2 Cor. 5:14), and not the love of rewards? Is not doing something for the purpose of obtaining a reward a far less worthy motive than doing it out of love and gratitude?

This view of ethics is sometimes called "disinterested benevolence." This is the atheistic ethic in which good is done only for the sake of the good, with no consideration of reward for the doing of it.[3] By forgetting the possibility of reward, man honors the ethic standard in its purity. The motivation for obedience is supposedly to be found only in the command itself. Only in this manner, maintains the atheist, can the selfishness of man be crushed and a pure altruism found. This motivation is "purely moral."

Regardless of how we feel about the matter, it seems very evident that the New Testament writers did not hesitate to use the motivation of future rewards as a central motivator for godly living. Certainly the motivation of thankfulness and grace was very important, but the vision of the future enhanced this stimulus.

Furthermore, they did not stagger to use the negative motivation of the loss of reward and exclusion from the joy of co-rulership. Jesus told His followers to lay up treasure in heaven (Mt. 6:9-21) and challenged them to discipleship on the basis of future rewards:

> Then Peter answered and said to Him, "Behold, we have left everything and followed You; what then will there be for us?" And Jesus said to them, "Truly I say to you, that you who have followed Me, in the regeneration when the Son of Man will sit on His glorious throne, you also shall sit upon twelve thrones, judging the twelve tribes of Israel. And everyone who has left houses or brothers or sisters or father

---

[3]See G. C. Berkouwer, *Faith and Justification* (Grand Rapids: Eerdmans, 1954), pp. 117ff., for strong refutation of this ethic.

or mother or children or farms for My names' sake, shall receive many
times as much, and shall inherit eternal life. But many who are first
will be last; and the last, first (Mt. 19:27-30 NASB).

Peter forthrightly asks what the benefit will be in the kingdom for a life of sacrifice now. Instead of rebuking him for striving for rewards, Jesus commends it and tells him that he will rule with Him.[4] The morality of the Bible is an offense to the "purely moral." It constantly urges us to look to the future. As Abraham wandered in Canaan, he "was looking forward to the city with foundations" (Heb. 11:10). Moses made his great decision to turn his back on the wealth of Egypt and endure suffering with the people of God "because he was looking ahead to his reward" (Heb. 11:26). Being stimulated by the reward he would receive is viewed as a praiseworthy motivation. Perhaps the Bible is a better judge of our nature and how to inspire it to zeal than the moral philosophers.

Part of our difficulty is the way we view these rewards. In their most general sense they refer to the joy of participating with Christ in God's eternal purposes, the inheritance. This eternal purpose is a good and wonderful purpose: to extend the glory and blessing of God to all creation. Whatever it involves, those who know Christ as their king must strive to have a share in this. It is not a striving so much for personal benefit but persevering in good works so that we can achieve the goal of sharing in the future reign of the servant kings. Whatever our role in that great future is, it will be magnificent. Because we love Him, we want to earn the right to rule with Him. So it is our love for Him and the joy set before us that motivates. We are not saying that the desire for future reward is to replace altruism as a motivator, only that it enhances it.

It is impossible to separate the motivation of love and the motivation derived from reward. They are, in the Bible at least, inextricably interrelated. This is so because to strive for the biblical inheritance requires that one strive "according to the rules." This means he must strive (1) with a heart motive that what he does is for Christ's sake and in response to Christ's love; and (2) with a realization that, once he has done all he can do, he still has only done his duty (Lk. 17:10); and (3) with an understanding that there is no strict contractual correspondence between a certain amount of work resulting in a certain amount of reward (Mt. 20:1-16). Since he has only done his duty, he understands that God rewards him not out of debt but out of grace. His work has not obligated God or placed God in his debt, but God in His grace has freely chosen to reward him even though there is no obligation placed upon Him to do so. This theoretical discussion can be clarified immediately with a simple illustration.

Consider a young mother of four. Her husband is a brutal alcoholic. He has on occasion abused her and heaped enormous debts on the family. In addi-

---

[4]See also Mt. 5:11-12; Lk. 6:35-38.

tion to the pain he causes, he is unfaithful and lets her know it. Now the Bible tells her to love this man in spite of the pain and hurt. She chooses to love for Christ's sake. After all, He first loved us. But in addition, she looks to the future. She knows that her Master will be greatly pleased and that she will be honored then, if not now. Her confidence that the universe is moral, that justice will one day prevail, and that her sufferings now equip her to reign with her king provide a greatly enhanced motivation to persevere. Even if the "purely moral" see this as selfish, the One before whom we will render an account clearly does not. When He exhorted us to show hospitality to those who cannot pay, He did not appeal to duty as the motive. Rather, He said, "Although they cannot repay you, you will be repaid at the resurrection of the righteous" (Lk. 14:14).

Performance and Unconditional Acceptance

Does this doctrine imply that God no longer accepts us unconditionally? Does this shift our attention from love and grace over to works? Does this mean that we must earn God's acceptance by performing correctly?

On the principles of the Experimental Predestinarians, the answer would seem to be yes. Their emphasis on obtaining assurance by means of works and their method of motivating, by warning that one may not be justified, has often led to an unhealthy introspection. The Experimental Predestinarian can never assure anyone that he has God's acceptance because that assurance cannot come until one has persevered to the final hour.

The Partaker, on the other hand, can be assured of God's unconditional acceptance. Furthermore, he can receive the warnings of the New Testament not as raising doubts about his acceptance with God but about his loss of reward. When he is warned, he falls back on the bedrock assurance of God's love and commitment to him, an assurance of which the Experimental Predestinarian can have only theoretical knowledge. Therefore, the warnings emerge out of a sense of grace, not uncertainty.

When we become Christians, the Scriptures affirm that we enter into two different relationships with Christ. The first, Paul called being "in Christ." This relationship is eternal and unchanging. It depends upon God alone and is received through faith on the basis of the justifying righteousness of Christ. We are born into His family and are the eternal objects of unconditional love.

The second relationship is often called "Christ in us," and it refers not to our eternal relationship but to our temporal fellowship. This relationship with Christ is changeable and depends upon our responses in faith to His love and grace. Within this relationship God requires performance in order to secure His approval and His future inheritance. As any father would, He disciplines His children. If our son disobeys us, we still love him, and he will always be our son. But our fellowship is broken until he confesses. Similarly, our fellowship with God is hampered and His blessing is withdrawn from the believer who refuses to respond to His grace displayed in justification:

Unless I wash you, you have no part with me (Jn. 13:8).

I write to you dear children, because your sins have been forgiven . . . Do not love the world or anything in the world. If anyone loves the world, the love of the Father is not in him (1 Jn. 2:12, 15).

If we confess our sins, he is faithful and just and will forgive us our sins (1 Jn. 1:9).

Your iniquities have separated you from your God; your sins have hidden his face from you (Isa. 59:2).

Husbands, in the same way be considerate as you live with your wives . . . so that nothing will hinder your prayers (1 Pet. 3:7).

To deny this is simply to deny that God holds us accountable for our behavior. If the Reformation placed too much emphasis on the fear of God, it is possible that our generation, inspired by the benevolent God of liberal theology and the narcissistic nature of our culture, has placed too much emphasis on God's love. Or at least we have defined love in a way that excludes accountability.

If this book has placed too much emphasis on accountability, it is only because of the widespread contemporary neglect of this biblical theme. We must emphasize, however, that our central focus should always be where the God of grace wants it--on His love and unconditional acceptance. Paul appeals not to duty to inspire his readers but to God's mercy. He asks for a response based not on obligation but upon heartfelt gratitude (Rom. 12:1-2). Luther once said, "A law-driver insists with threats and penalties; a preacher of grace lures and incites with divine goodness and compassion shown to us; for he wants no unwilling works and reluctant services, he wants a joyful and delightful service to God."

In his farewell speech to the Ephesians elders, the apostle Paul declared, "I commend you to God and to the word of His grace, which is able to build you up and give you an inheritance among all those who are sanctified" (Acts 20:32). It is grace that builds and motivates. Let us think of His wonderful death for our sins and His love for us before we think of our accountability. Then, and only then, can the doctrine of final accountability be seen in its biblical context.

The Purpose of the Messianic Kingdom

It is vitally important that the purpose and nature of this rulership be understood. Only then can our doctrine be properly defended from critics who degrade the glorious joint-heirship as too "carnal." Some prefer an indefinite and unexplained reign of the saints, either in heaven now or in the new heaven and new earth. To them it is material and carnal to talk of an earthly kingship. It is difficult to see how such a view could ever emerge from the plain intent of these wonderful predictions. To reign jointly with Christ is the most precious and glorious future that can be set before the mind of man.

What is the purpose of this great future? The design of this glorious reign of the metochoi is to deliver the world from the results of sin and to fill it with blessing and glory! These metochoi are not ruling for themselves but for others. Part of our problem is that in the present world, rulership nearly always implies the appropriation of power due to selfish motives. It has the connotation of "lording over " others. But the King Himself has taught us about another kind of rulership, servant rulership. The metochoi of King Jesus are not above their Master. They too are servant rulers.

> *The kings of the Gentiles lord it over them; and those who exercise authority over them call themselves Benefactors.* **But you are not to be like that.** *Instead, the greatest among you should be like the youngest, and the one who rules like the one who serves. For who is greater, the one who is at the table or the one who serves? Is it not the one who is at the table? But I am among you as one who serves* (Lk. 22:25-27).

How are such rulers developed? It is only through undergoing the trials of sin and suffering that true compassion can emerge. This is the theme of Heb. 2 where our great High Priest is said to have learned obedience by the things He has suffered, and He is leading many sons along a similar path to glory. Indeed the kingdom has been postponed and delayed for several thousand years precisely for this purpose, to raise up a body of rulers who will sustain it with dignity, purity, compassion, and selflessness worthy of the Messiah Jesus. The reason that the kingdom was not established under Moses or David or the first advent is surely to be explained by the apparent fact that man was not yet prepared for it. A period of time is necessary to prepare the future rulers. God has predetermined the number of those who will share in the reign of David's Greater Son, and until this number (known only to God) is completed, the kingdom itself will not be established.

If the metochoi are to enjoy these unspeakable privileges, they must be trained in obedience, suffering, temptation, and trial just as their Captain was. They are so elevated simply because they have learned these lessons and have persevered in them to the end of life. The King has told them that in the kingdom those who are the greatest servants now will be the greatest rulers then! When they finally inherit this kingdom, the wisdom of the divine plan will be evident. Their constant contact with evil and trial now uniquely fits them for their future positions. It will not only enhance their relationships to each other but will bring them into sympathy with the nations of earth. They will know and understand the struggle with sin which engages their subjects, the mortal inhabitants of the millennial earth. The experience gained now fits them to be wise, intelligent kings and sympathetic and loving priests. Their goal is not to exert authority but to serve those over whom they have been placed. They will model their Master's servant heart and will be greatly loved and respected by their subjects. They think only of the good they can do for others and the ways in which they can extend the glory and blessing of God to the created order. They will be universally honored for their love, graciousness, and friendship, as well as for their authority.

We may view the present world as the training ground for the aristocracy of the future kingdom, the ruling class of the world to come. A man may be in abject poverty now and completely ignored by the leaders of this world. He may be despised and without means to adequately provide for his family. Yet he is now a prince and will one day inherit his kingdom. Then he will obtain a position far higher and with more grandeur than that of any human ruler who ever lived. This truth is based upon numerous promises in Scripture **which God intends to fulfill!**

Security and Significance

It is doubtful than anyone would disagree with the observation that two of the most important needs of man are for security and significance.[5] The interplay of these emotions are obviously crucial in our motivations. Larry Crabb defines them this way:

> **Security:** *A convinced awareness of being unconditionally and totally loved without needing to change in order to win love, loved by a love that is freely given, that cannot be earned and therefore cannot be lost.*

> **Significance:** *A realization that I am engaged in a responsibility or job that is truly important, whose results will not evaporate with time, but will last through eternity, that fundamentally involves having a meaningful impact on' another person, a job for which I am completely adequate.*[6]

It is vitally important for our mental wholeness that we feel both secure and significant with God. As this book has attempted to prove, contrary to the Arminian and the Experimental Predestinarian, God does not threaten His children's security as a means of motivating them. But God does deal seriously with His children in terms of the final significance.

---

[5]For the discussion to follow, the writer is indebted to Ken Quick, "Living for the Kingdom" (D.Min. thesis, Dallas Theological Seminary, 1989), pp. 4-27.

[6]Lawrence Crabb, *The Marriage Builder* (Grand Rapids: Zondervan, 1982), p. 29.

Our need for security. It is certainly arguable that the most fundamental of human needs is secure love. Children who lack this are often scarred for life. Marriages without it are often full of anguish. Intimacy in marriage requires it. If one spouse fails to meet the need the other has for security, the likely result is divorce.

If this is true in all human relationships, how much more so is it in our relationship to God. And God for Christ's sake has granted us freely this thing we need and desire most from Him, primary security. Salvation is unconditional. The man who believes in Christ and has accepted His offer of forgiveness has:

1.   No fear of loss of salvation (Rom. 11:28; Eph. 1:13).

2.   No fear of eternal condemnation (Jn. 5:24; Col. 2:13-14).

3.   No fear of divine rejection as His child (Jn. 10:27-28; Rom. 8:34ff.).

4.   Positive assurance:
       We can know we are God's children forever.
       We can know He loves and accepts us, no matter what.

RESULT: Our primary security is established by God.[7]

Yes, our eternal security depends upon God and that is why it is secure indeed. No matter what our sin, no matter how far we wander, no matter how fruitless our lives or difficult our struggle, God always remains committed to us.

God's acceptance and adoption gives us a basis for life. As an earthly parent always loves his child, so our heavenly parent remains committed to us. Like an earthly parent, however, our heavenly parent does not always approve of our actions, and He will hold us accountable for them. In some cases He will deal severely with our willful failures.

Our need for significance. In order for us to be motivated in what we do, we need to feel that our task and our lives are significant and that there is a final accounting for what we do. Without that feeling work is a burden, and our lives lack focus and meaning. That this is so can be seen in numerous life situations.

A housewife cares for her family, fixes meals, and stays up until 2:00 AM talking with her teenage children. She chooses to stay home and commit twenty years of her life to being a mother instead of having a career. If she does not see fruit from her labor, if she does not see her children turning out well, if she is not

---

[7]Quick, p. 11.

affirmed by them and by her husband, she will lose motivation. She perceives that what she is investing her life in is not significant.

A secretary in a large Christian missionary organization labors daily behind the scenes. Because she is there, the teachers and evangelists are able to minister more freely. Yet if the organization fails to affirm the importance of her role, she loses the vision. She will no longer connect the computer on which she labors with conversions in the field. She no longer feels her work is significant, and she loses motivation.

A highly successful civil engineer has invested many years of his life in building buildings and bridges. One day he surveys what he has done and reasons, All that I have built will perish. I want to build things which will last for eternity. He has concluded that his work no longer has significance. He loses his motivation. His view is, of course, incorrect. What makes a task significant is the motive for doing it and the one for whom it is done. Nevertheless, in his motivational system, having concluded that this work is not significant, he leaves his job to become a foreign missionary.

A systems analyst has put together numerous computer systems for large corporations. One day he looks at what he has done and concludes there must be more to life than helping a business make more money. He no longer feels what he is doing is significant, and his motivation wanes.

Examples could be multiplied. It is self-evident that our motivation to accomplish a given task is directly related to how significant we feel the task is. When Paul said, "Whatever you do, work at it with all your heart, as working for the Lord, not for men, since you know that you will receive an inheritance from the Lord as a reward," (Col. 3:23-24) he was appealing to this same motivational force. This verse reveals a central aspect of what makes us feel something is significant: a task will be viewed as significant if the people who matter to us value it as so. In this case since it is God who determines the ultimate significance of the work, it will be perceived as highly important: "Always give yourselves fully to the work of the Lord, because you know that your labor in the Lord is not in vain" (1 Cor. 15:58).

Ken Quick observes, "Security says, I am accepted for who I am no matter what I do. Significance says, What I do is both of value and fulfilling, and is recognized and rewarded as such."[8]

But one more thing is needed for us to feel that our work is truly significant. There must be recognition and affirmation by someone else. Someone other than ourselves, someone who has expertise and authority to affirm that a particular task is valuable must give his affirmation. This recognition could be

---

[8]Ibid., p. 15.

given with a plaque, a word of praise, a compliment, a promotion, or a dinner in the person's honor. "But in some way one must receive the proof from the people who matter that he has done well."[9]

What is evident in the interpersonal relationships in this life can now be applied to our eternal relationship with God. He is the ultimate one who will evaluate my work and will pronounce the desired "Well done." And He is the one who matters more than anyone. Our eternal security gives us freedom to pursue our significance. We do not have to worry about rejection or about loss of salvation. But even though we cannot lose our justification, the warnings in the Bible tell us we can forfeit the inheritance, we can lose our eternal significance. The promises that our life can matter motivate us to make sacrifices, to take risks, to work hard, knowing that our work is not in vain in the Lord. God values **whatever** we do for Him. The warnings that we can lose reward inspire the fear of the Lord in our hearts and cause us to labor to avoid that terrible consequence. The other side of significance is final accountability.

We see then that there are two sides to the motivational influence. Positively, there is the legitimate desire for Christ's approval and for eternal significance. Negatively, there is a legitimate fear of Christ's displeasure and the loss of eternal significance.

Our lives can matter. They can make a difference. Through service to Him we can attach eternal value to the life we have lived. Some of us will pursue this goal more diligently than others. Some Christians, to their great shame and eternal loss, will not pursue this worthy goal at all. The differences will become evident when we stand before Him at the judgment seat of Christ.

Love could not grow between a father and son where the father throughout the son's life deals with his disobedience by (1) raising questions whether or not the young man was really his son (Experimental Predestinarian) or (2) threatening him with exclusion from the family (Arminian). However, love is possible in the midst of disobedience when the father affirms his love for his son and assures him he can never be put out of his family but then disciplines him. In extreme situations he may warn him of possible disinheritance. "The Lord disciplines those He loves and He punishes everyone He accepts as a son. . . . If you are not disciplined then you are illegitimate children and not true sons" (Heb. 12:6-8).

Differences in Eternity Future

Will these differences remain? The answer seems to be yes. However, the biblical picture of the eternal state is of full joy for all who are there:

---

[9]Ibid., pp. 13-14.

And there shall no longer be any curse; and the throne of God and of the Lamb shall be in it, and His bond-servants shall serve Him; and they shall see His face, and His name shall be on their foreheads and there shall no longer be any night and they shall not have need of the light of a lamp nor the light of the sun, because God shall illumine them, and they shall reign forever and ever (Rev. 22:3-5 NASB).

And He shall wipe away every tear from their eyes; and there shall no longer be any death; there shall no longer be any mourning or crying, or pain; the first things have passed away (Rev. 21:4 NASB).

It seems that on the authority of these and similar verses, when combined with the passages which stress differing rewards, we may confidently affirm that in eternity everyone's cup will be full, but the cups will be of different sizes. No one will enter eternity future with regret or mourning or pain. No one will feel like a second-class citizen of heaven because they were unfaithful now. While the faithful Christian will enjoy richer relationship and privilege with His King throughout eternity than the unfaithful, the predominate feeling for all will be joy and gratitude.

After all, we worship a God of grace. He who died for us will also wipe away every tear and remove all crying and sorrow.

Final Accountability

In his book *The Closing of the American Mind* Allan Bloom, professor of social thought at the University of Chicago, makes a disturbing observation of our university culture:

There is one thing a professor can be absolutely certain of: almost every student entering the university believes, or says he believes, that truth is relative. If this belief is put to the test, one can count on the student's reaction: they will be uncomprehending. That anyone should regard the proposition as not self-evident astonishes them, as though he were calling into question 2 + 2 = 4.[10]

These are things, says Bloom, which we no longer need to think about. For them the relativity of truth is a moral postulate. To deny it is to place yourself in the same category as a man who believes in witches or that the earth is flat. The study of world history teaches them that men were mad in past ages. Men always thought they were right, and that is what led to war. The answer: elimi-

---

[10]Allan Bloom, *The Closing of the American Mind* (New York: Simon and Schuster, 1987), p. 25.

nate the demon of absolutism, and inculcate relativity in our academic curriculum. The virtue of our modern society is "openness."

While no one questions the necessity of generous attitudes in a pluralistic society, the way we have arrived at this condition has revealed that the price was too high, the removal of any sense of final accountability. Perhaps not coincidentally the student's moral outrage against the evils of absolutism tended to correspond to their own desires to be free from all the restraints which a moral absolute imposed. At any rate, in our society today the removal of moral absolutes has brought with it the removal of any sense of final accountability for one's actions.

Even the absolute God of the Bible has seemingly acquired this virtue of openness. He understands our sin and will make exceptions. While it has always been sadly true that the evils of the society are eventually adopted by the church, the ease with which the modern church has accepted the values of the surrounding culture has surprised many. There are only minor statistical differences now between the divorce rates among Christians and non-Christians. Premarital sexual activity among our Christian young people has for many of them, like their non-Christian counterparts, become a "non-issue." Marriage is no longer "till death do us part" but "till difficulties do us in!"

Why has the church, which is supposedly a bastion of absolutism in the surrounding sea of relativism, so easily accepted the values of the encircling culture? This is a question with which church and cultural historians will wrestle, but it is quite clear that a profound theological error is near the heart of the matter. The doctrines of Westminster Calvinism, while designed to promote a high degree of moral purity, have virtually robbed the church of any sense of final accountability.

This is true for three reasons. First, an emphasis on evidences of regeneration as the true test of salvation has lead many who are not regenerate to look at some meager evidence that they are and conclude that they are saved when they are in truth on the highway to hell.

But just as serious, the misguided emphasis upon the practical syllogism has all but eliminated the central scriptural motivations for moving carnal Christians back to the path of growth to maturity. The Bible does not tell them they are not saved. Rather, it tells them that, if they are, they are going to miss out on the final destiny of man. It does matter to God that we live inconsistently with the faith we claim to possess. One day there will be a reckoning, and for some there will be weeping . . . and shame. Because these negative consequences of a carnal life have rarely been defined, many Christians do not live with a **healthy** fear of God. They often take the grace of God for granted because Experimental Predestinarians have told them they will all be rewarded, only some not as much as others. No doubt, many settle back into a life of lukewarmness under such teaching.

Third, their system emasculates the numerous warnings of their force. The warnings, we are told, do not apply to true Christians but to professing Christians. Since the lukewarm Christian in the pew is already assured of his saved status on the basis of looking at some evidences of works in his life, he concludes that the warnings do not apply to him. There is no danger. He is further told that he cannot lose salvation and will be rewarded anyway.

A combination of these three errors have so permeated our Christian culture that to raise the issue of disinheritance (which the Bible everywhere does!) draws gasps of surprise. Like the students in Bloom's university classroom, these are things that you do not need to talk about. As a result this theology has contributed unintentionally to the very spiritual lethargy against which it constantly rails.

To counteract this, Experimental Predestinarians can only point professing Christians to the opposite extreme and raise questions about their justification. For example, Buswell insists:

> *So long as a professing Christian is in the state of carnality, no pastor, no Christian friend, has the slightest ground for holding that this carnal person has ever been regenerated. . . . It is the pastor's duty to counsel such a person, "You do not give evidence of being in a regenerate state."*[11]

But the Scriptures do not point such men to examine the fruits of regeneration in their lives to ascertain whether they are Christians or not. They point them to the great future. Instead of threatening them with the fear of hell, the Scriptures warn them of profound regret and millennial disinheritance in the future. The danger is missing the Master's "Well done!" This is a healthy and ennobling fear which inspires men to growth and discipleship. The continual challenge to reconsider whether or not one is saved can hardly compare with this for spiritual incitement. Indeed, it leads backward to introspection and legalism instead of forward to confidence and freedom in Christ. Love and grace have always been higher and more powerful motivators than fear of hell, but the Experimental Predestinarian cannot offer these incentives because a carnal lifestyle suggests to him that the man in question has not experienced the love and grace of God at all. All that is left in his bag of motivational influences is to warn the man that he may not be saved and is in danger of perishing. Rarely do the

---

[11]J. Oliver Buswell, *Systematic Theology*, 2 vols. (Grand Rapids: Zondervan, 1962), 2:147.

Experimental Predestinarians attempt to motivate by means of appeal to the magnificent future.[12] In fact, they often disparage it as "some millennial crown."

Numerous examples of the devastating effects of this theology can be culled from the everyday life of the church. Not long ago a businessman related to this writer how he was leading a Bible study using a recent book written by a well-known Experimental Predestinarian Bible teacher. The thrust of this book was to challenge professing Christians that they cannot be sure of their salvation unless they live up to the demands of discipleship taught by Christ. When one man, who had faithfully attended for years failed to continue, he asked him what was wrong. The man revealed that the book had a strong negative impact on his spiritual motivation because it seemed impossible to love or to be loved by a God who demanded such perfection in order to be accepted into His family. He had many business and personal trials in life at that time, and he could not find the needed comfort he needed from his relationship with God when he was continually exposed to such introspective perfectionism.

The Experimental Predestinarian has a genuine and biblical concern. He does not want the grace of God to be taken for granted. It therefore grieves him to contemplate that a permanently carnal Christian could ever be the object of God's saving grace. He is concerned that a man who embraces the Partaker view of eternal security will reason this way: "I realize that my life of sin will exclude me from the future destiny of man, but I really don't care about that anyway. Even if I experience profound regret, it will only be temporary, and in the final analysis, in eternity future, I will have a full cup, even if it is not as large as others."

We reply that such a response is possible but would not be typical. Usually when Christians are challenged with the great future and reminded of the love of God, their hearts incline toward discipleship. Normally grace, love, and reward are powerful motivators. However, it is possible that men will take the grace of God for granted. Indeed, who of us does not do this every day! It is possible that some will argue, "Let us continue in sin that grace may abound." The apostle Paul was criticized for this very thing (Rom. 6:1). Any doctrine of grace which cannot be so misunderstood is not a biblical doctrine of grace. Grace is, after all, **unmerited favor**. This is one of the most obvious objections to the Experimental Predestinarian view of eternal security. It is impossible that their view of perseverance (i.e., that it is inevitably and necessarily linked with justification) could ever result in the accusation "Let us continue in sin that grace may abound." Their view, then, differs from the apostle Paul's. Westminster Calvin-

---

[12]In John MacArthur's recent Experimental Predestinarian book in which he is attempting to motivate the church to godliness, he devotes only one line of text to the subject of rewards! The remaining 253 pages are devoted to proving that a man with insufficient evidences of regeneration is in fact not a Christian at all (John MacArthur, *The Gospel According to Jesus* [Grand Rapids: Zondervan, 1988], p. 146).

ism could never be open to the charge of antinomianism because any antinomian is by definition in their system not a believer at all.

But the Bible is more realistic. Men like Saul, Solomon, and Alexander were all regenerate, but they did not persevere in either faith or well doing to the end of life. They presumed upon the grace of God.

While it is true that Westminster Calvinism could never be accused of teaching antinomianism, it nevertheless indirectly promotes the very antinomianism it abhors. It seems that Experimental Predestinarians have removed future accountability from the life of the Christian. The judgment seat of Christ is like the Super Bowl, and salvation is a ticket. Moses and Paul will be seated on the fifty yard line. Even if we are in the last row of the seats in the end zone, at least we are there. The difference between Moses and us will be irrelevant in the coming kingdom.[13] Would it not follow that many who embrace this view of eternal security would begin to lapse into spiritual dullness? Without consequence and accountability people simply feel that the commands are negotiable.

The writer is aware that his Experimental Predestinarian friends will reply that, by exhorting their congregations to examine themselves to see if they are really saved, they have in fact introduced accountability. The fear that one is not really saved is supposedly a strong motivator to do good works. Apart from the fact that this approach is noticeably absent from the Scripture, it doesn't work anyway. When confronted with such preaching, the average Christian does not reason, My works are not good enough. Therefore, I am not saved, and I must make a new beginning. Rather, he assures himself, I **KNOW** I am saved. Therefore, my works **MUST** be good enough! He intuitively senses the very thing the Experimental Predestinarian knows full well. It is impossible to define a certain level of works which are adequate to calm the claims of conscience and establish that one is saved. From Augustine to the truly saved carnal Christian there is a continuum that is impossible to draw a line across. Therefore, such preaching is simply ignored, as it should be. Thus assured, he continues in his lethargy.

It is granted that in the Partaker view of eternal security, in eternity future the differences between Moses and us will not be an occasion of regret, and we will know joy unspeakable. However, for the unfaithful believer the future kingdom will be a time of profound regret. The negative incentives of millennial disinheritance and missing the Master's "Well done!" will be deeply felt. The vast body of evangelical believers sitting under the Experimental Predestinarian system have concluded that, based on the fact they have believed and have glimmerings of life, they are born again. Simultaneously, they are taught that, if they are born again, they cannot lose salvation. Furthermore, they are taught that the warnings, such as Hebrews, chapter 6, do not apply to them but to professing

---

[13]Illustration from an excellent book on this subject by Walt Henrichson, *The Profit Motive* (Knoxville, TN: Vision Foundation, 1989), p. 30.

Christians. Having trusted in glimmerings of works in their lives, these Christians conclude they are saved and that they cannot lose salvation and that it will make no significant difference at the second coming anyway.

Furthermore, most of the Experimental Predestinarian objections to the Partaker view of eternal security is focused too narrowly upon the relative few who might take the grace of God for granted. They seem to reason that any system which allows a few to be saved who have presumed upon grace could not be biblical. They are preoccupied with the few. Partakers, on the other hand, are more preoccupied with the many. They worry about the vast majority of Christians who do not intend to take the grace of God for granted but who have lost their sense of accountability at the judgment seat of Christ because Experimental Predestinarians have assured them there is no danger if they are truly born again. The warnings do not apply to them.

We believe the great neglect of Western Christianity is not that our pulpits have failed to warn people who claim the name of Christ that they are perishing. Our neglect is that we have not sufficiently explained the great future joy of sharing in the coming messianic partnership and the danger of forfeiting this inheritance. If such a vision were consistently held before our congregations, the love and fear of God would be greatly increased. Surely many of those fifty million reported by the Gallup poll who claim to be born again would begin to act like it.

Conclusion

We now come to the end of the matter. The Lord promises to all who really know Him and see Him that they will enjoy unspeakable privilege in the final kingdom of David's Greater Son. That great future must constantly be set before the vision of all who name the Lord Jesus as their King. We should daily be evaluating our lives, our priorities, and our hearts in view of how we will feel about our decisions ten thousand years from now. Only those who live like this and who finish their course with the flag at full mast will share in the future reign of the servant kings. Let us "lay aside every encumbrance, and the sin which so easily entangles us, and let us run with endurance the race that is set before us."[14] After all, we "have become partakers of Christ, if we hold fast the beginning of our assurance firm until the end."[15]

---

[14]Heb. 12:1.
[15]Heb. 3:14.

Let us hear the conclusion of the whole matter,
Fear God and keep His commandments,
For this is the whole duty of man
For God will bring every work into judgment,
Including every secret thing,
Whether it is good or whether it is evil.[1]

---

[1]Ecc. 12:12-14

Epilogue

"Now, I understand," said the archangel Michael, many years later as he reflected on the amazing grace revealed in the divine plan. "How appropriate, that the co-heirs should find their ultimate significance by following the same path as their Savior."

"How typical of the Father," he thought, "that He would rebuke the Satan's rebellion in a way which would cost Him the sacrifice of His beloved Son."

"How wise and how unexpected, that He would establish the inferior creatures as the aristocracy of the future kingdom."

The Lord of Hosts had forever demonstrated the superiority of servanthood. The inferior creature, man, through the victory of **THE MAN** had recovered through obedience and dependence that which the Satan had stolen in independence and unbelief. Truly, there was no place for pride in the eternal purpose. God not only achieved this purpose but through the incarnation of His Son became the principle illustration of the life of love and service necessary for its accomplishment:

"Oh, the depth of the riches of the wisdom and knowledge of God! How unsearchable His judgments, and His paths beyond tracing out! Who has known the mind of the Lord? Or who has been His counselor?"[1]

The future reign of the servant kings is a central theme of the Bible. Everything relates in some way to the establishment of the kingdom of heaven. McClain has well said, "If there be a God in heaven, if the life which He created on the earth is worth-while, and not something evil *per se*, then there ought to be in history some worthy consummation of its long and arduous course."[2]

Without an earthly kingdom history becomes a staircase, and nothing more, a stairway that goes no place. It is a loaded gun which, when the trigger is pulled, fires a blank cartridge. "Such a philosophy of history not only flies in the face of the clear statements of Scripture, but also runs contrary to the reason of

---

[1]Rom. 11:33-34.

[2]Alva J. McClain, *The Greatness of the Kingdom* (Chicago: Moody Press, 1959), p. 530.

man in his finest moments and aspiration."[3] Yet this is exactly where many interpreters of the Bible have ended the story: centuries of misery and incomplete progress, then a sudden catastrophic finish to the whole of it!

This incomplete philosophy of history will never satisfy the deepest longings of man. No! History finds its meaning and significance in the future reign of the servant kings. Within history meaning and direction can be found. The fall of man and creation occurred within history, and it is essential that the redemption of man and creation occur within that process as well.

"What's wrong, Michael?" asked one of the other angels. The archangel seemed dejected.

"If only they would listen," he said.

"What do you mean?" the concerned angel replied.

"I have been thinking about the joy of the metochoi at the final gathering. What an unspeakable privilege to be there and to be entrusted with the accomplishment of the Father's eternal purpose. Yet some of those saved by the Son's sacrifice seem completely indifferent to eternal verities. They live as if the only reality is affluence and personal peace."

"Their ingratitude does become tiring," said Michael's colleague.

But then the archangel's face brightened when he remembered the millions who have persevered. Men and women to whom he had ministered, unknown to history, but faithful in the outworking of the eternal purpose. He warmly remembered the labors of the twelve apostles, the preaching of Whitefield and Wesley, the scholarly labors of John Calvin, the faithfulness of Adoniram Judson in Burma, of Hudson Taylor in China, and William Carey in India. He thought of the millions who have lived the life of discipleship in the workplace, of mothers in the home, of faithful pastors shepherding their flocks. He paused and thanked the Father for the privilege of encouraging such men and women in the accomplishment of their final destiny.

Then servant that he was, Michael turned from his reflections and redoubled his efforts to serve "those who will inherit salvation."[4]

---

[3]Ibid., p. 531.
[4]Heb. 1:14.

BIBLIOGRAPHY

Bibles and Scripture Versions

Hodges Zane, and Farstad, Arthur, eds. *The Greek New Testament According to the Majority Text*. 2d ed. Nashville: Nelson, 1985.

Holy Bible, New King James Version. Nashville: Nelson, 1982.

New International Version. New York: Oxford University Press, 1967.

Ryrie, Charles C. *The Ryrie Study Bible: New American Standard Translation*. Chicago: Moody Press, 1978.

Scofield, C. I. *The Scofield Reference Bible*. New York: Oxford University Press, 1967.

Septuagint Version, With Apocrypha - Greek and English. London: Samuel Bagster & Sons, 1851; reprint ed., Grand Rapids: Zondervan, 1978.

Language Resources

Abbott-Smith, G. *A Manual Greek Lexicon of the New Testament*. Edinburgh: T. & T. Clark, 1937.

Alford, Henry. *The Greek Testament*. Edited by Everett F. Harrison. 4 vols. Chicago: Moody Press, 1968.

Arndt, William F., and Gingrich, F. Wilbur. *A Greek-English Lexicon of the New Testament and Other Early Christian Literature*. Chicago: University of Chicago Press, 1957.

Barr, James. *The Semantics of Biblical Languages*. London: Oxford University Press, 1961.

Brown, Colin, ed. *The New International Dictionary of New Testament Theology.* 3 vols. Grand Rapids: Zondervan, 1975-78.

Brown, Francis; Driver, S. R.; and Briggs, Charles A. *Hebrew and English Lexicon of the Old Testament.* London: Oxford University Press, 1966.

Cremer, Hermann. *Biblio-Theological Lexicon of New Testament Greek.* Edinburgh: T. & T. Clark, 1895.

Dana, H. E., and Mantey, Julius R. *A Manual Grammar of the Greek New Testament.* New York: MacMillan, 1955.

Girdlestone, Robert. *Synonyms of the Old Testament.* Grand Rapids: Eerdmans, n.d.

Gramcord Analytical Computer Concordance. Gramcord Institute. Paul Miller, Director. 2065 Half Day Road, Deerfield, IL, 60015.

Harris, R. Laird; Archer, Gleason L., Jr.; and Waltke, Bruce K., eds. *Theological Wordbook of the Old Testament.* 2 vols. Chicago: Moody Press, 1980.

Hatch, Edwin and Redpath, Henry. *A Concordance to the Septuagint.* 2 vols. Reprint ed., Grand Rapids: Baker, 1983.

Jay, Eric G. *New Testament Greek: An Introductory Grammar.* London: S.P.C.K., 1958.

Kittel, Gerhard and Friedrich, Gerhard, eds. *Theological Dictionary of the New Testament.* Translated by Geoffrey W. Bromiley. Index compiled by Ronald E. Pitkin. 10 vols. Grand Rapids: Zondervan, 1964-76.

_____. *Theological Dictionary of the New Testament.* Translated and abridged in one volume by Geoffrey W. Bromiley. Grand Rapids: Eerdmans, 1985.

Lexicon Webster Dictionary. 2 vols. English Language Institute of America, 1971.

Liddell, Henry George and Scott, Robert. *A Greek-English Lexicon.* 1907; reprint ed., revised and augmented by Henry Stuart Jones and Robert McKenzie. Oxford: Clarendon Press, 1968.

Louw, J. P. *Semantics of New Testament Greek.* Philadelphia: Fortress; Chico, CA: Scholars Press, 1982.

Moule, C. D. F. *An Idiom Book of New Testament Greek.* 2d ed. Cambridge: University Press, 1959.

Moulton, James Hope, ed. *Grammar of New Testament Greek.* 3 vols. Edinburgh: T. & T. Clark, 1963.

_____, and Milligan, George. *The Vocabulary of the Greek Testament.* One-vol. ed. 1930; reprint ed., Grand Rapids: Eerdmans, 1974.

Moulton, W. F., and Geden, A. S. *A Concordance to the Greek Testament.* Edinburgh: T. & T. Clark, 1963.

Robertson, A. T. *A Grammar of the Greek New Testament in the Light of Historical Research.* Nashville: Broadman, 1934.

_____. *Word Pictures in the Greek New Testament.* 6 vols. Nashville: Broadman, 1933.

Thayer, J. H., ed. *Thayer's Greek-English Lexicon of the New Testament.* Reprint ed., Grand Rapids: Associate Publishers and Authors, n.d.

Trench, Richard Chenevix. *Synonyms of the New Testament.* London: 1880; reprint ed., Grand Rapids: Eerdmans, 1953.

Vine, W. E. *Expository Dictionary of Old and New Testament Words.* Reprint ed., Old Tappan, NJ: Revell, 1981.

_____. *An Expository Dictionary of New Testament Words.* 1939; reprint ed., Nashville: Nelson, n.d.

Webster's Ninth New Collegiate Dictionary. Springfield, MA: Merriam-Webster Inc., 1987.

Bible Dictionaries and Encyclopedias

Bromiley, Geoffrey W., ed. *International Standard Bible Encyclopedia.* Rev. Ed. 4 vols. Grand Rapids: Eerdmans, 1980-88.

Buttrick, George Arthur, ed. *The Interpreter's Dictionary of the Bible.* 4 vols. Nashville: Abingdon, 1962.

Douglas, J. D. *New Bible Dictionary.* Grand Rapids: Eerdmans, 1962.

Ewell, Walter A., ed. *Evangelical Dictionary of Theology.* Grand Rapids: Baker, 1984.

Harrison, Everett F., ed. *Baker's Dictionary of Theology*. Grand Rapids: Baker, 1960.

Hastings, J. ed. *Dictionary of Christ and the Gospels*. 2 vols. Edinburgh: T. & T. Clark, 1913.

Orr, James, ed., *International Standard Bible Encyclopedia*. 5 vols. Grand Rapids: Eerdmans, 1929.

Tenney, Merrill C., ed. *Zondervan Pictorial Dictionary of the Bible*. 5 vols. Grand Rapids: Zondervan, 1975.

Theology

Arminius, Jacobus. *Works of Arminius*. 3 vols. London, 1875, 1828, 1875.

Barnhouse, Donald G. *The Invisible War*. Grand Rapids: Zondervan, n.d.

Bell, M. Charles. *Calvin and Scottish Theology: The Doctrine of Assurance*. Edinburgh: The Handsel Press, 1985.

Berkhof, Louis. *Systematic Theology*. London: Banner of Truth, 1958.

Berkouwer, C. G. *Faith and Perseverance*. Grand Rapids: Eerdmans, 1958.

_____. *Faith and Justification*. Grand Rapids: Eerdmans, 1954.

Buswell, James Oliver. *A Systematic Theology of the Christian Religion*. 2 vols. Grand Rapids: Zondervan, 1962.

Calvin, John. *Concerning the Eternal Predestination of God*. 1961.

_____. *Institutes of the Christian Religion*. Translated by Henry Beveridge. 2 vols. Grand Rapids: Eerdmans, 1964.

Chafer, Lewis Sperry. *Systematic Theology*. 8 vols. Dallas: Dallas Seminary Press, 1948.

_____. *Major Bible Themes*. Rev. ed. Edited by John F. Walvoord. Grand Rapids: Zondervan, 1974.

Chrisope, Alan T. *Jesus is Lord*. Hertfordshire, England: Evangelical Press, 1982.

Cotton, John, *A Treatise on the Covenant of Grace*, 1659.

Dabney, Robert L. *Lectures in Systematic Theology*. Grand Rapids: Zondervan, 1972. Orig. pub. 1878.

Hodge, Charles. *Systematic Theology*. 3 vols. London: James Clarke & Co.

Hodges, Zane. *Dead Faith: What is it*. Dallas: Redencion Viva, 1987.

_____. *Grace in Eclipse*. Dallas: Redencion Viva, 1985.

_____. *The Gospel Under Siege*. Dallas: Redencion Viva, 1981.

_____. *Absolutely Free*. Grand Rapids: Zondervan, 1989.

Kaiser, Walter C., Jr. *Toward an Old Testament Theology*. Grand Rapids: Zondervan, 1978.

Kendall, R. T. *Calvin and English Calvinism to 1649*. Oxford: Oxford University Press, 1979.

_____. *Once Saved Always Saved*. London: Hodder and Stoughton, 1984.

Ladd, George Eldon. *A Theology of the New Testament*. Grand Rapids: Eerdmans, 1974.

Lightner, Robert P. *The Death Christ Died: A Case for Unlimited Atonement*. Des Plaines, IL: Regular Baptist Press, 1967.

Long, Gary. *Definite Atonement*. Grand Rapids: Presbyterian and Reformed, 1976.

Marshall, I. Howard. *Kept by the Power of God*. Minneapolis: Bethany House, 1969.

MacArthur, John. *The Gospel According to Jesus*. Grand Rapids: Zondervan, 1988.

McClain, Alva J. *The Greatness of the Kingdom*. Chicago: Moody Press, 1959.

Mueller, John Theodore. *Christian Dogmatics*. St. Louis: Concordia, 1955.

Murray, John. *The Collected Writings of John Murray*. 2 vols. Edinburgh: Banner of Truth, 1977

_____. *Redemption Accomplished and Applied*. London: Banner of Truth, 1961.

Owen, John. *The Death of Death in the Death of Christ*. Reprint ed., London: Banner of Truth, 1963.

Pentecost, J. Dwight. *Things to Come*. Grand Rapids: Dunham, 1958.

Perkins, William. *The Works of that Famous and Worthy Minister of Christ in the University of Cambridge, Mr. William Perkins*. 1608-1609.

Peters, George N. H. *The Theocratic Kingdom*. 3 vols. New York: Funk and Wagnalls, 1884; reprint ed., Grand Rapids: Kregel, 1972.

Pink, Arthur. *Eternal Security*. Grand Rapids: Baker, 1974.

Ryrie, Charles C. *So Great Salvation*. Wheaton, IL: Victor Books, 1989.

Schaff, Philip, ed. *The Creeds of Christendom*. 3 vols. Grand Rapids: Baker, 1985.

Sellers, C. Norman. *Election and Perseverance*. Miami Springs, FL: Schoettle, 1987.

Shank, Robert. *Life in The Son: A Study of the Doctrine of Perseverance*. Springfield, MO: Westcott, 1961.

Shedd, William G. T. *Dogmatic Theology*. 3 vols. New York: Charles Scribner's Sons, 1889; reprint ed., Minneapolis: Klock and Klock, 1979.

Smith, Wilbur. *The Biblical Doctrine of Heaven*. Chicago: Moody Press, 1968.

Swete, Henry Barclay. *The Holy Spirit in the New Testament*. Macmillan, 1910; reprint ed., Grand Rapids: Baker, 1964.

Thiessen, Henry Clarence. *Lectures in Systematic Theology*. Rev. ed. Revised by Vernon D. Doerksen. Grand Rapids: Eerdmans, 1979.

Warfield, Benjamin B. *Biblical and Theological Studies*. Philadelphia: Presbyterian and Reformed, 1968.

Commentaries and Studies

Allen, Ronald B. "Numbers." *The Expositor's Bible Commentary*. Edited by Frank E. Gaebelein. 11 vols to date. Grand Rapids: Zondervan, 1976--.

Ames, William. *An Analytical Exposition of Both the Epistles of the Apostle Peter, Illustrated by Doctrines out of Every Text*. 1641.

Barclay, William. *The Daily Study Bible. The Gospel of Matthew.* Philadelphia: Westminster, 1958.

Barnhouse, Donald G. *Messages to the Seven Churches.* Philadelphia: Eternity Book Service, 1953.

_____. *Revelation: An Expository Commentary.* Grand Rapids: Zondervan, 1971.

Beecher, Willis J. *The Prophets and the Promise.* New York: Thomas Y. Crowell, 1905; reprint ed., Grand Rapids: Baker, 1975.

Blum, Edwin A. "1 Peter." *The Expositor's Bible Commentary.* Edited by Frank E. Gaebelein. 11 vols. to date. Grand Rapids: Zondervan, 1976--.

Boice, James Montgomery. *The Sermon on the Mount: An Exposition.* Grand Rapids: Zondervan, 1972.

Bruce, F. F., gen. ed. *The New International Commentary on the New Testament.* 15 vols. to date. Grand Rapids: Eerdmans, 1959--.

_____. *Romans.* London: Tyndale, 1963.

Buchanan, George Wesley. "To the Hebrews." *The Anchor Bible.*

Burton, Ernest De Witt. *The Epistle to the Galatians. The International Critical Commentary.* Edinburgh: T. & T. Clark, 1921.

Bush, George. *Notes on Numbers.* Ivison & Phinney, 1858, reprint ed., Minneapolis: Klock & Klock, 1976.

Calvin, John. "The Epistles of Paul to the Romans and Thessalonians." *Calvin's New Testament Commentaries.* Translated by R. MacKenzie. Grand Rapids: Eerdmans, 1973.

_____. "Hebrews and 1 and 2 Peter." *Calvin's New Testament Commentaries.* Translated by W. B. Johnston. Grand Rapids: Eerdmans, 1963.

Cranfield, E. B. *A Critical and Exegetical Commentary on The Epistle to the Romans.* 2 vols. *The International Critical Commentary.* Edinburgh: T. & T. Clark, 1975-79.

Davidson, A. B. *The Epistle to the Hebrews.* Edinburgh: T. & T. Clark, 1959.

Denzer, George A. "The Pastoral Letters." *Jerome Biblical Commentary.* Edited by Raymond E. Brown, Joseph A. Fitzmeyer, and Roland E. Murphy. Englewood Cliffs, NJ: Prentice-Hall, 1968.

Dibelius, Martin. *James*. Revised by Heinrich Greeven. Translated by Michael A. Williams. Edited by Helmut Koester. *Hermeneia*. Philadelphia: Fortress, 1976.

Eadie, John. *Commentary on the Epistle of Paul to the Galatians*. Edinburgh: T. and T. Clark, 1884; reprint ed., Minneapolis: James and Klock, 1977.

Fairbairn, Patrick. *Pastoral Epistles*. T. & T. Clark, 1874; reprint ed., Minneapolis: James and Klock, 1976.

_____. *Typology of Scripture*. 1845-47; reprint ed., New York: Funk and Wagnalls, 1900.

Farrar, F. W. *The Epistle of Paul the Apostle to the Hebrews* in *Cambridge Greek Testament for Schools and Colleges*. Cambridge: Cambridge University Press, 1984.

Fitzmeyer, Joseph A. "First Peter." *The Jerome Biblical Commentary*. Edited by Raymond E. Brown, Joseph A. Fitzmeyer, and Roland E. Murphy. Englewood Cliffs, NJ: Prentice-Hall, 1968.

_____. "Romans." *The Jerome Biblical Commentary*. Edited by Raymond E. Brown, Joseph Fitzmeyer, and Roland E. Murphy. Englewood Cliffs, NJ: Prentice-Hall, 1968.

Godet, Frederic. *Commentary on First Corinthians*. Edinburgh: T. & T. Clark, 1889; reprint ed., Grand Rapids: Kregel, 1977.

_____. *Commentary on the Epistle to the Romans*. 1883; reprint ed., Grand Rapids: Zondervan, 1969.

Haldane, Robert. *Exposition of the Epistle to the Romans*. Reprint ed., Edinburgh, 1974.

Hawthorne, Gerald F. "Philippians." *Word Biblical Commentary*. Edited by David A. Hubbard and Glenn W. Barker. Waco, TX: Word, 1983.

Hodge, Charles. *St. Paul's Commentary on the Epistle to the Romans*. Grand Rapids: Eerdmans, 1950.

Hoekema, Anthony A. *The Bible and the Future*. Grand Rapids: Eerdmans, 1979.

Hogg, C. F., and Vine, W. E. *The Epistle To The Thessalonians*. Reprint ed., Grand Rapids: Kregel, 1959.

Hughes, Philip Edgecomb. *A Commentary on the Epistle to the Hebrews*. Grand Rapids: Eerdmans, 1977.

_____. *Paul's Second Epistle to the Corinthians*. Grand Rapids: Eerdmans, 1962.

Johnstone, Robert. *Lectures Exegetical and Practical on The Epistle of James*. Oliphant Anderson & Ferrier, 1871; reprint ed., Minneapolis: Klock and Klock, 1978.

Käsemann, Ernst. *Commentary on Romans*. Grand Rapids: Eerdmans, 1980.

Kaiser, Walter C., Jr. *The Uses of the Old Testament in the New*. Grand Rapids: Zondervan, 1988.

Kelly, J. N. D. *The Pastoral Epistles*. London: Adam and Charles Black, 1963.

Kuyper, Abraham. *The Work of the Holy Spirit*. New York: Funk and Wagnalls, 1900; reprint ed., Grand Rapids: Eerdmans, 1958.

Lang, G. H. *Pictures and Parables*. Miami Springs, FL: Conley and Schoettle, 1985.

_____. *Firstborn Sons, Their Rights and Risks*. London: Samuel Roberts, 1936; reprint ed., Miami Springs, FL: Conley and Schoettle, 1984.

_____. *The Epistle to the Hebrews*. Miami Springs, FL: Conley and Schoettle, 1985.

Lange, John Peter. *Lange's Commentary on the Holy Scriptures*. Translated and edited by Philip Schaff. 12 double vols. 1868-70; reprint ed., Grand Rapids: Zondervan, 1960.

Lenski, R. H. *The Interpretation of I and II Corinthians*. Minneapolis: Augsburg, 1963.

_____. *The Interpretation of St. Matthew's Gospel*. Minneapolis: Augsburg, 1961.

_____. *The Interpretation of the Epistles of St. Peter, St. John, and St. Jude*. Minneapolis: Augsburg, 1966.

Liddon, H. P. *Explanatory Analysis of St. Paul's Epistle to the Romans*. London: Longmans, Green, 1899; reprint ed., Minneapolis: James and Klock, 1977.

Lightfoot, John. *St. Paul's Epistle to the Philippians*. London: Macmillan, 1913; reprint ed. Grand Rapids: Zondervan, 1953.

Lloyd-Jones, D. Martin. *The Sons of God: Exposition of Romans 8:5-17*. Grand Rapids: Zondervan, 1975.

_____. *Romans Chapter 8:17-39: The Final Perseverance of the Saints*. Grand Rapids: Zondervan, 1976.

_____. *The New Man: Exposition of Romans 6*. Grand Rapids: Zondervan, 1973.

_____. *The Sons of God, Exposition of Romans 8*. Grand Rapids: Zondervan, 1973.

Longenecker, Richard N., and Tenney, Merrill C., eds. *New Dimensions in New Testament Study*. Grand Rapids: Zondervan, 1974.

_____. *Paul, Apostle of Liberty*. New York: Harper and Row, 1964.

MacArthur, John. *Hebrews*. Chicago: Moody Press, 1983.

Mounce, Robert H. *The Book of Revelation. The New International Commentary on the New Testament*. Edited by F. F. Bruce. 15 vols. to date. Grand Rapids: Eerdmans, 1959--

M'Neile, Alan Hugh. *The Gospel According to Matthew*. Reprint ed., London: Macmillan, 1961.

Meyer, Heinrich August. *A Critical and Exegetical Hand-book to The Epistle To The Romans*. T. & T. Clark, 1883; reprint ed., Winona Lake, IN: Alpha Publications, 1979.

Montefiore, Hugh. *A Commentary on the Epistle to the Hebrews*. London: Adam and Charles Black, 1969.

Morgan, G. Campbell. *A First Century Message to Twentieth Century Christians*. New York: Revell, 1902.

Morris, Leon. *The Epistle to the Romans*. Grand Rapids: Eerdmans, 1988.

Newell, William R. *Romans: Verse by Verse*. Chicago: Moody Press, 1938.

Hawthorne, G. G., ed. *Current Issues in Biblical and Patristic Interpretation*. Grand Rapids, 1975.

Nicoll, W. Robertson, gen. ed. *Expositor's Greek Testament*. 5 vols. Reprint ed., Grand Rapids: Eerdmans, 1967.

Owen, John. *Hebrews*. Cited by Arthur Pink, *An Exposition of Hebrews*. Grand Rapids: Baker, 1968.

Pink, Arthur. *An Exposition of Hebrews*. Grand Rapids: Baker, 1968.

Plummer, Alfred. "The Gospel According to Luke." *The International Critical Commentary*. New York: Charles Scribner's Sons, 1914.

Ramm, Bernard. *Protestant Biblical Interpretation*. Boston: W. A. Wilde, 1956.

Ramsay, W. M. *The Letters to the Seven Churches of Asia*. London: Hodder and Stoughton, 1904.

Robertson, Archibald and Plummer, Alfred. *A Critical and Exegetical Commentary on the First Epistle of St. Paul to the Corinthians*. 2d. ed. *The International Critical Commentary*. Edinburgh: T. & T. Clark, 1914.

Ryle, J. C. *Expository Thoughts on the Gospels*. 4 vols. Grand Rapids: Zondervan, n.d.

Sanday, William and Headlam, Arthur C. *A Critical and Exegetical Commentary On The Epistle To The Romans*. *The International Critical Commentary*. Edinburgh: T. & T. Clark, 1902.

Sauer, Eric. *In the Arena of Faith*. Grand Rapids: Eerdmans, 1966.

_____. *From Eternity to Eternity*. Grand Rapids: Eerdmans, 1963.

Selwyn, Edward Gordon. "The First Epistle of St. Peter." *Thornapple Commentaries*. Grand Rapids: Baker, 1981.

Shedd, William G. T. *Commentary on Romans*. New York: Charles Scribner's Sons, 1879; reprint ed., Grand Rapids: Zondervan, 1967.

Smith, J. B. *A Revelation of Jesus Christ*. Scottsdale, PA: Mennonite Publishing House, 1961.

Tasker, R. V. G., gen. ed. *The Tyndale New Testament Commentaries*. 20 vols. London: Tyndale, 1957-65.

Toussaint, Stanley D. *Behold the King: A Study of Matthew*. Portland: Multnomah, 1980.

Trench, Richard C. *Notes on the Miracles and Parables of the Lord*. 2 vols. in 1. Reprint ed., Westwood, NJ: Revell, 1953.

Waltke, Bruce. *Creation and Chaos*. Portland: Western Conservative Baptist Press, 1974.

Walvoord, John F., and Zuck, Roy, gen. eds. *The Bible Knowledge Commentary*. 2 vols. Wheaton, IL: Victor, 1983.

Westcott, B. F. *The Epistle to the Hebrews*. London: Macmillan, 2d. ed., 1892; reprint ed., Grand Rapids: Eerdmans, 1965.

Books

Alexander, Archibald. *Thoughts on Religious Experience*. Reprint ed., London: Banner of Truth, 1967.

Ames, William. *The Marrow of Sacred Divinity*, 1643.

Bloom, Allan. *The Closing of the American Mind*. New York: Simon and Schuster, 1987.

Bonar, H. *God's Way of Holiness*. Chicago: Moody Press, n.d.

Bridges, Jerry. *Trusting God*. Colorado Springs: NavPress, 1988.

Carroll, Lewis. *Alice Through the Looking Glass*. London: Macmillan, 1880.

Covey, Stephen R. *The Seven Habits of Highly Effective People*. New York: Simon and Schuster, 1989.

Crabb, Lawrence. *The Marriage Builder*. Grand Rapids: Zondervan, 1982.

Foxe, John. *Foxe's Christian Martyrs of the World*. Chicago: Moody Press, n.d.

Gallup, George, Jr., and Poling, David. *The Search For America's Faith*. Nashville: Abington, 1980.

Henrichson, Walt. *The Profit Motive*. Knoxville, TN: Vision Foundation, 1989.

Lovelace, Richard. *Dynamics of Spiritual Life: An Evangelical Theology of Renewal*. Downers Grove, IL: InterVarsity, 1979.

Nee, Watchman. *The Normal Christian Life*. Fort Washington, PA: Christian Literature Crusade, 1961.

Redpath, Alan. *Victorious Christian Living*. Old Tappan, NJ: Revell, 1955.

Sagan, Carl. *Cosmos*. New York: Random House, 1980.

Sproul, R. C. *Pleasing God*. Wheaton, IL: Tyndale, 1988.

Stott, John R. *Men Made New*. Downers Grove: InterVarsity, 1966.

Thomas, W. Ian. *The Saving Life of Christ*. Grand Rapids: Zondervan, 1961.

Weinburg, Stephen. *The First Three Minutes*. New York: Basic Books, 1977.

Journals and Magazines

Atwood, Alan. "Case of the Phantom Rabbits." *Time*, December 5, 1988.

Edgar, Thomas R. "The Meaning of 'Sleep' in 1 Thessalonians 5:10." *Journal of the Evangelical Theological Society* 22 (December 1979): 345-349.

Ferguson, Sinclair B. "The Assurance of Salvation." *The Banner of Truth* 186 (March 1979).

Fuller, J. William. "I Will Not Erase His Name from the Book of Life (Revelation 3:5)." *Journal of the Evangelical Theological Society* 26 (1983).

Howard, Tracy L. "The Meaning of 'Sleep' in 1 Thessalonians 5:10 - A Reappraisal." *Grace Theological Journal* 6.2 (1985).

Howe, Frederick R. "Review of *Birthright*, by David Needham." *Bibliotheca Sacra* 141 (January-March 1984): 68-78.

Inglis, James. "Simon Magus." *Waymarks in the Wilderness*, 5 (1867): 35-50. Reprinted in *Journal of the Grace Evangelical Society* 2 (Spring 1989): 45-54.

Johnson, H. Wayne. "The 'Analogy of Faith' and Exegetical Methodology: A Preliminary Discussion on Relationships." *The Journal of the Evangelical Theological Society* 31 (March 1988): 69-80.

Marshall, John E. "'Rabbi' Duncan and the Problem of Assurance." *The Banner of Truth*, 1980.

McCoy, Brad. "Secure Yet Scrutinized, 2 Timothy 2:11-13." *Journal of the Grace Evangelical Society* 1 (Autumn 1988): 21-33.

Murray, Iain H. "Will the Unholy Be Saved." *The Banner of Truth* 246 (March 1984).

Oberholtzer, Thomas. "The Eschatological Salvation of Hebrews 1:5-2:5." *Bibliotheca Sacra* 145 (January-March 1988): 83-97.

_____. "The Thorn-Infested Ground in Hebrews 6:4-12." *Bibliotheca Sacra* 145 (July-September 1988): 319-328.

Roberts, Maurice. "Final Perseverance." *The Banner of Truth* 265 (October 1985).

Rosscup, James E. "The Overcomers of the Apocalypse." *Grace Theological Journal* 3 (Fall 1982): 261-86.

Wilkin, Robert N. "Repentance and Salvation, Part 2: The Doctrine of Repentance in the Old Testament." *Journal of the Grace Evangelical Society* 2 (Spring 1989): 13-26.

Theses, Dissertations, and Papers

Benedict, Richard Reagan. "The Use of **Nikao** in the Letters to the Seven Churches of Revelation." Th.M. thesis, Dallas Theological Seminary, 1966.

Brown, William E. "The New Testament Concept of the Believer's Inheritance." Th.D. dissertation, Dallas Theological Seminary, 1984.

G. Michael Cocoris, "John MacArthur's System of Salvation: An Evaluation of the Book, The Gospel According to Jesus." Los Angeles, CA: By the Author, 1989

Pattillo, Jerry Lee. "An Exegetical Study of the Lord's Logion on the 'Salvation of the *Psyche*.'" Th.M. thesis, Dallas Theological Seminary, May 1978.

Quick, Ken. "Living for the Kingdom." D.Min. dissertation, Dallas Theological Seminary, 1989.

Sauer, R. C. "A Critical and Exegetical Reexamination of Hebrews 5:11-6:8." Ph.D. dissertation, University of Manchester, 1981.

Other

Durant, Will. *The Life of Greece* in *The Story of Civilization* 11 vols. New York: Simon and Schuster, 1966.

Publishers often become personally involved with their writers. Schoettle Publications found it interesting that during the past nine years, while Dr. Dillow was working on this book, he was directing a covert biblical training ministry behind the Iron Curtain. We thought many readers might have an interest in this unique ministry, and we have therefore included a brief description of it below.

Biblical Education by Extension, or **BEE**, has been operating in Eastern Europe and the former Soviet Union for the past fourteen years. Conceived as an inter-mission cooperative project, BEE has expanded to a twelve-mission coordinated effort designed to bring advanced biblical training to church leaders in closed countries.

The goal of BEE is the establishment of indigenous church-based training systems in each targeted country. As of the date of the publication of *The Reign of the Servant Kings*, nearly five thousand laymen in Russia, Czechoslovakia, Hungary, Romania, Poland, and Bulgaria are systematically working through the nineteen-course BEE curriculum which has been translated into each language.

Each course consists of twelve lessons and requires fifteen weeks to complete. This involves weekly self-study in the workbooks and textbooks, and a six-hour monthly seminar conducted by traveling members of the BEE team based in Vienna, Austria.

If you would like more information about the ministry of BEE and possible ways in which you could be involved in this worldwide effort to assist the church in closed countries, write Dr. Dillow at:

BEE International
405 West Shore
Richardson, TX 75080

MONUMENTAL WORKS
BY DODSON, GOVETT, LANG, MAURO,
NEIGHBOUR, PANTON, PEMBER, STANTON AND WILSON

KENNETH F. DODSON
THE PRIZE OF THE UP-CALLING

ROBERT GOVETT
GOVETT ON ISAIAH
GOVETT ON THE PARABLES
GOVETT ON JOHN (2 vols. in 1)
GOVETT ON ROMANS
GOVETT ON GALATIANS
GOVETT ON EPHESIANS
GOVETT ON PHILIPPIANS
GOVETT ON COLOSSIANS
GOVETT ON THESSALONIANS
GOVETT ON II TIMOTHY
GOVETT ON HEBREWS
GOVETT ON I JOHN
GOVETT ON REVELATION (4 vols. in 2)
CALVINISM BY CALVIN
CHRIST'S JUDGMENT OF HIS SAINTS
CHRIST'S RESURRECTION AND OURS
ENTRANCE INTO THE KINGDOM
ESAU'S CHOICE
ETERNAL SUFFERING OF THE WICKED
    AND HADES
GOSPEL ANALOGIES

HOW INTERPRET THE APOCALYPSE?
IS SANCTIFICATION PERFECT HERE BELOW?
KINGDOM OF GOD FUTURE
KINGDOM STUDIES
LEADING THOUGHTS ON THE APOCALYPSE
REWARD ACCORDING TO WORKS
SINS BEFORE FAITH AND SINS AFTER FAITH
SOWING AND REAPING
THE BEST MODE OF PRESENTING THE GOSPEL
THE CHURCH OF OLD: I CORINTHIANS 12, 13, 14
THE FUTURE APOSTASY
THE JEWS, THE GENTILES, AND THE CHURCH OF
    GOD IN THE GOSPEL OF MATTHEW
THE NEW JERUSALEM
THE PROPHECY ON OLIVET
THE SAINTS RAPTURE
THE SERMON ON THE MOUNT
THE THREE EATINGS: EDEN, PASSOVER &
    THE LORD'S SUPPER
THE TWO WITNESSES
TWO VIEWS OF THE SUPPER OF THE LORD

G.H. LANG
AN ORDERED LIFE
ANTHONY NORRIS GROVES
ATONING BLOOD
BALANCED CHRISTIANITY
COMING EVENTS
DEPARTURE
DIVINE GUIDANCE
FIRSTBORN SONS
FIRSTFRUITS AND HARVEST
GOD AT WORK ON HIS OWN LINES
GOD'S PLAN, CHRIST'S SUFFERING,
    AND THE SPIRIT'S POWER
IDEALS AND REALITIES
ISRAEL'S NATIONAL FUTURE
PICTURES AND PARABLES
PRAYER: FOCUSED AND FIGHTING
PRAYING IS WORKING
THE CHURCHES OF GOD

THE CLEAN HEART
THE DISCIPLE
THE EARLIER YEARS OF THE MODERN TONGUES
    MOVEMENT
THE EPISTLE TO THE HEBREWS
THE FIRST RESURRECTION
THE GOSPEL OF THE KINGDOM
THE HISTORY & DIARIES OF AN INDIAN
    CHRISTIAN
THE HISTORIES AND PROPHECIES OF DANIEL
THE LAST ASSIZE
THE LOCAL ASSEMBLY
THE MODERN GIFT OF TONGUES
THE NEW BIRTH
THE REVELATION OF JESUS CHRIST
THE SINNER'S FUTURE
THE UNEQUAL YOKE
WORLD CHAOS

PHILIP MAURO
GOD'S APOSTLE AND HIGH PRIEST

R.E. NEIGHBOUR
IF BY ANY MEANS
IF THEY SHALL FALL AWAY

D.M. PANTON
RAPTURE
THE JUDGMENT SEAT OF CHRIST
THE PANTON PAPERS

G.H. PEMBER
MYSTERY BABYLON THE GREAT
THE ANTICHRIST BABYLON AND
    THE COMING OF THE KINGDOM
THE GREAT PROPHECIES Vol. I

THE GREAT PROPHECIES Vol. II
THE GREAT PROPHECIES Vol. III
THE GREAT PROPHECIES Vol. IV
THE LORD'S COMMAND

GERALD B. STANTON
KEPT FROM THE HOUR

A. EDWIN WILSON
SELECTED WRITINGS

Available Through Your
Local Christian Book Store or Consult Publisher